16.71

PAGE 44

ON THE ROAD

YOUR COMPLETE DESTINATION GUIDE
In-depth reviews, detailed listings and insider tips

PAGE 301

SURVIVAL GUIDE

VITAL PRACTICAL INFORMATION TO HELP YOU HAVE A SMOOTH TRIP

Language

THIS EDITION WRITTEN AND RESEARCHED BY

Ryan Ver Berkmoes
Stuart Butler, Amy Karafin

welcome to Sri Lanka

The Undiscovered Country

You might say Sri Lanka has been hiding in plain sight. Countless scores of travellers have passed overhead on their way to someplace else, but years of war and challenges such as tsunamis have kept Sri Lanka off many itineraries.

But now – as you've probably heard – the war is over and Sri Lanka's looking up. If you've 'done' India, grown blasé about Southeast Asia or simply want to explore a place whose appeal and pleasures are myriad, then it's time you dropped in.

So Much in So Little

Sri Lanka's attributes are many. Few places have as many Unesco World Heritage Sites (eight) packed into such a small area. Its 2000-plus years of culture can be discovered at ancient sites filled with mystery. Legendary temples boast beautiful details crafted by artisans through the centuries.

Across whole swaths of the country, that thing that goes bump in the night might be an elephant heading to a favourite waterhole. Safari tours of Sri Lanka's pleasantly relaxed national parks encounter leopards, grouchy water buffaloes, all manner of birds and a passel of primates.

Endless beaches, timeless ruins, welcoming people, oodles of elephants, killer surf, cheap prices, fun trains, famous tea, flavourful food – need I go on? – describe Sri Lanka.

(left) Procession toward Gangaramaya Temple (p53), Colombo
(below) Beach at Mirissa (p111)

When you're ready to escape the tropical climate of the coast and lowlands, head for the hills, which are verdant, virescent and virally infectious with allure. Impossibly green tea plantations and rainforested peaks beckon walkers, trekkers or just those who want to see it on a spectacular train ride.

And then there are the beaches. The beaches! Dazzlingly white and all so often untrod, they ring the island so that no matter where you go, you'll be near a sandy gem. Should you beat the inevitable languor, you can surf and dive world-class sites without world-class crowds.

It's So Easy

Distances are short: see the sacred home of the world's oldest living tree in the morning (Anuradhapura) and stand awestruck by the sight of hundreds of elephants gathering in the afternoon (Minneriya). Find a favourite beach to call your own, meditate in a 2000-year-old temple, exchange smiles while strolling a mellow village, marvel at birds and wildflowers, try to keep count of the little dishes that come with your rice and curry. Stroll past colonial gems in Colombo and then hit some epic surf.

Sri Lanka is spectacular, it's affordable and it's still mostly uncrowded. Now is the best time to discover it.

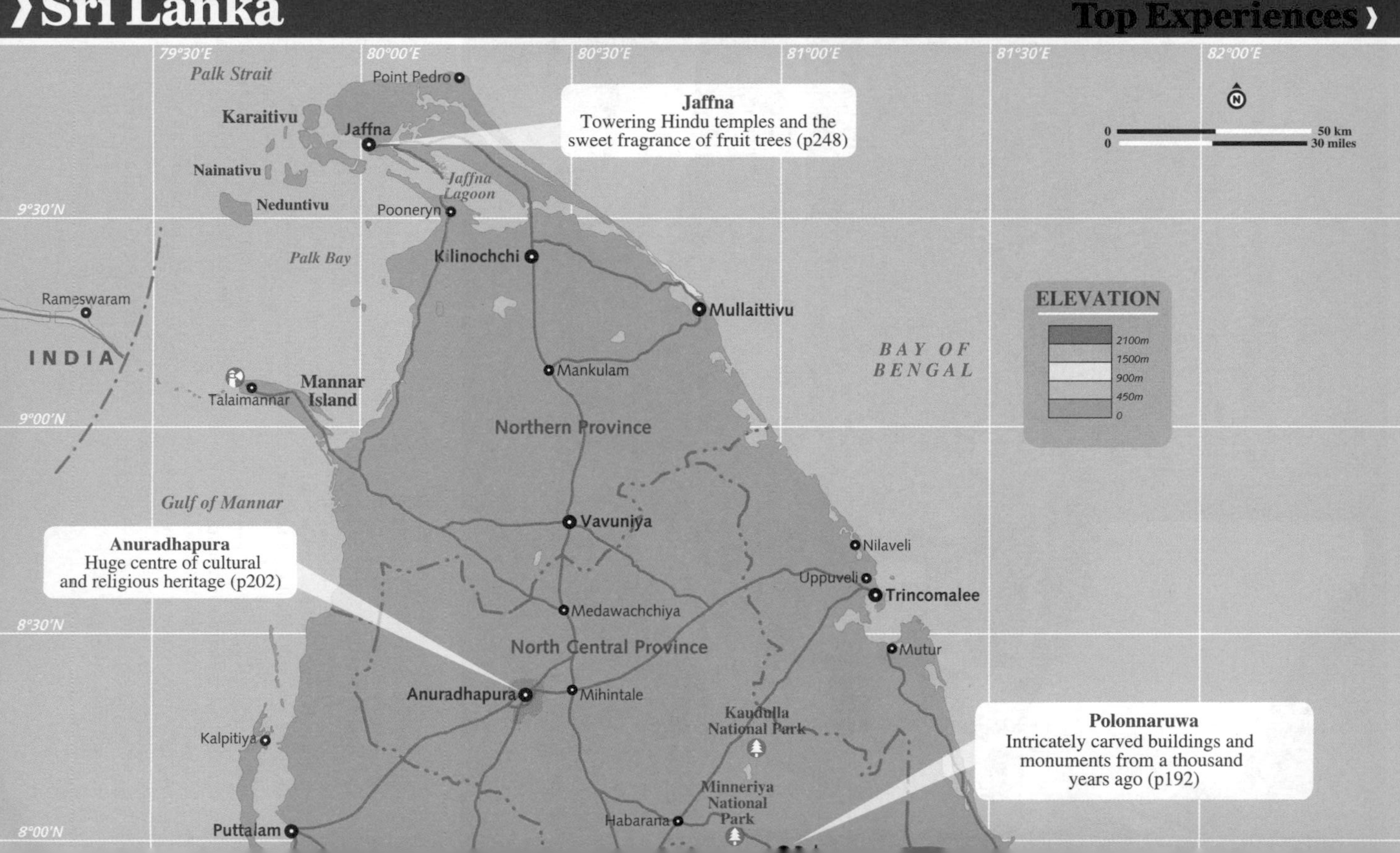
Jaffna
Towering Hindu temples and the sweet fragrance of fruit trees (p248)
Anuradhapura
Huge centre of cultural and religious heritage (p202)
Polonnaruwa
Intricately carved buildings and monuments from a thousand years ago (p192)
79°30'E
80°00'E
80°30'E
81°00'E
81°30'E
82°00'E
9°30'N
9°00'N
8°30'N
8°00'N
Palk Strait
Point Pedro
Karaitivu
Jaffna
Nainativu
Neduntivu
Jaffna Lagoon
Pooneryn
Palk Bay
Kilinochchi
Mullaittivu
Rameswaram
INDIA
Talaimannar
Mannar Island
Mankulam
Northern Province
BAY OF BENGAL
Gulf of Mannar
Vavuniya
Nilaveli
Uppuveli
Trincomalee
Medawachchiya
North Central Province
Mutur
Anuradhapura
Mihintale
Kaudulla National Park
Kalpitiya
Minneriya National Park
Habarana
Puttalam
ELEVATION
2100m
1500m
900m
450m
0
0
0
50 km
30 miles
N

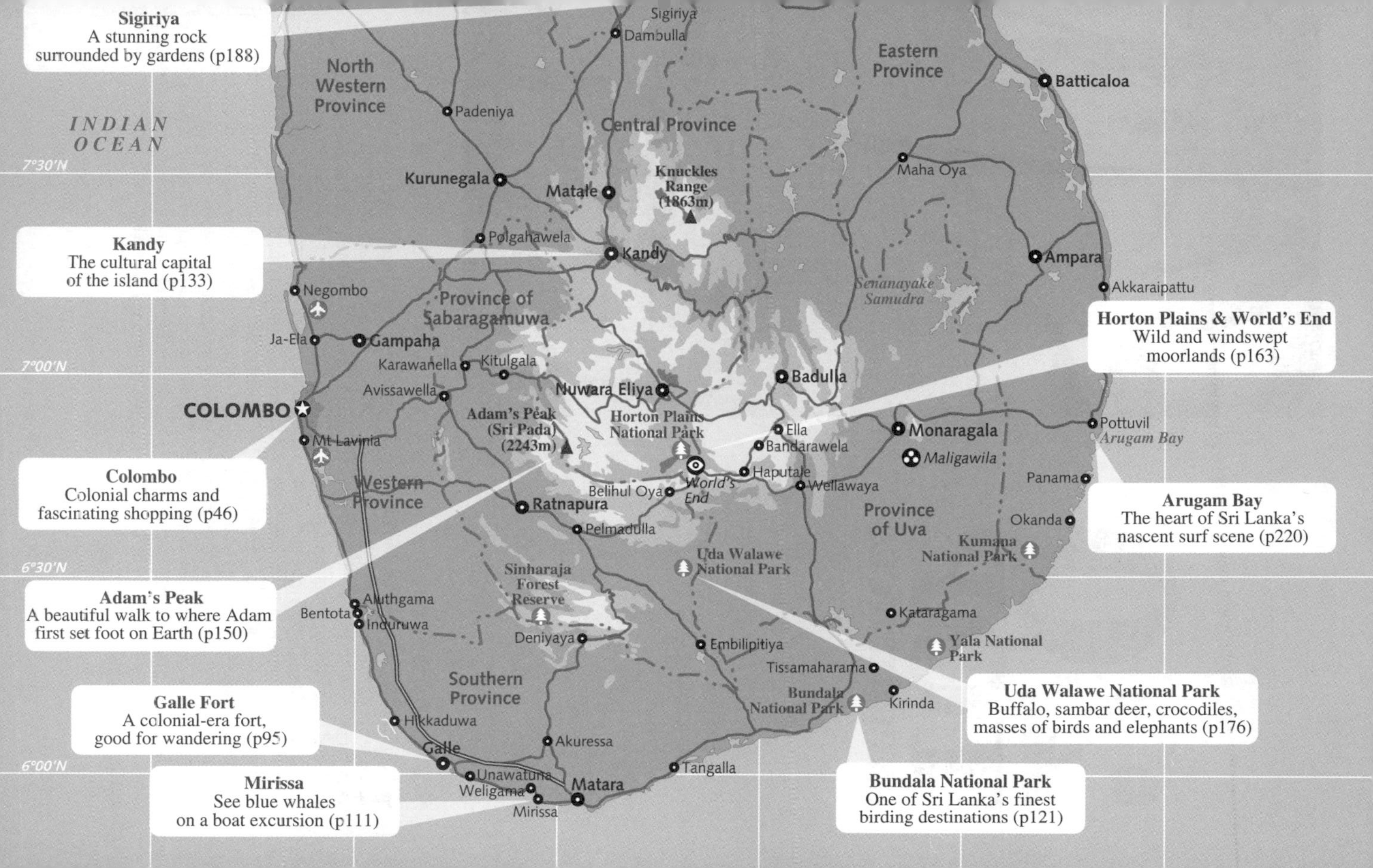
Sigiriya
A stunning rock surrounded by gardens (p188)
Kandy
The cultural capital of the island (p133)
Colombo
Colonial charms and fascinating shopping (p46)
Adam's Peak
A beautiful walk to where Adam first set foot on Earth (p150)
Galle Fort
A colonial-era fort, good for wandering (p95)
Mirissa
See blue whales on a boat excursion (p111)
Horton Plains & World's End
Wild and windswept moorlands (p163)
Arugam Bay
The heart of Sri Lanka's nascent surf scene (p220)
Uda Walawe National Park
Buffalo, sambar deer, crocodiles, masses of birds and elephants (p176)
Bundala National Park
One of Sri Lanka's finest birding destinations (p121)
INDIAN OCEAN
7°30'N
7°00'N
6°30'N
6°00'N
North Western Province
Central Province
Eastern Province
Province of Sabaragamuwa
Western Province
Southern Province
Province of Uva
Sigiriya
Dambulla
Padeniya
Kurunegala
Matale
Knuckles Range (1863m)
Polgahawela
Kandy
Negombo
Ja-Ela
Gampaha
Karawanella
Kitulgala
Avissawella
COLOMBO
Mt Lavinia
Adam's Peak (Sri Pada) (2243m)
Nuwara Eliya
Horton Plains National Park
World's End
Belihul Oya
Ratnapura
Pelmadulla
Sinharaja Forest Reserve
Aluthgama
Bentota
Induruwa
Deniyaya
Hikkaduwa
Galle
Akuressa
Unawatuna
Weligama
Mirissa
Matara
Tangalla
Embilipitiya
Uda Walawe National Park
Tissamaharama
Bundala National Park
Kirinda
Kataragama
Yala National Park
Kumana National Park
Okanda
Panama
Pottuvil
Arugam Bay
Akkaraipattu
Ampara
Batticaloa
Maha Oya
Senanayake Samudra
Badulla
Ella
Bandarawela
Haputale
Wellawaya
Monaragala
Maligawila

20 TOP EXPERIENCES

Stunning Beaches

1 There are long, golden-specked ones, there are dainty ones with soft white sand, there are wind- and wave-battered ones, and ones without a footstep for miles. Some have a slowly, slowly vibe and some have a lively party vibe, but whichever you choose, the beaches of Sri Lanka really are every bit as gorgeous as you've heard. And we guarantee that after you've returned home, every time you sit in rush-hour traffic on a wet and cold Monday morning, an image of palm trees and azure Sri Lankan waters will float into your mind! Tangalla (p117)

Travelling by Train

2 Sometimes there's no way to get a seat on the slow but oh-so-popular train to Ella (p170), but with a prime standing-room only spot looking out at a rolling carpet of tea, who cares? Outside, the colourful silk saris of Tamil tea pickers stand out in the sea of green; inside, you may get a shy welcome via a smile. At stations, vendors hustle treats, including some amazing corn and chilli fritters sold wrapped in somebody's old homework paper. Munching one of these while the scenery creaks past? Sublime.

1

KEVIN CLOGSTOUN / LONELY PLANET IMAGES ©

2

JULIET COOMBE / LONELY PLANET IMAGES ©

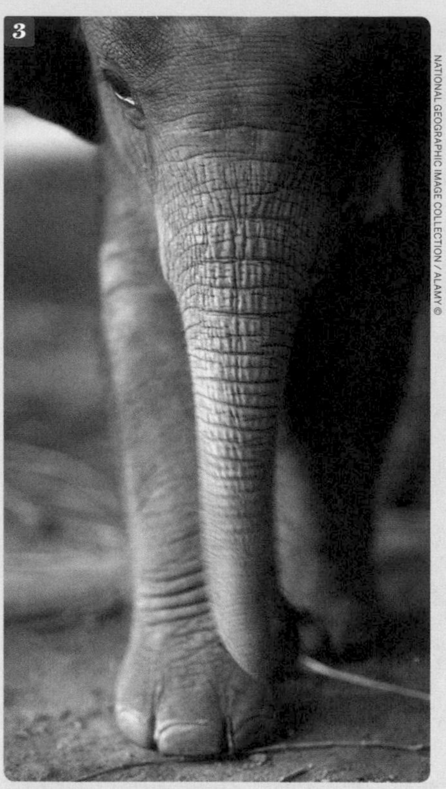
3

NATIONAL GEOGRAPHIC IMAGE COLLECTION / ALAMY ©

4

Uda Walawe National Park

3 This huge chunk of savannah grassland centred on the Uda Walawe reservoir is the closest Sri Lanka gets to East Africa. There are herds of buffalo (although some of these are domesticated!), sambar deer, crocodiles, masses of birds, and elephants – and we don't just mean a few elephants. We mean hundreds of the big-nosed creatures. In fact, we'd go so far to say that for elephants, Uda Walawe (p176) is equal to, or even better than, many of the famous East African national parks.

Ancient Anuradhapura

4 Here, big bits of Sri Lanka's cultural and religious heritage sprawl across 3 sq km. In the centre is the world's oldest tree, the Sri Maha Bodhi (more than two thousand years old). That it has been tended uninterrupted by record-keeping guardians for all those centuries is enough for shivers down the spine. The surrounding fields of crumbling monasteries and enormous dagobas (stupas) attest to the city's role as the seat of power in Sri Lanka for a thousand years. Biking through this heady past is a thrilling experience (p202).

Ruvanvelisaya Dagoba (p205)

Soaring Sigiriya Rock

5 If it was just the rolling gardens at the base of Sigiriya (p188), they would still be a highlight. Ponds and little man-made rivulets put the water in these water gardens and offer a serene idyll amid the sweltering countryside. But look up and catch your jaw as you ponder this 370m rock that erupts out of the landscape. Etched with art and surmounted by ruins, Sigiriya is an awesome mystery, one that the wonderful new museum tries to dissect. The climb to the top is a wearying and worthy endeavour.

5

MARGIE POLITZER / LONELY PLANET IMAGES ©

Bundala National Park

6 With all the crowds heading to nearby Yala National Park, the Ramsar-recognised Bundala National Park (p121) often gets overlooked. But with the park's huge sheets of shimmering waters singing to the sound of birdsong, skipping it is a big mistake. Bundala has a beauty that other parks can only dream of and is one of the finest birding destinations in the country. Oh, and in case herons and egrets aren't glam enough for you, the crocodiles and resident elephant herd will put a smile on your face. Cattle egret

6

NANDANA DE SILVA / ALAMY ©

Adam's Peak Pilgrims

7 For over a thousand years, pilgrims have trudged by candlelight up Adam's Peak (Sri Pada; p150) to stand in the footprints of the Buddha, breathe the air where Adam first set foot on earth, and see the place where the butterflies go to die. Today tourists join the throngs of local pilgrims and, as you stand in the predawn light atop this perfect pinnacle of rock and watch the sun crawl above waves of mountains, the sense of magic remains as bewitching as it must have been for Adam himself. View from Adam's Peak

Kandy: Cultural Capital

8 Kandy (p133) is the cultural capital of the island and home to the Temple of the Sacred Tooth Relic, said to contain a tooth of the Buddha himself. For the Sinhalese this is the holiest spot on the island, but for tourists Kandy offers more than just religious satisfaction: there's a pleasing old quarter, a pretty central lake, a clutch of museums and, in the surrounding vicinity, some beautiful botanical gardens. In case you need further blessings from the gods, there's also a series of fascinating ancient temples. Temple of the Sacred Tooth Relic (p133)

DREAMSTIME.COM ©

RICHARD ROSS / LONELY PLANET IMAGES ©

GREG ELMS / LONELY PLANET IMAGES ©

LOOKINGLOST / ALAMY ©

MARGIE POLITZER / LONELY PLANET IMAGES ©

Beloved Galle Fort

9 Man and nature have joined forces in Galle Fort (p97) to produce an architectural work of art. The Dutch built the streets and buildings, the Sri Lankans added the colour and style, and then nature got busy covering it in a gentle layer of tropical vegetation, humidity and salty air. The result is an enchanting old town that has recently become home to dozens of art galleries, quirky shops, and boutique cafes and guesthouses. For tourists, it's without doubt the number-one urban attraction in the country.

Surfing at Arugam Bay

10 The heart of Sri Lanka's nascent surf scene, the long right break at the southern end of Arugam Bay (p220) is considered Sri Lanka's best. From April to September you'll find surfers riding the waves; stragglers catch the random good days as late as November. Throughout the year you can revel in the surfer vibe: there are board-rental and ding-repair joints plus plenty of laid-back cheap hangouts offering a bed on the beach. And if you need solitude, there are fine breaks at nearby Lighthouse and Okanda.

Feeling the Healing: Ayurveda

11 If you start to feel the burden of the centuries while in Sri Lanka, you might appreciate an irony while you feel the tensions melt out of your body in an Ayurvedic sauna: the design is more than 2500 years old. Ayurveda is an ancient practice and its devotees claim enormous benefits from its therapies and treatments. Herbs, spices, oils and more are used on and in the body to produce balance. Some people go on multiweek regimens in clinics, others enjoy a pampering afternoon at a luxury spa (p306). Ayurvedic medicine

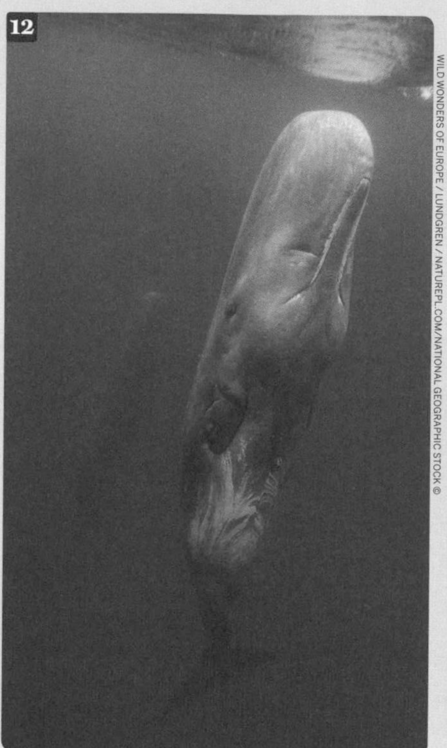

Whale-Watching at Mirissa

12 People once visited the beaches of southern Sri Lanka to laze under palm trees and maybe go and peer at a few little fish on a diving excursion. Then somebody realised that the deep blue was home to more than just a few little fish. It turns out that the waters off Sri Lanka are home to the planet's biggest creature, the blue whale (not to mention the slightly smaller sperm whale). Now, every morning in season, boats leave Mirissa (p111) in search of creatures like no other. Sperm whale

Exploring Undiscovered Beaches

13 Off limits due to war, inaccessible due to bad roads, not really on the map: these are all factors that have kept some truly magnificent east-coast beaches off traveller itineraries. But just take one look at these beautiful ribbons of sand and you won't want to leave. And you may well have the strands to yourself. A few areas to consider: Navalady (p230), Vakarai (p234), the islands near Batticaloa Lighthouse (p234), beaches down the strip from Uppuveli and Nilaveli (p238). Beach at Uppuveli

Richly Spiced Food

14 Venture into the entertaining pandemonium of a large Sri Lankan market, such as those found in Colombo and Kandy, and you'll soon see and smell the rich diversity of foods and flavours that come from the fertile land. An average Sri Lankan cook spends hours each day tirelessly roasting and grinding spices while mincing, slicing and dicing all manner of foods. A seemingly humble rice and curry can consist of dozens of intricately prepared dishes, each redolent of a rich and, yes, at times fiery goodness (p294). Selection of spices, including nutmeg, cinnamon and cloves

Horton Plains & World's End

15 The wild, windswept Horton Plains (p163), high, high up in Sri Lanka's Hill Country, are utterly unexpected in this country of tropical greens and blues, but they are far from unwelcome. You'll need to wrap up warm (a morning frost isn't uncommon) for the dawn hike across these bleak moorlands – it's one of the most enjoyable walks in the country. And then, suddenly, out of the mist comes the end of the world and a view over what seems like half of Sri Lanka. Horton Plains from World's End

Visiting a Tea Plantation

16 It wasn't really all that long ago that Sri Lanka's Hill Country was largely a wild and ragged sweep of jungle-clad mountains, but then along came the British and they felt in need of a nice cup of tea. So they chopped down all the jungle and turned the Hill Country into one giant tea estate, and you know what? The result is mighty pretty! Sri Lankan tea is now famous across the world, and visiting a tea estate and seeing how the world's favourite cuppa is produced is absolutely fascinating (p288). Tea picker at Nuwara Eliya (p156)

15

16

Jaffna & the Rediscovered North

17 In Jaffna (p248), everything seems different, especially the language: the rapid-fire staccato of spoken Tamil is a real change from singsong Sinhala. So too the cuisine: singularly spiced and, in season, complemented by legendary mangoes. And perhaps even the light: it has a distinctive quality, reflected as deep garden greens in Jaffna's suburbs. Revel in the uniqueness of Jaffna, from the towering, ornate Hindu temples to colourful saris draped over women on bicycles. Hindu temple decoration

Colonial Legacy

18 Yes, the Brits were chased out at independence in 1948, but their legacy lives on in much more than an often impenetrable bureaucracy addicted to forms. Colombo has wide, tree-shaded streets where you'll see the structures of the empire at its most magnificent. The National Museum building (p53) is redolent with empire. Look around a little and you'll find the colonial legacies of the Dutch and Portuguese as well. Just head to Fort and wander a bit, pausing at the new sensation: the restored Old Dutch Hospital (p49). Arcades of Cargills, Colombo

HEMIS / ALAMY ©

JOCHEN TACK / ALAMY ©

Polonnaruwa's Stupendous Structures

19 Arrayed around a vast grassy quadrangle like the chess pieces of giants, these intricately carved buildings and monuments offer a visitor-friendly briefing on what was the centre of the kingdom some thousand years ago. Handy plaques are loaded with information, although you may find the buildings too extraordinary to switch your concentration to signage. Catch sight of the ruins at sunrise and sunset, when the rosy rays of light bathe the complex in a romantic glow (p192). Gal Vihara (p196)

Shopping in Colombo

20 Part of the magic of Colombo – yes, you read that right – is going on a retail binge. We don't necessarily mean the kind where you buy more than will fit in a fleet of three-wheelers; rather we mean binging on the experience itself. Even as parts of the world race to a big-box future, Colombo's markets in Pettah (p49) heave and hurl with goods and offers and just general chaos. And if you'd like something a bit more stylish, Colombo has a growing collection of chic boutiques and stores (p68). Pettah market

need to know

Currency

» Sri Lankan Rupee (Rs)

Language

» Sinhala, Tamil and English

When to Go

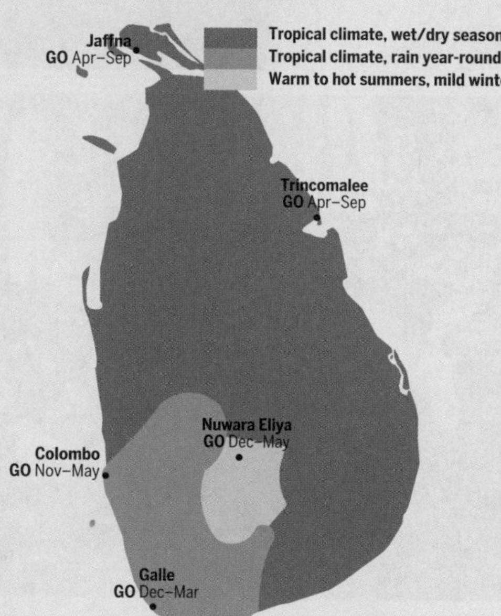

High Season (Dec–Mar)

» The Hill Country plus west- and south-coast beaches are busiest – and driest

» With beds in demand, prices peak

» The Maha monsoon season (October to January) keeps the East, North and Ancient Cities wet

Shoulder (Apr & Sep–Nov)

» April and September offer the best odds for good weather countrywide

» New Year's celebrations in mid-April cause transport to fill beyond capacity

» A good time to wander without a set schedule of bookings

Low Season (May–Aug)

» The Yala monsoon season (May to August) brings rain to the south and west coasts plus the Hill Country

» The weather in the North and East is best

» Prices nationwide are at their nadir

Your Daily Budget

Budget less than

Rs 3500

» Simple guesthouse: Rs 1000-2500

» A delicious rice and curry: Rs 200-400

» Bus fares: under Rs 300 per day

Midrange

Rs 3500 -16,000

» Double room in a nice midrange place: Rs 2500-8000

» Meals at hotel: Rs 1500-2500

» Hire bikes, ride trains and use a car and driver some days: average per day Rs 2500

Top end over

Rs 16,000

» Top-end hotel: Rs 8000 and up

» Meals at top-end hotels: from Rs 3000

» Daily use of car and driver: from Rs 5500

Money

» ATMs available in cities and large towns. Credit cards accepted at some midrange and all top-end hotels

Visas

» Thirty-day visitor visas cost US$20, apply in advance online (www.eta.gov.lk)

Mobile Phones

» Local SIM cards cheaply available for unlocked phones

Transport

» Buses go everywhere often and cheaply, trains are less convenient but fun; hire cars with drivers are popular and affordable

Websites

» **Lonely Planet** (www.lonelyplanet.com/sri-lanka) Destination information, hotel bookings, traveller forum and more.

» **Ceylon Today** (www.ceylontoday.lk) News, sports, entertainment and a handy ticker with exchange rates.

» **Gossip Lanka** (www.english.gossiplankanews.com) Gossip and entertainment news.

» **Indi.ca** (www.indi.ca) An excellent blog covering news, opinion and culture.

» **Kottu** (www.kottu.org) Aggregates content from over 1000 Sri Lankan blogs.

Exchange Rates

Australia	A$1	Rs 123
Canada	C$1	Rs 115
Europe	€1	Rs 151
Japan	¥100	Rs 148
New Zealand	NZ$1	Rs 95
UK	UK£1	Rs 181
USA	US$1	Rs 114

For current exchange rates see www.xe.com.

Important Numbers

All regions have a three-digit area code followed by a six- or seven-digit number. Mobile numbers usually begin with 07 or 08 and have up to 12 digits.

Country code	☎94
International access code	☎00

Arriving in Sri Lanka

» **Bandaranaike International Airport**
Sri Lanka's one main airport is 30km north of Colombo, see p310.
Taxis to Colombo
Prepaid Rs 2600, with a meter about Rs 2100; one to two hours to Fort.
Hotel car & driver to Colombo Rs 3000 to Rs 4000; one to two hours to Fort.
Bus to Colombo
Regular/air-con buses Rs 70/100; with connections one to three hours to the city.

What to Bring

You can get basic items you might need in Colombo and the major tourist towns, but many essentials and conveniences are best brought from home:

» Raincoat, waterproof jacket or umbrella – for when you run into a monsoon

» A good pair of earplugs – in case you end up staying near a busy strip such as Colombo's Galle Rd

» Sunglasses – if you wear prescription glasses or contacts, get the sunglasses in your prescription so they can be backup glasses

» Bottle opener – for those times you're on a lovely beach with a cold bottle of Lion lager

» Mosquito repellent – very hard to find in Sri Lanka (unlike mosquitoes)

» Sunscreen – another surprisingly hard-to-find item

» Tampons – impossible to find outside Colombo

what's new

For this new edition of Sri Lanka, our authors have hunted down the fresh, the transformed, the hot and the happening. These are some of our favourites. For up-to-the-minute recommendations, see lonelyplanet.com/sri-lanka.

Renovations in Colombo

1 The 17th-century Old Dutch Hospital in Colombo's historic Fort is leading the way for renovations across the city. Its restaurants and shops bring a dash of style to the capital (p49).

Maritime Museum, Galle

2 Galle is kindling an interest in its maritime past, present and future with this new state-of-the-art museum full of flashing lights and nautical displays (p97).

New Dolphin Tours, Kalpitiya

3 A huge project is underway to turn the area around Kalpitiya into a major package-tour hotspot. But a better reason for venturing here is the newly launched dolphin boat safaris (p76).

World Buddhism Museum, Kandy

4 Kandy's latest attraction is a flash new museum that uses photographs, maps and artefacts to showcase Buddhism around the planet (p137).

Gregory Lake

5 Gregory Lake has long been a forgotten expanse of water on the fringes of Nuwara Eliya, but no more! A new walkway has brought it firmly into town life (p157).

The A9 to Jaffna

6 Not only is this road open, but you no longer need permission from the Ministry of Defence to travel it. Same goes for most (but not all) of the North (p247).

Keerimalai Spring & Tellippalai, Jaffna Peninsula

7 The road to the ancient healing waters of Keerimalai spring – through a fascinatingly creepy militarised zone – is open for the first time in 20 years (p259).

Jaffna Music Festival

8 Jaffna hosts this new biennial festival in March of odd-number years. Folk music and dances from across the North and East are performed (www.jaffnamusicfestival.org; p254).

HMS Hermes, Batticaloa

9 Dives to this WWII wreck, not far from charming Batticaloa, have recently started up, run by a great dive school–guesthouse combo (p231).

New Highways

10 The new Southern Expressway to Galle shaves hours off the journey down the west coast. It's the first of new roads that will shrink travel times around the island (p313).

New Places to Stay

11 Visitors to popular Sigiriya can choose from great new guesthouses that are a cut above the norm; and it's happening in other popular spots like Ella and Galle, too (p197).

if you like...

Beaches

If Sri Lanka looked outlined in white from space, it's due to the beaches that encircle the island. You can rarely travel any part of the coast for long without coming upon a simply stunning stretch of sand. More amazing is that many are almost empty.

Thalpe For Galle expats, Thalpe, with its smattering of boutique guesthouses and quiet sands, is the new Unawatuna – and not a moment too soon (p108)

Marakolliya Beach So what if the swimming isn't always safe; for us this beach is simply stunning (p120)

Arugam Bay Classic hangout for surfers and anyone who likes mellow, easy vibes (p220)

Uppuveli & Nilaveli Beautiful beaches near the old front line; the location has kept them quiet and natural (p238)

Batticaloa Most of the coasts around here are totally isolated; for explorers, adventurers and dreamers only (p230)

Diving & Snorkelling

Sri Lanka's diving scene is developing along with its tourist scene. Excellent places for diving and snorkelling can be found right around the coast but most are still seldom visited. The west coast south of Colombo has been the centre of diving but other, better, areas are ready to take off as the infrastructure develops.

Bar Reef Little-exploited and near-pristine reefs where dolphins play in their hundreds (p76)

Great Basses Reefs It's tricky to access and conditions are very fickle but this might be the finest dive site in Sri Lanka (p126)

Pigeon Island National Park A shallow coral reef with tons of fish and sharks that's equally satisfying to snorkel or dive (p240)

Batticaloa The HMS *Hermes*, a WWII-era wreck, is for Tec divers, but the rock dives around here are for everyone (p231)

Walking

Sure it's a bit hot during the day and it might rain but there are oodles of places where you can stretch your legs and appreciate Sri Lanka's remarkable natural beauty, rich culture, ancient monuments or maybe just go shopping.

Colombo The main streets may be choked but other roads in the capital are tree-lined and have a genteel charm. Stroll from the buzzing neighbourhoods from Cinnamon Gardens to Galle Face Green (p48)

Polonnaruwa The ancient monuments here are in a lush park-like setting that rewards walkers ready to explore (p193)

Adam's Peak On Adam's Peak you can walk in the footsteps of the Buddha with hundreds of pilgrims (p150)

Knuckles Range Rain soaked and densely vegetated, the Knuckles Range is no walk in the park, but it offers the most exciting hiking in the country (p150)

» Pilgrims at the Temple of the Sacred Tooth Relic (p133), Kandy

Buddhist Temples

More than 2000 years of religious heritage can be found in the temples great and small that dot this small island. Time your visit to a festival for an extraordinary experience.

Colombo Gangaramaya Temple is one of several temples in the capital that have high-profile celebrations through the year (p53)

Mulkirigala Hiding inside a series of cleft-like caves and dangling off a rocky crag is this beautiful and little-visited temple (p119)

Temple of the Sacred Tooth Relic Containing a tooth of the Buddha, this is the heart and soul of Sri Lankan Buddhism (p133)

Sri Maha Bodhi The world's oldest documented living tree is the focus of this very sacred site in the heart of Anuradhapura (p205)

Mihintale This temple of legends has over 1800 legendary steps to its mountaintop location (p211)

Nagadipa A simple temple on a little island in the far north where the Buddha, legend goes, once visited (p262)

Wildlife

The island may be small but the animals are big, especially the herds of Asian elephants that live inside and outside the national parks. Leopards and water buffaloes are just some of the other creatures.

Yala National Park Still drawing crowds like only a spotty big cat can, a leopard safari in Yala National Park is a Sri Lankan highlight (p127)

Uda Walawe National Park If you've ever wanted to see a wild elephant, you're unlikely to find a better place to do so than this park (p176)

Minneriya National Park Already a good place to see elephants and other animals, this park is the site of 'the Gathering', when over 400 pachyderms gather in an awesome spectacle (p201)

Kumana National Park Leopards, elephants and birds galore at this park that's much less crowded than its popular neighbour, Yala (p228)

Pottuvil Lagoon safaris may bring you titillatingly close to elephants, monitor lizards and crocodiles (p226)

Shopping

Being a lush country, it's not surprising that some of Sri Lanka's best goods are what it grows. Tea is an obvious purchase, all manner of spices another. In addition there are various handicrafts and a growing range of designer items.

Colombo Of course the capital has good shopping. What's surprising is just how good it is. Stylish designer boutiques, galleries and all manner of markets sell just about anything you might want, with plenty of surprises on offer (p68)

Negombo Charming and ramshackle Negombo has a busy town centre full of shopping Sri Lankans and a beachfront lined with tourist souvenir shops (p78)

Galle With a surfeit of classy little galleries, independent clothes shops and boutique bric-a-brac shops, Galle is a fascinating place for shoppers to explore (p102)

Hill Country At tea plantations and factories you can buy excellent teas – many hard to find elsewhere – at good prices (p130)

If you like... fabulous local food, you can never go wrong ordering the national staple: rice and curry. Family-run guesthouses often serve the best versions (p295)

Ayurveda

Ayurveda is an ancient system of medicine and therapies designed to heal and rejuvenate. Ayurveda is widely used in Sri Lanka for a range of ailments and draws many visitors each year; some book into clinics and spas and stay for weeks.

Colombo The backstreets of the old market district of Pettah have some Ayurveda shops where you can browse the vast range of unguents, ointments, oils, scrubs and many other potions (p49)

Siddhalepa Ayurveda Hospital South of Colombo, this is a full-service clinic where you can stay for a week or more getting treatments (p58)

Suwamadura You can cleanse your mind on walks around the lush hills of lovely Ella, then head to this noted spa to get your innards cleansed and your kinks removed (p170)

Sanctuary Spa A hard day swimming in the energetic surf of Unawatuna can be followed by long sessions getting your inner balance restored (p105)

Heritage Sites

Unesco has recognised eight World Heritage Sites in Sri Lanka, an impressive number for a small island.

Galle The Dutch Fort forms Sri Lanka's most beautiful urban environment: stroll the walls at sunset (p94)

Kandy The Royal City and temples are the heart of culture (p133)

Sinharaja Forest Reserve One of the last remaining slabs of dense montane rainforest in Sri Lanka is a birdwatcher's dream (p178)

Dambulla The cave temples and their extraordinary paintings are works of art (p185)

Sigiriya The rock monastery which, yes, many people still think was a fort or temple; on a clear day you can almost see forever from the top (p188)

Polonnaruwa A vast range of surviving structures of the medieval capital (p193)

Anuradhapura The sacred and the secular come together in a sprawling precinct that spans centuries of history (p203)

Central Highlands The forests and peaks of Sri Pada Peak Wilderness, Horton Plains and Knuckles Range house outstanding biodiversity (p38)

Colonial Architecture

The Dutch, the Portuguese, the British, the Klingons, er, not them. Many of the world's great colonial powers had their way with Sri Lanka at one point. Their legacies are today's atmospheric sights.

Colombo The Dutch-built Old Dutch Hospital is just one of many colonial beauties you can enjoy in the capital. The National Museum is in an old British compound (p49)

Galle Fort Walls Take a sunset walk along the perimeter of Galle's Dutch-built Fort walls and you can almost feel history seep out of the ground around you (p95)

Nuwara Eliya Stay in one of the grand old hotels of Sri Lanka's favourite colonial hill station and the days of the Raj seem to come flickering back to life (p159)

Jaffna Nineteenth-century homes and Portuguese-era churches, though damaged in the war, pepper the city's suburbs (p249)

month by month

Top Events

1. **Aurudu (New Year)**, April
2. **Kandy Esala Perahera**, August
3. **Duruthu Perahera**, January
4. **Vesak Poya**, May
5. **Maha Sivarathri**, March

January

At the peak of the tourist season when crowds are at their largest, many popular towns have special events such as the fast-growing literary festival at Galle.

Duruthu Perahera

Held on the *poya* (full-moon) day at the Kelaniya Raja Maha Vihara in Colombo and second in importance only to the huge Kandy *perahera* (procession), this festival celebrates Buddha's first of three visits to Sri Lanka.

Thai Pongal

Held in mid-January, this Hindu winter-harvest festival honours the sun god Surya. It is important to Tamils in Sri Lanka and South India. Look for the special sweet dish, *pongal,* which is made with rice, nuts and spices.

Galle Literary Festival

An annual event held in mid- to late January, this five-day festival (www.galleliteraryfestival.com) brings together renowned Asian and Western writers. It is well regarded and attracts big names. A parallel fringe festival covers current issues and other creative pursuits.

Kala Pola Art Market

The original Kala Pola Art Market is an annual event held the third Sunday of January. Up to 500 artists from across Sri Lanka display their work. It's a kaleidoscope of creativity and has spawned a smaller weekly version.

February

The tourist crowds continue strong, with wintering Europeans baking themselves silly on the beaches. This is a busy month for Sri Lankans, with an important national holiday.

Independence Day

Sri Lanka gained independence on 4 February 1948 and this day is commemorated every year with festivals, parades, fireworks, sporting events and more across the nation. In Colombo, motorcades shuffle politicians from one event to the next.

Navam Perahera

First celebrated in 1979, Navam Perahera is one of Sri Lanka's biggest and flamboyant *perahera*s. Held on the February *poya,* it starts from the Gangaramaya Temple and travels around Viharamahadevi Park and Beira Lake in Colombo.

March

This is an important month for many of Sri Lanka's Buddhists and you'll see observance of Maha Sivarathri in the Ancient Cities areas and portions of the west coast where they are in the majority.

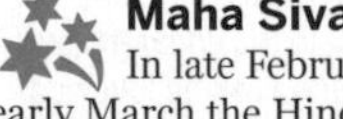

Maha Sivarathri

In late February or early March the Hindu festival of Maha Sivarathri commemorates the marriage of Shiva to Parvati with all-night vigils and more. It's the most important day for Shaivites, who comprise the majority of Sri Lanka's Hindus.

April

Although Christians comprise only 6% of Sri Lanka's population, secularised versions of Christian holidays are popular. Don't be surprised when you see an Easter bunny at the mall.

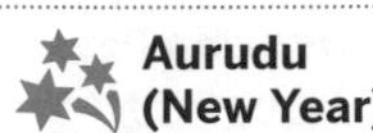

Aurudu (New Year)

New Year's Eve (13 April) and New Year's Day (14 April) are non-religious holidays. There is a period between the old and new year called the 'neutral period'; all activities are meant to cease, otherwise buses and trains are jammed.

Art Trail

As if Galle wasn't enough of a work of art, the whole Fort area virtually becomes one giant artist's easel during the Art Trail (www.gallearttrail.com), a bi-annual event (the next is due to be held in 2013).

May

The southwest monsoon blows in for five months, bringing huge rains from the Indian Ocean that drench the Hill Country and the beach towns in the southwest.

Vesak Poya

This two-day holiday – *poya* day and the day after – commemorates the birth, enlightenment and death of the Buddha. Amid the festivities, the high point is the lighting of paper lanterns and oil lamps outside of every Buddhist home, shop and temple.

June

Sri Lanka's Buddhists barely have a chance to catch their breath after Vesak before another major religious event occurs – and they'll want to catch their breath...

Poson Poya

The Poson *poya* day celebrates the bringing of Buddhism to Sri Lanka by Mahinda. In Anuradhapura there are festivities in the famous temples, while in nearby Mihintale thousands of white-clad pilgrims ascend the 1843 steps to the topmost temple.

July

Light-bulb vendors do a huge business as Buddhists gear up for Esala Perahera, which begins at the end of the month. Light displays are an integral part of the Kandy festivities, with a parade of light-bulb-decorated elephants.

Vel

This festival is held in Colombo and Jaffna. In Colombo the gilded chariot of Murugan (Skanda), the god of war, is ceremonially hauled from Pettah to Bambalapitiya. In Jaffna the Nallur Kandaswamy Kovil has a 25-day festival.

Kataragama

Another important Hindu festival is held at Kataragama, where devotees put themselves through a whole gamut of ritual masochism. It commemorates the triumph of the six-faced 12-armed war god Skanda over demons here.

August

The Kandy Esala Perahera is important but smaller versions are held across Sri Lanka. Many celebrations feature dancers and other performers such as stilt-walkers who practise all year.

POYA

Every *poya* (full-moon) day is a holiday. *Poya* causes buses, trains and accommodation to fill up, especially if it falls on a Friday or Monday. No alcohol is supposed to be sold on *poya* days, and some establishments close. Some hotels and guesthouses discreetly provide their thirsty guests with a cold beer 'under the table'.

Note that the official full-moon day for *poya* does not always coincide with the same designated full-moon day in Western calendars. Because of the religious time used to calculate the exact moment of full moon, the *poya* day may be a day earlier or later than that shown on regular calendars.

For more on these important days, see p286.

Kandy Esala Perahera

The Kandy Esala Perahera, Sri Lanka's most spectacular and prominent festival, is the climax of 10 days and nights of celebrations during the month of Esala. This great procession honours the sacred tooth relic of Kandy and starts in late July.

Nallur Festival

Jaffna's Nallur Kandaswamy Kovil temple is the focus of an enormous and spectacular Hindu festival over 25 days in July and August, which climaxes on day 24 with parades of juggernaut floats and gruesome displays of self-mutilation by entranced devotees.

October

This is a month of meteorological mystery as it falls between the two great monsoon seasons. Rains and squalls can occur almost any place at any time.

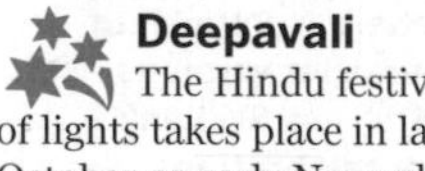

Deepavali

The Hindu festival of lights takes place in late October or early November. Thousands of flickering oil lamps celebrate the triumph of good over evil and the return of Rama after his period of exile.

November

The second-to-last month of the year is a time of waiting: waiting for the tourist throngs, waiting for Christmas, waiting for the coming monsoon rains in the dry North and East.

European Film Festival

Sri Lanka's nascent film industry gets its chance to show off during this new festival (www.europeanfilmfestsrilanka.com) held at venues across the island, including Jaffna, Kandy, Colombo and Galle. It's held in either October or November.

December

The other great monsoon season of the year begins this month and lasts until March. Winds come from the northeast and that's just the part of the island that sees huge rains.

Adam's Peak

The pilgrimage season, when pilgrims of all faiths (and the odd tourist) climb Adam's Peak near Ella, starts in December and lasts until mid-April. The trek begins shortly after midnight so that everyone can be in place for sunrise.

Unduvap Poya

This full-moon day commemorates Sangamitta, who brought a cutting from the sacred Bodhi Tree in India in 288 BC to Anuradhapura. The resulting tree, the Sri Maha Bodhi, is considered the oldest living tree in the world. The ceremonies attract thousands in their finest.

Christmas

Outside of Sri Lanka's Christian communities – mostly around Colombo – this day has become a popular secularised holiday. Ersatz versions of Western Christmas traditions can be found across the nation, from bone-thin Santas in strange masks to garish artificial trees.

itineraries

Whether you've got six days or 60, these itineraries provide a starting point for the trip of a lifetime. Want more inspiration? Head online to lonelyplanet.com/thorntree to chat with other travellers.

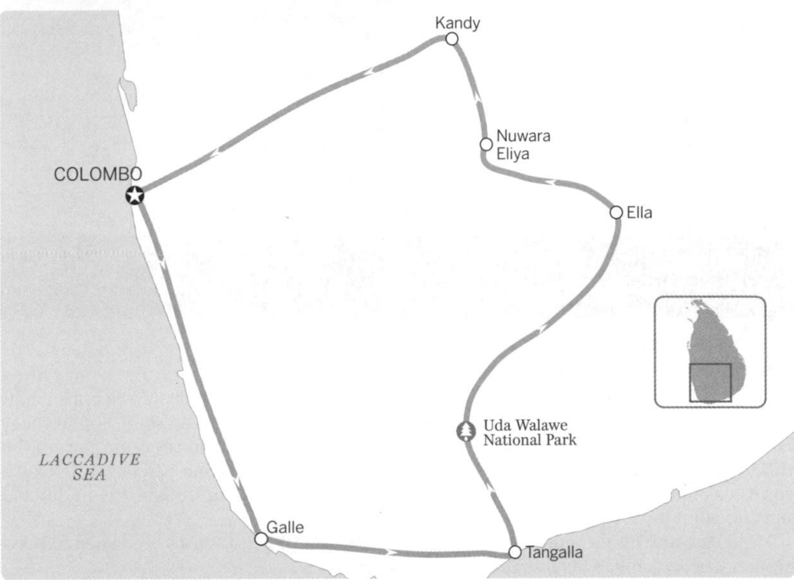

Two Weeks

Capital, Coast & Hill Country

Start in **Colombo**, exploring the markets and visiting the city's vibrant Buddhist temples. Then take the new Southern Expressway south and you'll be in **Galle** in no time, avoiding the often traffic-clogged road on the west coast and the ho-hum towns along it. Explore the languid streets of Galle's 17th-century Dutch city-within-a-fort.

From Galle, go get some beach time. **Tangalla** has a growing selection of groovy beach places on its lovely and uncrowded ribbon of sand. Head inland and venture up to **Uda Walawe National Park**, where you'll see dozens of elephants and many other animals. Take the winding road up in the heart of the Hill Country and put down roots for a few days in **Ella**, a cool town with a fun travellers' vibe. Walk to waterfalls and mountain peaks.

Take one of the world's most beautiful train rides to the stop for the British colonial heritage town of **Nuwara Eliya**, where you'll enter a time warp. Visit tea plantations and stop in iconic **Kandy** for temples and gardens. From here it's an easy jaunt back to Colombo or the airport.

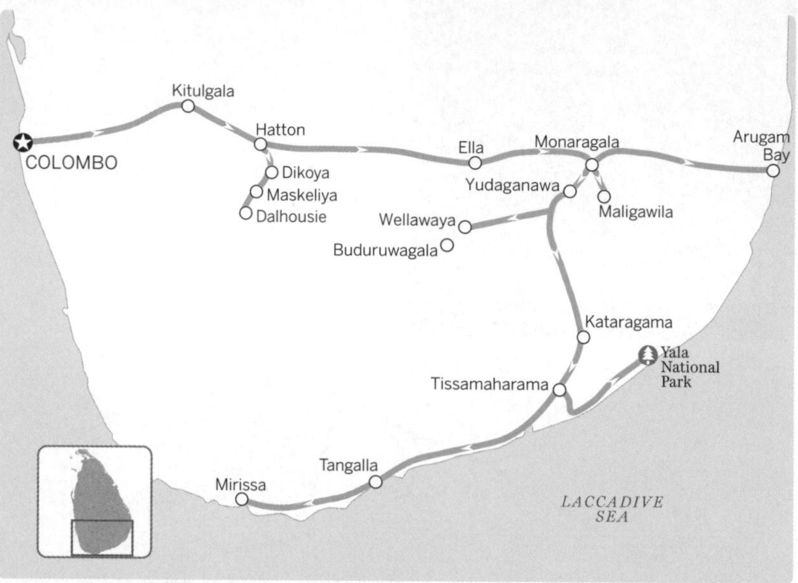

Three Weeks

Hilltops & Beaches

Start in **Colombo**, where you can absorb some of Sri Lanka's newfound energetic vibe before you head right off the map – almost. **Kitulgala** is a gateway for rafting the Kelaniya Ganga, as well as for jungle hikes and birdwatching. Movie buffs might recognise scenes from *Bridge on the River Kwai* here. Take the short hop to misty **Hatton**, **Dikoya** and **Maskeliya**, three small towns in some of the most scenic parts of the Hill Country. Spend a few days tasting fragrant single-estate teas and bed down in luxurious ex-colonial tea planters' bungalows, or cosy guesthouses in **Dalhousie**, the traditional starting point for the pre-dawn ascent of Adam's Peak.

Head east to **Ella** for more hiking, wonderful views and guesthouses renowned for having some of Sri Lanka's tastiest home-cooked food.

Travel southeast to **Monaragala**, a low-key gateway to the east and the jumping-off point for one of Sri Lanka's most atmospheric ancient Buddhist sites at **Yudaganawa**. Also nearby, **Maligawila** is home to an 11m-tall standing Buddha that's over a thousand years old.

Continue east to **Arugam Bay**, with its easygoing surfers' vibe, excellent seafood and few travellers compared with the southern beaches. It's easy to spend an extra day or three here, swinging in a hammock at one of the beach guesthouses. Don't miss a boat trip exploring the nearby Pottuvil Lagoon. After a few days on the beach, veer back inland via Monaragala to **Wellawaya**, and find time for a brief detour to Sri Lanka's tallest standing Buddha at **Buduruwagala**. Soak up the beauty of the tiny lakes and listen to the birds.

Descend from Wellawaya to the coastal plains of **Kataragama**, the terminus of the Pada Yatra, a pilgrimage that begins at the other end of the island. One of Sri Lanka's oldest and most venerated dagobas (stupas) is in nearby **Tissamaharama**, which is also a convenient entry point for forays into **Yala National Park**, where you can spot most of Sri Lanka's iconic critters. From 'Tissa', beach-hop via **Tangalla** along the south coast to laid-back **Mirissa**, a good base for whale-watching.

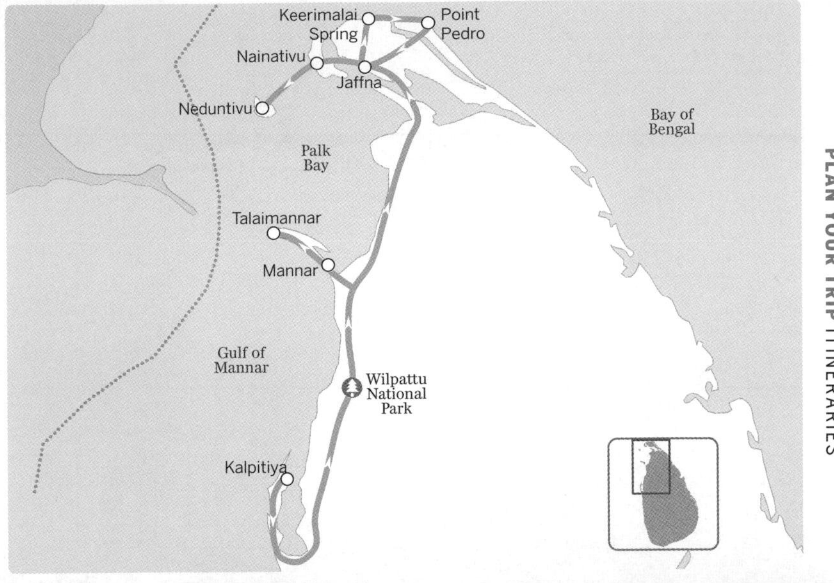

Two Weeks

Emerging Sri Lanka

With peace, parts of Sri Lanka that were off limits – or almost off limits – for decades are opening up to visitors, who will be warmly welcomed. Start at **Kalpitiya**, the main town on the long finger of land that juts up into the Indian Ocean. The beaches here are just OK but the kitesurfing and reef diving are spectacular. Hook your way around north to **Wilpattu National Park**. This treasure was closed for years during the war but is now returning to life. It has all of Sri Lanka's iconic animals and is very quiet.

Next, explore another spit of Sri Lanka extending into the sea: **Mannar** is technically an island but feels like a peninsula. It has white beaches, wild donkeys and incredible beauty. The remote town of **Talaimannar** feels like the end of the world. Here a chain of reefs and islets almost form a land bridge to India.

Hook around again to the Jaffna peninsula. **Jaffna** bears scars of the war, which still seems like a recent memory here. But the rich Tamil culture is returning and charming temples on shady backstreets await exploration.

Roads closed for years have reopened and you can visit **Keerimalai spring**, a sacred site with legendary bathing pools. It's close to the Naguleswaram Shiva Kovil, which traces its past to the 6th century BC.

Your next destination is **Point Pedro**, which is still shaking off the 2004 tsunami but holds onto traces of a colonial past. There is a long swath of the whitest beach you can imagine here.

Jaffna has nearby islands well worth exploring for their sheer minimalistic beauty. There's actual sights on **Nainativu**, which you reach via increasingly unsubstantial causeways and a ferry. Buddhist and Hindu temples draw the pious to this tiny speck of sand.

Another ferry ride – which is half the fun – takes you the 10km to **Neduntivu**, which some still call by its old Dutch moniker Delft. It's a windswept place beyond the end of the road and wild ponies roam seemingly deserted streets.

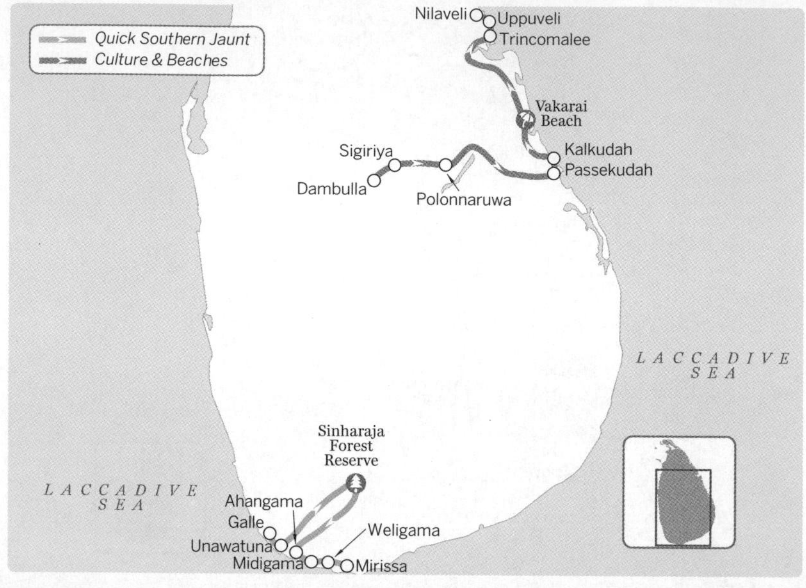

One Week
Quick Southern Jaunt

This fast trip will warm even the most frost-bitten visitor escaping a frigid winter elsewhere in the world. Begin your jaunt in **Galle**: founded by the Portuguese in the 16th century, it is one of Southeast Asia's best-preserved, fortified colonial cities. Walk the walls at sunset and enjoy the many cafes cropping up along streets lined with renovated and delightfully dilapidated old buildings.

Hit the beach at nearby **Unawatuna**, which has an alluring crescent of sand, cafes overlooking the surf and perfectly blue waters luring you in. Now find your inner Tarzan (many of the movies were shot in Sri Lanka) at the Unesco-recognised **Sinharaja Forest Reserve**, Sri Lanka's last major tropical rainforest.

Back on the south coast, Sri Lanka has a fast-breaking surf scene and you'll find lessons, board rentals and cheap surfer dives in **Ahangama** and **Midigama**.

Another short jaunt east brings you to **Weligama**, which has beach resorts and a lively fishing village with fascinating markets. Not far away is the sandy gem of the south, **Mirissa**, where cute little places to stay are hidden in the palms.

One Week
Culture & Beaches

This tour covers the uncrowded middle of Sri Lanka. Start in **Dambulla**, with its series of cave shrines painted with vivid Buddhist murals. From here it's a short jaunt to **Sigiriya**, a 200m-tall rock outcrop that was once a monastery and is truly one of the island's most amazing sights.

Further northeast the former royal capital of **Polonnaruwa** offers an inspiring collection of Buddhist sculptures and monastery ruins dating back nearly a thousand years. Head due east to the coast and the beaches at **Kalkudah** and **Passekudah**. The former is a deserted and beautiful broad strip of sand. The latter is also beautiful and draws locals by the busload.

Continue your beach adventures 20km north at one of Sri Lanka's hidden gems, **Vakarai Beach**. You're really off the grid here at this paradise and only have electricity a few hours at night.

Go north again and you are on the idyllic natural harbour of **Trincomalee**. It has a rich history going back centuries that the recent war couldn't erase. Finally, end your cultural and sandy trek at the dual beach towns of **Uppuveli** and **Nilaveli**. There's much debate about which is better: you decide.

Sri Lanka Sun, Sea & Sand

Best Beaches

Talk about opening a can of worms, but in the interest of sun-lounger debates across Sri Lanka here's our pick of the nation's finest stretches of sand.

Tangalla Tranquil tropical coves and endless sweeps of white sand mean Tangalla has something for everyone (p117).
Mirissa Many people's favourite south-coast beach resort and the best whale-watching base (p111).
Uppuveli Beach Stunning Uppuveli is the beach of choice on the east coast (p238).
Arugam Bay The best surf spot in the country and the most developed east-coast beach resort (p220).
Bentota An empty swath of golden sand backed by boutique hotels (p83).
Unawatuna Hardly undiscovered but undeniably beautiful and with a huge range of facilities (p103).

When to Go

Sri Lanka is pretty much a year-round beach destination. When it's raining in the East it's normally sunny in the West and vice versa.

» The main tourist season coincides with the northeast monsoon, which runs from December to March. At this time the beaches on the west and south coasts are bathed in sunshine and the tourist industry for this part of the country is in full swing. The east coast, by contrast, is often wet and many hotels are closed.

» Between May and September, when the stronger southwest monsoon hits the island and the southwest coast is drenched, head straight for the east coast, which sits in the rain shadow of the highlands and will be sunny and idyllic.

» Don't take the seasons as gospel, though: even during the height of the southwest monsoon it can often be sunny in the morning on the west-coast beaches before the afternoon thunderstorms roll in.

» The north of the island is generally much drier so you could come here any time and get your beach towel out.

Beaches

For many people the beach is Sri Lanka, and small though the island is, it really is no slouch in the sand and sea department.

» The west coast is the most developed beach area and is where the majority of the package-tour resorts can be found; but don't let that put you off because some of the beaches here are up there with the best in the country.

BEACH CULTURE IN THE NORTH & EAST

By and large Sri Lankans are an easygoing and accepting lot and on the south and west coasts they are also very used to foreign tourists and their skimpy beachwear. For much of the East and North, though, the situation is a little different: women in bathing suits, even modest one-piece numbers, can attract a lot of unwelcome attention. Even in the increasingly popular east-coast beach resorts such as Arugam Bay and the beaches north of Trincomalee the attention can be excessive (and there have been sexual assaults). On these beaches and especially in more remote locations, women will not want to travel alone, and should consider wearing a T-shirt and shorts into the water.

» With its stunning beaches, good selection of accommodation and activities that range from diving to sunning to surfing, it's no surprise that the south coast of the island is the most popular area with beach-bound independent travellers.

» War and unrest have kept the east-coast beaches largely off the radar of all but the most adventurous, but with peace big changes are afoot here and some absolute corking beaches are starting to get travellers' tongues wagging.

» Finally, there's the far north, where a beach to yourself isn't just a possibility but more of a given. However, only explorers need pack their beach things.

Safe Swimming

Every year drownings occur off Sri Lanka's beaches. If you aren't an experienced swimmer or surfer, it's easy to underestimate the dangers – or even to be totally unaware of them. There are few full-time lifesaving patrols, so there's usually no one to jump in and rescue you. A few common-sense rules should be observed:

» Don't swim out of your depth. If you are a poor swimmer, always stay in the shallows.

» Don't stay in the water when you feel tired.

» Never go swimming under the influence of alcohol or drugs.

» Supervise children at *all* times.

» Watch out for rips. Water brought onto the beach by waves is sucked back to sea and this current can be strong enough to drag you out with it. Rips in rough surf can sometimes be seen as calm patches in the disturbed water. It's best to check with someone reliable before venturing into the water.

» If you do get caught in a rip, swim *across* the current towards the breaking waves. The currents are usually less where the waves are actually breaking and the surf will push you shoreward. Never try and swim against the current. If it's too strong for you to do this, keep afloat and raise a hand so that someone on shore can see that you are in distress. A rip eventually weakens; the important thing is not to panic.

» Exercise caution when there is surf.

» Beware of coral; coming into contact with coral can be painful for the swimmer and fatal for the coral. Always check with someone reliable if you suspect the area you're about to swim in may have coral.

BEST BEACH FOR....

» **Diving & snorkelling** Pigeon Island (p240) off Nilaveli beach offers crystal waters, shallow reefs, colourful fish, and diving and snorkelling that's great for a beginner or the experienced.

» **Whale-watching** Whales can be seen all along the Sri Lankan coast but Mirissa is the best base for seeing the blue whales that splash past Dondra Head (p112).

» **Indulgence** Bentota beach (p83) has an unrivalled collection of sublime boutique hotels, and when you're done with pampering the beach itself ain't bad.

» **Solitude** We almost want to keep this one to ourselves, but seeing as you asked nicely... Talalla beach (p116) is utterly empty and utterly divine – for the moment.

» **Safe swimming** Unawatuna (p103), Passekudah (p234) and Uppuveli (p238) all vie with one another for title of calmest, safest swimming beach.

BEST DIVE SPOTS

» **Great Basses Reefs** (p126) Several kilometres off the southeast coast, these remote reefs are ranked by divers as about the best in the country. Eagle rays and white-tip sharks are the big fish to see here. And just in case you're interested, treasure from sunken ships has been found here too... But take note – it's for experts only.

» **Bar Reef** (p76) These offshore reefs in the northwest of the country offer pristine reef systems, masses of fish and dolphins and whales to boot, but again it's experienced divers only.

» **Pigeon Island** (p240) Accessible for beginners but still rewarding for experts, the beautiful, colour-splashed reefs off this pinprick of an island put a smile on everyone's face. Around 300 species of fish and other marine life has been seen in the waters around here. Also a great snorkelling spot.

» **Unawatuna** (p103) It's all about wreck diving here – one boat was even sunk exclusively for the purpose of improving the diving. Several dive schools, lots of facilities and good for all levels of experience.

» **Batticaloa** (p230) Calm waters and exploring the wreck of HMS *Hermes*, a WWII British naval ship.

» Never dive into the water. Hazards may be lurking under the surface or the water may not be as deep as it looks. It pays to be cautious.

Surfing

Sri Lanka has consistent surf year-round, but the quality of waves is far lower than the nearby Maldives and Indonesia. You visit Sri Lanka more for the culture, climate and ease of travelling than for the chance to get barrelled. Sri Lanka is, however, a superb place to learn how to surf or for intermediate surfers to get their first reef-break experiences. Many of the spots are very close to shore and surf access couldn't be easier, and this also makes Sri Lanka an ideal destination for a surfer with a non-surfing partner.

» Sri Lanka's best-known wave is Arugam Bay (p220) on the east coast. Surf's up at this long right point from April to October.

» Weligama (p110), on the south coast, seems custom-made for learning to surf and a number of surf schools and camps have recently sprung up there.

» On the west and south coasts, the best surfing is from November to April, with the start and end of this season more consistent than January and February (when, bizarrely, most surfers choose to visit).

» The reefs of Hikkaduwa (p87) on the west coast are a long-time favourite, although more for the ease of living than for the quality of the waves.

» The Midigama area (p108) is the best spot along the south coast, with a mellow left point, a nearby consistent beach break and a short and sharp right reef, which offers about the only frequently hollow wave in Sri Lanka.

» Boards can be hired (expect to pay Rs 300 to 500 per hour) and lessons are available at most beach towns; courses start at around €30.

» **Low Pressure Stormrider Guides** (www.lowpressure.co.uk) offers good advice on surfing Sri Lanka.

White-water Rafting, Canoeing & Boating

You don't have to be a beach babe to enjoy Sri Lankan water sports. High up in the hills, rivers tumble down mountains to produce some memorable rafting conditions.

» Currently the best-known white-water rafting area is near Kitulgala (p154), where a number of different operators can take you out on gentle river meanders (around US$30 per person) or, for experienced rafters, exciting descents of Class 4-5 rapids.

» **Adventure Sports Lanka** (☎011-279 1584; www.actionlanka.com) is the biggest player in Sri Lankan rafting and organises rafting expeditions to Kitulgala and elsewhere from its Colombo base.

» The Belihul Oya (p165) area of the Hill Country is also gaining a reputation for kayaking and other river-borne sports.

DREAMSTIME ©

» (above) Colourful underwater spectacle
» (left) White-water rafting outside Kitulgala (p153)

Back on salty water you can organise boat or catamaran trips for sightseeing, bird-watching or fishing around Negombo, Bentota and most east-coast beach resorts.

Windsurfing & Kitesurfing

Sri Lanka isn't renowned for its windsurfing or kitesurfing but that doesn't mean there's no action. Negombo (p79) has a well-run kitesurfing school that runs kiting trips up and down the coast. Further north, the Kalpitiya area (p76) is gaining a reputation for kitesurfing. Winds tend to be more consistent up here but for the moment facilities are few and far between.

On that note, the far north of Sri Lanka, around Munnar Island and the islands off Jaffna, have good windsurfing potential, but they remain very much off the beaten track.

Some top-end hotels and a couple of private water-sport operators around the Bentota area (p83) hire beaten-up sailboards. It's a good place for learners and lessons are possible; windsurfing courses cost around Rs 10,000.

Whale-watching & Dolphin-watching

Sri Lanka is fast gaining a reputation for being a world-class whale-watching location. The big attraction is big indeed – blue whales, the largest of all creatures. Mirissa (p111) is the best place from which to organise a whale-watching trip. On the east coast, Uppuveli (p238) and Nilaveli (p240) offer quieter but less-reliable whale-watching and in the northwest the Kalpitiya area (p76) is the new whale in town, although here schools of dolphins are more common than whales.

In all these places local boat tours are available, but it pays to go with someone who really knows what they're doing. In this respect **Jetwing Eco Holidays** (☎011-238 1201; www.jetwingeco.com; 46/26 Navam Mawatha, Colombo) and **Eco Team Sri Lanka** (☎011-583 0833; www.srilankaecotourism.com; 20/63 Fairfield Gardens, Colombo) are first-rate and offer whale-watching (and dolphin-watching) tours to all of these places.

The season for whales (and dolphins) off the south coast and Kalpitiya is from January to April, while on the east coast it runs from May to October.

RESPONSIBLE DIVING

Please consider the following tips when diving and help preserve the ecology and beauty of reefs:

» Never use anchors on the reef, and take care not to ground boats on coral.

» Avoid touching or standing on living marine organisms or dragging equipment across the reef. Polyps can be damaged by even the gentlest contact. If you must hold on to the reef, only touch exposed rock or dead coral.

» Be conscious of your fins. Even without contact, the surge from fin strokes near the reef can damage delicate organisms. Take care not to kick up clouds of sand, which can smother organisms.

» Practise and maintain proper buoyancy control. Major damage can be done by divers descending too fast and colliding with the reef.

» Take great care in underwater caves. Spend as little time within them as possible as your air bubbles may be caught within the roof and thereby leave organisms high and dry. Take turns to inspect the interior of a small cave.

» Resist the temptation to collect or buy corals or shells or to loot marine archaeological sites (mainly shipwrecks).

» Ensure that you take home all your rubbish and any litter you may find as well. Plastics in particular are a serious threat to marine life.

» Do not feed fish.

» Minimise your disturbance of marine animals.

Diving & Snorkelling

There are plenty of opportunities to live like a fish in Sri Lanka. Dive schools can be found all along the coast (except the far north) and you can slap on a snorkel almost anywhere. Diving and snorkelling in Sri Lanka is more about the fish than the reefs, but there are a few exceptions and wreck diving is also possible. Sri Lanka has the full dose of tropical Indian Ocean fish species including such pretty little numbers as angel fish, butterfly fish, surgeon fish and scorpion fish. Higher up the gnashing-teeth scale come the black- and white-tip sharks.

Along the west coast, the best time to dive and snorkel is generally from November to April. On the east coast, the seas are calmest from April to September. But at none of these times can underwater visibility be described as breathtaking.

Diving shops can be found in Colombo and in the major west-coast resorts. They hire and sell gear, including snorkelling equipment. PADI courses cost around €250 to €300 and are also available with the following respected dive schools:

» **Poseidon Diving Station** (p88), Hikkaduwa

» **Unawatuna Diving Centre** (p104), Unawatuna

» **Sport Diving** (p110), Weligama

» **Sri Lanka Diving Tours** (p231), Batticaloa

» **Poseidon Diving School** (p241), Nilaveli

Safety Guidelines for Diving

Before embarking on a scuba-diving or snorkelling trip, carefully consider the following points to ensure a safe and enjoyable experience:

» Possess a current diving certification card from a recognised scuba-diving instructional agency (if scuba diving).

» Be sure you are healthy and feel comfortable diving.

» Obtain reliable information about physical and environmental conditions at the dive site (eg from a reputable local dive operation).

» Dive only at sites within your realm of experience; if available, engage the services of a competent, professionally trained dive instructor or dive master.

National Parks & Safaris

Best Wildlife Experiences

Blue Whales Scan the horizon on a boat safari in search of the biggest creature ever to live (boxed text p112).

The Gathering Gasp as several hundred elephants gather on the banks of the Minneriya Lake in August (boxed text p201).

Dolphins Smile at the sight of playful schools of spinner dolphins hundreds strong (p76).

Turtles Watch baby turtles take their first uncertain steps in life as they scramble down the beach and swim out to sea (p117).

Leopards Creep slowly towards a leopard in Yala National Park (p127).

Bird Wave Learn the secrets of the bird wave in Sinharaja (p178).

Sri Lanka is one of the finest wildlife-watching countries in South Asia. The island may be small in size, but the variety of habitats, and the wildlife found there, would do justice to a country many times its size. Even a visitor with only the most casual of interest can't help but be overawed by the sight of great herds of elephants, enormous whales, elusive leopards, schools of dolphins, hundreds of colourful birds, and reefs teeming with rainbow-coloured fish.

The Sri Lankan tourism industry hasn't been slow to cotton onto the country's wildlife-watching potential and an impressive array of national parks, protected zones and safari options exist that allow anyone, from dedicated naturalist to interested lay person, to get out there with a pair of binoculars and make the most of the Sri Lankan wilderness.

Wildlife

For its size, Sri Lanka boasts an incredible diversity of animalia: 92 mammal species, 242 butterflies, 435 birds, 107 fish, 98 snakes and more. Given the fragility of the environment in which they live (see p280), it should come as no surprise that quite a few are vulnerable.

BEST PLACES FOR ELEPHANTS

» **Uda Walawe National Park** With around 500 elephants present year-round, this park offers the most reliable elephant-spotting in the country (p176).

» **Minneriya National Park** Each August hundreds of elephants home in on this park in an elephant spectacle known as 'the Gathering' (p201).

» **Kaudulla National Park** Over 250 elephants call this park home (p201).

» **Bundala National Park** Consistent elephant sightings in a beautiful watery setting (p121).

» **Yala National Park** Lots of elephants but surprisingly hard to see (p127).

» **Gal Oya National Park** Arguably the best park in the east for elephants (p229).

Mammals

Sri Lanka's mammals include some of the most easily observable of the country's animal species, as well as some of the most invisible. Hard to spot are the solitary and mostly nocturnal leopard, Sri Lanka's top predator; the scavenging golden jackal; the shaggy sloth bear; the civet (a catlike hunter related to the weasel); the mongoose; and the shy, armour-plated Indian pangolin, with overlapping scales made from modified hair.

Very audible but not always visible are troops of tree-bound cackling primates, like common langurs, also known as Hanuman or grey langurs; endemic purple-faced langurs; hairy bear monkeys; and toque macaques, notable for their distinctive 'dos – a thatch of middle-parted hair. The slow movements of the slender loris belie its ability to snatch its prey with a lightning-quick lunge.

More often crossed, albeit at different times of the day, are the majestic Asian elephant; the omnivorous and tusked wild boar of Sri Lanka; and cervine creatures like the big, maned sambar and smaller white-spotted Axis deer. The bushy-tailed, five-striped palm squirrel is commonly seen scurrying around gardens and town parks. These are often also the locations of the large trees in which Indian flying foxes (large fruit-eating bats) camp by the hundreds.

Mammals don't just hide out in the forests and savannahs. The biggest of all mammals are to be found in the waters off Sri Lanka. Blue whales and slightly smaller sperm whales swim along migration corridors off the coast here. The area around Dondra Head, at the southern tip of the country, is being hyped as the best place in the world to see blue whales.

Birds

A tropical climate, long isolation from the Asian mainland and a diversity of habitats have helped endow Sri Lanka with an astonishing abundance of birdlife. There are more than 400 species, 26 of which are unique to Sri Lanka; others are found only in Sri Lanka and adjacent South India. Of the estimated 198 migrant species, most of which are in residence from August to April, the waders (sandpipers, plovers etc) are the long-distance champions, making the journey from their breeding grounds in the Arctic tundra.

Birders may wish to contact the **Field Ornithology Group of Sri Lanka** (www.fogsl.net), the national affiliate of Birdlife International.

Tips for Birdwatchers

» Visit a variety of habitats – rainforest, urban parks and bodies of water in the dry zone – to see the full diversity of birdlife in Sri Lanka.

» February to March is the best time for birdwatching. You miss the monsoons, and the migrant birds are still visiting.

» Waterbirds are active for most of the day.

» Although morning is always the best time to go birdwatching, in the evening you will see noisy flocks of birds preparing to roost.

» A pair of binoculars is an invaluable tool to help with identification. Small models can be bought cheaply duty-free, and don't weigh much.

» Consider taking a tour with a specialist if you're keen to see the endemic species and achieve a healthy birdwatching tally, particularly if time is short.

Planning Your Safari

Where to Go

Where to go depends entirely on what you want to see and what kind of safari you want to take. For example Yala National Park (p127) in the far southeast is the most popular overall park and is fantastic for leopards, but it's also very busy and can become something of a circus with minibuses chasing each other around in search of cats. If you want your leopard-spotting quieter (and less certain) try Wilpattu National Park (boxed text, p77), although you'll have to cope with much more basic facilities.

National Parks & Reserves

More than 2000 years ago, enlightened royalty declared certain land areas off limits to any human activity. Almost every province in the ancient kingdom of Kandy had such *udawattakelle* (sanctuaries). All animals and plants in these reserves were left undisturbed.

Today's system of parks and reserves is mostly an amalgamation of traditionally protected areas, reserves established by the British, and newly gazetted areas set aside for things like elephant corridors. There are more than 100 of these areas under government guard, covering approximately 8% of the island. They are divided into three types: strict nature reserves (no visitors allowed), national parks (visits under fixed conditions) and nature reserves (human habitation permitted). Sri Lanka also has two marine sanctuaries – the Bar Reef (west of Kalpitiya peninsula) and Hikkaduwa National Park (see p88).

Off the Beaten Track

A full 82% of Sri Lanka's land is controlled by the state in some form or another, and is therefore subject to a raft of legislation to combat destructive activity and protect sensitive areas like the scores of natural forests. The boxed text on p38 only includes information about 11 of the 20 national parks and three other green spaces from among the 63 sanctuaries, a long list of forest reserves and countless wetlands both with and without official titles.

Given the overcrowding at some of the better-known natural areas, new attention has been directed to other deserving national parks, such as Lunugamvehera (which serves as a link between Yala and Uda Walawa National Parks, allowing elephants to pass freely between the two) as an alternative to Yala, and Wasgomuwa instead of Gal Oya or Minneriya.

Sri Lanka is a signatory to the Ramsar Convention on Wetlands, which currently recognises three coastal zones: Bundala National Park (p121); the 915-hectare Madu Ganga Estuary near Balapitiya, 80km south of Colombo on the A2, site of one of the last pristine mangrove forests in Sri Lanka; and the Annaivilundawa Tanks Wildlife Sanctuary, just west of the A3 about 100km north of Colombo, a cluster of ancient, manmade, freshwater reservoirs that are now a safe haven for awesome wetland biodiversity.

For further listings of out-of-the-way green escapes, contact the government conservation departments or consult *LOCALternative Sri Lanka – a responsible travel map* (www.localternative.com).

When to Go

Sri Lanka is a year-round wildlife-watching destination but generally the best times correspond with the main November-to-April tourist season. At this time of year all the big parks are open and the dry conditions mean that animals start to gather around water holes, making them easier to spot (this is

BEST PLACES FOR BIRDS

- **Sinharaja Forest Reserve** A slab of rainforest with around 160 bird species (p178).
- **Knuckles Range** Little-known montane forests filled with hill-country and forest birds (p150).
- **Bundala National Park** This wetland park is the classic Sri Lankan birdwatching destination (p121).
- **Yala & Kumana National Parks** Superb low country birdwatching with around 150 species present (p127 and p228).
- **Muthurajawela Marsh** Excellent wetland birding close to Colombo (p82).
- **Pottuvil Lagoon** Numerous waders and waterbirds in this little-visited east-coast wetland (p226).

MAJOR NATIONAL PARKS & RESERVES

PARK	AREA	FEATURES	BEST TIME TO VISIT
Bundala National Park (p121)	62.2 sq km	coastal lagoon, migratory birds, elephants	year-round
Gal Oya National Park (p229)	629.4 sq km	grasslands, evergreen forest, deer, Senanayake Samudra (tank), elephants, sloth bears, leopards, water buffaloes	Dec-Sep
Horton Plains National Park (p163)	31.6 sq km	Unesco World Heritage Site, montane forests, marshy grasslands, World's End precipice, sambars	Dec-Mar
Kaudulla National Park (p201)	66.6 sq km	Kaudulla Tank, evergreen forest, scrub jungle, grassy plains, elephants, leopards, sambars, fishing cats, sloth bears	Aug-Dec
Knuckles Range (p150)	175 sq km	Unesco World Heritage Site, traditional villages, hiking trails, caves, waterfalls, montane pygmy forest, evergreen forest, riverine forest, grasslands, scrub, paddy fields, 31 mammal species	Dec-May
Kumana National Park (p228)	181.5 sq km	grassland, jungle, lagoons, mangrove swamp, waterfowl	May-Sep
Lunugamvehera National Park	235 sq km	grasslands, reservoir, elephants	May-Sep
Minneriya National Park (p201)	88.9 sq km	Minneriya Tank, toque macaques, sambars, elephants, waterfowl	May-Sep
Sinharaja Forest Reserve (p178)	189 sq km	Unesco World Heritage Site, sambars, rainforest, leopards, purple-faced langurs, barking deer, 147 recorded bird species	Aug-Sep, Jan-Mar
Sri Pada Peak Wilderness Reserve (p150)	192 sq km	Unesco World Heritage Site, Adam's Peak, hiking trails	Dec-May
Uda Walawe National Park (p176)	308.2 sq km	grassland, thorn scrub, elephants, spotted deer, water buffaloes, wild boar	year-round
Wasgomuwa National Park	393.2 sq km	evergreen forest, hilly ridges, grassy plains, elephants, leopards, sloth bears	Jun-Sep
Wilpattu National Park (boxed text, p77)	1317 sq km	dense jungle, scrub, saltgrass, elephants, leopards, sloth bears, deer, crocodiles	Jan-Mar
Yala National Park (p127)	141 sq km	tropical thornforest, lagoons, elephants, sloth bears, leopards, water buffaloes, lesser flamingos	Nov-Jul

especially so between February and early April). If you come in the May-to-October southwest monsoon season, head to the parks around the Ancient Cities and in the east of the island.

The north of the country remains much more of an unknown quantity for wildlife viewing, and there are currently no protected areas open to the public, but that is likely to change fast.

FIELD GUIDES & WILDLIFE BOOKS

There are plenty of good field guides out there. These are some of our favourites:

» **A Photographic Guide to Mammals of Sri Lanka** (Gehan de Silva Wijeyeratne) This well-known Sri Lankan naturalist has also published extensively on the country's birds and butterflies, among other things. The same author has also written *Sri Lankan Wildlife*, published by Bradt Travel Guides.

» **A Selection of the Birds of Sri Lanka** (John and Judy Banks) A slim, well-illustrated tome that's perfect for amateur birdwatchers.

» **A Field Guide to the Birds of Sri Lanka** (John Harrison) A pricier hardback with colour illustrations; one of the best field guides available.

» **The Nature of Sri Lanka** With stunning photographs by L Nadaraja, this is a collection of essays about Sri Lanka by eminent writers and conservationists.

» **What Tree Is That?** (Sriyanie Miththapala and PA Miththapala) Contains handy sketches of common trees and shrubs in Sri Lanka, and includes English, Sinhala and botanical names.

How to Book

For all the major national parks and other protected areas organising a safari couldn't be easier. Groups of safari jeep drivers can normally be found in the nearest town or gathered outside the gates, and hotels can also organise a safari. It's normally just a case of turning up the evening before and discussing a price and your needs. Entry fees to all parks are paid directly at entrance gates. See under each park in the On The Road section for more detailed information.

Department of Forest Conservation (☎011-286 6632; forlib@sltnet.lk; 82 Rajamalwatta, Battaramulla) Administers some areas, like Sinharaja and the Knuckles Range.

Department of Wildlife Conservation (☎011-256 0380; 382 New Kandy Rd, Malambe) Manages all national parks; direct all enquiries and park lodging requests (circuit bungalows or campsites) here.

Eco Team Sri Lanka (☎011-583 0833; www.srilankaecotourism.com; 20/63 Fairfield Gardens, Colombo) Eco Team and Jetwing are the best tour operators in Sri Lanka, and can organise tours before you leave home.

Jetwing Eco Holidays (☎011-238 1201; www.jetwingeco.com; 46/26 Navam Mawatha, Colombo)

Naturetrek (www.naturetrek.co.uk) UK-based company worth noting for its highly regarded tours that include such unusual holidays as a butterfly-watching tour and endemic birds tour as well as more standard wildlife-watching tours. There are many other international wildlife-watching tour companies also operating in Sri Lanka.

Travel with Children

Best Regions for Kids

Colombo

Yes it's chaotic and at times noxious but the capital also has plenty of cool things that kids, albeit older kids, will enjoy, such as the mad markets of Pettah.

West Coast

It's beaches, baby, all along this sandy coast. There are all manner of relaxed resorts where you can relax and maybe build a castle or two.

The South

More beaches plus the cool environs of the Fort. (It's a *real* fort!) And in the west there's elephants.

The Hill Country

Waterfalls are literally cool places to hang out. Plus the mild temperatures are a good respite from the heat elsewhere. Tea plantations and trains are an unbeatable day out.

The Ancient Cities

Ancient temples, forts, ruins, jungle and elephants. Hello Indiana Jones!

Sri Lanka for Kids

Like a good rice and curry, Sri Lanka offers a dazzling array of choices. This is obviously not a first-world country, so the child who expects a packaged Disneyland experience won't be happy. It's the real world, but a real world it is. There's enough to see and do to keep a family busy for weeks.

Although practical details may be a challenge at times, your time will be eased by the Sri Lankans themselves. They love children and they'll go out of their way to help you if you're travelling with kids. We've watched a grimly serious driver suddenly melt and start playing the silliest games with a client's youngster.

Eating with Kids

Sri Lankan hospitality means that people will go to any length to please young and finicky eaters; most places have a few Western-style dishes.

To ease your children into Sri Lankan food, try a breakfast of *pittu*. The coconut-rice combination will be kind to their palates. Also try hoppers, especially the string variety or, nice and mild *rotti*.

The profusion of fresh and exciting varieties of fruit should mean that everybody will find something they like.

TRAVELLING WITH A TODDLER *STUART BUTLER*

We travelled with our 22-month-old son around the west and south coasts and the Hill Country. I'd be lying if I said it was all plain sailing and if I said it was always a perfectly relaxing holiday! However, it was certainly rewarding and travelling with him was a real ice-breaker with both local people and other tourists, plus our son absolutely adored Sri Lanka.

A few points to note: few places have baby beds. We knew this and came with our own but we met many other couples with young children who ended up sleeping in the same bed as their toddler for the whole time. It was, in their words, 'Not as romantic a holiday as we hoped!' You should also bring a mosquito net to cover them as hotels rarely have spares.

Always order your child's meal well in advance, otherwise by the time the food arrives they'll be too tired to eat. Our son loves curry, fruit, fish and curd so we had no issues getting him to actually eat. If yours won't eat this then pasta is normally available in tourist areas.

Some people travel by public transport but we hired a car and driver for the duration, which had the added bonus of meaning we had a babysitter on hand!

Without any doubt it was easier to travel along the coast than the hills (where attractions are more for adults). If you really want to make things easy for yourself then just choose one beach, make a base and take day trips from there.

Nappies (diapers), even if they're the same brand you use at home, don't seem to work as well and rarely made it through the night. The size scale is also smaller, so if you buy mediums at home you'll need large in Sri Lanka.

Children's Highlights

There aren't many attractions dedicated solely to children in Sri Lanka, but there are a lot of sights they'll love.

» **Pinnewala Elephant Orphanage** Near Kandy, a home for elephants with up to 80 ready to interact with visitors.

» **Millennium Elephant Foundation** A smaller, grassroots version of Pinnewala (which is nearby), with fewer pachyderms and smaller crowds.

» **Uda Walawe** One of the best national parks for wildlife-spotting safaris.

» **Elephant Transit Home** Not far from Uda Walawe, this is a well-regarded halfway house for injured and orphaned elephants.

» **Minneriya** A national park renowned for its herds of elephants.

» **Turtle hatcheries** On the west coast, these are popular.

» **Polhena** Near Matara, the beach here is safe and shallow for little ones.

» **Polonnaruwa** Kids can literally run themselves silly at the vast and car-free ancient heritage sites such as this one, with their very cool ruins.

» **Three-wheelers** Buzzing, blowing and completely unlike any ride anyplace else, these ubiquitous transport options are good for a thrill.

» **Backwater boat trips** These will also keep kids amused.

Planning & Practicalities

» Sri Lankan hotels and guesthouses invariably have triple and family rooms, plus extra beds are supplied on demand. Most restaurants don't supply highchairs.

» For very young children, a dilemma is to bring either a backpack carrier or a pram/stroller. If you can, bring both. Prams have tough going on uneven or nonexistent footpaths but are worthwhile in Colombo and Kandy.

» Check if your hired car (with driver) has a child's seat. If not, you can get one in Colombo.

» Buy pharmaceutical supplies, imported baby food and disposable nappies at Cargills Food City and Keells supermarkets throughout the country.

» Breastfeeding in public is accepted, but parents will struggle with finding dedicated baby-changing rooms. It's not a major problem as it's acceptable for toddlers to be naked in public.

» Rabies and animal-borne parasites are present in Sri Lanka, so keep children away from stray animals, including cats, dogs and monkeys.

» Bring suncream and children's mosquito repellent with you because you won't find it in Sri Lanka.

regions at a glance

Colombo

Sunsets ✓✓
Urban Life ✓✓✓
Shopping ✓✓

Sunsets
Built right up to the shores of the Indian Ocean, Colombo faces west into the setting sun. Many evenings begin with an explosion of magenta and purple on the horizon that you can share with others at a hotel bar or with the real people along the shore.

Urban Life
The first time you almost get run down by a madman with a cart full of goods in the markets of Pettah, you may regret your decision to come. But soon you'll be in the chaotic thick of things and on the ride away, you'll be urging your three-wheeler driver to go faster, faster!

Shopping
From artworks to tea, you can find unique and desirable goods and gifts in Colombo, especially along the leafy streets of Cinnamon Gardens.

p46

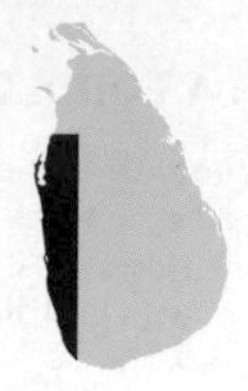

West Coast

Beaches ✓✓
Activities ✓✓✓
Lodging ✓✓

Beaches
From all-inclusive package-tour resorts to former hippy hangouts and little-visited sands, the beaches of the west coast span all the spectrums and keep everyone happy.

Activities
Ride the waves and dive the reefs of Hikkaduwa, birdwatch on the marshes, explore the back blocks and see the dolphins in the north and get pampered in a spa and take a boat safari around Bentota.

Accommodation
The beaches around Bentota are home to some breathtaking boutique hotels that rank among the finest in the country. Cheerful Negombo also contains some memorable accommodation.

p74

The South

Beaches ✓✓✓
Activities ✓✓✓
Wildlife ✓✓✓

Beaches
There are beaches here with lots going on and a real traveller vibe or there are beaches with barely another person in sight, but the uniting factor is that they're almost all stunning.

Activities
In these parts it's all about surfing and diving. The area between Galle and Matara is arguably the finest slice of surf country in South Asia; for divers there's everything from wrecks to reefs to big fish.

Wildlife
Monkeys crash through the trees, whales splash through the seas, leopards slink through the night, birds flap through the skies, turtles emerge on the beach and naturalists can't stop smiling.

p93

The Hill Country

Walking ✓✓
Wildlife ✓✓✓
Eating ✓✓✓

Walking
Hack through jungles, shiver over high plateaus, traipse to vertigo-inspiring viewpoints, tip-toe through tea plantations and walk in the footsteps of gods.

Wildlife
No other part of Sri Lanka offers such varied wildlife habitats. There's steamy rainforests filled with noisy birds, grassland savannahs ruled by elephants, and highland forests covered in delicate lichens and moss.

Eating
Eating in Sri Lanka is rarely anything but a pleasure but it's in the Hill Country where the preparation, and consumption, of food becomes an art form, and the best food comes from your guesthouse kitchen.

p130

The Ancient Cities

Monuments ✓✓✓
Temples ✓✓✓
Cycling ✓✓

Ancient Monuments
The Polonnaruwa Quadrangle, the ancient quarter of Anuradhapura, the jaw-dropping sight of the rock monastery at Sigiriya: just some of the remarkable ruins ready for exploration.

Temples
Amid the leaf-shrouded ruins of Anuradhapura is Sri Maha Bodhi, a tree that has seen history and devotion for 2000 years. Other temples, such as the one up over 1800 steps in Mihintale, will inspire your own devotion.

Cycling
The ruins of the Ancient Cities are sited within much larger parks and reserves. You can pedal between the wonders along palm-shaded paths and never see a car. Guesthouses have bikes for hire.

p181

The East

Beaches ✓✓✓
Activities ✓✓✓
Wildlife ✓

Beaches
Most of the east coast's miles upon miles of beaches are untouched, but even those that are developed are sandy wonderlands, with just the right amounts of palm trees, white sands and low-key scenes.

Activities
The East generously provides activities to alternate with napping on beach hammocks. The ocean here isn't just calm and gorgeous, but it has the reefs and wrecks for great snorkelling and diving, and the right waves for surfing.

Wildlife
Kumana National Park doesn't have the size (or the leopard population) of its neighbour Yala. However, it also lacks Yala's tourist population, which means the leopards, elephants and birds here are all yours.

p217

Jaffna & the North

Rediscovery ✓
Temples ✓✓✓
Islands ✓✓✓

Off the Beaten Path
All but shut down to travel for years, the North is now ready to be explored. The going is rough and rocky, but seeing glimpses of war history is powerfully moving.

Temples
Hindu gods and goddesses painted in exquisite riots of colours animate towering temple gateways all over the North. Even better, though, are the friendly priests and devotees who will welcome you to *puja* (prayer).

Islands & Seashores
Seemingly endless coastlines curl around the Jaffna region's mainland and islands. Coast roads, causeways and wooden-boat rides to isolated islands are only second to the islands' sublime beauty.

p243

Every listing is recommended by our authors, and their favourite places are listed first

Look out for these icons:

TOP CHOICE Our author's top recommendation

A green or sustainable option

No payment required

See the Index for a full list of destinations covered in this book.

On the Road

Colombo

☎ 011 / POP 2.4 MILLION

Includes »

Best Places to Eat

- AVP Restaurant (p64)
- Hotel De Pilawoos (p65)
- Gallery Cafe (p65)
- Bu Ba (p67)

Best Places to Stay

- Lake Lodge (p60)
- Cinnamon Grand Hotel (p60)
- Havelock Place Bungalow (p62)
- Casa Colombo (p62)

Why Go?

Colombo is rapidly emerging from the bad rap it has carried for decades. No longer just the sprawling city you have to endure on your way to the southern beaches, it has become a worthy destination in its own right. New restaurants, designer shops and other attractions open constantly.

The legacies of colonial Colombo are still very much intact along its often shady boulevards. Fort is in the midst of widespread historic restoration while Pettah brims with markets and rampant commerce.

Even traffic-clogged Galle Rd is getting spiffier, while the seafront benefits from new roads that are spurring hotel construction. Colombo's cosmopolitan side supports stylish cafes, interesting stores, galleries and museums. Surprises abound in its old quarters. You can easily spend a couple of days exploring this vibrant city and a visit here is an excellent start – or finish – to your Sri Lankan adventures.

When to Go

Colombo

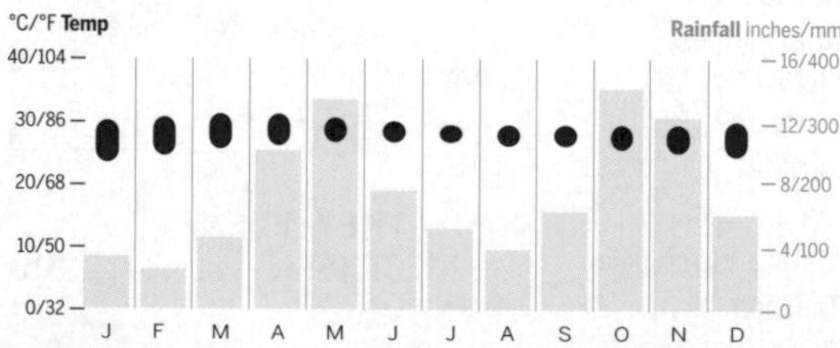

Jan–Mar The driest season, with night-time cool breezes. More tourists, so book hotels in advance.

Apr Colombo feels empty around the Sinhalese New Year as people return to their home villages.

Dec Although Christians are a minority, Christmas is popular and decorations are everywhere.

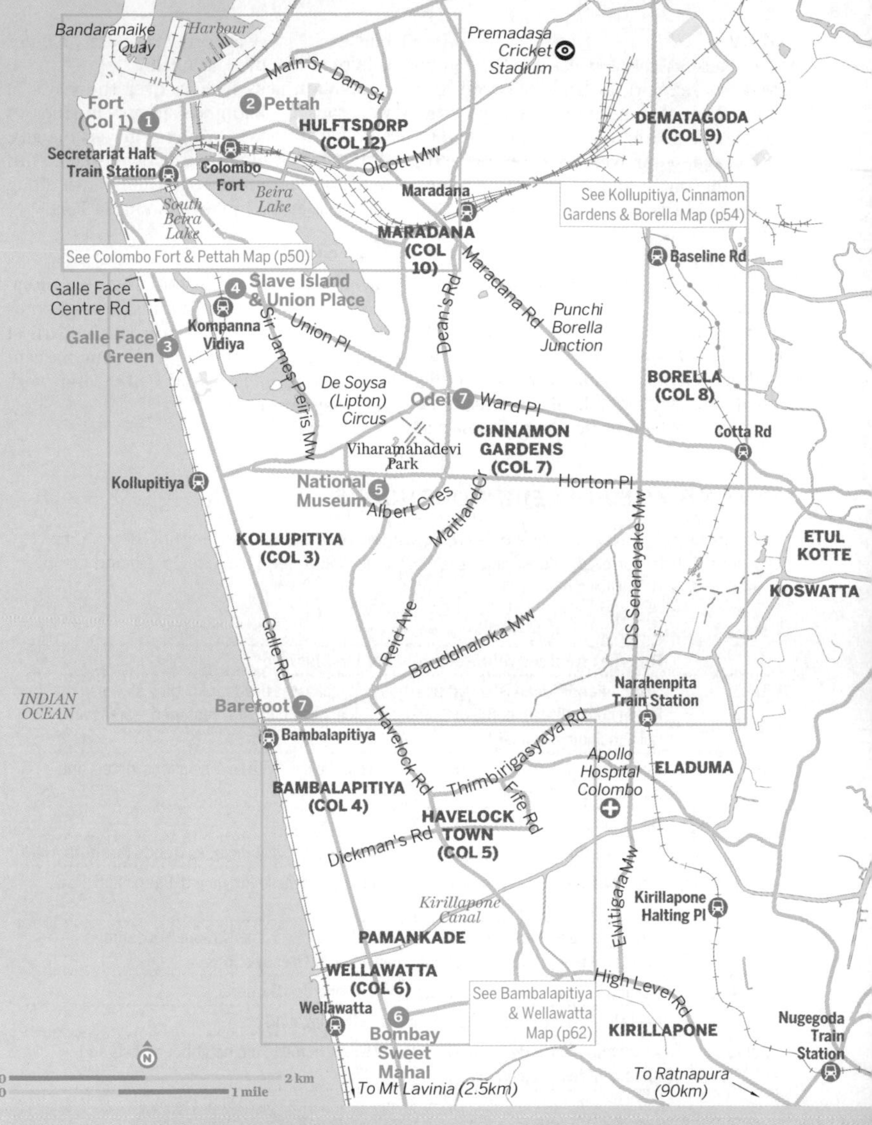

Colombo Highlights

1. Revelling in the restoration of the historic **Fort area** (p49)

2. Plunging into the commercial madness of the shops, stalls and markets of ages-old **Pettah** (p49)

3. Catching a sunset amid families and courting couples on Colombo's front lawn, **Galle Face Green** (p51)

4. Strolling the ancient quarters of **Slave Island** and **Union Place** (p52) before they fall to new glitzy developments

5. Walking through Sri Lanka's history in the remarkable **National Museum** (p53), which is right in the city's heart near Viharamahadevi Park

6. Enjoying a traditional Indian sweet at **Bombay Sweet Mahal** (p66), one of many locally beloved candy shops along Galle Rd

7. Shopping at creative local stores such as **Odel** and **Barefoot** (p69), where you can browse some of Sri Lanka's most interesting merchandise

History

As far back as the 5th century, Colombo served as a sea port for trade between Asia and the West. During the 8th century Arab traders settled near the port, and in 1505 the Portuguese arrived. By the mid-17th century the Dutch had taken over, growing cinnamon in the area now known as Cinnamon Gardens, but it wasn't until the British arrived that the town became a city. In 1815 Colombo was proclaimed the capital of Ceylon.

During the 1870s the breakwaters were built and Fort was created by flooding surrounding wetlands. Colombo was peacefully handed over when Sri Lanka achieved independence in 1948. A new parliament was built in Sri Jayawardenepura-Kotte, an outer suburb of Colombo, in 1982.

Bomb attacks in Fort over the years of war caused Colombo's major businesses and institutions to disperse across the city. With peace, Colombo is growing fast, with much development north and south along the coast and a building boom in Fort.

Sights

Lacking signature must-see sights, Colombo's real appeal lies in its many neighbourhoods, which span an era from the earliest colonial days to the city's present nascent boom. Start in Fort and Pettah and work your way south.

COLOMBO'S MAIN NEIGHBOURHOODS

Colombo is split into 15 postal-code areas, which are often used to identify the specific districts. Pettah, for example, is also referred to as Colombo 11 (or just Col 11) and so on. The main areas of interest:

ZONE	SUBURB
Col 1	**Fort** The revitalised centre of the city, historic and chic
Col 2	**Slave Island** Not an island at all (though it really was used for keeping slaves in the Dutch colonial era); some of Colombo's oldest – and most threatened – areas are here, including Union Pl
Col 3	**Kollupitiya** The dense commercial heart of the city, with myriad shops, hotels and businesses along Galle Rd
Col 4	**Bambalapitiya** An extension of Col 3
Col 5	**Havelock Town** Gentrifying southern extension of Col 4 includes trendy Stratford Ave
Col 6	**Wellawatta** More commercial sprawl south along Galle Rd. Inland, Pamankade is a newly stylish enclave
Col 7	**Cinnamon Gardens** Colombo's swankiest district has the National Museum, Viharamahadevi Park, old colonial mansions and trendy shops
Col 8	**Borella** The quieter eastern extension of Cinnamon Gardens
Col 11	**Pettah** Old quarter just east of Fort, with thriving markets
Col 13	**Kotahena** Alongside the port north of Pettah, home to old neighbourhoods and important religious buildings

Navigating Colombo

Colombo's spine is Galle Rd, which starts just south of Fort and runs all the way to its namesake city in the south. Along the way, it passes the old beach resort of Mt Lavinia, which isn't officially part of Colombo but is definitely within its urban sprawl. Development is also frenzied all the way to the airport 30km north.

Note that street numbers start again each time you move into a new district. Thus there will be a '100 Galle Rd' in several different neighbourhoods.

Some Colombo streets have both an old English name and a post-independence Sinhala name. Ananda Coomaraswamy Mawatha is also known as Green Path, for example, while RA de Mel Mawatha is still known as Duplication Rd. For longer stays, the 96-page *A-Z Street Guide* is useful; Google Maps are up to date and accurate.

COLOMBO IN...

One Day

Start at the bustling markets of **Pettah**, taking time for small Hindu temples and the **Dutch Period Museum**. Head west to **Fort** and pause to appreciate the restoration of colonial gems like the **Old Dutch Hospital**. Have an excellent local lunch at **AVP Restaurant**.

In the afternoon visit the eclectic Buddhist **Gangaramaya Temple** and wander down to **Viharamahadevi Park**. Later, take a stroll along the oceanfront with Sri Lankan families at **Galle Face Green** as the sun sets and enjoy a snack from a vendor.

Two Days

Grab a *kotthu* (a *rotti* chopped and fried with a variety of ingredients) at **Hotel De Pilawoos** before tackling the excellent **National Museum**. Afterwards, go shopping at the many excellent stores and boutiques in leafy **Cinnamon Gardens** and **Kollupitiya**. For dinner, join the smart set at **Gallery Cafe** or crack your way into shellfish sitting on the sand at **Beach Wadiya**.

FORT

During the European era Fort was indeed a fort, surrounded by the sea on two sides and a moat on the landward sides. Today it's literally at the centre of Colombo's resurgence, with grand old colonial-era buildings being restored amid a mix of modern structures, such as the World Trade Center.

Security remains in evidence in this area as the president's official residence and various government ministries are here. You may have to detour around a bit but it's a compact area and can be appreciated on a short stroll. Start at the **Old Galle Buck Lighthouse** (Map p50), which has excellent seafront views. It was built in 1954 and is surrounded by old canons.

Just north, look for the large white dagoba (stupa) of **Sambodhi Chaitiya** (Map p50), perched about 20m off the ground on stilts – a landmark for sea travellers. The **clock tower** (Map p50) at the junction of Chatham St and Janadhipathi Mawatha (once Queen St) was originally a lighthouse that was built in 1857.

Chatham St is seeing a lot of renovation of old buildings, one of the grandest being the old colonnaded **Central Bank** (Map p50). Just north, Sir Baron Jayatilaka Mawatha has the grandly restored **Lloyd's Buildings** (Map p50), which are in sharp contrast to the battered old hulk on the east side. Local retail giant Cargills once had its **main store** (Map p50) on York St: the now mostly empty ornate red building still shows its faded elegance in its long arcades that still have old store signage such as the one noting 'toilet requisites'.

The busy harbour on the north side of Fort is mostly walled off but you can enjoy sweeping views from the tiny terrace of the otherwise humdrum top-floor cafe of the **Grand Oriental Hotel** (Map p50; 2 York St, Col 1; ⏲7am-9pm).

TOP CHOICE **Old Dutch Hospital** HISTORIC BUILDING
(Map p50; Bank of Ceylon Mawatha, Col 1) Centrepiece of the newly vibrant Fort, this colonial-era complex dates back to the early 1600s. Lavishly restored, it is home to shops, cafes and restaurants run by some of Colombo's best operators. Enjoy a pause for a cold drink amid the incredibly thick columns of its arcades.

St Peter's Church CHURCH
(Map p50; ⏲7am-5pm) Reached along the arcade on the north side of the Grand Oriental Hotel, this church was converted from the Dutch governor's banquet hall and was first used as a church in 1821. Inside it has an original wood ceiling and myriad plaques attesting to its work with seamen through the years.

PETTAH

Immediately inland from Fort, the bustling bazaar of Pettah is one of the oldest districts in Colombo and one of the most interesting places to spend a few hours. It is the most ethnically mixed place in the country. Large religious buildings represent a plethora of faiths, while more earthly pursuits can be found in market stalls and shops selling seemingly everything.

Colombo Fort & Pettah

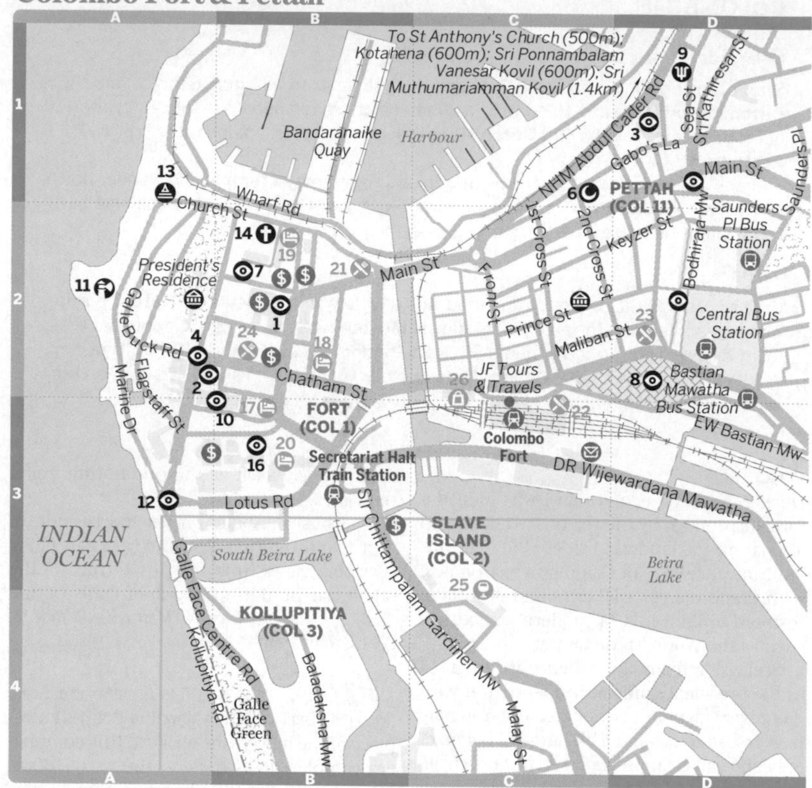

Many thoroughfares have their own shopping specialities:

1st Cross St at Bankshall St	plastic flowers
2nd Cross St at Bankshall St	lace & ribbons
2nd Cross St	jewellery
Gabo's Lane at 5th Cross St	Ayurvedic medicines
Dam St	bicycles

The crowds in Pettah can become overwhelming during the morning and late-afternoon rush hours but the streets are still thronged during most daylight hours. Vendors hurrying with carts piled with impossible loads, zooming three-wheelers, cars trying to fit down narrow lanes and people rushing hither and yon can make for an exhausting experience. Your best bet is to find a shady spot out of traffic and just observe the timeless swirl around you. Wolfendhal Lane is a typical side-street refuge: wander past its pirated-DVD and textile stores and exchange gentle 'hellos' with the locals.

TOP CHOICE Old City Hall HISTORIC BUILDING

(Map p50; Main St, Col 11; ⌚8am-5pm Mon-Sat) Dating to 1865, this municipal building from the British era is mostly empty today, save for some old trucks and municipal equipment on display in the ground-floor galleries. But let the attendants (tip them Rs 100) lead you up the vintage mahogany stairs and you'll discover a virtual waxworks in the old council chambers. There, covered in dust, are replicas of the town's first councillors in 1906. It's slightly comic and ghoulish, especially given the green glow from the stained glass. Views from the windows put you above the hubbub outside.

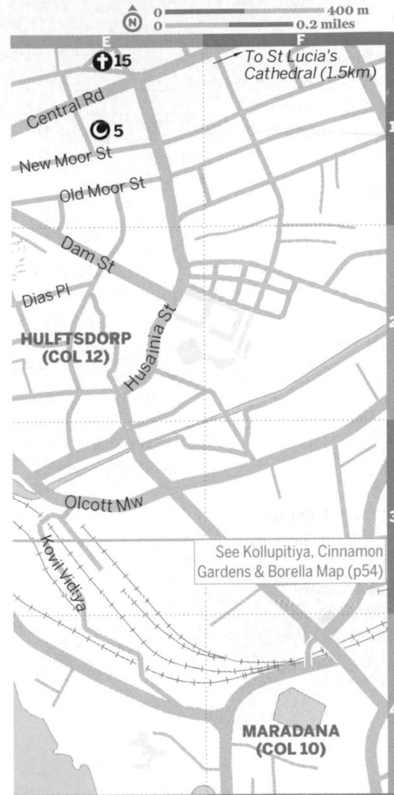

Markets MARKETS

(Map p50) The concentrated and manic commerce of Pettah is concentrated even further in its markets. Just east of Fort train station, **Manning Market** is ripe with everything grown in Sri Lanka. It's the city's wholesale fruit and veg centre and is a monkey's dream of bananas. The **Federation of Self Employees Market** stretches along 5th Cross St and is a hive of household goods and food. Much of the same can be found in the five floors of the **Central Market**.

Dutch Period Museum HISTORIC MUSEUM

(Map p50; 95 Prince St, Col 11; adult/child Rs 500/300; ⌚9am-5pm Tue-Sat) This unique museum was originally the 17th-century residence of the Dutch governor and has since been used as a Catholic seminary, a military hospital, a police station and a post office. The mansion contains a lovely garden courtyard and has a nice faded feel since a 1977 restoration. Exhibits include Dutch colonial furniture and other artefacts.

Hindu Temples TEMPLES

(Map p50) Known as *kovils,* Hindu temples are numerous in Colombo, with a particularly high concentration in Pettah. All the following *kovils* are open from 6am to 6pm. On Sea St, the goldsmiths' street, **Old Kathiresan Kovil** and **New Kathiresan Kovil**, both dedicated to the war god Murugan (Skanda), are the starting point for the annual Hindu Vel festival held in July/August, when the huge *vel* (trident) chariot is dragged to various *kovils* on Galle Rd in Bambalapitiya.

Mosques MOSQUES

(Map p50) In the heart of Pettah, the decorative 1909 **Jami-Ul-Alfar Mosque** (cnr 2nd Cross & Bankshall Sts, Col 11) is a show-stopper with its candy-striped red-and-white brickwork. Guards will usually let you in for a look, except during peak prayer times on Fridays. The modern **Grand Mosque** (New Moor St, Col 11) is the most important of Colombo's many mosques.

Wolvendaal Church CHURCH

(Map p50; Wolvendaal Lane, Col 11; ⌚9am-4pm) The 1749 Wolvendaal Church is the most important Dutch building in Sri Lanka. When the church was built, this area was a wilderness beyond the city walls. The Europeans mistook the packs of roaming jackals for wolves, and the area became known as Wolf's Dale, or Wolvendaal in Dutch. The church is in the form of a Greek cross, with walls 1.5m thick, but the real treasure is its Dutch furniture. The Dutch governors had a special pew made with elegant carved ebony chairs, and the workmanship in the wooden pulpit, baptismal font and lectern is just as beautiful. The stone floor includes the elaborate tombstones to long-forgotten Dutch governors and colonists.

GALLE FACE GREEN

Colombo's front porch is immediately south of Fort. **Galle Face Green** (Map p54) is a long stretch of lawn facing a narrow beach and the sea. It was originally cleared by the Dutch to give the cannons of Fort a clear line of fire. Today its broad lawns and seaside promenade are a popular rendezvous spot; on weekdays it's dotted with kite flyers, canoodling couples and families, and (especially Sunday evenings) **food vendors** (Map p54) at the south end along the surf offer up

Colombo Fort & Pettah

Top Sights
- Dutch Period Museum ... C2
- Federation of Self Employees Market ... D2
- Old City Hall ... D1

Sights
- 1 Cargills Main Store ... B2
- 2 Central Bank ... A2
- 3 Central Market ... D1
- 4 Clock Tower ... A2
- 5 Grand Mosque ... E1
- Grand Oriental Hotel ... (see 19)
- 6 Jami-Ul-Alfar Mosque ... C1
- 7 Lloyd's Buildings ... B2
- 8 Manning Market ... D2
- 9 New Kathiresan Kovil ... D1
- 10 Old Dutch Hospital ... B3
- 11 Old Galle Buck Lighthouse ... A2
- Old Kathiresan Kovil ... (see 9)
- 12 Pelicans ... A3
- 13 Sambodhi Chaitiya ... A1
- 14 St Peter's Church ... B2
- 15 Wolvendaal Church ... E1
- 16 World Trade Center ... B3

Activities, Courses & Tours
- Spa Ceylon ... (see 10)

Sleeping
- 17 Colombo City Hotel ... B3
- 18 Colombo YMCA ... B2
- 19 Grand Oriental Hotel ... B2
- 20 Hilton Colombo ... B3

Eating
- 21 AVP Restaurant ... B2
- Colombo Fort Cafe ... (see 10)
- Curry Leaf ... (see 20)
- 22 Lion Cafe ... C3
- Ministry of Crab ... (see 10)
- 23 New Palm Leaf Hotel ... D2
- 24 Pagoda Tea Room ... B2

Drinking
- 25 7° North ... C3
- Brewery by O! ... (see 10)

Entertainment
- Blue Leopard ... (see 19)

Shopping
- 26 Bazaar ... C2
- Sri Lanka Gem & Jewellery Exchange ... (see 16)

all manner of deep-fried and briny snacks. Kids jump from the small **pier** (Map p54) into the rather dubious waters below. Note the **pelicans** (Map p50) perched atop the light poles at the north end.

The remaining structures of the 19th-century **Colombo Club** (Map p54) face the green from the grounds of Taj Samudra hotel; the club's rooms are still used for functions. At opposite ends of the green are the delightful old Galle Face Hotel and the monolithic and ageing hotels of Fort. A new wave of luxurious digs is planned for the area east of Galle Face Centre Rd.

SLAVE ISLAND & UNION PLACE

After Pettah, Colombo's oldest neighbourhoods are found here. Slave Island was once mostly surrounded by water and it's where the Dutch kept slaves during colonial times. Largely a backwater during the war, its proximity to Fort and Galle Face Green make it an area ripe for development. Now it's good for the still-quiet strolls along **South Beira Lake** (Map p54).

With large modern office buildings at its south end, Union Place is not likely to remain the same for long. But until bulldozers arrive, its narrow lanes pulse with life little changed in centuries. Start at the row of **colonial storefronts** (Map p54) on Union Pl and then plunge into the neighbourhood by walking south on Malay St and then Church St. Tiny shopfronts sell goods of uncertain provenance and each alley holds a surprise. Wind your way south until you reach Nawam Mawatha and South Beira Lake.

SOUTH BEIRA LAKE & AROUND

South Beira Lake is a pretty centrepiece to the city. Pelicans vie with rental paddle boats in the shape of huge swans for space on the water. The latter are popular with courting couples looking for a little privacy.

Seema Malakaya Meditation Centre SPIRITUAL PLACE

(Map p54; ⏲6am-6pm) One of Colombo's most photographed sights is on an island on the east side of the lake. This small but captivating meditation centre was designed by

Geoffrey Bawa (see boxed text, below) in 1985 and is run by Gangaramaya Temple. The pavilions – one filled with Thai bronze Buddhas, the other centred on a bodhi tree and four Brahmanist images – are especially striking when illuminated at night.

Gangaramaya Temple BUDDHIST TEMPLE
(Map p54; Sri Jinaratana Rd, Col 2; ⌚5.30am-10pm) Run by one of Sri Lanka's more politically adept monks, this bustling temple complex has a library, a **museum** (donation Rs 100) and an extraordinarily eclectic array of bejewelled and gilded gifts presented by devotees and well-wishers over the years. Gangaramaya is the focus of the Navam Perahera (p59) on the February *poya* (full-moon) day each year. You might pray for the welfare of the sad-looking elephant chained up in one corner of the grounds.

KOLLUPTIYA

This long commercial strip along traffic-choked Galle Rd is jammed with all manner of shops, businesses and hotels both modest and grand. It makes for a good stroll as surprises abound. Several places popular for snacks are along here as well: see p65. Improvements to Marine Dr should spark a boom in waterfront development.

Saskia Fernando Gallery ART GALLERY
(Map p54; www.saskiafernandogallery.com; 61 Dharmapala Mawatha, Col 3; ⌚10am-7pm Mon-Fri) Some of the best contemporary Sri Lankan artists are displayed in the white-washed compound.

CINNAMON GARDENS

About 5km south of Fort and inland from Kolluptiya, Cinnamon Gardens is Colombo's most gentrified area. A century ago it was covered in cinnamon plantations. Today it contains elegant tree-lined streets with posh mansions, embassies, stylish cafes and shops, sports grounds, and a cluster of museums and galleries.

Colombo's white-domed 1928 **Old Town Hall** (White House; Map p54) overlooks the area's heart, Viharamahadevi Park. To the south is the striking new Performing Arts Theatre.

The bustling **De Soysa (Lipton) Circus** (Map p54) is an important crossroads. One corner of the roundabout is occupied by the highly recommended Odel Unlimited department store. Opposite is the **Cinnamon Gardens Baptist Church**, which dates to 1877. Located just south of the church is the **Dewata-Gaha Mosque** (Map p54), a crumbling sun-bleached structure dating to 1802 that bustles with people following the Friday afternoon prayers. You won't be able to miss the ragtag confection of red and white bricks that was once the **Eye Hospital** (Map p54) and which now awaits rescue from ruin.

TOP CHOICE **National Museum** MUSEUM
(Map p54; Albert Cres, Col 7; adult/child Rs 500/300; ⌚9am-6pm) A large 9th-century stone Buddha greets you with an enigmatic smile as you enter Sri Lanka's premier cultural institution. In galleries dating back as far as 1877,

GEOFFREY BAWA – 'BRINGING POETRY TO PLACE'

The most famous of Sri Lanka's architects, Geoffrey Bawa (1919–2003) fused ancient and modern influences in his work. Architect Ranjith Dayaratne described it as 'bringing poetry to place'.

Using courtyards and pathways, Bawa developed pleasing connections between the interior and exterior of his structures. These connections frequently included contemplative spaces, as well as framed areas that enabled glimpses of spaces yet to be entered.

His designs were based within the environment. And he was not averse to the environment claiming his structures – at times he encouraged jungle growth along walls and roofs.

While Bawa created aesthetic beauty, he was also concerned with the functional aspects of architecture, opening and exposing structures to air and light while ensuring shelter and protection from harsh climatic elements.

His approach was important not only for its originality but also for its influence on architecture in Sri Lanka and abroad.

Bawa's work included the parliament house in Colombo and the Kandalama Hotel near Dambulla.

The historic building that houses Colombo's Gallery Cafe used to be Bawa's office and is now used as an exhibition space for art and photography. You can also see his gem-like Seema Malakaya Meditation Centre.

Kollupitiya, Cinnamon Gardens & Borella

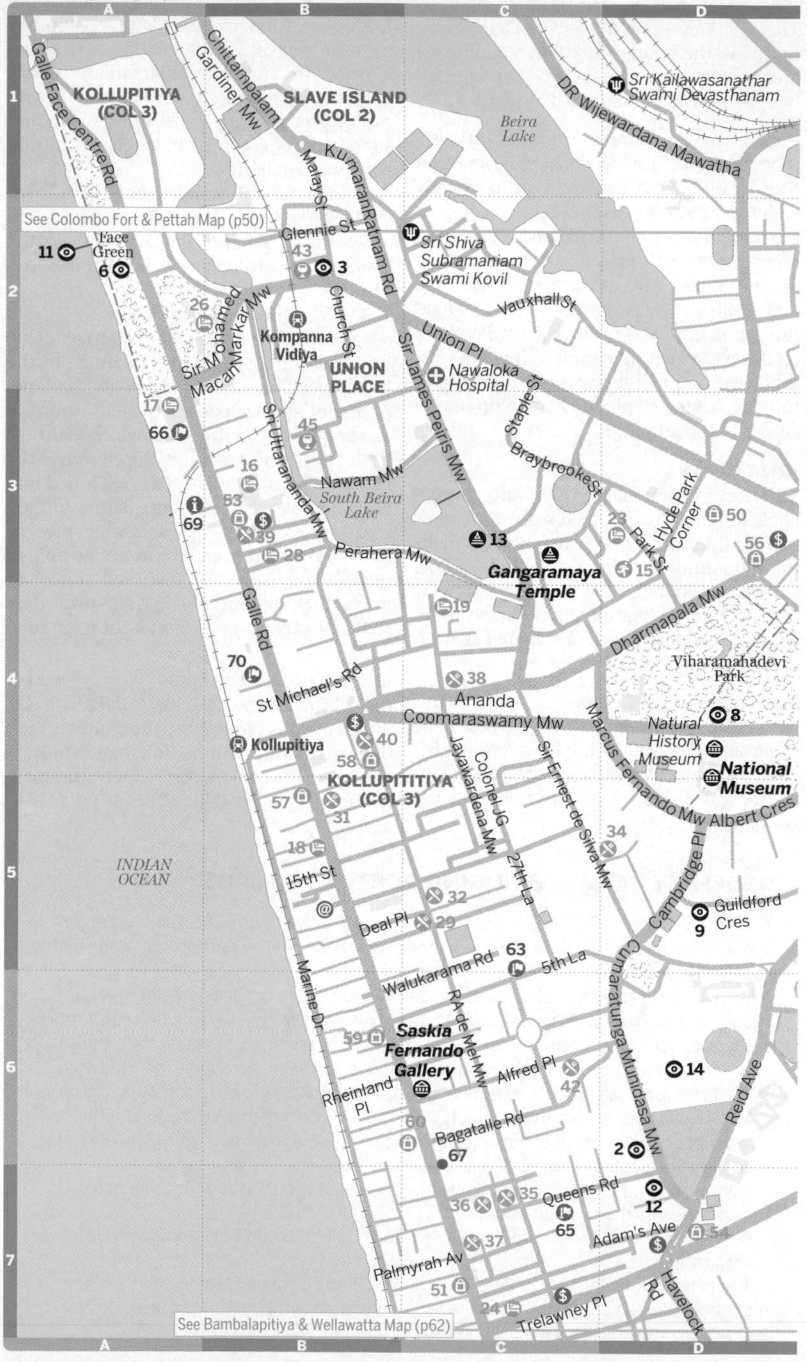

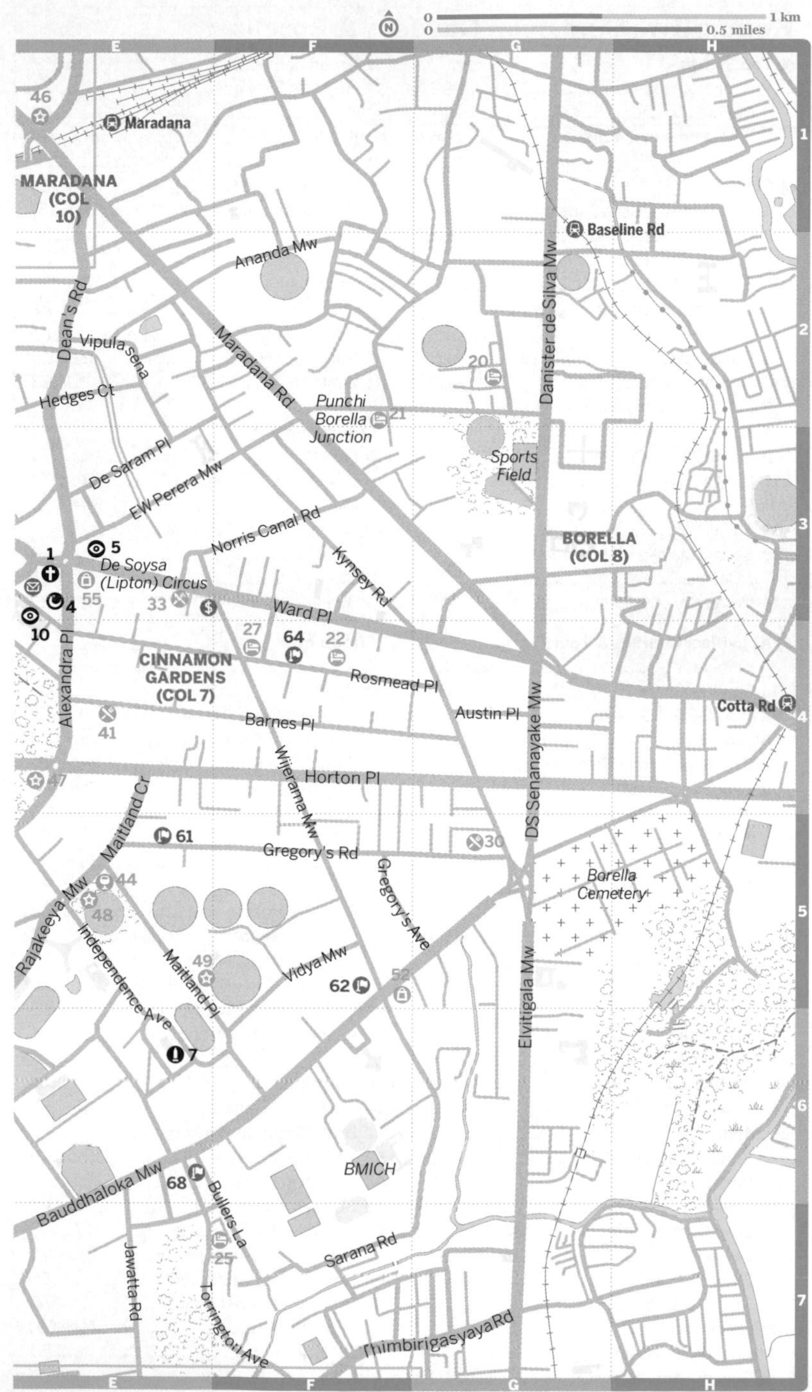
0 1 km
0 0.5 miles
E
F
G
H
1
2
3
4
5
6
7
Maradana
MARADANA (COL 10)
Baseline Rd
Ananda Mw
Dean's Rd
Vipulasena
Hedges Ct
Maradana Rd
Punchi Borella Junction
Danister de Silva Mw
Sports Field
De Saram Pl
EW Perera Mw
Norris Canal Rd
Kynsey Rd
BORELLA (COL 8)
De Soysa (Lipton) Circus
Ward Pl
CINNAMON GARDENS (COL 7)
Rosmead Pl
Alexandra Pl
Austin Pl
Cotta Rd
Barnes Pl
Wijerama Mw
DS Senanayake Mw
Horton Pl
Maitland Cr
Gregory's Rd
Gregory's Ave
Borella Cemetery
Rajakeeya Mw
Independence Ave
Maitland Pl
Vidya Mw
Elvitigala Mw
BMICH
Bauddhaloka Mw
Bullers La
Sarana Rd
Jawatta Rd
Torrington Ave
Thimbirigasyaya Rd

Kollupitiya, Cinnamon Gardens & Borella

Top Sights

Gangaramaya Temple ... C3
National Museum ... D4
Saskia Fernando Gallery ... C6

Sights

1 Cinnamon Gardens Baptist Church ... E3
2 College House ... D6
Colombo Club ... (see 26)
3 Colonial Storefronts ... B2
4 Dewata-Gaha Mosque ... E3
5 Eye Hospital ... E3
6 Food Vendors ... A2
7 Independence Memorial Hall ... E6
8 Kala Pola Art Market ... D4
9 Lionel Wendt Centre ... D5
10 Old Town Hall ... E3
11 Pier ... A2
12 Saifee Villa ... D7
13 Seema Malakaya Meditation Centre ... C3
14 University of Colombo ... D6

Activities, Courses & Tours

Kemara ... (see 41)
15 Spa Ceylon ... D3

Sleeping

16 Cinnamon Grand Hotel ... B3
17 Galle Face Hotel ... A3
18 Hotel Renuka & Renuka City Hotel ... B5
19 Lake Lodge ... C4
20 Mrs Chitrangi de Fonseka's ... G2
21 Mrs Swarna Jayaratne's ... F2
22 Parisare ... F4
23 Park Street Hotel ... D3
24 Pearl City Hotel ... C7
25 Ranjit's Ambalama ... F7
26 Taj Samudra ... A2
27 Tintagel ... F4
28 YWCA National Headquarters ... B3

Eating

Barefoot Garden Cafe ... (see 51)
29 Bars Cafe ... C5
30 Bayleaf ... G5
Boulevard ... (see 55)
31 Carnival ... B5
32 Chesa Swiss ... C5
33 Coco Veranda Cafe ... E3
34 Commons ... D5
35 Cricket Club Cafe ... C7
36 Gallery Cafe ... C7
37 Green Cabin ... C7
38 Hotel De Pilawoos ... C4
39 Keells ... B3
40 Keells ... B4
41 Milk & Honey Cafe ... E4
Paradise Road Cafe ... (see 56)
Park Street Mews ... (see 15)
42 Raffles ... C6

Drinking

43 Castle Hotel ... B2
44 Clancy's Irish Pub ... E5
Galle Face Hotel ... (see 17)
45 White Horse ... B3

Entertainment

46 Elphinstone Theatre ... E1
Lionel Wendt Centre ... (see 9)
Mojo ... (see 26)
47 Nelum Pokuna Performing Arts Theatre ... E4
48 Silk ... E5
49 Sri Lanka Cricket ... E5

Shopping

50 Arpico ... D3
51 Barefoot ... C7
52 Buddhist Book Centre ... F5
53 Crescat Boulevard ... B3
Dilmah Tea Shop ... (see 53)
Dilmah Tea Shop ... (see 55)
KT Brown ... (see 15)
54 Laksala ... D7
Mlesna Tea Centre ... (see 53)
55 Odel ... E3
56 Paradise Road ... D3
57 Photo Technica ... B5
58 Photo Technica ... B4
59 Sri Lanka Cashew Corporation ... B6
60 Sri Lanka Tea Board Shop ... C6
Vijitha Yapa Bookshop ... (see 53)

Information

61 Australian Embassy ... E5
62 British High Commission ... F5
63 Canadian Embassy ... C5
64 French Embassy ... F4
65 German Embassy ... C7
66 Indian High Commission ... A3
67 Indian Visa Office ... C6
68 Netherlands Embassy ... E6
69 Sri Lanka Tourist Board ... A3
Tourist Police ... (see 69)
70 US Embassy ... B4

you'll encounter all manner of art, carvings and statuary from Sri Lanka's ancient past, as well as swords, guns and other paraphernalia from the colonial period. There are fascinating 19th-century reproductions of English paintings of Sri Lanka, and an excellent collection of antique demon masks. Look for the magnificent royal throne made for King Wimaladharma in 1693 as well as the 9th-century bronze Bodhisattva Sandals. The grounds are shaded by magnificent banyan trees.

Viharamahadevi Park PARK
(Map p54) Colombo's biggest park was originally called Victoria Park but was renamed in the 1950s after the mother of King Dutugemunu (see p123). It's notable for its superb flowering trees, which bloom in March, April and early May. Working elephants sometimes spend the night in the park, chomping on palm branches.

National Art Gallery ART GALLERY
(Map p54; 106 Ananda Coomaraswamy Mawatha, Col 7; admission free; ⌚9am-5pm, closed poya days) The grandest thing about the National Art Gallery is the name. Next to the National Museum, it has a small permanent collection of portraits and landscapes shown without labels or air-conditioning.

Lionel Wendt Centre ARTS CENTRE
(Map p54; ☎269 5794; www.lionelwendt.org; 18 Guildford Cres, Col 7; ⌚9am-1pm & 2-5pm Mon-Fri, 10am-noon & 1-5pm Sat & Sun) Has a constantly changing lineup of cultural events with regular art exhibitions as well as performances. It's worth turning up just to see what's on.

University of Colombo UNIVERSITY
(University of Ceylon; Map p54) The 50-acre University of Colombo campus, which originally opened as the Ceylon Medical School in 1870, is surrounded by long tree-lined avenues lined with colonial-era mansions. Of note is Cumaratunga Munidasa Mawatha along the southwest side of the sporting green. Ponder the gracious lives of the people who built the Italianate Baroque **Saifee Villa** in 1910 and the nearby turreted **College House** in 1912. (And spare a thought for the hard lives of the servants.)

Independence Memorial Hall MONUMENT
(Map p54; Independence Square, Col 7) Really a large memorial building to Sri Lanka's 1948 independence from Britain, the huge stone edifice is loosely based on Kandy's Audience Hall. This is a good place to escape Colombo's crowds as it always seems almost empty.

DON'T MISS

KALA POLA ART MARKET

Every Sunday morning the broad avenue Ananda Coomaraswamy Mawatha south of Viharamahadevi Park comes alive with colour as local artists display their works. This weekly explosion of colour is an outgrowth of the original **Kala Pola Art Market** (Map p54), an annual event still held the third Sunday of January when up to 500 artists display their work. The market is a kaleidoscope of creativity from across the nation and you might just find a bargain-priced treasure.

SOUTHERN COLOMBO

South of Kollupitiya and Cinnamon Gardens is more of the same, only less so. The commercial strip of Galle Rd continues south through Bambalapitiya and Wellawatta. Inland, Havelock Town is a more relaxed version of Cinnamon Gardens. It has many comfy midrange hotels. The one area here with buzz is **Pamankade**, which has some interesting shops and cafes along Stratford Ave.

Puppet Museum MUSEUM
(☎573 5332; www.puppet.lk; Anagarika Dharmapala Mawatha, Dehiwala; admission Rs 500, performance prices vary; ⌚9am-5pm) Puppet shows were long a part of traditional entertainment in Sri Lankan villages. Performing troupes would stage shows with intricate plots that lasted for hours. This engaging museum keeps the traditional puppet arts alive. Dozens and dozens of colourful puppets – some quite huge – are displayed. Many are surprisingly animated even when still. Call to find out if you can catch a performance (or to get directions). It's about 200m east of Galle Rd, about midway between Wellawatta and Mt Lavinia.

MT LAVINIA

Long Colombo's beach retreat, Mt Lavinia makes for a good close-in respite from the city's cacophony and fumes. The **beach** is not bad, although some rivers just north empty dodgy water into the ocean after rains and the undertow can be prohibitive. If you're heading to the famous beaches south there's no need to stop here. Otherwise

Mt Lavinia's many beachside cafes are good places to laze away the hours until sunset.

KOTAHENA

Kotahena, immediately northeast of Pettah, is closely linked to Colombo's port, which forms the west boundary. It's not as rampant with commerce as Pettah but also boasts many old buildings and streets. You could easily visit the sights listed here with the services of a taxi or three-wheeler.

Hindu Temples TEMPLES

During the harvest festival of Thai Pongal (held in January), devotees flock to **Sri Ponnambalam Vanesar Kovil** (off Map p50; Srimath Ramanathan Mawatha), which is beautifully built of South Indian granite, and **Sri Muthumariamman Kovil** (off Map p50; Kotahena St, Col 13). The latter's namesake goddess is thought to be responsible for many miracles.

St Anthony's Church CHURCH

(off Map p50; St Anthony's Mawatha, Kotahena; ⏲6am-6pm) One of the city's most interesting shrines is St Anthony's Church. Outside it looks like a typical Portuguese Catholic church, but inside the atmosphere is distinctly subcontinental. There are queues of devotees offering *puja* (offerings or prayers) to a dozen ornate statues; a statue of St Anthony said to be endowed with miraculous qualities is the centre of devotions from people of many faiths. Mothers often bring pubescent daughters here to pray for protection from evil spirits that might take advantage of the girls' nascent sexuality. Photography is frowned upon.

St Lucia's Cathedral CHURCH

(off Map p50; St Lucia's St, Kotahena; ⏲5.30am-noon & 2-7pm) The enormous, 1887 cathedral lies in the Catholic heart of the Kotahena district. The biggest church in Sri Lanka, it can hold up to 5000 worshippers in its rather plain interior.

NORTH & NORTHWEST OF COLOMBO

The busy road linking Colombo with Negombo, the airport and the north is often traffic-choked and is lined with an untidy mishmash of strip malls aimed at Sri Lanka's burgeoning middle class. It's much the same for the first few kilometres of the road to Kandy, although lush green landscapes soon provide relief.

Kelaniya Raja Maha Vihara BUDDHIST TEMPLE

It's believed Buddha visited the site of this temple on his third visit to Sri Lanka. Suitably grand and labyrinthine, it has a dramatic past. The original temple was destroyed by Indian invaders, restored and destroyed again by the Portuguese in the 16th century. The Dutch restored it again in the 18th century in order to curry favour locally. The dagoba, which (unusually) is hollow, is the focus of the Duruthu Perahera in January each year. The complex is some 7km northeast of Fort, just off the Kandy Rd.

Activities

Ayurveda & Spas

Ayurveda spas and clinics are popular with many visitors to Sri Lanka. For more details about these ancient treatments and therapies, see p306.

Spa Ceylon SPA

(www.spaceylon.com) Old Dutch Hospital (Map p50; ☎566 5599; Fort, Col 1; ⏲10am-11pm); Park St Mews (Map p54; ☎230 7676; Park St, Col 2; ⏲10am-11pm) This chain of luxury spas offers both Ayurveda treatments and regular spa services in chic surrounds.

Kemara SPA

(Map p54; ☎269 6498; www.kemaralife.com; 12 Barnes Pl; ⏲10am-8pm) Holistic health treatments and luxurious beauty and health products, many based on fruits and herbs. A long list of therapies and spa treatments is available.

Siddhalepa Ayurveda Hospital SPA

(off Map p64; ☎273 8622; www.siddhalepa.com; Templers Rd, Mt Lavinia) This full-service Ayurvedic health centre offers treatments and therapies that take an hour or a week. It even has a herb of the month (ginger when we were there).

Swimming

Skip the polluted waters off Galle Face Green; the only place you might consider an ocean dip is at Mt Lavinia, and even there you might think twice.

Rather, if you are staying someplace without a pool – or just want a change of scenery – consider paying to swim at a hotel with a pool. Most will allow you to use the facilities for a fee of Rs 500 to 1000. Two good choices are the outdoor saltwater pool right by the seafront at Galle Face Hotel and the magnificently positioned pool at Mount Lavinia Hotel.

Meditation

Kanduboda Meditation Centre SPIRITUAL RETREAT

(☎240 2306; www.metta.lk/temples/kandubodha/) Located 25km outside Colombo in Delgoda, this is a major centre for meditation instruction in the style of the late Mahasi Sayadaw. Accommodation and meals are offered free of charge, though donations are expected. Most meditators stay for an initial three-week training period, after which they can meditate on their own for as long as they like. The Pugoda bus 224 passes the centre and can be caught from the Central Bus Station on Olcott Mawatha.

Tours

Colombo City Tour BUS TOUR

(☎281 4700, 077 759 9963; www.colombocitytours.com; tour Rs 2850; ⏲8.30am Wed, Sat & Sun) Tour Colombo's sprawl from high above the traffic in an old open-top double-decker bus. The narration is in English and snacks and water are included. The four-hour tours cover the city and stops include the National Museum.

Colombo Walking Tour WALKING TOUR

(☎077 683 8659; www.sriserendipity.com; tours from US$20) Quirky historic walking tours reveal the secrets and unique spots of central Colombo. The guide is the author of guidebooks about Colombo and elsewhere in Sri Lanka, Juliet Coombe.

Festivals & Events

Special events, such as street rally races and open-air concerts by the ocean, are blossoming in Colombo.

Duruthu Perahera RELIGIOUS FESTIVAL

Held at the Kelaniya Raja Maha Vihara on the January *poya*.

Navam Perahera RELIGIOUS FESTIVAL

On the February *poya* and led by 50 elephants; it starts from Gangaramaya Temple and is held around Viharamahadevi Park and South Beira Lake.

Vel RELIGIOUS FESTIVAL

During the Vel in July/August, the gilded chariot of Murugan (Skanda), the Hindu war god, is ceremonially hauled from the Kathiresan *kovil* to a *kovil* at Bambalapitiya.

Sleeping

Like many other aspects of life in the capital, the accommodation scene in Colombo is awakening from a long slumber. New top-end hotels are being built and older ones refurbished. Luxurious boutique hotels are proliferating in the city's leafier neighbourhoods and there's a new selection of high-quality midrange places. New budget guesthouses are also opening.

Amid this new hostelry energy, some older properties continue to limp along on past glories. Fort and Galle Rd in particular have shabby properties that are little changed – or improved – in decades. As tourist numbers in Sri Lanka soar, it's worth booking ahead – especially for that first night in Colombo – so you don't end up at an inferior option.

Negombo (p79) is a short drive from Bandaranaike International Airport and has a full range of sleeping options, many right on the beach.

FORT & PETTAH

Fort is home to international-style highrise hotels, some of which are decidedly long in the tooth. This is also where you can find historic hotels with rates that make their miscues palatable.

Hilton Colombo HOTEL $$$

(Map p50; ☎249 2492; www.hilton.com; 2 Sir Chittampalam A Gardiner Mawatha, Col 2; r standard/executive US$147/236; ❄@📶🏊) This large international business-class hotel buzzes with activity around the clock. It has 382 rooms in regular- and executive-floor flavours, six restaurants, a pub, a 24-hour

DON'T MISS

SUNSET

The Indian Ocean can yield up sunsets so rich in vivid colours that your eyes and brain can't quite cope. Many people opt for the outdoor bars in the cloistered surrounds of the Galle Face Hotel, but you can have a much more authentic experience joining Colombo's great and many on Galle Face Green. Nature's beauty is a moment best shared with others and you can enjoy a local snack from the many vendors. The beachside cafes of Mt Lavinia are also good sunset venues. Note that the day's weather is no indication of sunset quality, a dreary grey day can suddenly erupt in crimson and purple at dusk.

business centre, a fully equipped sports-and-fitness club and an attractive garden and pool area.

Grand Oriental Hotel HOTEL $$
(Map p50; ☎232 0391/2; www.grandoriental.com; 2 York St, Col 1; r US$60-90; ❄📶) Opposite the harbour, this was Colombo's finest hotel 100 years ago, a place to see and be seen. Although it's no longer the case, there's a certain frumpy charm here. Most rooms have been stripped of original features and given a vaguely low-end Mediterranean motif. There are superb harbour views from the 4th-floor restaurant and terrace; go for a drink, skip the food.

Colombo City Hotel HOTEL $$
(Map p50; ☎534 1962; www.colombocityhotel.com; Level 3, 33 Canal Row, Col 1; r US$35-70; ❄📶) This hotel has reasonable rates and a fine location next to the Old Dutch Hospital. The 32 rooms have fridges but are rather small and most lack decent views. Also, the hotel can be very noisy and service is unpolished; against these demerits consider that rates are often cheap online and it's a short walk to Fort station. The sea views from the restaurant roof are outstanding, even if the food is not.

Colombo YMCA GUESTHOUSE $
(Map p50; ☎232 5252; 39 Bristol St, Col 1; dm Rs 180, r Rs 550-1200) This old Y is kind of depressing, but if you've been robbed and need a place to crash – or you're on a very tight budget – this could be it. It offers male-only dorms, and a few single and double rooms that are open to both men and women: some share bathrooms and some have fans.

KOLLUPITIYA

Colombo's best large hotels are in this central area, near the ocean and noisy Galle Rd. On back roads to the east you'll find numerous interesting choices.

TOP CHOICE **Lake Lodge** GUESTHOUSE $$
(Map p54; ☎232 6443; www.taruhotels.com; 20 Alvis Tce, Col 3; ❄📶) This hotel gets everything just right. The 13 rooms are well equipped and stylish in a minimalist way. Long concrete counters are good for work or simply sorting through your luggage. The rooftop terraces have views of South Beira Lake and are fine places for breakfast or an evening drink. Service is excellent and the hotel is well managed. You can easily walk to much of what's interesting in Colombo.

Cinnamon Grand Hotel HOTEL $$$
(Map p54; ☎243 7437; www.cinnamonhotels.com; 77 Galle Rd, Col 3; r US$100-180; ❄@📶🏊) Colombo's best large hotel has a central location well back from Galle Rd. It buzzes with energy as there always seems to be an elite wedding on while some high-profile politician strolls the huge, airy lobby. The 501 rooms are large; ask for a high floor to enjoy views. Service is excellent. There's a fitness centre, a big outdoor swimming pool, several top-notch restaurants and a lobby confectionary. It even has a small, re-created Sri Lankan village that's a hidden gem. It's attached to the smallish Crescat Boulevard Plaza shopping mall.

Park Street Hotel BOUTIQUE HOTEL $$$
(Map p54; ☎243 9977; www.asialeisure.lk; 20 Park St, Col 2; r from US$270; ❄📶🏊) The sort of place you might have lived if you owned a plantation, this hotel is in a beautiful colonnaded 250-year-old mansion. The 10 rooms and two suites are very large and open onto breezy arcades and overlook gardens and the pool. Antiques and artwork set off the minimalist modern furniture. The hotel is close to the centre and excellent shopping.

Galle Face Hotel HOTEL $$$
(Map p54; ☎254 1010-6; www.gallefacehotel.com; 2 Kollupitiya Rd, Col 3; hotel r US$80-160; ❄@📶🏊) Location, location, location. The *grande dame* of Colombo faces Galle Face Green to the north and the sea to the west. The sweeping stairways, high ceilings and trademark checked-tile floors look much as they did when the hotel opened in 1864. Sunset drinks are popular with visitors to Colombo. But the Galle Face also shows its years in many ways (the newish Regency Wing is superior) and service can be barely adequate. Look for the huge plaque near the entrance with the names of the famous who've bedded down here, from Noel Coward to Richard Nixon to 'Carrie Fisher "Star Wars"'.

Taj Samudra HOTEL $$$
(Map p54; ☎244 6622; www.tajhotels.com; 25 Galle Face Centre Rd, Col 3; r US$90-150; ❄@📶🏊) Part of the well-regarded Indian chain, this vast edifice has elegant public areas and a well-tended 11-acre garden. The hotel has a 24-hour coffeeshop (with an excellent Rs 1000

buffet) and several more restaurants and bars. The 270 rooms are comfortable and modern.

Pearl City Hotel HOTEL $$

(Map p54; ☎452 3800; www.pearlcityhotel.net; 17 Bauddhaloka Mawatha, Col 4; r Rs 5600-7000; ❄📶) Standard rooms at the Pearl City are a little boxy and basic, but slightly better deluxe rooms are comfortable enough, although all have a rather naff brocaded look. It's just off Galle Rd, which helps with noise (but still get a room in the rear). The 69 rooms are served by an elevator and have fridges. The excellent staff are very professional.

Hotel Renuka & Renuka City Hotel HOTEL $$

(Map p54; ☎257 3598; www.renukahotel.com; 328 Galle Rd, Col 3; r US$45-80; ❄📶) An excellent midrange hotel, the Renuka is bifurcated into two different buildings. Its 81 rooms are well maintained and have safes, fridges and 24-hour room service. Decor is somewhat basic; get a room not facing Galle Rd (and ask to see a couple). The staff are good, as is the Palmyrah restaurant, known for its Jaffna dishes.

YWCA National Headquarters GUESTHOUSE $$

(Map p54; ☎232 3498; natywca@sltnet.lk; 7 Rotunda Gardens, Col 3; dm Rs 550, r Rs 3300-5500; ❄@) This place has eight tidy, basic rooms (most fan-only) that surround a leafy courtyard. It's a secure refuge for female travellers; men can stay if they're with a female companion. There are women-only rooms with shared bathroom, while mixed rooms have private bathrooms. There's a cheap cafeteria (meals Rs 150 to 350), open from Monday to Saturday for breakfast, lunch and dinner.

CINNAMON GARDENS

The tree-lined streets here offer at least the allusion of genteel charm.

Parisare HOMESTAY $

(Map p54; ☎269 4749; 97/1 Rosmead Pl, Col 7; s/d Rs 1500/2500) It's not the most luxurious guesthouse in town, but it's probably the most interesting. Parisare is a modern split-level home with few walls so that many of the common spaces are open-air. It's cluttered but clean and down a small alley off a leafy street. Parisare is good value and very popular – book ahead.

Ranjit's Ambalama GUESTHOUSE $$

(Map p54; ☎250 2403, 071 234 7400; www.ranjitsambalama.com; 53/19 Torrington Ave, Col 7; r Rs 4000-6000; ❄📶) This guesthouse is modern and airy, with a small leafy courtyard and a wealth of books on Buddhism. There are six rooms, two with private bathrooms. All rooms have air-con (an extra Rs 1500). Finding the house is a bit tricky. Coming down Torrington Ave from Bauddhaloka Mawatha, look for the mosque on the right, then take the first left at a small playground and then the first right. It's the second house on the left.

Tintagel BOUTIQUE HOTEL $$$

(Map p54; ☎460 2122; www.tintagelcolombo.com; 65 Rosmead Pl, Col 7; r US$250-450; ❄@📶🏊) Set inside an old mansion that once was home to a prime minster's family, this ultra-chic hotel dazzles with its dark, minimalist design, elegant contours and idiosyncratic artworks. It's owned by Shanth Fernando, the same designer who created Gallery Cafe. Each of the 10 rooms is unique and some include private splash pools. Unfortunately someone didn't get the memo that cool doesn't mean frigid: when we were here staff were openly rude.

BORELLA & MARADANA

These middle-class neighbourhoods are both quiet and rather far from the rest of Colombo to the west.

Mrs Swarna Jayaratne's HOMESTAY $

(Map p54; ☎269 5665, 077 731 4977; indcom@sltnet.lk; 70 Ananda Rajakaruna Mawatha, Col 8; s/d Rs 1800/2200, air-con Rs 700 extra; ❄) Mrs Jayaratne's guesthouse features two clean rooms with a shared bathroom. There's an attached guest sitting area with satellite TV, a balcony and a small patch of lawn. To get here catch bus 103 or 171 (Rs 10 from Fort train station) and get off at Punchi Borella Junction.

Mrs Chitrangi de Fonseka's HOMESTAY $$

(Map p54; ☎269 7919; www.gardenguesthousecolombo.com; 7 Karlshrue Gardens, Col 10; r US$60-80; ❄📶) This is a modern home bubbling with eccentricity, including chintzy decor, lots of porcelain and an indoor fountain. The three spacious rooms have TVs and a pink colour scheme that would delight a preteen girl. Bus 103 or 171 from Fort will take you nearby; get off at Punchi Borella Junction.

BAMBALAPITIYA, HAVELOCK TOWN & WELLAWATTA

South of the centre, you realise some savings in both money and, at least on the side streets, noise.

TOP CHOICE **Havelock Place Bungalow** GUESTHOUSE $$$
(Map p62; ☎258 5191; www.bungalow.lk; 6-8 Havelock Pl, Col 5; r US$95-140; ❄@📶🏊) This appealing guesthouse has seven rooms spread across two colonial houses. Modern luxury is matched with antiques and it feels authentic to the period. It's on a quiet lane and has lush gardens and a small lap pool. The outdoor cafe here is a good place to while away the hours on the comfy wicker furniture. The air is scented with cinnamon.

Casa Colombo BOUTIQUE HOTEL $$$
(Map p62; ☎452 0130; www.casacolombo.com; 231 Galle Rd, Col 4; US$200-500; ❄📶🏊) This vast 200-year-old mansion sits in isolated splendour behind a row of shabby storefronts on Galle Rd. Protected from the noise, it's an urban refuge with huge old trees and a rather infamous pink-hued swimming pool. There are 12 large suites, all decorated in colonial colours that mix modern and minimalist with an eye-catching punch. Service is excellent.

Hotel Sunshine HOTEL $$
(Map p62; ☎451 7676; sunshine.shrubbery@gmail.com; 5A Shrubbery Gardens, Col 4; r Rs 1700-4800; ❄📶) This small budget hotel is tall and narrow and hemmed in by even taller neighbours. It has 23 clean but plain rooms at reasonable rates (cheaper ones are fan-only), just a half-block from the sea. The staff are professional and the lobby is a tiny gem.

Tropic Inn GUESTHOUSE $$
(Map p62; ☎250 8838; www.tropicinn.com; 19 De Vos Ave, Col 4 ❄📶) A new good-value guesthouse from the owners of the well-run hotel of the same name in Mt Lavinia. The five rooms here are in a three-storey house that

Bambalapitiya & Wellawatta

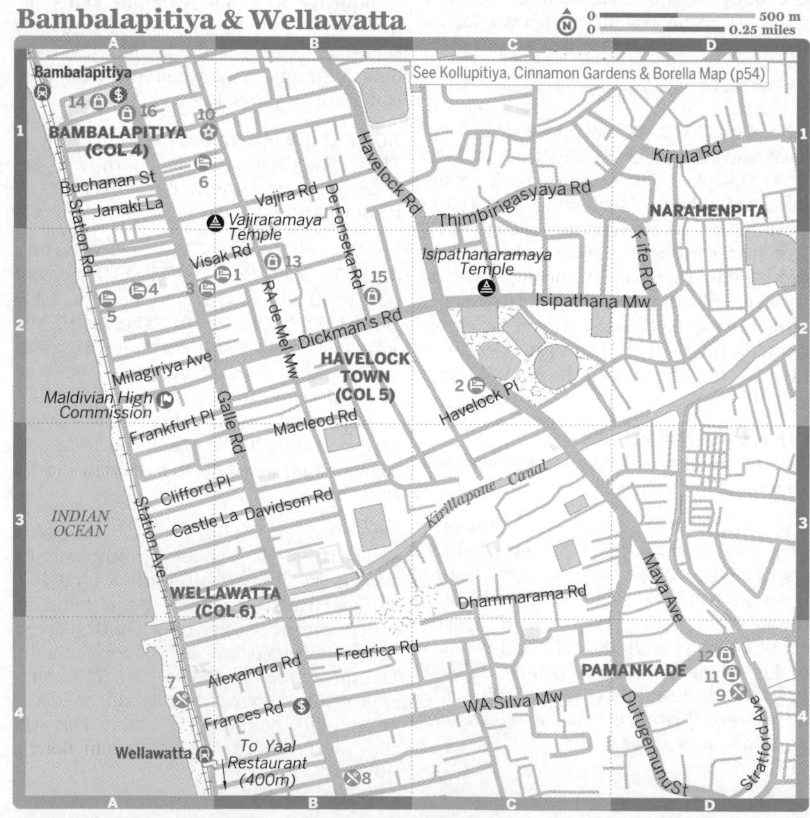

hides behind a gate off a small lane. Everything is tidy and basic.

Mrs Marie Barbara Settupathy's HOMESTAY $
(Map p62; ☎258 7964; jbs@slt.lk; 23/2 Shrubbery Gardens, Col 4; r US$22-30, air-con extra US$6; ❄) The voluble Mrs Settupathy offers four clean and tidy rooms (three with private bathroom). There's a sitting area with a TV, a full guest kitchen and a minuscule pebble courtyard. To find the Settupathys' house, look for the Church of Christ on the left as you come down Shrubbery Gardens (a name irresistible to Monty Python fans).

Hotel Atlantic HOTEL $
(Map p62; ☎720 2315, 454 2846; 237 Galle Rd, Col 4; r Rs 2200; ❄📶) Close to various diversions, this Galle Rd cheapie is well run, albeit with nine very basic rooms. Ask for a quiet one. The budget prices for a night's sleep are matched by the cheap beer prices in the popular – and dark – bar.

MT LAVINIA

If you're looking for a quieter alternative to Colombo but don't want to go as far as large beach towns like Negombo, Mt Lavinia is a 30-minute drive from Fort and has a rather modest beachy charm. There are numerous simple guesthouses aimed at local weekend travellers along the aptly named Hotel Rd as well as De Saram and College Rds. Inspect a couple before deciding. The Mt Lavinia train station is central to all the hotels listed here.

Haus Chandra BOUTIQUE HOTEL $$
(Map p64; ☎273 2755; www.plantationgrouphotels.com; 37 Beach Rd; r Rs 6400-8000; ❄@📶🏊) Tucked along a quiet lane, this colonial-era residence-turned-hotel has 30 rooms spread across two buildings that span a quiet lane. Other options include a charming villa that sleeps six and a suite with antique furnishings, carpets and a fully equipped kitchen that's a good choice for tropical fantasies. The pool has ocean views.

Mount Lavinia Hotel HOTEL $$$
(Map p64; ☎271 5221-7; www.mountlaviniahotel.com; 100 Hotel Rd; governor's wing s US$120-160, d US$140-180; ❄🏊) Part of this grand seafront hotel dates to 1806, when it was the residence of the British governor. About a third of the hotel – the appropriately named 'governor's wing' – has colonial decor and rather small rooms; the remainder is modern and the rooms have balconies. There's a private sandy beach and a beautifully positioned pool and terrace.

Tropic Inn GUESTHOUSE $$
(Map p64; ☎273 8653; www.tropicinn.com; 30 College Ave; r US$40-45; ❄@📶) This multistorey hotel features 16 clean rooms in a simple, stylish building. There's an internal courtyard and many of the rooms have a balcony; all rooms have cable TV. The engaging staff are helpful.

Blue Seas Guest House GUESTHOUSE $
(Map p64; ☎271 6298; 9/6 De Saram Rd; r Rs 1700-2800; ❄) This large house down a quiet lane has 14 clean, simple and spacious rooms, some with balconies. There's a large sitting room decked out with colonial furniture, and a garden. Most rooms are fan-only.

Eating

Colombo boasts a great and growing selection of restaurants. In addition to good Sri Lankan food, you'll find food from across the region and further afield. There are upscale and stylish cafes aimed at the well heeled but perhaps even more interesting are the many high-quality places aimed at

Bambalapitiya & Wellawatta

Sleeping
1 Casa Colombo ... B2
2 Havelock Place Bungalow ... C2
3 Hotel Atlantic ... A2
4 Hotel Sunshine ... A2
5 Mrs Marie Barbara Settupathy's ... A2
6 Tropic Inn ... A1

Eating
7 Beach Wadiya ... A4
8 Bombay Sweet Mahal ... B4
9 Cafe Che ... D4

Entertainment
10 Rhythm & Blues ... A1

Shopping
11 Cottage Craft ... D4
Dilmah Tea Shop ... (see 14)
12 Gandhara ... D4
13 House of Fashion ... B2
14 Majestic City ... A1
Mlesna Tea Centre ... (see 14)
Photo Technica ... (see 14)
15 Raux Brothers ... B2
16 Vijitha Yapa Bookshop ... A1

Dehiwala & Mt Lavinia

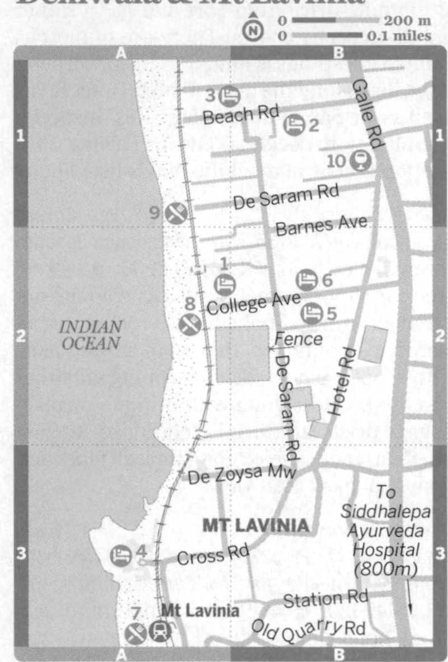

Dehiwala & Mt Lavinia

Sleeping

1 Berjaya Mount Royal Beach Hotel A2
2 Blue Seas Guest House B1
3 Haus Chandra A1
4 Mount Lavinia Hotel A3
5 Mrs Lyn Mendis' B2
6 Tropic Inn B2

Eating

7 Bu Ba A3
8 Golden Mile A2
9 La Voile Blanche A1

Drinking

10 Lion Pub B1

Colombo's burgeoning middle class. Here you'll find local food at its freshest.

For cheap, tasty food it's hard to beat a lunch packet (about Rs 150). Sold between about 11am and 2pm on street corners and from carts all over the city, the lunch packet contains rice and curry, usually made from vegetables, with fish or chicken as optional extras. Also look for open-front shops with short eats (snacks to eat on the go) fresh from the kitchen on display.

The website www.lankarestaurants.com is a good source of updated reviews.

FORT & PETTAH

Hordes of office workers, traders, commuters and residents support excellent snack stands and restaurants, most aimed at the masses. In the Fort's high-profile Old Dutch Hospital you'll find an array of chic restaurants and outdoor cafes run by noted locals.

TOP CHOICE AVP Restaurant SRI LANKAN $

(Map p50; 50 Baron Jayathilaka Mawatha, Col 1; mains Rs 100-500; ⏲7am-5pm Mon-Fri) Occupying the triangular-shaped ground floor of a classic colonial-era flatiron building, this huge restaurant has vast windows that flood the dining area with light. This is good as you'll want to admire your food, whether a simple rice and curry or something like fish cooked to order. Everything is excellent, as confirmed by the flock of local workers who line up here at lunch. Don't miss one of the myriad fresh juices.

Colombo Fort Cafe BISTRO $$$

(Map p50; Old Dutch Hospital, Col 1; mains Rs 600-1500; ⏲10am-11pm) Tapas standards, spicy local nibbles, burgers, salads and much more are created in the open kitchen that backs the long bar of this vaguely Mediterranean-themed bistro. Good beers on tap, many wines and an excellent coffee bar provide refreshment.

Ministry of Crab SEAFOOD $$$

(Map p50; ☎234 2722; www.ministryofcrab.com; Old Dutch Hospital; Col 1; mains Rs 800-4000; ⏲5-11pm) Crabs are a major income earner for Sri Lanka's fishing industry but most are exported and you don't often see crab on menus. This high-profile restaurant (two owners are former captains of the Sri Lanka cricket team) rectifies this loss in a major way by celebrating the crustaceans in variations ranging from Singaporean chilli crab to locally spiced crab curry. Depending on the catch, not everything is always available.

Curry Leaf SRI LANKAN $$$

(Map p50; Hilton Colombo, 2 Sir Chittampalam A Gardiner Mawatha, Col 1; buffet Rs 2500; ⏲7pm-midnight) Tucked away in a lovely garden that has the motif of an idealised traditional village, the buffet here has a vast range of Sri Lankan foods prepared with top-quality ingredients.

New Palm Leaf Hotel SRI LANKAN $
(Map p50; 237 Olcott Mawatha, Col 11; mains Rs 150-200; ⏲6am-10pm) Like elsewhere in Sri Lanka, 'hotel' here means 'simple eating place'. Across the very busy road from the Fort station and close to Pettah's market madness, pause here for a tea and cake or a short eat.

Pagoda Tea Room BAKERY $
(Map p50; ☎232 5252; 105 Chatham St, Col 1; mains Rs 100-150; ⏲9am-8pm) Hungry like the wolf? Duran Duran filmed its classic 1980s video for that very song in this venerable establishment (watch it on YouTube; sadly, there are no monkeys or snake charmers at Pagoda these days). Although a variety of regional dishes are on the menu, the main focus is on inexpensive pastries.

Lion Cafe SRI LANKAN $
(Map p50; 62A Olcott Mawatha, Col 11; snacks Rs 100; ⏲6am-10pm) On a strip of simple cafes along a road on the east side of Fort station commonly called Station Way, this tidy vendor serves up fresh short eats and excellent *kotthu* (*rotti* chopped and combined with vegetables and meat). Nearby choices have Indian veggie food.

KOLLUPITIYA

Old favourites can be found along Galle Rd; head east for restaurants and cafes along quieter and often tree-lined streets.

TOP CHOICE **Hotel De Pilawoos** SRI LANKAN $$
(Map p54; 417 Galle Rd; meals Rs 300-400; ⏲24hr) Just known as Pilaroos, this open-fronted purveyor of short eats is renowned for what may be the best *kotthu* in town. Expect the mighty and the humble to drop by anytime to grab one; take our advice and have the cheese version. Service is snappy.

Gallery Cafe ASIAN FUSION $$$
(Map p54; ☎258 2162; www.paradiseroad.lk; 2 Alfred House Rd, Col 3; mains from Rs 800; ⏲11am-11pm; 📶) The trim colonial bungalow that houses Shanth Fernando's Gallery Cafe used to be the office for Sri Lanka's most famous architect, Geoffrey Bawa (see boxed text, p53). The open-air dining area looks over an intimate courtyard and reflecting pool, while the lounge is where Bawa's old office used to be (his desk is still there). The decor is stunning and the Sri Lankan–inspired dishes focus on fresh ingredients and bold, clean flavours. Curries made with black pork and prawns are popular.

Chesa Swiss CONTINENTAL $$$
(Map p54; ☎257 3433; www.chesaswiss.com; 3 Deal Pl, Col 3; mains Rs 1000-2500; ⏲lunch 11am-2pm, dinner 5-11pm; ❄) This classy restaurant serves classically prepared meals with a European accent. Steaks, roasts and seafood are among the best in the city; in fact Chesa outclasses the top-end hotel dining rooms. Dine in the elegant garden or inside in air-con splendour. There are Swiss classics such as fondue and you can purchase a wide range of European deli items. La Brasserie at Chesa is the lunch incarnation and features simpler fare.

Bars Cafe CAFE $$
(Map p54; 24 Deal Pl, Col 3; mains Rs 400-800; ⏲11am-11pm; ❄📶) Dine on the shady terrace or inside the Euro-styled dining area at this smart cafe that serves excellent casual fare. Linger over drinks and work up an appetite for the burgers, steaks and artistic rendition of rice and curry. The desserts are sumptuous.

Green Cabin SRI LANKAN $
(Map p54; 453 Galle Rd, Col 3; mains Rs 150-400; ⏲7.30am-11.30pm) An institution in the local restaurant trade, Green Cabin is well known for baked goods and an inexpensive array of rice and curry variations, all served in a leafy dining room that's a refuge from Galle Rd. The lunchtime buffet is excellent value – the mango curry, if it's on, is very good. For a snack try the short meals from the bakery area such as vegetable pastries or the deep-fried peppers.

Barefoot Garden Cafe CAFE $$
(Map p54; 704 Galle Rd, Col 3; meals Rs 600-800; ⏲10am-11pm) Located in the courtyard of the splendid Barefoot gallery, this casual but stylish cafe serves sandwiches, salads and daily specials that usually include Sri Lankan and Asian dishes. The wine list is good and some nights there's special events like trivia contests or book readings.

Cricket Club Cafe PUB $$
(Map p54; 34 Queens Rd, Col 3; meals Rs 600-900; ⏲11am-11pm) This colonial-style bungalow with a garden and deeply shaded colonnaded veranda celebrates its namesake sport. Autographed cricket bats line the walls along with other oval-related memorabilia. Options range from pasta to seafood to burgers with salad and chips. There's a small air-con pub and an excellent selection of beers and wines.

Park Street Mews CAFE $$

(Map p54; 50/1 Park Rd, Col 2; mains Rs 500-2200; ⌚11am-11pm; 📶) The namesake cafe of the smart little lane of designer shops has a suitably hip vibe with an industrial motif and pillows on the concrete floor for lounging – along with tables, chairs and more traditional butt-rests. The menu mixes burgers, salads and Asian fare, with most items under Rs 800. Pastas and steaks are pricier.

Raffles FUSION $$$

(Map p54; ☎255 2837; www.rafflescolombo.com; 35 Bagatalle Rd, Col 3; mains Rs 500-1200; ⌚10am-11pm; ❄📶) This cosy colonial-style restaurant in an old gated mansion includes several areas for a drink, and multiple dining rooms for a quiet dinner. Pastas, salads and seafood dominate the menu, which also has steaks. The weekday lunch buffet is popular.

Carnival ICE CREAM $

(Map p54; 263 Galle Rd, Col 3; cones under Rs 100; ⌚10am-9pm) Unchanged in decades, you don't visit Carnival for the ice cream (which is more icy than creamy) but rather for the timeless ice-cream-parlour surrounds. Still, where else can you get your sundae topped with a banana for only Rs 20?

Keells SUPERMARKET $

(Map p54); Crescat Blvd (89 Galle Rd, Col 3); Liberty Plaza (RA de Mel Mawatha, Col 3) Western-style supermarket popular for its large selection of imported goods.

CINNAMON GARDENS

Stylish little cafes and more ambitious restaurants can be found along the genteel streets of Colombo's classiest district.

Milk & Honey Cafe HEALTH FOOD $$

(Map p54; 12 Barnes Pl, Col 7; meals Rs 300-500; ⌚9am-6pm Mon-Sat) Eating well never tasted so good; in a simple house shared with a kids' bookstore and Kemara spa, this groovy little cafe has an ever-changing menu of fresh fare such as slow-roasted veggies with pesto and a scrumptious mushroom and cream cheese focaccia. Enjoy one of many fresh juices outside in the garden.

Commons BISTRO $$

(Map p54; 39A Sir Ernest de Silva Mawatha, Col 7; meals Rs 400-600; ⌚7.30am-midnight; ❄📶) This cafe has a strong following among Colombo's iPad-wielding set. Customers lounge in soft seats arranged around low tables and feast on an array of dishes, including popular *rotti*, burgers, pastas and wraps. The breakfasts are very good and the desserts are spot on. The garden at the back is a shady urban retreat.

Coco Veranda Cafe CAFE $$

(Map p54; 32 Ward Pl, Col 7; meals Rs 500-900; ⌚8am-midnight; ❄📶) In a small building with designer clothing shops, this cool little cafe has an extraordinarily long menu of teas, coffee drinks, frappes and fresh juices. There are burgers, sandwiches and pasta as well as very alluring desserts. This is a good late-night stop for snack.

Boulevard FOOD COURT $

(Map p54; Odel, 5 Alexandra Pl, Col 7; meals Rs 200-600; ⌚9am-6pm) Right in front of the entrance to the popular and chic Odel department store is this silver-hued swath of food stalls in a sleek outdoor food court. Outlets of well-known local vendors serve up sandwiches, Indian fare, health food, pizza, various snacks and much more. It's an ideal stop if you're walking – or shopping.

Paradise Road Cafe CAFE, DELI $$

(Map p54; 213 Dharmapala Mawatha, Col 7; meals Rs 250-500; ❄) Part of the designer shop of the same name, this smart cafe serves coffee drinks, milkshakes, cakes and a plethora of teas. You can enjoy a sandwich or pasta but be sure to leave room for the double chocolate cheesecake or one of the other desserts from the cafe's renowned sibling, the Gallery Cafe. Get upscale picnic fare from the deli and enjoy it in Viharamahadevi Park.

Bayleaf ITALIAN $$$

(Map p54; ☎269 5920; 79 Gregory's Rd, Col 7; mains Rs 800-1700; ⌚noon-3pm & 6-11pm) In a beautiful old colonial mansion in one of Colombo's most exclusive streets, this refined restaurant specialises in Italian fine dining. The menu could be a direct import from Milan, although the tables in the lush tropical garden are all Sri Lanka.

WELLAWATTA

Local favourites dominate the options of this southern quarter, which has Galle Rd as its spine. Look for a dose of hip over on Stratford Ave in Pamankade.

TOP CHOICE **Bombay Sweet Mahal** CANDY $

(Map p62; 195 Galle Rd, Col 6; treats from Rs 50; ⌚9am-7pm) Galle Rd boasts many vendors of Indian sweets but this tiny open-fronted shop is the best. An array of candies and treats sits colourfully in the display cases.

We especially like the thick and chewy *nut musket*. Buy by weight to go (and they'll wrap your sweets uber-carefully) or enjoy on the spot. Grab a cool juice at a table at the back. The engaging staff are happy to explain the many offerings.

Beach Wadiya SEAFOOD $$$
(Map p62; ☎258 8568; www.beachwadiya.com; 2 Station Ave, Col 6; mains Rs 500-1600; ⏰noon-3pm & 6-11pm) Renowned for its seafood, Beach Wadiya has attracted a popular following for decades, including various celebrities. The location is a tropical dream: cross the train tracks at the seashore and enter a walled enclave. Waiters describe what's fresh – there's always crab, prawns and lobster – then enjoy something cold while your fish is cooked. Expect to get messy as you'll be doing your own shell-cracking and extracting. Book a few days ahead.

Cafe Che INTERNATIONAL $$
(Map p62; 60 Stratford Ave, Col 6; Mains Rs 500-1000; ⏰11am-11pm; ❄) Just down the street from the trendy shops of Stratford Ave, this appealing cafe has a long menu with a diversity that would no doubt please its eponymous revolutionary. There's a few Cuban items along with burritos, pasta, pizza and more. The dining room shuts out the hurly-burly of traffic outside.

Yaal Restaurant JAFFNA $$
(off Map p62; 56 Vaverset Pl, Col 6; mains Rs 300-500; ⏰10am-10pm) The unique spicy cuisine of Jaffna's Tamils features at this simple yet very tidy restaurant across from the seashore. The speciality is the truly unique *odiyal kool*, a famous Jaffna dish consisting of vegetables and seafood combined in a creamy porridge. Or opt for the tasty garlic curry.

MT LAVINIA

The beachfront here is lined with cafes offering up drinks, simple meals and seafood in settings from common to grand. Sunset is prime time for a beverage followed by a meal as the skies go dark.

TOP CHOICE **Bu Ba** CAFE $$
(Map p64; Mt Lavinia beach; mains Rs 800-3200; ⏰8am-midnight) With candlelit tables right on the sandy beach, this seafood pub is the less-vaunted alternative to Seafood Wadiya. In the heat of the day you can retreat under the grove of palm trees, at night let the sky open overhead and the starlight rain down. Weekend dance parties are sometimes held here. To find it, walk south alongside the tracks from Mt Lavinia train station – about 100m.

La Voile Blanche CAFE $$
(Map p64; 43/10 Beach Rd; mains from Rs 300; ⏰11am-11pm) Amid the often rather shabby Mt Lavinia beachfront cafes, this vision in white stands out. Under seven iconic palm trees, a range of comfy chairs and loungers beckons. The drinks list is long and the menu offers up sandwiches, pasta and seafood. Look for the cafe across the tracks behind the Mount Breeze Hotel.

Golden Mile SEAFOOD $$$
(Map p64; ☎273 3997; 43/14 College Ave; mains Rs 1400-2000; ⏰11am-midnight) The setting at this beachside restaurant is romantic and you'll often get live music in the evenings. It specialises in Western-style seafood, with a variety of cooked prawns and a fine seafood platter. It's a cut above the other nearby cafes and there's a lookout tower so you can try to spot pirates – or whales.

Drinking

Finding a spot for sunset drinks is an essential experience (try Galle Face Green or Mt Lavinia), otherwise many of the best places to eat also are good for a drink (notably Bars Cafe, Barefoot Garden Cafe, Cricket Club Cafe). Note that last call comes early: technically 11pm, although some places keep pouring later.

Brewery by O! PUB
(Map p50; Old Dutch Hospital, Col 1; ⏰5pm-midnight) Beer fresh from the pub's owner (the local brewer Lion) is the highlight at this English-style pub in the Old Dutch Hospital. This is a good place to find beers like Sinha Stout on tap.

Galle Face Hotel HOTEL BAR
(Map p54; 2 Kollupitiya Rd, Col 3; ⏰11am-midnight) The venerable hotel has the iconic Veranda bar area with its trademark checkered tiles and lawn tables under palms. Popular with tourists, service can be mediocre.

Clancy's Irish Pub LOUNGE
(Map p54; 29 Maitland Cres, Col 7; ⏰7am-3am Mon-Sat) A rollicking bar popular with Colombo's nouveau rich and expats, there are frequent drink specials, views of the nearby cricket oval, live music and club nights. Part of a

club zone, the pub's Soprano's karaoke bar has 14,000 songs for punters to mangle.

White Horse PUB

(Map p54; 2 Nawam Mawatha, Col 2; ⏲10am-2am) White Horse is a hugely popular place for a drink before setting off for further adventures. On Friday nights the mixed crowd of locals and expats from the surrounding office buildings often spills out onto the street. The fish fry is justifiably popular.

7° North COCKTAIL BAR

(Map p54; Cinnamon Lakeside Hotel, 115, Sir Chittampalam A Gardiner Mawatha, Col 2; ⏲5pm-1am) The one compelling reason to visit this otherwise forgettable hotel is this sprawling posh bar that overlooks Beira Lake from a large deck. Enjoy high-end cocktails under the stars.

Castle Hotel BAR

(Map p54; Masjid Jamiah Rd; ⏲10am-11pm) Right off gritty Union Pl, this timeless boozer offers up cheap drafts of Lion in once-posh surrounds that have borne witness to generations of drinkers, from politicians to railway workers. It's a genial place, good for catching up on current Colombo events.

☆ Entertainment

Colombo has not traditionally been a mecca for after-dark entertainment but that's changing as new venues – especially a huge new performing arts centre – open.

Nightclubs

Colombo's club scene is burgeoning with the rest of the capital's nightlife. Although hotel dance clubs dominated the scene for years, indie locations are beginning to thrive.

Silk CLUB

(Map p54; 41 Maitland Cres, Col 7) Near other nightspots like Clancy's Irish Pub, this club is among the city's most popular. It has a rooftop dining venue called Lemon.

Rhythm & Blues LIVE MUSIC

(R&B; Map p62; 19/1 Daisy Villa Ave, Col 4) This place has live music nightly. It can get rowdy at the pool tables. Despite the Daisy Villa Ave address, it's on RA de Mel Mawatha.

Blue Leopard CLUB

(Map p50; Grand Oriental Hotel, 2 York St, Col 1) Somewhat gritty, with a few sailors from the nearby harbour.

Mojo CLUB

(Map p54; ☎077 311 1113; Taj Samudra Hotel, 25 Galle Face Centre Rd, Col 3; ⏲Wed-Sun) Glossy; wait until after midnight, call to book a table.

Performing Arts

Nelum Pokuna Performing Arts Theatre VENUE

(Map p54; www.lotuspond.lk; Ananda Coomaraswamy Mawatha, Col 7) The big news in Colombo's cultural circles is this glossy new venue built largely with Chinese aid and located in a high-profile spot south of Viharamahadevi Park. Its stunning design is based on the Nelum Pokuna, the 12th-century lotus pond in Polonnaruwa. Look for important productions here. Note that politicians such as Mahinda Rajapaksa have tried to get their names added to the building.

Elphinstone Theatre THEATRE

(Map p54; ☎243 3635; Maradana Rd, Col 10) This restored 80-year-old theatre maintains a busy program that includes music, theatre and films.

Lionel Wendt Centre CULTURAL CENTRE

(Map p54; ☎269 5794; www.lionelwendt.org; 18 Guildford Cres, Col 7; ⏲9am-1pm & 2-5pm Mon-Fri, 10am-noon & 1-5pm Sat & Sun) Among other cultural events, this gallery occasionally hosts live theatre.

Sport

Sri Lanka Cricket CRICKET

(Map p54; www.srilankacricket.lk; 35 Maitland Pl, Col 7; ⏲ticket office 8.30am-5.30pm) The top sport in Sri Lanka is, without a doubt, cricket. You can buy tickets for major games from Sri Lanka Cricket, at the office near the oval.

Casinos

Gaming is legal in Colombo, but only for holders of foreign passports. Most of the clientele is from the region and the casinos – despite adopting names familiar to Vegas high rollers – are very modest affairs with no connection to their famous namesakes.

Shopping

Colombo's markets (p51), with their vast selection of everyday goods, are much more compelling as places to visit than venues for finding goods to take home. Otherwise, Colombo has many good stores making that extra bag essential.

Shopping Malls

Expect a wave of new shopping malls to open in Colombo as the economy booms. In the meantime the city has several rather tatty large malls. Your best bets are the following pair.

Crescat Boulevard MALL
(Map p54; 89 Galle Rd, Col 3) Small upscale mall next to the Cinnamon Grand Hotel.

Majestic City MALL
(Map p62; Galle Rd, Col 4) Large mall with a wide range of stores.

Large Stores

TOP CHOICE **Odel** DEPARTMENT STORE
(Map p54; www.odel.lk; 5 Alexandra Pl, Col 7) A high-profile department store that combines international and top local brands in one glitzy labyrinth. From fashions to homewares to cosmetics and gift items, Odel's selection is tops.

Arpico SUPERSTORE
(Map p54; Hyde Park Corner) A huge store good for replacing almost anything you left at home. Imported foods (get your Oreos), cosmetics, sunscreen, a pharmacy, gear such as plug adaptors and much, much more.

Handicrafts & Collectables

Barefoot also produces a large range of appealing handicrafts.

Paradise Road HOMEWARES
(Map p54; 268 6043; 213 Dharmapala Mawatha, Col 7) In addition to a variety of colonial and Sri Lankan collectables, you'll find a good selection of original homewares and designer items in this high-style boutique. Paradise Road's Gallery Cafe Shop is part of the noted restaurant and is tightly packed with small, artistic goods. Both are excellent places to look for small gifts to take home.

Cottage Craft HANDICRAFTS
(Map p62; 40 Stratford Ave, Col 6) Rather than clichéd carved elephants, this tiny shop sells paper items made from elephant dung. There's no smell and the items such as travel journals are exquisite. Everything sold here is made in Sri Lankan villages using eco-friendly techniques. Look for the batiks and artworks.

Gandhara HOMEWARES
(Map p62; 28 Stratford Ave, Col 6) This stylish designer shop on the trendy stretch of Stratford Ave sells everything from candles to coffee tables. Gift items pegged to the season are displayed in profusion and there is a good section of books on Sri Lankan art.

Raux Brothers HOMEWARES, ANTIQUES
(The Colonial; Map p62; 533 9016; 7 De Fonseka Rd, Col 5) This 48-year-old antiques showroom, located in a large, beautiful colonial house, stocks an impressive range of furniture and artworks crafted from wood. There are genuine antiques and handcrafted new pieces. This is possibly the best antiques house in the city.

Fabrics & Clothing

Sri Lanka has a thriving weaving industry that produces both hand- and machine-woven fabrics, and is a major garment manufacturer. All manner of clothing, ranging from beachwear to padded jackets, is sold in Colombo.

TOP CHOICE **Barefoot** TEXTILES
(Map p54; 258 0114; www.barefootceylon.com; 704 Galle Rd, Col 3) Designer Barbara Sansoni's beautifully laid-out shop, located in an old villa, is justly popular for its bright hand-loomed textiles, which are fashioned into bedspreads, cushions, serviettes and other household items (or sold by the metre). You'll also find textile-covered notebooks, lampshades and albums, and a large selection of stylish, simple clothing.

House of Fashion CLOTHING
(Map p62; 250 4639; cnr RA de Mel Mawatha & Visak Rd, Col 4) This three-storey surplus outlet for the nation's garment industry is the place to go for serious clothes shopping. It's always crowded; many items are hugely discounted.

KT Brown CLOTHING
(Map p54; Park St Mews, 48A Park St) Noted local designer Kanchana Thalpawila offers a range of women's clothing, from casual garb to haute couture. Her inspirations are traditional fabrics and costumes.

Tea

Ceylon tea is sold in just about every place that sells foodstuffs, from minimarts to supermarkets. For the best quality and selection, however, visit a specialist shop.

TOP CHOICE **Sri Lanka Tea Board Shop** TEA
(Map p54; 574 Galle Rd) A large but unflashy shop which has many of the smaller brands of Ceylon tea that can be hard to find. It

also has the full range of top brands such as Mackwoods and all sorts of tea-related merchandise.

Mlesna Tea Centre TEA
Crescat Boulevard (Map p54; 89 Galle Rd, Col 3); Majestic City (Map p62; Galle Rd, Col 4) High-end boutiques with teas and tea-making wares.

Dilmah Tea Shop TEA
Cinnamon Gardens (Map p54; Odel, 5 Alexandra Pl, Col 7); Crescat Boulevard (Map p54; 89 Galle Rd, Col 3); Majestic City (Map p62; Galle Rd, Col 4) Sri Lanka's top tea brand has its own posh shops.

Gift Items

Most of the shops listed in this entire Shopping section can yield excellent gift items.

TOP CHOICE **Sri Lanka Cashew Corporation** FOOD
(Map p54; 518 Galle Rd, Col 3) Cashews were brought by the Portuguese to Sri Lanka from Brazil in the 16th century. They've clearly found the climate agreeable as the nuts are now a major export item. This small shop is packed full of fulsome cashews of a size and quality that are usually hard to find, especially in that dodgy bag of mixed nuts.

Laksala SOUVENIRS
(Map p54; 215 Bauddhaloka Mawatha, Col 7) A large outlet of the government-run chain of souvenir shops popular with groups. Cheap carved elephants, well-crafted handicrafts and handmade clothing compete for attention.

Bazaar SOUVENIRS
(Map p50; Col 11) A large collection of stalls just west of Fort station, selling items aimed at tourists.

Bookshops

In addition to the shops listed here, Odel has a small but good book department.

Barefoot BOOKS
(Map p54; www.barefootceylon.com; 704 Galle Rd, Col 3) Within the much-lauded designer shop is an excellent book department. This is where you'll find a carefully selected range of locally published books such as Juliet Coombe's excellent books about Sri Lanka and Colombo, the full range of Michael Ondaatje's works and much more.

Vijitha Yapa Bookshop BOOKS
Crescat Boulevard (Map p54; 89 Galle Rd, Col 3); Unity Plaza (Map p62; Galle Rd, Col 4) Stocks a comprehensive collection of foreign and local novels, guidebooks and pictorial tomes on Sri Lanka.

Buddhist Book Centre BOOKS
(Map p54; 380 Bauddhaloka Mawatha, Col 7) Filled with books on Buddhism; about a third of the stock is in English.

Gems & Jewellery

For high-end shops, head to the Crescat Boulevard mall. **Sri Lanka Gem & Jewellery Exchange** (Map p50; 4th & 5th fl, East Low Block, World Trade Center, Bank of Ceylon Mawatha, Col 1) has dozens of small shops.

Photo Supplies & Repairs

Photo Technica CAMERAS
Kollupitiya (Map p54; 288 Galle Rd, Col 3); Liberty Plaza (Map p54; RA de Mel Mawatha, Col 3); Majestic City (Map p62; Galle Rd, Col 4) Near the Kollupitiya location there is also a visa photo service at 262 Galle Rd.

Information

Dangers & Annoyances

CRIME Violence towards foreigners is uncommon, although you should take the usual safeguards. Solo women should be careful when taking taxis and three-wheelers at night; if, as sometimes happens, your taxi turns up with two men inside, call another.

SCAMS & TOUTS Colombo has its share of touts and con artists. You may be approached by someone who, after striking up a conversation, asks for a donation for a school for the blind or some such cause – these people are invariably con artists. Galle Rd is the main hunting ground for these characters, although they are easily ignored. Street offers for guides and 'special' tours should also be shunned.

Emergency

Fire & Ambulance (242 2222)

Medi-Calls Ambulance (257 5475)

Police (119, 243 3333)

Tourist Police (Map p54; 242 1451; 80 Galle Rd, Col 3; 24hr)

Internet Access

Most cafes in Colombo offer wi-fi, often for free.

Berty's Cyber Cafe (Map p54; 380 Galle Rd, Col 3) is a central internet cafe.

Media

The daily English-language newspapers, the *Daily Mirror*, the *Daily News* and the *Island* all have local news and entertainment listings.

Good websites:

Ceylon Today (www.ceylontoday.lk) News, sports and entertainment.

Daily Mirror (www.dailymirror.lk) Best of the newspaper websites.

Gossip Lanka (www.english.gossiplankanews.com) Gossip and entertainment news.

Indi.ca (www.indi.ca) An excellent blog covering news, opinion and culture.

Kottu (www.kottu.org) Aggregates content from over 1000 Sri Lankan blogs.

Medical Services

Avoid government hospitals, such as Colombo General.

Nawaloka Hospital (Map p54; ☎254 4444, 557 7111; www.nawaloka.com; 23 Sri Saugathodaya Mawatha, Col 2) This private hospital has a good reputation and English-speaking doctors.

Money

There are banks and ATMs all over the city. Exchange services are in the arrivals hall at Bandaranaike International Airport, in Fort and along Galle Rd.

Post

Sri Lanka Post (Map p50; DR Wijewardana Mawatha, Col 1; ⊙7am-6pm, poste restante 7am-9pm, stamps & telephone 24hr) offers poste restante and can hold mail for two months – call ☎232 6203 to see if there's anything awaiting you.

The major international express shipping services all have locations in Colombo.

Tourist Information

Sri Lanka Tourist Board (SLTB; Map p54; ☎243 7059; www.srilanka.travel; 80 Galle Rd, Col 3; ⊙9am-4.45pm Mon-Fri, to 12.30pm Sat) The country's national tourism office. Staff can book hotels among other services.

Travel Agencies

Colombo's plethora of travel agencies can organise tours across Sri Lanka. See p315 for details of the main operators. There are numerous travel agent offices on Chatham St in Fort.

 Getting There & Away

Although Bandaranaike International Airport is at Katunayake, 30km north of the city, it is called Colombo (CMB) in airline schedules. Arriving by air – especially late at night – it is easiest to spend your first night in the city. You can then easily move on by road, rail or bus.

Note that the roads in and around Colombo are very congested; however, new highways should provide a speedier alternative. See the boxed text on p72 for details.

HAVE YOUR SAY

Found a fantastic restaurant that you're longing to share with the world? Disagree with our recommendations? Or just want to talk about your most recent trip?

Whatever your reason, head to lonelyplanet.com, where you can post a review, ask or answer a question on the Thorntree forum, comment on a blog, or share your photos and tips on Groups. Or you can simply spend time chatting with like-minded travellers. So go on, have your say.

Air

For details on Bandaranaike International Airport, see p310.

Bus

Colombo's bus stations may be chaotic, but there are frequent buses going in all directions. The city has three main bus terminals, all just east of Fort train station on the south edge of Pettah. Long-distance buses leave from **Bastian Mawatha station** (Map p50) and **Saunders Pl station** (Map p50); **Central Bus Station** (Map p50) on Olcott Mawatha is where many suburban buses start and stop. The following table details which buses leave from which station:

FROM BASTIAN MAWATHA	FROM SAUNDERS PL
Ambalangoda	Anuradhapura
Galle	Badulla
Hikkaduwa	Haputale
Kandy	Jaffna
Kataragama	Kurunegala
Matara	Negombo
Nuwara Eliya	Ratnapura
Tangalla	Polonnaruwa
	Trincomalee

Check fares and other details in the destination chapter listings.

A new bus service, the **Southern Expressway Bus** (already being called the SEX bus; Rs 400, every 30 to 60 minutes), travels the new Southern Expressway (p313) to Galle in about 90 minutes. The comfy air-con buses leave from the **Maharagama bus stand** (☎770 6286) near the

COLOMBO'S NEW EXPRESSWAYS

During rush hour it can take up two hours or more to get from the airport to the beginning of the new **Southern Expressway** at its start in Makumbura, some 12km southeast of Colombo's centre. From Fort, getting there can take almost as long.

Two new toll-road projects should greatly speed travel times:

» **Colombo–Katunayake Highway** Running some 25km from the airport to a point just northeast of Fort, this could cut travel times to under 30 minutes. It should be open in 2013.

» **Outer Circular Highway** This beltway will link the Colombo–Katunayake Hwy with the Southern Expressway, putting Galle and the south within two hours of the airport, which will revolutionise travel patterns. It should be fully open by 2015.

southern suburb of Kottawa. It's very close to the start of the Southern Expressway.

Train

The main train station, **Colombo Fort** (Map p50), is very central. Trains in transit often stop only for two or three minutes. See p315 for details of services and routes.

JF Tours & Travels (Map p50; ☎244 0048; ⏰9am-5pm) has an office at the front of Fort station; the helpful staff know everything about transport in and out of Colombo. Or you could try the information desk in the station. There is **left-luggage storage** (per bag per day Rs 60; ⏰4.30am-11.30pm) at the extreme left-end as you face the station.

Getting Around

To/From the Airport

Completion of the Colombo–Katunayake Hwy will speed travel times from Bandaranaike International Airport to the city. Until then, however, expect a car or taxi to take one to two hours.

Any domestic flights that are operating are likely to depart from Colombo's Ratmalana Air Force Base; for details, see (p312).

BUS Buses to the airport (regular/air-con Rs 70/100) depart from Bastian Mawatha station every 15 minutes from 6am until 9pm. The bus stops about 1km from the airport; a free shuttle takes you the rest of the way.

From the airport, catch the free shuttle from outside the arrivals area. Buses to Colombo often begin their journey elsewhere, so you may find the bus crowded and little space for luggage. The journey can take one to three hours.

CAR You can arrange an airport car with most Colombo-area hotels for Rs 3000 to 4000. In fact hotels as far as Galle and beyond can often arrange airport transport. Whether a hotel car or a driver you've booked in advance, expect to be met in the arrivals area of the airport.

TAXI Convenient and as quick as traffic allows. There is a taxi stand right outside the arrivals building. Compared to previous years, getting a taxi is relatively hassle-free. Expect to pay about Rs 2100 to Colombo (one to 1½ hours), Rs 1500 to Negombo (30 minutes) and Rs 5000 to Kandy (two to three hours). Don't take a three-wheeler between the airport and Colombo; it's a long, exhaust-fume-choked journey. Taxis to Colombo prepaid at desks in the arrivals area cost Rs 2600.

Public Transport

BUS The *A-Z Street Guide* contains a detailed table and a map showing bus routes in Colombo, but the best way to find out which bus to take is just to ask people at the nearest stop. Buses going down Galle Rd from Fort or Pettah include 100, 101, 102 and 400. Fares vary from Rs 5 to 40, depending on distance. Service is frequent; there is usually an English-language destination sign on the front of the bus.

TAXI Most taxis are metered, but often the driver won't use the meter – agree on the fare before setting off. A taxi from Fort train station to Galle Face Hotel (a little over 2km) should cost about Rs 200; Mt Lavinia should cost around Rs 1200.

Cabs dispatched by radio are becoming very popular as the companies use meters and the service is both more comfortable and cheaper than regular cabs or three-wheelers. Call the dispatch number and a cab will usually arrive within 15 minutes. Reliable companies:

Ace Cabs (☎281 8818)

Budget Taxi (☎729 9299)

Kangaroo Cabs (☎258 8588)

TRAIN You can use the train to get to the suburbs dotted along Galle Rd – Kollupitiya, Bambalapitiya, Wellawatta, Dehiwala and Mt Lavinia; as a bonus, the line follows the seashore. Timetables are clearly marked at the stations, though service is frequent. If you board the train at Fort train station, double-check that it stops at all stations or you may end up in Galle. Train fares are about the same as bus fares.

THREE-WHEELER Also known as tuk-tuks and tri-shaws, these smoke-spewing Indian-made creations are ubiquitous. Although you're likely to get wet if it rains and the cramped back seats have limited views out, a ride in a three-wheeler is part of the Colombo experience. Drivers dart fearlessly between huge buses, an experience that might be called exhilarating by some and reckless by others.

Agree on a price before you get in (stop drivers along the road; those waiting will charge the most). You may need to bargain with a couple. Although the general rule is Rs 50 to 100 per kilometre, it can be hard as a visitor to get this rate. From Fort, expect to pay Rs 400 to get to Cinnamon Gardens, Rs 600 to Bambalapitiya and Rs 1000 to Mt Lavinia. Metered taxis are cheaper.

A recent innovation in Colombo is metered three-wheelers, which carry signage advertising themselves as such. If you see one, hail it on the street and (!) confirm that it has a working meter. These can be the very cheapest means of getting around.

West Coast

Includes »

Best Places to Eat

» Lords (p80)
» Basil (p91)
» Kandoori (p86)
» Spaghetti & Co (p91)

Best Places to Stay

» Villa Araliya (p79)
» Club Villa (p84)
» Saman Villas (p85)
» Ice Bear Guest House (p79)

Why Go?

You don't have to be on Sri Lanka's west coast for long to realise that this coastline has something of a multiple personality. North of the capital is Negombo, a cheerful beach town crowned with church spires that is, thanks to its proximity to the airport, a staple of almost every visitor's Sri Lankan journey. Head further north, though, and you enter a wild and little-visited region that seems to consist of nothing but coconut plantations and lagoons, sparkling in the sun and filled with dolphins.

South of Colombo's chaos is a world that oscillates between the dancing devils of traditional Sri Lankan culture in Ambalangoda, the chic boutique hotels and uncluttered golden sands of Bentota, and the down-at-heel but ever-popular backpacker party town of Hikkaduwa.

Whichever side of the west coast you choose you can be sure you'll end up spending longer here than planned.

When to Go

Negombo

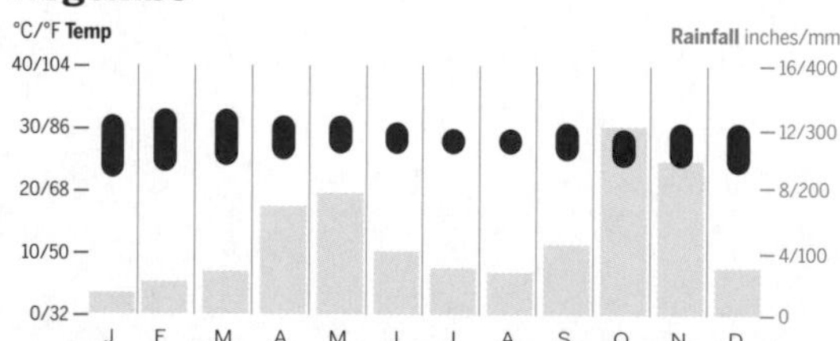

Jan Schools of dolphins party in Dutch Bay and packs of backpackers party nightly in Hikkaduwa.

Mar–Apr Sri Lanka's Christians stage Easter passion plays in Negombo and Talawila.

Nov If you prefer your beaches (almost) tourist-free then November is the month to come.

West Coast Highlights

1. Scanning the horizon for schools of playful dolphins in the waters off **Kalpitiya** (p76)
2. Finding your feet after a long flight in charming but ramshackle **Negombo** (p78)
3. Feeling the stress levels drop under the palm trees of lovely **Bentota** (p83), and booking in for a pampering in one of the area's boutique hotels
4. Ticking off egrets and herons during a waterborne birdwatching safari through the **Muthurajawela Marsh** (p83)
5. Learning the secrets behind the devil masks in **Ambalangoda** (p91)
6. Getting all green-fingered in the **Brief Garden** (p84) near Bentota
7. Raising a toast to the sunset after a hard day's diving and surfing in lively **Hikkaduwa** (p87)

NORTH OF COLOMBO

Leaving Colombo most eyes look south, but for those with time on their hands and a sense of curiosity, or for those on the slow road towards Anuradhapura, then the northbound A3 heads out of Colombo, skirts some charming old Dutch canals, slides past some sandy beaches and gets utterly lost among a matted tangle of coconut groves. It all adds up to a wonderful sense of discovery. For the moment, aside from workaday Negombo, which sits close to Bandaranaike International Airport, much of this area remains completely unexplored by tourists and the chances of finding an untarnished beach is high, but things are on the cusp of change. The government, inspired by the kind of high-end, exclusive beach tourism of the neighbouring Maldives, has embarked on an ambitious tourism project around the town of Kalpitiya at the end of the long peninsula that separates Dutch Bay from the ocean.

We start our coverage in the far north and work southwards.

Kalpitiya & Dutch Bay

Kalpitiya and Talawila are the two main towns on the long finger of land that separates Dutch Bay from the Indian Ocean. For the moment this is an intensely rural backwater that until recently saw very few visitors. Things are starting to change, though, and the government is engaged in a project to turn the peninsula and its string of offshore islands into one of Sri Lanka's prime beach tourism destinations. The blueprints call for businesses to invest in projects as diverse as luxury accommodation with beds for 10,000 people, a domestic airport, theme parks and an underwater amusement park (!), golf courses, high-speed boat safaris and much more besides. If reading that just made you raise your eyebrows in alarm then you're not alone. Environmentalists are concerned about the impact these projects will have on the populations of dolphins, sperm whales and dugongs who use the waters around Dutch Bay.

Maybe more importantly, though, a large number of local people are concerned that their needs are being overlooked in favour of grandiose tourist developments, and by the banning of fishing in certain areas. They also have concerns about the development process itself (the Minister of Economic Development has admitted that land deeds have been forged in some places). Local people have even gone so far as to stage protests in Colombo, but despite these protests many projects are already underway.

Considering, though, that the beaches here tend to be wind exposed, and the waters both within Dutch Bay and around the surrounding ocean are quite brown in comparison to the crystal-blue waters of the south coast (and most of the accommodation is vastly overpriced), many of these projects may end up mere white elephants.

An essential port of call in these parts is the excellent Dutch–Sri Lankan run **Tourist Information Centre** (☎032-561 2041; Kalpitiya; ⏰9am-5pm). This private tourist office can offer impartial advice on accommodation, ferries to outer islands, sights and activities in the area, and it organises some worthwhile boat trips and village visits.

Sights & Activities

Before we paint too grim a picture, there are some reasons for venturing up here. At **Talawila**, halfway up the peninsula, there's a Catholic shrine to St Anne. The church features satinwood pillars and is pleasantly situated on the seafront. Thousands of pilgrims come here in March and July, when major festivals honouring St Anne are held. The festivals include huge processions, healing services and a fair.

For most people, though, the biggest draw in this area is the dolphins. **Dolphin boat tours** are operated by the Tourist Information Centre in Kalpitiya. It charges Rs 9000 for up to five people for a half-day tour, but as government permits are required you must give them at least a day's notice. Two highly regarded Colombo-based operators that offer slightly more expensive but very professional dolphin-watching packages up here are **Jetwing Eco Holidays** (☎011-238 1201; www.jetwingeco.com; 46/26 Navam Mawatha, Colombo) and **Eco Team Sri Lanka** (☎011-583 0833; www.srilankaecotourism.com; 20/63 Fairfield Gardens, Colombo). Dolphins (and even whales) are seen around 80% of the time in the October-to-May season.

Snorkelling and **diving** on the spectacular offshore reefs are also possible. The prime dive site is the spectacular **Bar Reef**. Sitting several kilometres off the northwest tip of the peninsula this pristine reef system

WORTH A TRIP

WILPATTU NATIONAL PARK & PUTTALAM

After years of security-issue-enforced closures, Wilpattu National Park is finally open again. At 1085 sq km it is Sri Lanka's largest national park and was once its most popular. For years the park was on or near the frontline in the war and men, from both sides of the conflict, with guns ranged across the park. Needless to say conservation was not top of anyone's list of priorities at this time: the park's infrastructure remains basic and wildlife numbers are only a fraction of what they once were, but the park's dense pockets of jungle scrub interspersed with small clearings and water ponds are still worth exploring by the dedicated naturalist. The park is home to up to 50 rarely seen elephants and 50 or more leopards, which are increasingly commonly seen. In addition there are spotted deer, sloth bears, wild pigs, crocodiles and lots of different birds.

The turnoff to the park on the rough but paved Puttalam–Anuradhapura road (A12) is 26km northeast of Puttalam and 20km southwest of Anuradhapura. A further 8km of rough road leads to the park entrance and office at the barely discernable village of Hunuwilagama.

Jeeps can be hired in the old trading, pearling and fishing town of Puttalam, which itself has a pleasant setting on the edge of a lagoon, and is the kind of seriously go-slow place in which nobody understands the need for a watch. There is some basic accommodation available in the town.

is said to be one of the finest dive sites in Sri Lanka. Despite its remote location it's also considered a good snorkelling spot. The Tourist Information Centre in Kalpitiya can help organise diving trips (again, with notice), as can various Colombo-based operators including those listed earlier.

The area is also gaining a reputation for **kitesurfing**. Currently it's very much a DIY kind of thing, but some of the bigger hotels have a range of gear to rent and the Kite Centre Negombo runs kitesurf safaris up here.

Sleeping

The price of accommodation in these parts is almost laughable. We visited a number of establishments offering nothing more than a palm-frond hut with no electricity, running water or other facilities and for which the owners were asking between US$40 and US$70 a person. In Kalpitiya itself you can find a couple of basic **homestays** (r Rs 1250). The **Taniya Hotel** (☎032-329 3031; r with/without air-con Rs 3500/2000), a few kilometres south of Kalpitiya, offers some of the best-value rooms around. Don't forget to take your camera for the 'elephants', 'giraffes' and 'deer' that frolic in the hotel gardens. Another good, but more expensive, option is the **Ruwala Resort** (☎032-329 9299; tent Rs 2500, cabana Rs 11,000, r Rs 12,500) on the lagoon shore a few kilometres before Talawila. It's a friendly, resort-style complex that also offers a range of adventure activities such as horse riding, fishing and climbing.

Getting There & Away

There are frequent buses to Colombo (regular/air-con Rs 200/350, four hours) and Puttulam (regular/air-con Rs 60/120, one hour).

Kalpitiya to Negombo

Although the A3 stays close to the coast, there are few ocean views from the road. Rather, when heading south to Negombo, you pass through an endless series of coconut plantations, which have their own rhythmic beauty.

The tiny village of **Udappuwa**, south of Puttalam, has a hectic morning fish market and an important Hindu temple with a large gorpum. A colourful festival is held here in August, when devotees test their strength by walking on red-hot coals. Nearby the village mosque and church glare at one another from opposite sides of the street.

Twelve kilometres to the south of Udappuwa, **Chilaw** has a strong Roman Catholic flavour, and has elaborate statues to religious figures and local cardinals in the centre.

Munneswaram, 5km to the east of Chilaw, has a rather interesting Hindu temple that is an important centre of pilgrimage. There are three shrines at this complex; the central one is dedicated to Shiva. A major festival, also featuring fire walking, occurs here in August. Few tourists come here, but that doesn't stop a possie of guides and touts attempting to wrangle some rupees out of you.

Buses are frequent all along the A3.

Negombo

031 / POP 121,933

Negombo is a modest beach town located close to Bandaranaike International Airport. With a stash of decent hotels and restaurants to suit all pockets, a friendly local community, an interesting old quarter and a reasonable (though polluted) beach, Negombo is a much easier place to get your Sri Lankan feet than Colombo.

Culture vultures will find bustling Negombo town a historically interesting place that's strongly influenced by the Catholic Church. For the more natural-minded the narrow strip of land to the south of the lagoon, as well as the many different canals, make for good birdwatching.

The Dutch captured the town from the Portuguese in 1640, lost it, and then captured it again in 1644. The British then took it from them in 1796 without a struggle. Negombo was one of the most important sources of cinnamon during the Dutch era, and there are still reminders of the European days.

The busy centre of Negombo town lies to the west of the bus and train stations. Most places to stay, however, line the main road that heads north from the town centre, running almost parallel to the beach.

Sights

Dutch Fort — RUINS

(Map p78) Close to the seafront near the lagoon are the ruins of the old Dutch fort, which has a fine gateway inscribed with the date 1678. Also here is a green, called the **Esplanade**, where cricket matches are a big attraction. As the fort grounds are now occupied by the town's prison, the only way you'll get a peek inside is by stealing something; though you'd need to be very interested in old Dutch forts to go this far.

Several old Dutch buildings are still in use, including the **Lagoon Resthouse** (Custom House Rd).

Fish Market — MARKET

(Map p78) Each day, fishermen take their *oruvas* (outrigger canoes) and go out in search of the fish for which Negombo is well known. They're a fine sight as they sweep home into the lagoon after a fishing trip. Fish auctions on the beach and sales at the fish market near the fort are a slippery and very smelly sight, but one that's well worth forgoing some swimming pool time for. The catch is not all from the open sea: Negombo is at the northern end of a lagoon that is renowned for its lobsters, crabs and prawns. Across the lagoon bridge there's a second fish market. If you can stagger out of bed at 6am, it's a good place to watch much bigger fishing boats return with their catches.

Religious Buildings — RELIGIOUS

Negombo is dotted with churches – so successfully were the locals converted to Catholicism that the town is sometimes known as 'Little Rome' (another reason for

Negombo (Town)

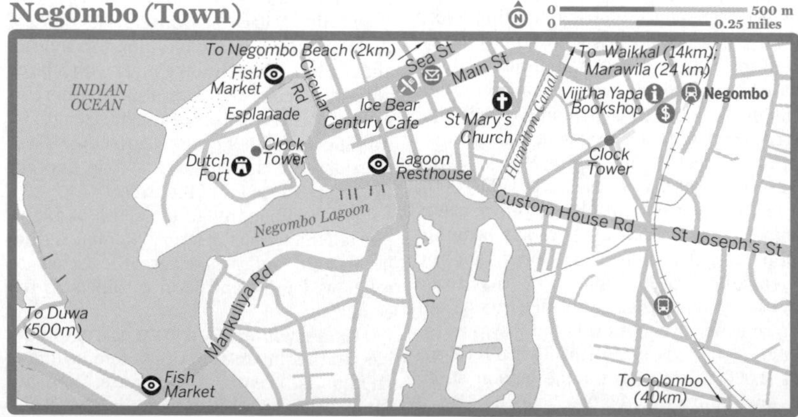

the moniker is that many of the residents receive money from relatives working in Italy). The fading pink chamber of **St Mary's Church** (Map p78), in the town centre, has some thunderous religious ceiling paintings covering the nave. East of town the **Angurukaramulla Temple**, with its 6m-long reclining Buddha, is also worth seeing. The island of **Duwa**, joined to Negombo by the lagoon bridge, is famed for its Easter passion play.

Canals CANALS

The Dutch showed their love of canals here like nowhere else in Sri Lanka. Canals extend from Negombo all the way south to Colombo and north to Puttalam, a total distance of over 120km. You can hire a bicycle in Negombo from various hotels and ride the canal-side paths for some distance, enjoying the views and small villages along the way. The road over the lagoon bridge continues as a small coastal road between lagoon and ocean almost all the way to Colombo.

Activities

Kite Centre Negombo EXTREME SPORTS

(Map p81; 077 746 1261; 13 Porutota Rd) If you want to get close to the ocean waters but, hopefully at least on this polluted stretch, not in it too much, then kitesurfing courses using decent equipment and run by experienced surfers are available through the Kite Centre Negombo based inside the Pearl guesthouse. A three-day course costs €349.

Lucky Tours BIRDWATCHING

(Map p81; 077 357 8487; lucky-tour55@hotmail.com; 146 Lewis Pl) Specialist birdwatching tours in the Negombo region including half-day tours to the Muthurajawela Marsh.

Sleeping

There are plenty of places along the beach in the budget and midrange categories. You can also find a couple of higher-priced places here and in Waikkal. Generally the closer the accommodation is to town, the rougher around the edges it is.

TOP CHOICE **Villa Araliya** BOUTIQUE HOTEL $$

(Map p81; 227 7650; www.villaaraliya-negombo.com; 154/10 Porutota Rd; r incl breakfast US$50-160;) This leading light in the Negombo hotel scene has a variety of modern rooms – some are all dashed up in multi-hued colours and others have exposed red-brick walls – but the uniting factor between all the rooms is that they are supremely comfortable with big beds, high ceilings and bathrooms that you'll be happy to splash about in – talking of splashing about, the pool will almost certainly entice you in for a few pre-breakfast laps. It's child-friendly (it has children's toys, cots and high chairs) and is on a quiet side street that's a five-minute walk from the beach.

TOP CHOICE **Ice Bear Guest House** GUESTHOUSE $$

(Map p81; 071 423 7755; www.icebearhotel.com; 103/2 Lewis Pl; r €29-59;) A gorgeous traditional villa with lots of colour and flair (or 'Swissness', as the sign says – to which you could also add 'and a little eccentricity'). This 'budget boutique' hotel has a variety of different types of rooms thrown about the beautiful dog- and duck-filled gardens. The rooms have flower-sprinkled beds, homey touches and hot water, and the pricier ones come with art-deco sinks and CD players. There's also a beachside cafe with tasty treats like homemade muesli, and classical music often wafts through the palms.

Angel Inn GUESTHOUSE $$

(Map p81; 223 6187; 189/17 Lewis Pl; r with/without air-con Rs 3000/2000) This is one of the most inviting cheap guesthouses in Negombo. Its six rooms might not have beach views, but in every other way it's truly excellent value with flawlessly clean and shiny rooms set around a small garden. It's family-run and that makes it friendly and caring.

Pearl GUESTHOUSE $$

(Map p81; 492 7744; www.pearl-negombo.com; 13 Porutota Rd; s/d €36/47;) This small beachfront pad might be discreet but it packs enough flair and comfort to gladden the heart of any weary traveller. The immaculate rooms are full of cheeky modern art and have DVD and CD players (with supplies). It's a base for kitesurfing around the west coast.

Beach RESORT $$$

(Map p81; 227 3500; www.jetwinghotels.com; Porutota Rd; s/d incl breakfast US$355/375;) With its imposing gateways, echoey corridors and vaguely Pharaonic murals, this place feels like a temple – a temple to minimalist luxury, that is. The rooms are close to perfect and the bathrooms, with walk-in showers and circular baths, actually are perfect. There's also a well-equipped spa and a pool that's lit up at night by flaming torches. There's even an in-house naturalist who will happily answer all of your birds-and-bees questions. The pool complex makes it a fantastic choice for children.

Ayurveda Pavilions BOUTIQUE HOTEL $$$
(Map p81; ☎227 6719; Porutota Rd; s/d villa incl breakfast from US$210/230; ❄@📶🏊) Beautiful mud-wall villas with minimalist, yet luxurious, furnishings. The bathrooms are the real highlight and soaking in one of the steamy, flower-petal-covered outdoor baths with someone special on a rainy afternoon is every bit as romantic as you hoped your holiday would be! There's a large range of treatments (available to nonguests from US$30), which are included in the room price.

Hotel Silver Sands HOTEL $$
(Map p81; ☎222 2880; www.silversands.go2lk.com; 229 Lewis Pl; r with/without air-con Rs 3630/1760;❄) An excellent, cheap beachfront option with neatly tiled rooms that have crazy tent-like mosquito nets and are decorated with bunches of plastic flowers. Fishy fans will love the rows of aquariums full of guppies, mollies and goodness knows what else.

Beach Villa Guest House GUESTHOUSE $
(Map p81; ☎222 2833; 3/2 Senavirathna Mawatha; tw Rs 800-3000; ❄) This backpacker classic has cheerful rooms, and is so close to the sea that you might want to consider snoozing in your swimwear. There's a cheap and pleasant cafe-restaurant and a wealth of travel advice. Cheaper rooms are fan only.

Sha Residence GUESTHOUSE $
(Map p81; ☎077 748 8746; www.sharesidence.com; 80 Cemetery Rd; s with/without air-con US$22/27, d with/without air-con US$30/35; ❄📶) This friendly seven-room place, a couple of hundred metres back from the beach and the main strip, is unusual in Negombo in that it's more of a homestay than a hotel. The spacious rooms come with hot water and there's a garden full of ducks and rabbits.

Camelot Beach Hotel RESORT $$
(Map p81; ☎222 2318; www.camelothotelnegombo.com; 345 Lewis Pl; s/d US$65/70; ❄@📶🏊) There's classic fun in the sun to be had at this good-value package-tour hotel, which at the time of our last visit was utterly festooned in Christmas decorations, lending a somewhat surreal edge to lying about under a palm tree. The rooms are bright and pleasant (even without the Christmas decorations), the facilities are numerous and there are two pools.

Jeero's Guest House GUESTHOUSE $
(Map p81; ☎223 4210; 239 Lewis Pl; r from Rs 2000) With latticework window frames, comfortably worn-in furniture and breezy balconies, this is a well-priced and friendly option set around a pleasing garden just back from the beach.

Dephani Guest House GUESTHOUSE $
(Map p81; ☎223 4359; dephani@slt.lk; 189/15 Lewis Pl; r Rs 2000; 📶) Prices are somewhat flexible at this personable little guesthouse, which has a shady garden full of sun-loungers and slightly gloomy, though spick and span, rooms. Cold-water showers only.

Goldi Sands Hotel RESORT $$$
(Map p81; ☎227 9021; www.goldisands.com; Lewis Pl; s/d US$115/125; ❄📶🏊) Recently renovated, this is a popular package-tour hotel, but don't let that put you off! Its modern, white rooms with black-and-white art offer fair value and it's a good base from which to recover from the long flight. Go for the room-only basis and pay for the breakfast separately as it works out US$10 cheaper than taking the B&B rate!

Eating & Drinking

There are lots of very so-so restaurants and cafes stringing the main road along the beach, with a few more-exciting options in between.

TOP CHOICE **Lords** FUSION $$$
(Map p81; 80B Porutota Rd; dishes Rs 850-1400) By far Negombo's most creative eating experience. Martin, the British owner of this half restaurant, half art gallery, brings a larger-than-life presence to the place and is a rare thing among expat restaurant owners in that he actually works on the floor and in the kitchen making sure that everything is just spot on. The food, which is so superbly prepared and presented that the thought of a free meal here was enough to get the president himself to come and open the restaurant, is a hybrid of Western and Eastern flavours. The gallery displays excellent contemporary work by local artists.

Alta Italia ITALIAN $$
(Map p81; 36 Porutota Rd; meals Rs 500-700) For a casual beach resort this is a surprisingly formal Italian-run place with a long menu that includes fresh pasta, seafood grills and thin-based pizzas. Try the authentic risotto and finish with a *limoncello* or grappa. Or

Negombo (Beach Area)

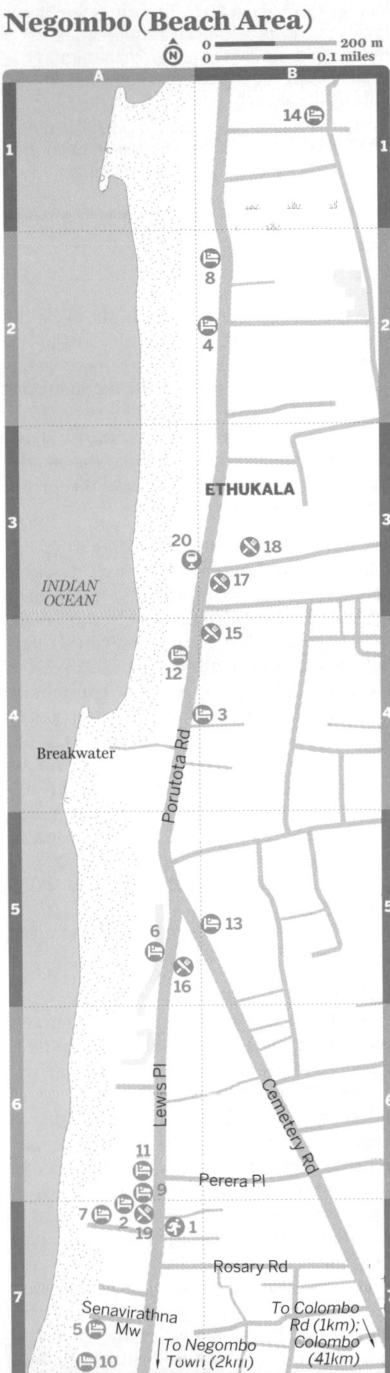

Negombo (Beach Area)

Activities, Courses & Tours

	Kite Centre Negombo	(see 12)
1	Lucky Tours	A7

Sleeping

2	Angel Inn	A7
3	Ayurveda Pavilions	B4
4	Beach	B2
5	Beach Villa Guest House	A7
6	Camelot Beach Hotel	A5
7	Dephani Guest House	A7
8	Goldi Sands Hotel	B2
9	Hotel Silver Sands	A6
10	Ice Bear Guest House	A7
11	Jeero's Guest House	A6
12	Pearl	A4
13	Sha Residence	B5
14	Villa Araliya	B1

Eating

15	Alta Italia	B4
16	Ammehula	A5
17	Bijou	B3
18	Lords	B3
19	Pancake House	A7

Drinking

20	Rodeo Pub	A3

sample from the espresso machine, steaming behind the counter.

Bijou INTERNATIONAL **$$**
(Map p81; Porutota Rd; mains Rs 300-1000) You'll know this place is Swiss-owned when you see fondue and other Swiss and German specialities on the menu. It mixes up such heavy dishes with a wide range of seafood.

Ammehula INTERNATIONAL **$$**
(Map p81; 286 Lewis Pl; meals Rs 400-600; ⌚10am-10pm) The young owners of this cafe claim that the name means 'Go Away!' and the menu features a cartoon turtle cussing about how all the good fish come here. Besides seafood dishes there are sandwiches, salads and a long breakfast menu that includes Dutch pancakes. There's a small library of books for swapping.

Ice Bear Century Cafe CAFE **$$**
(Map p78; 25 Main St; mains Rs 500; ⌚9am-6pm) In a lovingly restored peach-pink colonial-era town house, this calm retreat in the heart of Negombo offers a touch of refined class and all manner of Sri Lankan brews,

mountains of homemade cakes and biscuits, and lunch specials such as Thai noodle soups and Hungarian goulash.

Pancake House INTERNATIONAL **$$**
(Map p81; 227 Lewis Pl; mains Rs 400) Busy traveller cafe with a mix of local curries and seafood as well as sloppy pasta, pizzas and, yes, pancakes (although the pancakes are pretty good).

Rodeo Pub PUB
(Map p81; 35 Porutota Rd; dishes Rs 700-1000; ⌚9am-midnight) Homesick expats and tourists drown their sorrows at this wannabe European bar, where graffiti's scrawled across the walls and bacon butties, pints of lager and cocktails with sexy names prop up the clientele.

Information

There are numerous internet and telephone offices scattered along Lewis Pl and Porutota Rd, as well as near the bus and train stations. If this is your first stop in Sri Lanka, hotels can fix you up with guides and drivers for trips elsewhere in the country. The following are all in the centre of town:

Bank of Ceylon (Map p78; Broadway)
Post office (Map p78; Main St)
Vijitha Yapa Bookshop (Map p78; 135 Broadway) Has English-language novels, magazines, guidebooks and maps.

Getting There & Away

Central Transport Board (CTB), private and intercity express buses run between Negombo town (Map p78) and Saunders Pl, Colombo (regular/air-con Rs 48/80, one to two hours, every 20 minutes). Long queues form at the bus station on weekend evenings, when day trippers return to the capital. There are also trains to Colombo (2nd/3rd class Rs 70/40, two hours), but they're slower and rarer than the buses. You can get a taxi between Negombo and Colombo for about Rs 3000. Any hotel, guesthouse or travel agent will arrange a taxi for you.

For Kandy, buses run between 4.30am and 5.15pm every hour (Rs 120); the journey takes three to four hours.

Getting Around

Bus 240, for the Bandaranaike International Airport (Rs 19, 45 minutes), leaves from the bus station in town every 15 minutes between about 6am and 7pm. A three-wheeler costs about Rs 500 from Negombo town or Rs 800 from Lewis Pl. A taxi costs around double this. The journey takes about 20 to 30 minutes and all hotels can arrange transport. Three-wheelers may not pick up passengers from the airport terminal, but you can catch one on the road outside the airport.

To get from the bus station to Lewis Pl or Porutota Rd, you can catch a Kochchikade-bound bus or splash out Rs 200 on a three-wheeler.

Around Negombo

WAIKKAL & MARAWILA

☎031

The towns of Waikkal and Marawila lie about 3km inland of the coast on the A3. There are several mostly upmarket waterside hotels, which are self-contained and walled off from Sri Lanka. It's a very different scene from the bars and tourist shops at Negombo. On the plus side, the nearby beaches are long and golden, and the terrain is flat and palm-covered.

Ranweli Holiday Village (☎227 7359; www.ranweli.com; s/d incl breakfast from US$140/152; ❄📶), on the coast near Waikkal, is a showpiece ecofriendly hotel that has won dozens of prestigious international environmental awards. Away from recycling, tree planting and community development, you'll find that the gentle punt over the canal separating it from the mainland sets a romantic mood. The rooms are not wildly exciting, but there's an unmistakable air of exclusivity to the place. All the vegetables served in the restaurant are organically grown in the local area. It organises an array of bird- and butterfly-spotting trips.

Most people reach Waikkal and Marawila by taxi or car and driver.

SOUTH OF NEGOMBO

The narrow belt of land between the gulf and lagoon south of Negombo is sometimes called **Pamunugama**, after its biggest settlement. It's a lovely strip of coconut palms, old Portuguese-style churches, cross-dotted cemeteries on dunes and pockets of tidy houses. There are some small hotels along here. Unfortunately, though, the beach is steep, with a sheer reef drop-off that makes swimming little short of perilous no matter what the sea state.

This is also home to one of the best stretches of the old and straight-as-an-arrow **Dutch Canal** (also known as the Hamilton Canal) that runs along this entire length of coast. It's lined with small factories, fishing villages, mansions, nature areas and more. Hiring a bike in Negombo is an ideal way to tour this area.

TOP CHOICE **Muthurajawela Marsh**, which evocatively translates as 'Supreme Field of Pearls', is a little-known gem of a wetland at the southern end of Negombo's lagoon. The area had been a rich rice-growing basin before the Portuguese constructed a canal that ruined the fields with sea water. Over the centuries, Mother Nature turned Muthurajawela into Sri Lanka's biggest saline wetland, home to purple herons, cormorants and kingfishers. However, the marsh is under pressure from encroaching industrial development.

The **Muthurajawela Visitor Centre** (☎011-483 0150; Indigaslanda, Bopitiya, Pamunugama; ⏲7am-4pm) is at the southern end of the road along Pamunugama, next to the Hamilton Canal. It has some moth-eaten displays and a 25-minute video on the wetland's fauna; but much more interestingly, it also runs boat trips. A two-hour **guided boat ride** (per person Rs 1000) through the wetland is highly recommended. The wetlands provide a home to some 75 bird species, as well as crocodiles, monkeys and even some very rarely seen otters. A percentage of the profits goes toward local conservation initiatives. It's a very good idea to call and reserve a boat ride in advance as it can get quite busy at weekends and on holidays.

Very close to the Muthurajawela Visitor Centre is **Villa Palma** (☎011-223 6619; www.villapalmasrilanka.com; Beach Rd, Pamunugama; s/d from Rs 5500/6000; ❄📶🏊), which has 18 large and simple rooms that are a bit musty and overpriced. It's popular with local wedding parties, which bring colour and life (whereas the rooms don't).

SOUTH OF COLOMBO

Escaping the frenetic and sticky capital for the road south is a giant sigh of relief. Out go the congested streets and dark clouds of carbon monoxide and in come the sultry beaches of the Sri Lankan dream. Most independent travellers focus on surf-obsessed Hikkaduwa, but the Bentota area offers quieter, and maybe even more stunning, beaches, as well as a bizarre twinning of package-holiday hotels and sumptuous boutique hideaways.

Aluthgama, Bentota & Induruwa

☎034

Protected from noisy Galle Rd by the sluggish sweep of the Bentota Ganga, the ribbon of golden sand that makes up Bentota beach is a glorious holiday sun-and-fun playground. While it's primarily dominated by big package hotels, it also has a number of smaller places catering to independent travellers. There are more such places in Aluthgama, a small town on the main road between Beruwela and Bentota.

Aluthgama has a raucous fish market, local shops and the main train station in the area. Induruwa doesn't really have a centre – it's spread out along the coast.

Sights

If it's a **beach** you want, then it's a beach you're going to get; the Bentota area is home to some of the best beaches in all the country. Yet there is something altogether odd about these magnificent stretches of sand – despite the huge number of hotels and the fact that most people come to Sri Lanka for the three S's of sun, sand and surf, the beaches at the southern end of this strip are remarkably empty of people. Quite why

THE SOUTHERN EXPRESSWAY

One of the banes of a beach-bound holiday in Sri Lanka used to be the sheer length of time it took to travel from the airport on the northern fringe of Colombo to the west- and south-coast beach resorts. But in November 2011 all that changed with the opening of the Southern Expressway, Sri Lanka's first ever toll road. Currently the road runs from Kottawa southeast of Colombo to Pinnaduwa, north of Galle. The drive takes 90 minutes, but if you're considering leaving your departure from the beach to the airport to the very last moment note that until connecting roads are completed you should allow at least two hours to get from Kottawa to the airport.

You can join and leave the road at a number of points along its length. For more, see p313.

this should be the case we're not sure, but if the sands of nearby Hikkaduwa are a bit too trodden for your liking, then Bentota might be the place for you. Further watery fun is also available on the calm waters of the **Bentota Ganga**, though pollution can be an issue here.

Aluthgama has a bustling **market** every Monday, located across the train line, towards Dharga Town. A few kilometres inland on the south bank of the river is the **Galapota Temple**, which is said to date from the 12th century. To reach it, cross the bridge and take the side road to your left after 500m.

Brief Garden GARDENS

(admission Rs 1000; ⌚8am-5pm) Ten kilometres inland from Bentota is the Brief Garden. A barely controlled riot of a *Jungle Book* garden, the grounds are a lovely place to get lost, while the house, which used to be the home of Bevis Bawa, brother of renowned architect Geoffrey Bawa, has an eclectic range of artwork on display – from homoerotic sculpture to a wonderful mural of Sri Lankan life in the style of Marc Chagall. The mural was created by Australian artist Donald Friend, who originally came for six days but stayed six years – definitely not the sort of house guest you want! Other, more short-term, guests included Vivien Leigh and Laurence Olivier, who stayed here during the filming of *Elephant Walk* in 1953. It's a good idea to plaster on some insect repellent as the gardens are a favourite of biting insects. To get here follow the road south from Aluthgama to Matagama Rd and turn inland to the Muslim village of Dharga Town. From here you will periodically see yellow signs saying 'Brief', but as everyone knows this place, it's easy enough to ask directions. There's no public transport.

Activities

The vast lagoon and river mouth make this an excellent area for water sports. Windsurfing, waterskiing, jet-skiing, deep-sea fishing and everything else watery are offered by local operators. **Sunshine Water Sports Center** (☎428 9379; River Ave, Aluthgama) and **SRP Watersports Centre** (☎077 623 7376; River Ave, Aluthgama) are independent operators that are both right on the riverfront. Besides renting out a wide range of equipment, they also run courses, which include windsurfing (Rs 10,000) and waterskiing (from Rs 1000). There are also snorkelling tours, canoeing, deep-sea fishing and diving courses.

Boat journeys along the **Bentota Ganga** (Rs 4500 per group) are a peaceful, popular and bird-filled way to pass a late afternoon. Tours travel through the intricate coves and islands on the lower stretches of the river, which is home to more than a hundred bird species, plus a wide variety of amphibian and reptile species. Most trips last for three hours. Both of the above companies organise trips, otherwise all hotels can point you to operators.

Sleeping

In among the package-holiday resort bubbles are a number of divine boutique hotels and guesthouses, as well as one or two very rare budget offerings.

ALUTHGAMA

Anushka River Inn GUESTHOUSE $$

(☎227 5377; www.jetwinghotels.com; River Ave; s/d €35/50; ❄) This hotel's large rooms contain wooden beds, dressing tables and hot-water showers. The rooms without river views, with their shiny new feel, are actually the better deal as some of the others have a musty odour. Big discounts are common.

Hotel Hemadan GUESTHOUSE $$

(☎227 5320; www.hemadan.dk; River Ave; s/d from Rs 2400/2700) A cosy Danish-owned guesthouse that has 10 large, clean rooms in an ageing building. There's a leafy courtyard and prime river-viewing opportunities. Better rooms have balconies. There are free boat shuttles across the river to the oceanside beach. There's a babycot for those travelling with little people.

BENTOTA

TOP CHOICE **Club Villa** BOUTIQUE HOTEL $$$

(☎227 5312; www.club-villa.com; 138/15 Galle Rd; s/d incl half board US$231/275; ❄@☎≋) Ever wondered what happened to the hippies who bummed across Asia in the 1960s and '70s? Well, while some dropped out of life completely, others went home and became investment bankers who now spend their dollars reminiscing in hotels like this Bawa-designed masterpiece. From the tie-dye pillows and cushions to the blissed-out Buddha and Shiva statues, everything about this place reeks of hippy chic. Even the giant catfish that haunt the numerous ponds seem to cruise about in a stoned state of permanent indolence.

TOP CHOICE Saman Villas BOUTIQUE HOTEL **$$$**
(☎227 5435; www.samanvilla.com; r from US$503; ❄@☜≋) We would love to tell you just how incredible this place is, but the simple truth is that no words have yet been invented to describe the sheer opulence of this hotel complex. How opulent? Well, some of the rooms have private swimming pools – inside the bathroom! If you prefer your swimming more communal, there's also a heavenly infinity pool that merges into an ocean horizon and everywhere you go you will literally

HATCHING TURTLES

Five species of sea turtles lay eggs along the coasts of Sri Lanka. The green turtle is the most common, followed by the olive ridley and the hawksbill. The leatherback and loggerhead are both huge, reaching 2m or more in length. During what should be long lives (if they don't end up in a net, soup pot etc), female turtles make numerous visits to the beaches of the south coast to lay eggs in the sand of the very beach they themselves were born on. A few weeks later, hundreds of baby turtles make, as the many lurid nature specials will tell you, a perilous journey back to the water.

Most of the tiny turtles are quickly gobbled up by birds, fish, people and other critters with gullets. And many never hatch at all, since human egg-poachers work overtime to satisfy the demand for turtle omelettes. The turtle hatcheries on the coast around Bentota and Kosgoda claim to increase the odds for the turtles by paying locals for the eggs at a rate slightly above that which they would fetch in the market. The eggs are then incubated by the hatchery until they hatch. After a short stay in a tank (supposedly for protection against parasites, although many biologists say these tanks actually increase disease and parasite infection), the babies are released under the cover of darkness (in a 'wild' state the babies also emerge at night).

The reality of the situation is that the turtle hatcheries might be doing more damage than good. When a baby turtle hatches it retains a part of the yolk from the egg, which acts as a vital energy source when the turtles first swim out to sea. By keeping the babies for even a short time in a tank they do not gain the benefit of this first food source. In addition, mature female turtles like to return to the beach they were hatched on in order to lay their eggs: again, if they have been born in captivity they will not have obtained a 'magnetic imprint' of their beach of birth and thus they are thought to be unable to return to shore to lay their eggs. For a truly sustainable turtle conservation effort it's better that the eggs are simply left on the beach where they were laid and given protection there. For more on this see www.srilankaecotourism.com/turtle_hatchery_threat.htm.

Although the conservation benefits of the hatcheries are limited, there's no denying that the turtles are awfully cute and make for an entertaining visit. Visits rarely last more than about 20 minutes. Expect to see babies, as well as veterans who have been injured by nets and other calamities.

Kosgoda Turtle Centre (admission Rs 300; ⌚8am-6pm) This basic place is hands-on and has some charming staff. There's an old albino turtle that has survived both man (nets) and nature (tsunami). Look for a sign on the west side of Galle Rd, 500m south of the 73km marker.

Kosgoda Turtle Conservation Project (admission Rs 300; ⌚8am-6pm) On the beach side of Galle Rd, just north of Kosgoda, this volunteer-run operation has been here for 18 years. It's a very simple affair.

Kosgoda Turtle Hatchery (admission Rs 300; ⌚7am-7pm) Turn down a small track at the 73km marker to find this operation, located in a quiet spot right on the beach. Arrive at 6.30pm and you can help release the day's hatchlings into the ocean.

Sea Turtle Project (www.seaturtleszone.com; Induwara; admission Rs 300; ⌚6am-6.30pm) This facility feels more commercial and established than the Kosgoda operations.

walk on flower petals. But the real clincher is the setting: sited on the headland at the southern end of Bentota beach, the sea views are simply overwhelming.

Paradise Road – The Villa BOUTIQUE HOTEL **$$$**
(227 5311; www.villabentota.com; 138/18 Galle Rd; r incl breakfast US$249;) Fabulous and intimate boutique hotel decorated like a zebra in black-and-white stripes and adorned in karma-enhancing Tibetan Buddhist artefacts. Talking of the Buddha, you can recline like him on one of the oh-so-soft sofas or you can swirl up the pool like a koi carp or just take things easy with a pot of tea in the shade of a garden pagoda.

Dedduwa Boat Hotel GUESTHOUSE **$$**
(492 2024; Dedduwa Junction; r Rs 5750;) Head inland a couple of kilometres and, in a lush, green lakeside setting of utter tranquillity, is this hidden little offering. The rooms are carefully tended and you could spend hours just watching the birdlife on the neighbouring lake or walking the squelchy tracks between houses full of smiling locals.

Amal Villa BOUTIQUE HOTEL **$$**
(943-422 70746; www.amal-villa.com; Galle Rd; s/d incl half board from €50/65;) Want the bad news first? This place is frequently full and is on the wrong side of the busy main road. And the good news? This beautifully maintained German-run villa merges tropical oriental vibes with central European efficiency, which leaves it as a standout choice. The simple rooms, full of pure white lines and an old-fashioned flavour, have views inland over the rice paddies and a stunning swimming pool. Oddly they don't have mosquito nets and the Bentota area is swarming with the buggers, so bring your own net if staying here.

Wunderbar Hotel and Restaurant HOTEL **$$**
(227 5908; www.hotel-wunderbar.com; Galle Rd; s/d incl breakfast €53/75;) In among the surrounding luxury is this solid, and much cheaper, midrange option that has spacious and well-thought-out rooms with a taste for vaguely erotic art. Some rooms have balconies with sea views, and the pool is more inviting than many others in town.

Hotel Sasantha GUESTHOUSE **$$**
(227 5324; s with/without air-con Rs 5750/4300, d with/without air-con Rs 6350/5150;) Shady gardens, traveller-savvy staff, easy access to the northern part of Bentota beach and colourful rooms make this a very popular place to drop your backpack for a few days.

Wasana Guest House HOMESTAY **$**
(227 5206; s/d Rs 1500/1800) Close to the massive Taj Exotica package-tour hotel, this century-old house has half-a-dozen very basic pink rooms, which on their own aren't up to much. However, the point of this place is that you're living with the host family, sharing meals and relaxing in the same garden; in a tourist town like this, that's a rare treat indeed. Rooms are, however, often taken by drivers connected to the nearby big hotels.

INDURUWA

Temple Tree Resort & Spa BOUTIQUE HOTEL **$$$**
(227 1944; www.templetreeresortandspa.com; Galle Rd; d incl breakfast from US$306;) Picture a minimalist (and very expensive) Manhattan apartment translocated to a tropical beach and you get the Temple Tree Resort. The grey-stone rooms with electric-white walls have whirlpool baths, rain showers and every possible comfort.

Royal Beach Resort HOTEL **$$**
(227 4351; www.royalbeachresortsrilanka.com; Galle Rd; s/d incl breakfast US$100/110;) This hotel's slogan is that it's a 'semi-boutique hotel'; well, at least it knows its place in the world! The rooms are comfortable, the staff are helpful and the beachside swimming pool is good for a splash but it's true that the place lacks wow factor.

Long Beach HOTEL **$**
(227 5773; Galle Rd; tw Rs 1980) The rooms might be basic but if you can't stretch to hotels with private pools, this place might just fit the bill. The rooms are located in the upstairs of a family house. There are green, shady gardens and, something that matches all the big-boy hotels, a gorgeous beach on the doorstep.

Eating

Almost all of the hotels and guesthouses have restaurants, and the seafood-heavy meals that most serve are generally good (though often very expensive). If you want to escape the confines of your accommodation for a while, then the following options are recommended.

TOP CHOICE **Kandoori** INDIAN **$**
(428 Galle Rd, Beruwala; mains from Rs 300) Being a couple of kilometres north of Aluthgama on the road to Colombo, this simple

canteen-like place is a bit of a hassle to get to but it's well worth the effort. The food is all rich North Indian, although most of this is only available in the evening. At lunchtime plump for one of the superb biriyanis and follow up with a *watalappam* (egg, coconut milk, cardamom and jaggery pudding) for dessert. It does a takeaway service.

Chaplon Tea Centre CAFE **$**
(Galle Rd, Bentota) For a break from bronzing on the sands, come to this tea centre. As well as buying some of Sri Lanka's finest tea, you can also sit in a wicker chair on the terrace and enjoy tea and biscuits.

Of the hotel restaurants, almost all the top-end package-holiday resorts have restaurants open to nonguests, though they are often overpriced. Otherwise the **Wunderbar Hotel and Restaurant** (227 5908; Galle Rd) has an enjoyable 1st-floor restaurant open to the sea breezes, and a decent selection of seafood and Western dishes (Rs 400 to 600).

Information

There are internet facilities in many of the more expensive hotels, and others are sprinkled throughout the towns. The Bentota resort centre has a post office.

Cargills Food City (331 Galle Rd, Aluthgama) Sells a wide range of goods and has a pharmacy.

Commercial Bank (339 Galle Rd) Just north of the river; has an international ATM.

Tourist office (091-393 2157; 8.30am-4.30pm Mon-Fri) Outside the Bentota Beach Hotel.

Getting There & Around

Beruwela and Bentota are both on the main Colombo–Matara railway line, but Aluthgama, the town sandwiched between them, is the station to go to as many trains do not make stops at these smaller stations. Aluthgama has five or six express trains daily to Colombo (2nd/3rd class Rs 110/55, 1½ to two hours), and a similar number to Hikkaduwa (2nd/3rd class Rs 70/35, one hour).

When you get off the train at the unusual middle-platform station, you'll hear the usual boring tales from the touts and fixers that the hotel of your choice is 'closed', 'vanished' or has 'magically turned into the Statue of Liberty'. Just ignore them.

Aluthgama is also the best place to pick up a bus, although there is no trouble getting *off* any bus anywhere along the Galle Rd. There is frequent service to Colombo (regular/air-con Rs 65/125, one to two hours depending on traffic).

Sri Lankan Air Taxi (www.srilankan.lk/airtaxi) runs scheduled flights to and from Colombo on Monday and Friday for around Rs 6500 and to and from Dambulla on the same days for around Rs 11,700.

Three-wheelers are available from Aluthgama; fees range from Rs 50 for a local trip to Rs 400 for the jaunt to Induruwa.

Hikkaduwa & Around

091

Down-at-heel Hikkaduwa is Sri Lanka's candy-floss and ice-cream beach resort par excellence. First 'discovered' by that much-maligned group of people, the hippies, back in the 1970s, Hikkaduwa has been a firm fixture on the tourist map ever since. This long exposure to international tourism has left it a little worse for wear. Uncontrolled and unplanned development has meant that the swaying palms of yesteryear have given way to an almost unbroken strip of cheap guesthouses and restaurants that vie among themselves to be the closest to the lapping waves. This in turn has led to terrible beach erosion, and in parts the once-famous sand has now been almost completely replaced with sand bags fighting a vain battle to retain what little beach remains. To make matters worse the appalling Colombo–Galle road, with its asphyxiating smog and crazy bus drivers, runs right through the middle of it all, which can make stepping outside of your guesthouse as deadly as a game of Russian roulette!

Bad as it sounds, though, there are glimmers of hope. Hikkaduwa still lives up to its reputation of providing cheap and cheerful fun in the sun. There's an increasing range of activities on offer and, with the town slowly waking up to its demise, an increasing number of higher-class places to stay and eat. Finally, and maybe most importantly, locals hope that with the recent opening of the new Southern Expressway, linking Colombo to Galle, and which runs some way inland, Hikkaduwa will be rid of another of its demons (although saying that we felt that while there is less traffic the difference is fairly negligible). None of that sounds enough? Then take solace in the fact that the sunsets remain as beautiful as ever.

Sights & Activities

For many people a visit to Hikkaduwa begins and ends on the beach and you can't really fault them for that! The widest bit of sand extends north and south from Narigama. Here you'll find a few simple lounge chairs that you can rent, or even use for free if they're part of a cafe. But don't expect a chaotic scene: there are a few vendors, but it's pretty relaxed.

The sands at Wewala are narrower and steeper, but this is where the best surf is.

Hikkaduwa National Park WILDLIFE RESERVE

(adult/child Rs 30/15; ⏲7.30am-6pm) Hikkaduwa's overexploited marine national park stretches along the northern end of the beach. Once upon a time this was a magnificent garden of fishy colours and flowering corals, but today the reef is sadly a shadow of its former self, with much of the coral dying and the fish flipping away to more pristine spots. One of the big reasons for this demise has been coral bleaching, caused by oceanic and atmospheric conditions (quite probably man-made), which struck the reef in 1998, affecting about half the coral. The tsunami caused some further damage, but the real problem, as always, has been poor human management.

It's easy to see the coral. Dive shops and many hotels and guesthouses rent out snorkelling gear for around Rs 500 a day, or less. Glass-bottomed boat rides (not an ideal way to see the reef) are available for Rs 1750 per half-hour. The boats can be hired from beside the National Park Ticket Office, which, as the name suggests, is where you buy your entrance tickets.

Scuba Diving

The diving season runs from November to April. Professional Association of Diving Instructors (PADI) courses (open water €265), plus a selection of dives such as wreck dives, night dives and trips for those who just want to try out diving, are available from **Poseidon Diving Station** (☎227 7294; www.divingsrilanka.com; Galle Rd).

Surfing

The conditions for surfing are at their best from November to April. The Wewala and Narigama areas of the beach have a handful of tame reef breaks, as well as a beach break, all of which are perfect for beginner- to intermediate-level surfers. These waves, combined with the energetic nightlife, has made Hikkaduwa easily the most popular surf spot in Sri Lanka. The waves here tend to be fairly slow breaking and weak and, combined with the normally heavy crowds, experienced wave riders will probably wish they'd gone to Indonesia instead!

A-Frame Surf Shop (www.mambo.nu; 434 Galle Rd), located in Mambo's Place, repairs boards and has a selection of surfing gear. It rents out a variety of boards from Rs 1000 per day. It also offers surfing tours throughout the island under the moniker 'Mambo Surf Tours'.

Many places to stay also rent out boards (Rs 300 per hour).

Inland Attractions

To take a break from the beach scene, just walk or cycle along any of the minor roads heading inland. They lead to a calmer, completely different, rural world.

Seenigama Vihara TEMPLE

About 2km north of Hikkaduwa is the Seenigama Vihara, perched on its own island. It's one of only two temples in the country where victims of theft can seek retribution. People who have been robbed visit the temple and buy a specially prepared oil made with chilli and pepper. With the oil they light a lamp in their homes and recite a mantra. Sooner or later, maybe within weeks, the thief will be identified when they're struck down with misfortune, such as having a bicycle accident or being hit on the head by a falling coconut.

Moonstone Mines MINE

(⏲8am-5pm) Have you ever wondered where that pretty little moonstone on your finger actually comes from? Head inland 7km to Mitiyagoda and you can descend (not literally) into the mucky world of mining – 18th-century style! Moonstone has been mined in these sweltering forests forever and the moonstone mines, little more than muddy rabbit holes, 6m or 7m long, are fascinating – as is the process of filtering out the precious stones, cutting them up and polishing them ready for sale. Entrance is free, but expect a hardcore sales pitch in the on-site shop afterwards. To get there head towards Kahawa and turn inland to Mitiyagoda, after which it's clearly signed.

Gangarama Maha Vihara TEMPLE

Just off Baddegama Rd is this interesting Buddhist temple that has lots of popular educational paintings that are the work of

Hikkaduwa & Around

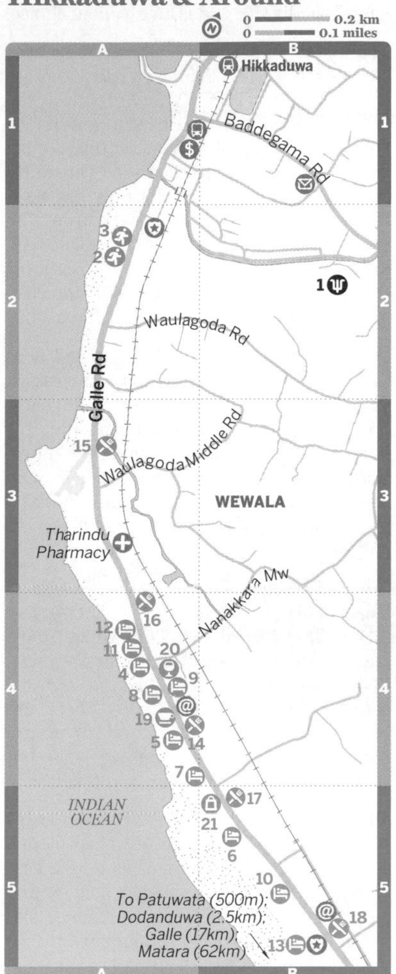

Hikkaduwa & Around

Sights
1 Gangarama Maha Vihara....................B2

Activities, Courses & Tours
A-Frame Surf Shop.......................(see 8)
2 Hikkaduwa National Park Ticket Office and Boat Hire A2
3 Poseidon Diving Station.......................A2

Sleeping
Anura Villa................................. (see 19)
4 Blue Ocean Villa A4
5 Hotel Moon Beam.................................A4
6 Hotel Rita B5
7 Lucky Dolphin..A4
8 Mambo's Place.......................................A4
9 Miga Villa...A4
10 Neela's..B5
11 Richard's Son Beach Villa...................A4
12 Time 'n' Tide Beach Resort A4
13 Top Secret B5
Why Not .... (see 7)

Eating
14 Basil A4
Chill Space Café..........................(see 8)
15 Cool Spot A3
Moon Beam Restaurant.............. (see 5)
16 No 1 Roti Restaurant A4
17 Rotty Restaurant B5
18 Spaghetti & Co B5

Drinking
19 Coffee Shop..A4
20 Sam's Surfers..A4

Shopping
21 Apsara Tailors B5

Information
Bookworm .... (see 5)

one man over nearly a decade. The monks are happy to show you around.

Hikkaduwa Lake LAKE
A further 2km from the temple along Baddegama Rd you come to Hikkaduwa Lake, home to monitor lizards and a lot of birdlife. Boat tours can sometimes be organised on the lake; ask around.

Sleeping

Virtually all of Hikkaduwa's accommodation is strung out along Galle Rd, but none of it is anything to write home about. The best way to find something to suit is simply to wander down the road (or beach) and look at a variety of rooms. All budget accommodation prices can be bargained over.

Most plots of land along the strip are quite narrow, which means that guesthouses will only have a few pricey rooms with views of the water. In contrast, rooms closest to the road get a lot of noise, so be sure to get a room well away from the traffic. Many places are jammed right up against each other.

Hotel Moon Beam HOTEL **$$**
(☎077 905 6954; hotelmoonbeam@hotmail.com; 548/1 Galle Rd; s incl breakfast Rs 4000-4500, d Rs 4500-6000; ❄) A smart midrange option with numerous spick-and-span rooms that are enlivened by pictures and wooden decorations. Piping-hot water gushes forth from the showers and some rooms have balconies with surf views. The restaurant is highly recommended.

Blue Ocean Villa HOTEL **$$**
(☎227 7566; blueocean@sltnet.lk; 420 Galle Rd; r Rs 2500-6000; ❄📶) Smart people rock up to this friendly place in the heart of all the action and score themselves a classy room that comes with wicker chairs, hot water and a rock-and-water-world fantasy in the reception area. The only real downside we could come up with is that some of the rooms suffer from road noise.

Mambo's Place GUESTHOUSE **$$**
(A-Frame; ☎545 8131; www.mambo.nu; 434 Galle Rd; s Rs 3500, d Rs 4500-6000; 📶) A growing empire, this is also home to the popular Chill Space Café and a well-informed surf shop. The dozen rooms here are brushed up in funky colours but only some have hot water. There's an Arabian-style lounge area on the 1st floor and incredible surf views from the 2nd.

Why Not GUESTHOUSE **$$**
(☎492 1261; Galle Rd; r Rs 1500-3000) Well, why not indeed? This place is good value, and you can choose from bright and cheerful mellow-yellow downstairs rooms or a more impressive tree-house-style raised cabana overlooking the surf (Rs 3000). There's a popular cafe with all your favourite creatures of the deep on the menu. Surfboards are available for rent.

Hotel Rita GUESTHOUSE **$$**
(☎227 7496; www.ritashotel.com; Galle Rd; r from US$25; ❄📶) Keeping passing travellers content for years, Rita's has tidy back rooms for those on a budget while midrange cruisers will find the fancier ocean-facing rooms, which are larger and have more attention to detail, to their pleasure. There's an in-house travel agency and a busy beachside restaurant.

Neela's GUESTHOUSE **$$**
(☎438 3166; neelas_sl@hotmail.com; 634 Galle Rd; r US$30-45) This place is reaching for the stars – it's got so many floors. Its many rooms are excellent value, with ocean-blue bathrooms and immaculately clean rooms. It has a friendly vibe and is an excellent choice.

Top Secret GUESTHOUSE **$$**
(The Harmony; ☎227 7551; www.srilanka-holiday.info; Galle Rd; r Rs 2000-3000; 📶) Right at the eastern end of the tourist strip, and on an appealing patch of beach, is this stylish guesthouse. The rooms themselves are fairly plain and like most places it only has cold-water showers, but move away from the rooms and you'll discover an Arabian-style lounge area and a decent bar-restaurant that pins up a useful five-day surf forecast. Minimum three-night stay in high season.

Lucky Dolphin GUESTHOUSE **$$**
(☎077 664 3785; 533 Galle Rd; r incl breakfast Rs 3500) With rooms that are as impeccably manicured as any Parisian poodle, this hotel represents real bang for your buck. Rooms come with four-posters, colourful windows, hot-water showers and a friendly management. Sadly, though, road noise is a real issue.

Richard's Son Beach Villa GUESTHOUSE **$**
(☎227 7184; Galle Rd; r Rs 1000) Unlike most places locally, this small single-storey guesthouse has a huge garden planted with coconut palms and other trees. There are hammocks hanging about, and an overall mellow vibe. The eight rooms are small but clean and about as cheap as things get.

Miga Villa GUESTHOUSE **$**
(☎077 591 7156; Galle Rd; r Rs 700) This colonial villa, set in gorgeous gardens, is pure eccentricity. Stuffed full of wooden statues and paintings of gods, animals and kings, and fluffed up with enormous bouquets of fake wedding-day flowers, it's virtually a museum in the making! It's normally used to host wedding parties and so can be noisy (though you'll probably end up being invited to dance along with everyone), but the basic, and none-too-clean, rooms (which are behind the main building) are open to all-comers.

Time 'n' Tide Beach Resort HOTEL **$$**
(☎227 7781; timentide@sltnet.lk; 412E Galle Rd; s/d Rs 2500/3500; 📶) A smart but sterile place that nevertheless offers excellent-value rooms. A big plus is the shady terrace and a grassy lawn. All rooms have fan only.

Anura Villa GUESTHOUSE **$$**
(☎071 774 3990; Galle Rd; r with/without air-con Rs 4500/2500; ❄) A brand-new mellow-

yellow villa with half-a-dozen fresh and clean rooms. The fan-only rooms are actually better value than those with air-con.

Eating & Drinking

Most of Hikkaduwa's best places to eat are connected to hotels and guesthouses. Down on the sandy shores of Narigama, you can table-hop from one spot to the next through the night. Many places are good just for a drink and a few stay open past 11pm – but don't expect any raves here.

Basil ITALIAN **$$**
(495 Galle Rd; meals Rs 700-900) The current hot spot of the moment. This new Italian restaurant receives rave reports from locals and travellers alike thanks to its homemade pastas, excellent pizzas and real Italian coffees. It's also a good spot for a slow European breakfast.

Spaghetti & Co ITALIAN **$$**
(Galle Rd; meals Rs 700-900) The lush gardens that surround this colonial-style villa go someway to hiding busy Galle Rd, which helps enhance the enjoyment of the ultra-thin-crust pizzas and creamy homemade pastas this spot serves.

Moon Beam Restaurant INTERNATIONAL **$$**
(☎545 0657; 548/1 Galle Rd; mains Rs 400-800) Hotel Moon Beam has easily the most attractive restaurant on the beach. It has a salty, open-air nautical decor, and tables where you can curl your toes in the sand. The seafood is truly excellent and it's also a good place for a sunset drink.

Cool Spot SEAFOOD **$$**
(327 Galle Rd; mains Rs 250-800) This family-run place has been serving up fresh seafood from a canary-yellow vintage roadside house at the north end of the strip since 1972. There's a cool veranda where you can peruse the blackboard menu and delight in specialities, such as garlic prawns and the bulging seafood platter. It's someway north of the main independent tourist strip.

Chill Space Café INTERNATIONAL **$$**
(434 Galle Rd; meals Rs 500-800) This almost comically surf-fashion-obsessed beachside cafe, which is situated in front of Mambo's Place, features reasonable shakes, snacks,

WORTH A TRIP

AMBALANGODA & AROUND

Ambalangoda is a sweaty and unattractive town, which, not surprisingly, is completely overshadowed by nearby Hikkaduwa as a tourist destination. The main reason for visiting – and it's a good one – is to dig under the surface of the Sri Lankan souvenir scene and discover the magical meanings behind the ubiquitous 'devil' masks. Genuine devil dances, which drive out spirits causing illness, still occur irregularly in the hinterland villages. Visitors are welcome, though you do have to expect more curiosity and less English from the villagers. The real catch is finding out about one of these dances, but ask around and count on good luck from the gods. In addition, this is also the best place in the country in which to buy these masks.

There are two mask shops (with free museums) on either side of the intersection of Galle Rd and Main St, 800m north of the train and bus stations. Each is owned by a son of the famous mask-carver Ariyapala. The **Ariyapala Mask Museum** (www.banduwijesooriyadanceacademy.org; cnr Galle Rd & Main St; ⏲8.30am-5.30pm) is the better museum, with dioramas and explanations in English. It also sells the booklet *The Ambalangoda Mask Museum*, if you want to delve into the mysterious world of dance, legend and exorcism, and the psychology behind the masks. **Ariyapala Traditional Masks** (432 Galle Rd; ⏲8am-7pm) is the other shop. The pieces on sale at both are rather expensive but utterly captivating.

Opposite, and aligned with, the Ariyapala Mask Museum is the **Bandu Wijesooriya Dance Academy** (☎225 8948; www.banduwijesooriyadanceacademy.org; cnr Galle Rd & Main St), which teaches the southern forms of dance such as *kolam* (masked dance-drama), Kandyan and Sabaragamu. Officially dance courses last a year but it's often possible for foreigners to arrange shorter one-on-one courses.

Ambalangoda is on the main transport route between Colombo and Hikkaduwa and buses and trains are frequent.

seafood and more, but basically you're paying for the atmosphere more than anything else. There are free beach chairs and occasional live music at night.

No 1 Roti Restaurant SRI LANKAN $
(373 Galle Rd; meals Rs 80-100) Away from the beach and a whole world away from the beach restaurant scene, this hole in the wall right on the road sells over 60 kinds of *rotti* (doughy pancake), ranging from garlic chicken to banana. There are also fresh shakes and lassis.

Rotty Restaurant SRI LANKAN $
(Galle Rd; rotti from Rs 100; ⌚8am-1am) Start off with a cheese-and-bacon *rotti*, wrap it up with a pineapple-and-banana *rotti*, and wash it all down with a mango juice at this simple and friendly place. It also does an excellent rice and curry.

Coffee Shop CAFE $
(Galle Rd) Real Italian coffees, including hangover-busting espressos, give a pre-surf morning boost at this fashionable cafe.

Sam's Surfers BAR
(Roger's Garage; 403 Galle Rd) A laid-back bar that shows recent movies every night at 7.30pm. It's very much a Brits-and-Aussies-abroad kind of place but is popular all the same.

Shopping

A good buy here is a pair of made-to-measure surfing board shorts (for men or women). Numerous tailors provide this service, but we were very impressed with the stitch work of **Apsara Tailors** (Galle Rd).

Information

There are numerous IDD telephone bureaus on Hikkaduwa's main street, many of them with internet facilities. From tourist libraries along Galle Rd (the Bookworm and the Sun Beam Tourist Library were favourites of ours) you can borrow books written in numerous European languages. There's usually a small fee (Rs 200) per read, plus a deposit (say Rs 300), which is refunded on the safe return of the book. Guidebook rental is more expensive.

Bank of Ceylon (Galle Rd)

Commercial Bank (Galle Rd) ATM.

Cyber Lounge Internet Cafe (Galle Rd; per hr Rs 120)

Main post office (Baddegama Rd)

Tharindu Pharmacy (238 Galle Rd)

Tourist Police Station (☎125 7222; Galle Rd)

Web House (Galle Rd; per hr Rs 120; ⌚7.30am-11pm)

Getting There & Away

Bus

There are frequent buses from Colombo (normal/luxury Rs 75/150, two to three hours). Buses also operate frequently to Galle (Rs 28, 30 minutes). Buses to Galle or beyond will drop you south of the bus station along the guesthouse strip. When leaving Hikkaduwa you stand more chance of a seat if you start at the bus station.

Car

There are two roads connecting Hikkaduwa with Galle and Colombo. The old Colombo–Galle road runs right through the middle of Hikkaduwa. Travelling along this road to central Colombo takes at least three hours and you should allow four or five hours to get to the airport (at quiet times you can do it faster than this). Galle is 30 minutes away. It's not worth taking the new Southern Expressway, which is the toll road running 15 minutes inland from the coast, to Galle, but you can shave a great chunk of time off the journey to the southern edge of Colombo. See p83 for more.

Train

The trains can get very crowded; avoid the really slow ones that stop everywhere. Check at the station for express departure times. Service on the coast line is fairly frequent; destinations include Colombo (2nd/3rd class Rs 140/80, two to three hours), Galle (2nd/3rd class Rs 40/20, 30 minutes) and beyond to Matara.

Getting Around

A three-wheeler from the train or bus stations to Wewala or Narigama costs about Rs 120.

The South

Includes »

Best Places to Eat

- » Mama's Galle Fort Roof Café (p101)
- » Galle Fort Hotel (p101)
- » King Fisher's Restaurant (p106)
- » Surya Garden (p117)

Best Places to Stay

- » Talalla Retreat (p116)
- » Mangrove Cabanas (p120)
- » Dutch House (p100)
- » Secret Garden (p105)
- » Fort Printers (p98)
- » Palm Villa (p111)

Why Go?

Southern Sri Lanka overwhelms the senses. The landscape is one of utter beauty; the radiant green rice paddies and forests of swinging palm trees contrast with beaches of ivory-coloured sand and an ocean of rich turquoise. The air is heavy with the scent of jasmine and the people drift past in clouds of bright colours.

No matter what you're after you'll find it here. You can dive across glowing coral reefs or learn to surf on gentle sandbars. The culturally inclined can soak up works of Buddhist-inspired art in lonely caves; for the naturalist there are huge whales splashing through offshore swells, and leopards moving like spirits in the night.

A sense of romance and wonder sweeps up all visitors to this coastline; after all, this is the land where people dance across fire on monsoon nights, fishermen float on stilts above the waves and turtles crawl up onto moonlit beaches.

When to Go

Galle

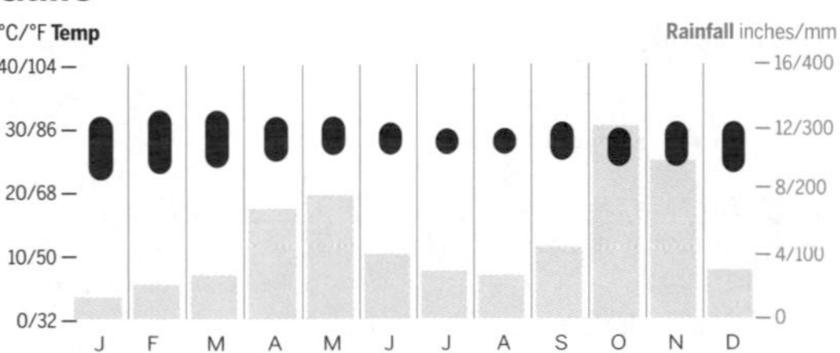

Jan Whales roll through the sea, the beaches buzz and Galle's literary festival is held.

Aug Pilgrims perform acts of self-mortification at the unforgettable Kataragama festival.

Nov The monsoon rains die out, beach resorts wake up and crowds are yet to arrive.

Galle

☎091 / POP 90,270

Galle (pronounced gawl in English, and *gaar*-le in Sinhala) is a town of colour, texture and sensation totally unlike anywhere else in Sri Lanka. It is at once endlessly exotic, bursting with the scent of spices and salty winds, and yet also, with its wonderful collection of slowly decaying Dutch-colonial buildings, vaguely familiar, like a whimsical medieval European town unexpectedly deposited in the tropics. Above all else Galle is a city of trade and, increasingly, art. Today the Fort is crammed full of little boutique shops, cafes and hotels owned by local and foreign artists, writers, photographers, designers and poets – a third of the houses are owned by foreigners.

Built by the Dutch, beginning in 1663, the 36-hectare Fort occupies most of the promontory that forms the older part of Galle and is an amazing collection of structures dating back through the centuries. Just wandering the streets at random yields one architectural surprise after another. Its glories have been recognised by Unesco, which has made the Fort a World Heritage Site.

A key part of the Fort's allure, however, is that it isn't just a pretty place. Rather, it remains a working community: there are administrative offices, courts, export companies, lots of regular folks populating the streets and a definite buzz of energy in the air.

Galle is easily reached as a day trip from Hikkaduwa and Unawatuna, but an increasing number of travellers are staying within the atmospheric walls of the Fort.

History

Although Anuradhapura and Polonnaruwa are much older than Galle, they are effectively abandoned cities – the modern towns

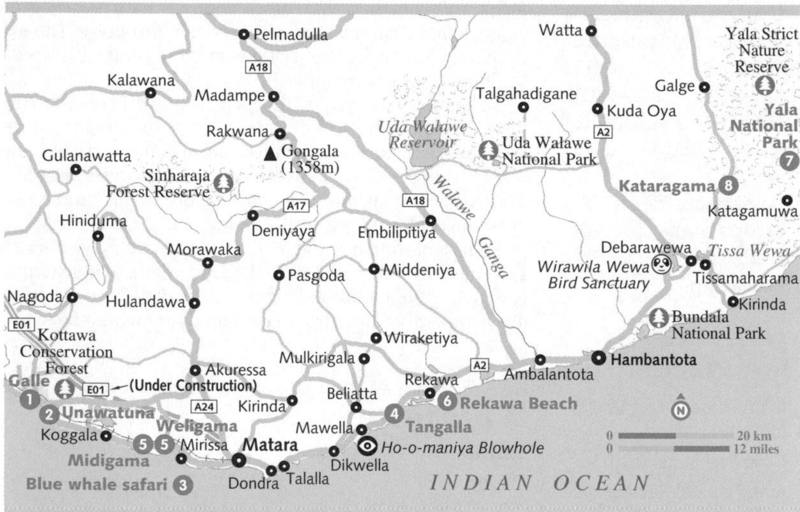

The South Highlights

1. Strolling the sculptured streets of arty and whimsical **Galle** (p94)
2. Slipping into the limpid, moonstone-coloured waters of **Unawatuna** (p103)
3. Staring in slack-jawed amazement at the biggest creatures ever to live during a **blue whale safari** (p112)
4. Oohing, ahhing and staying forever on the perfect beaches of **Tangalla** (p117)
5. Speeding through the tube at **Midigama** (p108) or learning to surf at **Weligama** (p110)
6. Watching the first faltering flipper-flaps of a tiny baby turtle on **Rekawa Beach** (p117)
7. Spotting a spotty leopard and listening out for big-eared elephants in **Yala National Park** (p127)
8. Walking on fire to make your peace with the gods at the spectacular **Kataragama festival** (p128)

are divorced from the ancient ruins. In contrast, both old and new Galle have remained vibrant.

Some historians believe Galle may have been the city of Tarshish – where King Solomon obtained gems and spices – though many more argue that a port in Spain seems a more likely candidate. Either way Galle only became prominent with the arrival of the Europeans. In 1505 a Portuguese fleet bound for the Maldives was blown off course and took shelter in the harbour. Apparently, on hearing a cock (*galo* in Portuguese) crowing, they gave the town its name. Another slightly less dubious story is that the name is derived from the Sinhala word *gala* (rock).

In 1589, during one of their periodic squabbles with the kingdom of Kandy, the Portuguese built a small fort, which they named Santa Cruz. Later they extended it with a series of bastions and walls, but the Dutch, who took Galle in 1640, destroyed most traces of the Portuguese presence.

After the construction of the Fort in the 17th century, Galle was the main port for Sri Lanka for more than 200 years, and was an important stop for boats and ships travelling between Europe and Asia. However, by the time Galle passed into British hands in 1796, commercial interest was turning to Colombo. The construction of breakwaters in Colombo's harbour in the late 19th century sealed Galle's status as a secondary harbour, though it still handles some shipping and yachts.

The 2004 tsunami hit Galle's new town badly and many people were killed around the bus station area. In contrast the solid walls of the Fort meant that damage was fairly limited in the old quarter.

For an interesting take on local history, buy a copy of *Galle: As Quiet As Asleep* by Norah Roberts, Galle's long-time librarian. Or, to learn more about the people of today's Galle, Juliet Coombe and Daisy Perry's book *Around the Fort in 80 Lives* should do nicely.

Sights

The Fort area is home to about 400 houses, churches, mosques, temples, and many old commercial and government buildings. To really experience it throw away all ideas of an itinerary and don't worry if you don't tick off every museum. Galle is an experience to savour, taste and touch rather than a list of prescribed sites, so wander those walls and streets at will, making your own discoveries as you go. And don't neglect the new town: there are all manner of interesting shops and markets along Main St and Matara Rd.

At the time of writing the government was due to start renovation work on some of the buildings in Galle Fort.

THE FORT WALLS

One of the most pleasant strolls you can take in town is the circuit of the Fort walls at dusk. As the daytime heat fades away, you can walk almost the complete circuit of the Fort along the top of the wall in an easy hour or two. You'll be in the company of lots of locals, shyly courting couples and plenty of kids diving into the protected waters.

The **Main Gate** in the northern stretch of the wall is a comparatively recent addition – it was built by the British in 1873 to handle the heavier flow of traffic into the old town. This part of the wall, the most intensely fortified because it faced the land, was originally built with a moat by the Portuguese, and was then substantially enlarged by the Dutch who split the wall in 1667 into separate Star, Moon and Sun Bastions.

Following the Fort wall clockwise you soon come to the **Old Gate**. The British coat of arms tops the entrance on the outer side. Inside, the letters VOC, standing for Verenigde Oostindische Compagnie (Dutch East India Company), are inscribed in the stone with the date 1669, flanked by two lions and topped by a cock. Just beyond the gate is the **Zwart Bastion** (Black Bastion), thought to be Portuguese built and the oldest of the Fort bastions.

The eastern section of the wall ends at the **Point Utrecht Bastion**, close to the powder magazine. The bastion is topped by an 18m-high lighthouse, which was built in 1938.

Flag Rock, at the end of the next stretch of wall, was once a Portuguese bastion. During the Dutch period approaching ships were signalled from the bastion, warning them of dangerous rocks – hence its name. Musket shots were fired from Pigeon Island, close to the rock, to further alert ships to the danger. On the **Triton Bastion** there used to be a windmill that drew up sea water, which was sprayed from carts to keep the dust down on the city streets. This part of the wall is a great place to be at sunset. There's a series of other bastions, as well as the tomb of a Muslim saint outside the wall, before you arrive back at your starting point.

Galle

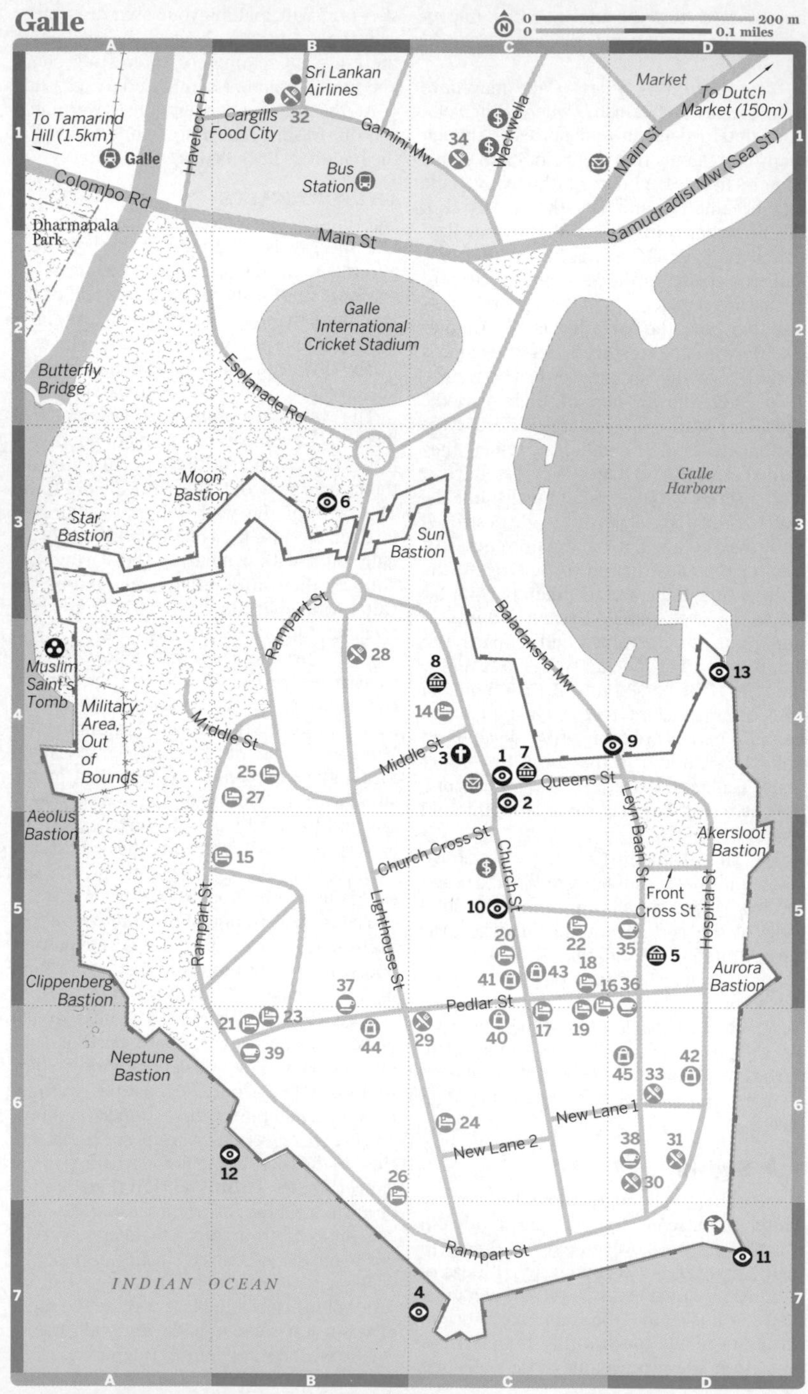

0 200 m
0 0.1 miles
To Tamarind Hill (1.5km)
Galle
Sri Lankan Airlines
Cargills Food City
32
Havelock Pl
Gamini Mw
34
Wackwella
Market
To Dutch Market (150m)
Main St
Samudradisi Mw (Sea St)
Bus Station
Colombo Rd
Main St
Dharmapala Park
Galle International Cricket Stadium
Butterfly Bridge
Esplanade Rd
Galle Harbour
Moon Bastion
Star Bastion
Sun Bastion
Rampart St
Baladaksha Mw
Muslim Saint's Tomb
Military Area, Out of Bounds
Middle St
Aeolus Bastion
Queens St
Leyn Baan St
Akersloot Bastion
Church Cross St
Church St
Lighthouse St
Front Cross St
Hospital St
Aurora Bastion
Clippenberg Bastion
Pedlar St
Neptune Bastion
New Lane 1
New Lane 2
Rampart St
INDIAN OCEAN

Galle

Sights

	Amangalla	(see 14)
1	Bell Tower	C4
2	Dutch Government House	C4
3	Dutch Reformed Church	C4
4	Flag Rock	C7
5	Historical Mansion	D5
6	Main Gate	B3
7	National Maritime Museum	C4
8	National Museum	C4
9	Old Gate	D4
10	Old Lloyd's Office	C5
11	Point Utrecht Bastion	D7
12	Triton Bastion	B6
13	Zwart Bastion	D4

Sleeping

14	Amangalla	C4
15	Fort Dew Guesthouse	B5
16	Fort Inn	C5
17	Fort Printers	C6
18	Frangipani Motel	C5
19	Frangipani Motel annex	C6
20	Galle Fort Hotel	C5
21	Hotel Weltevreden	B6
22	Mango House	C5
23	Mrs Khalid's Guest House	B6
24	Mrs ND Wijenayake's Guest House	C6
25	New Old Dutch House	B4
26	Ocean View Guest House	B6
27	Seagreen Guest House	B4

Eating

28	Anura's Restaurant	B4
	Galle Fort Hotel	(see 20)
29	Heritage Cafe	C6
30	Mama's Galle Fort Roof Cafe	D6
31	Nescafe Shop	D6
32	Ruhunupura Pastry Shop	B1
33	Serendipity Arts Cafe	D6
34	South Ceylon Bakery	C1

Drinking

35	Café Nicos@Olanda Antiques	D5
36	Janahitha Teashop	D5
37	Pedlar's Inn Cafe	B5
38	Royal Dutch Cafe	D6
39	Sunset Cafe	B6

Shopping

40	Barefoot	C6
41	Exotic Roots	C5
	Olanda Antiques	(see 35)
42	Orchid House	D6
43	PS Weerasekara Fashion Jewellery	C5
44	Shoba Display Gallery	B6
45	Suthuvili Gallery	D6

INSIDE THE FORT

Most of the older buildings within the Fort date from the Dutch era. Many of the streets still bear their Dutch names, or are direct translations. The Dutch also built an intricate sewer system that was flushed out daily by the tide. With true Dutch efficiency, they then bred musk rats in the sewers, which were exported for their musk oil. There's a large Muslim community living and working inside the Fort, particularly at the southern end of the walled town. Many shops close for a couple of hours around noon on Friday for prayer time.

Near the Dutch Reformed Church are a **bell tower** (built in 1901) and the old **Dutch Government House**. A slab over the doorway bears the date 1683 and Galle's ubiquitous cock symbol. Look for the **Old Lloyd's Office**, with its preserved ship arrival board, in the 19th-century commercial building just north of Galle Fort Hotel.

National Maritime Museum MUSEUM
(adult/child US$5/2.50; ⏲9am-4.30pm) Entered via the Old Gate, the newly refurbished National Maritime Museum is probably the most modern and high-tech museum in the country. Its beeping, flashing exhibits include lots of film and child-friendly interactive displays that illuminate the town's maritime past, present and future.

National Museum MUSEUM
(Church St; adult/child Rs 300/150; ⏲9am-5pm Tue-Sat) The National Museum is housed in an old Dutch building near the Main Gate. The museum, with just a little more effort, would be superb; however, as it is, it has sad displays of traditional masks, information on the lace-making process, a few examples of the luxury items that once passed through the port, and religious items, including a relic casket.

GALLE TOURS

Author and photographer **Juliet Coombe** (☎077 683 8659; www.sriserendipity.com; tours Rs 1500, cooking tours US$20) leads small-group or individual tours of Galle. As well as standard historical tours she and her team also run more unusual Mystical Fort tours, which delve into the legends and myths of the Fort; a Meet the Artists tour (24 hours' notice required), which introduces you to the town's large artist community; and a range of culinary tours. Perhaps the most interesting for exhausted parents are the children's tours, which include cooking lessons and meeting the town's last traditional storyteller. Juliet can be contacted through the Serendipity Arts Cafe (p101).

Historical Mansion MUSEUM
(31-39 Leyn Baan St; ⏲9am-5.30pm Mon-Thu, Sat & Sun, 10am-noon & 2-5.30pm Fri) If you think you've got a lot of clutter filling up the shelves at home, then just wait until you get a load of the Historical Mansion, which is the private collection of one serious hoarding squirrel. Set in a well-restored Dutch house, it's not really a museum, as many of the exhibits have price tags. It's a junkyard of colonial artefacts, including collections of antique typewriters, VOC china, spectacles and jewellery. There's also a gem shop.

Dutch Reformed Church CHURCH
(Groote Kerk, Great Church; cnr Church & Middle Sts; ⏲9am-5pm) Near the Amangalla hotel, this church was originally built in 1640, but the present building dates from 1752 to 1755. Its floor is paved with gravestones from the old Dutch cemetery (the oldest dates from 1662); the friendly caretaker will tell you where remains are held in the walls and under the floor. The organ from 1760 still sits in the building and the impressive pulpit, made from calamander wood from Malaysia, is an interesting piece. Services are held each Sunday.

Amangalla HISTORIC BUILDING
The ultra-posh hotel Amangalla was built in 1684 to house the Dutch governor and officers. As the New Oriental Hotel it was the lodging of choice for 1st-class P&O passengers travelling to and from Europe in the 19th century. Today it's the lodging of choice for 1st-class airline passengers.

Activities

Adventure Asia International HOT-AIR BALLOONING
(☎011-586 8468; www.ad-asia.com; adult/child €160/120) Hot-air ballooning is a romantic and wonderful way to see Galle and its surroundings from an entirely new angle.

Festivals & Events

HSBC Galle Literary Festival CULTURAL FESTIVAL
(www.galleliteraryfestival.com) An annual event held in mid- to late January, this festival brings together renowned Asian and Western writers. It's one of the best-regarded events of its type in Asia.

Art Trail ART FESTIVAL
(www.galleарttrail.com) As if Galle wasn't enough of a work of art, the whole Fort area virtually becomes one giant artist's easel during the Art Trail, a bi-annual event (the next one is due to be held in 2013) that takes place in April.

Sleeping

Galle has an ever-increasing number of truly amazing places to stay, but be warned: the European architecture comes with near European prices, so travellers of all budgets will need to splash out more cash here than in most other parts of the country.

FORT

TOP CHOICE **Fort Printers** BOUTIQUE HOTEL $$$
(☎224 7977; www.thefortprinters.com; 39 Pedlar St; r US$140-150; ❄@📶🏊) This 18th-century mansion was once used by printers, and you can still see the enormous wooden beams used to support the presses. Unlike most of Galle's boutique hotels, they've done something a bit different here; rather than recreating the colonial highlife, they've filled the magnificent rooms and public spaces with colours and styles as brash as the modern art that coats the walls. It's a place of utter calm and tranquillity and the only thing likely to disturb you will be the flutter of frangipani petals falling to the ground around you as you laze beside the pool.

TOP CHOICE **Frangipani Motel** GUESTHOUSE $$
(☎222 2324; www.frangipanigroup.com; 32 Pedlar St; r with air-con Rs 2500-3500, with fan Rs 2000-2500; ❄📶) Modern and kitsch in the most

perfect of ways, this family-run guesthouse is rapidly expanding into quite an empire of hotels (it now has an annex over the road at number 32 and has teamed up with the Mango House, p99). The two downstairs rooms are neat and clean with hot-water bathrooms, while the larger rooms upstairs are airy and bright, with spicy ocean breezes billowing through the roof slats and a flower-bedecked bed. There's a garden full of songbirds, where you can eat and relax, but for us the best bit was the plastic indoor garden, complete with waterfalls and fish ponds.

Fort Dew Guesthouse GUESTHOUSE **$$**
(☎222 4365; fortdew@yahoo.com; 31 Rampart St; r Rs 4000) Set close to the ancient city walls, next to a patch of parkland from which resonates the eternal thunk of ball on cricket bat, this guesthouse is a real find. It's whitewashed in a classic Mediterranean style and beautifully maintained. The rooftop terrace cafe and bar with stunning views help make this one of the best deals in town. It should be noted, though, that the hot showers do require a degree in engineering to operate.

Seagreen Guest House GUESTHOUSE **$$**
(☎224 2754; www.seagreen-guesthouse.com; 19B Rampart St; r Rs 4500;) A fab new guesthouse with just five whitewashed rooms with colourful Indian textiles. The bathrooms are some of the best in this price range and the rooftop terrace has sublime sunset views off over the ramparts and far, far away over a salt-spray Indian Ocean.

Galle Fort Hotel BOUTIQUE HOTEL **$$$**
(☎223 2870; www.galleforthotel.com; 28 Church St; r from US$201;) This former 17th-century Dutch merchant's house has been transformed into a breathtaking boutique hotel. The rooms are all different, with each room's design reflecting the part of the L-shaped structure it occupies. Some have two levels and others stretch across entire floors. Linens are exquisite and there are antiques everywhere. What you won't find are distractions like TVs – rather, you can enjoy the large courtyard pool and the hospitality of the accommodating owners and staff. The restaurant serves excellent food and the bar is a stylish meeting place. The hotel also rents out several luxurious villas and has its own spa.

Fort Inn GUESTHOUSE **$**
(☎224 8094; rasikafortinn@yahoo.com; 31 Pedlar St; r with/without air-con Rs 2500/2000;) The ever-beaming owner of this three-room guesthouse will obligingly offer neatly attired rooms with hot showers and a perfect people-watching balcony. There's also a very enjoyable terrace cafe-restaurant with a Chinese-influenced menu that includes noodle soups (Rs 500 to 600).

Amangalla BOUTIQUE HOTEL **$$$**
(☎223 3388; www.amanresorts.com; cnr Middle & Church Sts; r from US$400;) The Aman resorts group has converted a 17th-century town house into the ultimate in colonial decadence. The opening scene is one of massive, polished wooden floors and spiffily dressed staff, who lead you like royalty into giant rooms with beds that contain the biggest and fluffiest pillows we've ever seen, as well as bathrooms with beautiful freestanding tubs. Books about fine art and 18th-century exploration line the numerous bookcases and outside you'll find a pool to die for. It also has private cottages, which start at around US$1400 a night – these are OK too. If this isn't in your budget, then you may at least want to hang out in the lobby for a drink.

Mango House GUESTHOUSE **$**
(☎224 7212; www.frangipanigroup.com; 3 Leyn Bann Cross St; r with/without air-con Rs 2500/2000;) Numerous wooden Buddhas greet you on entering this guesthouse and his calming influence seems to permeate everything here. The rooms are smart and spacious and there's a large lawn shaded by, you guessed it, mango trees.

New Old Dutch House BOUTIQUE HOTEL **$$**
(☎223 2987; www.newolddutchhouse.lk; 21 Middle St; r incl breakfast US$45-55;) All you really need to know is that this friendly place might well be the most immaculate and sparkly clean guesthouse in all of southern Sri Lanka. The spacious rooms have creaky, polished wooden floors and lovely soft beds, and breakfast can be enjoyed under the courtyard's pawpaw trees. The eight rooms are modern and all white, and come with satellite TV and fridge.

Mrs ND Wijenayake's Guest House GUESTHOUSE **$**
(Beach Haven; ☎223 4663; www.beachhaven-galle.com; 65 Lighthouse St; r Rs 1000-3500;) The wonderful Mrs Wijenayake has been playing host to grateful backpackers forever and her knowledge of their needs shows in this superb guesthouse. Rooms range from the clean and simple with shared bathrooms to fancier air-con rooms. The family still talk of

VILLAS IN PARADISE

If a fancy boutique hotel isn't exclusive enough for you, then the answer might lie in one of the string of extraordinarily lavish villas that have sprung up over the past couple of years along the south coast. The Fort area of Galle has a particular glut of such places, but make no mistake about it – when we say these are lavish, we really mean lavish. Fine modern art adorns the walls, heavenly swimming pools fill the courtyards and private cooks and butlers are on hand with a G&T at just the right moment. Needless to say, such a lifestyle doesn't come cheap and for most of these places you're looking at around US$500 a night, with a three- or four-night minimum stay. However, as they often comfortably sleep four or five, if you're travelling with friends it can actually work out as an economical way to live like the other half – even if only for a while. For more see www.villasinsrilanka.com or www.lankarealestate.com.

the extended stay by Lonely Planet cofounder Tony Wheeler in 1977.

Ocean View Guest House GUESTHOUSE **$$**
(☎224 2717; www.oceanviewlk.biz; 80 Lighthouse St; r US$40-45; ❄) The small and pleasingly old-fashioned rooms come in as many styles and flavours as there are curries in Sri Lanka. The real clincher, though, is the beautiful rooftop garden, complete with luminous flowers, a bouncy lawn and one very happy tortoise (which oddly enough is bright green). The guesthouse is entered from Rampart St.

Hotel Weltevreden GUESTHOUSE **$**
(☎222 2650; piyasena88@yahoo.com; 104 Pedlar St; r Rs 1500-2500) A heritage-listed Dutch building, the Hotel Weltevreden has basic rooms painted in daring colours set around a well-loved courtyard garden. Plenty of friendly chit-chat with the elderly owner is included in the room price. Cheaper rooms have shared bathrooms.

Mrs Khalid's Guest House GUESTHOUSE
(Huize Bruisen de Zee; ☎223 4907; sabrik@sltnet.lk; 102 Pedlar St) For years this old place has been a classic backpacker hangout but at the time of research it was closed and undergoing a major refurbishment. It will have reopened by the time this book is printed.

OUT OF TOWN

TOP CHOICE **Dutch House** BOUTIQUE HOTEL **$$$**
(☎438 0275; www.thedutchhouse.com; 23 Upper Dickson Rd; ste incl breakfast US$397; ❄📶🏊) Cruise up to this 18th-century Dutch admiral's palace in your very own 1920s Rover, and live life like you're the star of a period drama. After a game of croquet on the lawn and a swim in the dreamy pool, retire to your room to write a novel or sketch a masterpiece on the artist's easel and then, if the high life gets tiring, take a break by clambering into the towering four-poster or by blowing bubbles of love in the bath. This award-winning hotel is seriously indulgent.

Sun House BOUTIQUE HOTEL **$$$**
(☎438 0275; www.thesunhouse.com; 18 Upper Dickson Rd; r incl breakfast from US$217; ❄📶🏊) This gracious old villa, built in the 1860s by a Scottish spice merchant, has been renovated with superb taste. Located on the shady hill above the new town, the hotel has wonderful views towards the Fort. The spearmint-striped rooms are so perfect, you feel as if you've intruded into a shoot for one of those house decoration magazines (and in fact during our last visit it was indeed being used in a photo shoot). Our favourite room is the red-and-white one with its mix of the old and new.

Tamarind Hill BOUTIQUE HOTEL **$$$**
(☎222 6568; www.asialeisure.lk; 288 Galle Rd; s/d incl breakfast US$160/180; ❄📶🏊) This 175-year-old former British Admiral's pad has been converted into a small boutique hotel with luxurious rooms, fine service and a jungle-fringed pool. However, the massive phone tower overlooking the property and the drive over what appears to be nothing but waste ground (and the crap piped music in the bar and restaurant) don't do a lot for the property. It's 2km west of town.

Closenberg Hotel HISTORIC HOTEL **$$$**
(☎222 4313; www.closenburghotel.com; 11 Closenberg Rd; s/d incl breakfast from US$150/175; ❄@📶) Built as a 19th-century P&O captain's residence in the heyday of British mercantile supremacy, this bougainvillea-bedecked hotel, east of the centre, sits out on a promontory with views over Galle beach

and the Fort. The rooms are all actually in a modern wing and have been decorated in a manner sympathetic to the overall feel of the place. The asking price is a bit steep, but fortunately discounts are as common as a sweaty afternoon in the Fort. Reaching the property involves driving through the port.

Eating

Many of the places to stay in Galle have good places to eat, but nightlife remains very subdued.

FORT

Mama's Galle Fort Roof Café SRI LANKAN **$$**
(76 Leyn Baan St; mains Rs 350) Eat under the twinkling star-lit sky with views of a spinning lighthouse at this guesthouse, which conjures up some of the most sensational curries in Galle – all at a great price. If the food really grabs you, ask about joining one of its cookery courses.

Galle Fort Hotel FUSION **$$$**
(28 Church St; set menu Rs 3720) The restaurant at this hotel serves superb, though very pricey, Asian fusion cuisine at tables set along the deep inner veranda. The dinner menu changes nightly. At other times there are baked goods, classic breakfast dishes, salads and sandwiches. The bar, overlooking Church St, feels like a colonial retreat, and is popular with the expat community.

Serendipity Arts Cafe INTERNATIONAL **$$**
(65 Leyn Baan St; meals Rs 200-500) This art-crammed cafe has a fusion menu that includes Western sandwiches and Eastern curries, brilliant juices and shakes, bacon-and-egg hoppers and proper filter coffee. Staff claim that some of the recipes are generations-old family secrets – though we're assured that the ingredients aren't as old! It's an ideal place for lunch or breakfast.

Anura's Restaurant INTERNATIONAL, SRI LANKAN **$$**
(9 Lighthouse St; mains Rs 300-600) This tiny, bright-orange, hole-in-the-wall place serves light curries, various pastas and even what are reputed to be Galle's best pizzas. The paintings on the wall give it a trendy cafe-gallery feel.

Heritage Cafe INTERNATIONAL **$$**
(53 Lighthouse St; mains Rs 300-600) Another in the array of boutique-style cafes that fill the streets of the Fort. This one stands out for its superb array of unusual salads and a menu that encircles half the planet in its culinary loveliness. Choose between eating on the sunny terrace, under the lazy interior fans or out in the courtyard garden.

Nescafe Shop SRI LANKAN **$**
(Rampart St; rotti from Rs 50; ⏲4.30am-6.30pm Mon-Fri, 10am-7pm Sat & Sun) There's no sign, but you can't really miss the *rotti*-slapping going on at this dark little cave of a cafe almost opposite the lighthouse. By far the cheapest place in the Fort to stuff your face.

NEW TOWN

South Ceylon Bakery SRI LANKAN **$**
(6 Gamini Mawatha; mains Rs 50-200) Opposite the bus station, this highly popular lunch spot, with its impossible-to-resist sweet and savoury short eats and gut-busting curries, is the most convenient place to eat in the new town.

Ruhunupura Pastry Shop ICE CREAM **$**
(26 P&J City, Gamini Mawatha; ice cream Rs 50) Despite the name, this place specialises in ice cream. It's hot out there under the sun. Indulge.

Drinking

Galle is awash in fancy Western-style coffee shops. The following are all in the Fort.

Café Nicos@Olanda Antiques CAFE
(30 Leyn Baan St; sandwiches Rs300-700) Now this is unexpected. Inside a fusty old antique shop is a thoroughly modern cafe serving real Italian-style coffee, plus juices and snacks.

Royal Dutch Cafe CAFE
(Leyn Baan St; meals from Rs 250; ⏲Sat-Thu) Mixing cinnamon cake with biryani and ginger tea with a shop full of batiks, this is a chilled spot for a light lunch.

Pedlar's Inn Cafe CAFE
(☎077 314 1477; 92 Pedlar St; meals Rs 200-350; ⏲8am-6pm Sat-Thu) A groovy little place in an old colonial house. Shakes, coffees and sandwiches can be enjoyed at long tables that are good for lounging. Doubles as a jewellery shop.

Janahitha Teashop CAFE
(cnr Pedlar & Leyn Baan Sts; ⏲6am-7.30pm) A world away from all the posh restaurants and arty cafes, this solidly locals-only teashop brews the best cuppa in the Fort.

Sunset Cafe CAFE
(Rampart St) A little roadside snack bar and cafe with a couple of tables set outside under the shadow of the fort walls. It's a relaxed place for a soft drink or ice cream as the sun goes down.

Shopping

Galle's history makes it a natural spot for antique shopping, and you'll find several places inside the Fort.

Look for the **Dutch Market** (Main St), selling Galle's freshest fruits and vegetables under a 300-year-old columned roof. There are other fresh food and spice markets along Main St, as well as a busy row of shops, many selling excellent merchandise at dirt-cheap prices. The entire area is worth a wander and a browse.

TOP CHOICE **Shoba Display Gallery** ARTS & CRAFTS
(www.shobafashion.org; 67 Pedlar St) Beautiful lacework made right here. The shop teaches local women dying crafts and ensures them a fair price for their work. Even if you're not buying, pop in to witness the process of making lace – amazing! If you're interested in a more hands-on approach, (with advance notice) they'll teach you how to weave your own lace.

Olanda Antiques ANTIQUES
(30 Leyn Baan St) A vast Aladdin's cave of antique furniture and clocks that stopped ticking in 1929 are among the treasures you'll find here. There's also an attached cafe.

Barefoot ARTS & CRAFTS
(www.barefootceylon.com; 41 Pedlar St) With its mixture of ethnic-style clothing, jewellery, high-quality house decorations, crafts, gifts and books (including an excellent selection of Sri Lanka–centric titles) this is a fine place to pick up some souvenirs.

Suthuvili Gallery ARTS & CRAFTS
(Leyn Baart St) This small shop has a breathtaking collection of elaborate and beautiful polychromatic masks.

Exotic Roots ARTS & CRAFTS
(32 Church St) French artist Catherine creates beautifully colourful bowls and house decorations while her daughter mixes up the colours in striking paintings.

PS Weerasekara Fashion Jewellery JEWELLERY
(Church St) Affordable and recommended jeweller that is several cuts (ahem) above the omnipresent gemstone vendors.

Orchid House JEWELLERY
(28A Hospital St) A teashop with a sideline in jewellery and the sweet smells of incense.

Information

Galle is a good source of supplies and other essentials for those heading east along the coast.

There is no shortage of banks with international ATMs, both in the Fort and the new town. For internet, most hotels have wi-fi access or there are a couple of internet cafes inside the P&J City shopping complex opposite the bus station.

Galle has a small band of bamboozlers, fixers, flimflammers and other characters looking to pull a scam. A firm 'I have no interest in anything you have to offer' should do the trick – at least by the fourth repetition.

Cargills Food City (3rd fl, 26 P&J City, Gamini Mawatha) This supermarket also has a pharmacy.

Commercial Bank (Church St) Has an international ATM.

Hatton National Bank (Wackwella St) Has an international ATM.

Main post office (Main St)

Post office (Church St) A small branch office.

Sampath Bank (Wackwella St) Has an international ATM.

Sri Lankan Airlines (☎224 6942; 3rd fl, 16 Gamini Mawatha) You can book flights here; it also offers a full range of travel services.

Getting There & Around

Bus

There are plenty of buses linking the towns along the coastal road. They leave from the bus station in the centre of Galle, opposite the cricket stadium. Major destinations:

Colombo regular/air-con Rs 115/230, three hours

Hikkaduwa Rs 28, 30 minutes

Matara regular/air-con Rs 52/110, one hour

Unawatuna Rs 16, 10 minutes

Air-con buses using the new Southern Expressway from Colombo (Rs 400) take 90 minutes and depart from the southern Colombo suburb of Maharagama near Kottawa, near the start of the new highway. For more on the new road see the boxed text, p313.

Car

Galle is currently the southern terminus of the new toll road, the Southern Expressway. It takes just under 90 minutes to travel from the Galle entrance to Kottawa (the current terminus and a short way northeast of Colombo). This saves at least two hours compared to taking the road along the west coast. Note that from the toll road entrance to the international airport near Negombo can take two hours but this will change in the next couple of years as new access roads are built.

Train

There are express passenger trains to Colombo's Maradana station (2nd/3rd class Rs 180/100, three hours) from the town's vaguely art-deco train station. Local trains serve Hikkaduwa (2nd/3rd class Rs 40/20, 30 minutes) and Matara (Rs 80/40, one to 1½ hours). There's a daily express to Kandy (Rs 320/175, 6½ hours).

Around Galle

Huge and glistening, the **Peace Pagoda** was the gift of a Japanese Buddhist monk in 2005. It can be seen on a precipice at the east end of the bay. Take the first turn after the water ends as you drive east and follow a tree-lined track for about 4km. Along the way, you can visit isolated **Jungle Beach**, which can be reached down a steep path that begins by a huge tree.

The road heading north passes the **Kottawa Conservation Forest**, a 14-hectare wet evergreen forest about 15km northeast of Galle. There are walking tracks in the forest, but first get permission from the forest department office near the gate. Wear good walking shoes and trousers: the leeches are ferocious. Trees are identified with their botanical names, making this a good opportunity to get to know your Sri Lankan flora. In the small-sized park is a swimming spot fed by a waterfall.

About 10km east of Kottawa the 10m-high seated Buddha at **Kaduruduwa Temple** (donation Rs 100) rises above the surrounding paddy fields.

Just 4km inland from Unawatuna the **Yatagala Raja Maha Viharaya** (donation Rs 100) is a quiet rock temple with a 9m reclining Buddha. The mural-covered walls are painted in the typical style of the Kandyan period. Monks have been living here for at least 1500 years.

WARNING

Sri Lankan authorities have pledged to remove structures built too close to the hightide line at beaches along the southwest coasts. Although this could include some cafes and even a few guesthouses, it should be noted that these actions have been discussed for years. In December 2011 authorities did remove a few cafe terraces built out over the water in Unawatuna, but even then the main structures – which were technically built too close to the water under rules put into effect after the tsunami – were left standing.

Be advised that should the authorities take more decisive action some listings in this chapter may be affected. Other areas where demolitions have been discussed include Mirissa and Hikkaduwa.

Unawatuna

091

Unawatuna is a place of dreams: a banana-shaped bend of boiling golden sand massaged by a gentle sea of moonstone blue. It's a place to dream of on drab Monday mornings at the office, a place to fantasise about when winter engulfs you, a place where life always seems slow and easy, and where there's never a bill to be paid or a mortgage payment to be made. The Resplendent Isle does not get any more resplendent than Unawatuna.

Unfortunately, even paradise is plagued with greed. Unawatuna was devastated by the 2004 tsunami and when rebuilding took place owners ignored plans for buildings to be set back from the water and rebuilt their places right on the sand. Some guesthouses sit directly on the high-tide mark and in fact, during big tides, they are now actually in the water. On some parts of the beach there is actually little beach at all left to play on.

Sights & Activities

Most people spend a lot of their time lying around the beach or slouching in cafes.

Water Sports

Unawatuna doesn't have a lot in the way of surf thanks to a fringing reef, though there

Unawatuna

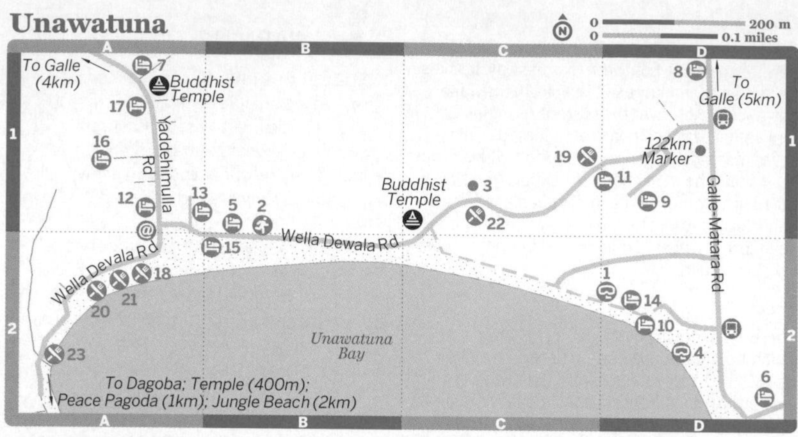

Unawatuna

Activities, Courses & Tours

1 Ocean Dive Centre D2
2 Sanctuary Spa B1
Sea Horse Scuba Diving Centre .... (see 14)
Secret Garden .... (see 13)
3 Sonjas Health Food Restaurant C1
4 Unawatuna Diving Centre D2

Sleeping

5 Amma's Guesthouse B1
6 Black Beauty Guest House D2
7 Dream House A1
8 Nooit Gedacht D1
9 Palm Grove D1
10 Peacock Hotel D2
11 Pipels House D1
12 Primrose Guest House A1
13 Secret Garden A1
14 Surfcity D2
15 Villa Hotel B2
16 Village Inn A1
17 Weliwatta House A1

Eating

Dream House .... (see 7)
18 Hot Rock A2
19 Jayasingha Tea Room C1
Jinas Vegetarian and Vegan Restaurant .... (see 19)
20 King Fisher's Restaurant A2
21 One Love Restaurant A2
22 Roti Shop C1
23 Shekira Restaurant A2

is a gentle right at the western end of the bay that a few locals ride.

You can hire snorkelling equipment from some of the beachfront places (or borrow it from guesthouses) to explore the reefs a short distance from the west end of the beach.

There are several interesting wreck dives around Unawatuna, as well as reef and cave diving. The wreck dives include the *Lord Nelson,* a cargo ship that was wrecked about 10 years ago; it has a 15m-long cabin to explore. The 33m-long *Rangoon* is one hour south of Unawatuna. The following places run diving courses and trips.

Ocean Dive Centre DIVING
(☎077 721 3559; www.oceandive.asia) Runs Professional Association of Diving Instructors (PADI) courses from €325. Also rents out equipment and offers single dives for €25.

Sea Horse Scuba Diving Centre DIVING
(☎228 3733; www.seahorsedivinglanka.com) A well-regarded and long-standing outfit. A PADI Open Water course costs €225 and a single dive for a qualified diver is €25.

Unawatuna Diving Centre DIVING
(☎224 4693; www.unawatunadiving.com) Runs PADI courses from €320. Also rents out equipment and offers single dives (€30). It's probably the most professional outfit in town and the only one with a decompression unit.

Walking

You can take some interesting walks over the rocks rising from the west end of the beach or up the hill behind Yaddehimulla Rd to catch views to the other side of the promontory. The rocky outcrop on the west end of the beach, **Rumassala**, is known for its protected medicinal herbs – legend has it that Hanuman, the monkey god, dropped herbs carried from the Himalaya here. The **temple** right on the promontory is fenced off, but you can wander up to the **dagoba** (stupa) on top of the hill and on to the huge **Peace Pagoda** and isolated **Jungle Beach**; see p103 for more details. A slightly different kind of walk (Rs 300) can be found at the **Mangrove Sanctuary**; a disorganised work in progress that is nevertheless a highly commendable local conservation effort protecting a swampy slab of mangrove forest a few minutes inland, filled with snails, crabs, birds and even monkeys. It's well worth taking time out from the beach to pace the raised walkways through the tangled roots and trees. To get there look for the yellowing signs along the Galle–Matara road and then ask and ask.

Courses

Sonjas Health Food Restaurant COOKING
(☎224 5815/077 961 5310) Highly recommended day-long cookery courses (Rs 3000) that tutor you in the finer points of Sri Lankan cuisine are run here. The course is led by the lovely Karuna and a trip to Galle market is included in the price. Book at least a day in advance. Several other restaurants along the same road also offer very similar courses.

Secret Garden YOGA
(Rs 1000) Find your inner peace – and muscles you never knew you had – on one of the recommended yoga classes held daily at 9am and 5pm in the yoga pavilion of the Secret Garden hotel. It's also open to non-guests of the hotel.

Sanctuary Spa MASSAGE
If a holiday means doing nothing more strenuous than being utterly pampered, the Sanctuary Spa should be music to your knotted muscles. A full treatment is around Rs 2800 and it has both male and female masseurs. It's also an Ayurveda centre.

Sleeping

Unawatuna is packed with budget places to stay. Decent midrange places are becoming more common and there are even a few fairly luxurious options springing up.

TOP CHOICE **Secret Garden** BOUTIQUE HOTEL $$
(☎224 1857; www.secretgardenunawatuna.com; cottages from US$50, r from US$66; ❄📶) Creak open the door and, like the name suggests, step into a hidden botanical wonderland full of crazy tropical flowers and mischievous monkeys. This beautifully renovated 140-year-old house has a range of rooms that are colour coordinated with the flowers outside. If the beautiful rooms are a bit pricey, try one of the simple but good-value cottages. Various yoga and Ayurvedic courses are on offer.

Nooit Gedacht HISTORIC HOTEL $$
(☎222 3449; Galle–Matara Rd; r incl breakfast US$60-80; ❄@🏊) A wonderful sense of blissful calm befalls anyone lucky enough to cross the threshold into this atmospheric 1735 Dutch colonial mansion, which is slightly tumbledown but perfectly enchanting. Rooms are divided into those in the old wing and those in a brand-new block (which are very slick indeed and well worth paying the extra for). There's a well-regarded Ayurvedic treatment centre and not one but two swimming pools.

Palm Grove GUESTHOUSE $$
(☎225 0104; www.palmgrovesrilanka.com; r with/without air-con US$40/32; ❄📶) Rummage through the masses of pot plants and hanging baskets and you'll discover a little English-run gem of a guesthouse. The spacious rooms have had lots of thought put into their layout and decoration, and upstairs is a roof terrace filled with hammocks from which you can lazily savour the view over Unawatuna's leafy back lanes.

Dream House BOUTIQUE HOTEL $$
(☎438 1541; dreamhouse@libero.it; s/d incl breakfast US$50/65; 📶) Set well back from the hustle of the beach, this Italian-owned house has four intimate rooms that have been restored and decorated in a Rome-meets-the-tropics fusion. There's nothing overstated or brash about this place – it's just pure and simple class. There's also a good restaurant.

Pipels House GUESTHOUSE $$
(☎077 428 3903; www.pipels.com; r incl breakfast Rs 3500, apt Rs 9000; 📶) This tiny place has vanilla-coloured rooms with flashy photos on the walls and modern metal furnishings. Some of the rooms share a pretty mosaic-patterned bathroom, while the apartment has its own kitchenette, bathroom and living room. The downstairs restaurant has

an Italian behind the stove – and that is a good thing!

Villa Hotel HOTEL $$
(☎224 7253; www.villa-unawatuna.com; s/d incl breakfast US$55/65; ❄@📶) A lovely waterfront hotel built in a traditional but very tall style. The twirling wooden window slats have an Arabic feel and the interiors of the rooms are attired in Indian art and ancient furnishings, while the bathroom is utterly modern. The highlight is the garden full of ornate 1920s English garden furniture.

Black Beauty Guest House GUESTHOUSE $$
(☎077 658 2909; www.black-beauty-sri-lanka.com; r with/without air-con Rs 4000/3000; ❄@📶🏊) Located away from the beach, there is nothing remotely black about this guesthouse, nor anything horsey, but there is plenty of beauty. The tranquil gardens provide a home to Spiderman and a flawless pool, and the bright-orange tower of a guesthouse has equally colourful rooms. It's good for people travelling with children as there are lots of kids toys about the place (although you do have to cross a busy road to reach the beach).

Surfcity Guest House HOTEL $$
(☎224 6305; www.surfcity1.net; with/without air-con s Rs 2000/1600, d Rs 2000/3500; 📶) The ever-expanding Surfcity emporium includes an internet cafe, coffee shop, restaurant, tour company and hotel, which has great-value clean rooms (three have hot water). Ravi, the owner, can arrange almost anything you might wish for, and the restaurant has nuexpected items such as hummus and flat bread on the menu.

Peacock Hotel HOTEL $$
(☎438 4998; www.peacockunawatuna.com; r incl breakfast with/without air-con Rs 4000/2500) The number of bronzing backpackers lounging around here indicates that this is a popular choice – and with good reason. There's a huge variety of well-tended rooms and all manner of traveller-related services. More expensive rooms have hot water.

Primrose Guest House GUESTHOUSE $$
(☎077 607 4428; primroseguest@hotmail.com; r with/without air-con US$45/40; ❄📶) Smart and spacious rooms that are impressively well maintained, with bedsheets tied into a knot of artistic brilliance. Each room has a little balcony overlooking a mass of bamboo plants. Good value.

Village Inn GUESTHOUSE $
(☎222 5375; unavillageinn@gmail.com; r Rs 1000) An idyllic garden retreat that can't be beaten on price. All rooms have bathrooms and a balcony or veranda, which are perfect for passing a lazy afternoon on.

Weliwatta House GUESTHOUSE $$
(☎222 6642; www.weliwatta.com; s/d incl breakfast old house Rs 2500/3500, new wing Rs 3500/4500) This century-old buttercup-yellow villa has a couple of spacious and tidy rooms with hot-water bathrooms in the main building and newer and more comfortable rooms behind. You'll love relaxing in the luxuriant garden in a comfy chair with a cold drink and good book to hand. There's also a reasonable restaurant.

Amma's Guesthouse GUESTHOUSE $
(☎222 5332; s/d Rs 1000/1500) The basic concrete cubicles inside this rambling old house, with its equally rambling garden, might not look too pretty, but it's cheap and just a few sandy paces from the beach.

Eating & Drinking

Almost all places to stay provide meals or have restaurants. The best way to choose from the many places on the beach may be to simply stroll around and see what you like. Most places are good for a drink – see which ones are in favour when you're there. Just don't expect much past midnight. The places listed here offer something a bit different or have a little more character than the rest.

King Fisher's Restaurant INTERNATIONAL $$$
(meals Rs 700-1000; ⏰9am-midnight Tue-Sun) This seafront restaurant is currently flavour of the month with both visitors and local expats. Although it cooks up a bit of pretty much everything, it's best known for its excellent Thai food and its prawns – grilled or fried to perfection.

Shekira Restaurant SEAFOOD $$
(meals Rs 300-600) With boats bobbing like ducks on the water just a few metres away, this romantic wooden fishermen's shack, with just a couple of candlelit tables, is perfect for a cold sunset beer and an ultracheap fried-fish dinner washed down with the owner's friendly banter. For the non-nautical among you it also has a few land-based Chinese dishes.

Dream House ITALIAN $$
(mains Rs 500-600) Eat alfresco while being serenaded by classical music at this authentic Italian restaurant. The owner is of true-blue Latin stock, so you can be sure the tomatoes have been placed in just the right spot and the perfect amount of fresh basil has been added.

One Love Restaurant SRI LANKAN $$
(meals Rs 250-400) This small and friendly place literally hangs above the water and the creaky wooden floorboards further enhance the sensation of being on a boat sailing across the seven seas. It's unusual in that its good range of curries allows you to eat like a local (a rarity in Unawatuna). Pumpkin curry is the house special.

Sunil Garden INTERNATIONAL $$
(☎0777 472441; meals Rs 400-600) Sunil, the owner, sets a festive mood while cooking up seafood, pasta and more. On many nights he leads live music. This is *the* place for a beer, but if that's too racy for you, there's also a straight-out-of-the-city coffee and smoothie bar.

Jinas Vegetarian and Vegan Restaurant VEGETARIAN $$
(meals Rs 500-600) This enjoyable garden restaurant offers a wide array of classic Indian dishes such as thalis and masala dosas as well as European vegetarian dishes, including veggie burgers, lasagne and the not very veggie-sounding peacock pie.

Hot Rock INTERNATIONAL $$
(☎224 2685; meals Rs 200-500) A classic beachside seafood restaurant with delightful owners and such vivid colours it looks like Joseph's amazing technicolour dream cafe.

Jayasingha Tea Room SRI LANKAN $
(meals Rs 150; ⏲noon-3pm) Remind yourself of what Sri Lanka is supposed to taste like with one of the superb rice and curries up for grabs at the back of this grocery shop. Locals can't get enough of the food here, but foreign tourists are as rare as a mild chilli.

Roti Shop SRI LANKAN $
(rotti Rs 200-250) Dozens of sweet and savoury *rotti* rammed full of cheeses, fruits and more make for an easy (but, it should be said, a very slow-to-make) lunch.

Information

For most goods and services you'll have to make the short trip to Galle, as there are only a couple of rudimentary huts selling bottled water and crisps. Many places offer internet access.

GG Happy Tours (☎223 2838; www.gghappytours.com; per hr Rs 240; ⏲9am-10pm) Internet access, and has also been recommended by a number of travellers for its tour and car-hire services.

Getting There & Away

Coming by bus from Galle (Rs 16, 10 minutes) you can get off at the small road that leads into town, or get off at the next stop, where the ocean meets the main road, and walk in along the beach. A three-wheeler to or from Galle costs between Rs 300 and 400.

Unawatuna to Koggala

☎091

Beyond Unawatuna the road runs close to the coast through Thalpe, Dalawella and Koggala, and on to Ahangama and beyond. With numerous beautiful stretches of virtually deserted beaches and many picturesque coves, this is a perfect place to stick a pin in the map and find an empty stretch of fantastic sand to suit.

Along this part of the coast you will see stilt fishermen perching precariously like storks above the waves at high tide. Each fisherman has a pole firmly embedded in the sea bottom, close to the shore, on which they perch and cast their lines. Stilt positions are passed down from father to son and are highly coveted. You'll be amazed at how fast they can get off those stilts and run up to you if you even vaguely wave a camera in their direction!

Sights & Activities

Koggala Lake LAKE
Next to the road, Koggala Lake is alive with birdlife and dotted with islands, one of which features a Buddhist temple that attracts many visitors on *poya* (full moon) days and another that contains an interesting cinnamon plantation. Guided two-hour boat rides (Rs 2500 to 4000; up to five people) are possible on the lake. To find the boatmen, look for the signs reading 'Bird Island' between Koggala and Ahangama.

Lagoon Herbal Garden GARDEN
(⌚8am-6pm) There are several spice gardens around the lake, and Lagoon Herbal Garden is a good one to visit. It will provide you with the chance to buy all manner of home remedies and to see how many of the plants are grown. It also offers boat trips on the lagoon (Rs 4000).

Martin Wickramasinghe Folk Art Museum MUSEUM
(admission Rs 200; ⌚9am-5pm) Near the 113km marker, west of Koggala, is this museum, which is set back from the road. It includes the house where respected Sinhalese author Martin Wickramasinghe was born. The exhibits are interesting and well displayed, with information in English and Sinhala. Among them is a good section on dance (including costumes and instruments), puppets, *kolam* (masked dance-drama) masks (including one of a very sunburnt British officer), kitchen utensils and carriages. The bookshop sells the author's works, many of which deal with local culture.

Kataluwa Purwarama Temple TEMPLE
Just east of Koggala, this feels like the temple time forgot. Dating from the 13th century, it has some recently restored murals. A friendly monk will open the building and explain the murals. Some of the Jataka tales (stories from the Buddha's lives) painted here are 200 years old. The turnoff to the temple is at Kataluwa – you'll see the signs on the inland side of the road. Continue a couple of kilometres inland and ask for directions.

Sleeping & Eating

THALPE

Thalpe is the new beach bolt-hole for Galle expats and those over the whole Unawatuna scene. There are a number of very exclusive places to stay as well as a few cheaper options. The beach is largely hidden from the road by a solid line of villas, houses and hotels, and there's little in the way of public access.

The Frangipani Tree BOUTIQUE HOTEL **$$$**
(☎228 3711; www.thefrangapanitree.com; r incl breakfast US$250; ❄📶🏊) Cement. It's not the most beautiful building material, but in this intimate boutique hotel you'll learn to love the stuff. It's everywhere – benches, floors, walls and showers – but my oh my have they turned the drab, grey stuff into a thing of utter beauty. The vast, cool rooms, with outdoor bathrooms set under the petal fall of tropical trees, are nothing short of perfect.

Era Hotel BOUTIQUE HOTEL **$$$**
(☎228 2302; www.jetwinghotels.com; s/d incl breakfast US$230/250; ❄📶🏊) Small boutique hotel where wood and stone combine to create a Zen-like sense of happiness (the beachside setting and gorgeous pool help out with this too). However, some rooms catch a little road noise and the welcome at reception isn't always that great.

KOGGALA

Koggala is home to a long, wide, but wave-lashed stretch of beach. The road runs quite close to the shore but most of the time it remains just out of sight.

The Fortress HOTEL **$$$**
(☎438 9400; www.thefortress.lk; r incl breakfast from US$360; ❄📶🏊) From the outside this vast place, with its high walls, looks exactly like a prison. However, we rather suspect that most Sri Lankan prisons do not come with infinity pools overlooking the Indian Ocean, whirlpool baths and rain showers, chic urban-style rooms, wi-fi and fine dining.

Ahangama & Midigama

☎091

The Ahangama and Midigama area are home to the most consistent, and possibly the best, surf in Sri Lanka. It's a very low-key area with plenty of cheap, surfer-friendly accommodation and a scattering of pretty beaches (though the road often runs very close to the shore). The first spot is the consistent beach break at Kabalana Beach, which normally has something to ride even when it's tiny elsewhere. In Midigama itself, a spicepot-sized village built beside a curve of sand, there are a couple of reef breaks. Lazy Left is the aptly named wave that bends around the rocks and into the sandy bay – it's perfect for that first reef experience. A few hundred metres further down is Ram's Right, a hollow, shallow and unpredictable beast. It's not suitable for beginners.

Note that the water covers lots of rocks, coral and other hazards. Also, besides a few guesthouses offering battered boards for rent (Rs 600 to 1000 per day), there are no places selling surf gear or offering repairs – you'll have to go to Hikkaduwa. If you are looking for **surf lessons**, Yannick, a Frenchman who has done much to help rebuild

RAMYADAVA GUNASEKARA – SURFING WITH RAM

Ramyadava (known to all and sundry as Ram) owns one of the long-standing surfer guesthouses in Midigama.

'I think the first surfers arrived in Midigama in 1977. I was very young and had never seen surfers before. One day six Australian surfers arrived. I thought they were very strange and everyone in the village came down to watch them surf. My parents told me not to go near them because they were hippies and it might make problems if I touched them, because everyone thought that hippies were dirty! These surfers were the first foreigners to stay in Midigama, but after they left it was several years before more came.

'Today people in the village know the surfers don't have germs and most people like them because they spend money here. They buy fruit from people, use the three-wheelers, eat at people's restaurants and so on. After the tsunami many of the surfers staying here gave money as well as books and clothing for the children. Some of them stayed on to help clean up and rebuild. Yannick, a French surfer, has done a lot for the village. He started a charity and obtained new boats for the fishermen and household utensils for everyone. But just after the tsunami a surfer was caught stealing people's stuff from the rubble. When he was caught he was beaten up by the other surfers and sent away. Before he did that I thought all foreigners were good people.'

Midigama after the tsunami, runs one of the better surf schools in the area in conjunction with the Subodinee Guesthouse. He charges €30 for a one-day course or €75 for a three-day course. He also has the best, and most expensive, range of boards for hire.

Sleeping & Eating

AHANGAMA

Many surfers stay in Ahangama and ride the waves in Midigama. The following are listed in the order you pass them coming from Unawatuna. There are no stand-alone tourist restaurants, but all the accommodation places serve food.

Kabalana Beach Hotel HOTEL **$$**
(☎228 3294; www.kabalana.com; s/d incl breakfast from US$55/65; ❄☜≋) At their best, the rooms here seem born of a local mother and a colonial father, and include latticework window frames, four-poster beds and antique Indian furniture. However, despite no price difference, room quality varies a lot, and if you get a dud one you'll feel cheated. There's a small pool and a painfully slow and bland restaurant. It's a very popular wedding destination so it can be noisy.

Ahangama Easy Beach HOTEL **$$**
(☎228 2028; s/d incl breakfast €32/34, d with air-con €39; ❄@☜) A Norwegian-run place that's popular with the new wave of surfers – connected permanently to their laptops and mobile phones. Mickey Dora would turn in his grave! The rooms are decent and have nicely tiled bathrooms and four-poster beds. Each time we've visited we've found the welcome quite cold.

MIDIGAMA

There is an array of cheap guesthouses here and one or two plusher places. If you don't surf there's not a lot of point in coming here.

The following are listed in the order you reach them when coming from Unawatuna.

Subodinee Guesthouse GUESTHOUSE **$**
(☎228 3383; www.subodinee.com; s/d from Rs 1000/1500, cabanas €35; @) Long ago when the first surfers showed up in Midigama, Jai and his wife Sumana had a small tea shop from which they served rice and curry to the strange newcomers. Today things have come a long way and they now have a huge range of rooms, which kick off as hot concrete cubes with shared bathrooms, and work their way up to pleasing individual cabanas or rooms in a new building over the road with hot water and all the trimmings. There's also a taxi service, surf school and board hire, and a restaurant that with notice (an hour or two) can whip up a rice and curry.

Rams Guesthouse GUESTHOUSE **$**
(☎225 2639; s Rs 900-1500, d Rs 1400-2500; @) The rooms at this eternally popular surfers' hangout are as basic as basic gets, but they are kept clean and have private bathrooms. The rooms in the ever-growing main block are slightly less dingy, though like all the

rooms they suffer from road noise. Many surfers barely leave here for months on end, which gives it a friendly community vibe. The welcome is very warm and it's located right in front of what is probably the best wave on the island. See the boxed text, p109, for the owner's experiences with surfers.

Villa Naomi HISTORIC HOTEL $$
(041 225 4711; www.naomibeach.com; s/d incl breakfast Rs 4000/4500;) Beautiful colonial villa with whitewashed rooms, antique furnishings, plush bathrooms and a veranda that's just crying out to have an evening G&T drunk on it. All up it offers exceptional value for money.

Villa Tissa HISTORIC HOTEL $$
(041 225 3434; www.villatissa.net; s/d incl breakfast Rs 5000/7000;) If you're a live-like-the-other-half surfer then the lovely Villa Tissa should float your board. Set in pleasant beachfront gardens, the huge rooms recall bygone days and are very well appointed. There's a good swimming pool and a narrow patch of beach out the front.

Getting There & Away

There are frequent buses along the southern coastal road connecting Ahangama and Midigama with other towns between Galle and Matara and points beyond. The bus from Galle costs Rs 30 to Midigama. Many Colombo–Matara trains stop at Ahangama. Only a few local trains stop at Midigama.

Sri Lankan Air Taxi (www.srilankan.lk/airtaxi) runs daily scheduled flights from Koggala airstrip to Colombo (around Rs 8700) and to Dambulla on Monday and Friday (around Rs 11,700).

Weligama

041

Weligama (meaning 'Sandy Village'), about 30km east of Galle, is an interesting and lively blend of international beach resort and raucous Asian fishing town. You can spend a happy day wandering around, getting a feel for local life, dipping your toes in the ocean and marvelling at the denizens of the deep, who end their days being hacked up and sold from the roadside fish stalls.

Close to the shore – so close that you can walk out to it at low tide – is a tiny island known as **Taprobane** (www.taprobaneisland.com). It looks like an ideal artist's or writer's retreat, which indeed it once was: novelist Paul Bowles wrote *The Spider's House* here in the 1950s. Even better, the island was once owned by the French Count de Maunay-Talvande. If you really like it you can stay here; though at well over US$1000 a night, it's probably beyond the budget of many.

Sights & Activities

Scenic though the bay is, Weligama Beach is a bit shabby and not geared for sunbathers. It's primarily a fishing village, with catamarans lining the western end of the bay. It's a very good place to learn to surf with soft, sandy beach waves that rarely exceed a metre. Among other places, both the Samaru Beach House and the Weligama Bay View, next door, rent boards and provide lessons.

Weligama is known for its **lacework**, and stalls are located on the main road along the coast.

Sport Diving DIVING
(225 0799; www.freewebs.com/padisportdiving) Snorkelling at Weligama is good, or you can scuba dive. This operation, close to the harbour at the western end of the beach, runs PADI courses (€300) as well as excursions such as wreck dives. It can also organise whale and dolphin diving and snorkelling trips.

Sleeping & Eating

Accommodation is spread out along the beach road, but compared with nearby Mirissa, most of it seems somewhat overpriced and poor value.

For eating, tuck into some fresh-from-the-ocean seafood at the waterfront **Dinesh Seafood Restaurant** opposite Taprobane Island and for dessert head to the **AVM Cream House** opposite the bus station, which some readers swear blind has the best fruit juices and salads around.

Samaru Beach House HOTEL $$
(225 1417; www.guesthouse-weligamasamaru.com; 544 New Matara Rd; r with/without air-con Rs 4000/3500;) Located at about the middle of the bay, this traveller-savvy place is right on the beach and has light and airy rooms that are sheltered from road noise. The better rooms have a veranda. Bikes and surfboards (Rs 300 to 400 per hour) may be rented and the owner can organise all manner of local tours and activities. Surf lessons are Rs 2500 per day.

Dilkini Guesthouse GUESTHOUSE $
(☎225 0281; s/d Rs 750/1000) On the edge of the village proper, this place has rooms that might be very ordinary, but there's a friendly welcome awaiting you and, in a town with unnaturally high room rates, the rock-bottom prices make this basic guesthouse the best value around. You wouldn't want to swim off the bit of beach it fronts.

Mandara Resort RESORT $$$
(☎567 6768; www.mandararesort.com; s/d incl breakfast US$215/230; ❄@☎≋) Weligama's most luxurious resort is, like almost everywhere in town, a bit overpriced but nevertheless its clean and utterly modern lines make this a very comfortable place to stay. Some rooms are so comfortable they even have private plunge pools!

Getting There & Away

There are frequent buses to Galle (Rs 40, one hour) and Matara (Rs 21, 30 minutes). Weligama is on the Colombo–Matara train line; destinations include Colombo (2nd/3rd class Rs 220/120, four hours), Galle (Rs 60/30, one hour) and Matara (Rs 30/15, 30 minutes).

Mirissa

☎041

Crack open a coconut, slip into a hammock and rock gently in the breeze, allowing the hours, days and even weeks to slip calmly by. Welcome to sleepy Mirissa, which is 4km southeast of Weligama, and a place so idyllic that only a fool would ever want to leave.

Of the big three south-coast beach resorts (Hikkaduwa and Unawatuna being the other two) Mirissa is easily the least developed and is a good glimpse of what Unawatuna must have been like 15 years ago. For the moment most of the foreshore remains the domain of coconut trees, and much of the tourist development remains hidden from view (although in 2010 a rash of flimsy, and illegally built, shack-like restaurants were constructed along the foreshore. These were quickly demolished by the authorities, but it could be a sign of the future).

You'll need to go to Matara for most services, although there are internet and phone places, and small markets near the 149km marker.

Sights & Activities

Mirissa is designed for sitting and being, not for doing. Having said that, the water is deliciously clear and, around the reefs and rocks at either end, it's excellent for snorkelling. Surfers will find an inconsistent but fun right point at the western end of the bay. Many of the guesthouses have snorkelling and surfing gear to rent.

If you do need to move, then there are some pleasant walks. One heads up a steep series of steps from the main road to the small **Kandavahari temple**, while the headland is a good spot to view Weligama Bay.

The one activity that almost every visitor to Mirissa takes part in is a whale-watching boat trip. See the boxed text, p112, for more.

Sleeping

Rooms only have cold water unless otherwise specified. Look for signs along the main road. Many places to stay serve meals.

TOP CHOICE **Palm Villa** GUESTHOUSE $$
(☎225 0022; palmvillamirissa@yahoo.com; r US$35-60; ❄☎) The French-speaking owner of this new guesthouse isn't an interior designer, but he probably should be. Each of the lovely rooms is uniquely decorated in a bright and modern fashion, and the bathrooms are a riot of mosaics. The more expensive rooms are set right on the beach and the garden is full of cock-a-doodling roosters and white bunny rabbits. There's an excellent inhouse restaurant where you can eat at a candlelit table under the twinkling stars. More-expensive rooms have air-con and hot water.

TOP CHOICE **Mirissa Hills** BOUTIQUE HOTEL $$$
(☎225 0980; www.mirissahills.com; incl breakfast s US$74-195, d US$92-244; ❄☎≋) OK, so there's no beach view, but instead you've got buffalo wallowing in the ever-green rice paddies, peacocks strutting their stuff, and high above, on a hill in the heart of a working cinnamon farm, you can live like a lord or lady in this renovated old villa. The main villa has antique saris on the walls, free-standing stone bathtubs and a glut of sculptures twisted out of rusty old metal. Cheaper rooms are in an annex down the hill and are equally artistic.

The Spice House HOMESTAY $$
(☎077 351 0147; thespicehousemirissa@gmail.com; 151 Galle Rd; s/d incl breakfast Rs 3500/4800; ☎)

SEARCHING FOR MOBY DICK

In 2006 rumours started spreading through conservation circles of something big lurking in the waters off southern Sri Lanka. That thing was the blue whale, the biggest creature ever to inhabit planet Earth, and the word was that there was more than one of them. In fact, scientists have quickly come to the startling realisation that Sri Lanka may well be the best place in the world to see this very rare gentle giant as well as its cousin the sperm whale. While whale-watching tours had long been popular off Trincomalee on the northeast coast, it was always understood that sightings were hit-and-miss up there. When experts realised that potentially large numbers of whales were migrating between the Bay of Bengal and the Arabian Sea, passing by the Sri Lankan coast very close to Dondra Head, they set out in search of them. They didn't have to look for long. Within 15 minutes of standing on Dondra Head and scanning the water with binoculars, they'd sighted the first blue whale. When they headed out to sea the sightings became even more spectacular, with up to five blue whales being seen within 8 sq km and an almost equally impressive tally of sperm whales, as well as numerous dolphins.

Within two years of those first sightings the first tentative whale-watching trips launched to great success, with whales being spotted almost every time. Nowadays almost anyone with a boat has started offering whale-watching safaris – even the Sri Lankan navy has got in the act and offers tours leaving from Galle (although these are mainly aimed at local school groups and they use large boats). Not surprisingly this free-for-all is leading to problems. Some boat operators will try and get their clients as close to the whales as possible (this can often be after they have been put under pressure to do so by their clients), but whales become very stressed when boats approach too close and if the harassment continues they may change their behaviour patterns or leave an area altogether. Therefore for the future of the whales, and the whale-watching industry in Sri Lanka, it pays to go with someone who really knows what they're doing.

Neither of the following two companies are all that cheap (think around US$110 per person depending on the exact package taken), but the quality is undoubted. Numerous cheaper operators, charging between Rs 4000 to 6000 depending on boat speed and quality, can be found in and around Mirissa, but it can be a very hit-and-miss experience using some of those.

Jetwing Eco Holidays (☎011-238 1201; www.jetwingeco.com; 46/26 Navam Mawatha, Colombo) It doesn't just organise superb trips – it was among the first to break the news about the whales and has done the most to study and launch conservation efforts.

Eco Team Sri Lanka (☎011-583 0833; www.srilankaecotourism.com; 20/63 Fairfield Gardens, Colombo) Also operates highly recommended whale tours (and other wildlife tours).

Raja and the Whales (☎077 695 3452) One local Mirissa operator we have had positive feedback about.

Classic contemporary Asian-chic rooms, heavy four-poster beds, thick mattresses, terracotta colours, a beautiful garden and a family who bend over backwards to make you feel at home all add up to make this one of Mirissa's best. Unfortunately, it's on the wrong side of the road to the beach and some rooms suffer from road noise.

Secret Root GUESTHOUSE **$$**
(☎077 329 4332; www.secretroot.yolasite.com; r with/without air-con Rs 4000/5000; ❄📶) Secreted away at the end of a jungle lane, a few moments inland from the eastern end of the beach, is this family-run sanctuary of calm. The rooms are impressively clean and the hot-water bathrooms are the most inviting in the village. There's an inhouse Ayurvedic centre (male masseurs only), which has helped lower many a traveller's stress levels (treatments from Rs 1000). Prices include breakfast.

Amarasinghe Guest House GUESTHOUSE **$$**
(☎225 1204; r Rs 1000-4000; @) For those who want to be consumed by nature, this

delightful place, adrift in a web of rural lanes five minutes back from the beach, is ideal. A range of agreeably ramshackle rooms (some with shared bathrooms) and cottages lie scattered throughout gardens where the only disturbance will be the croaking of frogs and the chirping of birds. The owners grow all their own organically produced vegetables and spices, and the food receives rave reports. If they're full they have a couple of other nearby properties.

Palace Mirissa RESORT **$$$**
(☎225 1303; www.palacemirissa.com; s/d half board from €60/70;) With the dominant position on the headland at the western end of the bay, this is the village's oldest and best top-end option. The raised cottages are decked out like a Hindu temple (although there are slightly more portraits of naked women than at the average holy site) and have black-and-white tiled bathrooms with hot water. There's a pleasant swimming pool and stunning views from the restaurant.

Rose Blossom HOMESTAY **$$**
(☎077 713 3096; s Rs 1500, d Rs 2500-3000) This cute little three-room place has cosy (read: cramped) but well-decorated rooms and the most charming of owners. It's a five-minute walk inland from the eastern end of the beach.

Katies Hideaway GUESTHOUSE **$$**
(☎071 342 1630; nalabank@yahoo.com; r with/without air-con Rs 3000/1500) Just a couple of years ago, Katies, which is hidden away down a dusty lane, was a simple two-room homestay. Today it has grown into a multi-storey guesthouse complex and although it's lost a lot of its earlier charm, it still remains a good-value place to bed down for a night or three.

Calidan HOMESTAY **$**
(☎077 754 7802; s Rs 1000-1200, d Rs 1200-1500) A short walk from the hurly-burly of the beach scene, this is a welcoming homestay where you'll find five rooms painted in cheery colours and big smiles from the owners.

Poppies GUESTHOUSE **$**
(☎077 794 0328; r Rs 1500-2000) Brand new at the time of research, the pristine rooms here are set around a grassy courtyard and would be a great deal were it not for the fact that they're on the wrong side of the road from the beach. The blurting of bus horns will break into your dreams.

Calm Rest HOTEL **$**
(☎225 2546; r/cabana Rs 2000/2500) In a quiet location just 50m back from the beach. Both the rooms and the wooden cabanas here are a little dark, but the flower-bedecked bedspreads help ease the gloom.

Eating

As far as food goes, there are around half a dozen beach-shack restaurants serving up almost identical seafood and traveller 'cuisine' to a reggae soundtrack. Two of the better ones are Sea Fresh Restaurant and Café Mirissa. Prices at both these are around 25% cheaper than in the hotel restaurants.

No1 Dewmini Roti Shop SRI LANKAN **$**
(rotti around Rs 200) There are several *rotti* shops in Mirissa catering to strange foreign tastes (chocolate *rotti* anyone?) but this one, five minutes inland of the beach and on the way to the Amarasinghe Guest House, is the original and still the best. It also produces *kottus* and (with notice) more substantial rice and curry-style dishes. The ever-smiling chef and owner organises cooking classes (around Rs 2000 for six curries).

Getting There & Away

The bus fare from Weligama is Rs 9; a three-wheeler costs Rs 250. From Matara the bus fare is Rs 17. If you're heading to Colombo, it's better to catch a bus to Matara and change, as many buses will be full by the time they pass through Mirissa.

Matara

☎041 / POP 76,254

Matara, 160km from Colombo, is a busy, sprawling commercial town that owes almost nothing to tourism. Ironically it's this very fact, and the opportunity it affords to see day-to-day Sri Lankan life unaffected by the hurly-burly of the nearby beach scenes, that make it worth visiting.

Matara's main attractions are its ramparts, a well-preserved Dutch fort and, most of all, its street life. If you really can't live without sand between your toes, then choose between people-watching and ice-cream munching on the main Matara Beach or snorkelling, surfing and lazing on the white sands of Polhena or the less picturesque sands of Meddawatta Beach.

Matara

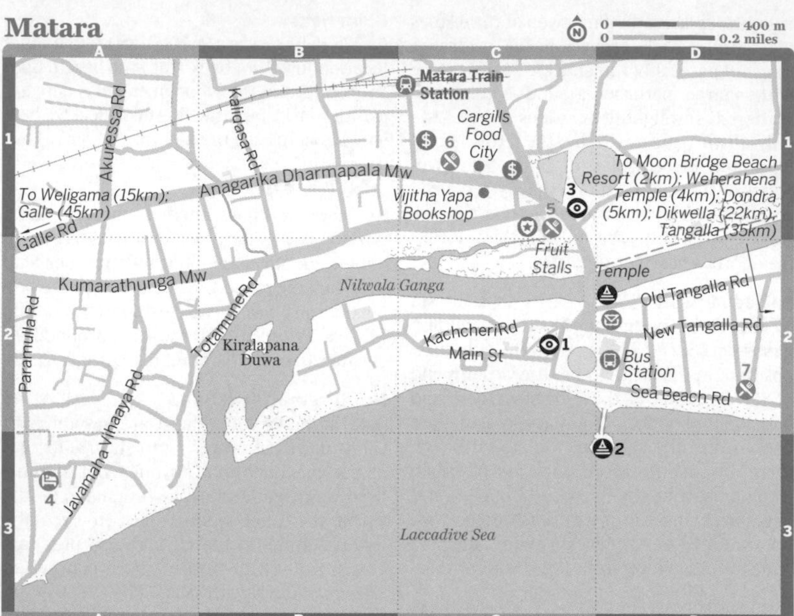

Matara

Sights
- 1 Dutch Rampart.....C2
- 2 Parey Dewa.....D3
- 3 Star Fort.....C1

Sleeping
- 4 Sunil Rest Guest House & Restaurant.....A3

Eating
- 5 Food Markets.....C1
- 6 Galle Oriental Bakery Restaurant.....C1
- 7 Mayura Beach Restaurant.....D2

Sights

Seeing all Matara has to offer shouldn't take more than an hour or two.

Parey Dewa TEMPLE

A pedestrian bridge near the bus station leads to a small island, Parey Dewa (Rock in Water), which is home to a tiny Buddhist temple with a very fancy modern bridge leading out to it. The beach on which it sits is a great place to go for an evening walk and have an ice cream with many of the town folk.

Dutch Rampart OLD TOWN

The smallish Dutch rampart occupies the promontory separating the Nilwala Ganga from the sea. Built in the 18th century to protect the VOC's kachcheri (administrative office), its structure is a little peculiar – it was originally meant to be a fort, but accountants, with their pesky cost-cutting exercises, dictated otherwise. Inside the rampart are quiet vestiges of old Matara. Wander the few streets and you'll see the odd colonial gem – though its real charm is that it is quieter than modern Matara.

Star Fort FORT

(10am-5pm) About 350m from the main rampart gate, Star Fort was built by the Dutch to compensate for deficiencies in the rampart. However, it's so small it could only have protected a handful of bureaucrats. The date of construction (1765) is embossed over the main gate, along with the VOC company insignia and the coat of arms of the governor of the day. Look for the two carved lions that guard the entrance gates. You can also spot the slots that once secured the drawbridge beams.

Sleeping

POLHENA

Many travellers stay in Polhena, southwest of the centre. Most places serve meals and have cold water and fans. Note that the area is a warren of small tracks, so you may need to ask for directions. A three-wheeler from Matara costs Rs 250.

Sunil Rest Guest House & Restaurant GUESTHOUSE $
(☎222 1983; sunilrestpolhena@yahoo.com; 16/3A Second Cross Rd; r Rs 1000;) An exceptionally friendly and helpful place, just back from the beach. The plain rooms in the main building are a bit run-down, but they operate a couple of other establishments with plusher rooms (up to Rs 5000) elsewhere in the neighbourhood. Staff can organise various excursions as well as diving trips. Note that they don't play the commission game, so many three-wheeler drivers will tell you it's closed down – it's not.

MEDDAWATTA

Medawatta beach is hidden around a small headland from the eastern end of the main town beach. The beach here is none too clean, but with consistent and gentle beach break waves it's a reasonably popular surf beach.

Moon Bridge Beach Resort HOTEL $$
(☎222 3717; www.moonbridge-resort.com; with/without air-con s Rs 2750/1320, d Rs 3850/1650;) Overlooking the waves but with otherwise fairly uninspiring rooms. The fan-only rooms are better value than those with air-con. There are a couple of other equally ho-hum places in the vicinity.

Eating

Just north of the bridge, on the main road, you'll see food markets and several fruit vendors with gorgeous displays of produce. Otherwise, dining choices are limited to some simple joints along the main road.

Galle Oriental Bakery Restaurant SRI LANKAN $
(41 Anagarika Dharmapala Mawatha; mains from Rs 100) The best central option is a classic old place with a wooden interior and display cases bulging with baked and savoury treats. The soups and curries are good.

Mayura Beach Restaurant SRI LANKAN $
(33 Sea Beach Rd; mains from Rs 100) This very popular locals' place has plate-glass windows overlooking the beach and (very spicy) curries.

Information

Cargills Food City Near Bandaranayaka Mawatha, this place has traveller supplies and a pharmacy.

Commercial Bank (Station Rd) Has an international ATM.

Post office (New Tangalla Rd) Near the bus station.

Sampath Bank (Anagarika Dharmapala Mawatha) Has an international ATM.

Vijitha Yapa Bookshop (25A 1/1 Anagarika Dharmapala Mawatha) Good selection of novels, magazines, maps and guidebooks.

Getting There & Away

Air

Sri Lankan Air Taxi (www.srilankan.lk/airtaxi) runs scheduled flights from nearby Dickwela to Colombo on Tuesday, Thursday, Saturday and Sunday for around Rs 10,000.

Bus

The Matara bus station is a vast multilevel place. Look for tiny destination signs over the queuing pens. As Matara is a regional transport hub, services are frequent in all directions. Some of the major destinations:

Amapara Rs 280, eight hours
Colombo regular/air-con Rs 210/310, four to five hours
Galle Rs 60, two hours
Ratnapura Rs 325, 4½ hours, morning only
Tangalla Rs 46, 1½ to two hours

Train

Matara's train station is the end of the coastal railway. Destinations include the following:

Colombo Rs 230/130, four hours
Galle 2nd/3rd class Rs 80/40, one to 1½ hours
Kandy Rs 360/195, seven hours
Vavuniya (for Anuradhapura) Rs 430/235, 10 hours

Matara to Tangalla

There are several other places of interest just off the road from Matara to Tangalla, including two superb examples of what one visitor labelled 'neo-Buddhist kitsch'.

Sights & Activities

Weherahena Temple TEMPLE
(admission by donation) Just as you leave the outskirts of Matara, a turn inland will take you to this gaudy temple, where an artificial cave is decorated with about 200

cartoon-like scenes from the Buddha's life. There's also a huge Buddha statue.

At the time of the late-November or early December *poya*, a *perahera* (procession) of dancers and elephants is held at the temple to celebrate the anniversary of its founding.

Dondra LIGHTHOUSE

About 5km southeast of Matara you come to the town of Dondra. Travel south from the main road for 1.2km and you'll reach the lighthouse at the southernmost point of Sri Lanka. There are good views from here, and there's a humdrum cafe nearby.

Buses from Matara will drop you in the centre of Dondra. From here you can three-wheel it or walk to the lighthouse.

Wewurukannala Vihara TEMPLE

(admission Rs 100) If the Weherahena Temple is 'Marvel Comics meets Lord Buddha', then here it's Walt Disney who runs into him. At the town of Dikwella, 22km from Matara, a road turns inland towards Beliatta. About 1.5km along you come to a 50m-high seated Buddha figure – the largest in Sri Lanka.

The temple is often thronging with worshippers. Before reaching the Buddha statue you must pass through a real hall of horrors full of life-sized models of demons and sinners. The punishments inflicted on these sinners include being dunked in boiling cauldrons, sawn in half and disembowelled. Finally there's the gigantic seated figure, which was constructed in the 1960s when kitsch was the name of the game.

Puja (literally 'respect'; offerings or prayers) is held every morning and evening.

You can reach the temple on any Matara–Tangalla bus that goes via Beliatta.

Ho-o-maniya Blowhole LANDSCAPE

About 6km northeast of Dikwella, near the 186km post, a road heads off for 1km to the (sometimes) spectacular Ho-o-maniya blowhole. During the southwest monsoon (June is the best time), high seas can force water 23m up through a natural chimney in the rocks and then up to 18m in the air. At other times the blowhole is disappointing. There's an admission fee (Rs 200) and lots of people after your money.

Sleeping & Eating

This little-known stretch of coast features some gobsmackingly perfect beaches but much of the accommodation is very much top end. Look for signs and watch the kilometre markers as you go; the following places are listed in the order you will reach them when travelling towards Tangalla.

Dickwella Resort RESORT **$$$**

(041-225 5271; www.dickwella.net; s/d half board US$140/168;) Fabulously nestled onto the tip of a low promontory, this classic

WORTH A TRIP

THE NEXT BIG THING?

Pssst! Want a tip-off on the next big name on the Sri Lankan beach scene?

If Unawatuna is too hectic for you, Mirissa past its best and Tangalla just so yesterday, then may we suggest Talalla? Just a few short kilometres east of Dondra and squirreled away down muddy dirt tracks, this is one of those near-pristine beaches that really do define all the tropical-beach postcard clichés. For the moment this 2km-long curve of sand is almost totally untouched by tourism development and has just two hotels hiding away under the palms at its western edge and a handful of brightly painted fishing boats pulled up onto its soft sand. To tell the truth this place is still so undiscovered that we faced a real dilemma about whether or not to tell you lot about it! Sounds good? Well you've only heard the half of it because not only is the beach breathtaking but it's also home to what we rate as one of the best beach hotels in Sri Lanka.

Talalla Retreat (041-225 9171; www.talallaretreat.com; Gandara; s/d incl breakfast US$118/142;) really couldn't be better named and everything about a stay here is designed to lull you into a state of utter bliss. It's set in large grounds filled with birdsong, frolicking squirrels and playful monkeys, and half the rooms here are completely open-plan, allowing you to live an alfresco life of outdoor showers and nights peering at the stars from your four-poster. The other rooms are just as romantic but offer slightly more privacy! Excellent yoga courses are available, the restaurant serves totally organic food, there's a beautiful pool and, should you feel the need to be more energetic, surf lessons are also available.

resort-style place has elegant whitewashed rooms with Indian Ocean vibes. There's a great pool complex and a restaurant serving up top-quality Italian dishes and seafood. Dickwella beach itself is a working beach and not all that special but the resort also fronts a second, much more enticing beach.

Claughton Villa BOUTIQUE HOTEL **$$$**
(077 772 0520; www.claughtonhouse.com; d half board US$185;) This beautiful colonial villa, with stunning views, sits on a knoll surrounded by rambling gardens which lead down to a heavenly pool and a beach that's even better. The rooms go for the white and minimal look but they aren't quite as flash as the price would indicate. The turnoff is 500m east of the 184km marker. It's not set up for casual drop-in visitors, so book in advance.

TOP CHOICE **Surya Garden** BOUTIQUE HOTEL **$$**
(0777 147818; www.srilanka-vacanze.com; s/d incl breakfast Rs 2500/3500, cabana US$55) Sri Lankan charm meats Italian flair at this personable little place, set 100m back from an idyllic beach. The three cabanas here could be described as imaginative and oh-so-very-chic mud huts. Don't worry though, there's nothing primitive about a stay here because the cabanas are beautifully kitted out and feature amazing outdoor bathrooms. There are also some cheaper rooms inside the main building. Not surprisingly, the restaurant menu features a lot of very tasty pastas and even if you don't stay here, it's well worth coming past for a meal (but telephone to let staff know beforehand). It's terribly signposted but the turnoff is at the 189km marker.

Amanwella BOUTIQUE HOTEL **$$$**
(047-224 1333; www.amanresorts.com; ste from US$550;) Easily the most luxurious resort in Sri Lanka, as well as one of the most expensive. Each of the 30 suites has its own private plunge pool and is comfortable to such an extent that you may need to be prised out on check out day. The modern design is dramatic; the open-air bathrooms are all natural stone. All of the units have ocean views, and some are right on the beach. Service is superb, and the food and beverages are as you'd expect. The resort entrance is near the 193km marker.

Tangalla

047

Quickly, look up at the rain beating against the window and feel the chill in your bones. Now, close your eyes and dream of somewhere else. What do you see? Is it a gently bending beach of coconut-coloured sand washed by lazy azure waters? If it is, then what you're dreaming about has a name. It's called Tangalla and it's the perfect medicine for the wintertime blues.

Sights & Activities

You come to Tangalla for the beach but should days of lethargy start to turn you a little stir crazy there are a couple of excuses to get out and about including some reminders of the colonial era on the knoll just south of the centre. The shady **Rest House** was once home to the Dutch administrators. It's one of the oldest rest houses in the country, and was originally built (as a plate on the front steps indicates) in 1774.

Turtle-Watching ECOTOUR
(adult/child Rs 1000/600) Rekawa Beach, some 10km east of town, has a growing reputation as a turtle-watching beach. From April to September, green, hawksbill and occasionally even leatherback turtles struggle ashore at night to lay their eggs. It's best to arrive well after dark and be prepared for a long wait – bring a torch, but remember that the turtles are easily disturbed by artificial lighting, and don't use camera flashes. Unlike the turtle hatcheries on the west coast (boxed text, p85) the eggs here are left undisturbed in the sand and are protected in situ. The entrance fee (which is refundable if you don't see any turtles) goes towards the **Turtle Conservation Project** (www.tcpsrilanka.org). A three-wheeler from Tangalla costs around Rs 1000.

Sleeping

There are several areas in and around Tangalla in which to stay.

GOYAMBOKKA

About 3km back towards Matara on the main road you'll come to a signposted turnoff at Goyambokka and a quiet, leafy road lined with several guesthouses. Any bus travelling between Matara and Tangalla will drop you at the turnoff. A three-wheeler from Tangalla bus station costs Rs 200.

Goyambokka Guest House CHALETS **$$**
(☎077 903 091; s/d incl breakfast Rs 2500/3500) Recently renovated, this whitewashed colonial villa set under a ceiling of dancing palm trees offers exceptionally pleasant and well-priced rooms, some of which come with romantic outdoor showers.

Palm Paradise Cabanas CHALETS **$$**
(☎224 0338; www.palmparadisecabanas.net; s/d incl breakfast €45/55; 📶) Set on a stunning sandy cove, the wooden cabanas are hidden behind a veil of trees and feel like something out of *Little Red Riding Hood*. Some of the cabanas are ageing a bit so ask to see a few first, but old cabana or new, being tucked up in your wooden hut listening to the waves is undeniably romantic. There is an in-house masseur.

Green Garden Cabanas & Resort CHALETS **$$**
(☎077 624 7628; lankatangalla@yahho.com; s/d incl breakfast US$25/35; 📶) Set back from the beach, this guesthouse has well-kept cabanas with wooden floors and tidy bathrooms that would seem more at home in a snowy mountain valley.

TANGALLA

The following options are above the beach, just southwest of the centre.

Moonstone Villas HOTEL **$$**
(☎077 675 8656; www.moonstonevillas.com; 336 Matara Rd; s/d US$50/62; ❄📶🏊) A new Canadian-run complex with modern and pleasantly decorated rooms, but they've tried to cram too many into too small a space with the result that you feel like you're living in your neighbour's pocket. It's one of the few hotels that charges for the loan of a baby cot (US$20).

Tangalla Bay Hotel HOTEL **$$$**
(☎224 0683; www.jetwinghotels.com; Mahawela Rd; s/d incl breakfast US$120/140; ❄📶🏊) It's hard to know what to make of this place. Designed to resemble a boat and plonked

Tangalla

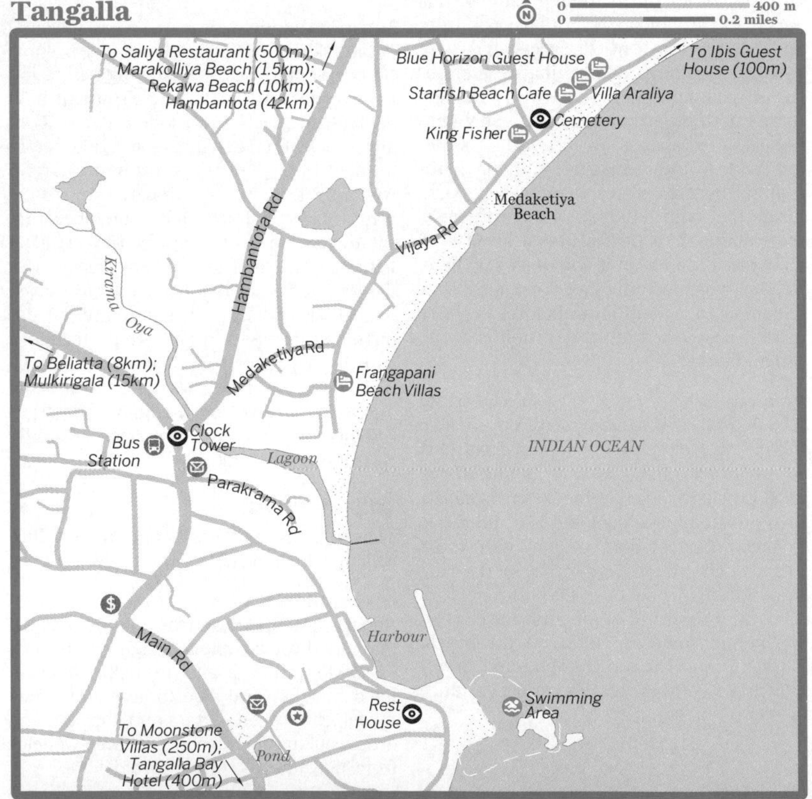

WORTH A TRIP

MULKIRIGALA

Dangling off a rocky crag, 16km northwest of Tangalla, and nestled away among a green forest of coconut trees are the peaceful rock temples of **Mulkirigala** (admission Rs 200; 6am-6pm). Clamber in a sweat up the many steps and you'll find a series of cleft-like caves sheltering a number of large reclining Buddha statues, together with other, smaller, sitting and standing figures. Vying with these for your attention are some fantastical wall paintings depicting sinners pleasuring themselves with forbidden fruit on Earth and then paying for it with an afterlife of eternal torture – apparently it was worth it! Further on up, and perched on top of the rock, is a small dagoba with fine views over the surrounding country.

Temples, in some form or another, have been located here for over 2000 years but the current incarnation, and their paintings, date from the 18th century. Nearby is a Buddhist school for young monks.

Pali manuscripts found in the monastic library here by a British official in 1826 were used for the first translation of the Mahavamsa (Great Chronicle), which unlocked Sri Lanka's early history for Europeans.

Mulkirigala can be reached by bus from Tangalla via either Beliatta or Wiraketiya (depending on the departures, it might be quicker to go via Wiraketiya than to wait for the Beliatta bus). A three-wheeler from Tangalla costs about Rs 1500 for a return trip.

atop an otherwise lovely headland, this hotel has long been considered a run-down blot on the landscape. It's still something of a blot but its recent take over by the Jetwing group means it has had a good scrubdown and is all ship-shape. However, it doesn't quite match the usual lofty standards set by Jetwing.

MEDAKETIYA BEACH

This is the most popular area with budget travellers, and a host of cheap-and-cheerful hotels and restaurants have sprung up to cater for them.

Frangipani Beach Villas GUESTHOUSE $
(071 533 7052; s/d Rs 2300/2500;) This is a fabulous new addition to the Tangalla guesthouse scene and it offers real value for money. The five rooms are in an ocean-coloured house and have bright bedspreads and sparkling bathrooms. The management is very enthusiastic and friendly, and organises a variety of activities. There's a traveller-style restaurant where fast friends are made.

Ibis Guest House GUESTHOUSE $$
(567 4439; www.guesthouse-ibis.de; r Rs 4500) Despite its chain-hotel name, this rambling place, way off at the far eastern end of Medaketiya Beach, offers a touch of unexpected class. The spacious rooms are filled with heavy wooden furnishings, four-poster beds and easy chairs. There's a secluded splash of sandy beach outside and a general lazy tropical ambience about the place.

Starfish Beach Cafe GUESTHOUSE $
(224 1005; starfish tangalle@gmail.com; r from Rs 2000;) Run by a bunch of energetic young guys, this is a good option, with large and airy rooms that are as neat as a pin. The bathrooms have a deep-blue nautical look. It's probably the most popular backpacker hangout on this strip and for good reason.

Blue Horizon Guest House GUESTHOUSE $
(077 651 0900; r incl breakfast Rs 1000-2500;) Rooms at this mustard-yellow multi-storey joint might be small but they've got loads of love packed into them. Every inch is crammed full of chairs, pictures, tables and decorations – and even a bed. The owner is backpacker-savvy and the attached restaurant is good.

Villa Araliya GUESTHOUSE $$
(077 715 1288; r from Rs 2500) Wallowing at the back of the luxuriant gardens are two bungalows crammed with old-fashioned furniture, including lovely carved wardrobes. There's also a family room with a private garden and semi-open-air bathroom. A friendly pooch will follow you everywhere you go.

King Fisher GUESTHOUSE $
(224 2472; s/d from Rs 800/1000) Thanks to being as electric blue as a kingfisher's feathers, and with toe-curlingly pink rooms, this

THE BEACH FILES

Tangalla marks the dividing line between the picture perfect tropical coves that dominate much of the south coast and the long, wind- and wave-lashed beaches that dominate the southeast of the island. There are three distinct beach zones around Tangalla, all with a range of accommodation and all with a different scene.

Goyambokka is the most westerly of the beach zones and Rekawa the most easterly.

Goyambokka

The beautiful little coves around Goyambokka, with their turquoise waters and gentle waves, are almost a cliché of what a tropical beach is supposed to look like. It's all very peaceful.

Tangalla

The town beaches are extraordinarily pretty but sadly the busy main road runs very close to the edge of the beach, meaning lots of fascinated bus passengers watching you lounge about in a bikini.

Medaketiya Beach

The long sandy beach here, which extends eastward away from the town, is very different in character to the beaches to its west. Sadly it isn't always as clean as it could be and dumping waves can make swimming dangerous.

Marakolliya Beach

Virtually a continuation of Medaketiya Beach, but much further out of town, the beach here is utterly breathtaking. Unfurling along the coast is a seemingly endless tract of soft sand backed by palms, tropical flowers and mangrove lagoons. At night, turtles lumber ashore to lay eggs; by day, a lucky tourist scours the sands for seashells. However, take note that the beach here suffers from treacherous dumping waves and undertows, and it's frequently too dangerous to swim.

Rekawa Beach

Around 10km east of Tangalla, this is another corker of a beach. Like Marakolliya, but much less developed, it's an endless stretch of wind- and wave-battered sand that isn't safe for swimming. It's the best beach for turtle-watching.

place certainly stands out from the pack. Rooms are adequate and, for the price, great value. The inhouse restaurant has seafood mains for Rs 500 to 600.

MARAKOLLIYA BEACH

Marakolliya Beach has the greatest concentration of quality midrange accommodation but it's all very low-key and peaceful.

TOP CHOICE Mangrove Cabanas CHALET **$$**
(☎077 790 6018; www.beachcabana.lk; cabana €36; wi-fi) Sitting slap-bang on a breathtaking stretch of near-deserted beach, this superb place has several rustic but chic cabanas hidden under the trees. Inside the cabanas it's all light and joy, and with virtually everything made of twisted driftwood there's no such thing as a boring straight line. The attached bathrooms are spirited away below ground level and have showers big enough to hold a party in. The restaurant produces fresh food that is as stunning as the accommodation. One US dollar per guest goes towards local conservation efforts, which has led to the planting of several hundred trees and mangroves.

TOP CHOICE Mangrove Chalets BUNGALOW **$$**
(☎077 790 6018; www.beachcabana.lk; bungalow €47) If your idea of paradise is sitting on a deckchair on a scruffy beach, then you're going to hate this place – the big-sister establishment of Mangrove Cabanas. If, however, your idea of paradise involves skipping across a creaky bridge and arriving among a gentle riot of palm trees on a sublime beach (with a natural pool perfect for kids) to find a series of romantic cottages painted in cool grey shades or sunburst Mediterranean colours then this almost-perfect place is for you.

TOP CHOICE Ganesh Garden CHALET **$$**
(☎224 2529; www.ganeshgarden.com; US$20-45; wi-fi) There's a very good reason why this is one of Tangalla's most popular places to

crash out. There's a whole array of different sizes and styles of cabanas – some have mud walls, some are built from twisted palm thatch and others are straight concrete, but all are comfortable and well designed and the place sucks in backpackers like a night out in a free bar!

Sandy's CHALET $
(☎077 622 5009; cabana Rs 1000-3500) This is one of those classic Robinson Crusoe–style beach hangouts with palm-thatch cabanas (the better ones have bedrooms open to the stars and the sea breezes) and lots of very contented backpackers. The beachside restaurant (mains around Rs 500 to 600) serves all the standards.

Nature Resort Tangalla RESORT $$
(☎224 0844; www.natureresorttangalle.com; r incl breakfast with/without air-con Rs 5500/6000; ❄📶🏊) This plush new place, with rooms that verge on luxurious, feels a little out of place in rustic Tangalla. The swimming pool is a tempting alternative to the often dangerous ocean and the price is good, but the gardens need time to mature before it really comes into its own.

Eating

Just about all guesthouses serve food. Of the hotel restaurants, the best are at the **Mangrove Cabanas** (mains Rs 300-600).

Nature Secret SEAFOOD $
(Marakolliya Beach; meals Rs 200) Cute little wooden cafe raised up on stilts and perched above the mangroves and waterways. With an H2O view like this it's not surprising that fish and seafood are big on the menu. Prices are notably lower than in the nearby hotel restaurants.

Saliya Restaurant SEAFOOD $
(Hambantota Rd; meals Rs 200-300; ⏲7am-10.30pm) Sitting on wobbly stilts a short way east of the town centre, this eccentric wooden shack, stuffed full of old clocks and radios, has great seafood as well as rice and curry.

Information

The main post office is west of the Rest House and there is an agency post office opposite the main bus station. **Commercial Bank** (Main Rd) has an international ATM.

Getting There & Away

Tangalla is serviced by bus. Following are some of the major destinations:

Colombo regular/air-con Rs 180/270, six hours
Galle Rs 95, two hours
Matara Rs 46, 1½ to two hours
Tissamaharama Rs 80, three hours

Bundala National Park

Much less visited than nearby Yala National Park (p127), **Bundala National Park** (adult/child US$10/5, plus per vehicle Rs 250, service charge per group US$8, VAT 12%) is a fantastic maze of waterways, lagoons and dunes that glitter like gold in the dying evening sun. This wonderland provides a home to thousands of colourful birds ranging from diminutive little bee-eaters to memorably ugly open-billed storks. It is a wetland sanctuary of such importance that it has been recognised under the Ramsar Convention on Wetlands. It shelters some 150 species of birds within its 62-sq-km area, with many journeying from Siberia and the Rann of Kutch in India to winter here, arriving between August and April. It's also a winter home to the greater flamingo, and up to 2000 have been recorded here at one time. If you're a birder, you'll want to devote a lot of time to this park (but from time to time the flamingos abandon the park for a year or two).

If you're after elephants, leopards and all the other big mammals, then you will be pleased to hear that Bundala National Park also has a small but very visible population of elephants (between 25 and 60 depending on the season), as well as civets, giant squirrels and lots of crocodiles. Between October and January, four of Sri Lanka's five species of marine turtles (olive ridley, green, leatherback and loggerhead) lay their eggs on the coast.

Bundala stretches nearly 20km along a coastal strip between Kirinda and Hambantota. Most people access the park (and hire jeeps) from Tissamaharama and Kirinda, and jeep hire rates are the same as for Yala (for more on this, see p123). Unlike Yala, Bundala is open year-round, allowing wildlife junkies to get a wet-season fix. There's an excellent new visitors centre at the main gate.

There's no accommodation in the park itself and most people stay in Tissamaharama, but you could do a lot worse than stay in the

Lagoon Inn (☎060-248 9531; lagooninn@yahoo.com; r Rs 1500-2650), a friendly home stay on the edge of the village of Weligathta (halfway between Tissamaharama and Hambantota, and an excellent alternative base for the park as it's only a couple of kilometres from the park's northern entrance gate). The upstairs rooms overlook the marshes, allowing you to birdwatch without leaving your seat. The owner is an experienced birdwatcher who can organise park tours.

Tissamaharama

☎047

In Tissamaharama (usually shortened to a less tongue-tying Tissa), eyes are automatically drawn upwards and outwards. Upwards to the tip of its huge, snowy-white dagoba and outwards, beyond the town's confines, to a wilderness crawling with creatures large and small. It's this wilderness that is most people's reason for visiting Tissa, and the town makes an ideal base for the nearby Yala and Bundala National Parks.

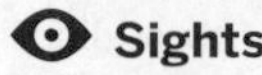

Sights

Tissa Wewa LAKE

The centrepiece of the town and its surrounds is the lovely Tissa Wewa (Tissa Tank), a huge man-made lake about 1.5km from the town centre. In the evening, check out the huge flocks of egrets that descend onto the trees around the lake to roost. Pleasant boat trips are possible around the lake from the Independent Jeep Association car park. Fight tooth and nail for a deal.

Yatala Wehera RELIGIOUS

Next to the Tissa–Deberawewa road is Yatala Wehera dagoba, built 2300 years ago by King Mahanaaga in thanks both for the birth of his son, Yatala Tissa, and for his safe escape from an assassination attempt in Anuradhapura.

There's a small **museum** (admission free) next to the dagoba; its hours vary. The museum contains an extraordinary range of treasures dug up from around the dagoba, including an ornate, ancient bidet, which – as well as containing an elaborate filtration

HAMBANTOTA

Until recently Hambantota was a dusty little workaday fishing town where nothing much ever happened. But today everything seems to be happening in Hambantota – this formally sleepy place is now the site of the biggest urban construction project Sri Lanka has ever seen. The show piece of the development project is a huge new port that the government claims will be the largest in South Asia on full completion.

The port, which has been built by Chinese companies and financed by Chinese government loans at a cost of US$1.4 billion, was officially opened in 2010, but since then the project has run into problems. A huge rock in the seabed has impeded access to the port (although at the time of writing the Sri Lankan government claimed to have removed this obstacle) and opposition ministers, as well as outside observers such as the Port of London Authority, have declared the port too shallow to be operationally viable for larger ships.

In addition to the port a new international airport large enough to handle the biggest passenger planes is scheduled to open in late 2012. The government hopes this will boost economic development in the area. As with the port project, though, there has been much criticism of the airport, with both being described as politically motivated projects (Hambantota is President Rajapaksa's home town). Environmentalists are understandably worried about the effect all these projects are likely to have on the surrounding environment; though the government claims the airport is an ecofriendly project, most environmentalists remain very concerned about the effect the projects will have on the nearby Bundala National Park and other wetland areas.

As if a new port and airport weren't enough, Hambantota is also home to a new international cricket stadium and is due to receive new roads, industrial parks and what is being described as a 'tele-cinema village'. Hambantota will also be connected to the Colombo–Matara railway line.

Needless to say, with all this construction work taking place Hambantota is currently one very dusty, noisy and unappealing place for tourists to find themselves.

Tissamaharama

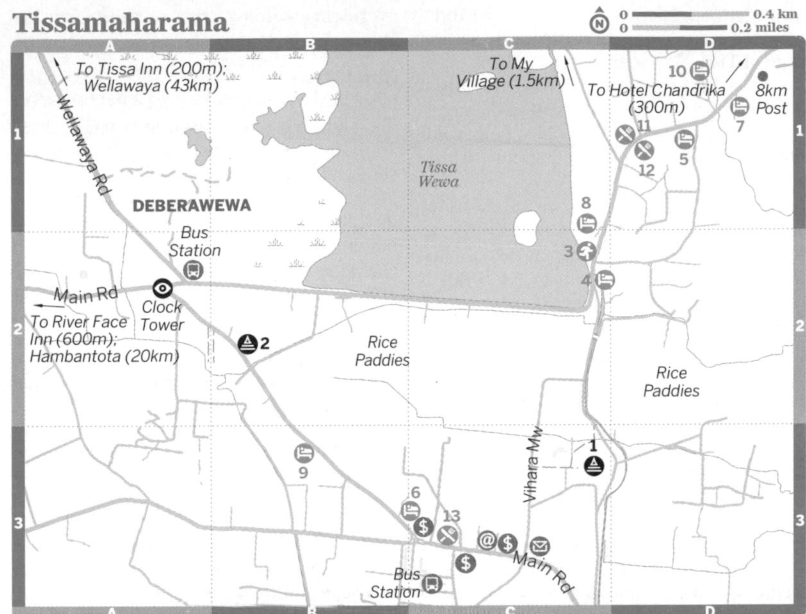

system that prevented any water pollution – had murals of ugly faces carved into it in order to stop the user thinking about sex!

At the time of research the museum was closed for renovations but you could still see the bidet outside the main entrance.

Tissa Dagoba — RELIGIOUS

The large white restored dagoba between Tissa town centre and the *wewa* is believed to have been built by Kavantissa, a king of the kingdom of Ruhunu, which centred on Tissamaharama. The dagoba has a circumference of 165m and stands 55.8m high. It is thought to have held a sacred tooth relic and forehead bone relic. It's attractively lit up at night.

Next to the dagoba is a statue of Queen Viharamahadevi. According to legend, Viharamahadevi was sent to sea by her father, King Devanampiya Tissa, as penance after he killed a monk. Unharmed, the daughter landed at Kirinda, about 10km south of Tissa, and subsequently married Kavantissa. Their son, Dutugemunu, was the Sinhalese hero who liberated Anuradhapura from Indian invaders in the 2nd century BC.

Nearby is the much smaller Sandagiri Wehera dagoba and the remains of a monastery complex thought to date back around 2000 years.

Tissamaharama

Sights

- Sandagiri Wehera ....(see 1)
- 1 Tissa Dagoba C3
- 2 Yatala Wehera B2

Activities, Courses & Tours

- 3 Independant Jeep Association C2

Sleeping

- 4 Hotel Lake Side Tourist Inn C2
- 5 Hotel Sun Sinda D1
- 6 Hotel Tissa C3
- 7 Priyankara Hotel D1
- 8 The Safari C1
- 9 Traveller's Home B3
- 10 Vikum Lodge D1

Eating

- 11 New Cabanas Restaurant D1
- 12 Refresh Hotel D1
- 13 Royal Restaurant C3

Tours

Tissa is by far the easiest place from which to arrange tours of Yala and Bundala National Parks. Almost every hotel organises safaris and this is the easiest way to go about arranging a jeep. Alternatively, you can go to the gathering of safari touts in the Independent Jeep Association car park on the edge of Tissa Wewa, but this can be a bit of a carnival-like experience. Despite the initial hassles, many of the guys who gather here are actually very knowledgeable about wildlife and genuinely concerned about making sure you have a good safari.

Most safari touts open negotiations at Rs 4500 per jeep for a half-day safari for up to four people (not including the raft of park fees), but they quickly drop to Rs 4000. If you're trying to save money then there's no need to hire both a guide and a driver, as the drivers tend to be fairly good at spotting animals (although they are of course concentrating on the road so don't expect them to see every movement in the bushes!).

Check out the jeep before you book a safari; obviously avoid rust buckets, but it's well worth plumping for one of the newer and grander models, which feature elevated, forward-facing open seats that help with spotting animals. Jeeps with sideways-facing benches are not ideal for use on a safari. Strictly speaking, a 4WD is not normally required (unless it's been raining heavily) but high clearance is. Good drivers provide binoculars.

Expect to leave your hotel about 5.30am so as to catch the animals at dawn and return around 10am. It's also possible to arrange dusk safaris and overnight trips to the animal-filled lands surrounding the park.

Sleeping

The cheaper places to stay are in the town centre, but there's no particular reason to be near the centre; if you can afford them, you might want to consider one of the midrange hotels around Tissa Wewa. Just about every place has a restaurant.

TOWN CENTRE

TOP CHOICE Traveller's Home GUESTHOUSE $
(☎2237958; www.yalasafarisrilanka.com; r Rs 1000-5000; ❄@☜) Surrounded by rice paddies, this traveller-aware guesthouse is just off Main Rd, about halfway between Tissa and Deberawewa. It's friendly, neat and good value, with a wide variety of rooms that range from cheapies with fans and cold water to ones that almost come across as posh. There are free bicycles for guests, a safari display, a great restaurant and somewhat expensive safaris (the owner can organise overnight camping trips in the vicinity of Yala).

Hotel Tissa GUESTHOUSE $
(☎223 7104; Main Rd; s Rs 1250, d Rs 2000-3000; @) Taking a room in this freshly painted and appealing town house will allow you to become fully immersed in Sri Lankan family life, as you'll be virtually adopted by the family who run it. The simple rooms in the main building provide all that is needed, and character is provided through the ample use of brass decorations. Out the back is a newer block with three swish, good-value rooms.

TISSA WEWA

Most of Tissa's accommodation is near the Tissa Wewa, about 1.5km from the centre of Tissa. It's easy enough to get into town by bus (Rs 15) or by three-wheeler (Rs 100) from this area.

My Village GUESTHOUSE $$
(☎077 350 0090; www.myvillagelk.com; Court Rd, Punchiakurugoda; r US$20-45; ❄☜) Arriving at this lovely little guesthouse, hidden away behind unassuming plain walls, you won't be surprised to learn that this is the dream creation of a local designer. There are only five rooms, all of which are slightly different. Two have curly and bendy walls full of glass, and another, the honeymoon room, has suitably passionate red walls, passionate stag antlers on the wall and slightly less passionate twin beds! There is a stylish open-plan cafe and communal area where the free breakfast is served. Guests can use bicycles for free. A three-wheeler from town is Rs 150.

The Safari LUXURY HOTEL $$$
(☎567 7620; www.ceylonhotels.lk; Kataragama Rd; s/d incl breakfast from US$144/155; ❄☜≋) This former government-run rest house has been reborn with private money and turned into Tissa's top accommodation option. Classical music floats through the sticky tropical air, a delicious swimming pool caresses the lakeshore, and the rooms? Well they're business-class plush, but kind of sterile.

Vikum Lodge GUESTHOUSE $
(☎071 464 7254; vikumlodge@gmail.com; off Kataragama Rd; r without air-con Rs 1800, s/d with air-con Rs 2000/2500; ❄) Hidden down a squelchy and muddy side street in a blissfully peaceful location is this flowery gem of a guesthouse. The rooms, which are lovingly cared for and come with private bathrooms,

are only half the story. It's the luxuriant, botanical bonanza that surrounds them that is the real star of the show. The lodge has a small restaurant with Chinese and Sri Lankan dishes (Rs 300 to 500).

Hibiscus Garden Hotel BUNGALOW **$$**
(☎223 9652; www.hibiscus-garden.com; off Kataragama Rd; s/d incl breakfast Rs 5600/6600; ❄📶🏊) A new place that needs time for the gardens to mature and add some character but otherwise it's a very good option with pleasing rooms in separate bungalow blocks. There's good birdwatching in the marshes and pools that surround the hotel, and afterwards the birds can watch you as you relax around the swimming pool. It's towards the northeastern end of the lake; to get there, head toward Hotel Chandrika and then follow the signs leading off to the left.

Hotel Sun Sinda HOTEL **$$**
(☎223 9078; Kataragama Rd; s/d incl breakfast Rs 4300/5400; ❄🏊) You're greeted by small vases full of flower petals floating in water, and ponds so full of colourful tropical fish you may well be tempted to don snorkel and mask – and if that doesn't appeal, there's an equally enticing pool. This is another reasonable option, but we have received complaints about broken air-con units and a dirty swimming pool (although it seemed clean enough when we visited). The rooms are airy and comfortable and the restaurant is stark and echoey.

Priyankara Hotel HOTEL **$$$**
(☎223 7206; www.priyankarahotel.com; Kataragama Rd; s/d incl breakfast US$110/120; ❄📶🏊) The rooms here, with their high wooden ceilings, languidly rotating fans, hardwood furnishings and modern bathrooms, have lots of colonial style as well as views over the gorgeous pool, which in turn has views over the gorgeous rice fields and duck-filled ponds. Sadly though, recent price hikes have made it seriously overpriced.

Hotel Lake Side Tourist Inn HOTEL **$$**
(☎493 1186; Tissawewa Rd; with/without air-con s Rs 3500/4000, d Rs 4000/4500; ❄📶🏊) This is a through-and-through tour-group hotel and is a bit old and drab, but if you're not up for the town's backpacker pads and not flush enough to afford the more expensive places, then here's your answer.

Peacock Reach Hotel GUESTHOUSE **$$**
(☎223 9095; peacockreach@sltnet.lk; Kataragama Rd; s/d Rs 3000/3500; ❄📶) This new place, a short way off the main road to the east, looks like one of those palace-like houses you see on Spanish and South American soap operas (and we suspect it's just as flimsily built as a film set!). If that's your kind of thing, then the combination of quiet location and fair price make it well worth considering.

Hotel Chandrika HOTEL **$$**
(☎223 7143; www.chandrikahotel.com; Kataragama Rd; s/tw US$74/80; ❄🏊) This slightly tacky hotel is very popular with tour groups and is a decent-enough option with comfortable, though sterile, rooms set around a palm-lined courtyard and good pool. The staff are very attentive and friendly and the restaurant, which does a tasty curry, has a stunning collection of 1980s power ballads.

DEBERAWEWA

River Face Inn GUESTHOUSE **$**
(☎077 389 0229; asamarasooriya@yahoo.com; off Hambantota Rd; r Rs 1500) At the time of research this was something of an ongoing project but it's one that's full of potential. The four tiled rooms are smart, spacious and in a peaceful location overlooking the river. The owner whips up some decent meals.

Tissa Inn HOTEL **$$**
(☎223 7233; www.tissainn.com; Wellawaya Rd; s/d Rs 2350/3000; ❄) About 1500m from the Deberawewa clock tower, this is a slightly rundown, in the most charming of manners, old hotel. It's worth checking out a few of the high-ceilinged rooms as quality varies, but at its best it's a spotless place of starched sheets and whirling fans.

Eating

Royal Restaurant SRI LANKAN **$$**
(Main St; mains Rs 200-300) You get a right royal welcome here and a right royal feast, with cheap and tasty curries that will leave you stuffed and happy. Lots of local families like to stop by for a big, noisy family lunch.

New Cabanas Restaurant SRI LANKAN **$$**
(Kataragama Rd; mains Rs 300-650) A simple, open-sided restaurant with well-priced rice and curry (Rs 650) and a comments book full of tales of culinary satisfaction.

Refresh Hotel INTERNATIONAL **$$$**
(Kataragama Rd; mains Rs 800-1000; ⏰11am-10pm) It seems that every tourist eats here

and as one of the only restaurants in the neighbourhood that's hardly a surprise, but the food is tamed down to suit Western tastebuds and is both bland in the extreme and highly overpriced. Despite this, it's one of the few places that actually feels like a Western-style restaurant.

Information

Nearly all the facilities are on Main Rd, where you'll find an agency post office. There's not much in the way of shopping, but there are some useful services. **Hatton National Bank** (Main Rd), **Commercial Bank** (Main Rd) and **Peoples Bank** (Main Rd) have international ATMs. **High Speed Internet** (Main Rd; per hr Rs 50; 7.30am-10pm) might not be as speedy as you hope but it's not bad either.

Getting There & Away

Few buses go directly to the Hill Country, and if you can't get one you'll need to change at Wirawila junction (Rs 19, 30 minutes) and/or at Wellawaya (Rs 80). There are no buses to Yala National Park. Other major bus destinations from Tissa:

Colombo regular/air-con Rs 250/380, nine hours

Galle regular/air-con Rs 130/210, four hours

Kataragama Rs 28, one hour

Tangalla Rs 75, two hours

Around Tissamaharama

WIRAWILA WEWA BIRD SANCTUARY

Between the northern and southern turn-offs to Tissa, the Hambantota–Wellawaya road runs on a causeway across the large Wirawila Wewa. This extensive sheet of water forms the Wirawila Wewa Bird Sanctuary. The best time for birdwatching is early morning.

KIRINDA

047

Tiny Kirinda, 10km south of Tissa, is a place on the edge. On one side its sandy streets and ramshackle buildings give way to a series of magnificently bleak and empty beaches (heavy undertows and dumping waves make swimming here treacherous) that are perfect for long evening walks. In the other direction, tangled woodlands and sweeps of parched grasslands merge into wildlife-filled national parks. The village itself centres on a Buddhist shrine piled atop some huge round rocks. Visible offshore are the wave-smashed **Great Basses** reefs with their lonely lighthouse. The diving out on these reefs is ranked as about the best in the country, but it's not for inexperienced divers – conditions are often rough and currents are strong. The window of opportunity for diving is also very narrow and basically confined to the period between mid-March and mid-April. For more on diving the Basses (and elsewhere), see www.divesrilanka.com. All of the accommodation places here can organise safaris to the national parks.

Sleeping & Eating

Suduweli GUESTHOUSE $$

(072 263 1059; www.beauties-of-nature.net; tw Rs 1000-1500, without bathroom Rs 500, bungalows Rs 2000-2500; @) Set on an old farm, this is a heavenly spot a little way out of the village. Accommodation consists of basic but clean rooms in the main house, or a handful of comfortable and quiet Swiss Alpine–style cottages in the gardens. There's a small lake on the grounds that attracts rainbow-coloured flocks of birds, and there are croaking frogs and scurrying lizards everywhere. However, you'd better like mosquitoes because there are great clouds of the beasts.

Temple Flower Guesthouse GUESTHOUSE $

(492 2499; templeflowerguest@yahoo.com; r Rs 1500-3000) A delicious little guesthouse with a wonderful green colonial-style veranda shared between several neatly attired rooms. Upstairs are further rooms, some with sunken walk-in showers, some with sea views and some with exposed stone walls. The food here is as delicious as the accommodation; there's real filter coffee and superb breakfasts and the owner is as friendly and helpful as can be.

Elephant Reach LODGE $$$

(567 7544; www.elephantreach.com; s/d from US$125/150;) A top-end establishment on the edge of the village. The stylish communal areas are stuffed full of contorted wooden furniture and the rooms are equally well thought out with huge showers, stone floors, hemp curtains, and TVs and DVD players in some rooms. Outside the lovely pool curls like a water snake around the gardens. If staff try to fob you off with an upstairs room at the back of the complex, then look elsewhere.

Getting There & Away

There is a bus from Tissa to Kirinda every half-hour or so (Rs 20) or a three-wheeler is Rs 500.

Yala National Park

With monkeys crashing through the trees, peacocks in their finest frocks and cunning leopards sliding like shadows through the undergrowth, Yala National Park (also known as Ruhunu) is the *Jungle Book* brought to glorious life. This vast region of dry woodland and open patches of grasslands is the big draw of this corner of Sri Lanka, and though it's far from Kenya, a safari here is well worth all the time, effort and cost.

Sights

Yala combines a strict nature reserve with a national park, bringing the total protected area to 1268 sq km of scrub, light forest, grassy plains and brackish lagoons. It's divided into five blocks, with the most visited being Block I (141 sq km). Also known as Yala West, this block was originally a reserve for hunters, but was given over to conservation in 1938.

With around 25 leopards thought to be present in Block 1 alone, Yala is considered one of the world's best parks for spotting these big cats. *Panthera pardus kotiya*, the subspecies you may well see, is unique to Sri Lanka. The best time to spot leopards is February to June or July, when the water levels in the park are low. Despite having around 300 elephants, they tend to keep away from the most visited parts of the park and Yala is not that well regarded for elephant sightings. With luck you'll get to see the shaggy-coated sloth bear or some of the fox-like jackals. Sambars, spotted deer, boars, crocodiles, buffaloes, mongooses and monkeys are here in their hundreds.

Around 215 species of birds have been recorded at Yala, many of which are visitors escaping the northern winter. These birds include white-winged black terns, curlews and pintails. Locals include jungle fowl, hornbills, orioles and peacocks by the bucketload.

Despite the large quantity of wildlife the light forest can make spotting animals quite hard; fortunately help is at hand in the form of small grassy clearings and lots of waterholes around which the wildlife congregates. The end of the dry season (March to April) is the best time to visit, as during and shortly after the rains the animals disperse over a wide area.

As well as herds of wildlife, Yala contains the remains of a once-thriving human community. A monastic settlement, **Situlpahuwa**, appears to have housed 12,000 inhabitants. Now restored, it's an important pilgrimage site. A 1st-century BC *vihara* (Buddhist complex), **Magul Maha Vihara**, and a 2nd-century BC chetiya (Buddhist shrine), **Akasa Chetiya**, point to a well-established community, believed to have been part of the ancient Ruhunu kingdom.

THE LONG WALK TO KATARAGAMA

Forty-five days before the annual Kataragama festival starts on the Esala *poya* (full moon), a group of Kataragama devotees start walking the length of Sri Lanka for the Pada Yatra pilgrimage. Seeking spiritual development, the pilgrims believe they are walking in the steps of the god Kataragama (also known as Murugan) and the Veddahs, who made the first group pilgrimage on this route.

The route follows the east coast from the Jaffna peninsula, via Trincomalee and Batticaloa to Okanda, then through Yala National Park to Kataragama. It's an arduous trip, and the pilgrims rely on the hospitality of the communities and temples they pass for their food and lodging. During the many recent periods when the war has been raging, the risks to them were great and the walk has not always been completed.

Pilgrims arrive in time for the festival's feverish activity. Elephants parade, drummers drum. Vows are made and favours sought by devotees, who demonstrate their sincerity by performing extraordinary acts of penance and self-mortification on one particular night: some swing from hooks that pierce their skin; others roll half-naked over the hot sands near the temple. A few perform the act of walking on beds of red-hot cinders – treading the flowers, as it's called. The fire walkers fast, meditate and pray, bathe in Menik Ganga (Menik River) and then worship at Maha Devale before facing their ordeal. Then, fortified by their faith, they step out onto the glowing path while the audience cries out encouragement. The festival officially ends with a water-cutting ceremony (said to bring rain for the harvest) in Menik Ganga.

Yala is a very popular park, perhaps too popular, and with little control on vehicle numbers the whole place can become something of a circus at busy times of the year. In an effort to get their clients to see all the big-name animals, safari drivers can often be seen careening about the park and any leopard or elephant silly enough to show its face will immediately be pounced on by dozens of safari jeeps who'll go after the poor creature until they physically can't follow it anymore. In late 2011 park authorities discovered a dead leopard that they believe was run over by a safari jeep.

In the interests of the wildlife it's best to ask your driver not to engage in chasing the animals around.

Sleeping

Although most of the park was untouched by the 2004 tsunami, two resorts near the shore were demolished (with the loss of 49 lives – a memorial today stands on the beach beside the remains of one of the resorts). Today there is no accommodation within the park and nor is there likely to be in the near future.

Chaaya Wild Yala LODGE **$$$**
(047-223 9449; www.chaayahotels.com; s/d full board US$264/298;) Just outside the entrance, Chaaya Wild Yala offers the ultimate in bush-chic accommodation. Rooms are in individual bungalows, which come with satellite TV, fridge and elephant bedspreads. Talking of elephants, they often pass through the lodge grounds at night and their not-so-soft footfalls are likely to break into your dreams. The hotel runs on solar power, some of the waste water is recycled, and there's a tree-planting scheme.

Information

The entrance fees for **Yala National Park** (adult/child US$15/8, jeep & tracker Rs 250, service charge per group US$8, plus overall tax 12%; 6am-6.30pm 16 Oct-31 Aug) are payable at the main office, which is near the entrance, some 21km from Tissa. There are a few displays here of the pickled and stuffed variety. The road from Tissa is rough but passable for any high-clearance vehicle. Realistically the only way to visit the park is as part of a safari (see p123).

Kataragama

047

Sheltered in the foothills, 15km northeast of Tissa, is Kataragama. A compelling mix of pomp and procession, piety and religious extravagance, this most holy of towns is a shot of oriental thrills at the end of an island-wide pilgrimage. Along with Adam's Peak (Sri Pada), this is the most important religious pilgrimage site in Sri Lanka and is a holy place for Buddhists, Muslims and Hindus alike. It is one of those wonderful places where the most outlandish of legends becomes solid fact and magic floats in clouds of incense. Many believe that King Dutugemunu built a shrine to Kataragama Deviyo (the resident god) here in the 2nd century BC, and that the Buddhist Kirivehera dagoba dates back to the 1st century BC, but the site is thought to have been significant for even longer.

In July and August, the predominantly Hindu **Kataragama festival** draws thousands of devotees who make the pilgrimage over a two-week period (see the boxed text, p127). Apart from festival time, the town is busiest at weekends and on *poya* days. At these times it may be difficult to find accommodation, and the place will be buzzing; at

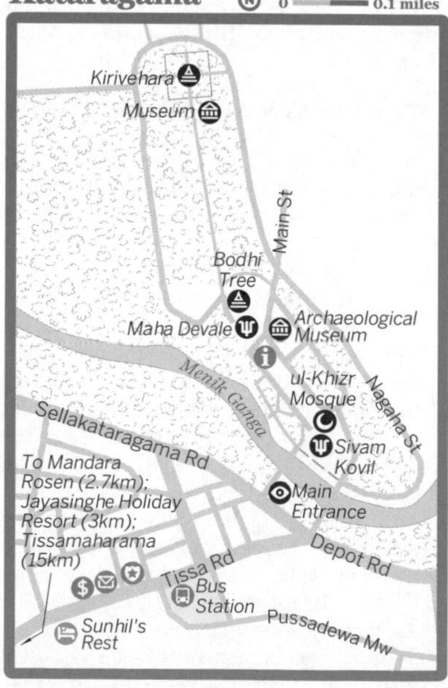

other times it can feel like a ghost town. If you're staying in Tissamaharama, you may just want to visit on a day trip.

Sights

The sacred precinct is set on the other side of Menik Ganga from the town, a chocolate-coloured (though not flavoured!) river in which pilgrims wash before continuing towards the shrines. The most important shrine is the **Maha Devale**, which contains the lance of the six-faced, 12-armed Hindu war god, Murugan (Skanda), who is seen as identical to the Kataragama Deviyo. Followers make offerings at daily *puja* at 4.30am, 10.30am and 6.30pm (no 4.30am offering on Saturday). Outside this shrine are two large boulders, against which pilgrims smash burning coconuts while muttering a prayer. The **Kirivehara** and **Sivam Kovil** shrines are dedicated to the Buddha and Ganesh (the remover of obstacles and champion of intellectual pursuits) respectively; there is also a **bodhi tree**.

Sitting beyond this temple complex is the **Kirivehara**, a large whitewashed Buddhist dagoba.

The Muslim area, close to the entrance, features the beautiful **ul-Khizr Mosque** with coloured tilework and wooden lintels, and tombs of two holy men.

Apart from the shrines, there are some other points of interest inside the temple complex. An **archaeological museum** (admission by donation; 10.30am-12.30pm & 6.30-9pm) has a collection of Hindu and Buddhist religious items, as well as huge fibreglass models of statues from around Sri Lanka. At the time of research this museum was temporarily closed. Another small **museum** has a display of Buddhist statues.

Sleeping & Eating

The accommodation in Kataragama is a sorry, and overpriced, lot and you'd do well to stay in Tissa and just make your visit a day trip.

Mandara Rosen BUSINESS HOTEL **$$$**
(223 6030; www.mandararesorts.com; Tissa Rd; s/d incl breakfast US$103/130;) The smartest address in town, Rosen was designed for the businessmen who never came. The quality of the rooms matches the price tag, but the hotel's best asset has to be the pool, which has an underwater music system – ask staff to play the *Jaws* theme tune!

Sunhil's Rest HOMESTAY **$$**
(567 7172; 61 New Town; r with/without air-con Rs 2800/1800;) This is a jolly little homestay on the edge of town. The rooms are brightly painted and all have an attached bathroom. It's a couple of minutes' walk from the bus station along the Tissa road.

Jayasinghe Holiday Resort RESORT **$$**
(223 5146; Tissa Rd; s/d incl breakfast Rs 4290/5060;) This place, 3km from town, feels depressingly like an English seaside holiday camp in winter, but if you want to stay the night in Kataragma then it's a fairly priced deal. The swimming pool is popular with frogs.

Information

There's a **Bank of Ceylon** (Tissa Rd), which has an ATM, and a **post office** (Tissa Rd). Don't expect much help from the information office in the religious complex.

Getting There & Away

There are frequent buses to Tissamaharama (Rs 28, one hour).

The Hill Country

Includes »

Best Places to Eat

» The Old Course Restaurant (p161)

» Sharon Inn (p139)

» Cafe Chill (Nescoffee Shop) (p172)

Best Places to Stay

» Lavender House (p155)

» The Kandy House (p149)

» Royal River Resort (p154)

» Waterfall Homestay (p170)

» Tea Trails (boxed text p153)

Why Go?

Picture Sri Lanka and visions of golden beaches probably dance before your eyes. But there's another side to this island. It's a side where mists slowly part to reveal emerald carpets of tea plantations and montane forests clinging to serrated ranges bookended by waterfalls. It's a side where you can wear a fleece in the daytime and cuddle up beside a log fire in the evening. It's a side where you can walk to the end of the world, stand in the footsteps of the Buddha, paddle a raft down a raging river, enjoy the drumbeat of traditional dance and be surrounded by a hundred wild elephants.

With a hit list like that it's perhaps hardly a surprise that when many visitors look back on their Sri Lankan adventures it's not the beaches that make them smile fondly, but rather it's memories of Sri Lanka's surging, rolling highlands.

When to Go

Nuwara Eliya

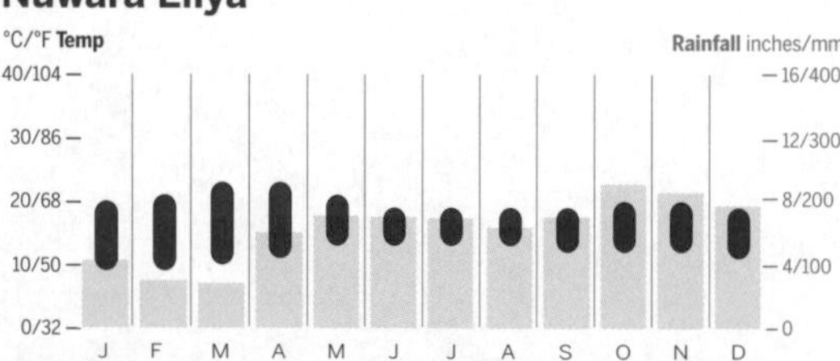

Jan Clear days, crisp nights and the pilgrimage up Adam's Peak.

Apr The Sinhalese New Year means horse racing and a hectic social calendar in Nuwara Eliya.

Jul–Aug Elephants put on their best frocks for the spectacular Kandy Esala Perahera festival.

The Hill Country Highlights

1 Experiencing the excitement of elephants, drummers and dancers at the **Kandy Esala Perahera** (p140)

2 Getting away from Sri Lanka's energetic buzz by trekking in the montane forests of the **Knuckles Range** (p150)

3 Joining devout pilgrims and following flickering torchlight to ascend the sacred heights of **Adam's Peak** (Sri Pada; p150)

4 Rattling and rolling with Tamil tea pickers on a slowly, slowly train journey from **Haputale to Ella** (p168)

5 Winding down in **Ella** (p170), combining excellent home-cooked food and spectacular walks

6 Discovering your inner birdwatcher amid the tangled perfection of the **Sinharaja Forest Reserve** (p178)

7 Rising before dawn for a view from the stunning heights of **World's End** (p163)

8 Counting elephants by the dozen in the **Uda Walawe National Park** (p176)

Colombo to Kandy

The **Henerathgoda Botanic Gardens** near Gampaha, off the Colombo–Kandy road about 30km northwest of Colombo, are where the first rubber trees planted in Asia were grown. Some original plantings dot the 37-acre gardens, together with 400 other plant varieties.

About 50km from Kandy is **Cadjugama**, famous for its cashew nuts. Brightly clad sellers beckon passing motorists with nuts they've harvested from the surrounding forest. At the 48km post is **Radawaduwa**, notable for woven cane items.

Kegalle, 77km from Colombo, is the nearest town to the **Pinnewala Elephant Orphanage**. Nearby is **Utuwankandu**, a rocky hill from where the 19th-century Robin Hood–style highwayman, Saradiel, preyed on travellers until the British executed him.

At **Kadugannawa**, just after the road and railway make their most scenic climbs – with views southwest to the large Bible Rock – is a tall pillar erected in memory of Captain Dawson, the English engineer who built the Colombo–Kandy road in 1826.

Cadjugama, Kegalle and Kadugannawa are on the A1, easily accessible by bus between Colombo and Kandy. Catch a train to Kadugannawa and the Henerathgoda Botanic Gardens at Gampaha.

PINNEWALA ELEPHANT ORPHANAGE

Almost nothing in Sri Lanka splits our readers' opinions more than this government-run elephant **orphanage** (adult/child Rs 2000/1000, video camera Rs 1500; ⌚8.30am-6pm), near Kegalle. Initially created to protect abandoned or orphaned elephants, it's one of Sri Lanka's most popular attractions, but today some people think it seems to have largely lost sight of its original aims and is more a zoo than anything else. Some people love the place and the opportunity it gives to get up close and cuddly with elephants, but many more find it an out-and-out rip-off with no conservational value whatsoever. Whichever category you fall into it's safe to say that nowhere else on the island, except at *peraheras* (processions), are you likely to see so many pachyderms at close quarters.

There are around 80 elephants of all ages. The creatures are largely well looked after, but the UK-based Born Free Foundation (www.bornfree.org.uk) has expressed some concern over the amount of contact elephants have with the public and the fact that the facility has been used for breeding, contrary to its status as an orphanage. Check its website and make up your own mind.

The elephants are controlled by their mahouts, who ensure they feed at the right times and don't endanger anyone. Otherwise the elephants roam freely around the sanctuary area. The elephants are led to a nearby river for bathing daily from 10am to noon and from 2pm to 4pm. Meal times are 9.15am, 1.15pm and 5pm. For Rs 250 you can bottlefeed a baby elephant (although take note of the point above about tourist-elephant contact). The afternoon light is better for photographs, but there are also more visitors at that time. If it's been raining heavily, bathing in the river is sometimes cancelled as the waters are too high.

Two kilometres from Pinnewala, on the Karandupona–Kandy road, the **Millennium Elephant Foundation** (www.millenniumelephantfoundation.org; admission Rs 600, elephant rides per 30min Rs 3000; ⌚8am-5pm) is similar but slightly different, with a number of elephants rescued from situations as diverse as aggressive mahouts and retirement from working in temples. Volunteers are welcome at the foundation and the facility also supports a mobile veterinary service. Volunteer placements last at least a month (Rs 150,000). Costs include all accommodation and food.

Several **spice farms** that are open to visitors line the road between the Millennium Elephant Foundation and Pinnewala. Colombo zoo is in the slow process of relocating to the area around Pinnewala.

Sleeping & Eating

Most people visit Pinnewala as a day trip, but there are also a few OK guesthouses at Pinnewala if it's too late to push on to Kandy from Colombo.

With both the hotels listed, if you come just for lunch then you will be made to pay the orphanage entrance fee as well (even though they're not actually inside the orphanage). If you stay the night at one of them you don't need to pay to watch the elephants frolicking in the river at lunchtime but you do need to pay to enter the orphanage proper.

Hotel Elephant Park HOTEL $$
(☎035-226 6171; www.pinnalanda.com; s/d incl breakfast Rs 5100/5450; ❄) Several smart, tiled rooms including some with views over elephants bathing in the river. The restaurant offers a wide range of average and overpriced Sri Lankan and Western dishes.

Hotel Pinnalanda HOTEL $$
(☎035-226 5297; www.pinnalanda.com; s/d incl breakfast Rs 3500/4200; ❄) Right opposite the Elephant Park and under the same management, this place offers a slightly better river view but much darker and drabber rooms.

Getting There & Away

The orphanage is a few kilometres north of the Colombo–Kandy road. From Kandy take a bus to Kegalle. Get off before Kegalle at Karandunpona Junction (Rs 45). From the junction, catch bus 881 (Rs 20) going from Kegalle to Rambukkana and get off at Pinnewala. A three-wheeler from the junction to Pinnewala is around Rs 300. It's about an hour from Kandy to the junction, and 10 minutes from the junction to Pinnewala. Buses also link Colombo and Kegalle.

Rambukkana station on the Colombo–Kandy railway is about 3km north of the orphanage and all trains travelling this route stop there. From Rambukkana get a bus (Rs 10) going towards Kegalle.

Kandy

☎081 / POP 112,000 / ELEV 500M

Some days Kandy's skies seem perpetually bruised, with stubborn mist clinging to the hills surrounding the city's beautiful centrepiece lake. Delicate hill-country breezes impel the mist to gently part, revealing colourful houses and hotels amid Kandy's improbable forested halo. In the centre of town, three-wheelers careen around slippery corners, raising a soft spray that threatens the softer silk of the colourful saris worn by local women. Here's a city that looks good even when it's raining.

And when the rain subsides – and it does with frequency and alacrity – Kandy's cobalt-blue skies reveal it as this island's other real 'city' after the brighter coastal lights of Colombo. Urban buzz is provided by busy spontaneous street markets and even busier bus stations and restaurants. History and culture are on tap, and 115km from the capital and at an altitude of 500m, Kandy offers a cooler and more relaxed climate.

Kandy served as the capital of the last Sinhalese kingdom, which fell to the British in 1815 after defying the Portuguese and Dutch for three centuries. It took the British another 16 tough years to finally build a road linking Kandy with Colombo. The locals still proudly see themselves as a little different – and perhaps a tad superior – to Sri Lankans from the island's lower reaches.

Kandy is renowned for the great Kandy Esala Perahera (boxed text p140), held over 10 days leading up to the Nikini *poya* (full moon) at the end of the month of Esala (July/August), but it has enough attractions to justify a visit at any time of year. Some of the Hill Country's nicest boutique hotels nestle in the hills surrounding Kandy, and the city is a good base for exploring the underrated terrain of the nearby Knuckles Range.

The *A-Z Street Guide,* available at Vijitha Yapa bookshop, contains a detailed map. The tourist office has a more rudimentary offering.

Sights

Kandy Lake LAKE
Dominating the town is Kandy Lake, which was created in 1807 by Sri Wickrama Rajasinha, the last ruler of the kingdom of Kandy. Several minor local chiefs protested because their people objected to labouring on the project. In order to stop the protests they were ruthlessly put to death on stakes in the lake bed. The central island was used as Sri Wickrama Rajasinha's personal harem. Later the British used it as an ammunition store and added the fortress-style parapet around the perimeter. On the south shore, in front of the Malwatte Maha Vihara, the circular enclosure is the monks' bathhouse.

A leisurely stroll around the lake, with a few stops on the lakeside seats, is a pleasant way to spend a few hours, although monoxide-spurting buses careening around the southern edge of the lake can mar the peace somewhat! The nicest part to walk along is the area around the Temple of the Sacred Tooth Relic. Note the warning (p145) for solo women travellers.

Temple of the Sacred Tooth Relic TEMPLE
(Sri Dalada Maligawa; adult/child Rs 1000/free, video camera Rs 300; ⏲5.30am-8pm, puja 5.30-6.45am, 9.30-11am & 6.30-8pm) Just north of the lake, this temple houses Sri Lanka's most important Buddhist relic – a tooth of

Kandy

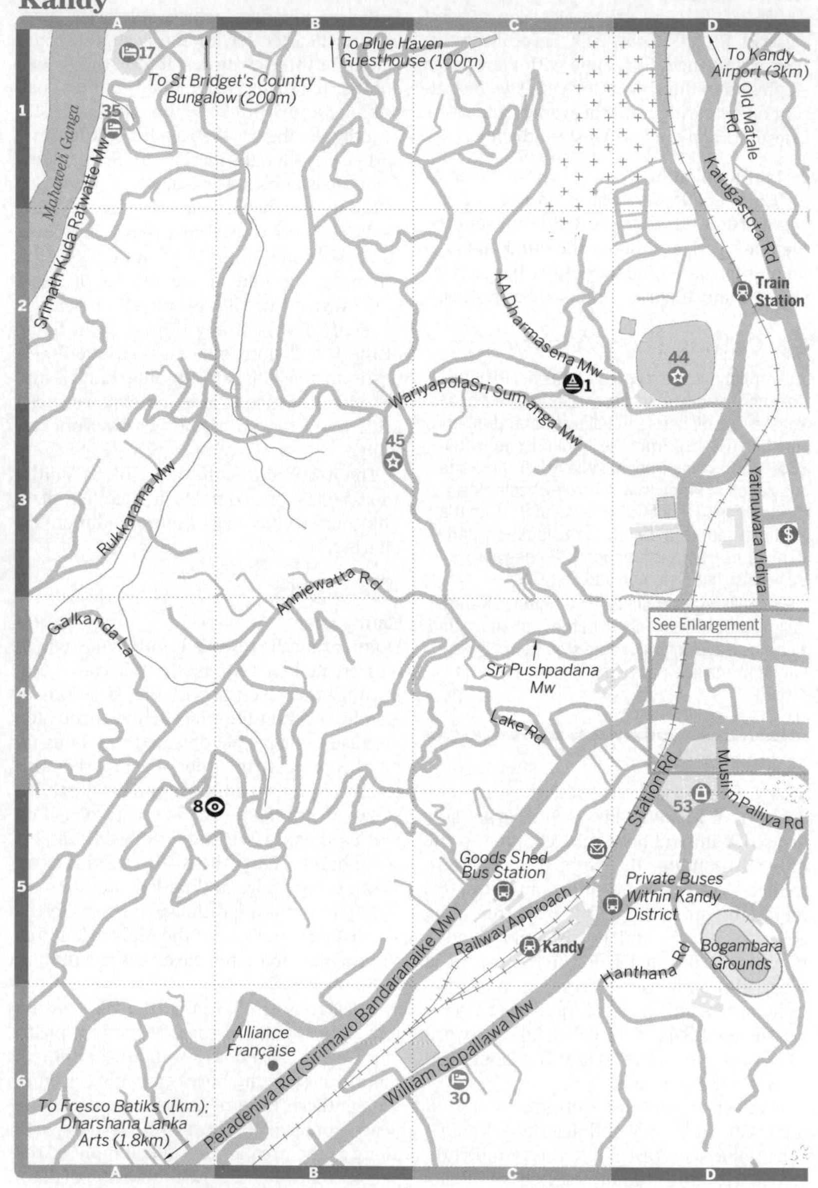

the Buddha. The temple was damaged when a bomb was detonated by the LTTE near the main entrance in 1998. The scars have been now repaired, but security remains high and there is significant screening of all visitors.

Freelance guides will offer their services for around Rs 500, and free audio guides are available at the ticket office. A newly installed elevator facilitates access for travellers with disabilities.

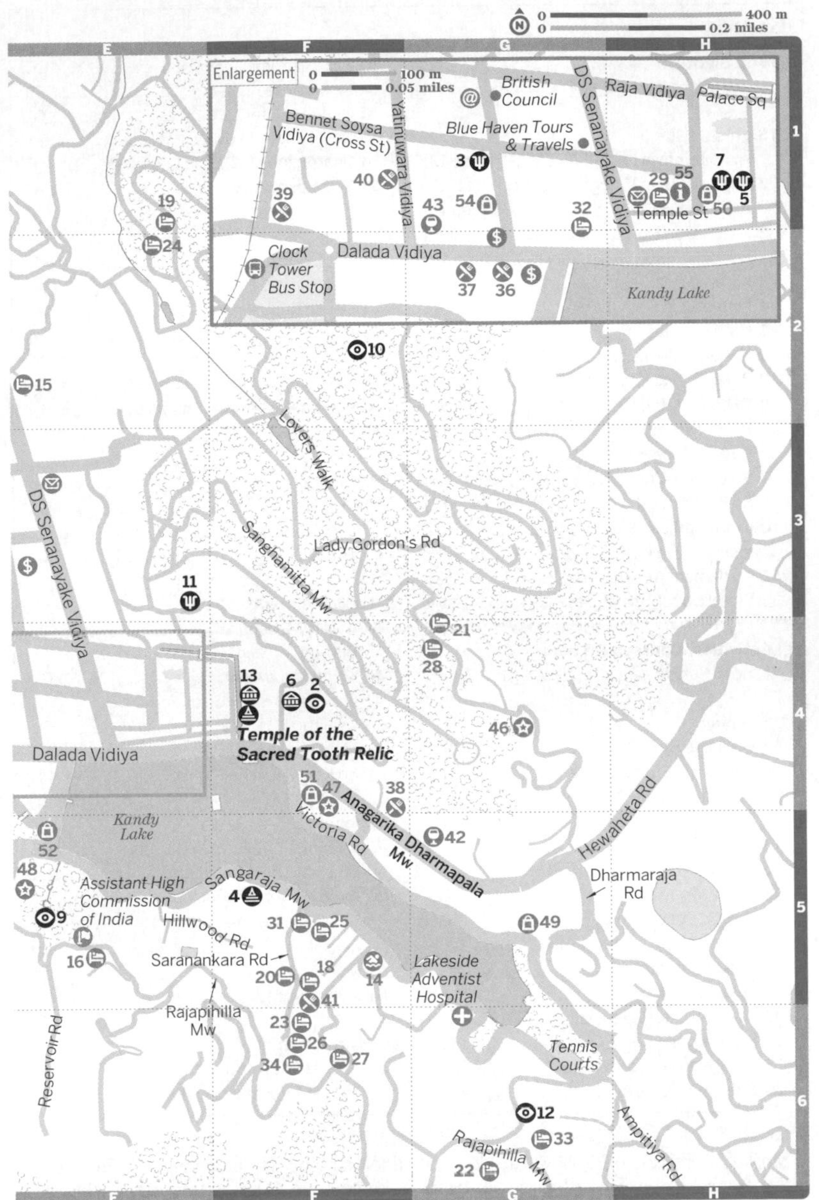

The shrine receives many worshippers and tourists, with fewer tourists in the morning. Wear clothes that cover your legs and your shoulders, and remove your shoes.

During *puja* (offerings or prayers), the heavily guarded room housing the tooth is open to devotees and tourists. However, you don't actually see the tooth. It's kept in a gold casket shaped like a dagoba (stupa), which contains a series of six dagoba caskets of diminishing size.

Kandy

Top Sights

Temple of the Sacred Tooth Relic F4

Sights

Alut Maligawa .... (see 13)
1 Asgiriya Maha Vihara C2
Audience Hall .... (see 13)
2 British Garrison Cemetery F4
Buddhist Publication Society ...... (see 49)
3 Kataragama Devale G1
4 Malwatte Maha Vihara F5
5 Natha Devale H1
6 National Museum F4
7 Pattini Devale H1
8 Queens Hotel A5
Rajah Tusker Hall .... (see 13)
9 Royal Palace Park E5
Sri Dalada Museum .... (see 13)
Sri Lanka Trekking .... (see 18)
10 Udawattakelle Sanctuary F2
11 Vishnu Devale E3
12 Wedamedura Ayurveda G6
13 World Buddhism Museum F4

Activities, Courses & Tours

14 Hotel Suisse F5

Sleeping

15 Burmese Rest E2
16 Castle Hill Guest House E5
17 Chaaya Citadel A1
18 Expeditor F5
19 Forest Glen E1
20 Freedom Lodge F5
21 Green Woods G4
22 Helga's Folly G6
23 Highest View F6
24 Kandy Cottage E2
25 Lake Bungalow F5
26 Lakshmi Guest House F6
27 McLeod Inn F6
28 Nature Walk Resort G4
29 Olde Empire Hotel H1
30 Palm Garden Guest House C6
31 Pink House F5
32 Queens Hotel G1
33 Royal Tourist Lodge G6
34 Sharon Inn F6
35 Villa Rosa A1

Eating

Bake House .... (see 43)
36 Cargills Food City G2
37 Devon Restaurant G2
38 History Restaurant F4
39 Kandy Muslim Hotel F1
Olde Empire Hotel .... (see 29)
40 Paiva's Restaurant F1
41 Restaurant F5

Drinking

42 PUB G5
Pub Royale .... (see 32)
43 The Pub G1

Entertainment

44 Asgiriya Stadium D2
45 Blackout B3
46 Kandy Lake Club G4
47 Kandyan Art Association & Cultural Centre F4
48 Mahanuwara YMBA E5
Sri Lanka Cricket Office .... (see 44)

Shopping

49 Buddhist Publication Society G5
50 Cultural Triangle Office H1
51 Kandyan Art Association & Cultural Centre F4
52 Laksala E5
53 Main Market D5
54 Vijitha Yapa G1

Information

55 Tourist Information Centre H1
Tourist Information Office .... (see 37)

Most visitors can only view the dagoba casket from the doorway, which is 3m from the actual altar. Guards keep the queue moving so no-one gets more than 15 seconds inside the shrine room.

Alut Maligawa

Behind the shrine stands the three-storey Alut Maligawa, a newer and larger shrine hall displaying dozens of sitting Buddhas donated by Thai devotees. The design resembles a Thai Buddhist shrine hall in tribute to the fact that Thai monks re-established Sri Lanka's ordination lineage during the reign of King Kirti Sri Rajasinha. The upper two floors of the Alut Maligawa contain the **Sri Dalada Museum** (7.30am-6pm), with a stunning array of gilded gifts to the temple. Letters and diary entries from the British time reveal the colonisers' surprisingly respectful attitude to the tooth relic. More recent photographs reveal the damage caused by the truck bomb in 1998.

Audience Hall

To the north inside the compound, and accessible only via the Temple of the Sacred Tooth Relic, is the 19th-century Audience Hall, an open-air pavilion with stone columns carved to look like wooden pillars. Adjacent in the **Rajah Tusker Hall** are the stuffed remains of Rajah, the Maligawa tusker who died in 1988 (see boxed text, p140).

World Buddhism Museum

(admission Rs 500; ⏲9am-8pm) Just behind the main temple, but still inside the complex, is the new World Buddhism Museum. Housed inside the former High Court buildings, the museum contains lots of photographs, models and displays illustrating Buddhism around the world. Note that a large number of the statues and other exhibits are actually reproductions.

TOP CHOICE **Tea Museum** MUSEUM

(Map p148; www.pureceylontea.com/teamuseum; admission Rs 400; ⏲8.15am-4.45pm Tue-Sun) An essential stop on any Sri Lankan tea tour, this museum occupies the 1925-vintage Hanthana Tea Factory, 4km south of Kandy on the Hanthana road. Abandoned for over a decade, it was refurbished by the Sri Lanka Tea Board and the Planters' Association of Sri Lanka. There are exhibits on tea pioneers James Taylor and Thomas Lipton (see boxed text, p164), and lots of vintage tea-processing paraphernalia. Knowledgeable guides can answer the trickiest of questions and there's a free cuppa afterwards in the top-floor tearoom.

National Museum MUSEUM

(adult/child Rs 500/300, camera Rs 160; ⏲9am-5pm Tue-Sat) This museum once housed Kandyan royal concubines and now features royal regalia and reminders of pre-European Sinhalese life. Sadly, it's all very poorly labelled, displayed and lit. One of the displays is a copy of the 1815 agreement that handed over the Kandyan provinces to British rule. This document announces a major reason for the event.

> ...the cruelties and oppressions of the Malabar ruler, in the arbitrary and unjust infliction of bodily tortures and pains of death without trial, and sometimes without accusation or the possibility of a crime, and in the general contempt and contravention of all civil rights, have become flagrant, enormous and intolerable.

Sri Wickrama Rajasinha was declared, 'by the habitual violation of the chief and most sacred duties of a sovereign', to be 'fallen and deposed from office of king' and 'dominion of the Kandyan provinces' was 'vested in... the British Empire'.

The tall-pillared audience hall hosted the convention of Kandyan chiefs that ceded the kingdom to Britain in 1815.

The National Museum, along with four *devales* (complexes for worshipping deities) and two monasteries – but not the Temple of the Sacred Tooth Relic itself – make up one of Sri Lanka's Cultural Triangle sites (see p145).

FREE **British Garrison Cemetery** CEMETERY

(⏲8am-5pm) This cemetery is a short walk uphill behind the National Museum. There are 163 graves. The most striking aspect of a visit to this melancholy place is just how young most people were when they died – if you made it to forty you were of a very ripe old age. Some of the deaths were due to sunstroke, elephants or jungle fever. The Cargills of supermarket fame lie here. James McGlashan survived the battle of Waterloo but later succumbed to mosquitoes. Donations are appreciated.

Devales TEMPLE

There are four Kandyan *devales* to the gods who are followers of Buddha and protect Sri Lanka. Three of the four *devales* are near the Temple of the Sacred Tooth Relic. The 14th-century **Natha Devale** is the oldest. It perches on a stone terrace with a fine *vahalkada* (solid panel of sculpture) gateway. Bodhi trees and dagobas stand in the *devale* grounds. Adjacent is the simple **Pattini Devale**, dedicated to the goddess of chastity. The **Vishnu Devale** on the other side of Raja Vidiya is reached by carved steps and features a drumming hall. The great Hindu god Vishnu is the guardian of Sri Lanka, demonstrating the intermingling of Hinduism and Buddhism.

Further away, the brightly painted tower gateway of the **Kataragama Devale** demands attention amid the bustle on Kotugodelle Vidiya. Murugan, the god of war, has six heads and 12 hands wielding weapons.

THE HISTORY OF THE TOOTH

The sacred tooth of the Buddha is said to have been snatched from the flames of the Buddha's funeral pyre in 483 BC and was smuggled into Sri Lanka during the 4th century AD, hidden in the hair of a princess. At first it was taken to Anuradhapura, then it moved through the country on the waves of Sri Lankan history before ending up at Kandy. In 1283 it was carried back to India by an invading army but it was retrieved by King Parakramabahu III.

The tooth gradually grew in importance as a symbol of sovereignty, and it was believed that whoever had custody of the tooth relic had the right to rule the island. In the 16th century the Portuguese apparently seized the tooth, took it away and burnt it with devout Catholic fervour in Goa. Not so, say the Sinhalese. The Portuguese had actually stolen a replica tooth while the real incisor remained safe. There are still rumours that the real tooth is hidden somewhere secure, and the tooth kept here is only a replica.

The Temple of the Sacred Tooth Relic was constructed mainly under Kandyan kings from 1687 to 1707 and from 1747 to 1782, and the entire temple complex was part of the Kandyan royal palace. The imposing pinky-white structure is surrounded by a moat. The octagonal tower in the moat was built by Sri Wickrama Rajasinha and used to house an important collection of *ola* (talipot-palm leaf) manuscripts. This section of the temple was heavily damaged in the 1998 bomb blast.

The main tooth shrine – a two-storey rectangular building known as the Vahahitina Maligawa – occupies the centre of a paved courtyard. The eye-catching gilded roof over the relic chamber was paid for by Japanese donors. The 1998 bomb exposed part of the front wall to reveal at least three layers of 18th- to 20th-century paintings depicting the *perahera* (boxed text p140) and various Jataka tales (stories of the Buddha's previous lives).

Sri Lankan Buddhists believe they must complete at least one pilgrimage to the temple in their lifetime, as worshipping here improves one's karmic lot immeasurably.

Monasteries TEMPLE

The principal *viharas* (Buddhist complexes) in Kandy have considerable importance – the high priests of the two best known, Malwatte and Asgiriya, are the most important in Sri Lanka. These temples are the headquarters of two of the main *nikayas* (orders of monks). The head monks also administer the Temple of the Sacred Tooth Relic. The **Malwatte Maha Vihara** is across the lake from the Temple of the Sacred Tooth Relic, while the **Asgiriya Maha Vihara** is off Wariyapola Sri Sumanga Mawatha, northwest of the town centre. It has a large reclining Buddha image.

Udawattakelle Sanctuary FOREST

(adult/under 12yr Rs 644/322; ⏲8am-6pm) North of the lake, this forest has huge trees, good birdwatching and loads of cheeky monkeys. Birdwatchers can arrange to enter the sanctuary at 6am in order to get the dawn chorus at its best.

Be careful if you're visiting alone. Muggers are rare but not unknown; solo women should take extra care.

Enter by turning right after the post office on DS Senanayake Vidiya. The last tickets are issued at 4.30pm

Activities

Visitors can learn or practise meditation and study Buddhism at several places in the Kandy area. Ask at the **Buddhist Publication Society** (p144) for details about courses. Many centres offer free courses, but a donation is appropriate and highly appreciated. See p147 for more information on nearby centres.

There are many walks around Kandy, including the **Royal Palace Park** (admission Rs 100; ⏲8.30am-4.30pm), constructed by Sri Wickrama Rajasinha and overlooking the lake. Further up on Rajapihilla Mawatha are even better views over the lake, the town and the surrounding hills. For longer walks, there are paths branching out from Rajapihilla Mawatha. Ask at your guesthouse.

Amaya Hills AYURVEDA

(Map p148; www.amayaresorts.com; Heerassagala; facial Rs 2500, oil massage & steam bath Rs 4000) Outside Kandy and the nicest Ayurveda centre in the area is the colourful ambience of the treatment centre at Amaya Hills. Also a resort (p149), Amaya Hills is high in the hills on a winding road. A three-wheeler from Kandy costs around Rs 1000 return. Make a day of it, have lunch and spend a few hours around the stunning pool.

Wedamedura Ayurveda AYURVEDA
(www.ayurvedawedamedura.com; 7 Mahamaya Mawatha; treatments Rs 1250-5000) Southeast of the lake, this is an Ayurvedic treatment facility with both male and female massage therapists. Residential packages (per week €700, including accommodation and food) are also available. It's a little dark and gloomy though, so if you're heading to Ella, visit the brighter Suwamadura (p170) instead.

Victoria Golf & Country Resort GOLF
(www.golfsrilanka.com; green fees Rs 5000-6500, caddy per round Rs 600) Located 20km east of Kandy and surrounded on three sides by the Victoria Reservoir, with the Knuckles Range as a backdrop; it's worth coming here for lunch at the clubhouse and to savour the views. Claimed to be the best golf course in the subcontinent, it's a fairly challenging 18 holes.

Sri Lanka Trekking HIKING
(☎602 996070; www.srilankatrekking.com) Based at Expeditor guesthouse. Sumone Bandara and Ravi Kandy at Sri Lanka Trekking can arrange trekking around Kandy and camping and trekking (and birdwatching) expeditions to the rugged Knuckles Range (p150). Sumone and Ravi can also arrange mountain-biking and rafting trips in other parts of the Hill Country.

Sleeping

Kandy has many good guesthouses, and the more comfortable hotels often occupy spectacular hilltop locations. There's an increasing range of smaller, boutique-style accommodation within around 45 minutes' drive of Kandy (see p149). These places enjoy quiet locations and make a good base for day trips. You will need your own transport, though.

At the time of the Kandy Esala Perahera, room prices can treble or quadruple, and usually book out in advance. Booking far ahead may secure you a better deal.

The highest concentration of accommodation is along or just off Anagarika Dharmapala Mawatha; buses 654, 655 and 698 will get you there (or just ask for 'Sanghamitta Mawatha' at the clock tower bus stop).

Most places have in-house restaurants.

TOP CHOICE **Sharon Inn** HOTEL $$
(☎220 1400; www.hotelsharoninn.com; 59 Saranankara Rd; r Rs 3000-4500; ❄@📶) One of Kandy's longest established guesthouses and still one of the best. Excellent views and scrupulously clean rooms decorated with Sri Lankan arts and crafts add up to a relaxing place to stay. Cheaper rooms share a bathroom. Not surprisingly it's one of the town's busiest traveller hotels and the owners are fully on the ball with travel information and can arrange cars and drivers. The nightly buffet dinner at 7.30pm (Rs 900) is a tasty shortcut to falling in love with Sri Lankan cuisine. Dinner is open to outside guests, so phone to make a booking.

TOP CHOICE **Villa Rosa** BOUTIQUE HOTEL $$$
(☎221 5556; www.villarosa-kandy.com; Asigiriya; s US$85-125, d US$125-180; ❄📶) Dotted with antiques, and with stunning views over a secluded arc of the Mahaweli River, Villa Rosa is the kind of place you'd build if you moved to Sri Lanka (and had deep pockets!). Spacious wooden-floored rooms in cool, neutral tones share the limelight with relaxing lounges and a what-do-I-read-next reading room. A separate pavilion houses yoga and meditation centres.

Freedom Lodge HOMESTAY $$
(☎222 3506; freedomomega@yahoo.com; 30 Saranankara Rd; s/d incl breakfast Rs 3000/3500; 📶) We really like this place! It's owned by a friendly family, surrounded by towering palm trees and has six spotless rooms, excellent food and an authentic family atmosphere. The bathrooms are what you'd expect from somewhere much flasher. When you take everything into account you can see why this has been considered one of Kandy's best guesthouses for many years.

St Bridget's Country Bungalow HOMESTAY $
(☎221 5806; www.stbridgets-kandy.com; 125 Sri Sumangala Mawatha, Asgiriya; s/d Rs 1960/2500; @) Hemmed in by jungly forest filled with birds, this gorgeous family house has eight pristine but small rooms (and the bathrooms are even tinier), a very warm welcome, superb home-cooking and a guestbook full of happy comments. It's a 20-minute uphill walk from town or Rs 150 in a three-wheeler.

Kandy Cottage GUESTHOUSE **$$**

(☎077 255 6487; www.kandycottage.com; 160 Lady Gordon Dr, Sri Dalada Thapowana Mawatha; s Rs 2200, d Rs 4136-6600; @) Tucked away in a forested valley, the coolly whitewashed Kandy Cottage has three rooms with chunky wooden furniture, polished concrete floors and a bohemian, artists' vibe. Central Kandy is just a 10-minute stroll away.

Queens Hotel HISTORIC HOTEL **$$$**

(☎223 3026; Dalada Vidiya; s/d incl breakfast from US$76/92; ❄ 📶 🏊) Ambience and location are the key reasons for checking in here. While other Asian hotel landmarks like Hanoi's Metropole or Galle's New Oriental have been gussied up, the Queens Hotel hangs in there with an array of old-school rooms with charming floral decor, shiny polished floorboards, and a lobby that's big enough for a one-day cricket match. Travellers have reported that hot water's sometimes off the agenda, but this is still *the* place to be during the Kandy Esala Perahera. It's only a short walk from the Temple of the Sacred Tooth Relic and Royal Palace compound. Next door is the cosy Pub Royale.

McLeod Inn GUESTHOUSE **$**

(☎222 2832; mcleod@sltnet.lk; 65A Rajapihilla Mawatha; r Rs 2500-2000; 📶) This spot could easily charge loads more for the stupendous lake views. Instead they focus on a relaxed family atmosphere, spotless rooms and perhaps Kandy's best balcony for the essential end-of-the-day combination: a good book and a cold drink.

Expeditor GUESTHOUSE **$$**

(☎223 8316; www.expeditorkandy.com; 41 Saranankara Rd; r Rs 1500-3500) Lots of potted plants, balconies with views and the opportunity to share the living areas with the guesthouse owners give Expeditor a cosy bed-and-breakfast feel. It's a good contact for trekking (p138).

Nature Walk Resort GUESTHOUSE **$$**

(☎222 4337; www.naturewalkhr.net; 9 Sanghamitta Mawatha; r Rs 2000-3000; ❄ 📶) Terracotta tiles and French doors lead to balconies with excellent forest views. The rooms are spacious and airy, and you can look forward to troops of monkeys in the morning and squadrons of bats at dusk.

KANDY ESALA PERAHERA

This *perahera* (procession) is held in Kandy to honour the sacred tooth enshrined in the Temple of the Sacred Tooth Relic (Sri Dalada Maligawa). It runs for 10 days in the month of Esala (July/August), ending on the Nikini *poya* (full moon). Kandy's biggest night of the year comes after these 10 days of increasingly frenetic activity. A decline in elephant numbers has seen the scale of the festival diminish in recent years – in earlier times more than 100 elephants took part – but it is still one of Asia's most fascinating celebrations.

The first six nights are relatively low-key. On the seventh night, proceedings escalate as the route lengthens and the procession becomes more splendid (and accommodation prices increase accordingly).

The procession is actually a combination of five separate *peraheras*. Four come from the four Kandy *devales* (complexes for worshipping Hindu or Sri Lankan deities, who are also devotees and servants of the Buddha): Natha, Vishnu, Kataragama and Pattini. The fifth and most splendid *perahera* is from the Sri Dalada Maligawa itself.

The procession is led by thousands of Kandyan dancers and drummers beating drums, cracking whips and waving colourful banners. Then come long processions of up to 50 elephants. The Maligawa tusker is decorated from trunk to toe, and carries a huge canopy sheltering, on the final night, a replica of the sacred relic cask. A trail of pristine white linen is laid before the elephant.

The Kandy Esala Perahera is Sri Lanka's most magnificent annual spectacle. It's been celebrated annually for many centuries and is described by Robert Knox in his 1681 book *An Historical Relation of Ceylon*. There is also a smaller procession on the *poya* day in June, and special *peraheras* may be put on for important occasions.

It's essential to book roadside seats for the main *perahera* at least a week in advance. Prices range from Rs 5000 to 6500. Once the festival starts, seats about halfway back in the stands are more affordable.

Castle Hill Guest House HOMESTAY **$$**
(☎222 4376; 22 Rajapihilla Mawatha; s/d Rs 3450/4200; @) This place has beautiful gardens with simply breathtaking views over the lake, town and distant mountain peaks playing peek-a-boo with the clouds. The guest rooms don't quite live up to the high expectations that the gardens instil but they're peaceful, well away from the tourist hustle and full of authentic 1930s architecture and decor.

Burmese Rest GUESTHOUSE **$**
(274 DS Senanayake Vidiya; s/d Rs 300/500) Considering the price (it's by far the cheapest place in Kandy) you might expect this former pilgrims' guesthouse to be awful, but in fact it's all very clean and well looked after and the building itself is an absolute gem. All the rooms share bathrooms. The monks are friendly, the courtyard is a slowly crumbling haven filled with tortoises and you can safely ignore the sign saying foreigners can only stay with permission from the Myanmar government (which effectively owns the place – which might be reason for some people to avoid it). It might be an idea to bring your own bed sheets.

Lake Bungalow HOMESTAY **$**
(☎222 2075; shiyan_duruwile@gmail.com; 22/2B Sangaraja Mawatha; r Rs 1800) The decor is a throwback to the 1970s, with frilly touches like at your Nana's house and a real homestay feel. With a full kitchen, this is a good option for self-caterers. You're perched above a preschool, so expect the occasional chorus of 'The wheels on the bus go round and round...' It has much less of a 'traveller' feel to it than many other places.

Royal Tourist Lodge GUESTHOUSE **$$**
(☎222 2534; royalxx@slt.lk; 201 Rajapihilla Mawatha; r Rs 2200; @📶) Cane furniture, garden patios and a warm family atmosphere combine to make this feel more like a homestay than a mere guesthouse. It's a particularly good bet for those staying a while who have more time to immerse themselves in Sri Lankan family life.

Lakshmi Guest House GUESTHOUSE **$**
(☎222 2154; www.lakshmipg2.lkguide.com; 57/1 Saranankara Rd; r from Rs 1650, without bathroom Rs 1100; @📶) One of the cluster of good guesthouses up Saranankara Rd, Lakshmi is a cheap, clean and cheerful option from the owners of Palm Garden. That means you're guaranteed good food and very friendly service.

Highest View GUESTHOUSE **$$**
(☎223 3778; www.highestview.com; 129/3 Saranankara Rd; r incl breakfast Rs 3000, without bathroom Rs 2000; @) It's not quite the 'highest view' – that honour probably goes to the McLeod Inn – but the views are pretty good. Pastel-coloured rooms, quiet shared areas, and a spacious restaurant and bar add up to a good choice on winding Saranankara Rd. Mr Thuvan, the manager, is a classic.

Forest Glen GUESTHOUSE **$$**
(☎222 2239; www.forestglenkandy.com; 150/6 Lady Gordon's Dr, Sri Dalada Thapowana Mawatha; r Rs 2000-3500) Simple, very quiet rooms feature at this wonderfully secluded family guesthouse on a winding road on the edge of Udawattakelle Sanctuary. It's popular with birdwatching types, and Kandy's bright lights are just a 10-minute walk away. The small children's playground helps make it a good family choice.

Green Woods GUESTHOUSE **$**
(☎223 2970; www.greenwoodskandy.com; 34A Sanghamitta Mawatha; r Rs 1800) Spend a few hours on the balcony of this welcoming spot with small and basic rooms, and you'll probably spy at least a few of the 45-plus bird species detailed in the guestbook. Surrounded by gardens and forest, Green Woods is a relaxing escape from Kandy's bustle. Chico the dog will probably wake you up early to tick off a few more feathered species.

Blue Haven Guesthouse GUESTHOUSE **$$**
(☎222 9617; www.bluehavenguesthouse.com; 30/2 Poorna Lane, Asgiriya; s/d Rs 2970/4400; 📶) The recently renovated rooms here, which are painted in all the colours of the rainbow, have fantastic views out over the Knuckles Range, but are undeniably a little overpriced. The proprietor, Mr Linton, is an entertaining host who can arrange car hire and tours of the country. The guesthouse is a Rs 200 three-wheeler ride from town.

Chaaya Citadel RESORT **$$$**
(☎Colombo 011-230 6600; www.chaayahotels.com; 124 Srimath Kuda Ratwatte Mawatha; s/d incl breakfast US$168/173; ❄📶🏊) Designer-chic rooms in chocolate tones and grey slate incorporate a riverside location with a breezy lobby and poolside bar at one of Kandy's nicest package-tour resorts. It's a little overpriced but even if you don't stay at least come for

lunch and use the pool (admission free with lunch). It's 5km west of Kandy; a taxi costs around Rs 600 one way.

Olde Empire Hotel HISTORIC HOTEL $
(☎222 4284; www.oldeempirehotel.com; 21 Temple St; r Rs 748-2200) Just a short stroll from the Temple of the Sacred Tooth Relic, the Olde Empire has hushed colonial hallways leading to basic rooms, some with attached bathroom. There's a balcony overlooking the lake, and a cheap and popular restaurant downstairs.

Pink House GUESTHOUSE $
(☎077 961 8552; 15 Saranankara Rd; r Rs 1300, without bathroom Rs 900) The Pink House is a throwback to the old days of overland travel. Tony Wheeler actually stayed here when he was researching the first Lonely Planet *Sri Lanka* guide. Almost 30 years on, you're still guaranteed an authentic family welcome – kids, dogs and, if we're honest, quite a lot of grime, but if you want a reminder of the days of the classic overland routes then this is the place.

Palm Garden Guest House GUESTHOUSE $$
(☎223 3903; www.palmgardenkandy.com; 8 Bogodawatte Rd, Suduhumpola; r Rs 2500-3500; 🛜@) There are no views at this modern guesthouse up the road from the train station, but the rooms are spacious and spotless and the rooftop restaurant-bar is staffed by some of the nicest folk in town. Rental cars and motorcycles are available. Just be ready for some road and train noise. Palm Garden is a Rs 100 three-wheeler ride from the centre of town.

Eating

Eating out in Kandy is pretty much a non-event. The town centre has a few basic eating establishments but nothing that could be called remotely fancy. Not surprisingly, most people end up eating in their guesthouse at night. Particularly good are **Sharon Inn** (☎222 2416; buffets Rs 900), with a buffet at 7.30pm, **Palm Garden Guest House** (buffets Rs 900) and St Bridget's Country Bungalow. Nonguests are welcome, but you need to book by mid-afternoon.

If you're staying on Saranankara Rd and don't feel like trudging into town, there's a simple no-name **restaurant** serving Sri Lankan standards for around Rs 150.

Devon Restaurant INTERNATIONAL $
(11 Dalada Vidiya; mains Rs 150-350) This large and busy restaurant and bakery has a long menu of Sri Lankan and Chinese staples, a few lacklustre Western offerings and some 'healthy' salads (the bacon, egg and chip butty 'salad' being a particularly healthy offering!). The main dining hall is a smart canteenlike affair that's a step up in the posh stakes from many of the other town-centre restaurants. It has high chairs and is popular with young families.

Kandy Muslim Hotel SRI LANKAN $
(Dalada Vidiya; mains Rs 100-350) No, it's not a hotel, but it is an always bustling eatery that offers Kandy's best samosas, authentically spiced curries and heaving plates of frisbee-sized, but gossamer-light, naan. Don't miss the frantic theatre of the guy making *kotthu* (*rotti* chopped and fried with meat and vegetables) out the front.

History Restaurant INTERNATIONAL $$
(27A Anagarika Dharmapala Mawatha; mains Rs 350-550; ⏲noon-11pm) With dishes from India, Italy, Thailand and Sri Lanka, this place could almost be called 'Geography'. The food's OK and there's a good selection of booze, but the real reason to go is for the interesting black-and-white pics of old Kandy. And no, you're not required to take notes during the Kandyan history PowerPoint presentation that runs silently in the background. It's a little hard to find but it's on the 2nd floor of a grey-brown building located above a bakery (which isn't bad either).

Paiva's Restaurant SRI LANKAN $$
(37 Yatinuwara Vidiya; mains Rs 300-400) The lunchtime rice and curry is a handy intro to Sri Lankan cuisine, with three different rices and a multi-plate array of curried accompaniments. In the evening choose between Chinese or North Indian à la carte menus. Both are good, and the friendly waiters will respect your request for 'spicy please?'. Just as well the beer is cold, eh?

Bake House SRI LANKAN $
(36 Dalada Vidiya; mains Rs 80-150) Downstairs from The Pub, Bake House is versatility plus, with tasty baked goodies out the front and a more formal dining room concealed under the building's whitewashed colonial arches. Pop in just after 3pm, when the second bake of the day comes out and the short eats are still warm.

DON'T MISS

HELGA'S FOLLY

If Gaudí and Dalí set to work on building a horror-house hotel, **Helga's Folly** (☎223 4571; www.helgasfolly.com; 32 Frederick E de Silva Mawatha; s/d incl breakfast US$200/210; ❄≋) would be the result. This 35-room hotel/art gallery/surrealist dream has to be the most over-the-top and truly extraordinary hotel in Sri Lanka. It's run and designed by the outlandish Helga da Silva, who grew up in a world of 1950s Hollywood celebrities, artists, writers, politicians and general intrigue, and she has to be one of the only hotel owners we've ever met who prefers her property not to be full! The rock band Stereophonics famously wrote a song about her and her creation has surely led to a thousand twisted nightmares for her guests. As extraordinary as it all is, once you've peeled through all the decorations you'll see that the place is actually looking pretty tatty. Rather than actually stay here we'd recommend just popping past for a poke about and a drink – for many people it's actually one of the most interesting sights in Kandy.

Olde Empire Hotel SRI LANKAN $
(☎222 4284; 21 Temple St; mains Rs 100-150) The modest dining hall at the Olde Empire Hotel is full of character and still serves rice and curry and lunch packets. The flowers on the tables are delivered fresh every day, but the food is only so-so.

Drinking

In this sacred city, the legislation for pubs, bars and discos is very strict. The typical Kandyan goes to bed early, but there are a few places for an end-of-day gin and tonic. All the top hotels also have decent bars.

The Pub BAR
(☎232 4868; 36 Dalada Vidiya; ⏲5pm-midnight) Does what it says on the pint glass, with Carlsberg and Lion Lager on tap, a few cocktails and the occasional Saturday-night jazz gig. The Western food (think chips, pasta, club sandwiches) is uninspired and overpriced, but the twilight view from the balcony onto Kandy's noisy rush hour is an enlivening end to any day.

Pub Royale BAR
(Dalada Vidiya; ⏲4pm-midnight) Beside Queens Hotel, this gloomy, dusty approximation of an English pub is a quiet escape from the diesel-infused intersection outside.

PUB BAR
(27A Anagarika Dharmapala Mawatha; ⏲5pm-midnight) Look for the giant red neon sign above the Bamboo Garden Chinese restaurant and you've found this place with shared wooden tables and great lake views.

Entertainment

Nightclubs

Kandy's two nightclubs are in hotels. At both, entry for women is free, for mixed couples Rs 500, and there's usually no entry allowed for unaccompanied men from outside the hotel. Long trousers, covered shoes and a collared shirt are mandatory for the lads.

Blackout NIGHTCLUB
(Swiss Residence Hotel, 23 Bahirawakanda; ⏲Thu-Sat) Located in the Swiss Residence Hotel, this is the only dance club within city limits. A three-wheeler should be around Rs 250 one way.

Le Garage NIGHTCLUB
(Map p148; ☎223 3521/2; Amaya Hills, Heerassagala; ⏲9pm-3am Sat) Thirty minutes' drive southwest of town by three-wheeler (Rs 500), the Amaya Hills disco is open Saturday night only.

Sport

The modest **Asgiriya Stadium**, north of the town centre, hosts crowds of up to 10,000 cheering fans at international one-day and test matches. The compact stadium is reckoned to be one of the most attractive used for international cricket. Ticket prices depend on the popularity of the two teams. India versus Sri Lanka matches are the most valued; seats in the grandstand can cost up to Rs 3000, while standing room in the public areas will cost Rs 200. Tickets are also sold on the day, or you can book grandstand seats up to a month in advance through the **Sri Lanka Cricket office** (☎223 8533) at the stadium.

Rugby is played between May and September at the Nittawella rugby grounds.

DON'T MISS

KANDYAN DANCERS & DRUMMERS

With elaborate costumes, gyrating dance moves and show-stopping fire-breathing stunts, a Kandyan dance performance is one of the defining experiences of a stay in Kandy. Calling it a traditional Kandyan dance performance is something of a misnomer as the shows are very much aimed at audience entertainment and contain dance routines and costumes from across the country, including the famous 'devil' dances of the west coast (which are sadly very hard to see in their home region).

There are three different venues. All have nightly performances at 5.30pm (get there 30 minutes in advance) and shows last an hour. All of them charge Rs 500.

» **Kandy Lake Club** (Sanghamitta Mawatha) Located 300m up Sanghamitta Mawatha. The front seats are usually reserved for groups, so for good seats arrive at least 20 minutes early. This show has arguably the most elaborate costumes.

» **Kandyan Art Association & Cultural Centre** (Sangharaja Mawatha) This is the busiest venue and it can be crammed with tour groups. The auditorium makes it easier to take photographs than at Kandy Lake Club. It's on the northern lake shore. Arrive early for a good look around the attached craft showroom and workshops.

» **Mahanuwara YMBA** (5 Rajapihilla Mawatha) Southwest of the lake, the YMBA guest-house is a much more low-key venue, but the performance is the equal of the others and the crowds somewhat less.

You can also hear Kandyan drummers every day at the Temple of the Sacred Tooth Relic (p133) and the other temples surrounding it – their drumming signals the start and finish of the daily *puja*.

Shopping

There's a government-run **Laksala** arts and crafts shop to the west of the lake that has lower prices than those of the Kandyan Art Association & Cultural Centre, but it has nothing on the big Laksala in Colombo.

Central Kandy has shops selling antique jewellery and silver belts, and you can buy crafts in the colourful **main market** (Station Rd).

Kandy has a number of batik manufacturers. Check out the original designs at **Upali Jayakody** (Peradeniya Rd) and **Fresco Batiks** (Peradeniya Rd). You'll find antiques showrooms nearby, including **Dharshana Lanka Arts** (923 Peradeniya Rd).

Kandyan Art Association & Cultural Centre HANDICRAFTS
(Sangharaja Mawatha) Has a good selection of local lacquerwork, brassware and other craft items in a colonial-era showroom covered in a patina of age. There are some craftspeople working on the spot.

Bookshops

Buddhist Publication Society BOOKS
(www.bps.lk; 54 Victoria Rd; ⏲9am-4.30pm Mon-Fri, 9am-12.30pm Sat) The Buddhist Publication Society, on the lakeside 400m northeast of the Temple of the Tooth, is a nonprofit charity that distributes the Buddha's teachings. Local scholars and monks occasionally give lectures, and there is a comprehensive library. See online for free information downloads. It's a good place to ask about meditation courses.

Cultural Triangle Office BOOKS
(⏲8am-4.15pm) Has a selection of books on the Ancient Cities for sale. *Kandy,* by Dr Anuradha Seneviratna, is an informative guide to the city's heritage. Also available is *The Cultural Triangle,* published by Unesco and the Central Cultural Fund, which provides background information on the ancient sites.

Vijitha Yapa BOOKS
(5 Kotugodelle Vidiya) Periodicals, newspapers (including foreign titles), maps, fiction and nonfiction.

Information

Cultural Centres

Alliance Française (642 Peradeniya Rd; ⏲8.30am-6pm Mon-Sat) The Alliance hosts film nights (often with English-subtitled films), and has books and periodicals. Good coffee is available. Non-members can browse in the library.

British Council (www.britishcouncil.org/srilanka; 88/3 Kotugodelle Vidiya; ⏲9am-5pm

Tue-Sat, 9am-2.30pm Sun) British newspapers, CDs, videos and DVDs, and occasional film nights, exhibitions and plays. Non-members may read newspapers on presentation of a passport.

Dangers & Annoyances

The back alleys of the town centre are worth avoiding after dark. Most habitués are local guys searching out gambling dens and late-night bars.

Touts mooch around the train station and the lake. You'll hear about guesthouses that have mysteriously 'closed', 'been shut down' or are now 'infested with cockroaches'. All these transparent lies are good reasons to book ahead with a guesthouse; most will pick you up from the Kandy train station. Beware also of guys saying 'I work at your hotel' or 'I met you yesterday'. Just ask for more specific information – like, 'Which hotel?' – and watch them drift away sheepishly.

While researching we also heard of solo women travellers being hassled around the lakeside at dusk and after dark. Get a three-wheeler back to your guesthouse to keep safe.

Internet Access

There are internet cafes throughout the town centre (Kotugodelle Vidiiya has a glut of such places). All charge around Rs 60 per hour. Many hotels also have wi-fi access.

Medical Services

Lakeside Adventist Hospital (☎222 3466; 40 Sangaraja Mawatha) Has English-speaking staff.

Money

The following all have ATMs and exchange facilities.

Bank of Ceylon (Dalada Vidiya)

Commercial Bank (Kotugodelle Vidiya)

Hatton National Bank (Dalada Vidiya)

HSBC (Kotugodelle Vidiya)

Post & Telephone

The main post office is opposite the train station. More central post offices include one at the intersection of Kande Vidiya and DS Senanayake Vidiya. There are numerous private communications bureaus for IDD calling.

Tourist Information

Cultural Triangle Office (⌚8am-4.15pm) Located in a colonial building near the tourist office. Books are available for sale, a scratchy DVD on Kandy's history is shown, and you can buy Cultural Triangle round trip tickets that cover many of the sites of the Ancient Cities. Within Kandy the round-trip ticket covers the four Hindu *devales* – for Kataragama, Natha, Pattini and Vishnu – two monasteries (Asgiriya and Malwatte) and the National Museum. It's also customary to make a donation (usually Rs 50 and upwards) at the *devales* and monasteries. For more information on these tickets, see p192.

Tourist Information Centre (☎222 2661; 9 Dalada Vidiya; ⌚8am-4pm) Located inside the Kandy City Centre Building.

Getting There & Away

Air

Sri Lankan Air Taxi (www.srilankan.lk/airtaxi) runs scheduled flights to and from Colombo on Monday, Wednesday, Friday and Sunday for around Rs 7000 one way.

Bus

Kandy has one main bus station (the manic Goods Shed) and a series of bus stops near the clock tower. The Goods Shed bus station has long-distance buses, while local buses, such as those to Peradeniya, Ampitiya, Matale and Kegalle, leave from near the clock tower. However, some private intercity express buses (to Negombo and Colombo, for example) leave from Station Rd between the clock tower and the train station. If you're still confused, ask someone to point you the right way.

For Sigiriya you must change in Polonnaruwa.

Taxi

Many long-distance taxi drivers hang around the Temple of the Sacred Tooth Relic. Your guesthouse or hotel can organise taxi tours, but you may be able to get a cheaper deal if you organise it through these guys. Cars can generally be hired, with a driver and petrol, for approximately Rs 5500 per day. For a whole van, expect to pay around Rs 6500 per day.

Some guesthouses advertise day trips to all three Cultural Triangle destinations (Sigiriya, Anuradhapura and Polonnaruwa), but this is an exhausting itinerary for both driver and passengers, and one that encourages manic driving. An overnight stay in Anuradhapura, Sigiriya or Polonnaruwa is a saner and safer option.

A taxi to Bandaranaike International Airport costs about Rs 4600, and to Colombo about Rs 5500.

Blue Haven Tours & Travels (☎077 737 2066; www.bluehaventours.com; 25 Trincomalee Rd) is one of a number of car-hire and tour companies. They charge US$50 per day for a car and driver.

Train

Kandy is a major railway station but is surprisingly disorganised (alright, maybe it's not that much of a surprise). Tickets can be bought and reserved up to 10 days in advance at the station (open 5.30am to 5.30pm).

Seats are very popular in the 1st-class observation saloon on the Badulla-bound train, which originates in Colombo and after Kandy stops in Hatton (near Adam's Peak), Nanu Oya (for Nuwara Eliya), Haputale, Ella and a number of other Hill Country stations. If you are unable to reserve a seat at the ticket window, enquire with the stationmaster, who can sometimes release further seating for tourists.

Trains run to the following:

Badulla 2nd/3rd class Rs 270/145
Bandarawela Rs 230/125
Colombo Rs 190/105
Ella Rs 240/130
Haputale Rs 210/115
Hatton Rs 110/65
Nanu Oya (for Nuwara Eliya) Rs 160/90

Getting Around

Bus

Buses to outlying parts of Kandy and nearby towns such as Peradeniya, Ampitiya, Matale and Kegalle leave from near the clock tower.

Taxi

With metered air-con taxis, **Radio Cabs** (223 3322) is a comfortable alternative to three-wheelers. You may have to wait some time for your cab, especially if it's raining and demand is heavy. With taxis (vans) that are not metered, settle on a price before you start your journey.

Three-Wheeler

The standard cost for a three-wheeler from the train station to the southeast end of the lake is Rs 100 to 150. Drivers will ask foreign tourists for much more, but if you stick to your guns you'll get something approximating the local price.

Around Kandy

081

There are a few things worth seeing around Kandy that can be done as a half-day trip.

Sights & Activities

TOP CHOICE **Peradeniya Botanic Gardens** GARDENS

(www.botanicgardens.gov.lk; adult/child Rs1100/550; 7.30am-5pm) At one time these beautiful botanical gardens were reserved exclusively for Kandyan Royalty. Today they're the largest botanic gardens in Sri Lanka, covering 60 hectares and bounded on three sides by a loop of the Mahaweli Ganga. Having blue blood is no longer an entry requirement.

There's a fine collection of orchids and a stately avenue of royal palms that was planted in 1950. A major attraction is the giant Javan fig tree on the great lawn. Covering 2500 sq metres, it's like a giant, living geodesic dome as imagined by Escher or Hundertwasser. A few lingering crows add a slightly sinister touch.

Cannonball trees and cabbage palms punctuate a couple of the elegant avenues, and the avenue of double coconut palms *(coco de mer)* has massive fruit up to 20kg.

In the spice garden near the entrance, see nutmeg, cinnamon and cloves without a salesperson looking over your shoulder. Nearby, the snake creeper is also worth a look. Seek out the giant bamboo and Assam rubber trees, and also take a closer look at the memorial trees, an interesting grab bag of trees planted by the famous and slightly less famous. Consider the trees' different growth rates with the historical legacy of those who planted them.

BUSES FROM KANDY

DESTINATION	BUS STATION	FARE (RS) AIR-CON	FARE (RS) NORMAL	DURATION (HR)
Colombo	Station Rd	240	121	3-4
Negombo	Station Rd	-	120	3-4
Nuwara Eliya	Goods Shed	180	93	2
Ratnapura	Goods Shed	-	134	6
Anuradhapura	Goods Shed	285	148	3-4
Polonnaruwa	Goods Shed	-	142	3

On weekends and holidays the gardens are packed with romantically inclined local tourists and it can be hard to move without tripping over yet another canoodling young couple!

If food is more a priority than love then you'll find an overpriced cafeteria (mains Rs 550 to 1000) about 500m north of the entrance, serving Western and Sri Lankan food on a roofed veranda. A better option is to stock up on picnic items. Just keep a close eye on the insistent posse of local dogs.

Bus 644 (Rs 15) from Kandy's clock tower bus stop goes to the gardens. A three-wheeler from Kandy is around Rs 700 return; a van is around Rs 1500. Many taxi drivers incorporate a visit to the gardens with the Pinnewala Elephant Orphanage or the Kandy temple loop.

Kandy Garrison Cemetery CEMETERY
(Deveni Rajasinghe; ⏲10am-noon & 1-6pm) This beautifully kept garden cemetery was founded in 1817 for the internment of British-era colonists and is managed by the Commonwealth War Graves Commission. Although there are many 19th-century graves, most date from WWII. The most famous is that of Sir John D'Oyly, a colonial official who planned the bloodless British capture of Kandy in 1815 and then succumbed to cholera in 1824. This cemetery is 2km southwest of Kandy. Donations are accepted.

Temples

There are several interesting temples around Kandy. Visiting them provides not just an insight into Sri Lankan religious culture but also a jolly good excuse for a romp around some exquisitely pretty countryside. This loop takes in three 14th-century Hindu-Buddhist temples and you'll pass by the entrance to the botanic gardens, allowing you to slot them into your busy day as well. There's a lot of walking involved, so you could narrow down your visit to one or two of the temples or take a three-wheeler trip to all three; expect to pay around Rs 3000 from Kandy. If you're combining walking and public transport you'll need to ask the way occasionally, as the loop is not signposted.

Embekka Devale TEMPLE
(admission Rs 150) Catch the frequent bus 643 (to Vatadeniya via Embekka) from near the Kandy clock tower. The village of Embekka is about 7km beyond the botanic gardens (about an hour from Kandy). From the village it's a pleasant rural stroll of about 1km to the 14th-century temple. The finely carved wooden pillars are reputed to come from a royal audience hall in Kandy. Carvings include swans, eagles, wrestling men and dancing women. A local *perahera* is held every September.

Lankatilake Temple TEMPLE
(admission Rs 300) From Embekka Devale to here is a 3km stroll beside rice paddies; you'll see the temple on the left. From Kandy you can go directly to the Lankatilake Temple on bus 644 or take a Kiribathkumbara or Pilimatalawa bus from the same stop as the Embekka buses. This temple is divided into two halves – one half Buddhist and one half Hindu. It features a Buddha image, Kandy-period paintings, rockface inscriptions and stone elephant figures. A caretaker will unlock the shrine if it's not already open. A *perahera* takes place in August.

The setting is as impressive as the temple.

Gadaladeniya Temple TEMPLE
(admission Rs 200) It's a further 3km walk to Gadaladeniya Temple, or you can catch a bus from Kandy; bus 644, among others, will take you there. Built on a rocky outcrop and covered with small pools, the temple is reached by a series of steps cut into the rock. This Buddhist temple with a Hindu annex is a similar age to the Lankatilake Temple and the Embekka Devale.

At the time of research scaffolding and a tin roof covered this temple in an effort to protect it from further rain-induced erosion.

The main Colombo–Kandy road is less than 2km from Gadaladeniya Temple – you reach the road close to the 105km post. It's a pleasant stroll, and from the main road almost any bus will take you to the Peradeniya Botanic Gardens or on to Kandy.

Meditation

Nilambe Meditation Centre MEDITATION
(www.nilambe.net) Close to Nilambe Bungalow Junction about 13km south of Kandy, Nilambe Meditation Centre can be reached by bus 633 (catch a Delthota bus via Galaha and get off at Office Junction); the trip takes about an hour. There are daily meditation classes and basic accommodation for 40 people. Stay for Rs 800 per day (including food). Blankets are supplied but you should bring a sleep sheet. There's no electricity, so bring a torch too. To reach Nilambe from Office Junction, you can walk a steep 3km through tea plantations or take a three-wheeler for Rs 250. A taxi from Kandy costs Rs 1400 one way.

Around Kandy

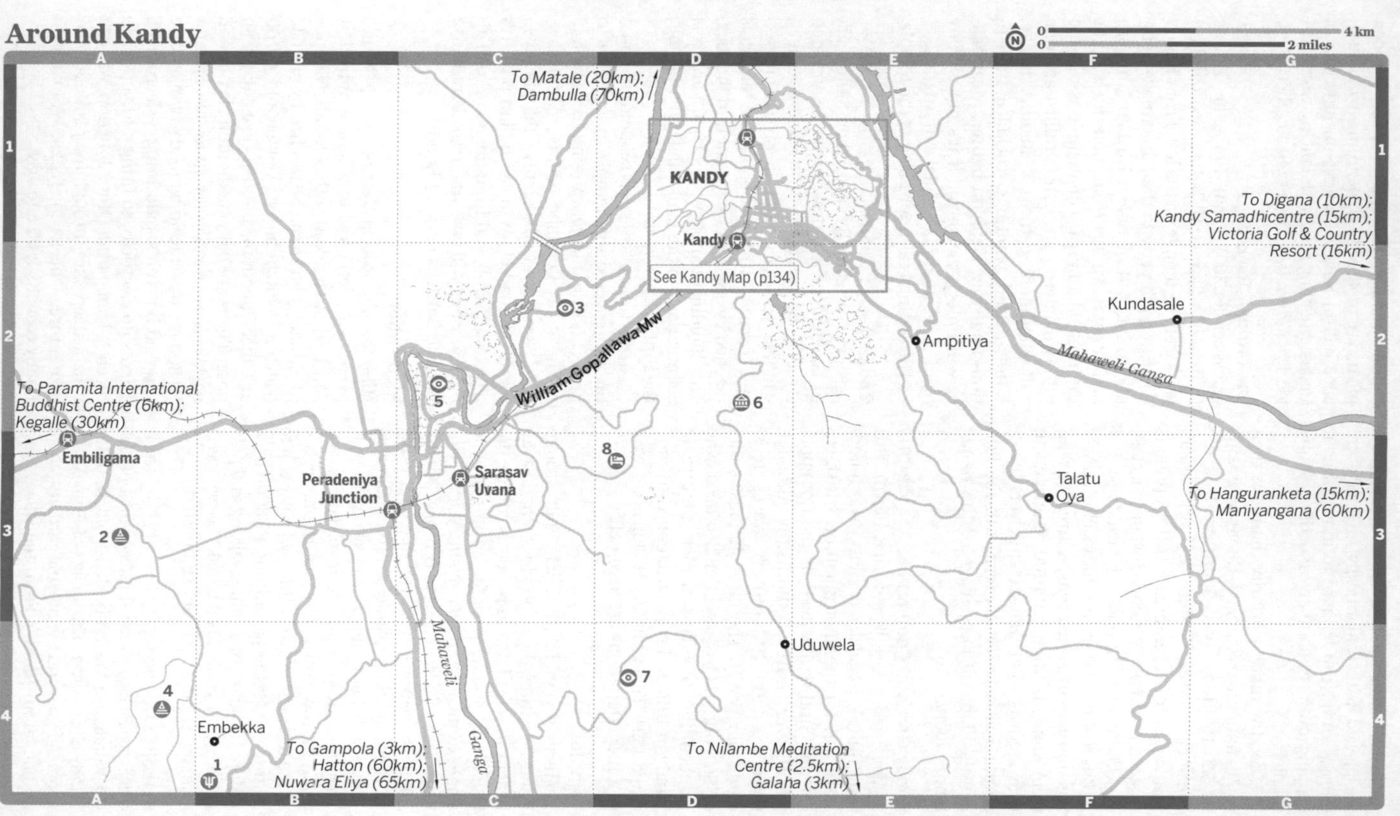

Around Kandy

Sights

Activities, Courses & Tours

Sleeping

Entertainment

Dhamma Kuta Vipassana Meditation Centre MEDITATION
(☎238 5774; www.kuta.dhamma.org; Mowbray, Hindagala) This centre offers free 10-day courses following the SN Goenka system of meditation. Booking ahead is mandatory. There's dorm accommodation for 90 students, with separate male and female quarters. Retreat schedules are posted at the Buddhist Publication Society in Kandy. Take a Mahakanda-bound bus from the clock tower bus stop in Kandy and get off at the last stop. It's a steep 2km walk; a three-wheeler costs Rs 250. A taxi from Kandy costs around Rs 900 to the bus stop.

Paramita International Buddhist Centre MEDITATION
(☎257 0732; www.paramitaibc.org) At the top of the Bolana Pass, 1km past Kadugannawa on the Colombo road, Paramita runs one-week courses, with clean accommodation for men and women, lush gardens and a library.

Sleeping

If you want quiet days spent wandering along shaded tracks, with views of rolling hills, then stay just out of Kandy. Accommodation skews to midrange and top-end properties; there are some lovely places worth splashing out for.

TOP CHOICE **The Kandy House** BOUTIQUE HOTEL $$$
(☎492 1394; www.thekandyhouse.com; Amunugama Walauwa; r incl breakfast from US$326; @☎≈) Almost two centuries ago, this beautiful courtyard villa housed the family of a local Kandyan chief. Now fully restored and decorated with colonial Dutch antiques, this divine boutique hotel ticks all the honeymoon requirement boxes. All rooms are named after local butterflies; the best suites have wonderfully private verandas. A garden infinity pool segues to emerald-green rice paddies. Note that rooms do not have air-conditioning and there's a two-night minimum stay.

Kandy Samadhicentre BOUTIQUE HOTEL $$$
(☎447 0925; www.thekandysamadhicentre.com; Kukul Oya Rd, Kandy; r US$200-300) Part boutique ecolodge and part Ayurvedic centre, this could be the most relaxing place to stay around Kandy. Thirteen pavilions dot a forested hillside, and each room is decorated with Asian textiles and four-poster beds. Simpler 'Mud House' rooms lack hot water but share the same serene ambience. Based on room quality alone we think it's overpriced but judging by the comments in the guestbook we're in the minority! Food is both organic and vegetarian, and no alcohol is served. Reiki and shiatsu massage (Rs 3500) is also available. Transport to the lodge (50 minutes east of Kandy) is Rs 2500; arrange pick-up when making your booking.

Amaya Hills RESORT $$$
(☎447 4022; www.amayaresorts.com; Heerassagala; s/d incl breakfast US$151/163; ❄@☎≈) Hats off to the architects for making the most of Amaya Hills' perfect location. Perched in the hills, 20 minutes' drive southwest of Kandy, this 100-room hotel incorporates a stunning open lobby, a clifftop swimming pool, and very comfortable rooms with lots of warm wooden tones and a Kandyan design motif. The well-equipped Ayurveda centre and Le Garage disco are both open to nonguests. It's a Rs 500 three-wheeler ride to Kandy, so you're better off having a driver.

East of Kandy

Kandy is an important transport hub, with most travellers going west to Colombo, north to the Ancient Cities, or south to the rest of the Hill Country. But it's also possible to go east to Mahiyangana and Badulla, and to Monaragala en route to Arugam Bay and Gal Oya National Park. Further northeast, Batticaloa can be reached by bus from Kandy.

The Buddha is said to have preached at Mahiyangana; a dagoba marks the spot. There are two roads to Mahiyangana. The A26 north road goes past the Victoria Golf Club and the

Victoria Reservoir to Madugoda, before twisting downhill through 18 hairpin bends to the Mahaweli lowlands and the dry-zone plains. It's one of the country's hairiest bus rides. Going up you worry about overheating, and going down it's all about the brakes. Many vehicles didn't make it and now lie in the jungle beneath.

Drivers prefer the road along the southern shores of the Victoria and Randenigala Reservoirs, which is much faster and in better condition. This road closes at dusk, however, because wild elephants from the nature reserve are attracted to headlights. To travel from Kandy to the hills of Uva Province (including towns such as Ella and Haputale), it's quicker to take this road and then the route south to Badulla than to go via Nuwara Eliya.

KNUCKLES RANGE

So named because the range's peaks look like a closed fist, this **massif** is home to pockets of rare montane forest. The area, which offers fabulous hiking and birdwatching possibilities, remains relatively unknown to foreign visitors and is one of the best areas in the Hill Country to get off the beaten tourist path.

If you are coming here in order to hike then you'll need to be well prepared. A knowledgeable guide is virtually essential.

Hotels in the Knuckles Range can organise guided hiking trips. In Kandy, see Sumone and Ravi at Sri Lanka Trekking (p139) or **Mr MG Nishantha** (077 918 8292). A guide for the high peaks is not just compulsory but also an essential as is some serious wet-weather gear as well as leech protection. For anything more ambitious than a couple of hours' stroll around the foothills you will need to be totally self-sufficient, with camping equipment and food (again, the people listed above can help).

The foothills of the Knuckles are covered in small villages and walking in this area is open to anyone. The high massif, though, is a protected zone and entrance is Rs 650. Tickets cannot be purchased at the gate itself, but will normally be obtained by your guide from a forestry department office.

A good source of information on the area is www.knucklesrange.org.

Sleeping & Eating

TOP CHOICE Rangala House BOUTIQUE HOTEL **$$$**
(081-240 0294; www.rangalahouse.com; 92B Bobebila Rd, Makuldeniya, Teldeniya; r incl breakfast US$156;) This former tea planter's bungalow ensconced on a steep forested hillside surrounded by spice trees is a fine example of the type of intimate and gorgeous boutique hotel that Sri Lanka is getting increasingly good at. There are just four double rooms, plus a large living and dining room with a fireplace and views – off over mountains, the jungles and the distant bright lights of Kandy – that just might be among the best on the island. The big swimming pool is solar-heated, and after dark the 15m-long veranda – complete with barbecue – is an essential end-of-day rendezvous point. Excellent trekking tours of the high Knuckles Range can be organised. Note that credit cards are not accepted.

Green View HOTEL **$$**
(081-567 1436; www.greenviewholidayresort.com; Karagahinna, Elkaduwa; s/d from Rs 2420/3300) This seven-room hillside lodge has spectacular views of a forested mountain valley and clean rooms with absolutely zero character. It's showing its age a little, but staff will happily lead you on easy low-level strolls or much tougher hikes around the edge of the Knuckles Range. Book ahead and they'll pick you up from Kandy.

Hunas Falls Hotel HOTEL **$$$**
(081-494 0320; www.hunasfallskandy.com; Elkaduwa; s/d full board from US$201/221;) Perched on the edge of a working tea plantation and spice garden, this package-tour hotel is popular with visitors from India and the Middle East, but frankly it's something of an ugly and impersonal blot on an otherwise stunning landscape.

Getting There & Away

A taxi from Kandy to Elkaduwa should cost Rs 1500. Alternatively, take a bus to Wattegama (from near the clock tower in Kandy), and then catch another to Elkaduwa.

Adam's Peak (Sri Pada)

ELEV 2243M

Located in a beautiful area of the southern Hill Country, this lofty peak has sparked the imagination for centuries and been a focus for pilgrimage for over 1000 years. King Parakramabahu and King Nissanka Malla of Polonnaruwa provided *ambalamas* (resting places to shelter weary pilgrims) up the mountain.

It is variously known as Adam's Peak (the place where Adam first set foot on earth after being cast out of heaven), Sri Pada (Sacred

VISITING THE VEDDAHS

Sri Lanka was inhabited long before the Sinhalese or Tamils arrived on the scene. These original inhabitants, known as the Veddahs (or hunters), are thought to have first arrived on the island some 18,000 years ago and until fairly recently they have lived alongside their fellow Sri Lankans without too many issues. Today though, as with aboriginal communities across South Asia, the remaining Veddah communities are under intense pressure and only a few hundred pure-blooded Veddah remain.

The last Veddah stronghold is in the countryside around the village of **Dambana**, which is east of the small town of **Mahiyangana**. If you want to meet the Veddah, then once in Dambana you need to find a translator-guide and then get to the pretty hamlet of **Kotabakina**, the most frequently visited Veddah village. Once here you will (for a fairly substantial sum) most likely be entertained with dancing, singing and a 'hunting' display by the Veddah people.

Perhaps not surprisingly the whole experience can feel rather staged, but it should also be borne in mind that the money tourism pumps into the villages, and the tourists' desire to see traditional tribal 'culture', might actually be enough to stop the last of Veddah from being swallowed up by mainstream Sri Lankan culture.

The best base for a visit to this area is Mahiyangana, a sprawling and sparsely settled town. The only highlight in the town itself is the **Mahiyangana dagoba** where, according to legend, the Buddha preached on his first visit to Sri Lanka.

There are a few lodging options in Mahiyangana, none of which are very accustomed to foreign guests, and there are buses to Kandy, Badulla and Polonnaruwa, among other destinations.

Footprint, left by the Buddha as he headed towards paradise), or perhaps most poetically as Samanalakande (Butterfly Mountain; where butterflies go to die). Some believe the huge 'footprint' crowning the peak to be that of St Thomas, the early apostle of India, or even of Lord Shiva.

The pilgrimage season begins on *poya* day in December and runs until **Vesak festival** in May; January and February are most busy. At other times the temple on the summit is unused, and between May and October the peak is often obscured by clouds. During the pilgrimage season pilgrims and a few tourists make the climb up the countless steps to the top.

Walkers leave from the small settlement of Dalhousie (del-*house*), 33km by road southwest of Hatton, which is situated on the Colombo–Kandy–Nuwara Eliya railway and road. In season the route is illuminated by a sparkling ribbon of lights. Out of season you will need a torch. Many pilgrims prefer to make the longer, more tiring – but equally well-marked and lit – seven-hour climb from Ratnapura via the Carney Estate because of the greater merit thus gained.

As dawn illuminates the holy mountain, the diffuse morning light uncovers the Hill Country rising in the east and the land sloping to the coast to the west. Colombo, 65km away, is easily visible on a clear day.

Adam's Peak saves its breathtaking coup de grâce for just after dawn. The sun casts a perfect shadow of the peak onto the misty clouds down towards the coast. As the sun rises higher this eerie triangular shadow races back towards the peak, eventually disappearing into its base.

Activities

You can start the 7km climb from Dalhousie soon after dark – bring a good sleeping bag to keep you warm overnight at the top – or you can wait until about 2am to start. The climb is up steps most of the way (about 5200 of them), and with plenty of rest stops you'll reach the top in 2½ to four hours. A 2.30am start will easily get you there before dawn, which is around 6.30am. Start on a *poya* day, though, and the throng of pilgrims might add hours to your climb. We've heard of some travellers taking up to nine hours on a *poya* day.

From the car park the slope is gradual for the first half-hour, passing under an entrance arch and then by the Japan–Sri Lanka Friendship Dagoba. The pathway then gets steeper until it becomes a continuous flight of stairs. There are tea houses all the way to the top; some open through the night. A few are open out of season. The authorities have banned litter, alcohol, cigarettes, meat and recorded music, so the atmosphere remains reverential.

The summit can be cold, so it's not worth getting there too long before dawn and then sitting around shivering. Definitely bring warm clothes, including something extra for the top, and pack plenty of water. If you're in Dalhousie in the pilgrimage season, stalls at the market sell warm jackets and headgear. Otherwise stop in at the market at Nuwara Eliya (p158) for outdoor gear at bargain prices. Some pilgrims wait for the priests to make a morning offering before they descend, but the sun and heat rise quickly, so it pays not to linger.

Many people find the hardest part is coming down. The endless steps can shake the strongest knees, and if your shoes don't fit well, toe-jam also kicks in. Walking poles or even just a sturdy stick will make the descent much less jarring on your legs. Take a hat, as the morning sun intensifies quickly. Remember to stretch your legs when you finish, otherwise you'll be walking strangely for a few days.

Between June and November, when the pathway isn't illuminated and there aren't many people around, travellers are urged to do the hike at least in pairs. Expect to pay around Rs 1000 for a guide.

Leeches may be about. A popular deterrent is an Ayurvedic balm produced by Siddhalepa Ayurveda Hospital. It costs only a few rupees and is available across Sri Lanka.

Sleeping & Eating

Dalhousie is the best place to start the climb, and it also has the area's best budget accommodation. Head to Dikoya (boxed text, opposite) for midrange and top-end options.

Out-of-pilgrimage-season buses may drop you off in Dalhousie's main square, but during the season buses stop near the beginning of the walk. In season there are a few tea shops, some of which stay open all night, where you can get an early breakfast or buy provisions for the climb.

Most guesthouses are on your left as you reach Dalhousie.

TOP CHOICE Slightly Chilled GUESTHOUSE $$
(☎051-351 9430; www.slightlychilled.tv; Dalhousie; r Rs 2500; @ wi-fi) Dalhousie's best option is Slightly Chilled in name and very chilled in nature. Spacious and colourful rooms with polished wooden floors have great views of Sri Pada, and there's an airy restaurant. Mountain bikes can be hired, there's lots of information on other trails in the area and at night there are occasional big-screen movies. It's on your left as you come into town.

Green House HOMESTAY $
(☎060-222 3956; Dalhousie; r Rs 600-800) Across the bridge at the start of the walking path, the Green House lives up to its name with a potplant-filled garden and a breezy gazebo restaurant. Some of the small rooms share a bathroom and all come with twee bedspreads. The friendly Tamil family can arrange trekking guides, and after your knee-wrecking descent from Sri Pada will prepare a herbal bath (Rs 300) for an essential après-pilgrimage soak.

White House HUT $
(☎077 791 2009; Dalhousie; r Rs 600-750) The White House has basic but clean accommodation inside creaky wooden huts – those with hot water cost more – run by a single guy and his friendly dog. It's a laid-back place with nice gardens and a natural swimming hole in the nearby river. Guiding services for walks across the tea gardens are available for Rs 2000 to 3000 per day.

River View Wathsala Inn HOTEL $$
(☎052-227 7427; Dalhousie; r Rs 2000-3200, without bathroom Rs 1500) Dalhousie's tour-group hotel of choice, this spot has 14 large rooms, some with shared bathrooms. Lots of balconies and nooks and crannies make it feel larger than it is, and it's easy to find a private space to take in the views. The trailhead is a 10-minute walk away.

White Elephant Hotel HOTEL $$
(☎051-350 7377; www.hotelwhiteelephant.com; Dalhousie; r Rs 3000; @ wi-fi) The town's flashiest digs, this new hotel has massive rooms with clean, tiled floors, but it's all a bit bling and is more popular with domestic tourists than foreign ones.

Information

There are no banking facilities in Dalhousie. The nearest ATMs are in Hatton.

For information on Adam's Peak visit www.sripada.org.

Getting There & Away

A taxi from Hatton to Dalhousie costs Rs 1500.

Bus

Buses run to Dalhousie from Kandy (from the Goods Shed bus station), Nuwara Eliya and Colombo in the pilgrimage season. Otherwise, you need first to get to Hatton or to Maskeliya, about 20km along the Hatton–Dalhousie road.

Throughout the year there are services to Hatton from Colombo, Kandy or Nuwara Eliya. There are also some direct buses from Nuwara Eliya and Colombo to Maskeliya.

There are buses from Hatton to Dalhousie via Maskeliya every 30 minutes in the pilgrimage season (Rs 60, two hours). Otherwise, you have to take a bus from Hatton to Maskeliya (Rs 30, last departure about 6pm) and then another to Dalhousie (Rs 30, last departure about 7pm).

Train

The *Podi Menike* and *Udarata Menike* trains from Colombo arrive in Hatton at 11.30am and 2.15pm respectively. These trains continue to Nanu Oya (for Nuwara Eliya), as do the local trains that leave Hatton at 7.35am and 4.20pm. In the other direction (to Colombo) the *Podi Menike* passes through Haputale and Nanu Oya and reaches Hatton at 2.13pm; the *Udarata Menike* leaves Hatton at 10.55am. Mail train 46 leaves at 10.52pm.

Kitulgala

036

Kitulgala is slowly gaining a reputation as the adrenalin-sports capital of Sri Lanka. For the moment most visitors are the young and energetic of Colombo, but more and more foreign visitors are starting to discover the

WORTH A TRIP

A TEA PLANTER'S LIFE

After ascending Adam's Peak most people take their strained leg muscles straight off for a well-deserved rest, and what better place to do so than in one of the delightful tea-estate bungalows that can be founded dotted about the beautiful countryside near Adam's Peak.

Castlereagh Family Cottages is along the main road between Hatton and Dikoya and can be reached by bus. Tea Trails can arrange pick-up for its guests in Colombo, Kandy or Hatton. A taxi from Hatton to any of these accommodations should cost around Rs 1200.

Castlereagh Family Cottages (051-222 3607; Norton Bridge Rd, Dikoya; cottages incl breakfast from Rs 3300) A series of nicely decorated cottages in a lovely spot under eucalyptus trees on the edge of the Castlereagh Reservoir. The smaller cottage has a double bed and a room with two bunks. The bigger one has three double rooms, plus a kids' room. Both have kitchens and hot water. Look for the sign for this place just after a bridge.

Castlereagh Holiday Bungalow (051-222 3688; www.castlereigh.net; Norton Bridge Rd, Dikoya; cottages incl breakfast from Rs 3800) Just up the hill from the Castlereagh Family Cottages. The property consists of a lovely stone bungalow surrounded by flower gardens. You can crash into a wicker chair and soak up the views before lighting a log fire in your room and pondering why they have Spanish bullfighting pictures on the walls.

Tea Trails (011-230 3888; www.teatrails.com; Dikoya; s/d full board €339/443;) For something altogether smarter, Tea Trails comprises a collection of four colonial-style bungalows built for British tea-estate managers in the late-19th and early 20th centuries. Completely refurbished, and the very definition of the words 'colonial luxury', the bungalows each have four to six large bedrooms, spacious dining and living areas, and verandas and gardens with views over Castlereagh Reservoir. Rates include Western and Sri Lankan meals prepared by a resident chef, along with complimentary wines and single-estate teas. Also on staff are an experienced guide who can lead hikes from bungalow to bungalow (or beyond), and a resident tea expert. If tea's not your tipple, have a single malt whisky or end-of-day G&T around your bungalow's roaring fire. The Tea Trails bungalows are one of Sri Lanka's finest places to savour the luxury and leisure of the British colonial experience.

delights of white-water rafting, jungle trekking, birdwatching and cave exploration.

The town's other main claim to fame is that David Lean filmed his 1957 Oscar-winning epic *Bridge on the River Kwai* here. You can walk down a pathway to the filming site along the banks of the Kelaniya Ganga. The pathway is signposted on the main road, about 1km from Plantation Hotel in the direction of Adam's Peak. It is virtually impossible to head down the path without attracting an entourage of 'guides' who expect a few rupees for their troubles. If you know the film you'll recognise some of the places. Apparently the actual railway carriages used in the movie now lie at the bottom of the river, after being sunk in an explosive conclusion. You'll have to bring your own scuba gear if you want a look.

A few kilometres from Kitulgala is a large **cave system** where the 28,500-year-old remains of early humans were discovered. Any of the hotels listed below can arrange a guide to the caves.

Activities

White-water Rafting RAFTING

The Kelaniya Ganga, the river that runs through Kitulgala, offers the best white-water rafting in Sri Lanka. The typical trip takes in seven Class 2-3 rapids in 7km for US$30 per person, including transport and lunch. You'll be on the water for around two hours. Experienced rafters can opt for more difficult Class 4-5 rapids by special arrangement. Almost every hotel can organise a rafting trip or there are several activity centres along the main road. All offer pretty much the same package for the same price.

The Kelaniya Ganga also has some good **swimming** spots; a popular hole is beside Plantation Hotel.

Jungle Trekking HIKING

The sheer hills surrounding Kitulgala are covered in dense forest and the area makes for some decent, but quite strenuous, day-long jungle hikes. You will need a guide (US$15), good footwear, waterproofs and leech repellent. Most hotels can arrange a guide and suggest a suitable route; Channa Perera at Rafter's Retreat (p154) is the most experienced 'jungle man' in the area and is knowledgeable on the local flora and fauna.

Birdwatching BIRDWATCHING

The area is famous for birdwatching – 23 of Sri Lanka's 27 endemic bird species inhabit the surrounding forest. Once again Channa Perera at Rafter's Retreat is the main man when it comes to birdwatching trips.

Sleeping & Eating

TOP CHOICE **Royal River Resort** BOUTIQUE HOTEL $$$

(Plantation Resort; 036-492 0790; www.plantationgrouphotels.com; Eduru Ella; s/d half board Rs 10,910/14,525;) Quick, future brides and bridegrooms! Get your 'I do's' over with and get out to this place for your honeymoon. Tucked away 6km from Kitulgala, in a haze of jungle and tea estates, this place is fantastically secluded. It has four old-fashioned (but actually new) timber cottages built around, onto and into a series of boulders and waterfalls. The rooms are pleasantly decorated in colonial shades and have stone floors, open wood fires and four-poster beds. There's a tasty little restaurant and a 'pool'. Ah, yes, the 'pool' – just wait until you see how amazing that is!

Rafter's Retreat HUTS $$

(228 7598; www.raftersretreat.com; incl half board s/d US$55/80;) A beautiful 85-year-old colonial bungalow serves as the hub for this rafting and birdwatching outfit that sprawls along the riverbank. The 10 eco-friendly, but slightly overpriced riverside cottages are basic but very private, and three rooms near the old house are clean and spacious with unbelievably high ceilings. The breezy riverside restaurant is a great place for a few beers, and the food is excellent. Ask the jovial owner Channa to show you around the wonderful colonial house that was originally built by his grandfather. All manner of tours and activities can be arranged.

Kitulgala Rest House HOTEL $$

(228 7233; www.ceylonhotels.lk; s/d incl breakfast Rs 6600/7480;) One corner of the dining room at this old rest house is a veritable shrine to the David Lean epic. Black-and-white stills punctuate a feature wall, and the hotel was actually used in the movie. The graceful colonial-style building is over 70 years old, and has 20 rooms with verandas facing the river. Satellite TV and minibars are more modern touches.

Plantation Hotel HOTEL $$$

(228 7575; www.plantationgrouphotels.com; Kalukohutenna; s/d incl breakfast Rs 7725/8710;) Comfortable but overpriced business-class rooms and a restaurant serving 'Western and Eastern' cuisine beside the river.

Getting There & Away

It's easy to stop at Kitulgala even if you are travelling by bus. If you're coming from Ratnapura, change at Avissawella, catch the bus to Hatton and get off at Kitulgala (Rs 50). When you're over Kitulgala, flag a bus on to Hatton from the main road (Rs 50).

Kandy to Nuwara Eliya

The road from Kandy to Nuwara Eliya climbs nearly 1400m as it winds through jade-green tea plantations and past crystalline reservoirs. The 80km of asphalt allow for plenty of stops at waterfalls and tea outlets.

Kothmale Reservoir (also known as Puna Oya Reservoir) can be seen further up the road. It's part of the Mahaweli Development Project and blamed by some locals for climatic quirks in recent years. **Ramboda Falls** (108m), about 1.5km from the road, is a spectacular double waterfall.

On the A5, 5km before Nuwara Eliya, the **Labookellie Tea Factory** (8am-6.30pm) is a convenient factory to visit as it's right on the roadside. Its tours are brief in the extreme and while it's worth stopping if you're passing by it's not worth the effort of a special visit. It is, though, a good place to buy well-priced quality teas and enjoy a cuppa with a slice of chocolate cake (Rs 60). Nearby the **Glenloch** and **Blue Field Tea Estates** offer a fairly similar deal, but with slightly fewer visitors.

Approaching Nuwara Eliya, roadside stalls overflow with all sorts of veggies – a legacy of Samuel Baker, who arrived in 1846 and made Nuwara Eliya his summer retreat. The veggie-loving Baker introduced many different varieties, including quite a few you vowed not to eat once you reached adulthood. Watch out on the steep roadside approach to Nuwara Eliya for children selling flowers. If you're travelling with a loved one, you know what to do.

Sleeping & Eating

TOP CHOICE Lavender House BUNGALOW $$$
(052-225 9928; www.thelavenderhouseceylon.com; s/d incl breakfast from US$300/325;) Of all the converted tea-estate bungalows in Sri Lanka this sublime old cottage is probably the finest. With grand old four-poster beds and portraits of Churchill hanging above the open log fire there's no doubting that it's got the old colonial tea planter thing down to a tee (if you'll excuse the pun), but it mixes this all up with fresh modern art, swish bathrooms, puffed-up pillows and an infinity pool that might have the best waterside view in all the Hill Country. It's not far from the Kothmale Reservoir. Advance bookings are essential.

Pussellawa Rest House HOTEL $$$
(077 351 9073; www.heritagepussellawa.lk; s/d incl breakfast US$110/122;) At Pussellawa, 45km from Kandy, this 120-year-old former government rest house has been recently privatised and renovated. It now offers somewhat overpriced, but otherwise very comfortable, rooms with plenty of old-fashioned grace to them.

Ramboda Falls Hotel HOTEL $$$
(052-225 9582; www.rambodafall.com; s/d half board US$61/71, cabanas s/d half board US$130/140) This motel-like place is 58km from Kandy and near Ramboda Falls and the Kothmale Reservoir. There are excellent views of the falls, especially from the restaurant. Rooms are clean and spacious, but the cabanas are insanely overpriced. The pricey restaurant serves a Sri Lankan buffet lunch (Rs 1000) and is a near-compulsory lunch stop for passing tour groups.

Maussawa Estate Eco Lanka Villa VILLA $$$
(051-223 3133; www.ecolanka.com; full board s €40-45, d €60-85) Combining ecotourism and an internationally recognised fair-trade garden, Eco Lanka Villa sits concealed on 50 acres of forest. Getting there from the main road joining Kandy and Nuwara Eliya is a rollicking adventure in itself. Once there, get busy trekking, birdwatching or bathing in the river. Afterwards relax in the main villa or the breezy garden restaurant. Everything is organic, vegetarian and very tasty. A percentage of profits is donated to the local village. Eco Lanka Villa is near the village of Pundaluoya, northwest of Nuwara Eliya. Advance reservations are essential.

TEA & SRI LANKA

Tea is not just central to life in the Hill Country, it is a vital part of the entire nation's culture, from its role as the hot beverage of choice to its place in the economy. For much more on tea, see p288.

Nuwara Eliya

052 / POP 25,966 / ELEV 1889M

Nuwara Eliya is often referred to by the Sri Lankan tourist industry as 'Little England'. And while the toy-town ambience does have something of an English country village to it, it comes with a disorienting surrealist edge. Three-wheelers whiz past red telephone boxes. Water buffalo daubed in iridescent dye for the Tamil festival of Thaipongal mingle outside a pink brick Victorian post office. A well-tended golf course morphs seamlessly into a rolling carpet of tea plantations. The dusty and bustling centre of town is a thoroughly Sri Lankan tangle, but scratch the surface a little to reveal colonial bungalows, well-tended hedgerows and pretty rose gardens.

In earlier times, Nuwara Eliya (meaning 'City of Light') was the favoured cool-climate escape for the hard-working and hard-drinking English and Scottish pioneers of Sri Lanka's tea industry. A rainy-day, misty-mountain atmosphere still blankets the town from November to February – don't come expecting tropical climes – but during April's spring release, the town is crowded with domestic holiday-makers enjoying horse racing and sports-car hill climbs and celebrating the Sri Lankan New Year. The cost of accommodation escalates wildly, and Nuwara Eliya becomes a busy, busy party town. For the rest of the year, the economy is based on tea, cool-climate vegetables, and even more tea. Treat yourself to a night at one of Nuwara Eliya's colonial hotels, play a round of golf and a few frames of billiards, and escape into the town's curious combination of heritage and the here-and-now.

The town has an abundance of touts eager to get a commission for a guesthouse or hotel. They'll intercept you on arrival at Nanu Oya train station with fabricated reports of accommodation being closed, cockroach-infested or just plain crooked. Just ignore them.

History

Originally an uninhabited system of forests and meadows in the shadow of Pidurutalagala (aka Mt Pedro, 2524m), Nuwara Eliya became a singularly British creation, having been 'discovered' by colonial officer John Davy in 1819 and chosen as the site for a sanatorium a decade later.

Later the district became known as a spot where 'English' vegetables and fruits, such as lettuce and strawberries, could be successfully grown for consumption by the colonists. Coffee was one of the first crops grown here, but after the island's coffee plantations failed due to disease, the colonists switched to tea. The first tea leaves harvested in Sri Lanka were planted at Loolecondera Estate, in the mountains between Nuwara Eliya and Kandy. As tea experiments proved successful, the town quickly found itself becoming the Hill Country's 'tea capital', a title still proudly borne.

As elsewhere in the Hill Country, most of the labourers on the tea plantations were Tamils, brought from southern India by the British. Although the descendants of these 'Plantation Tamils' (as they are called to distinguish them from Tamils in northern Sri Lanka) have usually stayed out of the ethnic strife endemic to Jaffna and the North, there have been occasional outbreaks of tension between the local Sinhalese and Tamils. The town was partially ransacked during 1983 riots.

At nearby Hagkala, there is a significant Muslim population, but internecine strife is not a problem.

Sights

TOP CHOICE Victoria Park PARK

(adult/child Rs 60/30; dawn-dusk) The lovely Victoria Park at the centre of town is one of the nicest, and best maintained, town parks in South Asia and a stroll around its manicured lawns is a pleasure indeed. The park comes alive with flowers around March to May, and August and September. It's also home to quite a number of hill-country bird species, including the Kashmir flycatcher, Indian pitta and grey tit.

At the far end of the park is a small children's playground and miniature train.

Pedro Tea Estate TEA ESTATE

(admission Rs 100; 8-11am & 2-4pm) To see where your morning cuppa originates, head to the Pedro Tea Estate, about 3.5km east of Nuwara Eliya on the way to Kandapola. Guided tours of the factory, originally built in 1885 and still packed with 19th-century engineering, run for a half-hour. However, you should note that due to the type of tea processed here (a very light tea), processing only takes place at night when it's colder and consequently you're unlikely to see much slicing and drying action taking place. Overlooking the plantations there's a pleasant tea house. Photography inside the factory is

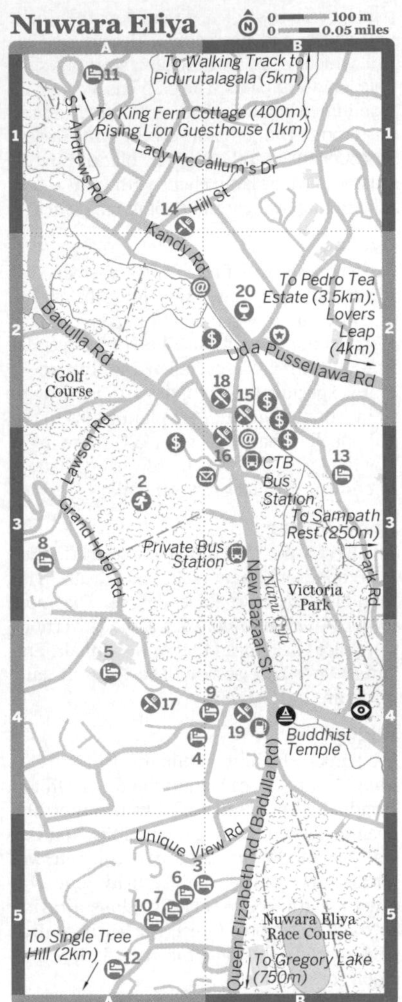

Nuwara Eliya

Sights

1 Victoria Park Ticket Office & Entrance B4

Activities, Courses & Tours

Hill Club ....(see 8)
2 Nuwara Eliya Golf Club A3

Sleeping

3 Alpine Hotel A5
4 Ceybank Rest A4
5 Grand Hotel A4
6 Grosvenor Hotel A5
7 Haddon Hill Hotel A5
8 Hill Club A3
9 Hotel Glendower B4
10 Single Tree Hotel A5
11 St Andrew's Hotel A1
12 Teabush Hotel A5
13 The Trevene B3

Eating

14 Cargills Food City A1
15 Central Market B2
16 De Silva Food Centre B3
Grand Hotel ....(see 5)
17 Grand Indian A4
Hill Club ....(see 8)
King Prawn Restaurant ....(see 9)
18 Milano Restaurant B2
Old Course Restaurant ....(see 11)
19 Restaurant Two B4

Drinking

Lakeview Pub ....(see 3)
20 The Pub B2

forbidden. A three-wheeler from Nuwara Eliya should cost Rs 350 return, including waiting time. Alternatively you could hop on a Ragalla-bound bus (bus 743) from the main bus station in Nuwara Eliya.

Gregory Lake LAKE

(admission Rs 10; ⌚dawn-dusk) The long-neglected Gregory Lake, at the southern end of town, has recently had some love and investment poured into it by the town council, and the newly paved walkways (stroller and wheelchair friendly) that fringe the lake have helped make it much more of a focal point of the town. In addition to a morning walk, you can hire **boats** (paddle boat Rs 1500 per 30min, motorboat Rs 2000 per 20min) or you can trot about the lakeshore on **horseback** (Rs 2500 per hr). There are also picnic tables and a small restaurant and snack bar.

Lovers Leap VIEWPOINT

From the Pedro Tea Estate a very enjoyable 5km (round-trip) walk can be made to the **Lovers Leap**, a spectacular viewpoint and waterfall. From the factory cross the main road and follow the signs to the tea manager's bungalow. From here take the left branch at the fork and continue walking for another quarter of an hour.

Hakgala Gardens GARDENS

(adult/child Rs 1100/550; ⌚8am-5pm) The pleasantly dishevelled Hakgala Gardens, 10km southeast of Nuwara Eliya (and about 200m lower), are a peaceful retreat. Legend has it that Hanuman, the monkey god, was sent by Rama to the Himalayas to find a particular medicinal herb. He forgot which herb he was looking for and decided to bring a chunk of the Himalayas back in his jaw, hoping the herb was growing on it. The gardens grow on a rock called Hakgala, which means 'jaw-rock'.

Unfortunately the Sri Lankan government (which manages the gardens) has quadrupled the price of entry in the past couple of years and made them absolutely not worth the cost of admission.

The Hakgala Gardens are a short bus ride from Nuwara Eliya (take a Welimada-bound bus).

Seetha Amman Temple TEMPLE

On the way to the Hakgala Gardens, near the 83km post, is the colourful Hindu Seetha Amman Temple at Sita Eliya. It's said to mark the spot where Sita was held captive by the demon king Rawana, and where she prayed daily for Rama to come and rescue her. On the rock face across the stream are circular depressions said to be the footprints of Rawana's elephant. Tamil wedding parties make it a point to stop here for *puja* (8am, 1pm, 2pm and 6pm).

Activities

The Grand Hotel, St Andrew's Hotel, the Hill Club and Hotel Glendower all have snooker rooms. Nonguests can play for around Rs 250 per hour.

Golf

Nuwara Eliya Golf Club GOLF

(☎223 2835; 18 holes green fees Rs 4000-5000, 10 holes Rs 3000-4000, caddie fee Rs 560) It didn't take the tea planters long to lay out land for drives and putts in their holiday town, and the club was founded in 1889. Spreading north from Grand Hotel Rd, Nuwara Eliya Golf Club is beautifully kept and has a retinue of languid sleeping dogs guarding more than a few of the greens.

Water hazards – in the form of rivers and streams – come into play on six holes. Temporary members pay Rs 500 per day. Hire golf clubs for Rs 1000 per day and golf shoes for Rs 150 per day. The club expects a certain dress code: for men, shirt with collar and pants or shorts (of a decent length), socks and shoes; and for women, 'decent' golf attire, which we assume means a skirt of a suitable length or pants. The club has a convivial wood-lined bar and a badminton hall and billiard room. Dinner in the **dining room** (mains Rs 450-950) includes classic bland English cuisine, such as lamb chops with mint sauce, and an increasing number of Asian dishes.

Cycling

Fat-tyre fans will find plenty of steep dirt trails radiating into the hills from the outskirts of town. Ask at the Single Tree Hotel about **mountain-bike rental** (per day Rs 1000). A relatively challenging, but undeniably spectacular, 10km day trip is through the verdant blanket of tea plantations to the Labookellie Tea Factory (p155). There are a few hills to climb, but the reward of swooping downhill makes it worthwhile.

Horse Racing

The **Sri Lanka Turf Club** (www.srilankaturfclub.com) sponsors horse racing at the 1875-vintage Nuwara Eliya Race Course. The most important event every year is the Governor's Cup race, held over the April Sinhala and Tamil New Year season. The races usually begin around 10.30am.

Hiking

Sri Lanka's highest mountain, **Pidurutalagala** (2524m), rises behind the town. On top stands the island's main TV transmitter; the peak is out of bounds to the public. You can walk about 4km up as far as a concrete water tank; beyond is a high-security zone. Follow the path from Keena Rd, along a ravine through eucalyptus forest (the town's source of firewood) and into the rare, indigenous cloud forest.

An alternative walk is up **Single Tree Hill** (2100m), which takes about 90 minutes. Walk south on Queen Elizabeth Rd, go up Haddon Hill Rd as far as the communications tower and then take the left-hand path. Guesthouses can supply you with a rudimentary map.

For longer hikes, ask at the Single Tree Hotel. Guided walks in the surrounding hills cost around Rs 1500 to 2000. Staff can also arrange longer camping trips.

If you need clothing for cooler weather or trekking, head to the **market** on New Bazaar St for brand-name outdoor gear from Sri Lankan garment factories at bargain prices.

Tennis

Hill Club TENNIS
(☎2222653; www.hillclubsrilanka.net; per hr Rs 500) There are four clay tennis courts here. The fee includes balls and racquet hire. Try not to lob a ball into the Sri Lankan president's residence next door.

Tours

Most hotels in town can arrange day trips by car or 4WD to Horton Plains National Park (p163). The standard price for up to five passengers is Rs 3500 (excluding park fees). One of the better 4WD tours organised by a cheap hotel is based at Single Tree Hotel. It's about an hour's drive to the park gates.

Single Tree can also arrange trips to the Pedro Tea Estate and Lovers Leap (Rs 1500). For the ultimate waterfall experience, join its waterfall day trip (per van Rs 3500) that takes in five different cascades and the Labookellie Tea Factory.

Sleeping

Nuwara Eliya's budget hotels can be on the dreary side, so it's worth being a little choosy where you stay. There's a good range of colonial-style places, but you will pay more for a heritage ambience. Unlike other parts of Sri Lanka, there isn't a good range of backpacker-oriented guesthouses. Two exceptions are the Single Tree Hotel and the excellent King Fern Cottage.

You'll need blankets to keep warm at night at almost any time of year. A few hotels will light a fire in the communal areas on cold nights – you won't find a toastier way to keep warm on drizzly Nuwara Eliya night.

During the 'season', around Sri Lankan New Year in April, rooms are three to five times their normal price. Prices also increase during long-weekend holidays and in August, when package tours descend from abroad.

TOP CHOICE **St Andrew's Hotel** HERITAGE HOTEL **$$$**
(☎222 3031; www.jetwinghotels.com; 10 St Andrew's Dr; r incl breakfast from US$130; @🛜) North of town on a beautifully groomed rise overlooking the golf course, this Georgian manor house was once a planters' club. Today it's far and away the most luxurious, and carefully renovated, of the colonial-style hotels. The rooms are a melange of the old and the new and the communal areas feature such gems as a graffiti-stained cocktail bar (happy hour is 7pm to 8pm), a library filled with dusty books and a roaring log fire, a billiards room and a superb restaurant, the Old Course Restaurant. There's an inhouse naturalist who leads excellent guided nature walks in and around the hotel grounds. Talking of which, the gardens, with their terraced lawns and white cast-iron furniture, seem custom designed for a cup of afternoon tea.

At nearby Ambewella, the same people also run **Warwick Gardens** (r incl breakfast from US$290), a beautifully restored planter's house with five bedrooms that redefine the words 'colonial glamour'.

TOP CHOICE **The Trevene** HISTORIC HOTEL **$$**
(☎222 2767; www.hoteltrevenenuwaraeliya.com; 17 Park Rd; s/d incl breakfast Rs 3500/4500; @🛜) Open the door of this beautiful colonial villa and you'll discover that it contains an excellent guesthouse. The rooms are filled with so much old-fashioned charm you'll struggle to fit yourself into them. That's not a huge problem though, because there's plenty of cosy hideaways in the communal areas where you can curl up with a book on a wet afternoon or, if it's sunny, head out into the gardens to enjoy the view. Sydney, the manager, is a jolly fellow.

King Fern Cottage GUESTHOUSE **$$**
(☎490 0503; nicetime@kingfern.com; 203/1A St Andrews Dr; s/d Rs 1100/1320; ⏲Nov-May; @🛜) Hands down Nuwara Eliya's funkiest place to stay, King Fern combines huge handmade beds, warm-as-toast bedspreads and a laid-back ambience that sometimes sees the owner breaking out his drums for an after-dark, fireside session. It's all wrapped up in a timber pavilion beside a bubbling stream and though it might sound a little rustic it's actually anything but, with immaculate and artistic rooms. Owner Nishantha is a qualified walking guide and will pick you up from Nanu Oya train station if you phone ahead.

Hotel Glendower HISTORIC HOTEL **$$$**
(☎222 2501; 5 Grand Hotel Rd; s/d incl breakfast from Rs 8450/9000; @🛜) This rambling colonial building has period-style rooms, though check a few first as some are better than others. If you get a good one then it's arguably the best-value heritage property in town. As well as bags of charm there's a pretty garden (complete with croquet set); a cosy bar, lined with bottles of spirits, that's well

worth propping up; and a billiards room with a full-size table. The attached King Prawn Restaurant does good Chinese.

Grosvenor Hotel HISTORIC HOTEL **$$**
(☎222 2307; 6 Haddon Hill Rd; s/d incl breakfast Rs 2750/3850) It's a century since it did service as the residence of the colonial governor, and the Grosvenor has expansive hallways, spacious rooms and period furniture that make it one of Nuwara Eliya's best-value colonial options. Thoroughly modern skylights illuminate the old library – a perfect spot to catch up on your travel diary. It's a good idea to take a look at a few rooms, as some were suffering badly from damp during our last visit.

Single Tree Hotel GUESTHOUSE **$$**
(☎222 3009; singletreehtl@sltnet.lk; 178 Haddon Hill Rd; s Rs 2000-2500, d Rs 2500-3500; @ 📶) The most popular backpacker guesthouse in town has a main building where the rooms have bright colours and loads of warm timber trim. The rooms in the annex building are a little darker and less inviting but still pretty good. The switched-on owners have a whole raft of suggestions for trekking, tours and transport. Some readers who've reserved in advance have complained that they haven't always got what they were promised.

Ceybank Rest HISTORIC HOTEL **$$**
(☎222 3855; s/d incl breakfast Rs 3300/5900; 📶) Recently taken over by the Bank of Ceylon (of all people), this was once a British governor's mansion, and has huge rooms – and even bigger suites – that are from the time when smart travellers journeyed with at least three steamer trunks. Teak furniture and a fine old bar make time travel to the 19th century very easy. It's a creaky old place though, so don't blame us if it inspires a few vivid dreams.

Teabush Hotel HISTORIC HOTEL **$$$**
(☎222 2345; 29 Haddon Hill Rd; s/d Rs 8700/10,060; @) Lots of antique furniture peppers this 140-year-old tea planter's bungalow. The heritage charm of the shared, public areas is tempered by slightly more prosaic rooms, but the restaurant views are superb. The grassy rooftop lawn – yes, you read that right – is the perfect spot for sundowners. Hiking and birdwatching excursions can be arranged with the resident naturalist.

Hill Club HERITAGE HOTEL **$$$**
(☎222 2653; www.hillclubsrilanka.net; 29 Grand Hotel Rd; r incl breakfast from Rs 12,500; @ 📶) Commanding its location with elegance and gravitas, the stone-clad Hill Club is the most profound evidence of Nuwara Eliya's colonial past. Up until 1970 it was reserved for British males, and one of its bars remained resolutely 'men only' until a few years ago. It's now open to Sri Lankans and women, and members retain reciprocal rights with London clubs. Temporary members (Rs 100 per day) are welcomed with open arms to ease the cash flow. Tennis courts are available to guests and nonguests, and the lawns and gardens are immaculate. The suites are spacious, but the regular rooms are small and have substandard furnishings given the price (head to the St Andrew's for better-value colonial accommodation). Dinner at the Hill Club is a thoroughly retro and unique experience. See the boxed text, p162.

Grand Hotel HERITAGE HOTEL **$$$**
(☎222 2881; www.tangerinehotels.com; Grand Hotel Rd; s/d incl breakfast US$176/189; ❄ @ 📶) Right by the golf course, this vast mock-Tudor edifice has immaculate lawns, a reading lounge and a wood-panelled billiards room. The rooms are spacious and comfortable, but if it all feels a bit plastic and forced that's because it is – the original building was merely a bungalow. It's very popular with visitors from the Middle East and India.

Sampath Rest GUESTHOUSE **$$**
(☎223 4690; 8A Wedderburn Rd; s/d incl breakfast Rs 2500-3500; @) This is an arresting little modern guesthouse. The dining room is full of wedding-day furnishings and the clean, airy rooms are painted a snotty green (don't worry, it's actually very pleasant!). It's run by a very friendly family and is well cared for.

Alpine Hotel HOTEL **$$$**
(☎222 3500; www.alpineecotravels.com; 4 Haddon Hill Rd; s/d incl breakfast Rs 6600/8250; ❄ @ 📶) The exterior of this inn is all twee wood panelling and glass and looks very impressive. The 25 rooms are decent enough but some can be decidedly musty. There's a large restaurant and pub with snooker and darts. Mountain bikes can be hired for Rs 1000 per day.

Rising Lion Guesthouse HOTEL **$$**
(☎222 2083; www.risinglionhotel.com; 3 Sri Piyatissapura; r Rs 2000-3000; @) Perched atop St Andrews Rd, and possibly the highest hotel in the land, this place has superb misty-

mountain vistas and an eclectic decor combining 1970s retro and numerous buffalo heads. It's all enough to make you forget you're in a tropical country. It's worth paying extra for a balcony with views.

Haddon Hill Hotel GUESTHOUSE $
(☎490 3675; 8B Haddon Hill Rd; r Rs 2000) It's back to basics here with simple rooms and the opportunity to use the shared kitchen. The thick blankets on the beds and the toe-warming carpets make it a cosy enough place for a fair price.

Eating & Drinking

For lunch there are plenty of good, cheap options in town, but for dinner you'll probably want to eat at your guesthouse or at one of the ritzier hotel eateries. Pubs open around 4pm but seldom serve after midnight.

Self-caterers should head for the central market for fresh produce and to **Cargills Food City** (Kandy Rd) for canned goods.

TOP CHOICE **The Old Course Restaurant** INTERNATIONAL $$$
(☎222 3031; 10 St Andrew's Dr; 4-course menu Rs 1800, mains Rs 1000-1600; ⊙noon-2.30pm & 6-10pm) The Old Course Restaurant, inside the St Andrew's Hotel, channels the culinary heritage of the British Empire with the Asian flavours of today, and the result is totally modern fusion food. The setting and service are superb and they have the largest wine cellar in Sri Lanka (but a bottle of wine is far from cheap with some bottles going for an eye-watering US$500). Although it's a formal restaurant there are none of the ridiculous dress codes of some of the town's other restaurants and the food is of a genuinely high standard.

TOP CHOICE **Grand Indian** INDIAN $$
(Grand Hotel Rd; mains Rs 400-600; ⊙11am-11pm) In front of the Grand Hotel, the surroundings are a bit cafeteria-like, but the food and the service here are top-notch – everyone is a fan of the thalis. Unlike a few other places around town, there's normally an energetic buzz about the place and in the evening you might have to wait for a table. Around the back is a decent bakery.

Hill Club WESTERN $$$
(☎222 2653; 29 Grand Hotel Rd; set menu Rs 1800; ⊙6-11pm) Dinner at the Hill Club is an event in itself. The five-course set menu focuses on hearty meals like roast beef, served, with all the trimmings, promptly at 8pm. The whole thing is carried off with faded colonial panache: gloved waiters, candles and linen tablecloths and serviettes. For the formal dining room, men must wear a tie and jacket – there is a very small selection on hand, but they sometimes run out – or Sri Lankan national dress. Women must also be suitably attired in a dress or dress slacks. The dress code at the Hill Club's à la carte, casual restaurant is not so strict. If you're not staying the night here, you'll have to pay a Rs 100 temporary joining fee. The food doesn't live up to everyone's expectations, especially with such a relatively high price tag, but it's still a great experience (see the boxed text p162). Come along an hour or so before dinner for a drink in the Hill Club's bars. It was only a few years ago that the 'Casual Bar' was resolutely enforced as 'men only'. In a new millennium all (well, OK, most) gender variations are now welcome, but we have heard reports that Sri Lankans of a certain 'class' are not always allowed.

Grand Hotel INTERNATIONAL $$$
(☎222 2881; Grand Hotel Rd; dinner menu Rs 2050) Five-course Asian and Western dinners are dished up by spiffy waiters serenaded by a grand piano, but like the hotel itself it all feels a bit over the top and fake. Smart, formal dress only.

King Prawn Restaurant CHINESE $$
(Hotel Glendower, 5 Grand Hotel Rd; mains Rs 400-600; ⊙noon-2pm & 6-10pm) Chinese is the overriding culinary influence here, all delivered in a dining room transplanted from 1930s England. Thai flavours also linger in some of the dishes, and there's a good array of seafood on offer. You're a few miles inland here, so expect to pay a hefty premium. Service is rather stiff and formal, but very prompt.

Milano Restaurant SRI LANKAN $
(94 New Bazaar St; mains Rs 180-380) This is a slightly classier version of the next-door De Silva Food Centre, with friendly service and a reliable menu of Sri Lankan, Western and Chinese dishes. Treat yourself to some sweet baked goodies and a coffee to set you up for the rest of the afternoon.

De Silva Food Centre SRI LANKAN $
(90 New Bazaar St; mains Rs 180-250) This inexpensive eatery located along a busy main street serves Sri Lankan and Chinese fare. A few vegetarian *rotti* make a good lunchtime snack.

TRAVELLING THROUGH TIME AT THE HILL CLUB *BRETT ATKINSON*

Built in 1885 by a homesick British coffee baron as a refuge from the heat of the Sri Lankan coast, the Hill Club is a melancholy monument to the British Empire's glory days. In the library, the only sound is the lonely tick...tick...ticking of a grandfather clock. Churchill's *History of the Second World War* sits under paintings of the royal family.

The hottest ticket in town is dinner in the shabbily genteel dining room. The club's arcane dress code is prescribed at reception. 'Dress is informal except from 7.00pm onwards when Gentlemen shall wear Tie and Jacket and Ladies shall wear suitable attire befitting the attire of Gentlemen. Sri Lankan National Dress is of course permitted.'

Feeling confident that my dusty travelling gear won't make the grade as Sri Lankan National Dress, I venture into a wardrobe that time forgot and throw together a snappy ensemble worthy of old-school silver-service dining. The selection is at least a generation old: I team a wide-lapelled crimplene jacket with a tie that should really come with a volume knob. Give me some well-trimmed sideboards and a Ford Capri, and I'd be a doppelgänger for Bodie or Doyle from the 1970s Brit cop show *The Professionals*.

Dinner goes back even further than the decade that taste forgot. The typed menu promises (apparently canned) chicken and sweetcorn soup, beef Holstien (sic), or roast mutton (actually goat) with mint sauce. Lyonnaise potato and leeks *au gratin* add a defiant, not to say desperate, international flavour. Attentive waiters drift around, perhaps wondering why so many of them have been rostered on. Orange mousse for dessert provides a minor highlight before I demolish the waiters with a few frames in the billiard room. Outside, it's the 21st century, but at this stage of the night, I'm really not sure.

Restaurant Two SRI LANKAN $

(Grand Hotel Rd; mains Rs 150-250) Cheap, simple semi-open-air place with a quiet setting next to the golf course. The food here can be fiery – you've been warned!

The Pub BAR $

(20 Kandy Rd; ⏲4pm-late) The cheapest place to drink in town, but not recommended for solo female travellers.

Lakeview Pub BAR $

(Alpine Hotel, 4 Haddon Hill Rd; ⏲4pm-late) Lots of moody, dark timber, billiards, darts and a lakeview terrace make this a popular spot.

ℹ Information

All the banks listed here have ATMs and exchange facilities.

Bank of Ceylon (Lawson Rd)

Commercial Bank (Park Rd)

Hatton National Bank (Badulla Rd)

Kavinro Internet Cafe (Kandy Rd; per hr Rs 60; ⏲8.30am-7pm) Reasonable connections.

People's Bank (Park Rd)

Post office (Badulla Rd)

Seylan Bank (Park Rd)

ℹ Getting There & Away

Air

Sri Lankan Air Taxi (www.srilankan.lk/airtaxi) runs scheduled flights to and from Colombo on Monday and Saturday.

Bus

The government CTB bus stand is by the main roundabout in the town centre and the private bus stand is just up the road. The trip from Kandy takes about four hours and costs between Rs 88 and Rs 190 depending on bus type. It's a spectacular climb. Buses leave every 30 minutes to an hour. There are also buses to/from the following:

Colombo normal Rs 190, intercity express Rs 380, six hours

Haputale Rs 85, 2½ hours

Matara intercity express Rs 360, seven to eight hours, departures between 7am and 9.40am

Welimada Rs 46, one hour

Train

Nuwara Eliya is served by the Nanu Oya train station, 9km along the road towards Hatton and Colombo. Buses meet the main trains (Rs 20 to Nuwara Eliya), so don't get sucked in by touts. Most Nuwara Eliya accommodation will pick you up – often for free – if you have already booked. A taxi from the station is around Rs 400.

Badulla 2nd/3rd class Rs 140/80

Bandarawela Rs 90/50
Colombo Rs 450/270
Ella Rs 110/60
Haputale Rs 80/40
Hatton Rs 60/30
Kandy Rs 160/90

A seat in the 1st-class observation carriage is a set Rs 750 no matter where you get on or off. The limited number of seats in this class are in high demand so try to book ahead. Not all trains have a 1st-class carriage.

Horton Plains National Park & World's End

Horton Plains (adult/child US$15/8, car Rs 125, jeep Rs 250, service charge per group US$8, VAT 12%) is a beautiful, silent, strange world with some excellent hikes in the shadows of Sri Lanka's second- and third-highest mountains, Kirigalpotta (2395m) and Totapola (2359m). The 'plains' themselves form an undulating plateau over 2000m high, covered by wild grasslands and interspersed with patches of thick forest, rocky outcrops, filigree waterfalls and misty lakes. The surprising diversity of the landscape is matched by the wide variety of wildlife.

The plateau comes to a sudden end at World's End, a stunning escarpment that plunges 880m. Unless you get there early the view from World's End is often obscured by mist, particularly during the rainy season from April to September. The early morning (between 6am and 10am) is the best time to visit, before the clouds roll in. That's when you'll spy toy-town tea plantation villages in the valley below, and an unencumbered view south towards the coast. In the evening and early morning you'll need long trousers and a sweater, but the plains warm up quickly, so take a hat for sun protection. The weather is clearest January to March.

Sights & Activities

World's End VIEWPOINT

This is the only national park in Sri Lanka where visitors are permitted to walk on their own (on designated trails only). The walk to World's End is 4km, but the trail loops back to Baker's Falls (2km) and continues back to the entrance (another 3.5km). The round trip is 9.5km and takes a leisurely three hours. Note that around 9am to 10am the mist usually comes down. All you can expect to see from World's End after this time is a swirling white wall. If you aim for a 5.30am to 6am departure from Nuwara Eliya or Haputale and get to World's End around 7am, you'll have a good chance of spectacular views.

Try to avoid doing this walk on Sundays and public holidays, when it can get crowded. And despite the signs, weekend groups of young Sri Lankan guys will do their utmost to make noise and inadvertently scare away the wildlife.

Guides at the national park office expect about Rs 750. There's no set fee for volunteer guides, but expect to donate a similar amount. Some guides are well informed on the area's flora and fauna, and solo women travellers may want to consider hiring one for safety's sake. One guide, who is genuinely enthusiastic about the park and unusually knowledgeable on the area's fauna and flora, is **Mr Nimal Herath** (☎077 618 9842; hrthnimal@gmail.com). He normally works as a guide/jeep driver through the Single Tree Hotel (p160) in Nuwara Eliya, but is available on a freelance basis as well.

Wear strong and comfortable walking shoes, a hat and sunglasses. Bring sunscreen, and food and water, as the eatery at the Farr Inn is expensive. Ask your guesthouse to prepare a breakfast package for you, and reward yourself with an alfresco brekkie once you reach World's End. The weather can change very quickly on the plains – one minute it can be sunny and clear, the next chilly and misty. Bring a few extra layers of warm clothing (it's very cold up here at 7am). It is forbidden to leave the paths. There are toilets at Farr Inn.

Note that there are no safety rails around World's End and there have been a couple of accidents where people have fallen to their deaths. If you have young children with you keep a very firm grip on them as you approach the cliff edge!

Although the main focus of the park is on World's End don't underestimate the joy of the walk across the grassland plains. It's also possible to do a shorter (3km), and less rewarding, walk to what has been dubbed Poor Man's World's End; the trail is just beyond the park entrance gate and normal park fees apply.

Wildlife WILDLIFE

As an important watershed and catchment for several year-round rivers and streams, the Horton Plains hosts a wide range of wildlife. The last few elephants departed the area in the first half of the 20th century, but there are still a few leopards, and sambar deer and wild boar are seen feeding in meadows at dawn and dusk. The shaggy bear monkey (or purple-faced langur) is sometimes seen in the forest on the Ohiya road, and occasionally in the woods around World's End (listen for a wheezy grunt). You may also come across the endemic toque macaque.

The area is popular with birdwatchers. Endemic species include the yellow-eared bulbul, the fantailed warbler, the ashy-headed babbler, the Ceylon hill white-eye, the Ceylon blackbird, the Ceylon white-eyed arrenga, the dusky-blue flycatcher and the Ceylon blue magpie. Birds of prey include the mountain hawk eagle.

A tufty grass called *Crosypogon* covers the grasslands, while marshy areas are home to copious bog moss (sphagnum). The umbrella-shaped, white-blossomed keena *(Calophyllum)* stand as the main canopy over montane forest areas. The stunted trees and shrubs are draped in lichen and mosses. Another notable species is *Rhododendron zelanicum,* which has blood-red blossoms. The poignant purple-leafed *Strobilanthes* blossoms once after five years, and then dies.

Farr Inn LANDMARK

A local landmark, Farr Inn was a hunting lodge for high-ranking British colonial officials, but now incorporates a restaurant and visitor centre with displays on the flora, fauna and geology of the park. A small souvenir stand nearby has books on the park's flora and fauna.

Tours

Almost every guesthouse in Nuwara Eliya and Haputale operates trips to Horton Plains and World's End. Expect to pay around Rs 3500 per van.

Sleeping & Eating

There are two basic Department of Wildlife Conservation bungalows where you can stay: Giniheriya Lodge and Mahaeliya Lodge. The bungalows have 10 beds each, and the charge for foreigners is US$16.80 per day plus park entry fees, Rs 75 per person for linen hire and a US$35 per group service charge. You must bring all of your own dry rations and kerosene. Dorm beds are also available for US$8 plus all the other charges listed above. The lodges open up only when people are staying, and you must book ahead through the **Department of Wildlife Conservation** (011-256 0380; 382 New Kandy Rd, Malambe) in Colombo.

Information

National Park Office (6am-6.30pm) Near Farr Inn, this is where you buy entrance tickets. Last tickets are sold at 4pm.

Getting There & Away

It takes about 1½ hours to get from Haputale to Farr Inn by road (Rs 3500 return). From Ohiya the road rises in twists and turns through forest before emerging on the open plains. Keep your eyes peeled for monkeys.

You can also drive to Farr Inn from Nuwara Eliya, a trip taking about an hour one way (around Rs 3500 return by van). This is the more popular access route. If taking a tour from Nuwara Eliya you can ask to be dropped afterwards at Pattipola train station in order to catch the afternoon train to Haputale and Ella (1.30pm).

SIR THOMAS LIPTON – ONE VERY CANNY SCOTSMAN

His name lives on in the hot-beverage aisle of your local supermarket, but Sir Thomas Lipton was a major success in business even before he became the biggest player in the global tea industry.

From 1870 to 1888 he grew his parents' single grocery shop in Glasgow to a nationwide chain of 300 stores. Recognising the potential of tea, he cannily bypassed the traditional wholesale markets of London, and went straight to the source by purchasing his own tea plantations in Sri Lanka. His network of 300 stores provided him with guaranteed distribution to sell tea at lower prices to an uptapped working-class market. It also inspired the winning advertising slogan, 'Direct from the tea gardens to the tea pot'.

Lipton's planet-spanning ambition wasn't only limited to trade. In 1909 he donated the Thomas Lipton Trophy for an international football competition 21 years before the first World Cup, and he was tireless in his (unsuccessful) attempts to win yachting's America's Cup. His well-publicised interest in the two sports ensured his brand became a household name on both sides of the Atlantic.

Taxi

A taxi from the Ohiya train station to/from Farr Inn (40 minutes one way) should cost about Rs 2000 return, including waiting time.

Train & Foot

You can walk to World's End, but it's a 30km round trip from Ohiya with some very steep ascents. Theoretically it would be possible to catch a night train to Ohiya and start the walk in the early hours, but as the trains are often delayed, you risk walking 15km up to World's End only to find the clouds have rolled in. It's better to arrive in Ohiya the day before if you really want to do the walk. The walk from Ohiya to Farr Inn is 11.2km, or 2½ to 3½ hours, along the road – you'll need a torch if you do it at night. Then you've got another 1½ hours to World's End. You'll need about two hours for the walk back down towards Ohiya. The trip up the main road has great views. A faster option is to catch a three-wheeler (Rs 2000) from Ohiya train station up to Farr Inn and the trailhead.

Keen walkers can also strike out for Farr Inn from Pattipola, the nearest train station to the park from Nuwara Eliya (a walk of about 10km along a 4WD track), or from Bambarakanda Falls, about four hours downhill from the plains (p165). To make this a longer two-day hike, start from Haputale.

Belihul Oya

☎045

Belihul Oya is a pretty hillside region worth passing through on your way to or from the Hill Country – it's 35km from Haputale and 57km from Ratnapura. From here you can walk up to Horton Plains, a seriously strenuous undertaking.

About 14km towards Haputale, near Kalupahana, are the **Bambarakanda Falls**. Ask the bus driver to let you off at Kalupahana Junction. From the main road it's another Rs 350 by three-wheeler up a barely-there track.

At 240m, the Bambarakanda Falls are the highest in Sri Lanka. March and April are the best months for viewing the falls, but any visit after heavy rainfall should be worthwhile. At other times the water may be reduced to a disappointing trickle. From near the falls the challenging four-hour trail runs to Horton Plains.

Bambarakanda Holiday Resort GUESTHOUSE **$**

(☎057-357 5699; www.bambarakanda.com; r half board Rs 1900) A few hundred metres before the falls is this homey and rustic resort. If you're really looking to get off the map for a few days, here's your chance. The rooms are very basic and a bit dingy, but with a setting close to the falls and a view like this that will hardly matter because you'll be outside the whole time enjoying nature in all her glory. Ideally you'll need your own transport to get here.

River Garden Resort RESORT **$$**

(☎228 0222; rivergardenbeli@gmail.com; chalets s/d US$48/60, safari tents per person incl full board US$50) Has three chalets with spotless rooms set in a shady terraced garden above a stream and comfortable 'safari' tents (permanent tents with beds) set in a shady area below the restaurant. There's also an 'eco lodge', 9km up the road, sleeping six (US$190). River Garden Resort can arrange multiday adventure programs incorporating canoeing, trekking, mountain biking, rock climbing and caving.

Haputale

☎057 / POP 5238 / ELEV 1580M

Perched at the southern edge of the Hill Country, the largely Tamil town of Haputale clings to a long, narrow mountain ridge with the land falling away steeply on both sides. On a clear day you can view the south coast from this ridge, and at night the Hambantota lighthouse pulses in the distance. On a not-so-clear day, great swaths of mist cling magnetically to the hillsides. Either way, it's a spectacular part of the country.

The town centre itself is a dusty ribbon of traffic, three-wheelers and small-scale commerce. But take a short walk and you'll be rewarded with extraordinary views. The railway hugs one side of the ridge in a minor victory for 19th-century engineering.

Haputale now mainly shows the influence of the Sinhalese and Tamil cultures, but the legacy of the British tea planters also lives on. Tea estates blanket the hillsides, punctuated by graceful planters' bungalows, all enveloped in a damp and heavy climate that must have made the British settlers feel right at home. The pretty Anglican church (St Andrew's) on the Bandarawela road has a graveyard filled with poignant memories of earlier times.

In recent years Haputale's popularity with tourists seems to have mysteriously diminished, but the town has an array of good, cheap accommodation and makes an excellent base for visiting Horton Plains National Park, exploring other places in the area or just taking pleasant walks in cool mountain air. Guesthouses arrange vans and 4WDs to Horton Plains for Rs 3500.

See the privately run website www.haputale.de for more information.

Sights

TOP CHOICE Dambatenne Tea Factory TEA ESTATE

(admission Rs 200; 8am-6pm daily Oct-Jul, Tue-Sat Aug-Sep) A few tea factories in this area are happy to have visitors. The most popular, Dambatenne, was built in 1890 by Sir Thomas Lipton, one of the most famous figures in tea history (see boxed text, p164). The tour through the works is an education on the processes involved in the fermentation, rolling, drying, cutting, sieving and grading of tea. The tea-factory tour here is probably the most comprehensive around, but sadly there's no opportunity for a cuppa afterwards. For further details about tea production, see p288.

Although it's 11km from Haputale, the factory is easily accessible. A bus for the estate workers goes from the bus station for Bandarawela to the factory and back again about every 25 minutes (bus *326*; Rs 23). A three-wheeler there and back costs about Rs 500.

TOP CHOICE Adisham Monastery MONASTERY

(admission Rs 100; 9am-12.30pm & 1.30-4.30pm Sat & Sun, poya days & school holidays) This beautifully calm Benedictine monastery is about 3km west of Haputale. Follow Temple Rd along the ridge until you reach the sign at the Adisham turnoff. The elegant stone-block monastery once belonged to tea planter Sir Thomas Lester Villiers. To recreate his English lifestyle, he developed some English country-cottage gardens and lawns amid the tropical surroundings and even had a Daimler car for transport, complete with an English chauffeur. Adisham is one of only 18 monasteries in the world belonging to the Sylvestrine Congregation, a suborder of the Benedictine fraternity founded in the 13th century. Inside, visitors are allowed to see the living room and library, which is filled from floor to ceiling with dusty, scholarly tomes on the lives of various British kings and colonial figures – the *Love Affairs of Mary Queen of Scots* was the raciest book we could find.

There's a small shop selling produce from the monastery's lovely gardens and orchards. Buy some real strawberry jam or wild guava jelly to enliven your next guesthouse breakfast.

A taxi should cost Rs 500 return, including waiting time. Before you reach Adisham the road passes through **Tangamalai**, a bird sanctuary and nature reserve, but there are no facilities.

Diyaluma Falls WATERFALL

Heading towards Wellawaya you'll pass the 171m-high Diyaluma Falls, Sri Lanka's third-highest waterfall, just 5km beyond the town of Koslanda. Cascading down an escarpment of the Koslanda Plateau, the stream is fairly small, but it quickly escalates after a downpour. By bus, take a Wellawaya service from Haputale and get off at Diyaluma (1¼ hours). The falls leap over a cliff face and fall in one clear drop to a pool below.

Climb up to some beautiful pools – ideal for swimming – and a series of minifalls at the top of the main fall. Walk about 500m down the road from the bottom of the falls and take the estate track that turns sharply back up to the left. From there it's about 20 minutes' walk to a small rubber factory, where you strike off uphill to the left. The track is very indistinct, although there are some white arrows on the rocks. Ask the locals to make sure you're going the right way. At the top the path forks: the right branch (more distinct) leads to the pools above the main falls, the left fork to the top of the main falls.

Other Attractions

For more spectacular views – weather permitting – take the train to **Idalgashinna**, 8km west of Haputale. Walk back beside the train tracks, enjoying a spectacular view with the terrain falling away on both sides.

Near the Dambatenne tea factory, the **Lipton's Seat** lookout rivals the views from World's End (and it's free). The Scottish tea baron Sir Thomas Lipton used to survey his burgeoning empire from here. Take the signed narrow paved road from the tea factory and climb about 7km through lush tea plantations to the lookout. From the tea factory the ascent should take about 2½ hours. The earliest bus leaves Haputale at 6.30am. Look forward to the company of Tamil tea pickers going off to work as you walk uphill to Lipton's Seat.

Some visitors hike along the train lines from Haputale to **Pattipola** (14km, an all-day hike), the highest train station in Sri Lanka. From Pattipola you can continue via foot or taxi to Ohiya train station, and from there to the Horton Plains.

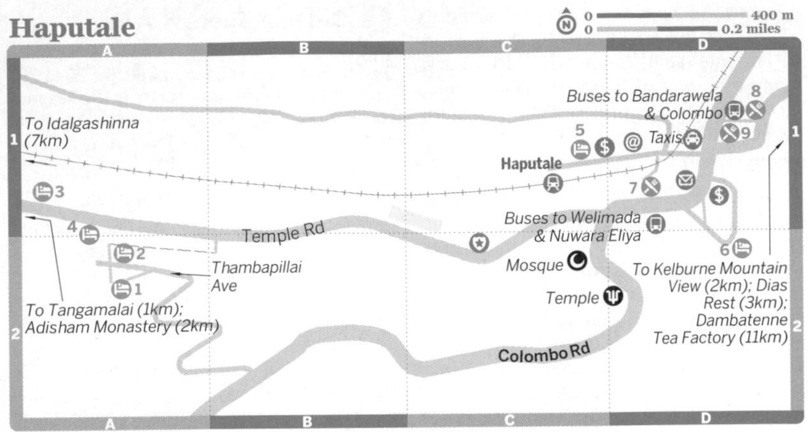

Sleeping

Sri Lak View Holiday Inn HOTEL $
(☎226 8125; www.srilakviewholidayinn.com; Sherwood Rd; s/d from Rs 900/1300; @) Haputale's best place to stay combines 16 spotless modern rooms with views that stretch a few hundred kilometres. If the weather's good, have an end-of-day beer on the grassy deck. Otherwise park yourself in the cosy restaurant. Multiple reader recommendations mean they must be doing something right.

Amarasinghe Guest House HOMESTAY $
(☎226 8175; Thambapillai Ave; r Rs 1500) With bright colours and a tranquil location, this is one of Haputale's longest-running and best guesthouses. There are eight simple rooms – most with balconies – and a comfortable downstairs restaurant. The surrounding garden is a riot of tropical vegetation and colourful flowers (and check out that vegetable garden!). Mr Amarasinghe will pick you up from the train station at no charge. If you walk, follow the directions to Bawa Guest House but continue on down the flight of steps, turn left and it's 10m away.

Olympus Plaza Hotel HOTEL $$
(☎226 8544; www.olympusplazahotel.com; Temple Rd; s/d incl breakfast Rs 4350/6000; @ wi-fi) This multistorey place brings a snazzy business-hotel feel to sleepy Haputale, and its modern rooms with abstract art on the walls, thick mattresses, hot-water showers and stellar views (from most rooms) offer good value if you're hanging out for a few away-from-home comforts. On weekends it's a popular wedding venue.

Haputale

Sleeping

1	Amarasinghe Guest House	A2
2	Bawa Guest House	A2
3	Hyacinth Cottage	A1
4	Olympus Plaza Hotel	A1
5	Royal Top Rest Inn	C1
6	Sri Lak View Holiday Inn	D2

Eating

7	Lanka Tea Centre	D1
8	Risara Bakers	D1
9	Sri Vani Vilas Hotel	D1

Kelburne Mountain View BOUTIQUE HOTEL $$$
(☎226 8029; www.kelburnemountainview.com; bungalows Rs 15,995) About 2km east of Haputale train station, Kelburne is a wonderful spot to relax for a few days, but only if you're in a group (each bungalow sleeps several people) otherwise you're paying a lot for what are actually fairly normal rooms. What does make the property stand out are the beautiful flower gardens and stunning views. Meals are also available from a resident cook. Advance bookings are essential.

Royal Top Rest Inn HOTEL $
(☎226 8178; 22 Station Rd; s Rs 750-1100, d Rs 850-1300) A short walk from the train station, this is a friendly place with pleasant views, a cheerfully gaudy living room and simple but clean rooms. There's a restaurant, a small outdoor area and a sunny shared balcony.

Hyacinth Cottage
HOMESTAY $

(☎226 8283; Temple Rd; r Rs 1000) This is a basic but cute family house with seven guest rooms that come with hot-water bathrooms. There's a small terrace to relax on and enjoy the views off over the escarpment.

Dias Rest
GUESTHOUSE $

(White Monkey; ☎568 1027; Thotulagala; r & cottage Rs 1200) Surrounded by a tea plantation and fruit trees 3km east of the train station, Dias Rest has a local atmosphere and two quite chilly double rooms and a family cottage – all with superb views that rival that of World's End on a clear day. The owner is an experienced guide and can advise on interesting local treks whatever the weather. A three-wheeler from the train station is around Rs 250.

Bawa Guest House
HOMESTAY $

(☎072 915 7616; 32 Thambapillai Ave; r from Rs 800) Housed in a sky-blue and spearmint-green villa, Bawa Guest House is now in its fourth decade of operation. After 30 years the friendly family has perfected their combination of homey, kitsch decor and a warm welcome. If you're arriving at the Bawa Guest House by foot, follow Temple Rd until you see a yellow Bawa Guest House sign to the south, just off the side of the road. Go down the first flight of stairs and head along the path for about 250m.

Eating

You're best off eating in your guesthouse, but there are a number of OK places for short eats, dosas (paper-thin pancakes), *rotti*, and rice and curry, including the **Lanka Tea Centre** (Temple Rd), opposite the Welimada and Nuwara Eliya bus stand, and the **Sri Vani Vilas Hotel** (Dambatenne Rd), near the Bandarawela bus stand.

Head to **Risara Bakers** for the town's best samosas. Pop in there when you get back from World's End in the early afternoon. A fresh batch of still-warm baked goodies usually appears around 2pm.

Information

Haputale has a **Bank of Ceylon** (Station Rd) and **People's Bank** (Colombo Rd), both with exchange facilities and ATMs. The post office is in the centre of town. **Website Link** (No 3 UC Complex, Station Rd) has internet (per hour Rs 60), Skype and international calling, and CD photo burning.

Getting There & Away

Bus

Destinations include Bandarawela (Rs 25 to 30 depending on route, one hour), Ella (Rs 72, one hour), Nuwara Eliya (Rs 80, 3½ hours, 8am and 2pm) and Tangalla (Rs 180, four hours).

Train

Haputale is on the Colombo–Badulla line, so you can travel directly by train to and from Kandy or Nanu Oya (for Nuwara Eliya). As always a 1st-class observation ticket is a set Rs 750 no matter where along the route you get off.

Bandarawela 2nd/3rd class Rs 20/15, 30 minutes

Colombo Rs 330/180, 8½ to nine hours

Ella Rs 50/25, one hour

Kandy Rs 210/115, 5½ hours

Nanu Oya Rs 80/40, 1½ hours

Ohiya Rs 30/20, 40 minutes

Bandarawela

☎057 / POP 7103 / ELEV 1230M

Bandarawela, 10km north of Haputale but noticeably warmer, is a busy market town that makes a good base for exploring the surrounding area. Due to its agreeable climate, it's a popular area to retire to. Each Sunday morning the town has a lively market. Otherwise Bandarawela has little to attract tourists except a fine old hotel dripping in colonial charm. It's also a good transport hub if you're heading east or further into the Hill Country.

Sights & Activities

Dowa Temple
TEMPLE

About 6km east of Bandarawela on the road to Badulla, the charming Dowa Temple is pleasantly situated close to a stream on the south side of the road. A beautiful 4m-high standing Buddha is cut into the rock face below the road. The walls of the adjacent cave shrine, cut from solid rock, are covered with excellent Sri Lankan–style Buddhist murals. The temple is like a smaller version of Dambulla (p185), and, like the Royal Rock Temple at Dambulla, King Valagamba (Vattajamini Ahhya) also took refuge here in the 1st century BC during his 14-year exile from Anuradhapura. Legend has it that a secret underground tunnel stretches from this temple all the way to Kandy. The temple is easy to miss (and the tunnel easier!) if you're coming by bus, so ask the bus conductor to tell you when to alight. A three-wheeler or taxi from Bandarawela should cost Rs 600 to 700 return, including waiting time. A donation is expected at the temple.

Sleeping & Eating

TOP CHOICE **Bandarawela Hotel** HISTORIC HOTEL $$$
(☎222 2501; www.aitkenspencehotels.com; 14 Welimada Rd; s/d incl breakfast US$85/100; wi-fi) Around 70 years ago they wisely stopped updating the furniture at this venerable tea planters' club. Now, in a new millennium, this hotel is a jolly fine show. So don your pith helmet, walk shorts, gloves and long socks and ease into one of the relax-at-all-costs easy chairs. There are spacious rooms with high ceilings, and a cosy bar and billiard saloon. The Bandarawela Hotel's elevated garden setting is a peaceful escape from the dusty city.

Orient Hotel HOTEL $$
(☎222 2407; 12 Dharmapala Mawatha; s/d incl breakfast US$70/90; wi-fi) The Orient's made a conscious effort to lift standards, with bright rooms and wall murals that give the impression of being in a children's nursery school. There's a billiard room and a sunny beer garden. Tour groups are occasionally seen lurking in the combined karaoke/lounge bar.

Vernon Guest House GUESTHOUSE $
(☎222 2328; www.vernonguesthouse.com; 32/9 Esplanade Rd; r Rs 1000-1500) Pleasant old villa at the end of a quiet lane sprinkled in fallen leaves. The rooms are sadly drab and dark but the price is good.

Mlesna Tea Centre CAFE $
(Welimada Rd) You're deep in tea country so buy some at this superb tea shop and cafe, which has high-quality leaves from across the hills.

Information

The post office is near the Bandarawela Hotel.

Bank of Ceylon (Badulla Rd) ATM.

Hatton National Bank (Badulla Rd) ATM.

Getting There & Away

Bus

Buses run to the following destinations:

Badulla Rs 45

Ella Rs 35

Haputale Rs 25 to 30 depending on route

Nuwara Eliya Rs 75

Welimada Rs 41

Long-distance services include Colombo (Rs 214, six hours), Tissamaharama, Tangalla and Galle. Buses to Tissa, Tangalla and Galle leave from the long-distance station on Esplanade Rd. Change at Wellawaya for buses to Tissa or the south coast.

Train

Bandarawela is on the Colombo–Badulla railway line. First-class observation tickets for all trains, except the one to Polonnaruwa, are Rs 750 no matter where you get off.

Badulla 2nd/3rd class Rs 60/30

Colombo Rs 340/185

Ella Rs 30/15

Haputale Rs 20/15

Kandy Rs 230/125

Nanu Oya (for Nuwara Eliya) Rs 90/50

Polonnaruwa Rs 440/240

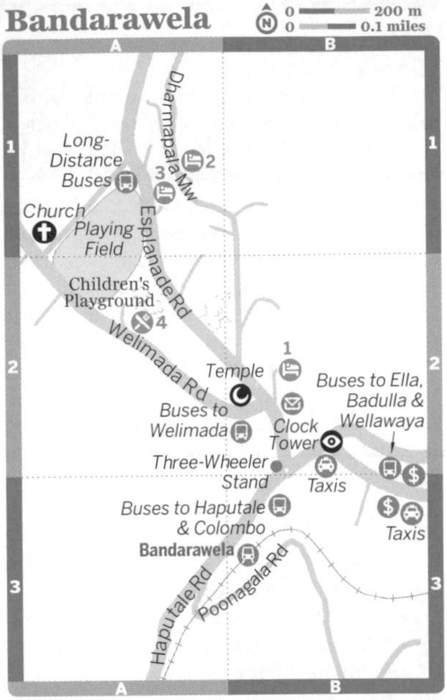

Bandarawela

Sleeping

1 Bandarawela Hotel B2

2 Orient Hotel A1

3 Vernon Guest House A1

Eating

4 Mlesna Tea Centre A2

Ella

☎057 / ELEV 1041M

Welcome to everyone's favourite hill-country village and the place to ease off the travel accelerator with a few leisurely days resting in your choice of some of the country's best guesthouses. The views through Ella Gap are stunning, and on a clear night you can even spy the subtle glow of the Great Basses lighthouse on Sri Lanka's south coast. Don't be too laid-back, though: definitely make time for easygoing walks through tea plantations to temples, waterfalls and viewpoints. After building up a hiking-inspired appetite look forward to Sri Lanka's best home-cooked food and the mini-splurge of an extended Ayurvedic treatment.

Activities

Suwamadura AYURVEDA

(☎567 3215; 25 Grand View, Passara Rd; 1hr treatment Rs 3000; ⏰8am-10pm) Spotless facility with trained staff offering a full range of treatment options, including massage, steam baths, herbal saunas, and the warm, soothing bliss of Shiro Dhara (see p306). The herbal sauna uses 50 different herbs, a few more than Colonel Sanders and probably a whole lot better for you. Treat yourself after a long day's walking. There are a number of other facilities in the village but this is the longest established.

Hiking

Ella is a great place for walking. Most accommodation can give you a hand-drawn map of local paths. Kick off with a stroll to what is locally dubbed **Little Adam's Peak**. Go down the Passara road until you get to the plant shop on your right, just past the 1km post. Follow the track to the left of the garden shop; Little Adam's Peak is the biggest hill on your right and is clearly signposted. Take the second path that turns off to your right and follow it to the top of the hill. Part of this path passes through a tea estate. The approximately 4.5km round trip takes about 45 minutes each way. The final 20 minutes or so is uphill, but otherwise it's an easy walk. Get an early start from your guesthouse – around 7am – and you'll meet Tamil families heading off to work in the tea plantations along the way. From atop Little Adam's Peak, waterfalls and a couple of tea factories shimmer from out of the mist that's often welded persistently to the surrounding hills.

Walking to **Ella Rock** is more demanding and a guide is a very good idea (it's easy to miss the turnoff from the railway track and get lost in the forest that covers the upper slopes). Most guesthouses can organise a guide for Rs 1500 per group. It's a three- to four-hour round trip and the views from the top are extraordinary.

An easier walk is the one along the train tracks (towards Bandarawela) for about 2.5km to the small **Rawana Falls**.

Sleeping

Touts might approach you on the train with tales that the hotel of your choice is too expensive, closed down or rat-infested. In fact, Ella has a high standard of accommodation, especially for guesthouses, so they're most likely telling fibs.

During the peak Christmas/New Year period prices can double from the standard high-season prices listed here.

TOP CHOICE **Waterfall Homestay** GUESTHOUSE $$

(☎567 8933; www.waterfalls-guesthouse-ella.com; s/d/tr incl breakfast Rs 3500/4000/5000; 📶) Delightfully secluded three-room homestay run by an Australian couple with a flair for art and design. The almost organic-seeming building melds perfectly into the hillside and offers fantastic views over the Rawana Falls, which seem to be perfectly framed by the trees surrounding the guesthouse. Each flamboyantly decorated room is different from the last and all the furnishings are of a high standard. Memorable meals are served on the terrace. It's 1.5km from town or a Rs 150 three-wheeler ride.

TOP CHOICE **Zion View** GUESTHOUSE $$

(☎072 785 5713; zionview@yahoo.com; r US$55-60; 📶) First-rate little 'boutique' guesthouse. Rooms have enormous glass panel windows, piping-hot showers and Mediterranean-style terraces strewn with hammocks and easy chairs. Eating breakfast on the sunny terrace with views down through the Ella Gap is as good as Ella moments get. Owner Sena, who trained in Switzerland, and his charming wife Rashinika know what travellers want and will go out of their way to help. The in-house restaurant serves a delicious rice and curry. If you're travelling with young kids then this is a good bet as they have all the gear as well as a playmate for your little 'un. At the time of research they were in the process of opening an Ayurveda centre.

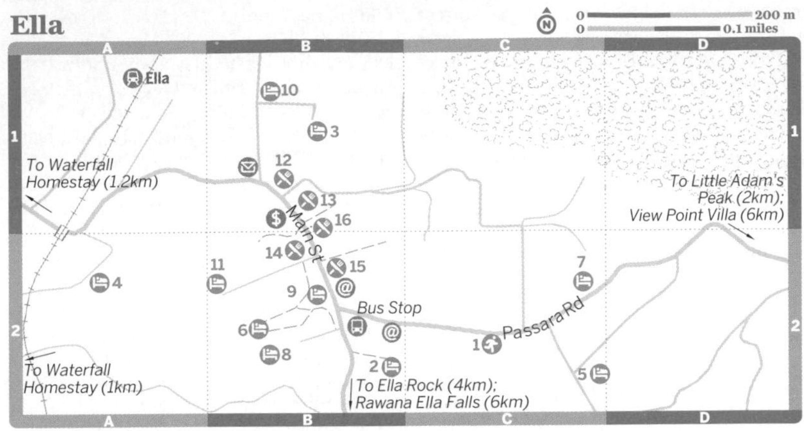

View Point Villa COTTAGE **$$**
(☎077 357 3851; www.viewpoint-villa-ella.com; 8 Mile Post, Passara Rd; cottage Rs 3500-5000;) A wonderfully isolated spot 6km from Ella on the Passara Rd, View Point has brightly coloured villas that combine soaring wooden ceilings with some of the best bathrooms in the Hill Country. Food comes courtesy of the adjacent organic garden, and there are great hill and tea plantation views from the breezy open verandas. A three-wheeler from Ella should cost around Rs 300. Motorcycles can be rented for Rs 600 per day for off-the-beaten-path exploring.

Little Folly CHALET **$$**
(☎222 8817; r Rs 1750, cottage Rs 2500-3000; @) Two quaint Little Red Riding Hood wooden cottages squirreled away in a forest that, if not the home of a big bad wolf, is probably home to a monkey or two. The cottages are airy, bright, clean and shinily new, and everything is made of wood. There's also one simple, little bright-green room in the main house as well as a top-notch tea and cake shop.

Eeshani Guest Inn HOMESTAY **$$**
(☎222 8703; r Rs 3000; @) This is a great new two-room homestay run by an endearing old couple who'll bustle you in and sit you down for a nice cuppa and a chat. The house is filled with sepia photos of the couple's sons and daughters on their wedding days and there's a pretty flower-filled garden. The bathrooms are fancy pants indeed – one has a huge curling, snakelike bath in it.

Ella

Activities, Courses & Tours

1 Suwamadura C2

Sleeping

2 Beauty Mount Tourist Inn B2
3 Eeshani Guest Inn B1
4 Ella Highest Inn A2
5 Green Hill C2
6 Hill Top Guest House B2
7 Little Folly C2
8 Rawana Holiday Resort B2
9 Rock View Guest House B2
10 Sun Top Inn B1
11 Zion View B2

Eating

12 Bakery B1
13 Cafe Chill (Nescoffee Shop) B1
14 Curd Shop B2
15 Down Town Rotti Hut B2
16 Dream Café B1
Little Folly Restaurant .... (see 7)

Information

Dream Café .... (see 16)

Green Hill GUESTHOUSE **$**
(☎578 6845; wemalasooriya@yahoo.com; s/d Rs 2200/2500; @) Two adorable little rooms with splendid views over Ella Gap. The rooms have bright-blue colour schemes and terracotta bathrooms. It's down a muddy lane five minutes' walk from the village. The food receives positive feedback.

Ambiente HOTEL $$

(☎222 8867; www.ambiente.lk; Kitalella Rd; r Rs 2640-3520, tr Rs 3080-4180; @) You get views of Ella's 'Big Three' – Little Adam's Peak, Rawana Waterfall and Ella Gap – at this motel-like place perched high on the edge of a working tea plantation. Rooms are comfortable and clean, but you are paying a premium for the stupendous views. Resident dogs Tim and Tina are your perfect canine walking guides. A three-wheeler from the train station should cost Rs 250. Don't even think about walking; it's very steep.

Hill Top Guest House GUESTHOUSE $$

(☎222 8780; s/d Rs 2250/2500; wi-fi) Immaculate rooms, views of Ella Gap to die for and a welcoming family add up to one of Ella's best. The house is surrounded by verdant gardens, giving a sense of privacy. Good Sri Lankan meals are available.

Sun Top Inn GUESTHOUSE $$

(☎222 8673; suntopinn@sltnet.lk; r incl breakfast Rs 2800-3600; @ wi-fi) This sunset-orange guesthouse (recommended by readers) is on a leafy side lane, an easy downhill stroll from the train station. Sun Top is run by a friendly family and has small and well-kept rooms. Bicycles are available for no charge, and there is a spacious and sunny shared lounge area.

Beauty Mount Tourist Inn GUESTHOUSE $

(☎222 8760; r Rs 1000, cottage Rs 1750-2000) Clean and simple rooms and more modern cottages cling to a forest-clad hill in the centre of Ella. The affable owner grows his own organic coffee, and the rice-and-curry dinners are a veritable feast. Follow the path across the river and up the hill.

Rawana Holiday Resort GUESTHOUSE $

(☎222 8794; nalankumara@yahoo.com; r Rs 1800-2500; wi-fi) Perched high on a hillside overlooking Ella, this family-run guesthouse contains six balcony rooms with views, plus four less-expensive interior rooms. Excellent food is served in the spacious open restaurant.

Rock View Guest House GUESTHOUSE $

(☎222 8561; r Rs 1500) Originally a Scottish tea planter's bungalow, Rock View combines spotless, freshly painted rooms with wooden floors and high ceilings, and new rooms with great Ella Gap views in an adjoining building. It's been in the same family for 50 years, and there are lots of poignant mementos dotting the walls.

Ella Highest Inn HOMESTAY $

(☎072 409 8725; r Rs 1000) More like a cosy bed and breakfast than a guesthouse, the Highest Inn has a shared lounge with Asian art, a stereo and DVD player, and clean and simple rooms. It's surrounded by a tea plantation and (assuming nobody builds on it – not as unlikely as it sounds) total seclusion. Trading standards may argue that it's not actually the highest guesthouse in Ella!

Eating & Drinking

Ella's guesthouses are great places to try excellent home-cooked food, perhaps some of the best eating you'll discover in all of Sri Lanka. All the guesthouses and hotels serve meals; they ask for around four hours' advance notice. Especially good is the food at Rawana Holiday Resort, Zion View, Beauty Mount Tourist Inn, Hill Top Guest House, Green Hill and Sita's Heaven – in many guesthouse restaurants you can even join the chef in the kitchen for a rice and curry–making class. At Rawana Holiday Resort you can look forward to around eight different dishes, including sweet-and-sour eggplant, spicy potato curry, and Rawana's signature garlic curry, made with whole cloves of the 'stinking rose' (it tastes much better than it sounds!). Just let them know by mid-afternoon.

In recent years, the sleepy village has spawned a couple of places that stay open for a few beers later at night. If you've been walking in the surrounding hills and tea plantations, you've probably earned a cooling end-of-the-day ale.

Curd (made with buffalo milk) and treacle (syrup from the *kitul* palm; sometimes misnamed 'honey') is a much-touted local speciality.

TOP CHOICE **Cafe Chill (Nescoffee Shop)** INTERNATIONAL $$

(Main St; meals Rs 300-700; wi-fi) This cool and compact roadside cafe-bar has the traveller-scene thing down to a tee – there's minty mojitos, cool tunes, sport on the TV, free wi-fi and easy conversations around the table. Oh, and the food? Well, that's pretty good as well, and you shouldn't leave without trying the *lamprais* (meat and vegetables wrapped in a banana leaf and very slowly cooked). At the time of research they were opening a new extension out the back, which should go some way to relieving the queues of people waiting for a table on busy evenings.

Curd Shop INTERNATIONAL **$**
(Main St; meals Rs 150-250) Tiny hole-in-the-wall spot near the bus stand that's good for breakfast – around 15% cheaper than the guesthouses – before or after an early-morning stroll to Little Adam's Peak. It's a classic backpacker-style place and is a good spot to try curd and honey or *kotthu rotti*. It's also handy for picking up sandwiches if you're going walking.

Dream Café INTERNATIONAL **$$**
(Main St; mains Rs 300-500; wi-fi) Multiple reader recommendations fly the flag for this main-drag place with a cool, shady garden. It's a cosmopolitan wee spot with good espresso coffee, well-executed Western dishes like tortilla chicken wraps, and smoothies and salads for the healthy traveller. Don't be too pious, though: the beers are nice and cold.

Little Folly Restaurant CAFE **$**
(cakes Rs 120) It's 3pm, you're in the Hill Country; that must mean it's time to have high tea and a slice of homemade lemon or chocolate cake. What better place to do so than this delightful forest-side cafe?

Down Town Rotti Hut SRI LANKAN **$**
(Main St; rotti around Rs 250) This place was just opening for business during our last visit, but our guess is they'll be wasting no time at all gaining a reputation for having some of the tastiest (and most amply proportioned) *rotti* in town.

Information

There's a post office, and the **Bank of Ceylon** has an ATM. Many guesthouses and some bigger restaurants have internet access (normally wi-fi). Cafe Chill (Nescoffee Shop) has a small selection of secondhand paperbacks.

Getting There & Away

Bus

The road to Ella leaves the Bandarawela–Badulla road about 9km out of Bandarawela. Buses change schedule fairly often, so ask for an update at either the Curd Shop (where many buses stop to collect passengers) or opposite, at Rodrigo Communications.

Buses go to Badulla (Rs 45), Bandarawela (Rs 35) and Wellawaya (Rs 55).

To or from Kandy you must change first at Badulla. Buses to Matara (CTB/intercity express Rs 150/278) stop at Ella around every hour from about 6.30am until about 2.30pm. The buses are likely to be quite full by the time they reach Ella, though the buses around noon are usually less busy. You can always catch a bus to Wellawaya and change there for a service to the south coast or for Monaragala (for Arugam Bay). A bus heads to Galle every morning at 8am (Rs 310).

Train

Ella is an hour from Haputale and Badulla on the Colombo–Badulla line. The stretch from Haputale (through Bandarawela) has particularly lovely scenery. Roughly 10km north of Ella, at Demodara, the line performs a complete loop around a hillside and tunnels under itself at a level 30m lower.

Ella's train station is quaint, and the fares and timetables are well posted. You'll probably be met by a few touts spinning fictional tales; Ella's guesthouse fraternity is perhaps the most competitive in all of Sri Lanka. Touts sometimes board the train a few stops before Ella. Observation class is a set Rs 750 and should be booked in advance.

Sample train fares:

Badulla 2nd/3rd class, Rs 40/20
Bandarawela Rs 350/410
Colombo Rs 350/190
Haputale Rs 50/25
Kandy Rs 240/130
Nanu Oya (for Nuwara Eliya) Rs 110/60

Around Ella

You can visit the **Dowa Temple** from Ella; see p168.

The **Uva Halpewaththa Tea Factory** runs tours (Rs 150). Catch a bus to Bandarawela, get off at Kumbawela junction, and flag a bus going to Badulla. Get off just after the 27km post, near the Halpe Temple. From here you've got a 2km walk to the factory. A three-wheeler from Ella will charge Rs 600 return.

The 19m-high **Rawana Ella Falls** are about 6km down Ella Gap towards Wellawaya. During rainy months the water comes leaping down the mountainside in what is claimed to be the 'wildest-looking' fall in Sri Lanka, but during the dry season it may not flow at all. There are vendors selling food and trinkets, and the invariable array of 'guides' wanting to point out the waterfall that's already blindingly obvious.

Further up the road and to your left as you approach Ella, a side road takes you to a little **temple** and a **cave** that is associated with the Ramayana story. You may visit the temple, which is part of a monastery, but remember to remove your shoes and hat, and to cover your legs and arms. The cave,

Around Ella

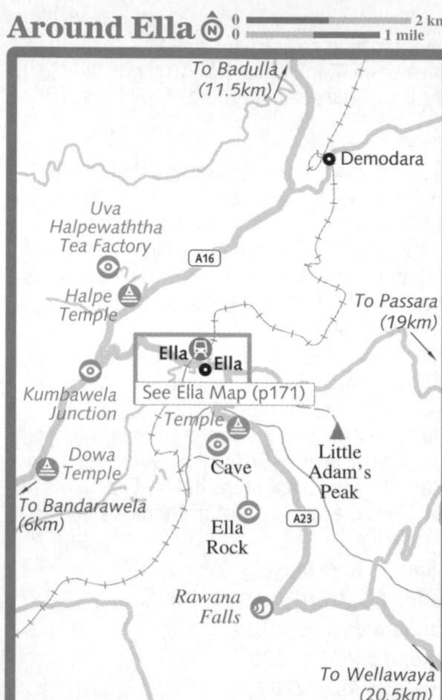

located in a cleft in the mountain that rises to Ella Rock, is reputed to be where the king of Lanka lived before capturing Sita. Boys will show you where the steep, overgrown and slippery track up to the cave starts.

Badulla

☎055 / POP 42,572 / ELEV 680M

Badulla marks the southeast extremity of the Hill Country and is a transport gateway to the east coast. It is one of Sri Lanka's oldest towns, occupied briefly by the Portuguese, who torched it upon leaving. For the British it was an important social centre, but beyond the pretty gardens and clock tower, any vestiges of a past that included a racecourse and cricket club are lost in Badulla's typical Sri Lankan bustle. The railway through the Hill Country from Colombo terminates here. In British times, it was an important hub for transporting plantation products to Colombo.

Sights

Most Sri Lankans visiting Badulla stop at either Muthiyagana Vihara or Kataragama Devale.

Muthiyagana Vihara TEMPLE

A large Buddhist complex that includes a whitewashed dagoba in spacious grounds in the southeast of town. During festivals the resident elephant may be paraded around.

Kataragama Devale TEMPLE

The main objects of veneration are statues of the gods Kataragama, Saman and Vishnu. Uniquely, the *devale* was constructed in Kandyan style rather than South Indian Tamil style, with a long wooden shrine hall painted with murals depicting a *perahera.*

St Mark's Church CHURCH

If you're a history buff, take a look through St Mark's Church and peruse the old headstones. Inside is a plaque commemorating the elephant hunter Major Rogers, who was killed by lightning. Legend has it that following a particularly severe thunderstorm in Haputale in 1845, Rogers stepped onto his veranda and proclaimed, 'It's all over now' to his wife. Ahh, not so fast, matey: one last bolt struck him dead. Relatives of the 1500 elephants he killed in a four-year stint probably trumpeted in glee. Rogers' actual gravestone near Nuwara Eliya is now cracked in half, reputedly by another bolt of celestial energy.

Dunhinda Falls WATERFALL

(admission Rs 200) Five kilometres north of Badulla are the 63m-high Dunhinda Falls. The best time to see them is June and July, but they're worth a visit at any time. It's a good spot for a picnic, but keep an eye out for light-fingered monkeys. Buses leave every 30 minutes from Badulla (Rs 30). From the bus stop the falls are about 1.5km along a clearly defined path. It's a bit of a scramble, so wear suitable shoes; note that you have to negotiate a plethora of little shops selling tack at the start of the walk.

You can see a lower waterfall on the walk, and there's a good observation spot at the end of the path. There are many snack places along the trail. Avoid public holidays and weekends, when the place can get packed. A three-wheeler from Badulla costs Rs 500 for the return trip.

Sleeping & Eating

In recent years, Badulla's cheaper guesthouses have developed a reputation for being hire-by-the-hour kinds of places. You're better off either paying a little bit more to ensure a good night's kip or just heading to Ella, which is less than an hour away. A few cheaper places hover around the train station if you're really counting your rupees.

There are many local eateries along Lower St, near the intersection with Bazaar St. Self-caterers can buy groceries at **Cargills Food City** (Post Office Rd), and the colourful **market** opposite the post office has a surprisingly wide range of fruit and veggies.

Hotel Onix HOTEL **$$**
(☎222 2426; 69 Bandaranayake Mawatha; r incl breakfast from Rs 3500; ❄✉) This popular wedding-venue place is overpriced, but its spacious rooms are about the best Badulla has to offer – which frankly isn't much!

Dunhinda Falls Hotel HOTEL **$$**
(☎222 3028; 69 Bandaranayake Mawatha; with/without air-con s Rs 2500/1250, d Rs 2950/2000; ❄) It's clean and friendly and while its motto 'Unparalleled Class' might well be true for Badulla, it does push the limits of believability elsewhere.

Information

Bank of Ceylon (Bank Rd) has an ATM and exchange facilities.

Getting There & Away

Bus

Colombo Rs 244 to 720 depending on bus type
Ella private bus Rs 46
Kandy Rs 200
Monaragala Rs 88
Nuwara Eliya Rs 94

Train

A 1st-class ticket in the observation carriage is a set Rs 750 no matter where you alight. Trains head to Colombo (2nd/3rd class Rs 370/205) and Kandy (Rs 270/145).

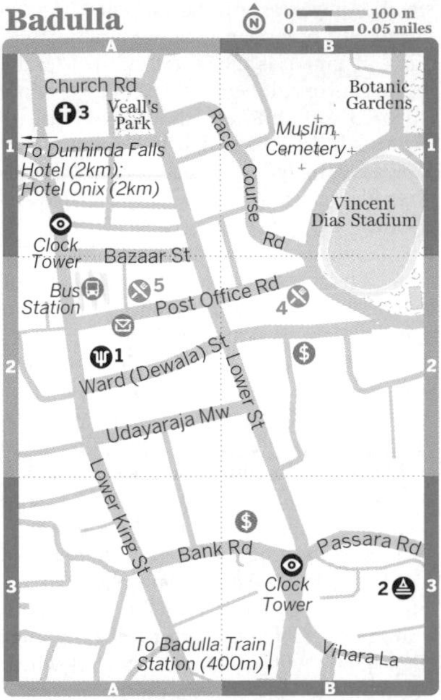

Badulla

Sights

1	Kataragama Devale	A2
2	Muthiyagana Vihara	B3
3	St Mark's Church	A1

Eating

4	Cargills Food City	B2
5	Market	A2

Wellawaya

☎055

By Wellawaya you have left the Hill Country and descended to the dry plains that were once home to the ancient Sinhalese kingdom of Ruhunu. Wellawaya is simply a small crossroads town and, apart from the nearby Buduruwagala carvings, there's not much of interest in the area. Apart from a quick three-wheeler dash to the Buddha figures at Buduruwagala, you'll be focused on sorting out onward transportation. Roads run north through the spectacular Ella Gap to the Hill Country, south to Tissamaharama and the coast, east to the coast and west to Colombo.

Sights

TOP CHOICE **Buduruwagala** MONUMENT
(admission Rs 200; ⌚9am-5pm) About 5km south of Wellawaya, a side road branches west off the Tissa road to the beautiful rock-cut Buddha figures of Buduruwagala. A small signpost points the way along a 4km road that crosses a series of delicate lakes. Keep an eye out for local birdlife, including many egrets and herons.

The name Buduruwagala is derived from the words for Buddha (Budu), images *(ruva)* and stone *(gala)*. The figures are thought to date from around the 10th century and belong to the Mahayana Buddhist school, which enjoyed a brief heyday in Sri Lanka during this time. The gigantic standing Buddha – at 15m, it is the tallest on the island – in the centre still bears traces of its original stuccoed robe, and a long streak of orange suggests it was once brightly painted.

The central of the three figures to the Buddha's right is thought to be the Mahayana Buddhist figure Avalokitesvara (the bodhisattva of compassion). To the left of this white-painted figure is a female figure thought to be his consort, Tara. Local legend says the third figure represents Prince Sudhana.

The three figures on the Buddha's left-hand side appear, to an inexpert eye, to be of a rather different style. The crowned figure at the centre of the group is thought to be Maitreya, the future Buddha. To his left stands Vajrapani, who holds a *vajra* (an hourglass-shaped thunderbolt symbol) – an unusual example of the Tantric side of Buddhism in Sri Lanka. The figure to the left may be either Vishnu or Sahampath Brahma. Several of the figures hold up their right hands with two fingers bent down to the palm – a beckoning gesture.

You may be joined by a guide, who will expect a tip. A three-wheeler from Wellawaya costs about Rs 500 return. Some people walk from the junction of the main road, which is very pleasant but also long and very hot.

Archaeological Museum MUSEUM
(admission free; ⏲8.30am-5pm Wed-Mon) Back on the corner of the main road from Wellawaya, the Archaeological Museum has stone and terracotta artefacts from nearby Buduruwagala. The artefacts are well lit and displayed but signage is in Sinhalese only.

Sleeping & Eating

There's a flurry of restaurants and snack stands across the road from the bus station.

Little Rose GUESTHOUSE $
(☎567 8360; www.littlerosewellawaya.com; 101 Tissa Rd; r Rs 1500-2000) Just 500m from the bus station, this is your best option if you're staying overnight waiting for onward transport. In a quiet rural setting, the country home is surrounded by rice paddies and run by a welcoming family. Good, inexpensive meals are available. The shoebox-size single room shares a bathroom. A three-wheeler from the bus station costs about Rs 100.

Getting There & Away

Wellawaya is a common staging point between the Hill Country and the south and east coasts. You can usually find a connection here until mid-afternoon. Buses to Ella cost Rs 55. For Tissamaharama, change at Pannegamanuwa Junction (Rs 70).

Embilipitiya

☎047

Embilipitiya is a good base for tours to Uda Walawe National Park, as it's only 23km south of the park's ticket office. It's a busy, modern town built to service the surrounding irrigated paddy fields and sugarcane plantations.

Around 1.5km south of the town centre, **Centauria Tourist Hotel** (☎223 0514; incl breakfast s/d US$74/85, cottage s/d US$100/115; ❄@📶🏊) combines a modern design with a languid, colonial ambience. The standard lakeside rooms are actually better value and more spacious than the cottages, but even so it's a bit overpriced. There is a good restaurant (mains Rs 440 to 660), but weekend entertainment may include a couple of guys in straw hats playing mediocre versions of Boney M songs you're trying to forget.

The bus station is in the centre of town, along with branches of **Hatton National Bank**, **Seylan Bank**, **People's Bank**, **Commercial Bank** and **Sampath Bank**. All have ATMs and exchange facilities and can arrange cash advances. There's an **internet cafe** opposite the central clock tower.

Buses leave regularly for most destinations from, or near, the bus station; destinations include Tangalla (Rs 50), Matara (Rs 100) and Ratnapura (Rs 100).

If you're staying at Embilipitiya and wish to organise a tour of Uda Walawe park, catch a bus to Tanamalwila (Rs 75) and ask to be dropped at the gate to the park.

Uda Walawe National Park

With herds of elephants, wild buffalo, sambar deer and leopards, **Uda Walawe National Park** (adult/child Rs 3375/900, service charge per group Rs 900, vehicle charge per group Rs 250, VAT 12%; ⏲6am-6pm) is the Sri Lankan national park that best rivals the savannah reserves of Africa. In fact, for elephant-watching, Uda Walawe often surpasses many of the most famous East African national parks. The park, which centres on the

308.2-sq-km Uda Walawe Reservoir, is lightly vegetated but it has a stark beauty and the lack of dense vegetation makes game-watching easy. It's certainly the one national park in Sri Lanka not to miss.

The entrance to the park is 12km from the Ratnapura–Hambantota road turnoff and 21km from Embilipitiya. Visitors buy tickets in a building a further 2km on. Most people take a tour organised by their guesthouse or hotel, but a trip with one of the 4WDs waiting outside the gate should be around Rs 3500 for a half-day for up to eight people with driver. Last tickets are usually sold at 5pm. A park guide is included in the cost of admission and these guys, who all seem to have hawklike wildlife-spotting eyes, are normally very knowledgeable about the park and its animals. A tip is expected.

Sights & Activities

There are about 500 elephants in the park in herds of up to 50. There's an elephant-proof fence around the perimeter of the park, preventing elephants from getting out and cattle from getting in. The best time to observe elephant herds is from 6.30am to 10am and again from 4pm to 6.30pm.

Besides elephants, sambar deer and wild buffalo (their numbers boosted by domesticated buffaloes), there are also mongooses, bandicoots, foxes, water monitor lizards, crocodiles, sloth bears and the occasional leopard. There are 30 varieties of snakes and a wealth of birdlife; northern migrants join the residents between November and April.

Wildlife in Udu Walawe is under threat for several reasons, including illegal settlement and the associated grazing of cattle, as well as significant numbers of visitors in private vehicles. Another problem is poaching and the use of 'Hakka Patas', small explosive devices that are concealed in food and left on the banks of the Uda Walawe Reservoir, where wild boar graze. Though the explosives target wild boar, several elephants have been severely injured in recent years.

All along the main road fringing the park, fruitsellers have set up shop selling fruit to passing motorists who then attempt to hand feed the wild elephants that gather along the edge of the park fence. Be aware that feeding the elephants encourages dependence and erodes their fear of humans, which frequently ends up leading to human–elephant conflict in which the elephants normally come out worse off. While the park rivals East Africa for its elephants, the Sri Lankan National Park authorities fall behind their competitors in Kenya and Tanzania in so far as good conservation practice goes.

Elephant Transit Home ZOO
(adult/child Rs 500/250; ⌚feedings 9am, noon, 3pm & 6pm) Helping to care for the area's injured elephants, this home is nearby on the main road about 5km west of the park entrance. Supported by the Born Free Foundation (www.bornfree.org.uk), the complex is a halfway house for orphaned elephants. After rehabilitation, the elephants are released back into the wild, many into the Uda Walawe National Park. At the time of writing 64 elephants had been rehabilitated at the Elephant Transit Home and subsequently released. A boisterous group of around 30 juvenile and teenage pachyderms gets fed four times a day. Unlike the Pinnewala Elephant Orphanage, you can't get up close and personal with the elephants, but feeding time is still a lot of fun, and the good work being undertaken is undeniable. Most 4WD operators include a visit to the Elephant Transit Home in their trips. For more about Sri Lankan elephants, see p281.

Sleeping & Eating

Accommodation in the vicinity of Uda Walawe is of poor value indeed.

Selara River Eco Resort LODGE $$
(☎077 643 2815; Walawe Handiya; s/d Rs 2500/3500) The adobe and stone bungalows found at this riverside location could be kept cleaner, but they have much more character than most options around here. Bathrooms are rustic designer-chic, with stone floors and natural waterfall-type showers. There's no air-con but still plenty of places to keep cool, including a two-storey tree-house bar that's crammed with home-built wooden furniture. The attached restaurant does great things with lake fish, so it's worth plumping for the half-board option. A friendly monitor lizard (around 1m long) sometimes mooches around for a feed. Turn right from Embilipitiya Rd into Walawe Handiya, and go a further 5km before turning right at the Selara sign.

Kottawatta Village RESORT $$
(☎047-223 3215; www.udawalawakottawattavillage.com; Uda Walawe Junction; r incl breakfast Rs 3000/6500; ❄) This modern resort-style place is professionally run and has

comfortable and well-maintained accommodation set in spacious gardens. It's 8km from the park in the direction of Embilipitiya.

Superson Family Guest GUESTHOUSE $
(☎047-347 5172; 90B CDE Place, Uda Walawe; r Rs 750-1200) This guesthouse has simple accommodation, a nice garden and good home-cooked food. Prices seem to be very flexible.

Sinharaja Forest Reserve

The last major undisturbed area of rainforest in Sri Lanka, this **forest reserve** (admission Rs 665, compulsory guide per person Rs 350) occupies a broad ridge at the heart of the island's wet zone. On most days the forest is shrouded by copious rainclouds that replenish its deep soils and balance water resources for much of southwestern Sri Lanka. Recognising its importance to the island's ecosystem, Unesco declared the Sinharaja Forest Reserve a World Heritage Site in 1989.

Sinharaja (Lion King) is bordered by rivers: the Koskulana Ganga in the north and the Gin Ganga in the south. An old foot track that goes past the Beverley Estate marks the eastern border, close to the highest peak in the forest, Hinipitigala (1171m). Towards the west the land decreases in elevation.

The reserve comprises 189 sq km of natural and modified forest, measuring about 21km east to west and 3.7km north to south. It was once a royal reserve, and some colonial records refer to it as Rajasinghe Forest. It may have been the last redoubt of the Sri Lankan lion.

In 1840 the forest became British crown land, and from that time some efforts were made toward its preservation. However, in 1971 loggers moved in and began selective logging. The logged native hardwoods were replaced with mahogany (which does not occur naturally here), logging roads and trails snaked into the forest and a woodchip mill was built. Following intense lobbying by conservationists, the government called a halt to all logging in 1977. Machinery was dismantled and removed, the roads gradually grew over and Sinharaja was saved. Much of the rest of Sri Lanka's rainforest stands on mountain ridges within a 20km radius of the forest.

There are 22 villages around the forest, and locals are permitted to enter the area to tap palms to make jaggery (a hard brown sweet) and treacle, and to collect dead wood and leaves for fuel and construction. Medicinal plants are collected during specific seasons. Rattan collection is of more concern, as the demand for cane is high. Sinharaja attracts illegal gem miners, too, and abandoned open pits pose a danger to humans and animals and cause erosion. There is also some poaching of wild animals.

The drier months (August and September, and January to early April) are the best times to visit. Hinipitigala stands for most of the year under drizzles and downpours. Sinharaja receives between 3500mm and 5000mm of rain annually, with a minimum of 50mm in even the driest months. There's little seasonal variation in the temperature, which averages about 24°C inside the forest, with humidity at about 87%.

Sights & Activities

Kotapola, 6km south of Deniyaya, has a superb early-17th-century **rock temple**. It's well worth the climb. The **Kiruwananaganga Falls**, some of the largest in Sri Lanka (60m high and up to 60m wide), are 5km east of Kotapola on the road towards Urubokka. The **Kolawenigama Temple**, 3km from Pallegama (which is 3km from Deniyaya), is of modest proportions but has a unique structure that resembles Kandy's Temple of the Sacred Tooth Relic. It was built by King Buwanekabahu VII in recognition of the protection given to the tooth relic by the villagers. The shrine has Kandyan-style frescoes.

Wildlife

Sinharaja has a wild profusion of flora. The canopy trees reach heights of up to 45m, with the next layer down topping 30m. Nearly all the subcanopy trees found here are rare or endangered. More than 65% of the 217 types of trees and woody climbers endemic to Sri Lanka's rainforest are found in Sinharaja.

The largest carnivore here is the leopard. Its presence can usually be gauged only by droppings and tracks, and it's seldom seen. Even rarer are rusty spotted cats and fishing cats. Sambar, barking deer and wild boar can be found on the forest floor. Groups of 10 to 14 purple-faced langurs are fairly common. There are three kinds of squirrels: the flame-striped jungle squirrel, the dusky-striped jungle squirrel and the western giant squirrel. Porcupines and pangolins waddle around the forest floor, mostly unseen.

WORTH A TRIP

RATNAPURA

Sitting in well-irrigated valleys between Adam's Peak and Sinharaja Forest Reserve, busy Ratnapura ('City of Gems' in Sanskrit) is a famous trading centre for the area's ancient wealth of gemstones. The region's wet and humid climate encourages the formation of riverbeds, which are the perfect environment for gemstones to develop.

There are several 'gem museums' that contain modest displays on gem lore, along with less-than-modest showrooms where you're encouraged to purchase 'local' gems at 'local' prices.

The outskirts of town are dotted with **gem mines** and, although none cater specifically to tourists, most guesthouses can arrange visits.

You can also observe **gem merchants** selling their wares along Saviya St northeast of the clock tower. The biggest local gem market, however, convenes most mornings (*poya* days being an exception) in **Newitigala**, a 40-minute drive away (hiring a taxi for half a day should cost around Rs 2500). Both markets are usually over by 3pm.

Another possible reason to visit Ratnapura is that it's the take-off point for one of the oldest routes up **Adam's Peak** (p150). Peak-baggers and pilgrims pick up the Gilimalai pilgrimage route from the road head at Carney Estate, 15km, or one hour, away from Ratnapura by bus. It takes six to eight hours to reach the top of the peak, and five to seven hours to descend. Leeches are a particular menace on this trail.

For a bed try **Ratna Gem Halt** (☎222 3745; www.ratnapura-online.com; 153/5 Outer Circular Rd; r Rs 800-2000), a family-run, seven-room guesthouse north of town. It has good Sri Lankan food and hospitality and fine views of emerald-green rice paddies. The cheapest rooms have no hot water and no views. It's run by a gem dealer who also runs gemmology courses and arranges half-day trips to the gem mines and markets.

Civets and mongooses are nocturnal, though you may glimpse the occasional mongoose darting through the foliage during the day. Six species of bat have been recorded here.

Sinharaja has 45 species of reptile, 21 of them endemic. Venomous snakes include the green pit viper (which inhabits trees), the hump-nosed viper and the krait, which lives on the forest floor. One of the most frequently found amphibians is the wrinkled frog, whose croaking is often heard at night.

There is a wealth of birdlife: 160 species have been recorded, with 18 of Sri Lanka's 20 endemic species seen here. The forest is renowned for its mixed 'bird wave'. This is when several different species of bird move in a feeding flock together. It's commonly seen in many parts of the world, but in Sinharaja it's worth noting for the length of time a flock can be viewed and the number of species (up to a dozen species) and it sometimes even contains mammals (such as ground squirrels).

Sinharaja has leeches in abundance. In colonial times the British, Dutch and Portuguese armies rated leeches as their worst enemy when they tried to conquer the hinterland (which was then much more forested), and one British writer claimed leeches caused more casualties than all the other animals put together. These days you needn't suffer as much because all guides carry anti-leech preparations.

Sleeping & Eating

It's most convenient to visit the reserve from Deniyaya if you don't have your own wheels.

DENIYAYA

Rainforest Lodge HOTEL $$
(☎492 0444; www.rainforestlodge-srilanka.de, in German; r Rs 2500) Located in perfect isolation up a 300m path bisecting a tea plantation, Rainforest Lodge has sparkling and spacious rooms with high-quality bathrooms. The views include a green trifecta of rainforest, rice paddies and tea gardens, and good food is served up by a welcoming local family. Forest trips cost Rs 4200 for one person or Rs 5500 for two people, including food, transport and guiding fees.

Sinharaja Rest GUESTHOUSE $
(☎041-227 3368; sinharaja_rest@yahoo.com; Temple Rd; r Rs 2000) Brothers Palitha and Bandula Rathnayaka are both certified forest guides, so staying here makes it easy to maximise your time. The six rooms at their home are fairly basic, but there's good

home-cooking and a lovely private garden. Day trips to the Sinharaja Forest Reserve cost Rs 3500 per person, including transport, guiding and lunch, but excluding park entrance fees. Trips are also open to nonguests. If you give the brothers a week's notice, they can arrange overnight stays in forest bungalows.

Deniyaya Rest House HOTEL **$**
(☎041-227 3600; r Rs 2000) Like most former government rest houses in Sri Lanka, this place has the best location in town, with great views over the countryside. The large rooms are fairly rundown but good value, and there's a bar and restaurant where you can tally up your leech bites over a stiff drink. It's just off the main road in the town of Deniyaya.

KUDAWA

The Forest Department at Kudawa has some bungalows with fairly basic accommodation. Contact the **Forest Department HQ** (☎011-286 6633; forest@slt.lk; 82 Rajamalwatte Rd, Battaramulla) in Colombo for information.

Rock View Motel HOTEL **$$**
(☎045-567 7990; Weddagala; s/d Rs 3300/4400) Functional and airy rooms with views over rolling hills of forest and tea bushes. It's let down by a cold welcome from the staff on reception. It's 2km east of Weddagala.

Boulder Garden BOUTIQUE HOTEL **$$$**
(☎045-225 5812; www.bouldergarden.com; Sinharaja Rd, Koswatta; s/d US$138/245; ❄) This brilliantly designed but somewhat down-at-heel eco-resort offers 10 rustic rooms – two of them in actual caves – built among boulders and streams. Meals are available in a beautiful garden restaurant (but be aware that they charge an astronomical US$69 for breakfast for a single traveller!). It's a little damp-smelling, but you are deep in the rainforest, after all. Activities on tap include kayaking, caving, birdwatching, abseiling and mountain biking.

Rainforest Edge LODGE **$$$**
(☎045-225 5912; www.rainforestedge.com; Balwatukanda, Weddagala; s/d incl breakfast US$173/244; ❄) Tucked up into the hills a kilometre or so from Weddagala, these seven rustic 'huts' are a bit too rustic for the high prices they charge. Still, the views from the terrace are stunning.

 Information

Tickets are sold at the main Forest Department office at Kudawa and at Deodawa, 5km from Deniyaya on the Matara road.

In Deniyaya, the **People's Bank** has an ATM and exchange facilities and internet access is also available in the village.

See www.sinharaja.4t.com for detailed information on the history, flora and fauna, and the challenges faced by the Sinharaja Forest Reserve.

Getting There & Away

There are several park access points, but the most relevant to travellers are those via Kudawa in the northwest and via Mederapitiya (reached from Deniyaya) in the southeast. At the time of writing the road via Mederapitiya was in reasonable condition, but the road via Kudawa was in serious need of repair and required 4WD access.

Wherever you start, try to get moving as early as you can because the roads are often damaged by flooding.

Bus

From Ratnapura to Deniyaya there are buses (Rs 110) roughly every hour from 6.45am until the afternoon. There are also several buses to and from Galle (Rs 120).

For Kudawa you can get a bus from Ratnapura to Weddagala (4km before Kudawa, Rs 100), and then change in Weddagala to a Kudawa-bound bus.

Car

If you have a car, the road through Hayes Tea Estate, north of Deniyaya en route to Madampe and Balangoda (for Belihul Oya, Haputale or Ratnapura), is very scenic. Trying to loop from the north to the south entrances of the park is also very scenic, but oh my is it slow and painful...

The Ancient Cities

Includes »

Best Places to Eat

» A&C Restaurant (p184)
» Ancient Villa Hotel (p190)
» Heritance Kandalama Hotel (p186)
» Milano Tourist Rest (p209)

Best Places to Stay

» Habarana Rest House (p200)
» Hotel Shalini (p209)
» Jetwing Vil Uyana (p191)
» Rice Villa Retreat (p198)

Why Go?

Crumbling temples, lost cities and sacred sites are reason enough to head up country. It was here on the hot central plains of Sri Lanka that ancient Sinhalese dynasties set up their capitals and supported massive artistic and architectural endeavours. Eventually these kingdoms fell, giving nature a chance to reclaim the land.

For more than a century archaeologists have been slowly shedding the many layers of history from this overgrown landscape. The Rock Fort at Sigiriya, the bulging dagobas of Polonnaruwa and the serene Buddhas scattered around Anuradhapura are but a few of the sites now considered national treasures.

The area covered in this chapter is commonly called the 'Cultural Triangle'. Besides the amazing ruins, save time for the national parks, which teem with elephants. Plan on spending several days here, wandering from town to town, making new discoveries daily.

When to Go

Dambulla

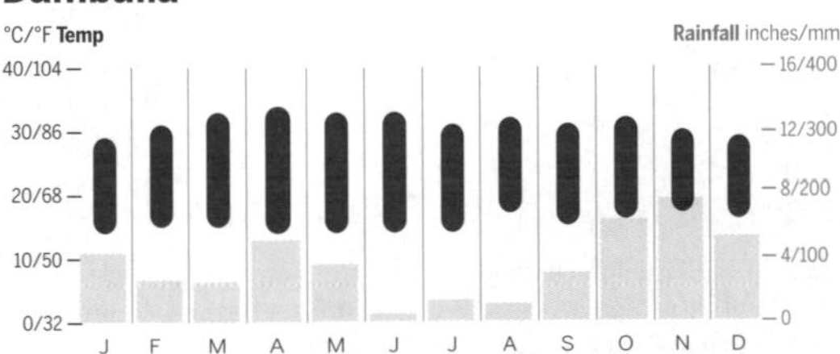

Jun A great festival, the Poson Poya, is held at Mihintale on the Poson full-moon night.

May–Sep Elephants abound in the central and easily visited Minneriya National Park.

Dec–Feb Coastal beaches are packed, but cultural sites offer a meaningful escape.

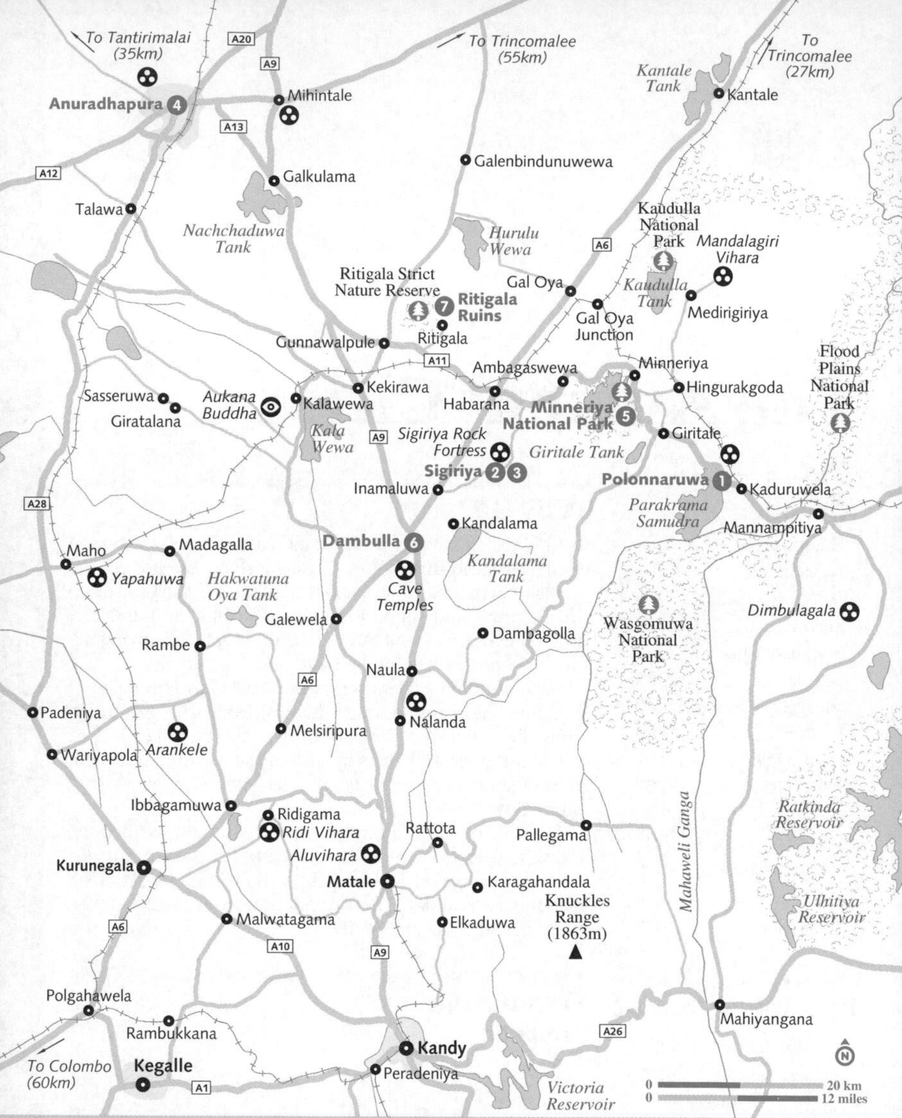

The Ancient Cities Highlights

1. Admiring the fine artwork carved into the fascinating **Polonnaruwa Quadrangle** (p194)
2. Scaling the rock monastery at **Sigiriya** (p188), known for its epic views, outstanding art and mind-boggling ruins
3. Getting lost for hours in Sri Lanka's best museum at **Sigiriya** (p188)
4. Cycling around the sprawling ruins of **Anuradhapura** (p202)
5. Spotting elephants and other wildlife in the lush **Minneriya National Park** (p201)
6. Going Buddha-spotting in **Dambulla** (p185), where rock caves contain some of Sri Lanka's most stunning paintings, temples and Buddhist images
7. Summoning your inner explorer at the mysterious ruins at **Ritigala** (p202)

 Information

Head to **Lonely Planet** (www.lonelyplanet.com/sri-lanka/the-ancient-cities) for planning advice, author recommendations, traveller reviews and insider tips.

CULTURAL TRIANGLE TICKETS

Tickets are needed to visit the major Cultural Triangle sites as well as a few of the minor ones. Most are run by the Central Cultural Fund (CCF), which has a good website (www.ccf.lk).

Until 2012 a Round Ticket was sold which covered all the main sites and offered substantial savings over individual admission tickets. Its withdrawal has not been popular, so it is worth checking to see if has been restored or replaced with a similar scheme.

Admission tickets to the main sites cost as follows:

Anuradhapura US$25
Dambulla US$10
Medirigiriya US$10
Nalanda US$5
Polonnaruwa US$25
Ritigala US$10
Sigiriya US$30

Getting Around

The towns and cities of the Cultural Triangle are well connected by public and private buses, and in some cases by train. Distances are not great and most roads are good, so getting around by public transport is relatively comfortable (although buses can be very crowded at certain times of day and during holiday periods). Departures between major towns and tourist sites are fairly frequent, so you needn't wait long for a ride.

As always the easiest way to tour, however, is with a car and driver. You can reach the area by train or bus and then arrange for a car and driver on a daily basis through your accommodation.

Matale

☎066 / POP 45,000

This midsize regional city at the heart of the island lies in a broad, fertile valley at an elevation of 300m. It's your likely gateway to the Ancient Cities, even if you won't linger long. The road to Kandy, 24km south, is not pretty and is lined with scruffy developments and lumber mills. However, once past Matale, look for plantations with vanilla, rubber, cinchona, jackfruit, cocoa and cardamom. The area is also famous for *kohila* (a type of watercress) and small, mild chillies.

A drive east through Knuckles Range, east of Matale, presents some remarkable mountain views. The B38 heads uphill from the north end of town to a pass near Rattota, while other roads head southwest to the hill villages of Elkaduwa and Karagahandala before winding down to Kandy and the Victoria Reservoir. For more details about Knuckles Range, see p150.

 Sights

Aluvihara MONASTERY

(admission Rs 200; ⏲7am-6pm) If the idea of a monastery built from a sheer rock wall sounds intriguing, make sure to pull off the road 3km north of Matale for a look at Aluvihara. This unique series of monastic caves are picturesquely situated among rocks that have fallen from the mountains high above the valley. Legend has it that a giant used three of the rocks as a base for his cooking pot, and the name Aluvihara (Ash Monastery) refers to the ashes from the cooking fire.

The first cave you come to contains a 10m reclining Buddha and impressive lotus-pattern murals on the ceiling. Another is filled with cartoon-like murals of the realms of hell – if you're considering straying from the straight and narrow, you may think twice after seeing the statues of devils meting out an inventive range of punishments to sinners in the afterlife. One scene shows a sexual sinner with his skull cut open and his brains being ladled out by two demons.

Up a flight of rock steps is a cave dedicated to Buddhaghosa, the Indian scholar who is supposed to have spent several years here while working on the Tipitaka. Although histories affirm that Buddhaghosa lived in Anuradhapura in the 6th century AD, there's no clear evidence he stayed at Aluvihara. Nonetheless the cave walls are painted with scenes showing Buddhaghosa working on *ola* (palm-leaf) manuscripts.

Stairs continue to the summit of the rock bluff, where you'll find a dagoba and sweeping views of the surrounding valley.

The Tipitaka was first transcribed from oral and Sinhalese sources into Pali text by a council of monks held at Aluvihara in the 1st century BC. Two thousand years later, in 1848, the monks' library was destroyed by British troops putting down a revolt. The long process of replacing the *ola* manuscripts still occupies monks, scribes and craftspeople today. You can see their **workshop** (payment by donation); the donation includes having your name inscribed on a small length of *ola*.

A three-wheeler from Matale to Aluvihara will cost about Rs 300 return, including waiting time, and a bus will cost Rs 10. If arriving by car, drive up and around the site to the left to avoid the first long set of stairs.

Matale Heritage Centre CULTURAL CENTRE
(☎222 2404; 33 Sir Richard Aluvihara Mawatha; admission free; ⌚9am-4pm Mon-Sat) About 2km north of Matale, this sleepy crafts centre draws on the rich traditions of the area, producing quality batik, embroidery, carpentry and brasswork. It occupies a sprawling compound of bungalows, workshops and gardens up in a forest. The centre's Aluvihare Kitchens does meals for groups of four (book by phone a day ahead); it costs Rs 1000 per person for a banquet of many rices and curries. A three-wheeler from Matale will cost about Rs 300 return, including waiting time.

Sri Muthumariamman Thevasthanam TEMPLE
(admission Rs 200;⌚6am-noon, 4.30-8pm) Just north of the bus stop for Kandy at the north end of town is this interesting Hindu temple. A priest will show you the five enormous, colourful ceremonial chariots pulled along by people during an annual festival.

Matale's pleasant **park** includes a monument to the leaders of the 1848 Matale Rebellion – one of the less-famous contributions to the Year of Revolutions! There are many **spice gardens** and several **batik showrooms** along the road between Matale and Aluvihara. Tours of the gardens include milkless cocoa tea sweetened with vanilla and banana, and various creams and potions claimed to make hair shine or cure flatulence. Prices at some spice-garden shops are higher than in city markets.

Sleeping & Eating

There's no compelling reason to stay in Matale but there a couple decent options should the day be late.

Sesatha Hotel GUESTHOUSE $$
(☎223 1489; 40 Kohombiliwela; r Rs 2500-3000; ❄) There are serene rice-field views from the balconies of the five rooms (all with fridges) at this small guesthouse. The decor is modern and everything is quite clean. There are frequent wedding receptions held here during the day but don't expect to get to kiss the bride. Food is available. Sesatha is 1.5km south of town, about 200m off the main road.

Matale Rest House GUESTHOUSE $
(☎222 2299; Park Rd; r Rs 800-1200, air-con extra Rs 1000; ❄) This is the old government-run guesthouse and has 14 somewhat acceptable rooms with hot water for the weary traveller. The rest house has a broad front lawn; Chinese and Sri Lankan meals at the restaurant cost around Rs 800.

TOP CHOICE **A&C Restaurant** SRI LANKAN $
(3/5 Sir Richard Aluvihara Mawatha; meals Rs 500-900; ⌚11am-3pm) The A&C is a real treat. The restaurant has been carved out of a local home, although the entire operation is rather slick. Tasty home-cooked Sri Lankan meals whipped up by the proprietors are varied and flavourful (when offered, the buffets are a great deal at Rs 800). It's on the same turnoff as the Matale Heritage Centre, but then take a sharp left rather than the road to the centre.

Bentota Bake House SRI LANKAN $
(77/A Kandy Rd; snacks from Rs 100; ⌚8am-8pm) At the south end of town, this is the place for a wide range of short eats (deep-fried snacks and other small bites). Its popularity means that food is fresh through the day.

Getting There & Away

Bus 593 runs from Kandy to Matale (normal/intercity express Rs 43/65, 1½ hours) every 10 minutes. Buses to Dambulla or Anuradhapura will drop you at Aluvihara (Rs 10) or the spice gardens. There are six trains daily on the pretty 28km spur line between Matale and Kandy (Rs 25, 1½ hours).

Nalanda

☎066

Nalanda is known for the venerable **Nalanda Gedige** (adult/child Rs 500/250; ⌚7am-5pm), about 25km north of Matale and 20km before Dambulla. Built in the style of a South Indian Hindu temple, it consists of an entrance hall connected to a taller *shikara* (holy image sanctuary), with a courtyard for circumambulations. There is no sign of Hindu gods, however, and the temple is said to have been used by Buddhists. This is one of the earliest stone buildings constructed in Sri Lanka.

The temple's richly decorated stone-block walls, reassembled from ruins in 1975, are thought to have been fashioned during the 8th to 11th centuries. The plinth bears some Tantric carvings with sexual poses – the only such sculptures in Sri Lanka – but before you get excited, the carvings are weather-beaten and it's difficult to see much.

The site is beside a tank (artificial lake) 1km east of the main road – a sign marks the turnoff near the 49km post. Anuradhapura buses from Kandy or Matale will drop you at the turnoff.

Dambulla

☎066 / POP 71,000

Dambulla's famed Royal Rock Temple is an iconic Sri Lankan image – you'll be familiar with its spectacular Buddha-filled interior long before you arrive in town. Despite its slightly commercial air, this remains an important holy place and should not be missed if you are anywhere nearby. You can visit it as a day trip on public transport from Kandy, or stop by on your way to or from Sigiriya.

Dambulla has ATMs, grocery stores and plenty of other shops.

Sights

TOP CHOICE **Cave Temples** TEMPLES

(adult/child Rs 1200/free; ⌚7.30am-6pm) The beautiful Royal Rock Temple complex sits 100m to 160m above the road in the southern part of Dambulla. The hike up to the temples begins along a vast, sloping rock face with steps in some places. There are superb views over the surrounding countryside from the level of the caves; Sigiriya is clearly visible some 20km distant.

The caves' history as a place of worship is thought to date from around the 1st century BC, when King Valagamba (Vattajamini Abhaya), driven out of Anuradhapura, took refuge here. When he regained his throne, he had the interior of the caves carved into magnificent rock temples. Further improvements were made by later kings, including King Nissanka Malla, who had the caves' interiors gilded, earning the place the name Ran Giri (Golden Rock).

There are five separate caves containing about 150 Buddha images. Most of the paintings in the temples date from the 19th century.

The ticket office is at the gate near the monstrous Golden Temple, and your receipt is checked at the entrance at the base of the hill. Photography is allowed inside the caves, but not of people.

Cave I (Devaraja Viharaya)

The first cave, the Temple of the King of the Gods, has a 15m-long reclining Buddha. Ananda, the Buddha's loyal disciple, and other seated Buddhas are depicted nearby. A statue of Vishnu is held in a small shrine within the cave, but it's usually closed.

Cave II (Maharaja Viharaya)

The Temple of the Great King is arguably the most spectacular of the caves. It measures 52m from east to west and 23m from the entrance to the back wall; the highest point of the ceiling is 7m. This cave is named after the two statues of kings it contains. There is a painted wooden statue of Valagamba on the left as you enter, and another statue further inside of Nissanka Malla. The cave's main Buddha statue, which appears to have once been covered in gold leaf, is situated under a *makara torana* (archway decorated with dragons), with the right hand raised in *abhaya mudra* (pose conveying protection). Hindu deities are also represented. The vessel inside the cave collects water that constantly drips from the ceiling of the temple – even during droughts – which is used for sacred rituals.

Cave III (Maha Alut Viharaya)

This cave, the New Great Temple, was said to have been converted from a storeroom in the 18th century by King Kirti Sri Rajasinghe of Kandy, one of the last Kandyan monarchs. This cave, too, is filled with Buddha statues, including a beautiful reclining Buddha, and is separated from Cave II by only a masonry wall.

Cave IV (Pachima Viharaya)

The relatively small Western Cave is not the most westerly cave – that position belongs to Cave V. The central Buddha figure is seated under a *makara torana,* with its hands in *dhyana mudra* (a meditative pose in which the hands are cupped). The small dagoba in the centre was broken into by thieves who believed that it contained jewellery belonging to Queen Somawathie.

Cave V (Devana Alut Viharaya)

This newer cave was once used as a storehouse, but it's now called the Second New Temple. It features a reclining Buddha; Hindu

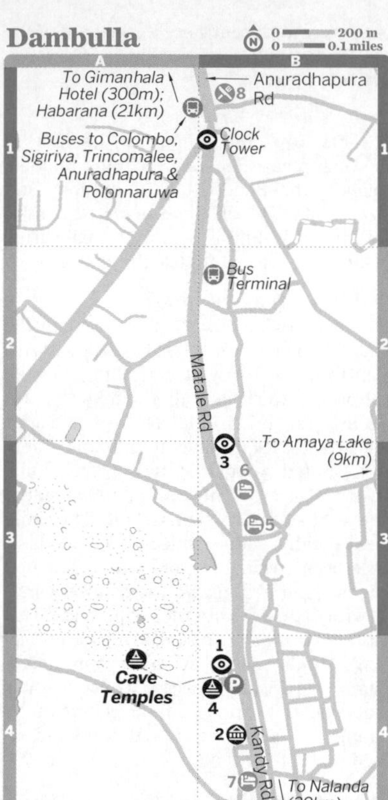

deities, including Kataragama (Murugan) and Vishnu, are also present.

Golden Temple TEMPLE

(www.goldentemple.lk; admission free) At the foot of the cave temples hill stands the modern Golden Temple, a kitschy structure completed in 2000 using Japanese donations. On top of the cube-shaped building sits a 30m-high Buddha image in the *dhammachakka mudra* (wheel-turning pose) and a huge neon sign.

Dambulla Museum MUSEUM

(adult/child Rs 230/115; ⏲7.30am-4.30pm) Recreations of art from the cave temples, artefacts and detailed English-language explanations are presented in a large building some 500m south of the main caves parking area. The displays are a good primer on Sri Lankan art from cave paintings to 18th-century frescoes. Staff are keen to show you around.

Dambulla

Top Sights

Cave Temples A4

Sights

1 Cave Temples Ticket Office B4
2 Dambulla Museum B4
3 Dambulla Produce Market B3
4 Golden Temple B4

Sleeping

5 Dambulla Guest House B3
6 Healey Tourist Inn B3
7 Sundaras B4

Eating

8 Bentota Restaurant B1

Dambulla Produce Market MARKET

(Matale Rd; ⏲noon-3am) Even if you're not looking to buy a truckload of bananas, this vast wholesale market south of the centre offers a fascinating look at the vast range of produce gown in Sri Lanka. What you see being carted about with manic energy (be careful and stay out of everybody's way) will be sold in Colombo tomorrow.

Sleeping & Eating

You have three main choices location-wise when deciding where to bed down in Dambulla: near the cave temples; north of town with various tour groups; and way out in the lush countryside by the Amaya Lake (which is a part Kandalama Wewa, a large old tank).

All the places to stay have places to eat; if going offsite, try the Dambulla Rest House or the vaunted Heritance Kandalama Hotel.

TOP CHOICE **Heritance Kandalama Hotel** RESORT HOTEL $$$

(☎555 5000; www.heritancehotels.com; r from US$170; ❄📶🏊) The Kandalama has a 'wow' factor thanks to its famous design by renowned architect Geoffrey Bawa (see boxed text, p53). The hotel emerges from the forest like a lost city, its walls and roofs covered in vines that allow it to blend into the natural environment. The award-winning 152-room hotel has an infinity pool overlooking the Kandalama Wewa and is renowned for its restaurants, which serve authentically fiery curries. Activities include birdwatching walks and 4WD safaris, and as at Amaya

Lake, there's a hotel-supported traditional village, Puranagama. It's 11km east of Dambulla.

Dambulla Guest House GUESTHOUSE **$$**
(228 4799; www.ceylonhotels.lk; Kandy Rd; r Rs 3900-7000;) With an attractive one-storey design, this former government rest house has been given a thorough revamp. The four comfortable rooms have a dark-wood and cream decor (three are large, one is small). The small restaurant has food a cut above the norm (mains from Rs 500) and you can enjoy a beer under trees out front while soaking up the roadside buzz.

Amaya Lake RESORT HOTEL **$$$**
(446 8100; www.amayaresorts.com; villas from US$130;) This huge, breezy complex has 126 stylish villas set in quiet gardens (wi-fi is lobby-only). Facilities include tennis courts, a gorgeous pool and an Ayurvedic spa. Adjacent to a traditional village are 11 'ecolodges', which were built with locally found natural materials and methods and have solar hot water. The Ayurvedic cuisine available in the restaurants uses herbs and vegetables cultivated in the village. To get here from Dambulla, follow the Kandalama road for about 3km, then veer left and continue for another 6km along the tank.

Sundaras GUESTHOUSE **$$**
(072 708 6000; www.sundaras.com; 189 Kandy Rd; s/d US$35/40;) Within a short walk of the caves and museum, this small, modern guesthouse has seven rooms spread over two floors. Furnishings are basic but there is hot water and a small garden. The busy compound of the family who owns the Sundaras is out back. Some budget guesthouses are nearby.

Healey Tourist Inn HOMESTAY **$**
(228 4940; 172 Kandy Rd; s/d Rs 1200/1500;) This place has the look and feel of an expanded family home. The five rooms are a little boxy but have hot water and there are common areas in which to chill. It's nothing luxurious, but the owners are a delight and it's within walking distance of the caves and bus station.

Little Dream GUESTHOUSE **$**
(072 289 3736; r fan-only Rs 1200, with air-con Rs 2500;) Out in the countryside just below the dam, the Little Dream is a great choice if you want to meet a local family and get to know life in rural Sri Lanka. It's close to the Kandalama tank, a great place to escape the oppressive afternoon heat. Snoozing in the hammock is just as pleasurable. It's about 8km along the road to Amaya Lake; a three-wheeler will cost about Rs 400 from the clock tower (ignore efforts by drivers to take you elsewhere).

Gimanhala Hotel HOTEL **$$**
(228 4864; gimanhala@sltnet.lk; 754 Anuradhapura Rd; r Rs 6000-7000; @) This solid midrange choice offers modern accommodation and a convenient location by the main road north of town. It's set back from the road in a compound and there's a swimming pool in a pretty garden. The hotel is popular with small groups and the 17 rooms have the expected comforts. The restaurant's daily buffets cater to tourists.

Pelwehera Village Resort HOTEL **$$**
(228 4281; www.pelweheraresort.com; Anuradhapura Rd; r US$60-90;) For solid no-frills comfort, try this two-storey hotel, just north of town. The 28 modern rooms have fridges, outdoor sitting areas and good beds. There is a spa and the pool is quite large: it will be a beacon of respite after a day surmounting the cave temples.

Bentota Restaurant SRI LANKAN **$**
(Anuradhapura Rd; meals from Rs 300; 8am-8pm;) At the centre of town, this outlet of the good local chain offers a wide range of short eats or more elaborate affairs (OK, rice and curry) in the dining rooms.

Getting There & Around

Dambulla is 72km north of Kandy on the road to Anuradhapura. The junction with the Colombo–Trincomalee road (Hwy 6) is in the centre of town.

The closest train station is in Habarana, 23km north. Frequent buses run from the modernistic bus terminal:

Anuradhapura Rs 80, two hours
Colombo Rs 150, five hours
Kandy Rs 74, two hours
Polonnaruwa Rs 74, 1¾ hours
Sigiriya Rs 27, 45 minutes

A three-wheeler around town will demand Rs 100; the drivers are especially aggressive at trying to steer you to favoured places to stay. Be firm.

Sigiriya

☎066 / POP 1500

The premier site of the Cultural Triangle, the soaring pillar of rock called Sigiriya doesn't disappoint, even from afar. For history buffs it has associations with both king and clergy. Art aficionados will appreciate the brilliant frescoes painted high up on its sheer walls. For casual tourists, Sigiriya is simply an awesome sight, with amazing views and impressive archaeological discoveries. Whatever attitude you bring to the rock, you won't be disappointed. The entire site is quite beautiful, from the lily-pad-covered moats to the quiet corners deep within the water gardens.

History

From a geologic point of view, Sigiriya is the hardened magma plug of an extinct volcano that long ago eroded away. Peppered with natural cave shelters and rock overhangs – supplemented over the centuries by numerous hand-hewn additions and modifications – the rock may have been inhabited in prehistoric times.

Popular myth says that the formation served royal and military functions during the reign of King Kassapa (AD 477–495), who allegedly built a garden and palace on the summit. According to this theory, King Kassapa sought out an unassailable new residence after overthrowing and murdering his own father, King Dhatusena of Anuradhapura.

After the 14th century the monastery complex was abandoned. British archaeologist HCP Bell discovered the ruins in 1898, which were further excavated by British explorer John Still in 1907.

Unesco declared Sigiriya a World Heritage Site in 1982.

Sights

Sigiriya (www.adstp.sltda.lk; adult/child US$30/15; tickets 8.30am-5.30pm) is a historic site. Since it is not a holy site, sarongs are not required. Expect a visit to take at least half a day.

Hopeful guides hang around the entrance to the site and will also approach you once you're inside. If you decide to use their services, negotiate very carefully.

An early or late ascent of the rock avoids the main crowds and the fierce heat. Allow at least two hours for the return trip, and more on very busy days. Bring plenty of water (there are drink vendors near the exit, once you're down) and wear a hat as it's often too windy near the summit to carry an umbrella. The 370m-ascent involves steep climbs, so if you're not fit it may be tough. Beware of 'helpers' who latch on to visitors offering assistance that turns to aggravation when they make outlandish demands for money. More charming are the ubiquitous monkeys with their pageboy hairdos.

TOP CHOICE **Sigiriya Museum** MUSEUM

(8.30am-5.30pm) It's not the spectacular ruins and rock, but this new museum is a show-stopper. Using detailed and engaging displays and models, exhibits provide an excellent introduction to the site and explain its cultural importance beyond the obvious natural beauty.

The verifiable theory that Sigiriya was always a Buddhist monastery is explained here, although locals insist on the more romantic notions that it was a palace or fortress. Hence the terms traditionally used to describe the various features on the rock city assume it was once a royal palace. Among the artefacts, the large buxom stone deity stands out.

The museum is near the main ticket booth, just outside the main Sigiriya site.

Royal Gardens GARDENS

The first major feature once you enter the site proper; vast landscaped gardens include water gardens, boulder gardens and terraced gardens. It's a beautiful place to wander away from crowds (and you may wish to return here *after* your climb). Find a quiet spot and listen to the gentle gurgle of water and the songs of birds.

The usual approach to the rock is through the western (and most elaborate) gate. This takes you through beautiful symmetrical **water gardens**, which extend from the western foot of the rock; bathing pools, little islands with pavilions that were used as dry-season palaces, and trees frame the approach to the rock. The rock rises sheer and mysterious from the jungle. A series of steps leads up through the boulders at its base to the western face, and then ascends it steeply.

The **boulder gardens**, closer to the rock, feature rocks that once formed the bases of buildings. The steplike depressions in the sides of boulders were the foundations of brick walls and timber columns. The cistern and audience hall rocks are impressive.

The base of Sigiriya has been landscaped to produce the **terraced gardens**.

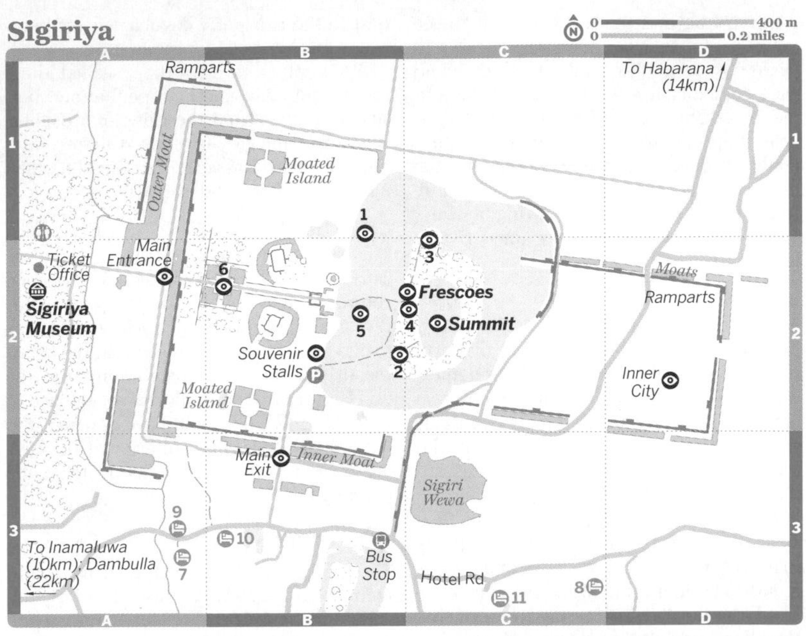

Sigiriya

Top Sights

- Frescoes C2
- Sigiriya Museum A2
- Summit C2

Sights

1. Boulder Gardens B1
2. Cobra Hood Cave B2
3. Lion's Paws & Stairs to Summit C2
4. Mirror Wall C2
5. Terraced Gardens B2
6. Water Gardens B2

Sleeping

7. Flower Inn A3
8. Hotel Sigiriya C3
9. Nilmini Lodge A3
10. Sigiriya Guest House B3
11. Sigiriya Village C3

Frescoes ART

Halfway up the rock there's an open-air spiral stairway leading up from the main route to a long, sheltered gallery in the sheer rock face.

In this niche is a series of paintings of buxom, wasp-waisted women, popularly believed to represent either *apsaras* (celestial nymphs) or King Kassapa's concubines. Modern theory suggests the female forms represent aspects of Tara – a bodhisattva and one of the most important figures in Tantric Buddhism. They are similar in style to the rock paintings at Ajanta in India, but have a specific character in their classical realist style. No one knows the exact dates of the impressive frescoes, though it's unlikely they date as far back as the 5th century (when King Kassapa reigned).

Protected from the sun in the sheltered gallery, the paintings remain in remarkably good condition, their colours still glowing. They're at their best in the late afternoon light. Flash photography is not allowed.

Mirror Wall ART

Beyond the fresco gallery detour, the path clings to the sheer side of the rock and is protected on the outside by a 3m-high wall.

This wall was coated with a smooth glaze upon which visitors of 1000 years ago felt impelled to note their impressions of the women in the gallery above – or so says local legend. The graffiti, inscribed between the 6th and 14th centuries, are of great interest to scholars because they show the development of the Sinhala language and script, and because they demonstrate an appreciation of art and beauty. You'll have to look hard beyond the modern mess to see the ancient messages.

One typical graffito reads, 'The ladies who wear golden chains on their breasts beckon me. As I have seen the resplendent ladies, heaven appears to me as not good.' Another reads, 'A deer-eyed young woman of the mountainside arouses anger in my mind. In her hand she had taken a string of pearls and in her looks she has assumed rivalry with us.'

Lion's Paws — CARVINGS

At the northern end of the rock the narrow pathway emerges on to the large platform from which the rock derives its later name – the Lion Rock, Sigiriya. HCP Bell, the British archaeologist responsible for an enormous amount of archaeology in Sri Lanka, found the two enormous lion paws when excavating here in 1898. At one time a gigantic brick lion sat at this end of the rock, and the final ascent to the top commenced with a stairway that led between the lion's paws and into its mouth. The lion symbolism serves as a reminder to devotees ascending the rock that Buddha was Sakya-Simha (Lion of the Sakya Clan) and that the truths he spoke of were as powerful as the sound of a lion's roar.

The 5th-century lion has since disappeared, apart from the first steps and the paws. Reaching the top means clambering up across a series of grooves cut into the rock; fortunately there is a handrail.

Summit — NATURAL FEATURE

The terraced top of the rock covers 1.6 hectares. At one time it was covered with buildings, but only the foundations remain today. With its commanding and obvious once-extensive development, it is easy to see how legends about a palace or even a fortress could replace the somewhat more mundane reality of the summit being the site of a monastery. A 27m-by-21m pond hewn out of the rock looks for all the world like a modern swimming pool, although it may have been used merely for water storage.

Dr Raja de Silva, Sri Lanka's former archaeological commissioner, has pointed out that there is no archaeological evidence of a palace-like structure anywhere on the summit. In particular there is a complete absence of stone bases, post holes, visible foundations for cross walls or window sashes, and a lack of lavatory facilities. Instead what you see is an enclosed terrace lying next to the ruins of a dagoba, suggesting it was a spot reserved for meditation.

A smooth stone slab (the so-called king's throne, possibly another meditation spot) sits 30m away from the ruins of a dagoba. You can sit and gaze far across the surrounding jungle as Kassapa – or the Buddhist monks – probably did over 1500 years ago.

Cobra Hood Cave — NATURAL FEATURE

This rocky projection earned its name because the overhang resembles a fully opened cobra's hood. Generally you will pass by this cave after descending the rock on your way to the south gate and the car park. Below the drip ledge is an inscription from the 2nd century BC that indicates it belonged to Chief Naguli, who would have donated it to a monk. The plastered interior of the cave was once embellished with floral and animal paintings.

 Tours

The land around the rock is loaded with animals and natural features. The large resorts, Elephant Corridor, Hotel Sigiriya and Jetwing Vil Uyana, all offer various **nature tours** from about Rs 2000. These are open to nonguests and usually include the services of naturalist.

Sleeping & Eating

Sigiriya's growing popularity means that new businesses are opening constantly. Hotels and guesthouses for all budgets can be found near the site itself and scattered along the road to Inamaluwa.

Guesthouses offer meals of tasty rice and curry for around Rs 500. For more elaborate affairs, consider the Ancient Villa Hotel, Jetwing Vil Uyana or Sigiriya Village. The small commercial strip near the site entrance has a basic cafe.

TOP CHOICE Ancient Villa Hotel — GUESTHOUSE $$

(077 630 2070, 077 857 0343; www.ancientvillasigiriya.com; Sigiriya Rd; s/d Rs 2500/3000;) This leafy compound about midway between Sigiriya and Inamaluwa backs up to a lovely little stream, which is often visited by thirsty elephants. There are five rooms (although there are plans to add more) in cottages – some shared – that include TVs and fridges. It's all excellent value but the real highlight here is the regular torch-lit barbecue dinners under the stars by the stream. Call to book if you're not staying here.

TOP CHOICE **Jetwing Vil Uyana** RESORT $$$
(☎228 6000; www.jetwinghotels.com; Kibissa; r from US$325; ❄📶🏊) Entering this open-air lodge you check in and enjoy a welcome drink while observing nature: crocodiles swim in the pond, monitor lizards dart through the grass and elephants come for an afternoon dip. The 25 individual chalets have a rustic look outside but inside are anything but. Well spaced around this vast naturalist property, some have private plunge pools. The resort includes a spa, and a resident naturalist is on hand to give walking tours.

Elephant Corridor RESORT $$$
(☎228 6951; www.elephantcorridor.com; Kibissa; r from US$300; ❄📶🏊) Hidden away on 200 acres of unfenced grasslands between the Kandalama Hills and Pothana Lake, this boutique resort takes its name from the wild elephants that often wander through the area. Each of the 23 high-ceilinged villas comes luxuriously equipped including binoculars, an artist's easel and pastels and a private plunge pool. Wi-fi is only in the lobby, which has a stunning view of the rock. The turnoff is 4km from the Inamaluwa junction en route to Sigiriya, down a dirt track.

Hotel Sigiriya HOTEL $$$
(☎228 6821; www.serendibleisure.com; Hotel Rd; s/d US$100/115; ❄@🏊) The hotel has 79 well-equipped rooms (minibars, safes), and there are great views of the rock from the dining room and large pool area (Rs 250 for nonguests). It's a pretty walk to Sigiriya from here, although many guests are in groups and ride a bus. Twitchers flock to this place, lured by its resident naturalist who leads much-lauded birdwatching trips (Rs 2000).

Sigiriya Village HOTEL $$$
(☎223 6803; www.sigiriyavillage.com; r US$120-150; ❄@📶🏊) This is one of the prettiest hotels in Sigiriya, thanks to its spectacular views of the rock that reflect off the shimmering swimming pool; nonguests can use the pool for Rs 250. This 124-room hotel also sets itself apart by growing organic vegetables for the attractive open-air restaurant. Make friends with the many resident geese. Only some rooms have wi-fi.

Grand Regent HOTEL $$
(☎567 0136, 482 2444; www.grandregenthotel.com; Sigiriya Rd; r 3500-4000; ❄) Deeply shaded, this small hotel has eight cabins set around frog-filled ponds. It's not as grand as the name suggests – the rooms are actually pretty average – but the common dining area is nice enough and it has Ayurvedic massage. It's about 4km from Inamaluwa junction.

Sigiriya Guest House GUESTHOUSE $$
(☎228 6299; www.ceylonhotels.lk; s/d Rs 5200/6000; ❄📶) This simple but tastefully designed rest house has lovely views of the rock and a peaceful atmosphere, especially when lounging on its long veranda. The 14 rooms are clean; the restaurant does nothing to compete with Sigiriya's inherent beauty. Wi-fi is expensive.

Hotel Eden Garden HOTEL $$
(☎228 6635; www.edengardenlk.com; Sigiriya Rd, Inamaluwa; r Rs 4000-6000; ❄📶🏊) Despite the rather ungainly facade, this is a good spot: 35 large, clean rooms, some with balconies, overlook a well-kept garden, and there's a pool (Rs 250 for nonguests). Cheaper options are fan-only. It's 100m from the junction, at Inamaluwa.

Nilmini Lodge GUESTHOUSE $
(☎567 0469, 077 306 9536; nilmini_lodge@yahoo.com; r Rs 800-2000; ❄📶) This guesthouse is small and basic (some rooms are fan-only and share bathrooms), but clean and comfortable enough for a short stay. It's close to the rock. Stay three nights and you can enjoy a free guided tour of the area in a half-century-old Morris Minor. It also lends out push bikes at no cost.

Flower Inn GUESTHOUSE $
(☎567 2197, 568 9953; r Rs 1200-2000) An obvious choice for travellers with a floral fetish, this centrally located small family home bursts with plants, both plastic and genuine. The nine rooms (some good for families, some with stuffed animals) are maintained by a friendly family that tries hard to please. Good Sri Lankan meals are hot, fresh and inexpensive.

Sigiri Holiday Inn GUESTHOUSE $
(☎228 6330; sholidayinn@yahoo.com; Sigiriya Rd; r Rs 1500-2200; ❄) This compact seven-room guesthouse is 500m from the Inamaluwa junction on Sigiriya Rd. With spotless bathrooms and an outdoor restaurant, it's a pleasant spot. Rooms downstairs are smaller and are fan-cooled with cold water.

Holiday Cottage GUESTHOUSE $$
(☎072 764 5477; Sigiriya Rd; r US$25-45; ❄📶) The two rooms at this huge property are well equipped, with fridges and comfy outdoor

sitting areas. Enjoy a beer out in the large garden and let the breezes blow in to save on the air-con surcharge.

Shopping

Sigiriya Crafts Complex HANDICRAFTS
(Sigiriya Rd) A hardy band of artisans and craftspeople soldier on at this government-run crafts village about midway between Inamaluwa and Sigiriya. Ignore the vacant buildings and concentrate on those where you'll find carvers, sculptors and more.

Information

Stock up on cash and supplies in Dambulla: the small village near the entrance to the site has just the bare essentials like bottled water.

Head to **Lonely Planet** (www.lonelyplanet.com/sri-lanka/the-ancient-cities/sigiriya) for planning advice, author recommendations, traveller reviews and insider tips.

Getting There & Around

Sigiriya is about 10km east of the main road between Dambulla and Habarana. The turnoff is at Inamaluwa. Buses to/from Dambulla run about every 30 minutes from around 7am (Rs 27, 45 minutes). The last bus to Dambulla leaves at around 7pm (but double-check this). Three-wheelers run from Dambulla to Sigiriya (about Rs 1000, negotiate).

Sigiriya and its surrounds are ideally explored by bike. Ask at your guesthouse or hotel about bike hire. Sigiriya Village rents mountain bikes to guests and nonguests for Rs 300 per hour.

DON'T MISS

EXPLORING AROUND SIGIRIYA

With a bike you can explore the entire region around Sigiriya, which has a wealth of lush forests, wild elephants, hundreds of bird species and no end of archaeological sites. One of the best places to start is **Pidurangala Rock**. About 1km north of the Sigiriya site, this important cultural spot includes a temple, a tiny museum and never any crowds. Most rewarding is the climb up the rock, where there are amazing views of the more famous rock looming to the south.

Another good ride follows backroads for 25km to Dambulla via Amaya Lake and Kandalama Wewa, the large tank (reservoir).

Polonnaruwa

027 / POP 110,000

Kings ruled the central plains of Sri Lanka from Polonnaruwa 800 years ago, when it was a thriving commercial and religious centre. From here, free-marketeers haggled for rare goods and the pious prayed at any one of its numerous temples. The glories of that age can be found in archaeological treasures which give a pretty good idea of how the city looked in its heyday. Exploring this compact archaeological park is an Ancient Cities must-experience. The Quadrangle alone is worth the trip.

That Polonnaruwa is close to elephant-packed national parks only adds to its popularity.

History

For three centuries Polonnaruwa was a royal capital of both the Chola and Sinhalese kingdoms. Although nearly 1000 years old, it's much younger than Anuradhapura and generally in better repair (though smaller in scale).

The South Indian Chola dynasty made its capital at Polonnaruwa after conquering Anuradhapura in the late 10th century: Polonnaruwa was a strategically better place to guard against any rebellion from the Ruhunu Sinhalese kingdom in the southeast. It also, apparently, had fewer mosquitoes! When the Sinhalese king Vijayabahu I drove the Cholas off the island in 1070, he kept Polonnaruwa as his capital.

Under King Parakramabahu I (r 1153–86), Polonnaruwa reached its zenith. The king erected huge buildings, planned beautiful parks and, as a crowning achievement, created a 25-sq-km tank, which was so large that it was named the Parakrama Samudra (Sea of Parakrama). The present lake incorporates three older tanks, so it may not be the actual tank he created.

Parakramabahu I was followed by Nissanka Malla (r 1187–96), who virtually bankrupted the kingdom through his attempts to match his predecessors' achievements. By the early 13th century Polonnaruwa was beginning to prove as susceptible to Indian invasion as Anuradhapura was, and eventually it, too, was abandoned and the centre of Sinhalese power shifted to the western side of the island.

In 1982, Unesco added the ancient city of Polonnaruwa to its World Heritage list.

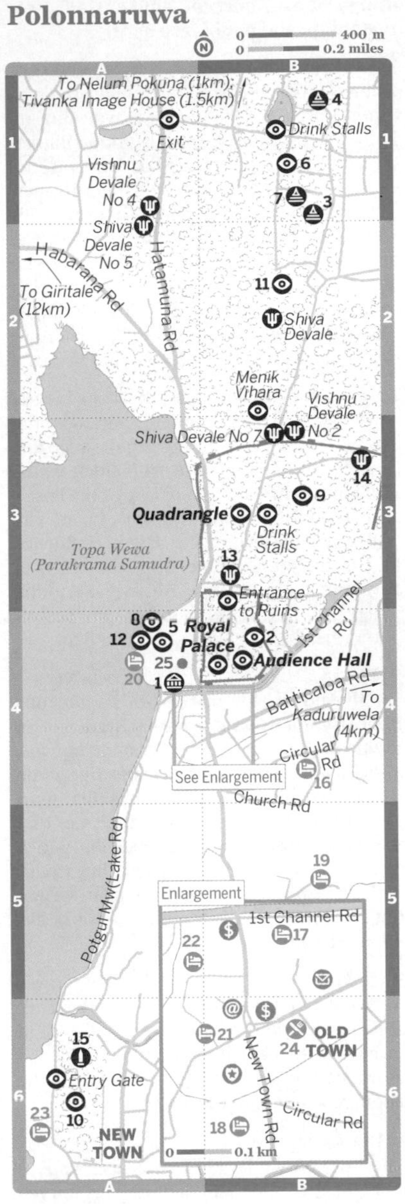

Polonnaruwa

Top Sights

- Audience Hall B4
- Quadrangle B3
- Royal Palace B4

Sights

1 Archaeological Museum A4
2 Bathing Pool B4
3 Buddha Seema Prasada B1
4 Gal Vihara B1
5 King's Council Chamber A4
6 Kiri Vihara B1
7 Lankatilaka B1
8 Nissanka Malla's Palace A4
9 Pabula Vihara B3
10 Potgul Vihara A6
11 Rankot Vihara B2
12 Royal Baths A4
13 Shiva Devale No 1 .... B3
14 Shiva Devale No 2 .... B3
15 Statue A6

Sleeping

16 Devi Tourist Home B4
17 Leesha Tourist Home B5
18 Manel Guest House B6
19 Palm Garden Guest House B5
20 Polonnaruwa Rest House A4
21 Samudra Guest House B6
22 Siyanco Holiday Resort A5
23 Village Polonnaruwa A6

Eating

Binora Restaurant .... (see 21)
24 Sathosa B6

Information

25 Ticket Desk A4

Sights

It is very easy to spend a day exploring the ruins, which can be conveniently divided into five groups: a small group near the Polonnaruwa Rest House on the banks of the tank; the royal palace group to the east of the Polonnaruwa Rest House; a very compact group a short distance north of the royal palace group, usually known as the Quadrangle; a number of structures spread over a wide area further north, known as the northern group; and the small southern group, towards the New Town. There are also a few other scattered ruins. The main sites all have informative info plaques.

A bike is an ideal way to explore the area. For details on admission policies, see p198.

Archaeological Museum MUSEUM

(9am-6pm) The Archaeological Museum is excellent. It's designed so that you walk from one end to the other, passing through a series of rooms, each dedicated to a

Polonnaruwa Quadrangle

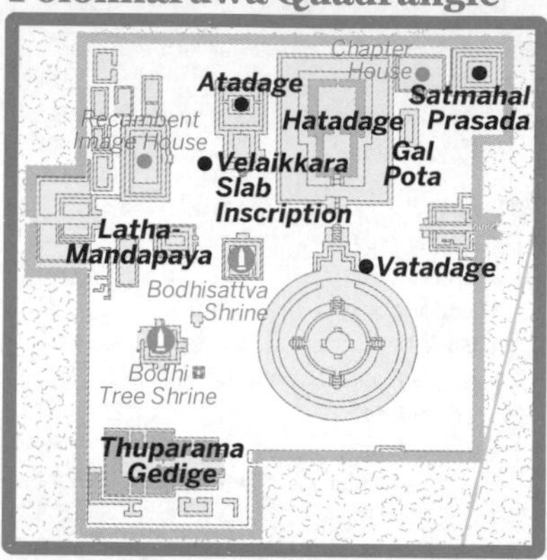

particular theme: the citadel, the outer city, the monastery area and the periphery, and Hindu monuments. The latter room contains a wonderful selection of bronzes. Of particular interest are the scale models of buildings, including the *vatadage* (circular relic house), which show how they might have looked in their heyday – if you follow the theory that they once had wooden roofs.

ROYAL PALACE GROUP

This group of buildings dates from the reign of Parakramabahu I. Parakramabahu's **Royal Palace** was a magnificent structure measuring 31m by 13m, and is said to have had seven storeys. The 3m-thick walls have holes to receive the floor beams for two higher floors; however, if there were another four levels, these must have been made of wood. The roof in this main hall, which had 50 rooms in all, was supported by 30 columns.

Parakramabahu's **Audience Hall** is notable for the frieze of elephants, each of which is in a different position. There are fine lions at the top of the steps.

In the southeast corner of the palace grounds, the **Bathing Pool** (Kumara Pokuna) has two of its crocodile-mouth spouts remaining.

QUADRANGLE

Only a short stroll north of the royal palace ruins, the area known as the Quadrangle is literally that – a compact group of fascinating ruins in a raised-up area bounded by a wall. It's the most concentrated collection of buildings you'll find in the Ancient Cities – an archaeologist's playpen. Besides the ruins described here, look for the **recumbent image house**, **chapter house**, **Bodhisattva shrine** and **bodhi tree shrine**.

Vatadage ANCIENT RUIN

In the southeast of the Quadrangle, the *vatadage* (circular relic house) is typical of its kind. Its outermost terrace is 18m in diameter, and the second terrace has four entrances flanked by particularly fine guardstones. The moonstone at the northern entrance is reckoned to be the finest in Polonnaruwa, although not of the same standard as some at Anuradhapura. The four entrances lead to the central dagoba with its four Buddhas. The stone screen is thought to be a later addition, probably by Nissanka Malla.

Thuparama Gedige ANCIENT RUIN

At the southern end of the Quadrangle, the Thuparama Gedige is the smallest *gedige* (hollow Buddhist temple with thick walls) in Polonnaruwa, but is also one of the best – and the only one with its roof intact. The building shows a strong Hindu influence and is thought to date from the reign of Parakramabahu I. There are several Buddha images in the inner chamber, but they're barely visible in the late afternoon light.

Gal Pota ANCIENT MONUMENT

On the north side of the Gal Pota (Stone Book) is a colossal stone representation of an *ola* book. It is nearly 9m long by 1.5m wide, and 40cm to 66cm thick. The inscription on it – the longest such stone inscription in Sri Lanka (and there are many!) – indicates that it was a Nissanka Malla publication. Much of it extols his virtues as a king, but it also includes the footnote that the slab, weighing 25 tonnes, was dragged from Mihintale, a mere 100km away.

Hatadage ANCIENT RUIN

Also erected by Nissanka Malla, the Hatadage is a tooth-relic chamber; it is said to have been built in 60 days. Stand at the entrance and admire the symmetry of the doors receding into the distance.

Latha-Mandapaya ANCIENT RUIN

The busy Nissanka Malla was also responsible for the Latha-Mandapaya. This unique structure consists of a latticed stone fence – a curious imitation of a wooden fence with posts and railings – surrounding a very small dagoba. The dagoba is encircled by stone pillars shaped like lotus stalks, topped by unopened buds. It is said that Nissanka

Malla sat within this enclosure to listen to chanted Buddhist texts.

Satmahal Prasada — ANCIENT MONUMENT

In the northeast corner stands the unusual ziggurat-style Satmahal Prasada, which consists of six diminishing storeys (there used to be seven), shaped like a stepped pyramid.

Atadage — ANCIENT MONUMENT

A shrine for the tooth relic, the Atadage is the only surviving structure in Polonnaruwa dating from the reign of Vijayabahu I.

Velaikkara Slab Inscription — ANCIENT MONUMENT

Just in case you thought that bureaucrats have evolved through the years, check out this 12th-century memorial slab with an equally lifeless slab of text tossing off credits in all directions.

AROUND THE QUADRANGLE

Along the road leading north from the Quadrangle, a gravel road branches off to the right just before you reach the city wall. Most of the following structures are on this road, as are many others. Several buildings in this area are Shiva Devales (Hindu temples), relics from the south Indian invasion of the 10th century.

Shiva Devale No 1 — TEMPLE

Just south of the Quadrangle, the 13th-century Hindu temple Shiva Devale No 1 displays the Indian influence that returned after Polonnaruwa's Sinhalese florescence. It is notable for the superb quality of its stonework, which fits together with unusual precision. The domed brick roof has collapsed, but when this building was being excavated a number of excellent bronzes, now in the Archaeological Museum, were found.

Shiva Devale No 2 — ANCIENT RUIN

Similar in style, Shiva Devale No 2 is the oldest structure in Polonnaruwa and dates from the brief Chola period, when the Indian invaders established the city. Unlike so many buildings in the Ancient Cities, it was built entirely of stone, so the structure today is much as it was when built.

Pabula Vihara — ANCIENT TEMPLE

Also known as the Parakramabahu Vihara, Pabula Vihara is a typical dagoba from the period of Parakramabahu I. It is the third-largest dagoba in Polonnaruwa.

NORTHERN GROUP

You will need a bicycle or other transport to comfortably explore these spread-out ruins, all north of the city wall. They include the Gal Vihara, probably the most famous group of Buddha images in Sri Lanka, and the Alahana Pirivena monastic group. The Alahana Pirivena group consists of the Rankot Vihara, Lankatilaka, Kiri Vihara, Buddha Seema Prasada and the other structures around them. The name of the group means 'crematory college' – it stood in the royal cremation grounds established by Parakramabahu.

Rankot Vihara — ANCIENT TEMPLE

The 54m Rankot Vihara dagoba, the largest in Polonnaruwa and the fourth largest on the island, has been ascribed to the reign of King Nissanka Malla. Like the other major dagobas in Anuradhapura and Polonnaruwa, the dome consists of earth fill covered by a brick mantle and plaster. The construction clearly imitates the Anuradhapura style. Surgical instruments found in a nearby ruined 12th-century hospital are said to be similar to those used today.

Buddha Seema Prasada — ANCIENT RUIN

The highest building in the Alahana Pirivena group, this was the monastery abbot's convocation hall. This building features a fine *mandapaya* (raised platform with decorative pillars).

Lankatilaka — ANCIENT RUIN

Built by Parakramabahu and later restored by Vijayabahu IV, the huge Lankatilaka

NAVIGATING POLONNARUWA

Polonnaruwa has three distinct areas:

Old Town has a small commercial centre, hotels, the main museum and is close to the archaeological site. It borders the waters of Topa Wewa (Topa Tank) and has a relaxed tropical vibe.

New Town is south of Old Town and also has hotels but is otherwise not very densely developed and has little of interest.

Kaduruwela is 4km east of Old Town and is the main commercial strip for the region. It has the main bus and train stations, banks and services and a lot of traffic and little beauty.

gedige has 17m-high walls, although the roof has collapsed. The cathedral-like aisle leads to a huge standing headless Buddha. The outer walls of the *gedige,* decorated with bas-reliefs, show typical Polonnaruwa structures in their original state.

Kiri Vihara ANCIENT TEMPLE

Construction of the dagoba Kiri Vihara is credited to Subhadra, King Parakramabahu's queen. Originally known as the Rupavati Chetiya, the present name means 'milk white' because when the overgrown jungle was cleared away after 700 years of neglect, the original lime plaster was found to be in perfect condition. It is still the best-preserved unrestored dagoba at Polonnaruwa.

Gal Vihara ANCIENT MONUMENT

This is a group of beautiful Buddha images that probably marks the high point of Sinhalese rock carving. They are part of Parakramabahu's northern monastery. The Gal Vihara consists of four separate images, all cut from one long slab of granite. At one time each was enshrined within a separate enclosure. You can clearly see the sockets cut into the rock behind the standing image, into which wooden beams would have been inserted.

The standing Buddha is 7m tall and is said to be the finest of the series. The unusual position of the arms and sorrowful facial expression led to the theory that it was an image of the Buddha's disciple Ananda, grieving for his master's departure for nirvana, since the reclining image is next to it. The fact that it had its own separate enclosure, along with the discovery of other images with the same arm position, has discredited this theory and it is now accepted that all the images are of the Buddha.

The reclining image of the Buddha entering parinirvana is 14m long. Notice the subtle depression in the pillow under the head and the wheel symbol on the pillow end. The other two images are both of the seated Buddha. The one in the small rock cavity is smaller and of inferior quality.

Nelum Pokuna POND

A track to the left from the northern stretch of road leads to unusual Nelum Pokuna (Lotus Pond), nearly 8m in diameter, which has five concentric, descending rings of eight petals each. The pool was probably used by monks.

Tivanka Image House ANCIENT MONUMENT

The northern road ends at Tivanka Image House. Tivanka means 'thrice bent', and refers to the fact that the Buddha image within is in a three-curve position normally reserved for female statues. The building is notable for the carvings of energetic dwarfs cavorting around the outside, and for the fine frescoes within – the only Polonnaruwa murals to have survived. Some of these date from a later attempt by Parakramabahu III to restore Polonnaruwa, but others are much older.

SOUTHERN GROUP

The small southern group is close to the compound of top-end hotels. By bicycle it's a pleasant ride along the bund of the Topa Wewa. You'll likely find more cows and their friends the ibises than you will people here.

Also known as the library dagoba, the **Potgul Vihara** is an unusual structure. A thick-walled, hollow, dagoba-like building, it is thought to have been used to store sacred books. It's effectively a circular *gedige,* and four smaller solid dagobas arranged around this central dome form the popular Sinhalese quincunx arrangement of five objects in the shape of a rectangle (one at each corner and one in the middle).

Another interesting structure in the southern group is the **statue** at the northern end. Standing nearly 4m high, it's an unusually lifelike human representation, in contrast to the normally idealised or stylised Buddha figures. Exactly whom it represents is a subject of some debate. Some say that the object he is holding is a book and thus the statue is of Agastya, the Indian Vedic teacher. The more popular theory is that it is a yoke representing the 'yoke of kingship' and that the bearded, stately figure is Parakramabahu I. Others claim that the king is simply holding a piece of papaya.

REST HOUSE GROUP

Concentrated a few steps to the north of the Polonnaruwa Rest House are the ruins of the **Nissanka Malla's palace**, which have almost been reclaimed by the earth. The **Royal Baths** are the ruins nearest to Polonnaruwa Rest House.

King's Council Chamber ANCIENT MONUMENT

Furthest north is the King's Council Chamber, where the king's throne, in the shape of a stone lion, once stood. It is now in Colombo's National Museum. Inscribed into each column in the chamber is the name of the minister whose seat was once beside it. The mound nearby becomes an island when the waters of the tank are high; on it are the ruins of a small summer house used by the king.

Sleeping

There's no reason not to stay right in the Old Town or nearby. There's a collection of tired large hotels in New Town. For a better selection overall, try Giratale.

TOP CHOICE Samudra Guest House GUESTHOUSE $
(222 2817, 077 692 8813; Habarana Rd; r Rs 700-2700;) A rambling old house with a charming owner, the Samudra offers pleasant service and basic rooms (the bargain cheapies have fans and cold water). The hosts can organise safari tours to Minneriya National Park and Kaudulla National Park for about Rs 4000 total for one to three people. Bicycles can be hired for Rs 200.

Devi Tourist Home HOMESTAY $
(222 3181; Lake View Watte; r Rs 1000-2500; @) Among the budget choices, this modest homestay is one of the best in terms of affability. It has five rooms (the cheapest are fan-only) arranged around a garden. It's about 1km south of Old Town and down Church Rd (there's a sign on the main road). The ebullient owner is a member of Sri Lanka's small Malay population. Bicycles are available for Rs 200 per day.

Palm Garden Guest House GUESTHOUSE $
(222 2622, 077 795 7595; a.mahavitana@hotmail.com; New Town Rd; r fan/air-con Rs 1000/1800;) Located down a quiet back road this place offers respite for the weary backpacker. You can get meals served on your room's terrace, rent a bike (Rs 200) or just relax in the shade of a palm tree. Call for pickup from the bus stop.

Leesha Tourist Home HOMESTAY $
(072 334 0591; 105/A New Town Rd; r Rs 1200) Near other budget choices, this new entrant in the bottom-end sweepstakes has three rooms in a most genial family compound just south of the Old Town. Rooms are straight-forward and sparkling clean. Long tables on the covered terrace are good for catching up on your journal or playing Parcheesi.

Manel Guest House GUESTHOUSE $
(222 2481; New Town Rd; r Rs 2000-3000; @) In a quiet spot just outside the Old Town wall, Manel's nine spacious rooms differ in price depending on whether you get a fan or air-con. Good meals are served under the veranda. The co-owner, Mr Bandula, trawls the town for backpackers, so you may meet him before reaching his place.

Polonnaruwa Rest House GUESTHOUSE $$
(222 2299; www.ceylonhotels.lk; Potgul Mawatha; r Rs US$60-80; @) Perched over Topa Wewa, this ageing rest house has some of the best views in town. Built in the early 1950s specifically for a visit by Queen Elizabeth II, the hotel has been a local landmark ever since. While renovation remains long overdue, you can concentrate instead on the languor that comes from sitting on the veranda or having a meal in the crazy, glassed-in dining room. The food is more plebeian than royal. Book well ahead, especially for the Queen's room.

Siyanco Holiday Resort HOTEL $$
(222 6868; 1st Channel Rd; r Rs 3500-7000;) Very central, this hotel has an older block of 15 rooms that are basic and often dark. But a new wing offers the best accommodation close to the museum. These 37 modern hotel rooms have fridges, TVs etc and are quite large. This newer section also outclasses the gaudy architecture of the original section.

Village Polonnaruwa HOTEL $$
(222 2405; Potgul Mawatha; r 2000-4000; @) This bland 1970s motel-style place is a bit tired, like others in New Town, but on the bright side, it's clean, relatively cheap (the cheapest rooms are fan-only) for having hotel services and close to the tank. It's about 2km south of the Old Town. As a non-guest, spend Rs 500 on drinks and/or food and the pool is yours.

Eating

There's little reason to venture far from your hotel or guesthouse for a meal as there are no stand-out selections locally.

Binora Restaurant SRI LANKAN $
(Habarana Rd; mains from Rs 200; 8am-9pm) Run by the same charmers who have the Samudra Guest House, this basic cafe on the Old Town main drag has good rice and curries, all manner of fried rice and various

mains 'devilled' (which means they are fried up with hot spices).

Sathosa GROCERY STORE $
(⏲24hr) Opposite People's Bank, this small market is the place to by snacks and picnic items for a shady spread at some far corner of the archaeological site.

Information

The museum's **Ticket Desk** (☎222 4850; www.ccf.lk/polonnaruwa/; adult/child US$25/12.50; ⏲7.30am-6pm) has some information.

The main archaeological site closes at 6pm, but in practice you can stay until after dark. You enter from Habarana Rd, about 500m north of the museum. Tickets are not checked at the Polonnaruwa Rest House group or at the southern group

Although tickets technically allow you only one entrance, you can ask a ticket collector to sign and date your ticket so you can return. This way you could visit the site in the morning, take a cool break over midday and return in the late afternoon. Laugh politely at the three-wheeler drivers who say you don't need a ticket if you travel with them.

Old Town and Kaduruwela have ATMs.

Post office (Batticaloa Rd) In the centre of the Old Town.

Sachira Communication Centre (70B Habarana Rd; per hr Rs 100; ⏲7.30am-10pm) Internet access.

Star Telecom (Kaduruwela; per hr Rs 100; ⏲9.30am-8pm) Internet access; in the bus station.

Tourist Police (☎23099; Batticaloa Rd) In Old Town at the main traffic circle.

Getting There & Away

Bus

Polonnaruwa's main bus station is in Kaduruwela, 4km east of Old Town on Batticaloa Rd. Buses to and from the west pass through Old Town, but to make sure you get a seat, start at Kaduruwela.

Service is frequent until about 4pm on main routes, which include the following:

Anuradhapura Rs 120, three hours

Colombo regular/air-con Rs 220/380, six hours

Dambulla via Habarana air-con Rs 73, one hour

Kandy regular/air-con Rs 80/150, three hours

Train

Polonnaruwa is on the Colombo–Batticaloa railway line and is about 30km southeast of Gal Oya, where the line splits from the Colombo–Trincomalee line. The train station is in Kaduruwela, near the bus station.

Trains include the following:

Batticaloa 1st/2nd/3rd class Rs 850/150/85, two hours, five daily

Colombo 1st/2nd/3rd class Rs 750/500/270, six to seven hours, three daily

Getting Around

Frequent buses (Rs 10) link Old Town and Kaduruwela. A three-wheeler will demand Rs 200.

Bicycles are the ideal transport for getting around Polonnaruwa's monuments, which are surrounded by shady woodland. Most guesthouses rent bikes for about Rs 200 per day. Follow Potgul Mawatha (Lake Rd) for a beautiful ride.

Giritale

☎027 / POP 14,500

Twelve kilometres northwest of Polonnaruwa on the Habarana road, Giritale is a sleepy village alongside the 7th-century Giritale Tank. Despite there being little here beyond places to stay, it's a good base for visiting Polonnaruwa and Minneriya National Park, especially if you have your own transport.

Sleeping

Overall, the sleeping choices in Giritale outclass Polonnaruwa.

TOP CHOICE **Rice Villa Retreat** GUESTHOUSE $$
(☎077 630 2070; dimuthu81@hotmail.com; 21st Mile Post, Polonnaruwa Rd, Jayanthipura; s/d Rs 2500/2750; ❄📶) This beautiful new guesthouse has two lovely little bungalows in a vast and verdant rice field. They have hot water, satellite TV and nice decks for enjoying the view. Air-con is Rs 750 extra per night; the caring owners will prepare scrumptious meals (breakfast/dinner Rs 350/650). Reserve in advance and arrange a pickup from the bus stop, it's 3.5km east of town.

Giritale Hotel HOTEL $$$
(☎224 6311; www.giritalehotel.com; r from US$90; ❄@) Up the hill from other upscale properties, every room at this genteel hotel has sweeping views of the tank. See if you can spot elephants across the waters. It's well managed, if a bit long in the tooth – the pool could use a revamp.

LOCAL KNOWLEDGE

NIMAL PIETHISSA – THE MAKING OF A MAHOUT

Nimal Piethissa is a mahout (elephant handler) living in Habarana. Nimal worked as an apprentice for three years in Kandy before beginning work as a freelance mahout. We met up with him at the Habarana watering hole where mahouts take their elephants for a daily scrub.

Why did you choose this career? I always liked elephants as a boy and thought about doing this job from a young age. My parents agreed and allowed me to leave school so I could become a mahout apprentice. The money is OK, I make around Rs 7000 per month, plus it's lots of fun. On the downside, it's not a very prestigious job. Westerners like to romanticise this work, but in Sri Lanka it's considered a dirty job. When I tell the local girls it's an instant turnoff, no one really wants to marry a mahout.

What is the most difficult aspect of the job? These animals are pretty temperamental, so the most difficult part of the job is controlling their temper and dealing with them when they become angry. Usually food, sweet food and fruits, will calm them down. They especially like sugar cane, pineapples and bananas. If that doesn't work, we rub them and push specific pressure points with a *hindua* (pole). If they are not feeling well we can give them medicine, usually leaves from the *cohomba* tree work wonders.

How do you control them? Mostly with the *hindua*. People get frightened when we hit them with it but they are so big that it doesn't affect them much – like someone whacking you with a chopstick. We also have 26 words that we use to control them; for example, '*daha*' is 'go' and '*ho*' is 'stop'.

How much do they eat? Up to 300kg a day – grass mostly but also coconut husk and fruit. They also need to eat at night, so we usually need to wake up around 2am and then again at 5am. Elephants can travel long distances for food if they need to. Their sense of smell is one of the best among mammals – they can smell food up to 15km away.

Which elephants are the best to work with? It's considered an honour to work with king elephants. These are the elephants you usually see in the temples. A king elephant must have seven parts that touch the ground – four feet, the tail, the trunk and the penis.

How long can elephant live? Some live up to 70 years – if they have a good mahout to take care of them!

Deer Park RESORT $$$
(☎224 6272; www.deerparksrilanka.com; r from US$120; ❄@☜≋) Large duplex rooms are the real appeal at this large resort property deep in the trees by the tank. All 77 cottages have lovely garden sitting areas, some have outdoor showers and the top units have views of Giritale Tank. Restaurants include one up in the tree tops. Various nature tours can be arranged and there is a spa.

Peacock Solitude Hotel GUESTHOUSE $$
(☎224 5454, 077 178 8683; peacocksolitude@hotmail.com; r s/d US$30/35; ❄☜) Before you say the name is for the birds, consider that this tidy guesthouse is set well back from the road in a little cove of lovely trees. In fact you just might make a nest or strut your stuff in one of the 10 basic yet comfortable rooms. It's 4km west of Giritale.

Wood Side Tour Inn GUESTHOUSE $
(☎224 6307; www.woodsidetourinn.com; Polonnaruwa Rd; r Rs 800-2000; ❄) A pretty garden setting and a big mango tree make this an attractive budget option. The 10 older fan-cooled rooms are bare but fine. Five newer rooms have air-con and colourful paint plus balconies for smelling the mangoes.

ℹ Getting There & Away

Frequent buses on the road between Polonnaruwa in the east and Habarana and various points west stop in the centre of what little passes for Giritale village. None of the places to stay is especially near the stop, so arrange for a pickup.

Mandalagiri Vihara

Near Medirigiriya, about 30km north of Polonnaruwa, is the Mandalagiri Vihara, a *vatadage* virtually identical to the one at Polonnaruwa. While the Polonnaruwa *vatadage* is crowded among many other structures, the Mandalagiri Vihara stands alone atop a low hill. The site is uncrowded, and the country back road out here is a pretty drive.

An earlier structure may have been built here around the 2nd century, but the one that stands today was constructed in the 7th century by Aggabodhi IV. A granite flight of steps leads up to the *vatadage,* which has concentric circles of 16, 20 and 32 pillars around the dagoba. Four large Buddhas face the four cardinal directions. This *vatadage* is noted for its fine stone screens. There was once a hospital next to the *vatadage* – look for the bath shaped like a coffin.

Admission tickets cost adult/child US$10/5, but it's rare for anyone to check your ticket.

Mandalagiri Vihara is best visited as a half-day trip from Giritale. There are no places to stay or eat, nor are there any worth mentioning in nearby Medirigiriya. Without your own transport, this trip is a nearly impossible odyssey.

Habarana

066

This small town serves as a regional crossroads as well as a base for safaris to Minneriya and Kaudulla National Parks. There is good accommodation to suit all budgets and good transport links; Habarana has the nearest train station to Dambulla and Sigiriya.

Elephant rides around the tank can be arranged for a pricey US$20 to US$30 per person per hour. In the creek near town you can watch mahouts scrubbing down their elephants; guides and most locals can point the way.

Sleeping & Eating

The Habarana Rest House is right at the main road junction; you can watch the safari guides try to rope in customers. The other places to stay listed here are about 500m south off the Dambulla Rd.

TOP CHOICE **Habarana Rest House** GUESTHOUSE $$
(227 0003; www.ceylonhotels.lk; r from Rs 3900;) This one-storey rest house, set in a pleasant garden, has four rooms fronted by a long shaded veranda. It's right on the crossroads and you can watch all the action from your porch. A recent revamp has given the property a dash of style, especially in the restaurant, where the wi-fi signal is best.

Cinnamon Lodge RESORT $$$
(227 0012; www.cinnamonhotels.com; r from US$135;) The 137 spacious rooms come in vaguely Portuguese-colonial-style duplexes, and are set in 11 hectares of lush landscaping. A nature trail leads to a treehouse platform for viewing birds and monkeys. There is a spa and, among the three restaurants, Lotus uses organic ingredients. It's run by Sri Lanka's best hotel group.

Chaaya Village RESORT $$$
(227 0047; www.chaayahotels.com; r from US$100;) This well-managed top-end resort offers 108 spacious terraced rooms with verandas. The restaurant looks over the swimming pool, and there are sports facilities and a spa. The lakefront setting makes for easy birdwatching before breakfast. It's next to the Cinnamon Lodge.

Habarana Inn GUESTHOUSE $
(227 0010; Dambulla Rd; r Rs 1500-3100;) This basic place is the town's cheapest place to sleep. The eight rooms are clean and simply furnished, most are fan-only. It's just past Cinnamon Lodge, on the Dambulla road. The restaurant serves Sri Lankan (rice and curry Rs 600), Western and Chinese dishes.

Getting There & Away

Bus

Buses stop at the crossroads outside the Habarana Rest House. Frequent services:

Anuradhapura Rs 82, two hours
Dambulla air-con Rs 40, 30 minutes
Polonnaruwa Rs 38, 30 minutes

Train

The train station is 1km north of town on the Trincomalee road. The infrequent train services include the following:

Batticaloa 2nd/3rd class Rs 180/100
Colombo 2nd/3rd class Rs 300/160
Polonnaruwa 2nd/3rd class Rs 90/50

The station at Palugaswewa, 6km west, is served by more and faster trains.

Around Polonnaruwa & Habarana

The national parks around Polonnaruwa and Habarana offer excellent access to elephants and other animals without the crowds of Yala National Park. On some days you won't need to enter the parks to see elephants as they freely roam the countryside, especially north of Sigiriya.

MINNERIYA NATIONAL PARK

Dominated by the ancient Minneriya Tank, this park has plenty of scrub and light forest in its 88.9 sq km to provide shelter for its toque macaques, sambar deer, leopards and elephants, to name a few. The dry season, from May to September, is the best time to visit. By then water in the tank has dried up, exposing grasses and shoots to grazing animals; elephants, which number 200 or more, come to feed and bathe during what is known as 'the Gathering'; and flocks of birds, such as little cormorants and painted storks, fish in the shallow waters.

The park entrance is on the Habarana Polonnaruwa road. A visitor centre near the entrance sells tickets and has a few exhibits about the park's natural history.

KAUDULLA NATIONAL PARK

This park stands on the fringe of the ancient Kaudulla Tank. It established a 66.6-sq-km elephant corridor between Somawathiya Chaitiya National Park and Minneriya National Park. Just 6km off the Habarana–Trincomalee road at Gal Oya junction, it is also a popular safari tour from Polonnaruwa and Habarana because of the good chance of getting up close and personal with elephants. In October there are up to 250 elephants in the park, including herds of juvenile males. There are also leopards, fishing cats, sambar deer, endangered rusty spotted cats and sloth bears. The best months for a visit are October to March, which dovetail nicely with Minneriya.

Information

To visit the parks you must be accompanied by a licensed guide and you must enter and leave by vehicle (which will be your guide's 4WD jeep or truck). Both parks are well served by tours: during busy times you'll find guides in jeeps waiting at the park gates. Typically, however, you'll arrange your trip with your guesthouse or hotel or hire a guide from those waiting at the main crossroads in Habarana. With guide fees – and the many park fees – expect to pay about US$40 per person for a four-hour safari.

Besides the guide you hire, a park ranger will accompany you. Although this service is technically free, each group should tip the ranger about Rs 500. The parks are open dawn to dusk; fees are as follows:

Minneriya National Park adult/child Rs 1800/900, service charge Rs 1000, charge per vehicle Rs 250

Kaudulla National Park adult/child Rs 1100/660, service charge Rs 900, charge per vehicle Rs 250

DON'T MISS

THE GATHERING

One of Asia's great wildlife spectacles occurs at Minneriya National Park in August and September. Known as 'the Gathering', 200 or more elephants gather for several weeks in one concentrated spot. Long thought to be driven by thirst during the dry season, only recently has it been learned that the natural factors behind the Gathering are much more complex.

The elephants surround the Minneriya Tank, the huge reservoir first built in the 3rd century AD. It was assumed that they were there for the water, as it remains wet even when smaller water holes dry up. However, biologists have discovered that the water's retreat from the land is what really lures the elephants. As the tank shrinks, it leaves behind vast swaths of muddy earth that are soon covered in rich, tender grass. It's a tasty feast for the elephants and they come in droves.

Unfortunately, like so much else in Sri Lanka, the Gathering is under threat. While the water authority had in previous years slowly drained the water from the tank into smaller ponds elsewhere, the tank was left mostly full in 2011 in order to preserve the water should the expanding nearby farms need it (they didn't). The result was a lot of elephants standing around looking for their food.

Ritigala Ruins

Possibly Sri Lanka's best Indiana Jones adventure: deep inside the **Ritigala Strict Nature Reserve** are the sprawling, jungle-covered ruins of an extensive monastic and cave complex. The 24-hectare site is isolated and almost deserted. The broken stone structures, fallen carvings and once-sacred caves lie on a hill, which at 766m isn't exactly high, but is nevertheless a striking feature in the flat, dry landscape surrounding it.

The true meaning of the name Ritigala remains unclear – *gala* means 'rock' in Sinhala, but *riti* may come from the Pali *arittha,* meaning 'safety'. Thus Ritigala was probably a place of refuge, including for kings, as long ago as the 4th century BC.

Ritigala also has a place in mythology. It's claimed to be the spot from which Hanuman (the monkey god) leapt to India to tell Rama that he had discovered where Sita was being held by the king of Lanka. Mythology also offers an explanation for the abundance of healing herbs and plants found in Ritigala: it's said that Hanuman, on his way back to Lanka with healing Himalayan herbs for Rama's wounded brother, dropped some over Ritigala.

Monks found Ritigala's caves ideal for an ascetic existence, and more than 70 such caves have been discovered. Royals proved generous patrons, especially King Sena I, who in the 9th century made an endowment of a monastery to the *pamsukulika* (rag robes) monks.

Ritigala was abandoned following the Chola invasions in the 10th and 11th centuries, after which it lay deserted and largely forgotten until it was rediscovered by British surveyors in the 19th century. It was explored and mapped by HCP Bell in 1893.

Sights

Ritigala has none of the usual icons: no bodhi tree, no relic house and no Buddha images. The only embellishments are on the urinals at the forest monastery – it's been conjectured that by urinating on the fine stone carving the monks were demonstrating their contempt for worldly things.

Near the Archaeology Department bungalow are the remains of a *banda pokuna* (artificial pond), which apparently fills with water during the rainy season. It's an evocative location, with the steep green mountain providing a backdrop like a verdant amphitheatre. From here it's a scramble along a forest path via a donations hall to a **ruined palace** and the **monastery hospital**, where you can still see the grinding stones and huge stone baths. A flagstone path leads upwards; a short detour takes you to what is often described as a stone fort – or, more accurately, a lookout.

The next group of ruins of note are the double-platform structures so characteristic of forest monasteries. Here you can see the **urinal stones**, although they almost certainly weren't always in this exact spot. Scholars think they were used for meditation, teaching and ceremony. You can actually spend hours scrambling around the hillside through the dense vegetation. Now might be the time for a machete.

Information

Few people make the trek out to the Ritigala ruins, which only adds to their allure. Individual tickets cost US$10/5 per adult/child.

There are some Archaeology Department staff on-site, but we've found them to be enigmatic at best. At least one will insist on accompanying you on a tour of the ruins (a tip of Rs 500 per group is more than sufficient), but if your interests extend beyond the most typically visited ruins, the 'guide' will leave you on your own – which you may welcome. You may have to agree to guiding services before the staff will allow you to see a map of the site.

Allow at least three hours to see the site and allow for driving time off the main road.

Getting There & Away

Ritigala is 14km northwest of Habarana and 42km southeast of Anuradhapura. If you're coming from Habarana, the turnoff from the Anuradhapura–Habarana road is near the 14km post. It's then 6.2km on a good paved road past rice fields to the entrance to the nature reserve. From here the road deteriorates rapidly over the final 2.3km through lush jungle to the parking area at the ruins. It may be impassable after heavy rains.

Anuradhapura

☎025 / POP 62,000

The ruins of Anuradhapura are one of South Asia's most evocative sights. The sprawling complex contains a rich collection of archaeological and architectural wonders: enormous dagobas, soaring brick towers, ancient pools and crumbling temples, built during Anuradhapura's thousand years of rule over

WORTH A TRIP

THE AUKANA BUDDHA

According to legend, the magnificent 12m-high standing **Aukana Buddha** (admission Rs 500) was sculpted during the reign of Dhatusena in the 5th century, though some sources date it to the 12th or 13th century. Aukana means 'sun-eating' and dawn, when the first rays light up the huge statue's finely carved features, is the best time to see it.

Note that although the statue is still narrowly joined at the back to the rock face it is cut from, the lotus plinth on which it stands is a separate piece. The Buddha's pose, *ashiva mudra*, signifies blessings, while the burst of fire above his head represents the power of total enlightenment.

You'll need a sarong to visit the statue; the ticket office is at the top of the first set of steep steps. A couple of vendors sell drinks (not always cold) near the parking area.

Getting There & Away

The Aukana Buddha is 800m from the village of Aukana. You can get a bus here from the junction town of Kekirawa (Rs 30, 30 minutes, every 30 minutes), which is on the busy Dambulla-Anuradhapura bus route.

Alternatively, Aukana is on the train line from Colombo to Trincomalee and Polonnaruwa. Four trains per day stop here: the station is 1km from the statue.

Sri Lanka. Today several of the sites remain in use as holy places and temples; frequent ceremonies give Anuradhapura a vibrancy that's a sharp contrast to the fairly moribund ruins at Polonnaruwa.

Current-day Anuradhapura is a rather pleasant albeit sprawling city. Mature trees shade the main guesthouse areas, and the main street is orderly compared to the ugly concrete agglomerations seen in many other regional centres.

History

Anuradhapura first became a capital in 380 BC under Pandukabhaya, but it was under Devanampiya Tissa (r 247–207 BC) – during whose reign Buddhism reached Sri Lanka – that it first rose to great importance. Soon Anuradhapura became a great and glittering city, only to fall before a South Indian invasion – a fate that was to befall it repeatedly for more than 1000 years. But before long the Sinhalese hero Dutugemunu led an army from a refuge in the far south to recapture Anuradhapura. The 'Dutu' part of his name, incidentally, means 'undutiful' because his father, fearing for his son's safety, forbade him to attempt to recapture Anuradhapura. Dutugemunu disobeyed him, and later sent his father a woman's ornament to indicate what he thought of his courage.

Dutugemunu (r 161–137 BC) set in motion a vast building program that included some of the most impressive monuments in Anuradhapura today. Other important kings who followed him included Valagamba (r 109–103 BC), who lost his throne in another Indian invasion but later regained it, and Mahasena (r AD 276–303), the last 'great' king of Anuradhapura, who was the builder of the colossal Jetavanarama Dagoba. He also held the record for tank construction, building 16 of them in all, plus a major canal. Anuradhapura was to survive for another 500 years before finally being replaced by Polonnaruwa, but it was harassed by invasions from South India again and again – invasions made easier by the cleared lands and great roads that were a product of Anuradhapura's importance.

Sights

You'll need a couple of days to properly explore the Unesco-recognised **Anuradhapura Heritage Site** (www.ccf.lk/anuradhapura/). See p210 for various important considerations in planning your visit.

The heritage site encompasses a large area; the main areas of interest are the following:

Mahavihara The spiritual centre of Anuradhapura with the truly amazing Sri Maha Bodhi.

Abhayagiri Monastery A series of ruins more than 2000 years old spread over a fairly large area to the north.

Citadel A compact collection of sites about a 1000 years old.

Jetavanarama A huge dagoba and important museum lie in a fairly small area.

Anuradhapura

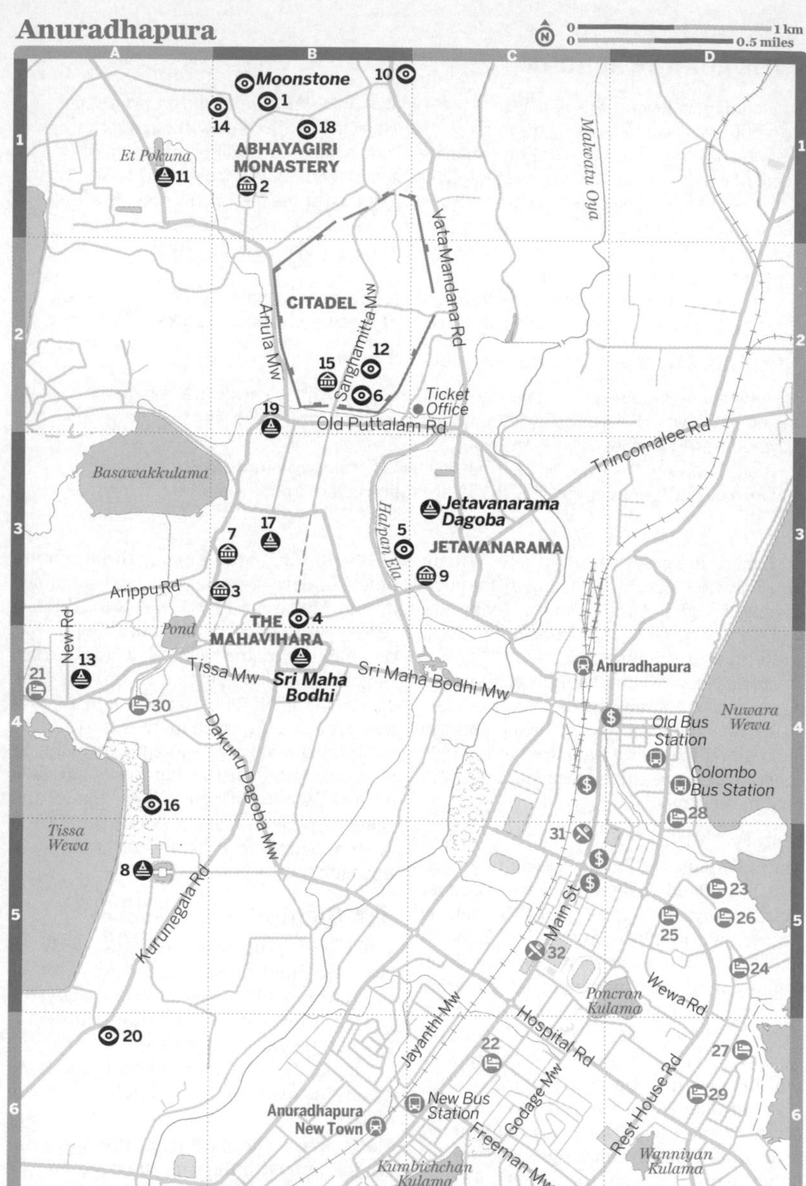

The main sights lie in an area about 3 sq km in size. You can appreciate individual areas such as the Citadel on foot but a bicycle is an ideal way to get around. There are pretty rides on car-free trails and walkways that link main sites. Bikes are also needed to visit the sites scattered to the west and south such as the Royal Pleasure Gardens.

A bike is also a good way to get from the main area of guesthouses in the east, which is separated from the main area of ruins by the commercial heart of Anuradhapura,

Anuradhapura

Top Sights

- Jetavanarama Dagoba ... C3
- Moonstone ... B1
- Sri Maha Bodhi ... B4

Sights

1 Abhayagiri Dagoba ... B1
2 Abhayagiri Museum ... B1
3 Archaeological Museum ... B3
4 Brazen Palace ... B3
5 Buddhist Railing ... B3
6 Dalada Maligawa ... B2
7 Folk Museum ... B3
8 Isurumuniya Vihara ... A5
9 Jetavanarama Museum ... C3
10 Kuttam Pokuna ... B1
11 Lankarama ... A1
12 Mahapali Refectory ... B2
13 Mirisavatiya Dagoba ... A4
14 Ratnaprasada ... B1
15 Royal Palace ... B2
16 Royal Pleasure Gardens ... A4
17 Ruvanvelisaya Dagoba ... B3
18 Samadhi Buddha ... B1
19 Thuparama Dagoba ... B2
20 Vessagiriya ... A6

Sleeping

21 Boa Vista ... A4
22 French Garden Tourist Rest ... C6
23 Grand Tourist Holiday Resort ... D5
24 Hotel Randiya ... D5
25 Hotel Shalini ... D5
26 Lake View Tourist Guest House ... D5
27 Milano Tourist Rest ... D6
28 Nuwarawewa Rest House ... D4
29 Saubagya Inn ... D6
30 Tissawewa Grand ... A4

Eating

31 Casserole ... C5
Family Super ... (see 31)
32 Salgado Hotel & Bakery ... C5

which in turn is bookended at the either end by the two main bus stations.

MAHAVIHARA

This is the heart of ancient Anuradhapura and is often the scene of religious ceremonies, which draw masses of people dressed in their finest along with all manner of vendors selling offerings, snacks, toys and refreshments. Relics here date from the 3rd century BC to the 11th century AD.

TOP CHOICE Sri Maha Bodhi SACRED TREE

(admission Rs 200) The Sri Maha Bodhi, the sacred bodhi tree, is central to Anuradhapura in both a spiritual and physical sense. The huge tree has grown from a cutting brought from Bodhgaya in India by the Princess Sangamitta, sister of Mahinda (who introduced the Buddha's teachings to Sri Lanka), so it has a connection to the geographical heart of the Sinhalese religion.

The sacred bodhi tree is the oldest historically authenticated tree in the world; it has been tended by an uninterrupted succession of guardians for over 2000 years, even during the periods of Indian occupation. There is not one but many bodhi trees here; the oldest and holiest stands on the top platform. The steps leading up to the tree's platform are very old, but the golden railing around it is quite modern. The railing and other structures around the trees are festooned with prayer flags. Thousands of devotees come to make offerings at weekends and particularly on *poya* (full-moon) days. April and December are particularly busy months as pilgrims converge on the site for *snana puja* (offerings or prayers).

For more on *poya*, see the boxed text, p23.

Brazen Palace HISTORIC SITE

So called because it once had a bronze roof, the ruins of the Brazen Palace stand close to the bodhi tree. The remains of 1600 columns are all that is left of this huge palace, said to have had nine storeys and accommodation for 1000 monks and attendants.

It was originally built by Dutugemunu more than 2000 years ago, but through the ages was rebuilt many times, each time a little less grandiosely. The current stand of pillars (now fenced off) is all that remains from the last rebuild – that of Parakramabahu around the 12th century.

Ruvanvelisaya Dagoba ANCIENT TEMPLE

Behind the Folk Museum, this fine white dagoba is guarded by a wall with a frieze of hundreds of elephants standing shoulder to shoulder. Apart from a few beside the western entrance, most are modern replacements for the originals from 140 BC.

This dagoba is said to be King Dutugemunu's finest construction, but he didn't live to see its completion. However, as he lay on his deathbed, a false bamboo-and-cloth finish was placed around the dagoba so that Dutugemunu's final sight could be of his 'completed' masterpiece. Today, after incurring much damage from invading Indian forces, it rises 55m, considerably less than its original height; nor is its form the same as the earlier 'bubble' shape. A limestone statue south of the great dagoba is popularly thought to be of Dutugemunu.

The land around the dagoba is rather like a pleasant green park, dotted with patches of ruins, the remains of ponds and pools, and collections of columns and pillars, all picturesquely leaning in different directions. Slightly southeast of the dagoba you can see one of Anuradhapura's many monks' refectories. Keeping such a large number of monks fed and happy was a full-time job for the lay followers.

Thuparama Dagoba ANCIENT TEMPLE

In a beautiful woodland setting north of the Ruvanvelisaya Dagoba, the Thuparama Dagoba is the oldest dagoba in Sri Lanka – indeed, probably the oldest visible dagoba in the world. It was constructed by Devanampiya Tissa in the 3rd century BC and is said to contain the right collarbone of the Buddha. Its 'heap-of-paddy-rice' shape was restored in 1862 to a more conventional bell shape and to a height of 19m.

The surrounding *vatadage*'s slender, capital-topped pillars, perhaps the dagoba's most unique feature, enclose the structure in four concentric circles. Impressions on the dagoba pediments indicate the pillars originally numbered 176, of which 41 still stand. Although some Sri Lankan scholars believe these once supported a conical wooden roof, there is no archaeological evidence for this theory, nor does it follow any known antecedent in South India, whose dagobas were the prototypes for virtually all Sinhalese dagobas.

ABHAYAGIRI MONASTERY

Lush jungle-like growth is always threatening to overwhelm this important area of ruins that date back a couple of millennia. Taking time to wander this precinct – and even losing your way on occasion – is one Anuradhapura's evocative pleasures.

Abhayagiri Dagoba ANCIENT TEMPLE

The huge Abhayagiri Dagoba (confused by some books and maps with the Jetavanarama), created in the 1st or 2nd century BC, was the centrepiece of a monastery of 5000 monks. The name means 'Hill of Protection' or 'Fearless Hill' (though some local guides mistakenly claim 'Giri' was the name of a local Jain monk). The monastery was part of the 'School of the Secret Forest', a heretical sect that studied both Mahayana and Theravada Buddhism. Chinese traveller Faxian (also spelt Fa Hsien) visited in AD 412.

The dagoba was probably rebuilt several times to reach its peak 75m height. It has some interesting bas-reliefs, including one near the western stairway of an elephant pulling up a tree. A large slab with a Buddha footprint can be seen on the northern side, and the eastern and western steps have unusual moonstones made from concentric stone slabs.

TOP CHOICE **Moonstone** HISTORIC SITE

A ruined 9th-century school for monks northwest of the Abhayagiri Dagoba is notable for having the finest carved moonstone in Sri Lanka; see how many species of animals you can find in its elaborate carvings. This is a peaceful wooded area full of butterflies, and makes a good place to stop and cool off during a tour of the ruins. It is often falsely described as Mahasena's Palace or the Queen's Pavilion. Look for the fine steps featuring plump little figures.

Ratnaprasada HISTORIC SITE

Follow the loop road a little further from the moonstones and you will find the finest guardstones in Anuradhapura. Dating from the 8th century, they depict a cobra king and demonstrate the final refinement of guardstone design. You can see examples of much earlier guardstone design at the Mirisavatiya Dagoba.

In the 8th century a new order of *tapovana* (ascetic) monks settled in the fringes of the city, among the lowest castes, the rubbish dumps and the burial places. These monasteries were large but unelaborate structures; ornamentation was saved for toilets, now displayed at the Archaeological Museum. The monks of Ratnaprasada (Gem Palace) monastery gave sanctuary to people in trouble with the authorities, and this led to a major conflict with the king. When court officials at odds with the king took sanctuary in the Ratnaprasada, the king sent his supporters to capture and execute them. The monks, disgusted at this invasion of a sacred place, departed en masse. The general populace, equally disgusted, besieged the Ratnaprasada, captured and executed the king's supporters and forced the king to apologise to the departed monks in order to bring the monks back to the city and restore peace.

To the south of the Ratnaprasada is the **Lankarama**, a 1st-century-BC *vatadage.*

Abhayagiri Museum MUSEUM

(⌚10am-5pm) The Chinese-funded Abhayagiri Museum, just south of the Abhayagiri Dagoba, commemorates the 5th-century visit of Chinese Buddhist monk Faxian to Anuradhapura. Faxian spent some time living at the Abhayagiri monastery translating Buddhist texts, which he later brought back to China. The museum, arguably the most interesting in Anuradhapura, contains a collection of squatting plates, jewellery, pottery and religious sculpture from the site. There is a bookshop selling Cultural Triangle publications.

Samadhi Buddha MONUMENT

After your investigations of guardstones and moonstones, you can continue east from the Abhayagiri to this 4th-century statue, seated in the meditation pose and regarded as one of the finest Buddha statues in Sri Lanka. Pandit Nehru, a prominent leader in India's independence movement, is said to have maintained his composure while imprisoned by the British by regular contemplation of a photo of this statue.

Kuttam Pokuna (Twin Ponds) WATER FEATURE

The swimming-pool-like Twin Ponds, the finest bathing tanks in Anuradhapura, are east of Sanghamitta Mawatha. They were likely used by monks from the monastery attached to Abhayagiri Dagoba. Although they are referred to as twins, the southern pond, which is 28m in length, is smaller than the 40m-long northern pond. Water entered the larger pond through the mouth of a *makara* (mythical multispecies beast) and then flowed to the smaller pond through an underground pipe. Note the five-headed cobra figure close to the *makara* and the water-filter system at the northwestern end of the ponds.

CITADEL

Although newer than other nearby ruins, the Citadel has almost entirely been reabsorbed by the earth. Little remains of the once-great walls that surrounded it.

Royal Palace HISTORIC SITE

About 1.5km south along Sanghamitta Mawatha from Kuttam Pokuna is the site of the Royal Palace. Built by Vijayabahu I in the 12th century after Anuradhapura's fall as the Sinhalese capital, the palace is indicative of the attempts made to retain at least a foothold in the old capital.

Close to it are a deep and ancient well and the **Mahapali refectory**, notable for its immense trough (nearly 3m long and 2m wide) that the lay followers filled with rice for the monks. In the Royal Palace area you can also find the **Dalada Maligawa**, a tooth-relic temple that may have been the first Temple of the Tooth. The sacred Buddha's tooth originally came to Sri Lanka in AD 313.

JETAVANARAMA

Jetavanarama Dagoba ANCIENT TEMPLE

The Jetavanarama Dagoba's massive dome rises from a clearing back towards the Sri Maha Bodhi. Built in the 3rd century by Mahasena, it may have originally stood over 100m high, but today is about 70m – similar to the Abhayagiri. When it was built it was the third-tallest monument in the world, the first two being Egyptian pyramids. A British guidebook from the early 1900s calculated that there were enough bricks in the dagoba's brick core to make a 3m-high wall stretching from London to Edinburgh.

Behind it stand the ruins of a monastery that housed 3000 monks. One building has door jambs over 8m high still standing, with another 3m underground. At one time, massive doors opened to reveal a large Buddha image.

Buddhist Railing HISTORIC SITE

A little south of the Jetavanarama Dagoba, on the other side of the road, there is a stone railing built in imitation of a log wall. It encloses a site 42m by 34m, but the building within has long disappeared.

Jetavanarama Museum MUSEUM

(⌚8.30am-5.30pm) A 1937 British colonial building provides a suitably regal venue for some of the treasures found at Jetavanarama. The objects displayed here show great craftsmanship and details, unlike what has been recovered and displayed from other sites. Look for the elaborate carved urinal in Room 1. In the fittingly named Treasure Room there are beautiful examples of jewellery, necklaces, carvings and pottery. Look for the 7th-century gold Buddhas.

MUSEUM QUARTER

Anuradhapura has one main museum, the Archaeological Museum, which covers most of the local sites. Two other museums, the Abhayagiri Museum and Jetavanarama Museum, are closely tied to their namesake sites.

TOP CHOICE Archaeological Museum MUSEUM
(⏲8am-5pm Wed-Mon, closed public holidays) The old British colonial administration building has been reused for this interesting collection of artworks, carvings and everyday items from Anuradhapura and other historic sites around Sri Lanka.

It has a restored relic chamber, as found during the excavation of the Kantaka Chetiya dagoba at nearby Mihintale, and a large-scale model of Thuparama Dagoba's *vatadage* as it might have been if a wooden roof (for which there is no physical or epigraphic evidence) had existed.

In the museum's grounds are the carved squatting plates from Anuradhapura's western monasteries, whose monks had forsaken the luxurious monasteries of their more worldly brothers. To show their contempt for the effete, luxury-loving monks, the monks of the western monasteries carved beautiful stone squat-style toilets, with their brother monks' monasteries represented on the bottom. Their urinals illustrated the god of wealth showering handfuls of coins down the hole. Look for other interesting and characterful sculptures scattered about the grounds.

Folk Museum MUSEUM
(admission Rs 100; ⏲8.30am-5pm Sat-Wed, closed public holidays) A short distance north of the Archaeological Museum there's a Folk Museum with dusty exhibits of country life in Sri Lanka's North Central Province.

OTHER SITES

South and west of the main historic and sacred areas are several more important sites.

Mirisavatiya Dagoba ANCIENT TEMPLE
Mirisavatiya Dagoba is one of three very interesting sites that can be visited in a stroll or ride along the banks of the Tissa Wewa. This huge dagoba, the first built by Dutugemunu after he captured the city in the 2nd century BC, is across the road from the Tissawewa Rest House. The story goes that Dutugemunu went to bathe in the tank, leaving his ornate sceptre implanted in the bank. When he emerged he found his sceptre, which contained a relic of the Buddha, impossible to pull out. Taking this as an auspicious sign, he had the dagoba built. To its northeast was yet another monks' refectory, complete with the usual huge stone troughs into which the faithful poured boiled rice.

Royal Pleasure Gardens HISTORIC SITE
If you start down the Tissa Wewa bund from the Mirisavatiya, you soon come to the extensive royal pleasure gardens. Known as the Park of the Goldfish, the gardens cover 14 hectares and contain two ponds skilfully designed to fit around the huge boulders in the park. The ponds have fine reliefs of elephants on their sides. It was here that Prince Saliya, the son of Dutugemunu, was said to have met a commoner, Asokamala, whom he married, thereby forsaking his right to the throne.

Isurumuniya Vihara ANCIENT TEMPLE
(admission Rs 200; ⏲8am-6pm) This rock temple, dating from the reign of Devanampiya Tissa (r 247–207 BC), has some very fine carvings. One or two of these (including one of elephants playfully splashing water) remain in their original place on the rock face beside a square pool fed from the Tissa Wewa, but most of them have been moved into a small museum within the temple. Best known of the sculptures is the 'lovers', which dates from around the 5th century AD and is built in the artistic style of the Indian Gupta dynasty of the 4th and 5th centuries. There is a lovely lotus pond in front.

Vessagiriya ANCIENT SITE
South of the Isurumuniya Vihara are extensive remains of the Vessagiriya cave monastery complex, which dates from much the same time.

Tanks WATER FEATURES
Anuradhapura has three great tanks. **Nuwara Wewa**, on the east side of the city, is the largest, covering about 12 sq km. It was built around 20 BC and is well away from most of the old city. The 160-hectare **Tissa Wewa** is the southern tank in the old city. The oldest tank, probably dating from around the 4th century BC, is the 120-hectare **Basawakkulama** (the Tamil word for tank is *kulam*) to the north. Off to the northwest of the Basawakkulama are the ruins of the **western monasteries**, where the monks dressed in scraps of clothing taken from corpses and,

it's claimed, lived only on rice. All are good for quiet bike rides and walks.

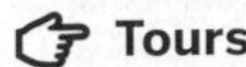

Tours

Freelance guides lurk throughout the heritage sites and generally are not worth the trouble. Most places to stay can arrange for licensed guides if you'd like – useful if you want a deep understanding of Anuradhapura and its rich history. Rates start at about Rs 1500 for two hours with you providing the transport.

One of the best local guides is **Charitha Jithendra Jith** (077 303 7835; charithjith@yahoo.com).

Sleeping

Anuradhapura is well endowed with budget and midrange accommodation choices and new ones are regularly opening as visitor numbers increase. The greatest concentration of places to stay is in the pleasant neighbourhood in and around Harischandra Mawatha near the Nuwara Wewa. If you're hot after a day touring, Nuwarawewa Rest House allows nonguests to use its large pool for Rs 500.

Note that commission-seeking room touts often board trains a few stations outside of town and hassle visitors. Three-wheeler drivers are often no better. Ignore them and be firm in your choice.

TOP CHOICE **Milano Tourist Rest** GUESTHOUSE **$$**
(222 2364; www.milanotouristrest.com; 40/596 JR Jaya Mawatha; r Rs 1500-3500;) One of the best deals in town, Milano is a comfortable and modern house with 11 rooms, comfy beds, fridges and satellite TV. The management and service are very professional. The restaurant is one of the best in town, with well-crafted Sri Lankan meals best enjoyed at a table in the garden. We didn't want to leave.

TOP CHOICE **Hotel Shalini** HOTEL **$$**
(222 2425; www.hotelshalini.com; 41/388 Harischandra Mawatha; r Rs 3500-4000;) This place has a cute gingerbread-house-like annex with a pleasant open-air restaurant, a rooftop garden and an internet cafe. Rooms all have windows and good ventilation; some have air-con. Tours of the ancient sites can be arranged. The delightful owners will arrange free transport to/from the bus and train stations with advance notice.

TEMPLE ETIQUETTE

Because so many of Anuradhapura's important sites are still considered holy it is important to be prepared to remove your shoes, wear a sarong or otherwise don modest dress as required.

Palm Garden Village Hotel HOTEL **$$$**
(222 3961; www.palmgardenvillage.com; Old Puttalam Rd, Pandulagama; r from US$100;) It's quiet at this modest resort, some 6km west of town. It has 63 large rooms in well-designed duplex units or separate villas, set in 38 hectares of gardens. Extras include tennis courts, an Ayurvedic spa and the occasional elephant. Wi-fi is only in the lobby. A three-wheeler from town costs Rs 400.

French Garden Tourist Rest GUESTHOUSE **$**
(222 3537; www.frenchgardenanuradhapura.com; 488/4 Maithrepala Senanayaka; r Rs 1800-2500;) A new place by the New Bus Station, this modern two-storey guesthouse has all the main amenities demanded by travellers. The rooms are very clean. The namesake garden is not large and plans call for a cafe to replace some of the greenery.

Tissawewa Grand HOTEL **$$**
(222 2299; www.quickshaws.com; r Rs US$85-100;) A Raj-era relic with a style all its own, the century-old Tissawewa is authentic right down to the shower railings and claw-foot bathtubs. Besides high-ceilinged lounge areas and verandas, it has 4.4 hectares of gardens with mahogany and teak trees. You can sit in an old cane lounger on the veranda and watch the peacocks strut. The downside is that it's almost a museum piece with minimal modern conveniences, and rates and extras are all pricey.

Hotel Randiya HOTEL **$$**
(222 2868; www.hotelrandiya.com; 19A/394 Muditha Mawatha; r Rs 4300-6500;) The 14-room Hotel Randiya looks good from the outside, with its *walawwa* (minor palace) bungalow-style architecture. Inside, rooms are a little small, although more expensive ones have fridges and nice bathrooms. Note the promise on their website: 'We give fullest corporation for the guest's meritorious affairs.'

Lake View Tourist Guest House GUESTHOUSE $
(☎222 1593; 4C/4 Lake Rd; r Rs 1500-2800; ❄) On a lane off Harischandra Mawatha, this is an agreeable place with 15 rooms, some with hot water and air-con. The ones in the front of the building looking out towards Mihintale are best. The owners are cheerful, and the Sri Lankan food is good. Bicycle hire is Rs 250.

Nuwarawewa Rest House HOTEL $$
(☎222 3265; www.quickshaws.com; Dhamapala Mw; r US$50; ❄@🛜🏊) Rooms are fairly bland, although the unrefurbished 1960s look is so retro it's almost chic. The rest house does have a decent lakeside location and a nice pool. Wi-fi only works in some rooms, and some rooms don't have patio furniture to take advantage of the lake views.

Saubagya Inn GUESTHOUSE $$
(☎222 3490; JR Jaya Mawatha; r Rs 2750-4000; ❄) It's worth bargaining at this simple guesthouse. Rooms are clean and basic, some fan-only.

Boa Vista GUESTHOUSE $$
(☎223 5052; www.srilankaboavista.com; 142 Old Puttalam Rd; r Rs 1500-5000; ❄@🛜) Ignore the jazzy website, the 15 rooms are modestly equipped; the pretty lakeside location is somewhat isolated.

Grand Tourist Holiday Resort GUESTHOUSE $$
(☎223 5173; thegranddami@yahoo.com; 4B/2 Lake Rd; r Rs 2500-4000; ❄) This is really a large special-event venue with eight rooms. Porches overlook Nuwara Wewa. Spend more for a room with air-con as the others can get hot.

Eating

As visitor numbers surge, it's likely that Anuradhapura will develop a few cafes and restaurants aimed at travellers. But until then choices are few. Milano Tourist Rest and the pricey Tissawewa Grand are the best options for looking outside your own lodging.

Casserole CHINESE $$
(279 Main St; mains Rs 70-250; ⏰7am-8.30pm; ❄) A busy and large 2nd-floor restaurant serving Sri Lankan, Chinese and Western meals. You'll find all the standards here. For a good dessert, try the *wattalappam* (egg, coconut milk, cardamom and jaggery pudding).

Salgado Hotel & Bakery SRI LANKAN $
(dishes Rs 150-300) This is an old-fashioned place serving Sri Lankan breakfasts, short eats and biscuits.

Family Super SUPERMARKET, BAKERY $
(279 Main St; mains Rs 100-250; ⏰7am-8.30pm) Anuradhapura's best supermarket has imported foods, sunscreen, mosquito repellent and a separate bakery area with good short eats and ice cream.

Information

In the commercial district, Main St and Dhamapala Mawatha have banks and ATMs as well as shops selling anything you might need.

Most guesthouses and hotels offer wi-fi or internet access and many will let nonguests log on for a fee.

Head to **Lonely Planet** (www.lonelyplanet.com/sri-lanka/the-ancient-cities/anuradhapura) for planning advice, author recommendations, traveller reviews and insider tips.

Tickets for Anuradhapura

A ticket for the main sites of Anuradhapura costs US$25/15 per adult/child.

Unfortunately the Anuradhapura ticket is good for only one day. To avoid having to buy more than one, you'll need to be strategic. Tickets are most closely inspected in the Abhayagiri, Citadel and Jetavanarama collections of sites and museums plus the main Architecture Museum. You could try to squeeze your touring of these important sites into one day and then use a second day for sites with their own entrance fees such as Sri Maha Bodhi and Mirisavatiya Dagoba. Obviously it would be best if the authorities ditched this hugely unpopular one-day rule – there's no evidence it gets people to spend more on admissions.

You can buy the Anuradhapura ticket at the Abhayagiri, Jetavanarama and Architecture museums. There's also a handy ticket office just east of the Citadel.

Getting There & Away

Bus

Anuradhapura has three bus stations which effectively bookend the commercial centre. Unless noted otherwise, daytime service in all directions is frequent.

COLOMBO BUS STATION Private air-con and 'semi-comfortable' (curtains, larger seats, no air-con) buses leave from this small station near the Old Bus Station. Services include the following:

Colombo Rs 420, five hours
Dambulla Rs 150, 1½ hours
Kandy Rs 285, three hours

NEW BUS STATION Better called the 'incomplete' bus station. Buses heading to points east and north start here. Services include the following:

Mihintale Rs 27, 20 minutes

Polonnaruwa Rs 120, three hours

Trinco Rs 170, 3½ hours, two daily

OLD BUS STATION Southbound buses start here and stop at the New Bus Station, by which time seats may be few. Services include the following:

Colombo via Dambulla Rs 220, five hours

Colombo via Negombo Rs 200, five hours

Dambulla Rs 80, 1½ hours

Kandy Rs 138, three hours

Train

Anuradhapura's main train station is an art-deco gem. Train services include the following:

Colombo 1st/2nd/3rd class Rs 520/290/160, five hours, four daily

Colombo Intercity Express 2nd class Rs 380, four hours, one daily

Kandy, changing at Polgahawela 1st/2nd/3rd class Rs 460/260/140, six hours, four connections daily

Getting Around

The city is too spread out to investigate on foot. A three-hour taxi tour costs about Rs 1200 and a three-wheeler about Rs 900. Bicycles are the best local means of transport and can be rented at most hotels and guesthouses (Rs 300 to 500 per day).

Numerous buses run between the Old and New Bus Stations via Main St.

Mihintale

☎025

This somnolent village and temple complex holds a special place in the annals of Sri Lankan lore. In 247 BC King Devanampiya Tissa of Anuradhapura was hunting a stag on Mihintale Hill when he was approached by Mahinda, son of the great Indian Buddhist emperor, Ashoka. Mahinda tested the king's wisdom and, considering him to be a worthy disciple, promptly converted the king on the spot. Mihintale has since been associated with the earliest introduction of Buddhism to Sri Lanka.

Mihintale is 13km east of Anuradhapura.

Each year a great festival, the **Poson Poya**, is held at Mihintale on the Poson full-moon night (usually in June).

Sights

Exploring Mihintale hill involves a massive climb, so you may wish to visit it early in the morning or late in the afternoon to avoid the midday heat. There are a few unctuous guides who charge about Rs 500 for a two-hour tour that is exhaustive in detail. If the guide follows you up the steps, you're committed, so make your decision clear before setting out. Single women are advised not to tour alone with a guide.

Stairway — STEEP CLIMB

In a series of flights, 1843 ancient granite slab steps lead majestically up the hillside (if you lose count, you have to go back to the bottom and start over). The first flight

SCULPTURAL SYMBOLISM

The four *vahalkadas* (solid panels of sculpture) at the Kantaka Chetiya are among the oldest and best preserved in the country and are the only ones to be found at Mihintale.

Vahalkadas face each of the four cardinal directions and comprise a series of bands, each containing some sort of ornamentation. The upper part usually contained niches in which were placed sculptures of divine beings. At either end of each *vahalkada* is a pillar topped with the figure of an animal, such as an elephant or a lion. How or why these sculptural creations came into being is subject to speculation, but one theory is that they evolved from simple flower altars. Others suggest they were an adaptation from Hindu temple design.

The cardinal points in traditional sculptural work are represented by specific animals: an elephant on the east, a horse on the west, a lion on the north and a bull on the south. In addition to these beasts, sculptures also feature dwarfs (sometimes depicted with animal heads), geese (said to have the power to choose between good and evil), elephants (often shown as though supporting the full weight of the superstructure) and *naga* (serpents, said to possess magical powers). Floral designs, apart from the lotus, are said to be primarily ornamental.

Mihintale

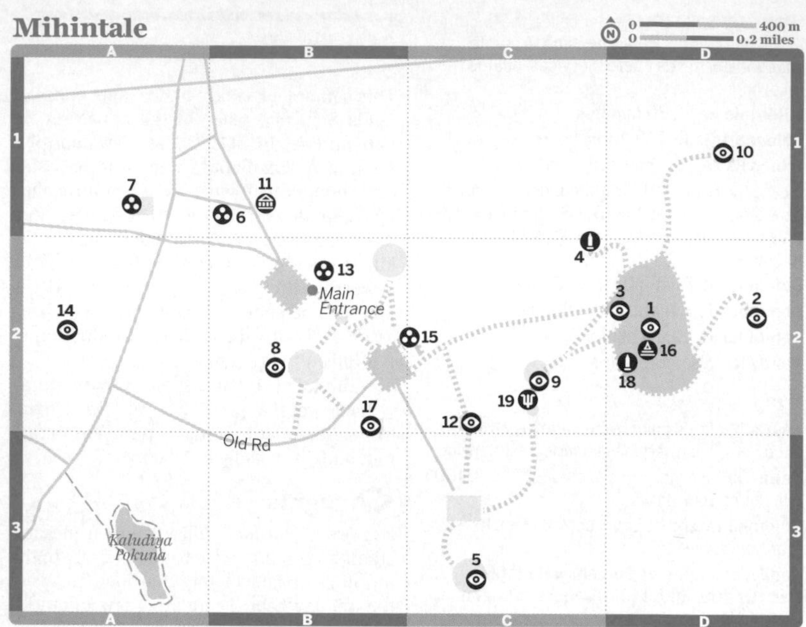

is the widest and shallowest. Higher up the steps are narrower and steeper. It's possible to avoid more than half the steps by driving up Old Rd.

Kantaka Chetiya ANCIENT TEMPLE

At the first landing a smaller flight of steps leads to this partly ruined dagoba off to the right. It's 12m high (originally it was higher than 30m) and 130m around at its base. A Brahmi inscription found nearby records donations for the dagoba. While exactly who built it is open to conjecture, Devanampiya Tissa (r 247–207 BC) had 68 cave monasteries built, and the dagoba would have been constructed near these. King Laji Tissa (r 59–50 BC) enlarged it. So the dagoba was built sometime in between, and is certainly one of the oldest at Mihintale. It is noteworthy for its friezes (see p211). Four stone flower altars stand at each of the cardinal points, and surrounding these are well-preserved sculptures of dwarfs, geese and other figures.

South of the Kantaka Chetiya, where a big boulder is cleft by a cave, if you look up you'll see what is thought to be the oldest inscription in Sri Lanka, predating Pali in Sri Lanka. The inscription dedicates the mountain's shelters to meditation, now and for eternity. Through the cave, ledges on the cliff face acted as meditation retreats for the numerous monks once resident here. There are around 70 different sites for contemplation.

TOP CHOICE **Monks' Refectory & Relic House** ANCIENT RUIN

On the second landing is the monks' refectory with huge stone troughs that the lay followers kept filled with rice for the monks.

Nearby, at a place identified as the monastery's relic house, are two inscribed stone slabs erected during the reign of King Mahinda IV (r 975–91). The inscriptions laid down the rules relating to the relic house and the conduct of those responsible for it. One inscription clearly states that nothing belonging to the relic house shall be lent or sold. Another confirms the amount of land to be given in exchange for a reliable supply of oil and wicks for lamps and flowers for offerings. Also known as the Mihintale tablets, these inscribed stones define the duties of the monastery's many servants: which servants gather firewood and cook, which servants cook but only on firewood gathered by others, and so on. There are also rules for monks: they should rise at dawn, clean their teeth, put on their robes, meditate and then go to have their breakfast (boiled rice) at the

Mihintale

Sights

1	Ambasthale Dagoba	D2
2	Aradhana Gala	D2
	Assembly Hall	(see 15)
3	Bodhi Tree	D2
4	Buddha Statue	C2
5	Et Vihara	C3
6	Hospital	B1
7	Indikatu Seya Complex	A1
8	Kantaka Chetiya	B2
9	Mahaseya Dagoba	C2
10	Mahinda's Cave	D1
	Monks' Refectory	(see 15)
11	Museum	B1
12	Naga Pokuna	C2
13	Quincunx	B2
14	Rajagirilena	A2
15	Relic House	C2
16	Sela Chetiya	D2
17	Sinha Pokuna	B2
18	Statue of the King	D2
19	Temple & Devale	C2

refectory, but only after reciting certain portions of the scriptures.

Assembly Hall ANCIENT RUIN

On the same level as the relic house, this hall, also known as the convocation hall, is where monks met to discuss matters of common interest. The most senior monk would have presided over the discussions, and the raised dais in the middle of the hall was apparently where this person sat. Sixty-four stone pillars once supported the roof. Conservation of this site began in 1948. The main path to the Ambasthale Dagoba leads from here.

Sinha Pokuna ANCIENT RUIN

Just below the monks' refectory on the second landing, and near the entrance if you are coming via Old Rd, is a small pool surmounted by a 2m-high rampant lion, reckoned to be one of the best pieces of animal carving in the country. Anyone placing one hand on each paw would be right in line for the stream of water from the lion's mouth. There are some fine friezes around this pool.

Ambasthale Dagoba ANCIENT TEMPLE

(admission Rs 500) The final steep stairway, lined with frangipani trees, leads to the place where Mahinda and the king met. The Ambasthale Dagoba is built over the spot where Mahinda stood. Nearby stands a **statue of the king** in the place where he stood. On the opposite side of the dagoba from the statue is a cloister and behind that, a large, white sitting **Buddha statue**. Stone pillars surround the dagoba and may once have been used to hold offerings (or if you believe the local theory, to support a wooden roof). You must remove your shoes and hat, and umbrellas aren't allowed.

The name Ambasthale means 'Mango Tree' and refers to a riddle that Mahinda used to test the king's intelligence (p214).

Nearby is the **Sela Chetiya**, which has a stone rendering of the Buddha's footprint. It's surrounded by a railing festooned with prayer flags left by pilgrims, who have also scattered coins here.

Mahaseya Dagoba ANCIENT TEMPLE

A stone pathway to the southwest of the Ambasthale Dagoba leads up to a higher dagoba (arguably the largest at Mihintale), thought to have been built to house relics of Mahinda. The **bodhi tree** to the left of the base of the steps is said to be one of the oldest surviving ones. From here there is a view over the lakes and trees to Anuradhapura, a horizon studded with the domes and spikes of all the massive dagobas. A small **temple** at the foot of the dagoba has a reclining Buddha and Technicolor modern frescoes – donations are requested. A room at the side is a **devale** (a complex designed for worshipping a Hindu or local Sri Lankan deity) with statues of major gods – Ganesh, Vishnu, Murugan (Skanda) and Saman.

Mahinda's Cave NATURAL FEATURE

There is a path leading northeast from the Ambasthale Dagoba down to a cave where there is a large flat stone. This is said to be where Mahinda lived and the stone is claimed to be where he rested. The track to the cave is hard on tender bare feet.

Aradhana Gala VIEWPOINT

To the east of Ambasthale Dagoba is a steep path over sun-heated rock leading up to a point with great views. A railing goes up most of the way. Aradhana Gala means 'Meditation Rock'.

Naga Pokuna ANCIENT RUIN

Halfway back down the steep flight of steps from the Ambasthale Dagoba, a path leads to the left, around the side of the hill topped

MAHINDA'S RIDDLE

Before Mahinda initiated King Devanampiya Tissa into Buddhism, he needed to gauge the king's intelligence. He decided to test the king with a riddle. Pointing to a tree, he asked him the name of the tree. 'This tree is called a mango,' replied the king. 'Is there yet another mango beside this?' asked Mahinda. 'There are many mango trees,' responded the king. 'And are there yet other trees besides this mango and the other mangoes?' asked Mahinda. 'There are many trees, but those are trees which are not mangoes,' said the king. 'And are there, besides the other mangoes and those trees which are not mangoes, yet other trees?' asked Mahinda. 'There is this mango tree,' said the king, who as a result passed the test.

by the Mahaseya Dagoba. Here you'll find the Naga Pokuna (Snake Pool), so called because of a five-headed cobra carved in low relief on the rock face of the pool. Its tail is said to reach down to the bottom of the pool. If you continue on from here, you eventually loop back to the second landing.

Et Vihara ANCIENT TEMPLE

At an even higher elevation (309m) than the Mahaseya Dagoba are the remains of a dagoba called **Et Vihara** (literally, 'Elephant Monastery'). The origin of the name is open to conjecture, but it may have been named after the monastery nearby. The Mihintale tablets mention Et Vihara and its image house.

Museum MUSEUM

There is a small museum on the road leading to the stairs; however, it is shut for an interminable refurbishment. It normally has a small collection of interesting artefacts.

Hospital ANCIENT RUIN

A ruined hospital and the remains of a **quincunx** of buildings, laid out like the five dots on a die, flank the roadway before the base of the steps to the temple complex. The hospital consisted of a number of cells. A *bat oruwa* (large stone trough) sits among the ruins. The interior is carved in the shape of a human form, and the patient would climb into this to be immersed in healing oils. Inscriptions have revealed that the hospital had its specialists – there is reference to a *mandova*, a bone and muscle specialist, and to a *puhunda vedek*, a leech doctor.

Indikatu Seya Complex ANCIENT RUIN

Back on the road leading to Old Rd and outside the site proper are the remains of a monastery enclosed in the ruins of a stone wall. Inside are two dagobas, the larger known as Indikatu Seya (Dagoba of the Needle). Evidence suggests that this monastery was active in fostering Mahayana Buddhism. The main dagoba's structure differs from others in Mihintale; for example, it's built on a square platform.

Nearby is a hill that's been dubbed **Rajagirilena** (Royal Cave Hill) after the caves found here with Brahmi inscriptions in them. One of the caves bears the name of Devanampiya Tissa. A flight of steps leads up to the caves.

Kaludiya Pokuna WATER FEATURE

Further south along the same road is the Kaludiya Pokuna (Dark Water Pool). This artificial pool was carefully constructed to look realistic, and features a rock-carved bathhouse and the ruins of a small monastery.

Sleeping & Eating

Hotel Mihintale HOTEL $$

(226 6599; www.ceylonhotels.lk; r Rs 3500-4000;) Although most people visit Mihintale on a day trip from Anuradhapura, you can spend the night at this pleasant 10-room inn. Oddly, the cheaper rooms are nicer as they have nice little outside terraces. The pavilion cafe at the front is a good place to pause for a stairway-to-hell refreshment.

Getting There & Away

Mihintale is 13km east of Anuradhapura. Buses run often (Rs 27, 20 minutes) from Anuradhapura's New Bus Station. A return taxi, with two hours to climb the stairs, costs about Rs 1200; a three-wheeler is about Rs 900. It takes less than an hour to cycle here.

Padeniya

About 85km south of Anuradhapura and 25km northwest of Kurunegala, where the Puttalam and Anuradhapura roads branch off, is the Kandyan-style **Padeniya Raja Mahavihara** (donations appreciated), which is worth popping into if you're passing by. It's a pretty, medieval temple with 28 carved pillars and a stunning elaborate door (said to be the largest in Sri Lanka) to the main shrine. There is also a clay-image house and a library, as well as a preaching hall with an unusual carved wooden pulpit.

Panduwasnuwara

Almost abandoned but with moody old canals and ruins, the 12th-century remains of the temporary capital of Parakramabahu I are worth a stop if you're heading past. The sprawling site, covering some 20 hectares, hasn't been fully excavated. The turnoff to the site is at Panduwasnuwara village, where there is a tiny **museum** (donation expected) that's a dusty cliché.

Near the entrance to the site is a moat, the massive citadel wall and the remains of a palace. Further on are image houses, dagobas and living quarters for monks. Follow the road past the school and veer left; you will shortly come to a restored tooth temple with a bodhi tree and, beyond that, the remains of a round palace (apparently once multistoreyed) enclosed in a circular moat.

There are many stories about who lived in this palace and why it was built. Legend has it that it kept the king's daughter away from men who would desire her; it had been prophesised that if she bore a son, he'd eventually claim the throne. Another story is that it was built to house the king's wives and, intriguingly, that there was once a secret tunnel that led from the king's palace and under the moat to the queens' palace. However attractive these stories are, historians have not been able to conclude why the palace was built.

Panduwasnuwara is about 17km southwest of Padeniya on the road between Wariyapola and Chilaw. It's best visited with your own transport.

DON'T MISS

YAPAHUWA

This **rock fortress** (admission Rs 500; 6am-6pm) rising 100m from the surrounding plain is quite impressive, despite being one-third the height of the much-more-visited Sigiriya. Ongoing restorations and archaeological digs are opening up this fascinating fortress and holy site.

The granite outcropping of Yapahuwa (pronounced yaa-pow-a), also known as Fire Rock, was used in the early 13th century as a defensible refuge against the invading South Indian armies. Between 1272 and 1284, King Bhuvanekabahu I used the rock as his capital and kept Sri Lanka's sacred Buddha tooth relic here. Indian invaders from the Pandavan dynasty captured Yapahuwa in 1284 and carried the tooth relic to South India, only for it to be recovered in 1288 by King Parakramabahu I.

Yapahuwa's **steep ornamental staircase**, which led up to the ledge holding the tooth temple, is one of its finest features. One of the lions near the top of the staircase appears on the Rs 10 note. The porches on the stairway had extraordinarily beautiful pierced-stone windows, one of which is now in the National Museum in Colombo; the other is in the museum right here.

The **museum** is off a parking area about 300m beyond the entrance to the steps. On display are stone sculptures of Vishnu and Kali, fragments of pottery and the carved stone screen. There are excellent displays in English that explain many of the details of this fascinating site.

Past the museum you can wander through the remains of the **ancient fortress**. It's a beautiful area, with little waterways and stone ruins. Near the stairs entrance, a **cave temple** contains some 13th-century frescoes and images of the Buddha made from wood and bronze. At various junctures monks or staff for the site may open things for you; a tip of Rs 100 is a worthy offering of thanks.

Getting There & Away

Yapahuwa is 6km from Maho railway junction, where the Trincomalee line splits from the Colombo–Anuradhapura line, and almost 9km from the Anuradhapura–Kurunegala road, which buzzes with buses. It's possible to take a three-wheeler round trip from the Anuradhapura–Kurunegala road or the train station to the site for about Rs 1000 with waiting time.

Ridi Vihara

Literally the 'Silver Temple', **Ridi Vihara** (donation Rs 200; ⏲7am-4pm) is so named because it was here that silver ore was discovered in the 2nd century BC. It makes for an interesting detour to see its wonderful frescoes and the unusual Dutch tiles from Neduntivu (Delft) in the main cave.

The main attraction here is the golden statue in the main cave, called the **Pahala Vihara** (Lower Temple). Also within the Pahala Vihara is a 9m recumbent Buddha that rests on a platform decorated with a series of blue-and-white tiles, which were a gift from the Dutch consul. The tiles depict scenes from the Bible, including Adam and Eve being banished from the Garden of Eden and the transfiguration of Christ.

The nearby **Uda Vihara** (Upper Temple) was built by King Kirthi Sri Rajasinghe. The entrance has a Kandyan-period moonstone. It's interesting to try to pick out some of the clever visual tricks used by the fresco artists; in one case, what appears at a distance to be an elephant reveals itself on closer inspection to be a formation of nine maidens. Hindu deities and images of the Buddha are represented in the caves.

Outside the temple complex you can see an abandoned dagoba at the top of a smooth rocky outcrop. On the way up, to your right, is an ancient inscription in the stone, said to have been etched on King Dutugemunu's behalf. An easy 10-minute walk starts to the right of this abandoned dagoba (as you are walking up to it). Head past a modern pavilion to an abandoned bungalow; nearby, on the top of the cliff, is a slab from which you get the most magnificent views.

Ridi Vihara is situated east of the Kurunegala–Dambulla road. If you are coming by car from Kurunegala, the turnoff to Ridigama village is on your right just past Ibbagamuwa village.

Kurunegala

☎037 / POP 32,000

Kurunegala is a busy market town and transport hub between Colombo and Anuradhapura, and Kandy and Puttalam. The town itself is not particularly interesting, but if you need a break from the car or a pause between buses, it has diversions.

There are ATMs on all the main roads around the bus station.

Sights

The large, smooth rocky outcrops that loom over the town are a striking feature of this city. Named for the animals they appear to resemble (Tortoise Rock, Lion Rock etc), the outcrops are, unsurprisingly, endowed with mythological status; it's said that they were formed when animals that were endangering the free supply of water to the town were turned into stone.

There's a road going up **Etagala**, a large black boulder on the eastern side of the city. The views are extensive from here. On the way up you pass a small shrine, **Ibbagala Vihara**, and at the head of the road there is a **temple** named after the rock itself.

Sleeping & Eating

There are limited accommodation options here, but then there's little reason to stay.

Hotel Viveka HOTEL **$**

(☎222 2897; www.hotelviveka.com; 64 North Lake Rd; r fan/air-con Rs 2200/2500; ❄) This 150-year-old one-storey villa has an elegant veranda overlooking the lake in a shady part of town. The five rooms are spartan cubes with modern bathrooms. Some interesting framed photos grace the main room, and the hotel has Kurunegala's most convivial bar and restaurant. Weddings are often held here on weekends.

TOP CHOICE **In & Out** SRI LANKAN **$**

(18 Puttalam Rd; snacks from Rs 100; ⏲7am-10pm; ❄) Close to the bus station, this bakery and cafe serves up a good array of Western and Sri Lankan dishes. Smoothies, omelettes and sandwiches are available. The rice and curry for Rs 150 is an excellent lunch deal. Short of time? The short eats are superb.

Getting There & Away

Buses depart from a chaotic bus station in the middle of a block in the very centre of town. Amid the exhaust-choked pandemonium, however, there are clear signs identifying the departure points for various destinations. Frequent services include the following:

Anuradhapura express Rs 200, two hours
Colombo express Rs 410, four hours
Kandy express Rs 80, one hour
Negombo Rs 150, 3½ hours

Trains depart from a station 2km southwest from the town centre.

The East

Includes »

Best Places to Eat

- Hideaway (p225)
- Palm Beach (p240)
- Crab (p240)
- Pigeon Island Beach Resort (p242)

Best Places to Stay

- Hideaway (p223)
- Chaaya Blu (p239)
- Palm Beach (p238)
- Kumana National Park (p228)

Why Go?

Tumbling out of the cool Hill Country, the world you enter is one of unexplored beaches stretching for mile after dazzling white mile and tropical lushness bursting with elephants and flamboyant peacocks. Gaudy Hindu temples are filled with bright celestial beings; scattered jungle ruins evoke the ghosts of kings, queens and monks of dynasties past; youthful villages thrive around perfect waves; and Muslim communities – which are the majority in the East – maintain traditions that survived the ancient trip from the Arab world.

It's a place where the sense of adventure is strong and, sadly, it's also a place that's been through a lot: still recovering from the horrors of war and the 2004 tsunami, people here are eager for a better tomorrow. Rebuilding – of homes and of spirit – is ongoing, and you'll find a region that makes up for its modest tourism infrastructure with raw, brilliant natural beauty.

When to Go

Trincomalee

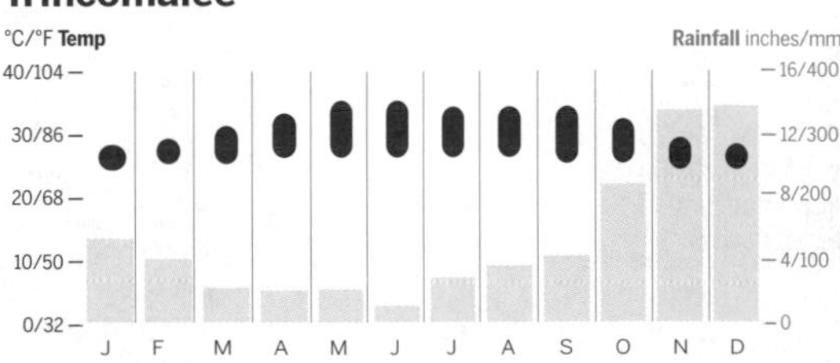

May–Jun Shoulder season; nesting season in Kumana and good elephant-spotting.

Jun–Jul Uppuveli, Nilaveli, Arugam Bay and the white-sand beaches in between are in their prime.

Aug–Sep Arugam Bay's international surfing competition is crowded, sunny and captivating.

The East Highlights

1. Hanging ten on the endless rights of chilled-out **Arugam Bay** (p220)
2. Chasing a skittish leopard – or monitoring the treetops for sleeping cats – in **Kumana National Park** (p228)
3. Snorkelling or diving with baby sharks around the reefs of **Pigeon Island National Park** (p240)
4. Building sandcastles on the divine sands of **Uppuveli** (p238) or **Nilaveli** (p240)
5. Listening to the quiet ripple of the water and watching rainbow-coloured kingfishers flit around mangroves on **Pottuvil Lagoon** (p226)
6. Napping in a hammock on a hill overlooking the sea at **Lighthouse Point** (p227)
7. Meandering around wild – and wildly empty – beaches in **Batticaloa** (p230) and **Vakarai** (p234)
8. Being bowled over by the massive Buddha at **Maligawila** (p220) or the quiet paintings at **Yudaganawa** (p219)

Monaragala

☎055

If you're coming from touristy Hill Country, then Monaragala will probably be your first stop in the east. With its frontier feel and warm welcome, it's a good introduction. If you're coming from the east and heading for the hills, you'll find foliage-packed Monaragala a refreshingly cool entry to the highlands. Its name means 'peacock rock' and it nestles beneath Peacock Rock, a round-topped forest-covered mountain.

Sights & Activities

An easy but beautiful hike starts near the bus station. Walk five minutes past a colourful little Hindu **Ganesh Temple** to the ageing rubber factory, then veer left to a rock-paved footpath that climbs between attractive boulder fields through Monaragala's famous rubber plantations. A much more demanding trek is the full-day round trip to the summit of the densely forested **Maragala Rock**. There is no set trail up the mountain and you'll need a guide, which can be organised through most guesthouses for Rs 1500 to 2500. From the summit you can check the surf at Arugam Bay on a clear day.

Sleeping & Eating

For very cheap meals there are various fly-friendly dives around the bus station.

Queens Inn GUESTHOUSE $
(☎227 7126, 071 836 0839; Obbegoda; s/d/tr Rs 1500/1800/2100) Six kilometres out of Monaragala in the direction of Pottuvil, in the blink-and-you'll-miss-it village of Obbegoda, is this charming little guesthouse run by an exceedingly friendly family. The five rooms surround a pleasant outdoor restaurant (mains Rs 150 to 350), which serves a memorable fried rice. If you call in advance they'll arrange a three-wheeler from town; otherwise one will cost Rs 300.

Victory Inn HOTEL $
(☎/fax 227 6100; Wellawaya Rd; s Rs 1500, d with/without air-con Rs 3500/2500; ❄) Rooms here (some with balconies) are pleasantly old-fashioned, well taken care of and comfortable, and the service is professional (with a 10% charge for it). The restaurant, with its pretty outdoor eating area and decent Rs 350 lunch buffet, is Monaragala's nicest place to eat.

Sunshine Guesthouse HOTEL $
(☎227 6313; Wellawaya Rd; s/d Rs 1500/2500) The sister hotel of the Victory retains its shiny, just-out-of-the-wrapper appearance after several years and has small, tidy rooms with nets and pint-size bathrooms. Staff don't always answer the phone, but rooms rarely fill up.

Information

Commercial Bank (Bus Station Rd) and several others along Wellawaya Rd have ATMs. In the market area, **Samudura Communications** (internet per hr Rs 50; ⌚8am-6.30pm) is the best internet cafe.

Getting There & Away

Monaragala is a convenient junction town between the East, the South and the Hills. Some handy bus routes:

Ampara Rs 160, 2½ hours, hourly
Colombo Rs 380, seven hours, hourly
Ella Rs 80, two hours, six daily
Kandy Rs 170, five hours, four daily
Kataragama Rs 90, two hours, four daily
Nuwara Eliya Rs 160, four hours, 9.15am
Panama (via Pottuvil and Arugam Bay) Rs 125, three hours, one to two daily
Pottuvil (for Arugam Bay) Rs 105, 2½ hours, four daily
Siyambulanduwa (for Ampara and Arugam Bay) Rs 50, one hour, frequent
Wellawaya (via Buttala; for the Hill Country) Rs 50, one hour, hourly

Around Monaragala

YUDAGANAWA

A massive and ancient dagoba (stupa) lies quietly hidden in a forest clearing at Yudaganawa, near the little village of Buttala. Only the bottom third remains, but the setting is charming and your imagination can run riot with thoughts of how amazing it must have looked back in its day. It's thought to have been an earthen stupa built 2300 years ago, though various alterations over the years – including an ongoing renovation that began in the 1970s – have obscured its history.

Much more interesting than the dagoba itself is the small building in front housing 300-year-old carved-wood Buddhas and some exquisite faded paintings probably from the 7th century.

Just before reaching the main site you'll pass the charming, moss-encrusted ruins of

WORTH A TRIP

TREE TOPS

Beautifully isolated at the base of the Weliara Ridge, 8km from Buttala, **Tree Tops** (☎077 703 6554; www.treetopsjunglelodge.com; per person all-inclusive US$140) is a nature wonderland. Here's your chance to bathe at a private open-air well with forest views, enjoy bright starlight, and listen for wild elephants in the ebony trees behind your mud hut or beneath your tree house. Food (mostly vegetarian) and drinks are included in the price, as are guided hikes around the area, including to **Arhat Kanda**, the scenic 'Hills of Enlightenment'. Reservations are required, preferably at least a week in advance, and rates are discounted for extended stays. Tree Tops also runs **Aliya Safari Camps** (www.aliyasafari.com), which conducts excursions to Yala National Park and the East's little-explored Gal Oya National Park (per person US$135, including transfers and lunch), near Ampara.

the much smaller 12th-century **Chulangani Vihara**, with a lovely, compact dagoba and fragments of a 7th-century Buddha.

Yudaganawa is 3km from Buttala town. If you want to stay in Buttala, try the family-run **Tourist Home** (☎227 3919; 10/7 Temple Rd; s/d/tr Rs 800/900/1200, mains Rs 175-300), which has large, good-value, if slightly musty, rooms in a large bungalow. Darmakirti, the manager, speaks good English and is relatively knowledgeable about the area.

Buses from Monaragala to Buttala (Rs 35) run hourly, and a three-wheeler from Buttala costs Rs 250 return. A three-wheeler from Monaragala costs Rs 1300 return, or Rs 3000 for both the Yudaganawa sites and Maligawila.

MALIGAWILA & DEMATAL VIHARA

Tucked away in a shady forest glade in Maligawila (mali-*ga*-wila) are the extensive 7th-century remnants of **Pathma Vihara** (admission free; ⏲dawn-dusk) and its two stunning Buddha statues. A little walk through the woods (bearing left) brings you to a magnificent 15m-tall **Buddha statue**, carved from a single piece of stone and weighing 100 tons. The figure was only discovered in the 1950s and restored (and reheaded) a few decades later. At its feet are usually offerings of flower petals left by pilgrims.

A few minutes' walk in the opposite direction is the 10m-high **Maitreya Bodhisattva** (Avalokitesvara), sitting high atop five stone terraces. It was found in pieces in the 1950s, then blown up by treasure-seeking looters, and then reconstituted in 1991. It's a beautiful statue despite the scaffolding harness and corrugated canopy.

Frequent buses run to Maligawila from both Monaragala (Rs 40) and Buttala (Rs 35). The journey to Maligawila from Monaragala, past jungles and paddy fields, is as much a highlight as the ruins themselves. If you're heading towards Buttala it's possible to hop off the bus at **Dematal Vihara**, a gorgeous temple lost in a sea of picturesque paddy fields.

A three-wheeler from Monaragala costs Rs 1800 return, or Rs 3000 return for a Maligawila–Yudaganawa loop.

Arugam Bay

☎063

Lovely Arugam Bay, a moon-shaped curl of soft sand, is home to a famed point break that many regard as the best surf spot in the country. If you're not a surfer, there are plenty of other draws: the village is packed with beachfront guesthouses and restaurants and has a mellow, swing-another-day-in-a-hammock kind of vibe that's totally removed from the brash west-coast beach resorts. Arugam Bay also makes a great base for several adventures in the surrounding hinterland. During the low season (November to April) things get very quiet and many places shut up shop altogether, but it can also be a beautiful time to visit, with few tourists and glistening green landscapes.

Activities

Surfing

The long right point break at the southern end of Arugam Bay is considered the best surf spot in Sri Lanka and offers consistent surf from April to September, with some good (and much quieter) days until November. (Some other points don't get going until May or June.) Locals, as well as some travelling surfers, might try and tell you that Arugam Bay is a world-class spot, or even that it's one of the 10 best surf spots in the world; both these statements are slightly fanciful to say the least. However, it consistently produces long and fairly fat slow-breaking waves that are ideal for intermediate surfers. Surf averages 1m to 1.5m, with a few rare 2m days. On small days it can be very shallow and sectiony while at any size there can be lots of boils and bumps to deal with. In season it can get dangerously busy, and learners should stick to the gentle beach break further inside of the point, also known as Baby Point.

There are many more breaks of similar quality, most of which need a decent-size swell, including, to the north, **Pottuvil Point**, which is a slow right-hander ideal for learners (it tends to be better later in the season), **Whiskey Point** and **Lighthouse Point**, both also good for beginners; and, to the south, **Crocodile Rock**, **Elephant Rock**, **Peanut Farm**, which has two breaks, one of which is advanced, **Panama**, which gets bad reviews, and **Okanda**, which is rumoured to be the best of the lot.

Several surf shops rent out boards, give lessons and do camping trips to some of the further points. Surf-camp tours allow you to start surfing first thing in the morning, and you don't have to worry about food or transport, but some surfers find it's just as easy, and cheaper, to make their own way.

A-Bay Surf Shop SURF SHOP
(bodyboards & surfboards per day Rs 500, lessons per hr Rs 3000; 8am-8pm) This long-standing surf shop has a good selection of old boards suitable for learners. In addition it offers expert ding-repair service, wax and sunscreen.

A Frame Surf Shop SURF SHOP
(Mambo's; 568 7983; bodyboards per hr Rs 200, short/long boards per day Rs 800/1000, lessons per hr Rs 2000; 7am-8pm) For a range of bashed-up boards, including some better suited to more experienced surfers, and not-helpful service.

Aloha SURF SHOP
(224 8379; www.aloha-arugambay.com; short/long boards per day Rs 1000/1300, lessons per hr Rs 2500; 6am-7pm) This guesthouse and surf school has newish boards and will hold beginners' hands getting started.

Surf N Sun SURF SHOP
(224 8600; www.thesurfnsun.com; short/long boards per day Rs 800/1000) The surf-savvy owners here organise excursions to Peanut Farm (Rs 4000) and Okanda (Rs 6000). The boards for hire aren't ideal for learners. Opening hours are erratic.

Surfing Sam SURF SHOP
(077 695 6160; surfingsam@ymail.com; bodyboards per day Rs 500, short/long boards per day Rs 800/1000, lessons per hr incl board Rs 3000; 6am-8pm) Sam has about 100 boards and runs all-inclusive trips to Elephant Rock (Rs 7000) Peanut Farm (Rs 8000) and Okanda (Rs 10,000).

Swimming

Seas are rough but OK for swimming, but ask locals before plunging in at lesser-known beaches, where rips might be strong. The safest swimming is at the southern end of Arugam Bay, where the beach bends around towards the point. However, though it's attractive, it's essentially a fishing beach and not ideal for lounging on.

Nature-Watching

Highly relaxing **mangrove tours** on Pottuvil Lagoon (p226) can be organised DIY or booked at the **Arugam Bay Surf Resort** (224 8189; www.arugambay.lk; tours per 2 people Rs 3000).

There's a good chance of seeing crocodiles and elephants around Crocodile Rock on Pasarichenai Beach, just south of Arugam Bay. For **birdwatching**, various nearby lagoons are marvellous for waterfowl and waders, while Brahminy kites regularly soar above the surf point. The choice twitching sites are Pottuvil Lagoon and the ponds and lagoons between Arugam Bay and Panama.

Yoga & Ayurveda

AccuYoga Wave Flow YOGA
(077 640 0618; www.waveflowyoga.com; classes Rs 700) This teacher team offers several classes a week at Stardust Beach Hotel and Mambo's in season. Class packages and special workshops are also available.

Traditional Ayur MediCare AYURVEDA
(071 883 6883; 8am-6pm) This is no luxe Ayurvedic spa; the tiny, authentic little clinic is staffed by a friendly Ayurvedic physician who is actually here to treat what ails you.

Festivals & Events

Arugam Bay hosts the **Sri Lankan Airlines Pro** (www.aspworldtour.com) every year in August/September. It's an important ASP event for both men (World Longboard Title division) and women (6 Star World Tour division). Events are held in the mornings at Arugam Bay's main point, and even though it gets really hot on the sand, thousands of people come – from the neighbourhood, the country and around the world – to watch. Accommodation is tight, so book ahead.

Sleeping

Many of the guesthouses listed here serve meals. The term 'cabana' refers to anything from ultrabasic plank or *cadjan* (coconut-frond matting) huts to luxurious full-facility

Arugam Bay

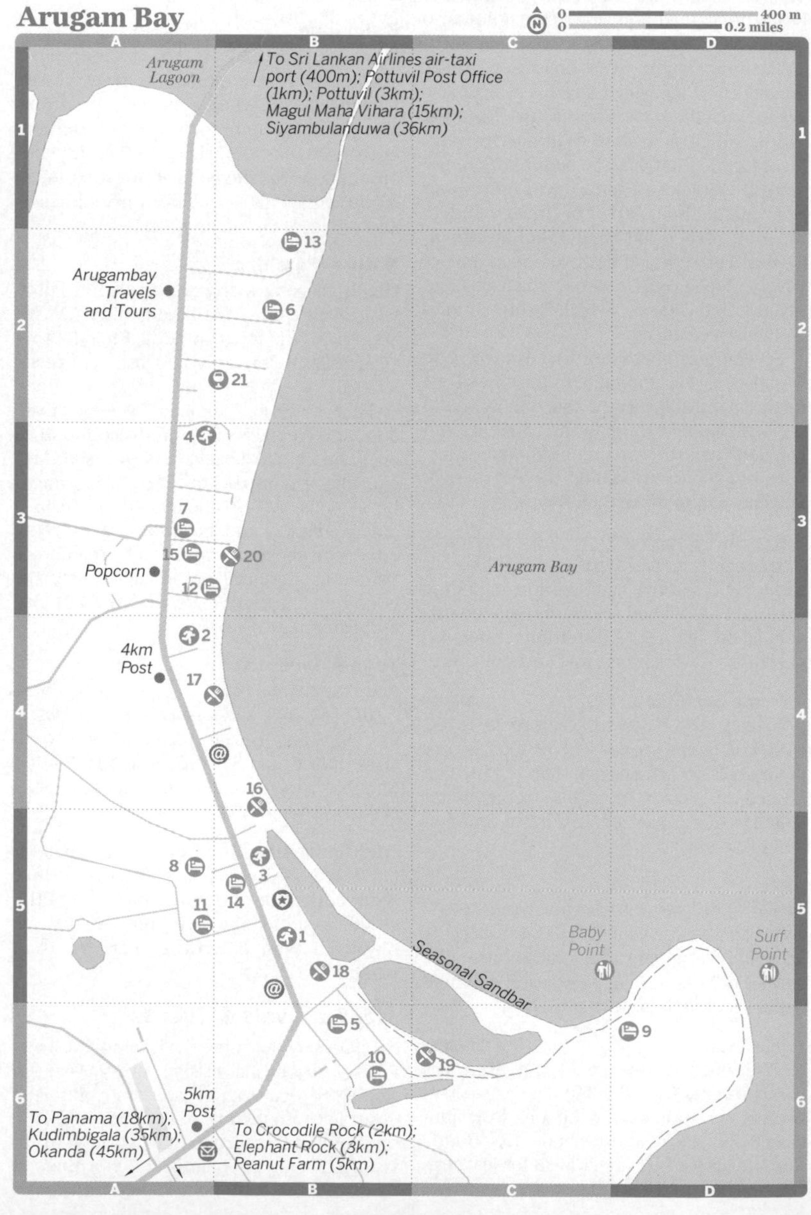

concrete bungalows. Low-season discounts of 20% to 35% are common.

TOP CHOICE Hideaway CABANA **$$**
(✆224 8259; www.hideawayarugambay.com; r/bungalows from Rs 5300/6500; ❄📶) The family-run Hideaway is something of a boutique guesthouse: the look is simple and organic, but full of poetic details. You'll find pomegranate seeds in your club soda, or a bird-of-paradise at your breakfast table; your toilet paper will be in a century-old brass bowl; and an affectionate snow-white cat with one blue and one green eye will nap on your terrace. Fresh bungalows are spread casually among the lush gardens, while an open-fronted colonial villa draped in bougainvillea has four atmospheric rooms and lounges with easy chairs and wood-beam ceilings. Charming, elegant and comfy all in one.

TOP CHOICE Galaxy Beach CABANA **$$**
(✆224 8415; www.galaxysrilanka.com; cabanas Rs 3000-4000) Elegant, spacious cabanas here are raised up into the palms, like a (designer) bird might do. Drop out of your perch into a private bougainvillea-filled outdoor garden bathroom. The ground-level cabanas are equally inspiring and have creaky wooden ladders leading up to roof terraces. The gardens are beautifully kept – earthy and shady but sophisticated – and the management is friendly.

Stardust Beach Hotel HOTEL, CABANA **$$**
(✆224 8191; www.arugambay.com; s/d/f cabanas US$30/35/65, d US$65-75; 📶) The only real resort-style place in town, this Danish-run hotel sits on a wild patch of beach at the end of the bay. Rooms are swish, with cool, modern touches, comfortable furniture, blue-and-white-tiled bathrooms, and views. The decor is clean and contemporary at the new colonial-style white building next door as well, where apartments have two doubles and an open-plan kitchen/living/dining space. Cabanas are a step above Arugam's other shacks. It's not the friendliest of places, though. Yoga classes and massages (Rs 4300 for one hour) are offered, and Stardust's partly alfresco restaurant (mains Rs 750 to 1200) is one of the more stylish places to eat, with treats like salads and hummus.

Happy Panda Homestay & Very Small Café GUESTHOUSE **$**
(✆077 299 0779; karikh@gmail.com; r Rs 1800; 📶) Tiny little Happy Panda has two simple, clean, artful rooms 50m from the beach and a very inviting porch-lounge area, complete with hammocks. Owner Natalia has plans for expansion that include a meditation room, which will perfectly balance out the

Arugam Bay

Activities, Courses & Tours

- A Frame Surf Shop .... (see 9)
- 1 A-bay Surf Shop B5
- 2 Aloha A4
- 3 Arugam Bay Surf Resort B5
- Surf N Sun .... (see 14)
- Surfing Sam .... (see 1)
- 4 Traditional Ayur MediCare A3

Sleeping

- 5 Freedom Beach Cabanas B6
- 6 Galaxy Beach B2
- Gecko .... (see 16)
- 7 Happy Panda Homestay & Very Small Café A3
- 8 Hideaway A5
- 9 Mambo's D6
- Nice Place .... (see 15)
- 10 PJ's B6
- 11 Ram's Place A5
- 12 Samantha's Folly A3
- Siripala Place Surf Cafe .... (see 19)
- 13 Stardust Beach Hotel B2
- 14 Surf N Sun B5
- 15 Tropicana Beach Hotel A3

Eating

- 16 Gecko B4
- Hideaway .... (see 8)
- 17 Lucky Beach Hotel A4
- 18 Perera Restaurant B5
- Samanthi's Restaurant .... (see 5)
- 19 Siripala Place Surf Cafe C6
- Surf N Sun .... (see 14)
- 20 Tsunami Beach Hotel B3

Drinking

- 21 Beach Hut B2
- Gecko .... (see 16)
- Mambo's .... (see 9)
- Siam View Beach Hotel .... (see 18)

excellent Italian coffee she makes (Rs 100). Happy Panda's also famous around town for its breakfasts (Rs 400, served 9am to 1pm), especially the French toast, which everyone always seems to be talking about.

Mambo's CABANA **$$**
(☎568 7983, 077 782 2524; www.mambo.nu; cabanas US$40-120; ❄📶) This surfer favourite is right next to the main surf point, allowing you to tumble out of bed and land in the lineup. But the solid bungalows and cabanas here are also excellent, with window screens, earthy, simple decor (think vegetable-dyed cotton curtains) and little porches, some with water views. Flagstone paths wind through cool patches of trees, and the attractive bar-restaurant has hammocks, good views of the waves, decent well-priced meals (Rs 300 to 1000) and Saturday-night parties. The only downside is the too-cool-for-school attitude.

Samantha's Folly CABANA **$$**
(☎077 338 7808; www.samanthasfolly.com; 'follies' Rs 1500, cabanas Rs 3000; @📶) Why even bother with a cabana at all? Samantha's pioneered the 'folly' – a giant four-poster-bed-like structure made of bamboo and topped with a thatch roof. Stow your stuff in giant, locked boxes and fall asleep among mirrored and jewel-colour fabrics and pillows; then watch the sun rise over the ocean through hanging sheer silks that billow in the sea breeze. There are also cabanas, a luxury 'royal tent' (Rs 3500) and chaise longues on the beach, along with a fun common area, a good restaurant (mains Rs 350 to 850) and board rental.

Surf N Sun CABANA **$$**
(☎224 8600; www.thesurfnsun.com; cottages incl breakfast US$35-45) Scattered across the lush, tropical gardens of this delightful place are a series of (slightly overpriced) wooden cottages with cosy rooms, hammocks swinging lethargically in the breeze and some crazy trees growing out of the showers. The grounds might be the most beautiful in town, with a waterfall, lush greenery and a shady lounge.

Freedom Beach Cabanas GUESTHOUSE **$**
(☎077 175 9620; www.wix.com/arugambay/freedombeachcabanas; r Rs 2500) Right on the beach by the main point, but tucked away in a garden, the relatively new, local-family-run Freedom Beach is one of Arugam Bay's better deals. Staff are warm and helpful, and rooms, though compact, are thoughtfully laid out and sparkling clean, with little porches. There's also, um, a castle (long story): a tall, skinny, funky structure that's sometimes available for Rs 1500. Freedom also rents out boards.

Tropicana Beach Hotel GUESTHOUSE **$**
(☎077 127 2677; d_asmin@yahoo.com; tw Rs 1200) The super-cute aquamarine cottages here are simple, but they're shown more love than many of the more expensive places. Rooms have only table fans, but the grounds have flowers and parakeets all around, and the nice couple who run it will involve you in family life.

Nice Place GUESTHOUSE **$**
(☎077 341 2240; r Rs 2500) The tiny rooms in this tiny guesthouse are a tad cramped, but the place has such good vibes that they're cute rather than claustrophobic. Rooms, front porches and a little garden are well maintained, and the food is homemade by the very friendly cook (reserve ahead).

Ram's Place GUESTHOUSE **$**
(☎567 0958; dm/r from Rs 400/1000) Run by Ram Sooriya, a sadhu lookalike (and live-alike), this hangout has extremely basic rooms, a scruffy male-only dorm and a 'bottle house', a tiny A-frame cottage whose facade is all glass bottles. It's all pretty rundown, but it's cheap, the vibe is right and there's a cool **library** (deposit Rs 400, lending Rs 100) and cafe where Mr Ram serves up excellent food. You have to order meals in advance and in person ('I want to see you,' he says). Discounts are given for longer stays. Ram's is behind Sooriyas Hotel.

Siripala Place Surf Cafe GUESTHOUSE **$**
(☎077 420 8765; r Rs 1500) Rooms here are very small and basic, but you come here for the location on the beach: open the door in the morning and there's the sea. Staff are friendly and discounts are given for long-stayers.

PJ's GUESTHOUSE **$$$**
(☎077 606 5765; www.onya.se; r from US$100; ❄📶) Right near Baby Point, PJ's aspires to luxury and is doing a good job so far: massive rooms have frosty air-con, sleek, gargantuan bathrooms, wi-fi and flat-screen TVs. (They also, somewhat incongruously, have bunk beds.) New 1st- and 2nd-floor rooms will be even plusher, with killer views. But it's all behind a walled enclosure, guarded

by dogs, and lacks local charm. Good if you want to be at the beach, without all the Sri Lanka.

Gecko CABANA **$$**
(☎224 8212; www.geckoarugambay.com; cabanas Rs 2800-4900, r/ste 3800/6900) Gecko is best known for its food and cool hangout spot, but the rooms aren't bad either: compact but smart, with pretty wall sconces, built-in desks and front-porch seating overlooking Gecko's cosy landscaped yard. Cabanas are standard for the neighbourhood but have great attached bathrooms, and the roomy suite is ideal for families.

Eating & Drinking

Note that most restaurants in Arugam Bay serve alcohol.

TOP CHOICE **Hideaway** INTERNATIONAL **$$$**
(☎224 8259; www.hideawayarugambay.com; mains Rs 900-1400, wine bottles Rs 2500-7500) The daily revolving menu here always includes fresh takes on local ingredients – some of which come from the organic garden out back, others from the ocean across the street. Dishes are heavy in Mediterranean influences – salad might be balsamic calamari and rocket, with vine-ripened tomatoes – and the atmospheric setting includes scattered bougainvillea flowers and the sounds of monkeys in the trees. Reserve ahead.

TOP CHOICE **Tsunami Beach Hotel** SRI LANKAN, EUROPEAN **$$**
(mains Rs 400-850; ⏲noon-4pm & 6pm-midnight) The name's unfortunate, but the Sri Lankan and Western food here is outstanding, especially the rice and curry, which is one of the best around. The lemon-butter chicken and Spanish-style prawns also come recommended. Both dining areas – the breezy front porch or beach tables under palm and pine trees – are made for lingering and sundowners. Order an hour in advance: everything's made from scratch.

Lucky Beach Hotel SRI LANKAN **$$**
(mains Rs 350-700; ⏲6am-1am) High above the sand, in a rickety stilted structure with fantastic views and heavenly breezes, Lucky Beach is a great place to watch the waves and eat some excellent fish. It might take an eon to be served, but the cooking here is good. It's also a popular place for happy hour and serves the local fave: arrack and Sprite.

Samanthi's Restaurant SRI LANKAN **$$**
(☎077 175 9620; Freedom Beach Cabanas; mains Rs 250-675) Samanthi's, at Freedom Beach Cabanas, is steps away from Main and Baby Points, and not only is the food great, but the place is run by a family of strong, cheerful local women. Order ahead for rice and curry (from Rs 350); other dishes are the standard A-Bay mix of Western and modified Sri Lankan. Try the fresh fruit with honey and buffalo curd: the yoghurt is a regional speciality.

Gecko INTERNATIONAL **$$**
(www.geckoarugambay.com; mains Rs 480-900) This chilled restaurant serves an excellent and varied menu for those with the homesick blues. Most of the dishes are homemade in their entirety and include salads, pasta, burgers, fish and chips, full English breakfasts, muesli and apple pie. Some ingredients come from Gecko's garden, a few kilometres away. Gecko also does a mean iced tea (Rs 140), oddly hard to find in Sri Lanka.

Siripala Place Surf Cafe SRI LANKAN **$$**
(mains Rs 400-850) Right next to the spot where the fish are first hauled out of the deep blue, so the seafood here is as fresh and tasty as can be. The views and breezes are the perfect backdrop.

Surf N Sun SEAFOOD, SRI LANKAN **$$$**
(www.thesurfnsun.com; mains Rs 600-1200) Some of the tables here are on the gorgeous outdoor deck lounge, with low-slung cushions, throw pillows, and candles and lanterns everywhere. The food is also good, with a focus on seafood and pizza and the occasional barbecue.

Perera Restaurant SRI LANKAN **$$**
(mains Rs 250-400) It can be hard to find a decent rice and curry around here, what with all the muesli and burgers everywhere. Perera offers homemade Sri Lankan meals, pure and simple.

Mambo's, Beach Hut, Gecko and **Siam View Beach Hotel** (www.arugam.com) all organise beach and full-moon parties in season, and are good spots for a drink on any night. Siam View brews its own beer and serves creative arrack cocktails on its pretty rooftop restaurant.

Information

The nearest ATMs are in Pottuvil.

Arugam Bay Information (www.arugam.info) Travel and local info.

CyberCafé (⊙9am-10pm; wi-fi/internet per hr Rs 100/150; ❄) Fast connections.

Lonely Planet (www.lonelyplanet.com/sri-lanka/the-east/arugam-bay) Planning advice, author recommendations, traveller reviews and insider tips.

Pasarichenai sub-post office (⊙8am-noon & 1-5pm Mon-Sat)

Tourist Police (☎011 308 1044) The Colombo number connects to the beach police station.

Xpress Café (⊙8am-10pm; internet or wi-fi per hr Rs 150)

Dangers & Annoyances

Women, especially if solo, might receive unwanted attention on the beaches: wearing a T-shirt over your swimsuit, or even a T-shirt and shorts, will make for much more pleasant swimming. Although it's not obvious in the tourist zone, this is a socially conservative area and it's considered respectful, for both men and women, to dress modestly. When off the beach, wear clothes.

There have been cases of attempted sexual assault in secluded areas, particularly south behind the surf point. There is a tourist police post on the beach.

Getting There & Around

AIR Arugambay Travels and Tours (☎224 8224; ⊙8am-9pm, to 1pm Fri) The local agent for Sri Lankan Airlines books tickets for Colombo air taxis, which, at research time, were about to commence.

BUS & THREE-WHEELER Buses arrive and depart from nearby Pottuvil, where you'll need to hop into a three-wheeler to Arugam Bay (Rs 150). The only exceptions are the rare buses from Pottuvil to Panama, which pass by Arugam Bay (one continues to Monaragala). Three-wheeler fares to local surf spots are given in the relevant sections.

CAR Private air-con taxis to Colombo cost Rs 16,000.

MOTORCYCLE & BICYCLE Arugam Bay Surf Resort (☎224 8189; www.arugambay.lk) Hires motorbikes (per day Rs 1200).

Popcorn (☎075 291 4800; ⊙8.30am-9.30pm, to 3.30pm Fri) Hires bicycles (per day/week Rs 500/1750) and scooters (Rs 1000 per day).

Tropicana Beach Hotel Bicycles for Rs 400 per day.

SIYAMBULANDUWA

Buses to Pottuvil – from anywhere – aren't frequent. But buses to Siyambulanduwa are, and so are buses from Siyambulanduwa to Pottuvil. By the transitive property, then, you can get to Arugam Bay most of the time if you layover here. Pottuvil buses run only until around 5pm, but the very well-run **Nethmini Hotel** (☎055-355 0891; www.nethminihotel.com; Ampara Rd; s with shared/private bathroom Rs 750/1050, d from Rs 1550; ❄) is 1km from the bus stand.

North of Arugam Bay

POTTUVIL

☎063

For most tourists Pottuvil is simply the transport hub for Arugam Bay, 3km further south. But Pottuvil has several ATMs near the bus stand, a decent market, a few low-key sights and excellent tours of its lagoon. Swing by **Dress Well** (⊙closed Fri) to buy one of Kalmunai's famous hand-woven cotton lungis (sarongs; Rs 1200).

Sights & Activities

Pottuvil Lagoon LAGOON

The mangroves, islands and waterways of Pottuvil Lagoon are a rich ecosystem teeming with giant monitor lizards, crocodiles, kingfishers, the occasional elephant (who does *not* like to be disturbed), eagles, peacocks, egrets and monkeys. Seeing them as you cruise along on a two-hour **mangrove ecotour** (www.arugambay.com/pages/eco.html; per 4-person boat Rs 2500; ⊙6am & 4pm), with only the sounds of the fisherman's pole in the water and animals in the trees, is both exciting and serene. The tours were designed to help conserve the mangrove forests and support local fishers and have been commended in international sustainable-travel awards. You can arrange a tour through Arugam Bay Surf Resort (p226), but if you can manage the language barrier (most boat conductors speak only Tamil), it's best for the fishers if you organise with them directly. Their **Hidiyapuram Fishermen's Cooperative Society** (☎075 097 0525, 077 861 9959) has an office on the south side of the lagoon; call and reserve as best you can, and someone will meet you there. A three-wheeler from Arugam Bay costs Rs 800 return.

Pottuvil Point BEACH

About 2km past the Cooperative Society's office, at the end of a scenic peninsula-like stretch of sand, is beautiful Pottuvil Point, which is a slow right-hander ideal for learners. There's a rustic **restaurant** (mains Rs 200-350) here, as well as a guesthouse that wasn't operational at research time. Pottuvil Point is Rs 800 return by three-wheeler.

Mudu Maha Vihara RUIN

Hidden away in Pottuvil's backstreets are the ancient ruins of Mudu Maha Vihara. This lovely little site, partly submerged in the encroaching sand dunes, features a fine 3m-high standing Buddha statue flanked by two bodhisattva figures. The **beach** just behind is wide, beautiful and undeveloped, but not safe for swimming.

Getting There & Away

Three-wheelers to Arugam Bay are Rs 150.

AIR At press time, **Sri Lankan Airlines** (☎1979; www.srilankan.lk) was planning regular seaplane service between Colombo and Arugam Lagoon (Map p222).

BUS In addition to buses listed here, two private, comfortable vans head to Colombo (Rs 500/700, eight hours, 4pm/7.30pm), along with a new air-con bus service (Rs 750, 9pm). You can also catch one of the more frequent Colombo departures in Monaragala. Useful private and Central Transport Board (CTB) bus services:

Ampara Rs 109, three hours, two daily
Batticaloa Rs 115, four hours, five daily
Colombo Rs 347, eight hours, two daily
Monaragala Rs 105, 2½ hours, hourly until 1pm
Panama (via Arugam Bay) Rs 25, one hour, five daily

WHISKEY POINT

Whiskey Point is a three-minute beach walk from Pottuvil Point but further by road. The point's good for beginners, and the waves are consistent from late April on. **SaBaBa Surf Café** (☎077 711 8132; mains Rs 350-900; ⏲7am-10pm) is Whiskey's pioneer cafe, with cosy cushions on its wooden deck, beds on the beach and Friday-night parties with fire-jugglers. Friendly owner Babaiya is also con structing cabanas. Reluctant to be listed in this book, he suggests that 'only those caring and sharing' should come.

Three-wheelers charge Rs 1200 to 1500 return, including three hours' waiting, from Arugam Bay (a 20-minute trip).

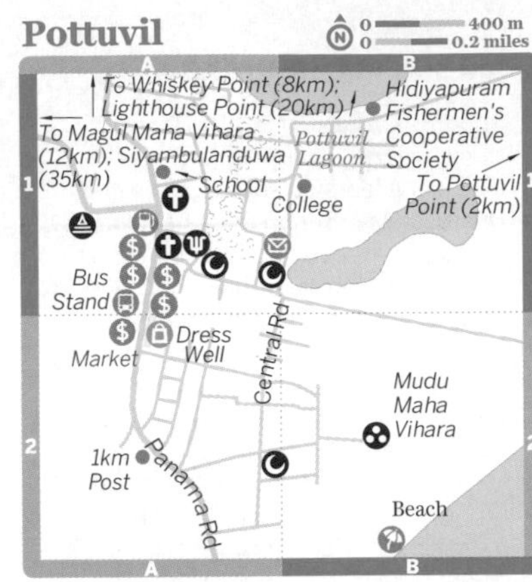

LIGHTHOUSE POINT

If you're caring and sharing but prefer quiet and simplicity, Lighthouse Point, another beginner/medium right-hander, might be your scene. The serene **Hilltop Beach Cabanas** (☎077 374 1466; dil0422@yahoo.com; cabanas with shared bathroom Rs 1000-1500), on a hill rising up from the beach, is run by the radiant Dilani, who is a fine cook (mains Rs 300 to 485) and a kind soul. Of the three cabanas, the one on stilts is best, with million-dollar views shining through seashell garlands. Rooms have minimal solar-powered electricity (lights only), and bathrooms are outside under the trees. Peak surfing starts in May or June; **Green House**, another point further north, is a 15-minute walk. Three-wheelers charge Rs 2000 return from Arugam Bay.

South of Arugam Bay

ARUGAM BAY TO PANAMA

Kilometres of untouched sandy beaches stretch south of Arugam Bay. Close-by surf points, reached via the coast road, include **Crocodile Rock** (Rs 400 return by three-wheeler), **Elephant Rock** (Rs 800) and **Peanut Farm** (Rs 1000). The lane to Panama stays somewhat inland but intersects with lagoons where you can spot waterfowl, wading birds, water buffalo and even elephants. It's a beautiful, savannah-like landscape. **Panama** itself is a dusty gathering of huts with an end-of-the-world atmosphere, whose only sights are an attractive white **dagoba** and a wide but unshaded arc of sandy beach a kilometre east of town. Heavy

WORTH A TRIP

MAGUL MAHA VIHARA

About 12km west of Pottuvil lies this evocative 5th-century-BC ruin, set in a peaceful forested spot. Built by King Dhatusena (473–453 BC), the ruin was probably part of a royal compound. At the foot of a former shrine is a beautiful and well-preserved moonstone; ringed with elephants, it's unusual for having little riders atop some of them. The site also has an elevated stupa, in good condition and guarded by stone lions, a *vatadage* (circular relic house) on a cross-shaped platform that – in a stroke of ancient trompe l'oeil – is 'supported' by the stone pillars and crouched lions around its base, and a crudely patched up headless Buddha. Note the streamlined elephant-trunk railings along the site's staircases. The site is 1km south of the A4 between 308km and 309km posts.

seas, however, mean that swimming is usually unsafe (and surfers won't have any joy on these dumpy shore breaks). At the northern end of the beach, close to the jellyfish-processing plant (jellyfish are sent to the Far East for use in cooking), is a fairly lame right-point break that is good for novice surfers. Arugam Bay three-wheelers charge Rs 1500 return, or you can wait for a rare bus. The road to Panama is low in places and may be underwater in the wet season.

PANAMA TO OKANDA

The superb 47-sq-km site of **Kudimbigala Forest Hermitage** is a jumble of forgotten Sigiriya-style outcrops set in dense jungle. Over 200 shrines and hermits' lodgings are set in caves or sealed rocky overhangs here (six Buddhist monks still live here). While none is individually especially interesting, the atmosphere is fantastic and the dagoba-topped summit of the highest rock offers vast panoramas across the eccentric landscape and forest canopy. There are glimpses of lagoon and sandbars towards the shore, and the far southwestern horizon is distantly serrated by the spiky Weliara Ridge. Kudimbagala is usually visited along with Kumana or Okanda; three-wheelers charge Rs 2500 return. As this is an active hermitage, quiet and modest dress are requested.

The Arugam–Okanda road ends at the entry gate for Kumana National Park. Immediately east of the gate is **Okanda**, a seasonal settlement for local fishers and home to the **Okanda Sri Murugan Kovil**. Though relatively small, the main temple has a colourful *gopuram* (gateway tower) and is a major point on the Pada Yatra pilgrimage to Kataragama (p127). Thousands of pilgrims gather here during the two weeks before the July *poya* (full moon) before attempting the last, and most dangerous, five-day leg of the 45-day trek from Jaffna. The temple is of great spiritual importance as it marks the supposed point at which Murugan (Skanda) and his consort Valli arrived in Sri Lanka on stone boats.

Just five minutes' walk from the temple is a sweeping beige-white beach with an excellent right point break popular with surfers fleeing the crowds at Arugam Bay.

KUMANA NATIONAL PARK & KUMANA RESERVE

This 357-sq-km **park** (☎063-363 5867; ⏲6am-6.30pm), often still referred to by its old name, Yala East, is much less frequently visited than its busy neighbour, Yala National Park. The result is a less 'zoolike' experience, although the range and density of animals are also less. Still, it's not rare to spot a leopard, along with elephants, peacocks, white cobras, wild buffalo and tons of birds. About a dozen bears live in the park, but they're rarely seen.

The park's best-known feature is the 200-hectare **Kumana bird reserve**, an ornithologically rich mangrove swamp 22km beyond Okanda. May to June is nesting season. There have been sightings of Sri Lanka's very rare black-necked stork, but more commonly spotted, even outside the bird reserve, are Malabar pied hornbills, green bee-eaters, blade-headed orioles and painted storks, among others.

Entry fees are myriad: US$10 per person, Rs 250 for your jeep and a US$8 service charge. Twelve percent of that sum is your tax. A mandatory guide (who may not speak English) accompanies each vehicle. Guesthouses in Arugam Bay can help arrange for a jeep and driver; the going rate is Rs 10,000 for the day. (It's not as expensive as it seems given the park's rough roads.) You can also try calling **Siddiq** (☎077 481 7774), whose driving and animal-spotting get rave reviews.

You can arrange **camping trips** within the park, which allow you to watch animals at dusk and dawn – the two best times. For this, the algorithm becomes even more complicated: US$20 per person, US$27 per group, Rs 250 per jeep, plus 12% tax. Drivers in Arugam Bay charge US$300 for two people, which includes the transport, evening and morning safaris, equipment and meals.

Ampara

063

Laid-back Ampara sits in the midst of succulent countryside dappled with paddy fields, lakes and palm groves. Though the town itself won't hold you, the area has a couple of low-key sights.

Sights

West of the clock tower and bus station, DS Senanayake Rd leads towards Inginyagala, passing scenic Ampara Tank. At the 1km post, the **Sri Manika Pillaiyar** (Inginyagala Rd) gives Ganesh a lovely view across the water. After a further 3km, a right turn brings you to the large, graceful **Japanese Peace Pagoda**, also known as Sama Chaitya. The incense-smoked **image room** near the entrance, with its Buddha statues and colourful altar, is far more interesting, especially when the friendly resident monk and nun are drumming and chanting. Plus, the nun often hands out sweets!

The main reason for coming here, though, is to see herds of passing **wild elephants**, but they've been shy in recent years and don't come by like they used to. Try your luck: at around 5pm to 6pm, the elephants may pass through a narrow passageway in front of the pagoda, or in the field behind it. Birdwatchers will also find the pagoda platform a handy perch for spotting hundreds of **waterbirds** that flit about the facing lake.

Chinese & Western Food Court and Tree Tops Jungle Lodge (p220) organise boat safaris in the exceedingly untouristed **Gal Oya National Park**, 22km west of town.

Sleeping & Eating

Ambhasewana Guest GUESTHOUSE $

(222 3865; 51st Ave; r with/without air-con Rs 1500/750;) When we arrived at this friendly little guesthouse, the owner was at the top of a big mango tree, attaching an antenna. He laughed at how funny it was to be having a conversation from a mango tree, which made his wife, in their little shop under the mango tree, laugh too. Good vibes all around. Plus: shade, flowering plants, and airy bargain-price rooms on a quiet side street just a couple of blocks from the town centre.

Monty Guest House HOTEL $$

(222 2169; www.montyhotel.com; 1st Ave; s/d/tr Rs 1500/2000/2250, with air-con from Rs 2500/3000/3250;) The Monty's contemporary lobby is all smooth concrete and warm woods. Rooms are not as sleek, but the newer ones do have modern furniture and clean lines. (Sadly, non-air-con rooms are only so-so.) The restaurant (mains Rs 250 to 600) serves a range of local and Western dishes on its cool outdoor terrace and in the tasteful dining room: the crumb-fried seer fish with fries – basically fish and chips – is shockingly good. Monty's is in a residential area a 10-minute stroll south of Commercial Bank.

Chinese & Western Food Court CHINESE, SRI LANKAN $$

(222 2215; terrelb@gmail.com; Stores Rd; mains Rs 250-650; 11am-10pm) Set in a little garden of potted plants, this is Ampara's most alluring place for a drink and dinner. Specialties include stir-fried cuttlefish and several dishes with *kankun,* a tasty leafy green related to morning glory. Even simple dishes like noodles with egg and tamarind are skilfully prepared. C&W also has rooms (from Rs 4250) that have lots of bells and whistles but are not well maintained.

New City SRI LANKAN $

(Keells New City Supermarket; mains Rs 100-150; 6am-9pm) The brightest and most characterful of several budget eateries around the clock tower, this place whips up rice and curry at lunchtime, rings with the deafening knife-work of the *kotthu*-maker each evening and has lots of short eats (deep-fried snacks and other small bites) for the times in between.

Indika Bakery & Sweet Delight FAST FOOD $

(Kachcheri Rd; short eats Rs 20-75; 6.30am-7.30pm) Also known as Indika Bakers with Sweet Delights, this place wins the prize for best names. It's a bright, clean, modern snack shop that's ideal for a cold drink.

Information

Several banks in town have ATMs, including **Commercial Bank** (DS Senanayake Rd).

SabeeCom.Net & Bookmart (Regal Junction; internet per hr Rs 50; ⌚8.30am-6.30pm Sun-Fri) is your internet hookup.

Getting There & Away

Ampara's bus stand has CTB and private services. For Arugam Bay you can also take a bus to Siyambulanduwa (Rs 75, eight daily) and change there, or minibus-hop via Akkaraipattu (Rs 47, hourly) to Pottuvil. For Batticaloa, you can minibus-hop via Kalmunai (Rs 40, frequent). Some useful services:

Batticaloa Rs 84, three hours, 6am

Colombo ordinary/semi-luxury Rs 370/490, 10 hours, nine/four daily

Kandy ordinary/air-con Rs 220/400, 5½ hours, frequent, especially in morning

Nuwara Eliya Rs 274, nine hours, 6.45am

Pottuvil (for Arugam Bay) Rs 109, three hours, 2pm

Around Ampara

BUDDHANGALA

At around 150m tall, the **Buddhangala Rock Hermitage** (donations accepted; ⌚6am-8pm) is the highest point in the area: from the top there's a wide panorama of views (travellers have reported spotting elephants at dusk). The site is said to be 1800 years old, and when the old temple, whose remains are to the left of the main shrine, was excavated in 1964, a gold casket containing a tooth of the Buddha was discovered. It's now housed inside the dagoba and is on view every June for three days around *poya* day.

Within an ancient cave overhang, interesting museum-style treasures include a human skeleton, used in meditation. The site is beautiful, but without a guide or English signage, its spiritual relevance is somewhat lost; English-speaking monks may be around to chat. Three-wheelers from Ampara, 7km away, cost Rs 700 return.

DEEGAWAPI

According to legend, Deegawapi (Dighavapi Cetiya) is the one place in southeastern Sri Lanka that the Buddha visited. The stupa was built during the reign of King Saddhatissa (137–119 BC) and patched up in the 2nd and 18th centuries AD before becoming lost in the jungle. Rediscovered in 1916, it has for decades been at the centre of disputes; many Sinhalese say the area's predominantly Muslim population deliberately settled on ancient dagoba (read: Sinhalese) land, while many Muslims, who have lived in the region for centuries, see the claim as a bridgehead for Sinhalese colonisation.

The site might not be interesting enough to warrant the lengthy detour: the vast central red-brick dagoba stub is massive, but it lacks the scenic forest setting of similar Yudaganawa. An excavation is under way, however, to be followed by a restoration of the stupa, which may make it more attractive (as well as fodder for more ethnic strife). The small, nearby **archaeological museum** (admission free; ⌚8am-5pm) has potential.

Batticaloa

☎065

Batticaloa, Batti for short, has no must-see sights. Nonetheless the vibe is right, and it has an intangible charm, magnified by the palm-filtered sunlight glancing off the nearby lagoons. Around town, the beaches are gorgeous if a bit desolate. Batticaloa has suffered from severe civil strife in the past, but it feels peaceful, even mellow, now. That said, the streets get very quiet at night, and locals don't recommend venturing out alone; take a three-wheeler.

Sights & Activities

Puliyanthivu NEIGHBOURHOOD

Puliyanthivu is pleasantly relaxed, and colonial edifices like **St Michael's College** (Central Rd) and the sturdy 1838 **Methodist Church** (Post Office Rd) are understated and charming. Of the dozens of churches, the most eye-catching are the vaguely Mexican, earth-toned **St Anthony's** (St Anthony's St) and the grand, turquoise **St Mary's Cathedral** (St Mary's St), which was rebuilt in 1994 following its partial destruction during fighting between Tamils and Muslims. Of the many Hindu temples, **Anipandi Sitivigniswara Alayar** (Hospital Rd) is visually the finest, with a magnificent *gopuram*. **Jami-Us-Salem Jummah Masjid** is among the town's prettier mosques.

Kallady & Navalady NEIGHBOURHOODS

Batti is linked by bridge to a long, beach-edged peninsula that has the Kallady and Navalady neighbourhoods. Kallady has a deserted strip of beach that's idyllic save for the tsunami evidence still all around. The **Thiruchendur Murugan Alayam temple**

(Navalady Rd), near the beach between Third and Fourth Cross Sts, was slammed by the tsunami, leaving its small colourful *gopuram* leaning at an alarming angle. Built in 1984 as a stopping point on the Pada Yatra pilgrimage to Kataragama, the temple's Murugan image is said to have opened its own eyes before the painter could do the job. You can swim at **Kallady beach**, which has a little boardwalk, or at beautiful **Navalady beach**, to the north, but it's not normally done and locals advise against going alone or straying too far off the beaten track.

Imperial Saloon SHRINE
(Trinco Rd; ⏲8.30am-8.30pm, to 1pm Sun) While you're in town, consider getting a haircut (Rs 300) at this salon, which is an amazing work of art. Every inch of it is covered in decorative painting, fake flowers, sequins, filigree, stained glass or tinsel garlands, and at the back of the salon, up towards the faux-sky ceiling, is an interfaith shrine, from where Durga, Mary and the Buddha keep an eye on things.

Dutch Fort FORT
(Bazaar St; ⏲8.30am-4.15pm) The 6m-thick walls of Batti's fort surround the rambling kachcheri (administrative office). The fort itself contains government offices and isn't very interesting, but it has a tiny **museum** with several intriguing items labelled, alas, only in Tamil. By the eastern entrance gate you'll find a couple of old canons guarding the District Secretariat Office. A great place to observe the fort is from across the water, beside the tiny **Auliya Mosque** (Lady Manning Dr), with its curious green minaret.

Sri Lanka Diving Tours DIVING
(☎031 371 7451, 077 061 5205; www.srilanka-divingtours.com; Navalady) This dive school, based at Deep Sea Resort, specialises in wrecks, and Batticaloa has a good one: the HMS *Hermes*, a British ship that was sunk by Japanese bombers in 1942. This dive is for certified Tec divers (the five-day certification course, for very advanced divers, is also offered here), but there are several other rock dives in the area for those less advanced. Dives cost US$40; the open-water course is US$335.

Batticaloa Market MARKET
(Lloyds Ave) Pick up the usual fruit as well as gifts for back home like spoons made from coconut shells and palmyra palm jaggery (raw sugar) in laid-back, hassle-free environs.

Sleeping

Many hotels are in Kallady, a Rs 150 three-wheeler ride from the town centre.

YMCA GUESTHOUSE $
(☎222 2495; Boundary Rd; s/d/tr from Rs 690/920/1150, with air-con Rs 1725/2300/2875; ❄) Oh, the Y. It's so cheap, the rooms are massive (especially in the new wing), the location is central but quiet, and staff are so friendly and eager to please that you might start to suspect something (they're really just helpful – don't worry). Rooms are not the cleanest, true, and there's no food onsite, but for the money, who cares?

Riviera Resort HOTEL $
(☎222 2164/5; www.riviera-online.com; New Dutch Bar Rd, Kallady; s/d from Rs 750/1200, d with air-con from Rs 3000; ❄@📶) Perched at the water's edge with lush gardens and views of Kallady Bridge and the lagoon, this peaceful spot less than 1km north of the bridge has a wide range of neat and clean bungalows. Cheaper rooms need painting but have hot water, mosquito nets and a touch of style, such as wood ceilings. The more expensive rooms are beautiful, with pretty bedspreads and small terraces. Benches are wisely set up by the lagoon for taking in views.

Deep Sea Resort GUESTHOUSE $
(☎031 371 7451, 077 061 5205; www.srilanka-divingtours.com; Navalady; r with/without air-con Rs 4000/2500; ❄@📶) Even if you're not diving with the on-site Sri Lanka Diving Tours, tiny Deep Sea Resort is an excellent, though remote, option. Located in quiet, sandy Navalady (about 5km from Kallady Bridge), the recently opened guesthouse has fresh, modern rooms and a lagoon-view gazebo restaurant (mains Rs 450 to 700) perfect for eating fresh seafood and writing your novel.

Subaraj Inn HOTEL $
(☎222 5983; 6/1 Lloyds Ave; r with air-con from Rs 2200; ❄📶) This comfortable and slightly quirky hotel is the kind of place where staff wear uniforms and rooms are old-fashioned and very orderly. (Avoid the Rs 990 non-air-con rooms, which are cramped and stuffy.) It's professionally run, has been around for ages and has a pleasant bar-restaurant.

Hotel Bridge View HOTEL $
(☎222 3723; www.hotelbridgeview.com; 63/24 New Dutch Bar Rd, Kallady; s/d/tr from Rs 1120/1300/1560; ❄) This garden hotel 1km from the bridge is charmingly old-school: think

Batticaloa

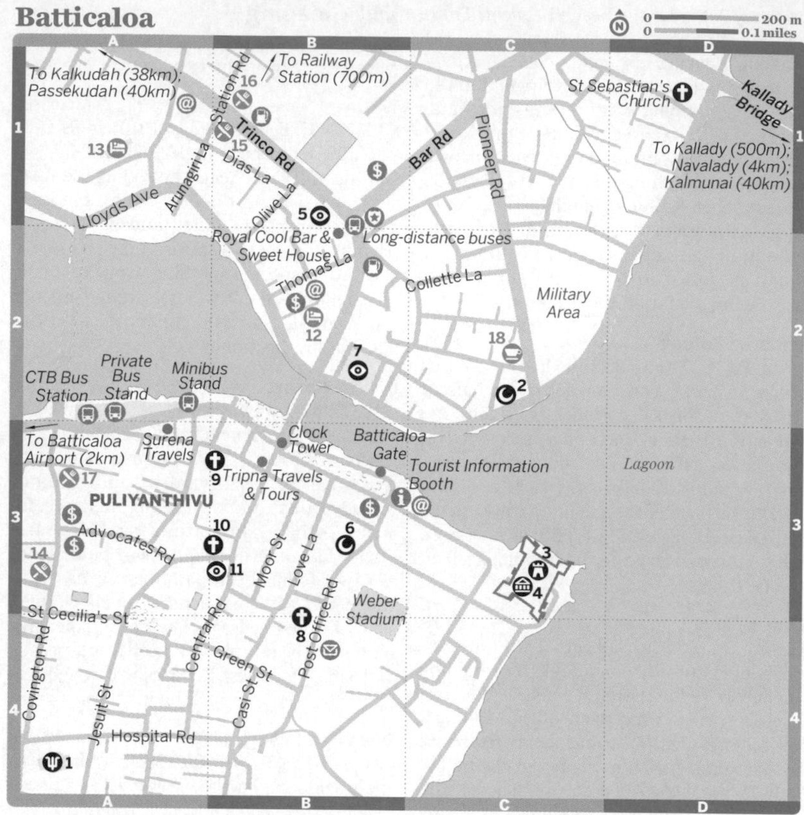

folding luggage racks and fresh white paint and potted plants everywhere. Rooms are surrounded by greenery, but oddly, those in the old wing are better than the newer ones. Any bridge views are imagined. The restaurant (mains Rs 250 to 450) has decent seafood and curries.

Railway Station GUEST ROOMS $
(☎222 4471; Station Rd; d/f Rs 700/1000) Batti's train station has infrequently used but surprisingly decent guest rooms for ticket-holders. Can't beat it for early trains.

Eating & Drinking

RN Buffet & Take Away SRI LANKAN $$
(42 Covington Rd; lunch buffets Rs 450; ⏲11am-2.30pm) This superclean little eatery above a grocery shop serves a delicious six-dish lunch buffet that's not excessively spiced. The restaurant also does a mean line in savoury pastries. It's run by a delightful couple who get their inspiration from a Delia Smith recipe book!

TD Foods & Takeaway SRI LANKAN $
(15 Covington Rd; mains Rs 150-320) Tiny TD is strung with coloured lights and Chinese lanterns and is next to a Tamil-film music shop – in other words, it has the best ambience ever. It's a favourite of families, who come for the excellent biryanis, noodles and *kotthu* (*rotti* chopped up and mixed with vegies).

Riviera Resort SRI LANKAN $
(☎222 2164/5; www.riviera-online.com; New Dutch Bar Rd; mains Rs 100-350; ⏲noon-3pm & 5-10pm) The old-fashioned Riviera sets you up with a drink on the porch, takes your order and then, an hour later, calls you into the dining room, set up with all manner of dishes and white-cloth napkins. The food is worth the wait: the Riviera is known for its crab curries (from Rs 200) and cashew curry (Rs 260).

Batticaloa

Sights

1 Anipandi Sitivigniswara Alayar A4
2 Auliya Mosque C2
3 Dutch Fort C3
4 Dutch Fort Museum C3
5 Imperial Saloon B1
6 Jami-Us-Salem Jummah Masjid B3
7 Market B2
8 Methodist Church B4
9 St Anthony's B3
10 St Mary's Cathedral B3
11 St Michael's College B3

Sleeping

12 Subaraj Inn B2
13 YMCA A1

Eating

14 RN Buffet & Take Away A3
Subaraj Inn .... (see 12)
15 Sun Shine Fast B1
16 Sun Shine Fast B1
17 TD Foods & Takeaway A3

Drinking

18 Café Chill C2

Seven Star SRI LANKAN $
(New Kalmunai Rd, Kallady; rice & curry Rs 100-200) A simple local joint with a fine rice and curry – one of the best around, in fact, as the lunchtime crowds will attest. Seven Star is just north of the clock tower.

Sun Shine Fast SRI LANKAN $
(315 Trinco Rd; mains Rs 160-250) With two locations across the street from each other, Sun Shine is doing a fine trade in lunchtime rice and curry, evening short eats and cakes, and night-time take-out noodles and fried rice. Good, simple comfort food.

Subaraj Inn SRI LANKAN $$
(6/1 Lloyds Ave; mains Rs 175-650; noon-3pm & 7.30-9.30pm) Maybe as a result of having been an expat hangout through the war, the bar and restaurant areas here are cosy and offer easy conversations. The menu favours local and Chinese food.

Café Chill CAFE $
(9 Pioneer Rd; drinks & snacks Rs 40-150; 9am-9pm) Coffee, tea, juices and lassis in a relaxed semi-alfresco setting with wind chimes, low-slung chairs and tables made from tree trunks. The ambience is great; the espresso is getting there.

Information

Bank of Ceylon (Covington Rd), **Commercial Bank** (Bar Rd) and **People's Bank** (Covington Rd) all have ATMs.

Google World (Station Rd; internet per hr Rs 40; 8.30am-8.30pm) Fastest internet in town.

Post office (Post Office Rd; 7am-8pm Mon-Fri, to 6pm Sat, to 5pm Sun)

Public Library (Bazaar St; internet per hr Rs 30; 9am-5pm, closed Wed & poya days)

SunNetCafe (Trinco Rd; internet per hr Rs 40; 8am-8pm)

Tourist information booth (Bazaar St; 9am-5pm)

Tripna Travels & Tours (St Anthony's St; 9am-5.30pm Mon-Fri, to 1pm Sat)

Getting There & Away

AIR The Sri Lankan Air Force's **Helitours** (011 311 0472, 011 314 444; www.airforce.lk, heli tours@slaf.gov.lk) conducts flights on military planes between Batticaloa's airport, 2km southwest of the bus stand, and Colombo's Ratmalana Air Force Base. Flights run in both directions on Tuesdays (one way Rs 6100). **Sri Lankan Airlines** (1979; www.srilankan.lk) may be running flights to/from Colombo by the time you arrive.

BUS CTB buses, private buses and minibuses have adjacent bus stations on Munai St, but many head out from the police station area; inquire in advance. Kalmunai is a major minibus junction town so if you can't find what you need in Batticaloa, inquire about Kalmunai. At press time, buses to Trinco were still taking the long way; the trip will be quicker once the coast road is repaired. Combined CTB and private departures:

Ampara Rs 84, three hours, two daily
Badulla Rs 205, six hours, five daily
Colombo Rs 275, nine hours, three daily
Jaffna (via Vavuniya) Rs 380, seven hours, 10 daily
Kalmunai Rs 60, 1½ hours, every 15 minutes
Polonnaruwa Rs 75, 1½ hours, hourly
Pottuvil (for Arugam Bay) Rs 125, five hours, 14 daily
Trincomalee Rs 201, seven hours, 10 daily
Valaichchenai (for Passekudah and Kalkudah) Rs 48, one hour, every 15 minutes

Most people prefer the private buses to Colombo:

Royal Cool Bar & Sweet House (Trinco Rd; 6am-10pm) For Colombo (ordinary/air-con

Rs 500/750, 9pm and 9.30pm) and Trincomalee (Rs 270, three daily).

Surena Travels (☎222 6152; Munai St; ⊙4.30-8.30pm) For Colombo (Rs 500, 10 hours, 8.30pm).

TRAIN Book at the helpful **railway office** (☎222 4471; ⊙8.30am-4pm), well in advance for Intercity trains.

Colombo Intercity express 3rd/2nd/1st class Rs 320/500/900, 7½ hours, 7.15am

Colombo semi-express 3rd/2nd class Rs 230/420, 7.15am (nine-hour journey) and 5.45pm (11-hour journey)

Trincomalee semi-express (transfer in Gal Oya) 3rd/2nd class Rs 150/280, five hours, 7.15am, 10.30am, 5.45pm and 8.15pm

Around Batticaloa

BATTICALOA LIGHTHOUSE

Batticaloa's **lighthouse** (Palameenmadu) and the coasts around it are a popular family excursion (avoid weekends). Swimming in the calm water, surrounded by sandbars and islands and inlets, is the main draw, though **boat trips** (Rs 350-3000; ⊙8am-7pm) can be good for bird- and crocodile-watching. The **Environmental Learning Centre** (☎065-306 4646; s/d Rs 750/1200), opposite the lighthouse, has tiny, immaculate rooms; brand-new **Sunrise Resort** (☎065-222 2451; sunrise_batti@yahoo.com; r from Rs 2500; ❄) has rooms and a restaurant.

Three-wheelers charge Rs 350 from Batticaloa, but plans are afoot to launch a boat service between Batticaloa Gate, in town, and the lighthouse, which will be a mad scenic ride. Ask at the tourist information booth for the status.

KALKUDAH & PASSEKUDAH BEACHES

Nuzzling either side of the palm-tipped Kalkudah headland, north of Batticaloa, are two breathtaking curves of sand. The hotels that once lined the road southwest from Kalkudah village all disappeared in the war or tsunami, but today tourism is making a major comeback. Passekudah Beach, the most northerly, is gorgeous and the water very shallow, but you'll often find busloads of Sinhalese tourists there. Try walking north along the shore to avoid the crowds.

Kalkudah Bay Beach, over the headland to the south, by contrast, is deserted. The ocean is rougher here, but it's a beautiful, broad beach. An army camp at the end of the Valaichchenai–Kalkudah road blocks the main approach; scoot around it and use the beach-access lane 800m further south.

Some of the best guesthouses are set back about 2km from the beaches on the Valaichchenai–Kalkudah road, like the **New Land Guesthouse** (☎065-568 0440; r Rs 1000, mains Rs 200-250), which has a shady terrace, gardens, clean, basic, airy rooms (ask for the big one!) and good vibes, and **Victoria Guest House** (☎065-077 957 8968; victoriaghouse@yahoo.com; s/d from Rs 1500/2000, mains Rs 250; 📶). Victoria is the owner's mum, who runs the Simla Inn next door and is legendary for her great curries and her perseverance through the war and tsunami. Today, however, daughter Mercy is running a tighter ship at her guesthouse, which is all fresh paint and fastidiousness. **Moni Guesthouse** (☎065-365 4742; d with/without air-con Rs 2500/1500) is in the midst of the throngs, but has a good family feel and is close to the beach.

WORTH A TRIP

VAKARAI

Kalkudah and Passekudah are pretty, but they don't compare to the white sands of Vakarai, about 20km north. The best way to enjoy them is with an unplugged, off-the-grid stay at **Tranquility Coral Cottages** (☎011-262 5404; http://tccvakaraisl.com; Sallithievu Rd, Pannichankerni; cottages incl meals Rs 4000-8000). Tranquility's location is out of a dream: at the edge of a headland, beside a defunct military base and in view of a lush island that's connected to the beach by a string of sand. There's only electricity at night, and the three cottages are simple; the best one is just steps from the water. A cook will prepare excellent meals with fish caught nearby, but note that she may be the only one around. Not surprisingly, it's tricky to get here without your own transport. From Batti, take a bus to Vakarai (Rs 107, three hours, six daily) and get down at the Sallithievu junction; Tranquility is 2km from here.

Batticaloa buses to Valaichchenai (Rs 48, one hour, every 15 minutes) go to a stand in Pethalai, where three-wheelers charge Rs 300 return, including waiting time, for the beach. Buses become less frequent after 5pm, in which case consider walking to the Valaichchenai junction on the A15 (Trinco Rd), about 1km from Valaichchenai market, to catch one of the many passing long-distance buses. Three-wheelers from the market area to the beach charge Rs 200/400 one way/return.

There is a train station called Kalkudah: it's tiny and very isolated, 2km southwest of Kalkudah Beach on the seldom-used shortcut road from Kumburumoolai. Should you jump off a train here, head north through the well-marked minefield towards the beach-access road.

Trincomalee

026 / POP 57,000

Trincomalee (Trinco) had a rough time in the war, but the fascinating town is beginning to thrive again. Sitting along one of the world's finest natural harbours, Trincomalee is old almost beyond reckoning: it's possibly the site of historic Gokana in the Mahavamsa (Great Chronicle), and its Shiva temple, that of Trikuta hill in the Hindu text the Vayu Purana. Most people just pass through the city on their way to the nearby beaches of Uppuveli and Nilaveli, but the town has some charm, lots of history and an interesting diversity of people.

Trincomalee's economic trump card is a superb deep-water port, which, historically, has made it the target for all manner of attacks: by the British takeover in 1795, the city had changed colonial hands seven times. Today the Sri Lankan armed forces control Fort Frederick, along with the British-built airfield China Bay, to the south.

Sights & Activities

Fort Frederick Area FORTRESS

Built by the Portuguese, Fort Frederick was rebuilt by the Dutch. Today, British insignias crown the tunnel-like gateway that pierces the fort's massively stout walls. Most of the fortress is under military jurisdiction, but you can stroll up to the big new standing **Buddha statue** at the **Gokana Temple**. The road continues up to scenic **Swami Rock**, a 130m-high cliff nicknamed Lovers' Leap, and the revered **Koneswaram Kovil** (6-11am, 11.30am-1.30pm & 4.30-7pm) – one of Sri Lanka's *pancha ishwaram,* the five historical Hindu temples dedicated to Shiva and established to protect the island from natural disaster. The temple houses the *lingam* (Hindu phallic symbol) known as the **Swayambhu Lingam**, making it one of Sri Lanka's most spiritually important Hindu sites. The original shrine may be much older, but the temple existed at least by 300 AD and was built up over the years by everyone from the Cholas to the Jaffna Kingdom (its *gopuram* was said to be visible to sailors at sea), until being destroyed by the Portuguese. The current structure dates to 1952. Outside the temple, check out the piece from the original temple sitting atop a boulder; it was used for worship before the new temple was built. *Puja* (prayers) is at 6.30am, 11.30am and 4.30pm. You'll need to check your shoes at the bottom of the hill (Rs 10).

Religious Sights RELIGIOUS

Kali Kovil (Dockyard Rd) has the most impressive, eye-catching *gopuram* of Trinco's many Hindu temples. Most others are outwardly rather plain, including the important **Kandasamy Kovil** (Kandasamy Kovil

RAWANA & THE SWAYAMBHU LINGAM

The radio-mast hill opposite Swami Rock is considered to be the site of the mythical palace of the 10-headed demon king Rawana. He's the Hindu antihero of the Ramayana, infamous for kidnapping Rama's wife, Sita. Along with Sita, he supposedly carried to Lanka the powerful Swayambhu Lingam, taken from a Tibetan mountaintop. This *lingam* became the object of enormous veneration. However, in 1624, the proselytising Catholic-Portuguese destroyed the surrounding clifftop temple, tipping the whole structure, *lingam* and all, into the ocean. It was only retrieved in 1962 by a scuba-diving team that included writer Arthur C Clarke, who described the discovery in *The Reefs of Taprobane*. For cameraman Mike Wilson, who first spotted the *lingam*, the experience proved so profound that he renounced his career and family to become Hindu Swami Siva Kalki (see http://kataragama.org/sivakalki.htm).

Trincomalee

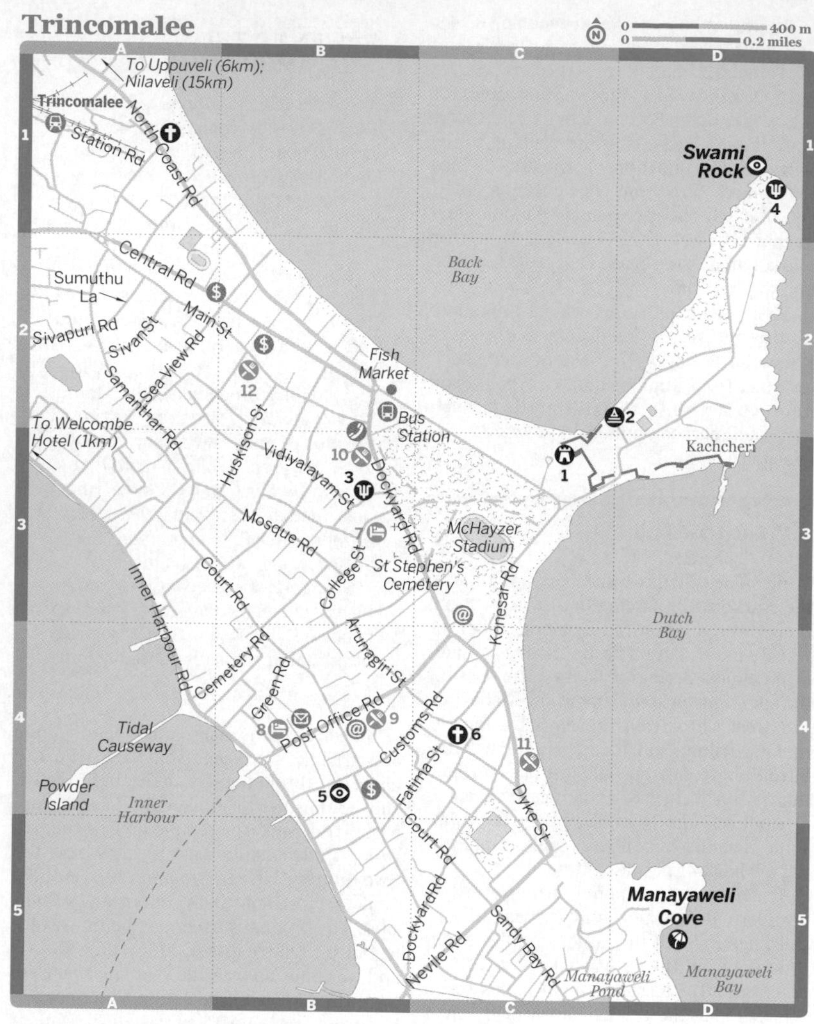

Rd), dedicated to Murugan. Of the churches, the 1852 Catholic **St Mary's Cathedral** (St Mary's St) is particularly attractive, with a sky-blue neobaroque frontage.

Beaches BEACHES

Trinco's most famous beaches are at nearby Uppuveli and Nilaveli, but picturesque **Dutch Bay** isn't bad. It's more a place for strolling, but swimming is possible despite sometimes dangerous undertows. **Manayaweli Cove** is an appealing curl of fishing beach where you can also swim; reach it by strolling past **Manayaweli Pond**, aka Dhoby Tank, where local washers do their laundry. Don't consider bathing in polluted **Inner Harbour**.

Sleeping

For good reason, most travellers prefer the accommodation in Uppuveli, just 6km north.

Silver Star Inn HOTEL $

(☎222 2348; fax 222 1889; 27 College St; tw/tr from Rs 1300/2000, tr/q with air-con Rs 3500/5000; ❄) The friendly Silver Star is the best deal in town, with tidy rooms with mosquito nets

Trincomalee

Top Sights
- Manayaweli Cove D5
- Swami Rock D1

Sights
- Buddha Statue .... (see 2)
- 1 Fort Frederick C3
- 2 Gokana Temple C2
- 3 Kali Kovil B3
- 4 Kandasamy Kovil D1
- 5 Koneswaram Kovil B4
- 6 St Mary's Cathedral C4
- Swayambhu Lingham .... (see 5)

Sleeping
- 7 Silver Star Inn B3
- 8 Sun Flower B4

Eating
- 9 Ajmeer Hotel B4
- 10 Anna Pooram Vegetarian Restaurant B3
- 11 Green Park Beach Hotel C4
- 12 New Parrot Restaurant B2

and helpful staff. Rooms in the three-storey building are pricier but have views; they're also away from the kitchen and wedding hall, which can be noisy on event nights (ask ahead).

Welcombe Hotel HOTEL **$$**
(☎222 3885/6; www.welcombehotel.com; 66 Orr's Hill Lower Rd; s/d from US$74/78; ❄📶🏊) It's starting to fade, but the Welcombe is Trincomalee's most architecturally interesting place to stay, with its quasi-Japanese modern angles and lines. The pool and balconies have water views, staff are friendly and prices may be negotiable; it's a nice little waterside escape (relative to Trincomalee). In a previous incarnation this site was a naval centre rumoured to have harboured a torture chamber. Sweet dreams!

Sun Flower HOTEL **$**
(☎222 7078; 154 Post Office Rd; tw with/without air-con Rs 2000/1000) A simple and quiet place located above a bakery where occasional wafts of slow-baking cakes (and sometimes wafts of slow-baking rubbish in the streets outside) will drift into your sleep. It's well maintained and quiet, the owners are friendly and the showers mildly tepid. Paradoxically, only air-con rooms have mosquito nets.

Eating & Drinking

Ajmeer Hotel SRI LANKAN **$**
(65 Post Office Rd; mains Rs 100-250; ⊙5.30am-10.30pm) This popular halal lunch place does excellent rice and curries (Rs 100 to 190) – even the veg version rocks. The refills seem to never end, portions are enormous and the vibe is friendly.

Anna Pooram Vegetarian Restaurant SOUTH INDIAN **$**
(415 Dockyard Rd; snacks Rs 15-80, rice & curry Rs 120-150) This simple little pure-veg eatery excels in *idlis* (rice cakes) and *sambar* (soupy lentil dish with veg), tea, and short eats, though it also does lunch. It has a couple of tables, but is hugely popular for its take-out.

Welcombe Hotel EUROPEAN **$$**
(☎222 2373; 66 Orr's Hill Lower Rd; mains Rs 450-750; ⊙11am-3.30pm & 7-9.30pm) There's appealing alfresco, harbour-view dining at this hotel restaurant, which serves some original and mostly successful Western dishes, including lamb chop in wine and rosemary, and jumbo prawns in lemon-garlic butter. It's also a good spot for a drink.

New Parrot Restaurant SRI LANKAN **$**
(96 Main St; mains Rs 100-300; ⊙noon-2pm & 5-8pm, closed dinner Sun) Reliably good fried rice, *kotthu,* noodles and 'devilled' dishes.

Green Park Beach Hotel INDIAN **$$**
(312 Dyke St; mains Rs 375-600; 📶) It has a vast menu of mainly North Indian dishes, but is mostly worth mentioning for the free wi-fi.

Information

Commercial Bank (Central Rd) and **HNB** (Court Rd) have the most reliable ATMs.

Khethush Internet Browsing Spot (380 Court Rd; internet per hr Rs 40; ⊙8am-8pm Mon-Sat)

Lonely Planet (www.lonelyplanet.com/sri-lanka/the-east/trincomalee) Planning advice, author recommendations, traveller reviews and insider tips.

Post office (Post Office Rd; ⊙7am-7pm Mon-Sat, 8.30am-4.30pm Sun)

Trincomalee Public Library (Dockyard Rd; internet per hr Rs 40; ⊙8.30am-5.30pm Tue-Sun) Fast internet in bright, friendly surrounds.

ZainabCom (Dockyard Rd; ⊙8.30am 8.30pm) For international calls (Rs 4 per minute).

Getting There & Away

AIR **Helitours** (011 311 0472, 011 314 444; www.airforce.lk, helitours@slaf.gov.lk), the Sri Lankan Air Force's commercial arm, conducts passenger flights on military planes between China Bay airfield, 13km south of town, and Colombo's Ratmalana Air Force Base. Flights run in both directions on Monday and Friday (one way Rs 4100, one hour).

At press time, **Sri Lankan Airlines** (1979; www.srilankan.lk) were also planning to launch an air-taxi service between Colombo and Trincomalee.

BUS The coast road to Batticaloa was still closed at research time; the trip will be shorter once the A15 is repaired. CTB and private bus departures:

Anuradhapura Rs 185, four hours, three daily in morning

Batticaloa (via Habarana and Polonnaruwa) Rs 200, seven hours, 10 daily

Colombo from Rs 240, seven hours, frequent

Colombo (air-con; book in advance) Rs 490, six hours, two in evening

Jaffna (via Vavuniya) Rs 270, seven hours, eight daily

Kandy Rs 210, five hours, 16 daily, plus two air-con (Rs 358) buses daily

Uppuveli/Nilaveli Rs 12/22, 20/30 minutes, every 20 minutes

TRAIN There are two trains daily between Trincomalee and Colombo Fort, including a direct overnight sleeper service. On either train, you can change at Gal Oya for Batticaloa, but the evening train isn't recommended: the layover is long and late. Reserve at **Trincomalee station** (222 2271; bookings 8am-noon).

Services from Trincomalee:

Batticaloa 3rd/2nd class Rs 150/280, five hours, 7am

Colombo sleeper 3rd-/2nd-/1st-class sleeper Rs 270/450/750, nine hours, 7.30am

Colombo unreserved (transfer in Gal Oya) 3rd/2nd class Rs 205/370, nine hours, 7am

Uppuveli & Nilaveli

026

Now that peace has settled in, more and more travellers are discovering Uppuveli and Nilaveli. The scene here is much mellower (and the guesthouses slightly pricier) than those in Arugam Bay. Folks in Nilaveli will say that the water in Uppuveli is not as clear as it is in Nilaveli, but Uppuvelians will be quick to point out the cosiness of their beach, in contrast to Nilaveli's wide-open spaces. Either way, everyone loves Pigeon Island, a pretty island and reef 1km from Nilaveli that makes for a perfect snorkelling or diving day trip.

UPPUVELI

Uppuveli, 6km from Trincomalee, is less spread out than Nilaveli and has more budget sleeping options, though some of them are overpriced concrete boxes that host all-night parties for local hotel staff. You can dive and snorkel from here, but it's less practical than Nilaveli.

Sights & Activities

Commonwealth War Cemetery CEMETERY
(Nilaveli Rd; dawn-dusk) For a break from the beach, stroll up to this beautifully kept cemetery. This is the last resting place for over 600 Commonwealth servicemen who died at Trinco during WWII, most of them during a 1942 Japanese raid that sank over a dozen vessels.

Salli Muthumariamunam Kovil TEMPLE
Beachfront Salli Muthumariamunam Kovil is 4km by road from Uppuveli but only a short hop by boat; it's across Fishermen's Creek, masked from view by green-topped rocks.

Sri Lanka Diving Tours DIVING
(222 1611, 071 132 3974; www.srilanka-divingtours.com; Chaaya Blu) Chaaya Blu's diving centre is one of the better ones in the area, with three-day open-water certification courses for US$410. It also offers several local dives and snorkelling trips – including to Pigeon Island (US$80 for two dives and US$40 for snorkelling) and, for advanced divers, to Swami Rock in Trincomalee and the Irakkandy shipwreck – as well as kids' diving instruction, and guided boating and fishing trips.

DIYers can snorkel, or even just swim around with goggles, at the northern end of Uppuveli beach, where exotic sea life is plentiful and travellers have reported glimpsing some rare fish.

Sleeping

TOP CHOICE **Palm Beach** GUESTHOUSE $$
(222 1250; d with/without air-con Rs 3800/3200, annex s with shared bathroom Rs 1500, d Rs 2700; closed Nov-Jan;) It's not just the tasteful rooms, with dark-wood furniture, pretty patterned curtains and quality mosquito nets that make Palm Beach the best place

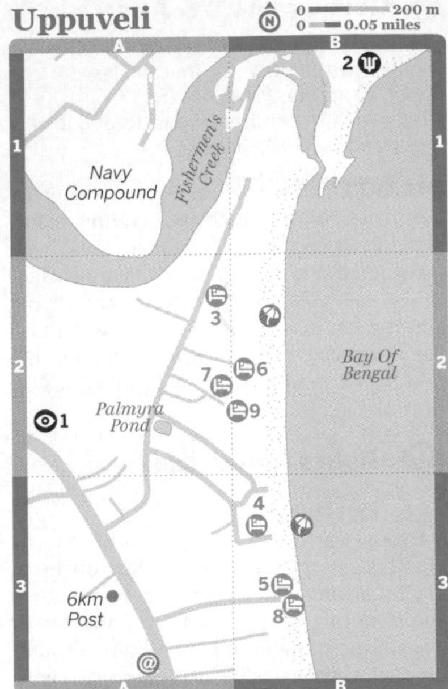

Uppuveli

Sights

1 Commonwealth War Cemetery..........A2
2 Salli Muthumariamunam Kovil...........B1

Activities, Courses & Tours

Sri Lanka Diving Tours................(see 3)

Sleeping

3 Chaaya Blu..A2
4 Coconut Beach Lodge.........................B3
5 French Garden Regish..........................B3
6 Golden Beach Cottage.........................B2
7 Jaysh Resort..A2
8 Palm Beach..B3
9 Sea Lotus Park......................................B2

Eating

Coconut Beach Lodge..................(see 4)
Crab...(see 3)
Palm Beach.....................................(see 8)
Sea Lotus Park...............................(see 9)

around. It's also immaculate (rooms are cleaned daily), is set amid peaceful, shady gardens just a few metres from the beach, and has awesome pets. Oh, and there's insanely good food and espresso. Even the rooms in the budget annex are bright, clean as anything, and charmingly monastic, with nets, wood furniture and fresh white paint. Book ahead.

TOP CHOICE **Chaaya Blu** RESORT $$$
(☎222 1611; www.chaayahotels.com; s/d incl breakfast US$215/230, s/d chalets incl breakfast US$245/260; ❄@🛜🏊) Chaaya's stunning decor couldn't go better with the bright sun and blue water outside: clean whites, whitewashes and rich blues are set off with punchy orange throw pillows, textile and mosaic art and, in the open-air lobby, massive columns tiled in mirror. Chic. Airy and comfy rooms and beachfront chalets have thoughtful touches and are spread along Uppuveli's finest stretch of beach. The food is excellent; book online for discounts.

Coconut Beach Lodge GUESTHOUSE $
(☎222 4888, 492 5712; sujeevah@yahoo.com; r with/without air-con from Rs 5000/2500) Not only does Coconut Beach have the beachfront location, along with porches and a gazebo from which to admire it at happy hour, but it's really trying to make it cosy. Standard rooms have touches like small artworks in the bathroom, while the air-con rooms in the main house have lofty wood-beam ceilings, art all around, and a homey vibe.

Sea Lotus Park RESORT $$$
(☎222 5327; www.lotustrinco.com; s/d Rs 8100/8700, bungalows Rs 6300/6775; ❄@🛜🏊) This poor-man's Chaaya Blu is sort of the PC to Chaaya's Apple – perfectly functional, with the mod cons, pool, and professional service, but without the style. Recently renovated rooms are somewhat contemporary, with flat-screen TVs and sea views, but the bungalows, though weathered, have beachfront porches and views you'll dream about for years to come.

Jaysh Resort GUESTHOUSE $
(☎320 7015; r from Rs 2500; ❄) Jaysh is starting to look older than its four years, but it's in an extremely quiet spot next to Sea Lotus Park. A path runs right to the beach.

Golden Beach Cottage GUESTHOUSE $
(☎721 1243; r from Rs 2000) The rooms are nothing special, but the grounds are OK, with picnic tables and a spot on a beautiful patch of beach south of Chaaya Blu.

French Garden Regish GUESTHOUSE $
(☎222 1705; r Rs 1200-1800) Even though it's right on the beach, the only thing to

recommend it is the price. Best of the French Garden lot.

Eating & Drinking

TOP CHOICE Crab INTERNATIONAL $$$

(Chaaya Blu; mains Rs 600-1300; noon-11pm) Chaaya Blu is known for the lunch and dinner buffets (from Rs 1650) at its main open-air restaurant. But its cafe, the Crab, has such inventive fusion entrees and creative light lunches – made with locally caught seafood – and such a perfect beachfront location, that we prefer it, especially on hot days. Try the fajita-fish wrap with fries and salad (Rs 680) for lunch, or the crab-and-corn fritters with cucumber relish, green salsa and fruity tomato gravy (Rs 1040). The bar menu is extensive, but drinks cost (a lot) extra. Service is in slow motion.

TOP CHOICE Palm Beach ITALIAN $$$

(222 1250; mains Rs 800-950; noon-2pm & 6.30-9pm, closed Nov-Jan) 'Palm Beach has really good Italian food,' one Italian traveller in Uppuveli said. 'And I don't mean good for Sri Lanka, I mean good for Italy.' Palm Beach's chef, Dona, creates a new menu daily based on what looks good at the market and in her garden, and whips up exquisite classics like spaghetti calamari tomato, opened with bruschetta, served with good wine, and ended with the best cappuccino you've ever had. Reservations required.

Sea Lotus Park INTERNATIONAL $$

(222 5327; mains Rs 400-800;) The menu has 10,000 things on it, but in reality, the restaurant specialises in anything that's fish, curry or a Sri Lankan version of pasta. It's also working on its steak, chicken cordon bleu et al. The beachfront dining is nice, either way.

Coconut Beach Lodge SRI LANKAN $

(222 4888, 492 5712; mains Rs 300-450) The relatively new Coconut Beach just has a few dishes on offer so far – rice and curry, fried rice etc – but they're prepared with love and served on a pretty candlelit patio. Reserve several hours in advance.

Information

Uppuveli has no banks; cash up in Trinco.

Jatheik GameNet Cafe (Nilaveli Rd; internet per hr Rs 60; 8.30am-8pm Mon-Sat)

St Joseph's Medical Service (Nilaveli Rd; 24hr) An around-the-clock medical centre.

Getting There & Away

Irakkandy–Trincomalee buses run every 20 minutes; flag one down for Trincomalee (Rs 12, 20 minutes) or Nilaveli (Rs 12, 10 minutes). Three-wheelers cost Rs 300 to Trinco and Rs 500 to Nilaveli.

NILAVELI

For years Nilaveli, with its bending palms swaying over the golden sand, has been considered one of Sri Lanka's best beaches. It also has excellent snorkelling and diving and a great dive school. But the beach also has a massive military camp plopped in the middle – a reminder that Nilaveli is not far from the old front line.

Sights & Activities

TOP CHOICE Pigeon Island National Park DIVE SITE

Floating in the great blue 1km offshore, Pigeon Island, with its powdery white sands and glittering coral gardens, tantalises with possibilities. The island, a breeding ground for rock pigeons, is beautiful enough, with rock pools and paths running through thickets, but it's the underwater landscape that's the real star. The reef here is shallow, making snorkelling almost as satisfying as diving, and it's home to dozens of corals, hundreds of reef fish (including blacktip reef sharks), and turtles. Going with a guide will cost more, but they'll be able to point out plants and creatures that you won't find on your own. They'll also help you to snorkel or dive less intrusively: although Pigeon Island became a natural park in 2003, there's not much regulation, and the recent surge in tourism is already damaging the reef and its populations.

The government has an assortment of charges for visiting Pigeon Island: entry fee adult/child US$10/5, service charge per group US$8 and charge per boat Rs 125. Add these up and take 12% of that figure to get the VAT. These are payable at the **Pigeon Island National Park ticket office** (320 3850; 6am-5.30pm), on the beach, before heading out, though if you go with Poseidon Diving School or one of the hotels, you'll stop on the way. In addition to the operators listed here, Chaaya Blu in Uppuveli also runs excursions to the island.

Note that the navy base in Trincomalee has a decompression chamber that can (allegedly) be reached by ambulance in 10 minutes.

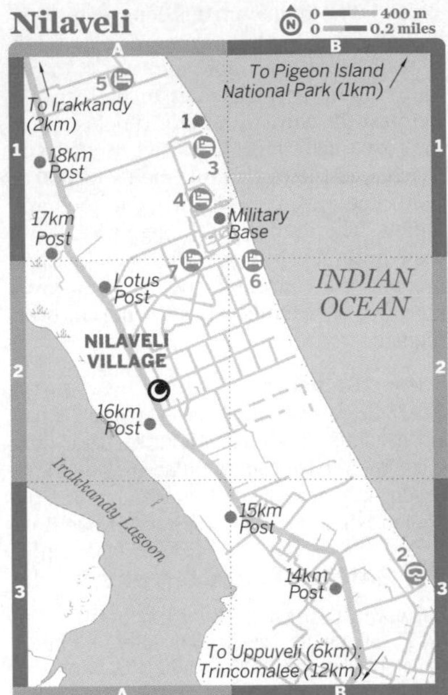

Nilaveli

Activities, Courses & Tours

Nilaveli Private Boat Service ....(see 1)
1 Pigeon Island National Park ticket office A1
2 Poseidon Diving School B3

Sleeping

3 Nilaveli Beach Hotel........ A1
4 Nilaveli Garden Inn........ A1
5 Pigeon Island Beach Resort A1
Pigeon Island View Guest House (see 2)
6 Seaway Hotel........ B2
7 Shahira A2

TOP CHOICE **Poseidon Diving School** DIVING
(☎077 706 9442; www.divingsrilanka.com) Our favourite dive operators charge €50 for three people, including equipment and boat, for Pigeon Island snorkelling trips. You can also rent snorkelling gear from them for Rs 800 per day. Open-water certification courses are €300, and single dives, to Pigeon Island or elsewhere, cost €30. Poseidon also offers **whale-watching trips** (per 3 people €130); you need to leave by 6am for the 10km trip.

Nilaveli Private Boat Service DIVING
(☎071 593 6919) The local boatmen's association has set prices for the Pigeon Island trip – Rs 1500 per two people, Rs 150 per additional person – which means you don't have to worry about haggling. You'll find captains at the beach by the ticket office; they can also help arrange snorkel-gear rental (Rs 250 for two hours). The Service also does **fishing trips** (Rs 2250) and **whale-watching trips** (per 4 people Rs 10,000).

Nilaveli Beach Hotel DIVING
(☎223 2295/6; www.tangerinetours.com) This reputable resort offers dive (€30) and snorkel (from Rs 2400) trips to Pigeon Island, open-water certification courses (€325) and fishing excursions (from Rs 2500).

Sleeping & Eating

Nilaveli's very spread out, and most accommodation is at least a 400m walk from the main road. All of the following serve food.

TOP CHOICE **Nilaveli Beach Hotel** RESORT $$$
(☎223 2295/6; www.tangerinetours.com; s/d with air-con incl breakfast from US$120/130, buffets breakfast/lunch/dinner Rs 1000/1800/2000; ❄☎≈) Nilaveli Beach Hotel definitely has the best grounds – sprawling, shady groves with hammocks and a gorgeous pool area – of any hotel in the area, as well as a beautiful stretch of beach, with views across to Pigeon Island. The architecture is organic and streamlined, with a creative use of fountains and concrete and a harmonious balance of contemporary and earthy – especially in the cottages. The restaurant is beloved for its buffets and specialises in pasta and seafood, but the beachfront-poolside dining area (mains Rs 800 to 1300) may be even better, for food, drinks and atmosphere.

Pigeon Island View Guest House GUESTHOUSE $$
(☎223 2238; d/tr from Rs 4000/5000; ❄) Right on the beach, the Pigeon Island View (which everyone will confuse with Pigeon Island Resort) is the nicest midrange place around and has the peacefulness, pretty beach, and island views of Nilaveli's more expensive options. Like many survivors around here, the owner patiently built up this three-storey house after the tsunami and has done well: rooms are plain but airy and well taken care of, and staff are friendly. It's an especially good choice if you're diving with Poseidon Diving School, based on-site.

Shahira GUESTHOUSE $

(273 3338, 567 0276; http://shahirahotel.com; d/tr Rs 2200/3300) Rooms at this cute little cheapie have front porches that wrap around a pretty garden, all with chairs for kicking back in. So what if it's set behind a military lookout tower with armed soldiers in it? Rooms have no air-con or hot water but are clean and big with antique touches and some character, which is rare for these parts.

Seaway Hotel HOTEL $$

(223 2212; r from Rs 3500;) The Seaway was brand new at the time of research, so we'll see how it holds up, but for now, it's looking good: huge, bright lemon-yellow rooms with porches set back from a beautiful, quiet bit of beach. Staff are friendly and the beachfront restaurant should be functioning by the time you arrive. The drawback: the creepy location, right next to the military base.

Pigeon Island Beach Resort HOTEL $$$

(492 0633; www.pigeonislandresort.com; s/d/tr with air-con incl breakfast from US$120/150/203,) The rooms in this long two-storey building aren't great for the price, and only suites have views (whose idea was it to run the building perpendicular to the beach?). But past the garden and large pool is one of the east coast's most attractive stretches of beach, and the restaurant (mains Rs 800 to 1200) gets rave reviews for its seafood and buffets. The dining and lounge areas, with their antique furniture, wicker lamps and breezes, are charming, too, so it's a great place for a drink or a meal if not an overnight stay.

Nilaveli Garden Inn HOTEL $$

(223 2228; www.hotel-garden-inn.de, in German; s/d/tr from Rs 2750/4100/4700;) It's a little scruffy and basic, but popular. It's not on the beach, but near it, and convenient for the Pigeon Island National Park ticket booth.

Getting There & Away

Flag down any passing bus for Trincomalee (Rs 22, 30 minutes, every 20 minutes). A three-wheeler will cost Rs 800; Rs 500 to Uppuveli.

Jaffna & the North

Includes »

Best Places to Eat

- » Manattrii (p256)
- » Mangos (p256)
- » Green Grass (p256)
- » Bastian Hotel (p256)
- » Malayan Café (p256)

Best Places to Stay

- » Theresa Inn (p254)
- » Morgan's Residence (p254)
- » Manattrii (p254)
- » Sarras Guest House (p255)
- » Baobab Guest House (p248)

Why Go?

With towering, rainbow Hindu temples, colourful saris draped effortlessly over women on bicycles, and warm breezes carrying the sweet fragrance of fruit trees, the North is a different world. Here the landscape is arid and the sun is hot and tough, with coastlines and sparkling aqua water everywhere. The light is stronger: surreal and white-hot on salt flats in the Vanni, bright and lucid on coral islands and northern beaches, and soft and speckled on Jaffna's leafy suburbs and its battle-scarred centre.

And of course there are the cultural differences. From the language to the cuisine to religion, Tamil culture has its own rhythms, and people here are proud of their heritage. It's still tense up here, and conversations easily veer from Tamil history to the military presence. But for now, the focus is on healing, rebuilding and reviving the rich traditions of northern life.

When to Go

Jaffna

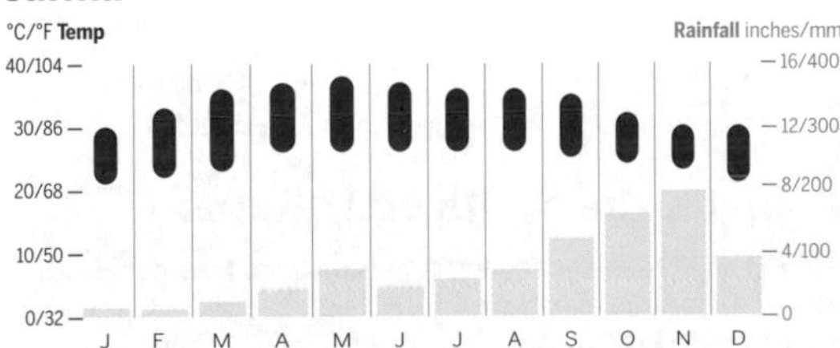

Feb A tiny post-monsoon, pre-unbearable-heat window; some drizzles still, but all is green.

Jun–Jul High season sees sunshine, moderate heat and Karuthakolamban mangoes.

Jul–Aug Jaffna's extraordinary 25-day Nallur festival is on: parades, ice cream and ritual self-mutilation.

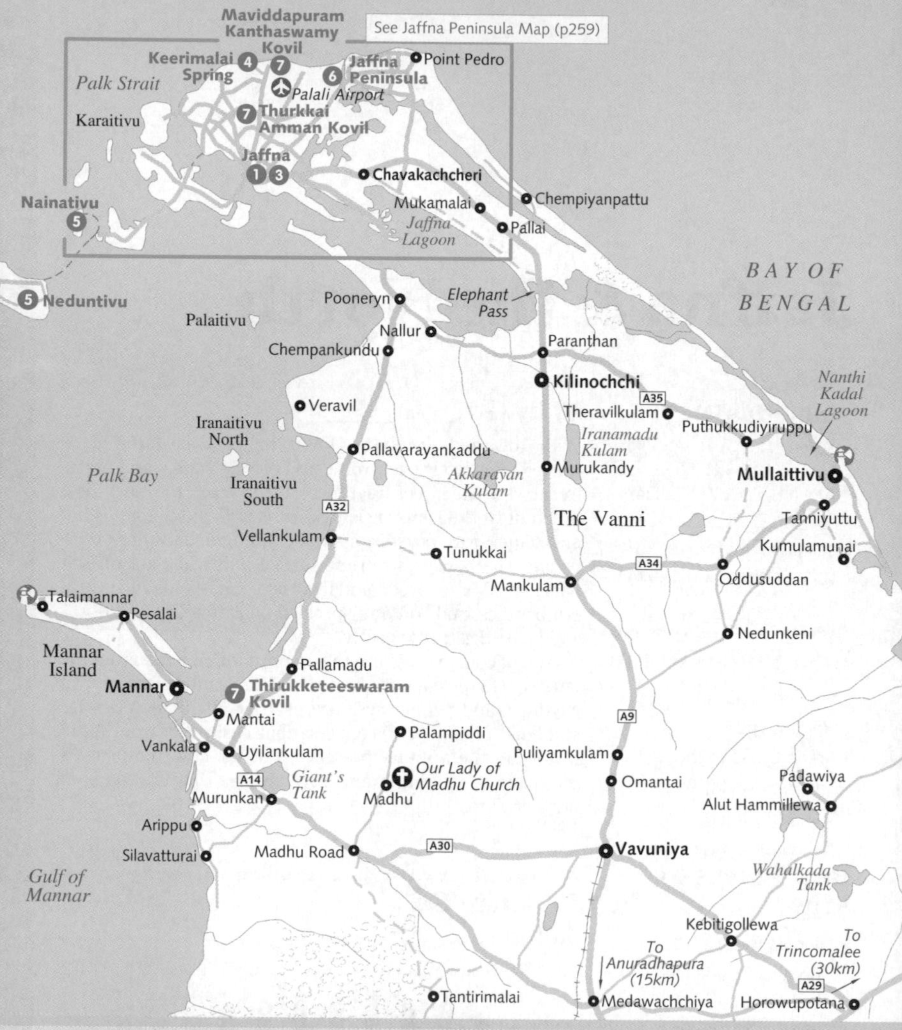

Jaffna & the North Highlights

1. Slipping into a trance during *puja* (prayers) at Jaffna's **Nallur Kandaswamy Kovil** (p249)

2. Observing the war's destruction of homes, temples and communities and appreciating the strength of its survivors

3. Exploring Jaffna's charming **market** (p257) and the smells of local coffee, fruit and cigars

4. Healing your ills in the sacred waters of **Keerimalai spring** (p260)

5. Gliding across the waters to the islands of **Nainativu** (p262) or **Neduntivu** (p263)

6. Riding along coastal roads in the **Jaffna peninsula** (p259), fringed by fishing boats, calm seas and quiet beaches

7. Learning about Hindu traditions at **Maviddapuram Kanthaswamy Kovil** (p260), **Thirukketeeswaram Kovil** (p248) or **Thurkkai Amman Kovil** (p259)

History

The North has always existed a bit apart from the rest of the island; even under colonial regimes the region remained highly autonomous. Jaffna, especially, has always been an important city, and one of the defining moments on the path to war came in 1981 when a group of Sinhalese burnt down Jaffna's library, seen as a violent affront to the Tamils' long and rich intellectual tradition. The war began two years later, and Jaffna continued to be a hotspot for violence throughout. The North became synonymous with violence – but also with peace: the war ended on the shores of Mullaittivu in 2009.

Climate

The North is made up of two distinct areas: the low-lying Jaffna peninsula and its islands, and the vast Vanni, a flat scrubby area. The region is extremely dry most of the year, except after the October–January northeastern monsoon, when the green erupts.

Vavuniya

☎024 / POP 75,000

Virtually all ground transport between Colombo and the North funnels through bustling Vavuniya (*vow*-nya). For travellers, a stay here is a convenient way to break up a trip from the South to Jaffna. It's a scruffy truckers' town with no real sights, but an afternoon here isn't unpleasant.

Sights

The town arcs around an attractive **tank** that's best observed from **Kudiyiruppu Pillaiyar Kovil**, a sprawling Ganesh temple. More photogenic is **Kandasamy Kovil** (Kandasamy Kovil Rd), a Murugan (Skanda) temple with a very ornate, if faded, *gopuram* (gateway tower) and a gold-clad image in its sanctum. The beautiful **Grand Jummah Mosque** (Horowapatana Rd) is awash in aqua, with shiny gold onion domes.

Vavuniya's **Archaeological Museum** (Horowapatana Rd; admission free; ⏰9am-5pm) is modest, but some of the 10th- to 15th-century terracotta figures are delightfully primitive, while the central hexagonal chamber has some fine 5th- to 8th-century Buddha statues in Mannar limestone.

The quietly charming **Madukanda Vihara** (Horowapatana Rd) is a Rs 150 three-wheeler ride from town, 3km along the A29. It was reputedly the fourth resting point in the 4th-century journey of the sacred Buddha tooth relic from India to Anuradhapura. The ancient ruins are upstaged by the white dagoba (stupa) and a 150-year-old bodhi tree. You can flag any passing bus to return to Vavuniya.

Sleeping & Eating

Hotel Swarkka GUESTHOUSE **$**
(☎222 1090; Soosapillaiyarkulam Rd; s/d from Rs 1750/2250, with air-con from Rs 2250/2750; ❄) The Swarkka has somewhat ordinary rooms with no hot water and a noisy temple across the street (visit at 5pm for *puja*). But the family running the place is so friendly that you'll feel right at home, and rooms are clean and have nets. The 'luxury' rooms are best value; avoid the 'economy' options (Rs 1250). Snacks are available and staff may be able to arrange bicycle hire.

Hotel Nelly Star HOTEL **$**
(☎222 4477; jerome.nellyrest@gmail.com; 84 2nd Cross St; r with/without air-con Rs 2700/1900, VIP Rs 3950, mains Rs 200-600; ❄≋) Snazzy architecture and pastel paint make Nelly Star seem a step above Vavuniya's other options, but it has severe attitude problems. Standard rooms don't live up to expectations but are the best in town. Ladies can forget about the swimming pool: it's full of gawking gents.

Pulley's Balmoral GUESTHOUSE **$**
(☎222 2364; Railway Station Rd; s/d from Rs 1300/1800, without bathroom Rs 850/1000, mains Rs 80-350; ❄) This old villa sits in a big, pretty palm garden opposite the train station. It's worn out (the shared bathrooms are dreary and the air-con rooms lack real windows) but friendly and conveniently located.

Ryana Restaurant SRI LANKAN **$**
(47/8 Kandasamy Kovil Rd; mains Rs 100-225) Ryana's *kotthu* (*rotti* chopped up and mixed with vegies) is so spicy it may knock your tongue off, but it's so good you won't even care. The little joint is cleaner than it looks and the staff are friendly. Vavuniya's local favourite.

Royal Garden Restaurant INDIAN, PIZZERIA **$$**
(☎492 2677; 200 Horowapatana Rd; meals Rs 140-350; ⏰10am-10pm) The cosy garden here has twinkling lights and little pavilions nestled amid ornamental trees. The Rs 300 mushroom *paneer* masala (mushroom and unfermented cheese curry) is richly delicious. It also delivers.

Vavuniya

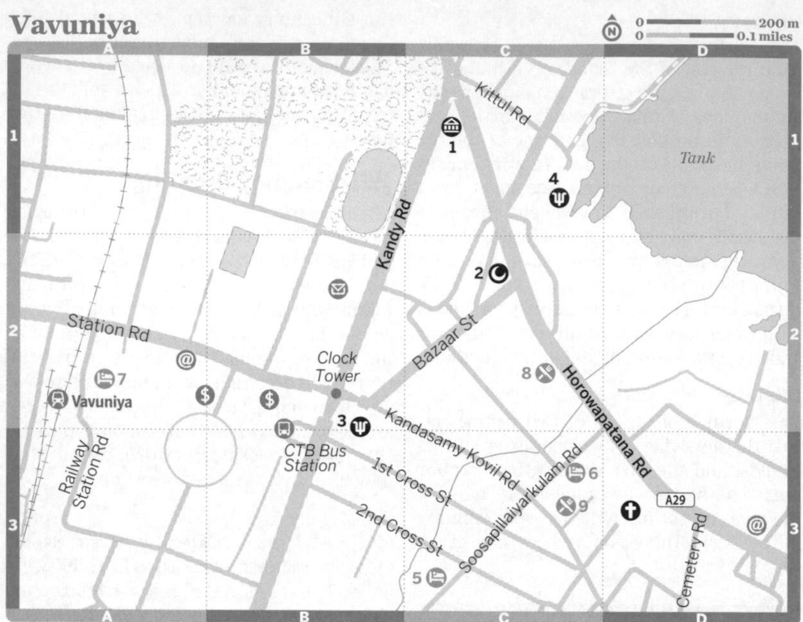

Vavuniya

Sights

1 Archaeological Museum C1
2 Grand Jummah Mosque C2
3 Kandasamy Kovil B2
4 Kudiyiruppu Pillaiyar Kovil C1

Sleeping

5 Hotel Nelly Star C3
6 Hotel Swarkka C3
7 Pulley's Balmoral A2

Eating

8 Royal Garden Restaurant C2
9 Ryana Restaurant C3

Information

Vavuniya is full of transient characters, and the streets get very quiet after dark. Solo women should exercise caution when going out at night. Vavuniya's also the entry town to the North's more conservative culture, so guys and gals should dress modestly.

Vavuniya's many banks with ATMs include Commercial Bank and HNB.

Post Office (Kandy Rd; 8am-8pm Mon-Sat)

SeeNet (395/1 Horowapatana Rd; internet per hr Rs 50; 8.30am-7pm Mon-Sat)

Vastec (1st fl, 65 Station Rd; internet per 15 min/hr Rs 15/40; 9.30am-8pm)

Getting There & Away

At the time of writing, only a passport photocopy was required to travel to Jaffna; check the latest before heading out.

BUS Vavuniya's Central Tourist Board (CTB) bus station is by the clock tower. Less well-organised private buses, with similar fares, line 2nd Cross St.

Anuradhapura Rs 60, one hour, every 30 minutes

Colombo CTB/private 'semi-luxury' Rs 250/360, seven hours, every 30 minutes

Jaffna Rs 148, four hours, every 30 minutes

Kandy Rs 170, five hours, 10 daily

Mannar Rs 89, two hours, hourly

Trincomalee Rs 105, four hours, hourly

TRAIN Call or visit Vavuniya's **railway booking office** (222 2271; 7-10am & 4-5pm) for current services; restoration of the rail line to Jaffna, destroyed in the war, was in progress at research time. Colombo–Vavuniya trains stop at Anuradhapura.

Anuradhapura 3rd/2nd/1st class Rs 50/90/160, one hour, 2.30pm and 10pm

Colombo intercity train 3rd/2nd class Rs 270/450, 3rd/1st class 'booking' Rs 345/700, seven hours, 5.45am

Colombo 'fast' train 3rd/2nd/1st class Rs 185/330/600, 9½ hours, 3.20am and 7am

Mannar Island & Around

023

Mannar Island is a beautiful, eerily dry near-peninsula with lots of white sand and palm trees, gulls and terns, wild donkeys, and little lanes and fishing boats. Jutting out into the Palk Strait, the island is only about 30km from India. Because of its location, Mannar Island was hard hit by the war: it was a major exit and entry point to and from India, and became a key host of refugees. The island's large Muslim population was driven out by the Liberation Tigers of Tamil Eelam (LTTE) in 1990, and some of the land is still mined. The Vavuniya–Mannar road was aggressively fought over, and most of the villages along it were abandoned; bunkers and watchtowers still dot the road at 50m intervals.

But despite all that, the town of **Mannar**, reached via a 3km-long causeway from the mainland, is a pleasant place. There's not much here for tourists, but it's quiet and more appealing than Vavuniya if you want to break up a Colombo–Jaffna trip. The town has a Portuguese-Dutch **star fortress**, which is an out-of-bounds military camp, and a big, exotic **baobab tree** (Palimunai Rd), 1.2km northeast of town. The tree is believed to have been planted in 1477 by Arab traders; it's shaped like a giant ball, with a 19m circumference.

About 38km from town, at the western end of the island is **Talaimannar**; long ago, ferries to Rameswaram, India, departed from a nearby pier. Offshore is **Adam's Bridge** – a chain of reefs, sandbanks and islets that nearly connects Sri Lanka to Rameswaram. In the Ramayana these were the stepping stones that the monkey king Hanuman used in his bid to help rescue Rama's wife Sita from Rawana, the demon king of Lanka. Along the coast, an abandoned lighthouse marks the start of Adam's Bridge. The navy now occupies this area and runs **boat trips** (per person Rs 500; 8am-4pm) to the first of the Bridge's sandbars.

In the other direction, about 13km from Mannar on the mainland, is **Thirukketeeswaram Kovil**. Like Naguleswaram Kovil, Thirukketeeswaram is one of the *pancha ishwaram,* the five historical Sri Lankan Shiva temples established to protect the island from natural disaster. It's an imposing site, with a towering, colourful *gopuram.* Ranged around the temple are pavilions containing five gigantic floats, called juggernauts, that are wheeled out each February for the impressive **Maha Sivarathiri festival**. Thirukketeeswaram Kovil is 4.5km down a side road off the Mannar–Vavuniya

THE ROAD TO JAFFNA

During the war, the A9 – when it was open at all – was often the only permitted land route across **Tamil Eelam**, the LTTE-controlled Vanni region. This flat, savannah-like area, sometimes nicknamed Tigerland, was effectively another country. Travellers stutter-stepped through Sri Lanka Army (SLA) and LTTE checkpoints, complete with customs and 'immigration' for LTTE-controlled territory, and the trip from Vavuniya to Jaffna took up to 16 hours.

Today, the trip takes four, and the nearest thing to a checkpoint is a little shack where government soldiers will take down your name and a copy of your passport. The stop takes about 10 minutes.

The rest of the trip may include a visit to Murukandy's tiny **Ankaran Temple**. Locals believe that a prayer here will ensure a safe journey, so many vehicles, including buses, make the stop.

Kilinochchi, once the administrative capital of Tigerland, is the only sizeable town en route. Tamil Eelam's capital suffered heavy damage before being captured by government forces in 2009. You may still see, on the ground, the massive water tower toppled during the fighting, as well as a tacky war memorial erected by the government (a nearby inscription reads that President Rajapaksa was 'born for the grace of the nation').

The final stretch of the journey runs through saltpans and across the **Elephant Pass**, a strangely beautiful 1km-long causeway that anchors the Jaffna peninsula to the rest of Sri Lanka. Possession of it was viciously fought over during the war.

At research time the A9 was undergoing a major repaving and expansion. By the time you visit, the trip may be even quicker through the former Tigerland.

OUR LADY OF MADHU CHURCH

This **church** (⏲6am-8pm) is Sri Lanka's most hallowed Christian shrine. Its walls shelter Our Lady of Madhu, a diminutive but revered Madonna-and-child statue brought here in 1670 by Catholics fleeing Protestant Dutch persecution in Mannar. The statue rapidly developed a reputation for miracles, and Madhu has been a place of pilgrimage – and, in modern times, refuge – ever since. The present church dates from 1872 and is a bit plain but has soaring central columns. Outside, the most striking feature is the elongated portico painted cream and duck-egg blue. The church attracts huge crowds of pilgrims to its 10 annual festivals, especially the one on 15 August.

Our Lady is 12km along Madhu Rd, which branches off the Vavuniya–Mannar road at the 47km post. Vavuniya–Mannar buses can let you down at Madhu Junction (Rs 55), where there's a tea stall and usually a three-wheeler (Rs 900 return including waiting time).

road between the 76km and 77km markers. Buses from Mannar are frequent; three-wheelers charge Rs 800 for the round trip.

Sleeping & Eating

Baobab Guest House GUESTHOUSE $
(☎222 3155; 70 Field St, Sinnakadai; s/d Rs 1000/1600, with air-con Rs 1800/2500; ❄) An exceedingly clean and organised place, Baobab has a comfy living room, kitchen and dining room that guests can use (a grocery store is across the street), and traditional red-oxide floors and window screens – screens! – throughout.

Mannar Red Rest GUESTHOUSE $
(☎222 2277; mannarbeo@redcross.lk; 4 Field Lane, Sinnakadai; s/d/tr Rs 750/1200/1800, with air-con Rs 1800/2000/2500; ❄@) Run by the Red Cross to subsidise its humanitarian work and provide local jobs, Red Rest is an excellent deal, with cute, simple rooms that have nets. It's also an ecofriendly place, and the manager is a great source of info: ask him if the bird sanctuary on the mainland, 8km from Mannar, has opened yet. Red Rest and Baobab are each a couple hundred metres from the bus stand, and both can arrange bicycles for hire.

Choice Hotel SRI LANKAN $
(Grand Bazaar; mains Rs 100-300) Choice looks dingy but is really just a simple place on a cute little Grand Bazaar alley with friendly service, Tamil films on the TV, good biryanis and a fine fish-curry-rice.

Hotel Pilawoos SRI LANKAN $
(Grand Bazaar; mains Rs 80-300; ⏲6am-midnight) Pilawoos, right at the main roundabout, is an ordinary eatery with lots of rice and curries, *kotthu,* and good hoppers for Rs 10 (be sure to get the 'sugar sambar' to go with them).

Information

Mannar has a **post office** (Field St) and a few banks with ATMs, including **Commercial Bank** (Main St).

Getting There & Around

The rail line from Colombo to Mannar, via Medawachchiya, was being restored at research time, and rumour had it that once trains were up and running, ferries to Rameswaram, India, would follow. By the time you arrive, the transportation situation may look very different; ask around. Meanwhile, buses from Mannar:

Colombo Rs 345, eight hours, three daily
Jaffna Rs 157, four hours, four daily
Tallaimannar Rs 54, one hour, hourly
Thirukketeeswaram Kovil Rs 19, 20 minutes, eight daily
Vavuniya Rs 89, two hours, hourly

Jaffna

☎021 / POP 111,000

Years of war, emigration, embargoes, and loss of life and property have chipped away at the art, culture and optimism of this historic Tamil town. It's also heavily militarised, and locals complain about harassment and infringement of property as well as livelihood. Peace and reconciliation are still works in progress.

But glimmers of hope are there, and Jaffna is also dusting itself off, welcoming back the many who left during the fighting, and looking to rise again as the bastion of Hindu tradition and creative culture that it was. It's an intriguing, unimposing and mostly untouristed place that rewards time taken to find the local rhythm. Palm-shaded colonial-era suburbs, peppered with beautiful temples, surround a compact commercial centre. You'll appreciate Jaffna more for its insights into the Tamil people and their struggle than for any specific points of interest, but it's a pleasant town and a good base for exploring the nearby islands and surrounding peninsula.

History

For centuries Jaffna has been Sri Lanka's Hindu-Tamil cultural and religious centre – especially during the Jaffna kingdom, the powerful Tamil dynasty that ruled from Nallur for 400 years beginning in the 13th century. But the Portuguese tried hard to change that. In 1620 they captured Cankili II, the last king (his horseback statue stands on Point Pedro Rd, near the Royal Palace ruins), then set about systematically demolishing the city's Hindu temples. A substantial wave of mass Christian conversions followed.

The Portuguese surrendered their 'Jaffnapattao' to the more tolerant Dutch a few decades later after a bitter three-month siege, and Dutch Jaffna, which lasted for almost 140 years, became a major trade centre. Jaffna continued to prosper under the British, who took over in 1795 and sowed the seeds of future interethnic unrest by 'favouring' the Jaffna Tamils (see p273).

The city played a crucial role in the lead-up to the war, and by the early 1980s escalating tensions overwhelmed Jaffna; for two decades the city was a no-go war zone. Variously besieged by Tamil guerrillas, Sri Lankan Army (SLA) troops and a so-called peacekeeping force (see p276), the city lost almost half of its population to emigration. In 1990 the LTTE forced Jaffna's few remaining Sinhalese and all Muslim residents to leave. Jaffna suffered through endless bombings, a crippling blockade (goods, including fuel, once retailed here for 20 times the market price – one reason so many residents ride bicycles), and military rule after the SLA's 1995 recapture of the town.

Then in the peace created by the 2002 accords, the sense of occupation was relaxed and Jaffna sprang back to life: domestic flights began; refugees, internally displaced persons (IDPs) and long-absent émigrés returned; and new businesses opened and building projects commenced.

Hostilities recommenced in 2006 and instability continued through the end of the war in 2009, but the rebuilding and sense of stability have resumed. The population of the Jaffna peninsula, however, is still well below its prewar figure, and as of 2011, NGOs estimated that the North still had more than 200,000 IDPs.

Sights

Commercial activity is crammed into the colourful hurly-burly of Hospital, Kasturiya and Kankesanturai (KKS) Rds. If you can get your hands on wheels, Jaffna is perfect for bicycle rides.

Nallur Kandaswamy Kovil TEMPLE
(Temple Rd; donations accepted; ⏲4am-7pm) Approximately 1.5km northeast of the centre, the Nallur Kandaswamy Kovil is the most impressive religious building in Jaffna and one of the most significant Hindu temple

STAYING SAFE

At press time, the country was peaceful, but some foreign governments, including those of New Zealand and Australia, were still issuing warnings against travel in the North. Occasional arrests and disappearances continue, and the root reasons for the civil unrest are far from resolved. Keep your wits about you.

Although NGOs have made enormous progress clearing land mines, some remain, along with tonnes of unexploded ordnance. Walk only on roads or very well-trodden paths. Do not wander on deserted beaches.

Locals may not want to speak openly about politics or the war; use sensitivity and tact. Also be careful not to take photographs of soldiers, military posts or potentially strategic sites like ports and bridges.

You're more likely to encounter army checkpoints, road closures or no-go zones than violence, but before visiting, research thoroughly and keep an eye on regional news and politics. For two very different perspectives, try www.defence.lk and www.tamilnet.com

Jaffna

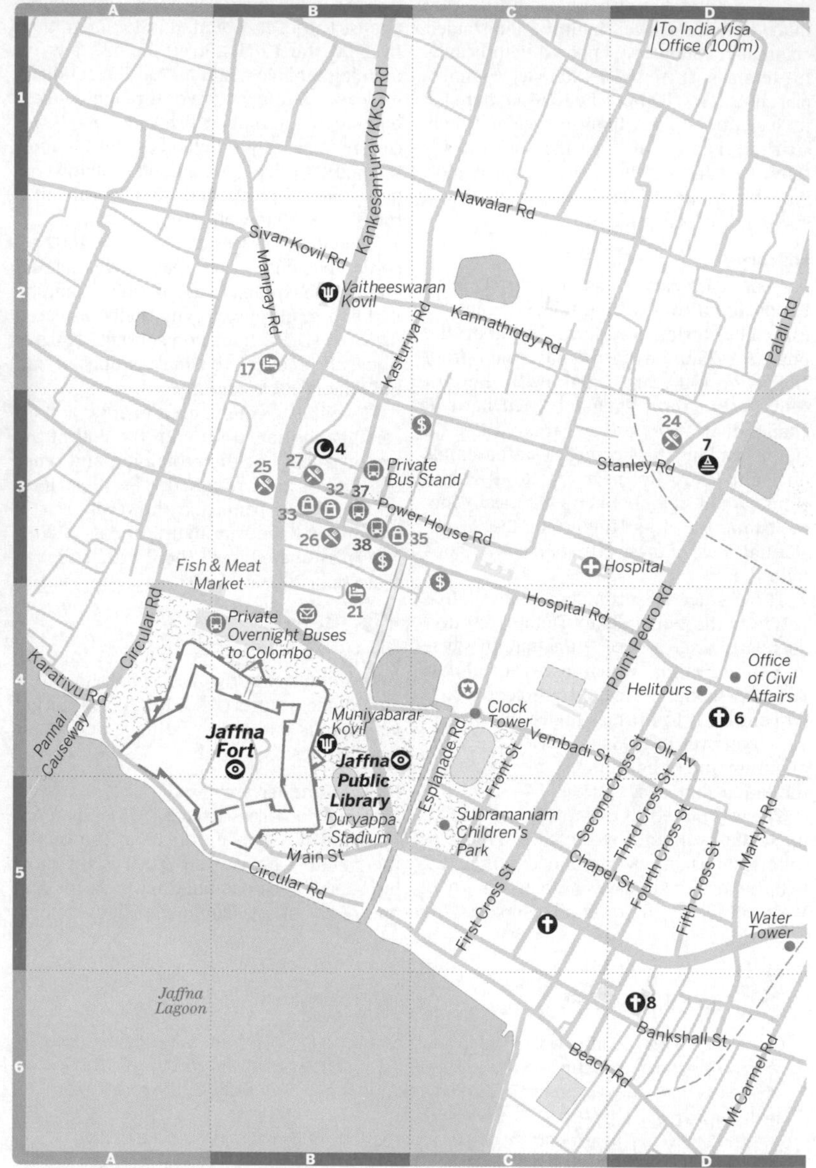

complexes in Sri Lanka. Its sacred deity is Murugan (or Skanda), and at cacophonic *puja* – at 5am, 10am, noon, 4.15pm (small *puja*), 4.30pm ('special' *puja*), 5pm and 6.45pm – offerings are made to his brass-framed image and other Hindu deities like Ganesh, Murugan's elephant-headed brother, in shrines surrounding the inner sanctum. You can also say a prayer at the sacred tree in the temple's southern courtyard anytime: get a piece of gold-threaded cloth from outside the temple, wrap some coins in

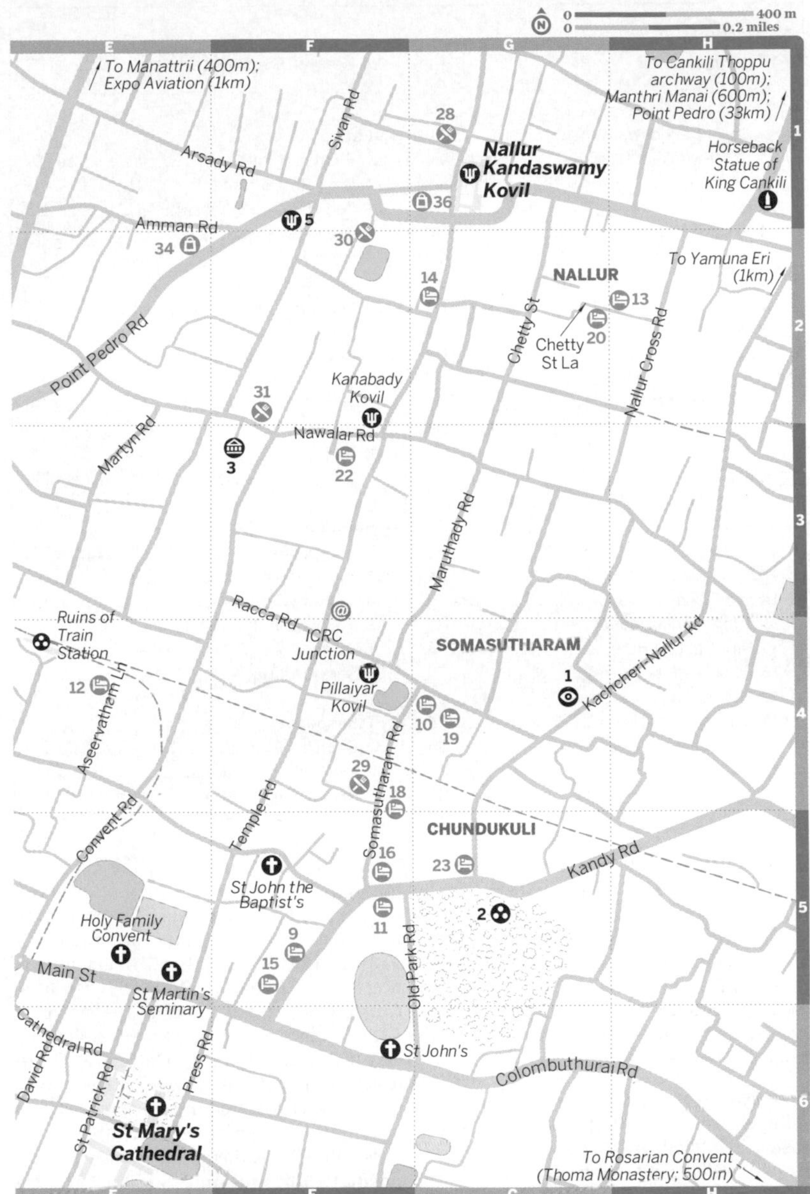

it, and tie it to the tree along with a prayer. Afterwards, ring the big brass bell.

The *kovil*'s current structure dates from 1734 (the 15th-century structure was destroyed by the Portuguese in 1620), and its large and airy space shelters decorative brasswork, larger-than-life murals, pillared halls and a colonnaded, stepped holy pool, all dominated by the god-encrusted, golden-ochre *gopuram* peering down one length of Point Pedro Rd. Several friendly priests, some of whom speak English, can answer

Jaffna

Top Sights

Jaffna Fort B4
Jaffna Public Library B4
Nallur Kandaswamy Kovil G1
St Mary's Cathedral E6

Sights

1 Alliance Française G4
2 Former Kachcheri G5
3 Jaffna Archaeological Museum F3
4 Jummah Mosque B3
5 Miralliamman Kovil F1
6 Our Lady of Refuge Church D4
7 Sri Nagavihara International Buddhist Centre D3
8 St James' D6

Sleeping

9 Bastian Hotel F5
10 Blue Haven G4
11 Expo Pavilion F5
12 Green Grass E4
13 Lux Etoiles H2
14 Morgan's Residence G2
15 New Bastian Hotel F5
16 Palan's Multicentre & Lodge F5
17 Pillaiyar Inn B2
18 Sarras Guest House F4
19 Theresa Inn G4
20 Thinakkural Rest G2
21 Tilko Jaffna City Hotel B4
22 Uthayan Guest House F3
23 YMCA G5

Eating

Bastian Hotel .... (see 9)
24 Cosy Restaurant D3
25 Food City B3
Green Grass .... (see 12)
26 Hotel Rolex B3
Lux Etoiles .... (see 13)
27 Malayan Café B3
28 Mangos G1
29 New Rest House F4
30 Rio Ice Cream F2
31 TCT Multi-Trade Centre F2

Drinking

Morgan's Residence .... (see 14)

Shopping

32 Anna Coffee B3
33 Jaffna Market B3
34 Ms Ruby Sorupan E2
35 Poobalasingham Book Depot B3
36 Saravana Tex G1

Transport

37 CTB Bus Stand B3
38 Minibus Stand B3
RB Booking Centre .... (see 32)

questions about the temple and its traditions. Visitors must remove their shoes; men need to remove their shirts as well.

The temple is the focus of an enormous and spectacular Hindu festival over 25 days in July/August, which climaxes on day 24 with parades of juggernaut floats and gruesome displays of self-mutilation by entranced devotees.

Houses of Worship RELIGIOUS

Jaffna's countless other **Hindu temples**, easily identified by their red-and-white-striped walls, range from tiny shrines to sprawling complexes featuring *mandapaya* (raised platforms with decorated pillars), ornate ponds and towering *gopuram*. **Miralliamman Kovil**, near Nallur, is particularly dazzling.

The city's abundance of **churches** isn't a reflection of its legions of Christian parishioners, now reduced from their 12% of the prewar population. Touring the many fine Catholic and Protestant structures is nevertheless an interesting excuse for discovering leafy backstreets. The grandest church is **St James'** (Main St), a classical Italianate edifice. From Hospital Rd, **Our Lady of Refuge Church** looks like a whitewashed version of a Gloucestershire village church. Built along classical lines, **St Mary's Cathedral** (Cathedral Rd) is astonishingly large and airy, with, curiously, corrugated-iron roofing held up by a masterpiece of wooden vaulting.

For Buddhists there's the solitary **Sri Nagavihara International Buddhist Centre** (Stanley Rd), quickly rebuilt after government forces retook Jaffna in 1995. The **Jummah Mosque** (Jummah Mosque Lane) is quirkily colourful.

Jaffna Public Library LIBRARY

(Esplanade Rd; 9am-7pm) Tellingly, one of the first major public buildings to be rebuilt after the 2002 ceasefire was the Jaffna Public Library. The earlier library was burnt by pro-government mobs (some say forces) after the violence-ridden Jaffna District Council elections of July 1981. Few acts were more significant in the build-up to civil war: Jaffna residents had long considered their city to be one of Asia's finest intellectual capitals, and the library was an important Tamil cultural centre and historic institution (it was inaugurated in 1841). Its destruction was interpreted as a cultural attack. The world-renowned collection had included more than 90,000 volumes, including irreplaceable Tamil documents such as the one surviving copy of *Yalpanam Vaipavama,* a history of Jaffna.

In its reconstruction, architects kept true to the original neo-Mughal design, and books were donated from around the world. Today it's a bright, spacious place that is building itself up again, while a statue of Saraswati – Hinduism's goddess of knowledge – sits out front.

Jaffna Fort FORT

Architecturally, Jaffna's fort is perhaps the best Dutch fort in Asia, and it's currently undergoing a massive restoration, funded mostly by the Dutch government, that will make it even more impressive. (Not all Tamils are happy about this, the fort having been used by several regimes, over several centuries, to rule over Jaffna.) It was built in 1680 over an earlier Portuguese original, and defensive triangles were added in 1792 to produce the classic Vaubanesque star form. But, while on a map the polygonal Dutch fort is a powerful presence, in reality its walls are currently hidden beneath overgrown slopes. During the war, government forces used it as an encampment, and in 1990 the LTTE – at the time in control of the rest of Jaffna – forced out government troops after a grisly 107-day siege. Much of the fort was destroyed. At research time, you could wander around the ruins and watch the progress of the rebuilding.

War Ruins RUINS

Jaffna is slowly rebuilding and repairing the damage left from the war. But east of the fort was Jaffna's former government district, and some ruined structures, like the **former kachcheri** (administrative office), remain, pockmarked by bullets and shrapnel, moss-encrusted and slowly folding in on themselves.

The fishing community between Beach Rd and the lagoon also suffered immensely in the fighting. It was a restricted area for years, and many fishermen had to pass through checkposts just to walk the few blocks to the water. Today the waterfront is scarred with damage from the war, but the neighbourhood is friendly, if unaccustomed to visitors.

Jaffna Archaeological Museum MUSEUM

(Nawalar Rd; donations accepted; ⌚8am-4.45pm Wed-Mon) This unkempt but interesting museum is hidden away at the end of a messy garden behind a concrete events hall. Asking locals for directions may elicit odd responses; the museum is a bit under the radar. At the door are a rusty pair of Dutch cannons from the fort and a set of whale bones. Inside, the most interesting items are some 15th-century Buddha torsos found at Kantarodai and a 14th-century 'seven-mouthed pot' – a clay pot that makes music when it's filled with water and its seven openings tapped with the palm of the hand.

Royal Palace RUINS

Nallur was the capital of the Jaffna Kingdom for 400 years, and a few weathered structures remain. They're worth the excursion if you have a good imagination. **Yamuna Eri** (off Chemmani Rd), a U-shape pool made of carved stones, is neglected but still intact. The king, the story goes, brought water from India's sacred Yamuna River to start the tank, and it's thought to have been the royal family's women's bathing pool. The tank is behind a playground on Chemmani Rd, about 500m from Kachcheri–Nallur Rd. Around the corner on Point Pedro Rd are **Cankili Thoppu archway**, one of the palace's original entrances, and the beautifully crumbling **Manthri Manai** (Minister's Quarters), once home to a prince before falling to the Portuguese.

Alliance Française CULTURAL BUILDING

(☎222 8093; alliancejaffna@yahoo.com; 61 Kachcheri–Nallur Rd; ⌚9am-5pm) In a cool, leafy part of town, the Alliance has a comfy lounge with English- and French-language newspapers, a library with books in English, French, Tamil, and Sinhalese, and various translations between them, and occasional film screenings.

Festivals

In addition to Jaffna's religious festivals, the city hosts the biennial **Jaffna Music Festival** (www.jaffnamusicfestival.org), in March of odd-number years. It showcases folk music and dances that have been sustained by families in the North and East over generations. The Alliance Française helps organise the excellent **European Film Festival** (www.europeanfilmfestsrilanka.com), held in Jaffna, Kandy, Colombo and Galle in October/November.

Sleeping

With the end of the war, opening of the A9 and elimination of travel permits, Jaffna has a gazillion new guesthouses. Most are in the leafy Chundukuli and Nallur districts. Book ahead.

TOP CHOICE **Theresa Inn** GUESTHOUSE $

(Do Drop Inn; ☎222 8615, 071 856 5375; calistusjoseph89@gmail.com; 72 Racca Rd; s/d/q Rs 1250/1500/2000, with air-con Rs 2000/2250/3500; ❄) Theresa Inn is a simple place that puts its energies in all the right places: rooms are super-clean and fresh, bathrooms have hot water and window screens, and the family running the place is welcoming and can help you set up anything from meals and tea to a car and driver. Bikes may be available for guests by the time you arrive. Rickshaw drivers may not know Racca Rd; tell them it's near ICRC Junction.

TOP CHOICE **Manattrii** GUESTHOUSE $$

(☎320 7665; www.manattrii.com; 250 Palali Rd, Kantharmadam; d with/without air-con Rs 3900/3500; ❄) Jaffna has some stunning architecture, but much of it was destroyed in the war and replaced with modern structures. Sherine Xavier started Manattrii to showcase and preserve traditional Jaffna architecture. The layout of the restored 19th-century home adheres to South Indian Vastu, with a central room that opens up to the sky (letting rain fall through and heat to escape), a prayer room (now a guest room), and an atmospheric porch and dining area that's cool as anything on a hot day. It's not perfect – showers are cold, and there's street noise – but it's a great way to immerse yourself in Old Jaffna.

Morgan's Residence GUESTHOUSE $$

(Maria's, UN Guesthouse; ☎222 3666; 103 Temple Rd; s/d with air-con Rs 3500/4000; ❄) With wood-beam ceilings, fresh white walls, antique four-posters with mosquito nets, little windowsills with seashells on them, stylish mirrors and a guest list that includes Angelina Jolie, this four-room place has far more character than Jaffna's other options. The two best rooms (including Angie's) have hot water and screened porches. Meals are available on request, and the backyard terrace is a favourite watering hole for NGO workers. The building is unmarked except for a small sign over the door. Book far ahead.

JAFFNA'S SLEEPING HOUSES

Although bodies of the deceased are generally cremated in Hindu tradition, those of LTTE fighters were buried instead, beneath neatly lined rows of identical stones. The fallen Tigers were called *maaveerar* – 'martyrs' or 'heroes' – and their cemeteries Maaveerar Thuyilum Illam (Martyrs' Sleeping Houses). The tradition of burial began in the 1990s, not long after the 1989 initiation of Maveerar Naal, Heroes Day, held each year since on 27 November. The cemeteries were controversial: many saw them as a natural way to honour those who died; for others, they were a propaganda tool.

When the Sri Lankan Army took control of the Jaffna peninsula in 1995, it destroyed many of the cemeteries, only to have the LTTE build them up again after the 2002 ceasefire. But when the SLA conquered areas in the East in 2006 and 2007, and then again after the war's end in 2009, all cemeteries (and other LTTE monuments) across the North and East were bulldozed anew – to the distress of many Tamils, especially family members of the deceased. The SLA went further in early 2011 by building a military base on the site of a cemetery at Kopay, just a few kilometres northeast of Jaffna. According to the BBC, the army claimed to be unaware of any 'unhappiness' over the site.

An online Maaveerar Thuyilum Illam, including the names and burial places of many Tigers, is maintained at www.maaveerarillam.com.

Sarras Guest House GUESTHOUSE $
(☎222 3627, 077 717 2039; 20 Somasutharam Rd; r with/without air-con from Rs 2500/2000; ❄) This charming guesthouse is in a thick-walled old colonial mansion with traditional red-oxide flooring, lots of white-painted wood slats and the most beautiful wooden spiral staircase you've ever seen. Each of the four rooms is unique and was undergoing renovation at research time. The top-floor doubles are fabulous, especially the one with three sides of windows, polished old floorboards and art-deco furniture. All have private bathrooms with hot water. Booking ahead is advised, either directly or through Theresa Inn.

Expo Pavilion HOTEL $$
(☎222 3790, 077 234 8888; expopavilion@expoavi.com; 40 Kandy Rd; s/d/tr with air-con incl breakfast Rs 6000/7500/9000; ❄📶) Among the most well decorated in town, the seven rooms in this pretty, rambling, yellow-and-white colonial house are done in dark woods and yellow ochres, with gleaming bathrooms (with hot water), air-con and, in some rooms, balconies. There's free wi-fi in the lobby, and Expo, the airline, also conducts flights to Colombo, so it's easy to coordinate plans. The only downside: 22% in service charges. Expo recently opened another property, in a restored 19th-century house, on the road to Palali.

Palan's Multicentre & Lodge GUESTHOUSE $
(☎222 3248; 71 Kandy Rd; tr/f Rs 2500/3500, with air-con Rs 3500/5500; ❄) Palan's is just a few rooms in a family home that are all fresh paint, squeaky-clean floors and bright, sparkling bathrooms. To keep it so spotless, you're asked to keep your shoes by the door, and the family supervision might be a bit much for some, but it's a dream for clean freaks. There's a pretty garden out front, too.

Tilko Jaffna City Hotel HOTEL $$
(☎222 5969; www.cityhoteljaffna.com; 70/6 KKS Rd; s Rs 2500-7500, d Rs 3500-8750; ❄@) This long-standing high-end favourite is set in a lovely large garden, complete with a silly dolphin fountain. The rooms are smart for the most part and the hotel aspires to full-service – with gym, business centre, sharply dressed staff etc – but the red-and-gold decor in the luxury rooms is overwrought and some of the furniture is starting to look tatty. Various room-and-board packages are available.

New Bastian Hotel GUESTHOUSE $$
(☎222 7374; 11 Kandy Rd; s/d/tr with air-con Rs 2500/3200/3800; ❄) Entered from beneath a pretty vine trellis, the New Bastian is a favourite of NGO types – and was a favourite throughout the war too: the owners describe it as a Hotel Rwanda–style safe space during the worst fighting. It's well taken care of and rooms are modern with TV, though not all of the bathrooms have hot water (upgrades forthcoming). No smoking or liquor is allowed on the premises.

Lux Etoiles HOTEL $$
(☎222 3966; www.luxetoiles.com; 34 Chetty St Lane; d with air-con Rs 4070-6270; ❄) Lux Etoiles wins the award for the most tightly tucked-in sheets in Jaffna. And maybe the cleanest rooms also. It's a tad overpriced, and rooms have no character, but the staff are super-motivated to make the place 'the best hotel in Jaffna', which counts for something. So do the bathtubs – small ones – in every room.

Thinakkural Rest HOTEL $
(☎222 6476; 45 Chetty Street Lane; tw with/without air-con Rs 2750/1650; ❄) Rooms here are spacious, though not cavernous, and homey, especially when combined with the warm welcome. Some fan rooms have detached, though not shared, bathrooms. The attached bar is totally without character; you'd do better to retreat to the hotel's breezy and peaceful upstairs terrace.

Pillaiyar Inn HOTEL $
(☎222 2829; www.pillaiyarinn.com; 31 Manipay Rd; s/d/tr from Rs 1800/2200/2800, with air-con Rs 2500/3500/4500; ❄@) Set back from the road in a pretty garden is this Jaffna institution. Friendly, old-fashioned and professionally run, it's the kind of place where you get a newspaper under your door each morning. It could use some better upkeep, though, especially in the older annex rooms. Go for the main building or the new wing, which has enormous (though characterless) rooms. The food is excellent if you live long enough for it to be served. The Pillaiyar also runs an air-con bus to Colombo.

Bastian Hotel GUESTHOUSE $
(☎222 2605; 37 Kandy Rd; d with shared bathroom from Rs 1500, s/d with air-con from Rs 2500/3200) The owners will nudge you over to the (more expensive) New Bastian, but the basic, presentably clean fan rooms here have some quiet personality, and the restaurant serves some seriously good food. The **bar** (⏰11am-2pm & 5-9pm), on the other hand, looks a bit sketchy.

YMCA GUESTHOUSE $

(☎222 2499; 109 Kandy Rd; tw with shared bathroom Rs 750) It's always full and not much English is spoken, but the rooms are cute and airy, with fresh paint and a Christian-missionary-style tidiness. The shared bathrooms are grim but passable and clean. Gals should check out the vibe – and any sketchy guests – before checking in. The **canteen** (⏰5am-7pm) next door is adorable, if grimy.

Uthayan Guest House GUESTHOUSE $

(☎222 2330; 392 Nawalar Rd; d with/without air-con Rs 2500/1500) Uthayan is somewhat generic-looking, but the friendly manager, quiet location and bright and airy rooms with white waffle-cotton bedspreads make up for it.

Blue Haven HOTEL $$

(☎222 9958; www.bluehavenjaffna.com; 70 Racca Rd; r Rs 3300; ❄📶🏊) The Blue Haven's rooms are not the best-maintained or -managed in the world, but they're big and newish and have air-con and hot water. The hotel's also worth considering for the pool and free wi-fi.

Green Grass HOTEL $$

(☎222 4385; www.jaffnagreengrass.com; 33 Aseervatham Lane, Hospital Rd; s/d/tr with air-con Rs 3000/3300/3850; ❄📶🏊) Rooms here have some personality, eg lime-green walls, but they're worn for the price. Still, they're in a pretty building surrounding a pool and gardens, and the hotel has an excellent bar-restaurant, free wi-fi and a Colombo bus service. Nonguests can use the **pool** (per hr Rs 200; ⏰8am-8pm).

Eating & Drinking

Jaffna is a good place to try South Indian-style cuisine. Red-hued *pittu* (a mixture of rice flour and coconut, steamed in bamboo moulds), *idiyappam* (string hoppers, or steamed rice noodles curled into a pancake of flat spirals) and *vadai* (deep-fried doughnut-shaped snacks made from lentil flour and spices) are local favourites. Boozewise, there are not many watering holes that don't feel dingy and surreptitious, and even fewer patronised by women, Jaffna being the conservative town that it is.

TOP CHOICE **Manattrii** SRI LANKAN $$

(☎320 7665; www.manattrii.com; 250 Palali Rd, Kantharmadam; mains Rs 300-600) Manattrii is not just interested in making good meals, though its food may be the best in Jaffna. The goals here are higher: dishes are cooked with an eye to preserving and reviving traditional Jaffna cooking, and so recipes, ingredients and techniques are sought out from across the region. Local toddy is added to the vegetable *koottu* (a kind of stew; Rs 200), along with coconut milk and seasonings. Be sure to start with the sublime 'Jaffna nachos' (Rs 250) – fried pappadum with a local take on guacamole that's even more addictive than the original.

Mangos SOUTH INDIAN $

(Nallalaxmy Ave, 359 Temple Rd; lunches Rs 180-240; ⏰10.30am-10pm) Always full with enormous Tamil families (and with more enormous Tamil families waiting for long rows of tables to clear), pure-veg Mangos does the best South Indian food in Jaffna. The *idlis* (rice cakes), dosas and *uttapam* (savoury rice pancake with onions, green chillies, coriander and coconut; Rs 70 to 160) shine, but the rice and curry lunch – an Indian–Sri Lankan hybrid – is also exceptional (and huge). And it's all served by friendly staff under a massive, thatch-roof gazebo just around the corner from the temple: good vibes all around.

Green Grass INDIAN, BAR $$

(www.jaffnagreengrass.com; 33 Aseervatham Lane, Hospital Rd; mains Rs 300-490; ⏰10am-10pm; 📶) You might hit up the Green Grass 'pool bar' because it's the most comfortable place to get a drink in Jaffna: even women will feel fine kicking back under a mango tree in the garden with a Lion (Rs 250). But the Jaffna, Indian and Chinese dishes are also excellent – it's a win-win. GG has an indoor restaurant (open 6.30am to 10pm) with the same food, but a dreary vibe.

Bastian Hotel SRI LANKAN $$

(1st fl, 37 Kandy Rd; mains Rs 200-400; ⏰9.30am-9.30pm) The incredibly good rice and curry here tastes homemade, and it is, in fact, cooked up to order by the Bastian's motherly owner. Some of Jaffna's best cooking, especially for vegies.

Malayan Café SRI LANKAN $

(36-38 Grand Bazaar; rice & curry Rs 100; ⏰7am-8.30pm) This popular, old-school eatery has marble-topped tables, long glass-and-wood cabinets and occasional blasts of incense to bless the in-house shrine. The cheap vegetarian fare – a divine rice and curry for lunch, light meals and snacks other times – is served on banana leaves and eaten by hand. When you're finished, fold up the leaf and post it through the waste chute in the hand-washing area. Ladies, if the mass of gents feels overwhelming, head to the family room in back.

Lux Etoiles SRI LANKAN **$$**
(☎222 3966; www.luxetoiles.com; 34 Chetty St Lane; mains Rs 650; ❄) The restaurant here prides itself on its Jaffna-style food, especially the crab *maruthuva* – or 'medicine' – curry: its secret combination of spices is supposed to have curative properties. Call ahead to book.

New Rest House SRI LANKAN **$**
(☎222 7839; 19 Somasutharam Rd; meals Rs 125-250; ⏲11-3pm & 5.30-9.30pm) This house-restaurant has great food in a simple, homey dining room. The rice and curry, though not ideal for vegies, is outstanding. Unusual for Jaffna, it also serves beer. New Rest also has three rooms (Rs 1500) that have lots of character but need a good cleaning.

Hotel Rolex SRI LANKAN **$**
(340 Hospital Rd; meals Rs 80-250) This cute little local eatery is done up in Kelly greens and is usually bustling with lots of curious men (there's a ladies' room in back). It has friendly management, a good range of food options and 'nuts ice cream'.

Cosy Restaurant NORTH INDIAN **$$**
(☎222 5899; 15 Sirampiyadi Lane, Stanley Rd; mains Rs 240-490; ⏲11am-11pm; ❄) The big attraction here is the tandoori oven, which starts at 6pm and churns out excellent fresh naan and a succulent chicken tikka (chicken marinated in spices and dry roasted; Rs 440). The long menu of alternatives – all halal – is mostly Punjabi and Chinese. It also delivers.

Rio Ice Cream ICE CREAM **$**
(448A Point Pedro Rd; ice creams & sundaes Rs 40-140; ⏲8am-10pm; ❄) For a typical Jaffna treat, head to the trio of popular ice-cream parlours behind the Nallur Kandaswamy Kovil. Rio is the local favourite.

Morgan's Residence BAR
(103 Temple Rd; ⏲6-10pm) The garden bar of this unsigned but characterful guesthouse is the unchallenged meeting place for NGO types. Lions are Rs 250; a bottle of wine, Rs 2750.

Jaffna Market is the best place to buy food, but if you need a supermarket, there's **Food City** (175 KKS Rd; ⏲8am-8pm) and **TCT Multi-Trade Centre** (327 Nawalar Rd; ⏲7am-9.30pm).

Shopping

Jaffna Market MARKET
(Hospital Rd) Jaffna's colourful fruit and vegetable market is west of the bus stand, but the greater market area encompasses several glorious blocks around it. In the market itself, visit **Mr M Chandresakaran's stall**, back by the bananas, to get a *suruthu* (Rs 3 apiece), Jaffna's famous traditional cigar (just bear in mind it's as bad for your health – maybe worse – than any Cuban). **Anna Coffee** (No 4, Modern Market; ⏲8.30am-6pm Mon-Sat) sells Sri Lankan coffee (Rs 700 per kg) and tea (from Rs 380 per kg) in its darling old shop. **Poobalasingham Book Depot** (Hospital Rd; ⏲8am-8pm Mon-Sat) has a good selection of newspapers.

Rosarian Convent WINE
(Thoma Monastery; 48 Colombuthurai Rd; ⏲8.30am-1pm & 2-5.30pm Mon-Sat) The convent makes Rosetto 'wine' (Rs 300 per bottle). Sweet and laced with cinnamon and cloves, it tastes like German *gluhwein*. There's startlingly-coloured grape 'juice' (Rs 180) and 'nelli crush' (Rs 180), both non-alcoholic, flavourful fruit cordial concentrates. These are all sold in Jaffna Market, too, at slightly higher prices. The convent is across from St Ann's Church.

Ms Ruby Sorupan CLOTHING
(☎320 5358; 89 Point Pedro Rd; ⏲10am-5pm) A kindly and competent seamstress, Ms Ruby Sorupan will whip you up a *salwar kurta* (dress-like tunic and trouser outfit) or *choli* (sari blouse) for about Rs 150. Shops around Nallur Temple sell 'salwar sets' and saris; those around the market do fabric by the yard. Only Mr Sorupan speaks English, so try to visit when he's around.

Saravana Tex TEXTILES
(526/529 Point Pedro Rd; ⏲8am-7.30pm Mon-Sat) The best of several fabric stores around Nallur Temple.

Information

The best of Jaffna's many ATMs are at **Commercial Bank** (Hospital Rd) and **HNB** (Hospital Rd & Stanley Rd).

Eelavar.com (www.eelavar.com/jaffna) This website, named for the residents of Tamil Eelam, is spotty but has some good sections on Jaffnese history and culture.

Jaffna Public Library (☎222 6028/5; Esplanade Rd; internet per hr Rs 30; ⌚9am-7pm Tue-Sun) Become a member (Rs 50) to use the internet, one of the city's best (and friendliest) connections.

Lonely Planet (www.lonelyplanet.com/sri-lanka/jaffna-and-the-north/jaffna) Planning advice, author recommendations, traveller reviews and insider tips.

Post office (Postal Complex, KKS Rd; ⌚7am-5pm Mon-Sat)

Selva Telecommunications Centre (124 Temple Rd; internet access per hr Rs 60; ⌚7.30am-8.30pm) Fastest connection in town, with good booths for international calls.

Getting There & Away

Air

Jaffna's Palali Airport is 17km north of town, deep within a high-security military zone.

Expo Aviation (☎222 3891, 222 6297; www.expoavi.com; 14F Palali Rd, Thirunelveli) flies twice daily to Colombo (one way/return Rs 10,000/19,100, 75 minutes) in its 12-seater Cessna. Airport shuttles leave from Expo's Thurnelveli offices.

Helitours (☎011 311 0472, 011 314 444; helitours@slaf.gov.lk; www.airforce.lk; Hospital Rd; ⌚10am-1pm), the commercial arm of the Sri Lankan Air Force, conducts passenger flights – on military planes – between Palali Airport and Colombo's Ratmalana Air Force Base. Flights run in both directions on Mondays, Wednesdays and Fridays (one way Rs 9550, 75 minutes). An obligatory shuttle bus departs from Helitours' town office. You need to arrive two hours ahead.

Bus

LONG-DISTANCE The well-organised **CTB bus stand** (☎222 2281) has both long-distance buses and those covering the peninsula. Most long-distance departures are in the morning or late afternoon. Useful long-distance services:

Anuradhapura Rs 200, five hours, one daily

Batticaloa Rs 410, nine hours, five daily

Colombo Rs 600, 11 hours, four daily

Kandy Rs 330, eight hours, seven daily

Mannar Rs 153, four hours, four daily

Trincomalee Rs 324, seven hours, three daily

Vavuniya Rs 148, four hours, every 30 minutes

Private buses follow similar schedules, with departures often alternating with those of CTB buses, at the chaotic private bus stand about 100m north of the CTB station, where few people speak English. Fares are similar.

COLOMBO Everyone and their dog operates an air-con overnight bus to Colombo. Dozens of them depart from the northern end of the Fort area in the evening, until about 9pm. You can just show up, or book ahead with **RB Booking Centre** (15 Grand Bazaar; ⌚8am-8pm). Most operators charge Rs 800/1100 for ordinary/air-con.

JAFFNA PENINSULA CTB routes around the peninsula (including the islands) are also served by identically numbered private minibuses; these leave from around the little blue cabin on Powerhouse Rd, or really from anywhere around the CTB station. These can get crowded, however, and locals warn that pickpocketing and wandering paws are common. Some services are infrequent; check return times before you head out. Useful CTB and minibus services:

Kairanagar (Karaithivu), via Vaddukkodai (782, 786) Rs 45, 1½ hours, every 30 minutes

Kayts (777) Rs 49, 36km, one hour, every 30 to 60 minutes (bus 780 also goes here but takes longer)

Keerimalai (private minibuses 82, 87, 89) Rs 36, one hour, every 20 minutes

Kurikadduwan (KKD; 776) Rs 61, 1½ to two hours, every 45 minutes

Point Pedro via Nelliady (750) Rs 58, 1½ hours, every 30 to 60 minutes

Point Pedro via Valvettiturai (VVT; 751) Rs 60, 1½ hours, every 30 to 60 minutes

Tellippalai via Chunnakam (for Thurkkai Amman Kovil, Kantarodai, Keerimalai spring; 769) Rs 25, every 30 to 40 minutes

Van

A convenient though pricey way to visit the Jaffna peninsula is to rent a van. Charges are about the same whether you go through a guesthouse or hire one off the street, though the latter are not always easy to find. Costs range between Rs 5000 and 6000 per day for up to 100km, including petrol. Add Rs 35 to 40 per kilometre for extra mileage. Around 130km covers virtually every 'sight' on the peninsula, not including the islands.

Getting Around

PUBLIC TRANSPORTATION From Chundukuli and Nallur, all buses and minibuses (from Rs 7) bound west and southwest on Kandy Rd and Point Pedro Rd, respectively, terminate at the CTB station.

To head out of town, take frequent bus 769 for Chundukuli or bus 750 for Nallur via Point Pedro Rd. Buses are much safer – in terms of both groping and theft – and less crowded than minibuses.

THREE-WHEELER At Rs 150 for short trips, or Rs 500 per hour to putt-putt around town, three-wheelers are more expensive in Jaffna than elsewhere in the country. At night, locals recommend calling one (or having someone call one for you) for security reasons. (If you find a good driver you like, get his number.) A couple of our favourite guys: **Baskar** (☎077 921 8122) and **Suman** (☎077 079 0317).

CYCLING Jaffna is perfect for cycling, but bicycles for hire are rare. Ask your guesthouse to lend or help you find one.

Jaffna Peninsula

☎021

Once you get beyond Jaffna's already rustic outer boroughs, you're plunged into fields of palmyra palms, Technicolor temples, holy springs and sunny coasts (surrounding several restricted military zones, of course). Few of the sights are individually outstanding, but together they make an interesting day trip or two, especially if you hire your own transport.

TOWARDS KEERIMALAI SPRING

Though a lot of the surrounding area is off limits, the road to Keerimalai spring was recently opened for the first time in 20 years. Kankesanturai (KKS), its endpoint, however, is still restricted.

From Jaffna, head first to Chunnakam and grab a three-wheeler (Rs 300 return) for the 3km squiggle of lanes leading west to the beautiful and mysterious **Kantarodai Ruins** (⏲8.30am-5pm) – two dozen or so dagobas, 1m to 2m in height, in a palm-fringed field. The 2000-year-old ruins were discovered in 1916 in a palmyra patch, and their origins are the subject of fierce controversy – part of the raging 'who was here first?' historical debate. Originally flat-topped and low to the ground, the stone structures were built upon by Sri Lanka's Department of Archaeology in 1978 – some say to restore the original dagoba shape that the ancient Buddhist community here had created; others say to impose a Buddhist history on an ancient culture that had its own set of traditions (maybe for burials). Many Buddhists refer to the site as Purana Rajamaha Vihara and appreciate the small Buddha temple constructed nearby and the SLA soldiers who watch over the site. Many Tamils, not so much. It's hardly a mind-blowing vista, especially as it's all behind a wire fence, but the structures are quite otherworldly-looking.

Beside the KKS road at the 13km marker, in the 'new' village of **Tellippalai**, the vast **Thurkkai Amman Kovil** (⏲5.30am-7pm, closed 1-3pm some days) is set behind a fairly deep, stepped pool. The temple celebrates the goddess Durga and draws relatively large crowds, of women especially, on Tuesdays and Fridays, when devotees pray for a good spouse. *Puja* is at 8am, 11am, noon and 4pm, and the priests are welcoming. The

Jaffna Peninsula

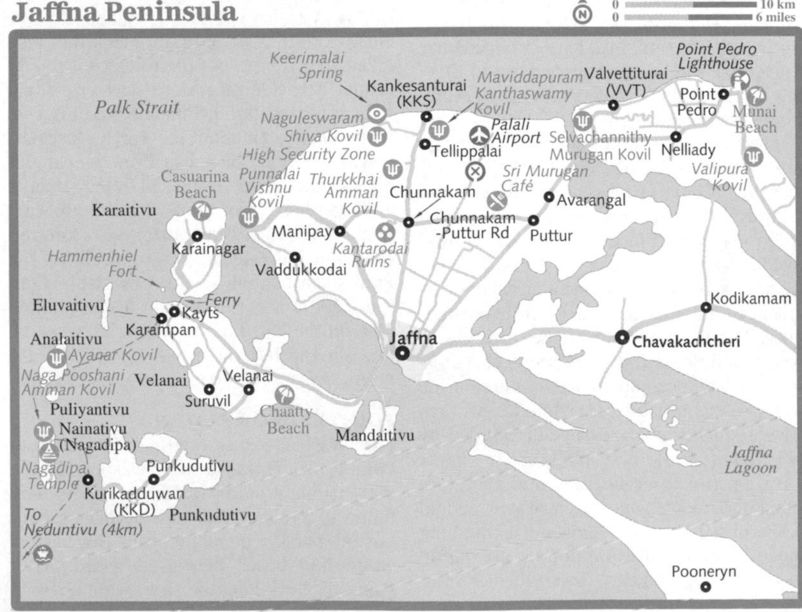

temple also runs an orphanage for 150 kids. The Tellippalai bus stand is just outside the temple; it's Rs 25 from Jaffna on the 769.

A kilometre further north lies the **Palali KKS Military Camp**, one of Sri Lanka's largest and perhaps most controversial High Security Zones. Between 1983 and 1993, the entire population (more than 25,000 families) was evicted from 58.5 sq km of prime agricultural land. Everything within the zone was either destroyed or converted for military use, including a limestone quarry that is now feared to be a major environmental problem. Since the war, the SLA has been returning small tracts of lands back to their owners, though local families we spoke to are wary of moving back just yet. You can now drive through the area to reach the Keerimalai spring (something you couldn't do for 20 years), and the sight of so many long-abandoned houses, roofless and with big trees growing through them, is very weird, to say the least.

At the turnoff for the Keerimalai spring is the **Maviddapuram Kanthaswamy Kovil**, which survived bombings and looting in the war; its devotees are making a valiant effort to get the place up and running. The priests here are very friendly and will probably do a *puja* for you if you like (otherwise, it's at 11.30am).

Just near the spring is the 6th-century-BC **Naguleswaram Shiva Kovil**, one of the *pancha ishwaram* (see p248). Only traces of the original buildings have survived, and the temple was bombed by the army in 1990, but it's undergoing repairs and is a peaceful place to wander around.

Legend has it that the sacred **Keerimalai spring** became famous after the 7th-century visit by a Chola princess: not only was her digestive disorder instantaneously healed when she bathed in the waters and prayed to Murugan, but so was her facial deformity, which, according to one source, had the 'likeness of a horse's head'. Even if your face doesn't look like a horse, the spring is a beautiful little spot: the men's side has a picturesque stepped pool of bright aquamarine water set against the sea, while the women have a smaller pool nearby surrounded by tall walls (for the best, really). The waters are supposed to be healing, and there are changing rooms on-site; women should bathe in a T-shirt and shorts or something modest. Jaffna buses/minibuses are Rs 30 to the spring, or get a three-wheeler from Tellippalai bus stand for Rs 300/600 one way/round trip.

If you're doing a one-day tour of the peninsula, then after visiting Keerimalai take Chunnakam–Puttur Rd towards Valvettiturai and Point Pedro and grab lunch at the excellent, old-fashioned **Sri Murugan Café** (Vakaiadi; rice & curry Rs 180; ⌚5am-9pm), 3km west of Puttur.

VALVETTITURAI

On the way to Valvettiturai (VVT) is the charming, waterfront **Selvachannithy Murugan Kovil** (also known as Sella Sannathy Kovil) in Thondaimanaru. Like so many places on the peninsula it was severely damaged in the war, but today the important Murugan temple is a scenic stop, with a lively *puja*.

The gorgeous coast road leads east to VVT, once a rich smuggling town but now most famous as the birthplace of LTTE leader Vellupillai Prabhakaran. Known for his extraordinary ruthlessness, charisma and single-minded strength of purpose, Prabhakaran's strong personality was considered by many to be the reason that the LTTE – of all the militant Tamil-rights groups that emerged in the 1970s – rose to prominence. Prabhakaran's death was reported during the final days of the war, but some believe he's hiding out abroad.

The green-walled **Prabhakaran family house** (Vampady Lane) was damaged by security forces in 1985, in an attack that also killed 70 civilians, but the ruins continue to attract a trickle of curious gawkers, along with graffiti in Tamil, Sinhalese and English. If you know a bit about the war, it's fascinating to see (don't be alarmed by the camouflaged watchtower at the end of the street!).

To get here from the VVT bus stop, walk west for 400m, passing **Muthumari Amman Kovil** with its fine *gopuram* – probably the Prabhakaran family's house of worship. Continue 200m and turn on the first asphalted lane on the left; Prabhakaran's house is the first on the left. Take bus 751 (Rs 60, 1½ hours, every 30 to 60 minutes) from Jaffna.

POINT PEDRO & AROUND

From VVT, the coast road curves around to Point Pedro. This area was devastated by the 2004 tsunami; locals say fishing boats were found 1km inland. The area has been rebuilt but is sparsely populated and the narrow white-sand beach here is deserted. It's a stunning ride along the shore, though, with its jetties, fishing boats and manta-ray fishers. (Look out for manta-ray butchering onshore; it's both disgusting and entrancing.)

Ramshackle **Point Pedro** is the Jaffna peninsula's second town; it has a few very faint hints of colonial style and a gorgeous, isolated beach to the east. From Point Pedro bus station walk 100m south and then east, passing a curious stone **tollgate** that locals claim dates from the Dutch era. Some 500m beyond, turn left towards the sea up St Anthony's Lane and past the town's two finest **churches**. The coast road continues 1km east to **Point Pedro Lighthouse** (off limits; no photos), beyond which the fishermen's beach becomes wider. The nicest area of **Munai Beach** is nearly 2km further on, as are some attractive views of Vadamaraadchi Lagoon. It was closed at research time, and the owners don't speak much English, but you may be able to stay overnight at **Gunam Lodge** (☎077 186 9015; 116/1 Nellandi Rd, Thumpalai; s/d Rs 500/750), across the street from the beach. Three-wheelers from central Point Pedro charge Rs 300 return for Munai Beach.

Further southeast is the much-revered **Valipura Kovil**, 5km from central Point Pedro. Its *gopuram* is painted in an unusually restrained colour palette and the temple interior has some very pretty Krishnas. It's famous for the boisterous, recently revived water-cutting festival in October, which attracts thousands of pilgrims. *Puja* is at 7am, 9.30am, noon, 4.15pm and, on Sunday, 6pm.

Jaffna's Islands

Southwest of the Jaffna peninsula is a clutch of low-lying islands, some attached to one another and the mainland by causeways. The main pleasure in exploring here is not any specific sight, but the hypnotic quality of the waterscapes and the escapist feeling of boat rides to end-of-earth removes.

There are a few day-trip possibilities. One is to loop around through Karaitivu (Karainagar), ferry-hop to Velanai and return via the causeway. The second option is an out-and-back excursion to Neduntivu (Delft) or sacred Nainativu (Nagadipa) via the causeways to Kurikadduwan (KKD) and a ferry.

The LTTE was once active on these waters, and the Sri Lankan Navy presence continues to be strong; in fact, the Navy itself conducts the ferry services.

KARAITIVU

Karaitivu has two main things going for it: access to Kayts and the trippy crossing from Jaffna across a long, water-skimming **causeway**, with views of fishers and shrimp traps. Look right at the start of the causeway to spy the towering *gopuram* of **Ponnalai Vishnu Kovil** through the palms. Karaitivu's popular-with-locals **Casuarina Beach** isn't great, but it's easy to reach and has a good family vibe, replete with a military-run ice-cream stand and kids in fancy outfits. It also has changing rooms and bathrooms (the usual T-shirt-and-shorts guidelines for gals applies). Less family-friendly is the unmarked **toddy shack** (⏲11am-2pm & 5-7pm, closed on poya days) nestled amid palms about 150m from the beach on the access road. Solo gals, or even groups of gals, may wish to stay away – not because it's dangerous but because it's full of staring drunks.

Half-hourly buses from Jaffna to **Karainagar** (782 and 786; Rs 45, 1½ hours) usually pass Casuarina Junction, 2km from the beach; ask before boarding. If not, get down at Vallenthallai Junction, about 1km away from Casuarina Junction. There are three-wheelers at both, but oddly, the guys at Vallenthallai charge less: Rs 300 return to the beach, including one hour of waiting time.

Buses and minibuses terminate close to the tiny **Kayts ferry** jetty, which is within a small naval zone. The free ferry (10 minutes, half-hourly except 12.30pm to 2pm) begins at 7am at Kayts; the last one leaves Karaitivu at 5.30pm.

VELANAI

Most people pass through Velanai – sometimes referred to as Leiden, its Dutch name, or Kayts, after the village on its northeast coast – on their way to either Punkudutivu or Analaitivu; it's a beautiful place but is sparsely populated and has a deserted feel thanks to the war.

If you approach Velanai from Jaffna, you'll see the turnoff for **Chaatty Beach** towards the island's eastern end. It's no white-sand wonder, but it's passable for swimming and easy to reach, just 11km from Jaffna. It has changing rooms, picnic gazebos and snack vendors. Bikinis are out of the question: women should swim in T-shirts and shorts. The spot is also noteworthy for **Chaatty Maaveerar Thuyilum Illam**, the LTTE cemetery that used to stand across the street (see p254). Any Kayts- or Kurikadduwan-bound bus from Jaffna can drop you at

ELEPHANT QUAY

Elephants were once indispensable to South Asian armies: they could transport troops through difficult terrain and waterways, carry heavy supplies, knock down the doors of forts and, when lined up with steel balls swinging from their trunks, scare the hell out of the enemy. Sri Lanka's elephants were known to be exceptionally strong, intelligent and large, and so the island became a major supplier to India – a practice that began around 300 BC and continued to the early 19th century.

Most elephants were caught in the Vanni, then marched through the Jaffna peninsula and shipped out from Elephant Quay, on Kayts. (Elephant Pass, linking the Jaffna peninsula to the rest of Sri Lanka, really was an elephant pass.) They were shipped in custom-made wooden elephant boats constructed in Kayts, and the town became renowned as an elephant port.

As powerful as the elephants were, however, they were frightened and confused by loud noises, so the arrival of firearms put an end to their war prowess and the Kayts elephant trade.

the Km 9 post; from here, follow the well-marked road 2km south to the beach.

If you approach Velanai from Karainagar, the ferry will drop you at eerie, semi-deserted **Kayts** between a dozen scuttled fishing boats. The town has three noteworthy churches near the jetty: walk straight up Sunuvil Rd and take your first right to get to the Portuguese **St James'**; if you turn left instead you'll hit **St Joseph's**; and if you continue up Sunuvil Rd, you'll see **St Mary's** on the left. Just beyond St Mary's, the first asphalt lane to the right leads 600m to a placid waterfront **cemetery** with views of offshore **Hammenhiel Fort**. The 17th-century fort was built by the Portuguese, then seized by the Dutch. It's now a navy camp, but there are rumours about it being converted into a resort. Buses from Jaffna (777 and 780; Rs 49, one hour) run every 30 to 60 minutes until 5.30pm. At the island's northwest is **Karampan**, where ferries depart for Analaitivu and Eluvaitivu.

NAINATIVU & NEDUNTIVU (DELFT)

The trip to these two remote islands passes through some beautiful sights. A long, delightful **causeway** links Velanai to the island of Punkudutivu. Notice the lagoon fishermen who use wade-out traps and sail little wind-powered canoes. **Punkudutivu** village, the scene of minor riots in December 2005, has one of Jaffna's most screechingly colourful Hindu temples, while many old houses lie in various stages of decay. Smaller causeways link Punkudutivu to the ferry port at **Kurikadduwan (KKD)** for boats to Neduntivu and Nainativu. Jaffna–KKD minibuses and buses (776; Rs 61, 1½ to two hours, every 45 minutes) start early and run until the last ferry has returned to KKD.

NAINATIVU (NAGADIPA)

Known as Nainativu in Tamil and Nagadipa in Sinhalese, this 6km-long lozenge of palmyra groves is holy to both Buddhist and Hindu pilgrims.

Right in front of you as you step off the jetty is the **Naga Pooshani Amman Kovil** complex, an airy Hindu temple set amid mature neem trees. The main temple deity is the *naga* goddess Meenakshi, a consort of Shiva. (The term *naga* refers variously to serpent deity figures and to the ancient inhabitants of the island.) Women wishing to conceive come here seeking blessings, delivered during the trance-inducing midday *puja*. Male devotees must remove shirts and shoes before entering. An impressive festival is held in June/July every year.

Walk 10 minutes south along the coast road to find the **Nagadipa temple**, the North's only major Buddhist pilgrimage site. According to legend, the Buddha came to the island to prevent war between a *naga* king and his nephew over ownership of a gem-studded throne. The solution: give it to the temple instead. The precious chair and original temple disappeared long ago, but today there is an attractive silver-painted dagoba. Just behind, three happy-looking Buddhas sit in a domed temple.

Poya (full-moon) days are observed by both Hindus and Buddhists on the island; expect crowds. Ferries (Rs 30, 20 minutes) depart KKD for Nainativu every 10 minutes or so, depending on the crowd, from 6.30am to 5.30pm.

NEDUNTIVU

The intriguing, windswept island of Neduntivu (Delft) is 10km across the water southwest of KKD. Thousands of people live here, but it feels deserted, with dirt roads running through coconut-palm groves, sun bouncing off aquamarine water and white sand, and a rich diversity of flora that includes neem, a rare, ancient **baobab tree**, and vines that you can swing from. Hundreds of field-dividing walls are hewn from chunks of brain and fan corals, most of it from Neduntivu's coral ground, while Delft ponies descended from Dutch mounts roam barren fields edged by rocky coral shores. There is a **giant rock** that is said to be growing and is therefore worshipped, and a small, very ruined **Dutch fort** is a short walk from the ferry dock. **Manal Kanuttadi** is a pretty beach 1km from the dock where you could camp with permission from the Navy. (There's a small shop near the dock selling water and snacks but little in the way of real food.) It would be difficult to see all the 'sights' on foot in one day; **Nelson** (☎077 844 8737) can arrange for a pickup-truck tour for up to eight people for Rs 3000.

Ferries (Rs 60, 40 minutes) depart KKD at 8.30am, 10am and 12.30pm, returning at 2pm (3pm on Sundays), 3.30pm and 5pm.

Understand Sri Lanka

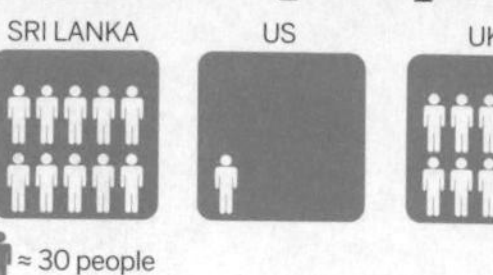

Sri Lanka Today

» Population: 20.8 million

» GDP: US$49.7 billion

» GDP per capita: US$5220

» Annual inflation: 5.9%

» Unemployment: 5.8%

Peace

The 26-year-long conflict between the Sri Lankan military and the Liberation Tigers of Tamil Eelam (LTTE) ended in May 2009 in a brutal end to a brutal war. Thousands of civilians in the North and East were killed as the Sri Lankan military launched all-out war on the areas controlled by the LTTE, and hundreds of thousands of civilians were put in refugee camps.

In the years since, a government reconciliation commission has heard testimony and verified the huge death toll in 2008 and 2009. The LTTE infiltrated refugee camps with its weapons, the military attacked those same refugee camps. The charges and counter-charges go on and on. But what's most important about the end of the war is just how ready the entire country is to move forward.

A pearl-shaped island of enormous natural wealth and potential, Sri Lanka has been a poster child for misfortune for far too long. An earlier effort at peace was upended by the 2004 Boxing Day tsunami, which killed tens of thousands and plunged the nation into a chaos that allowed the war to erupt again.

Progress

'Everyone agrees, they'd rather die than live through the war again', one Sri Lankan said to us, and the truth to that is palpable. Decades of delay in investment and progress are being made up for with vengeance. New roads and airports are being built across the nation. A great deal of work is being done in the former LTTE areas to try to mend the wounds.

The economy is booming and Colombo, which for years was a capital under siege from terrorists, is turning into a building site, and newfound wealth is translating into new shops and restaurants, restored historic buildings and huge public events such as pop-music concerts and fireworks.

Top Reads

Running in the Family A comic and reflective memoir by Michael Ondaatje of his Colombo family in the 1940s.

Monkfish Moon Nine short stories, by Booker Prize–nominated Romesh Gunesekera, provide a diverse glimpse of Sri Lanka's ethnic conflict.

The Foundations of Paradise Features places remarkably like Adam's Peak and Sigiriya. The author, Arthur C Clarke (1917–2008), wrote *2001: A Space Odyssey* and lived in Sri Lanka.

Local Guides

» *Sri Lanka's Other Half* is a collection of features and travel info for the top half of Sri Lanka, including the North and East. There's also a Colombo book and others in the series.

belief systems
(% of population)

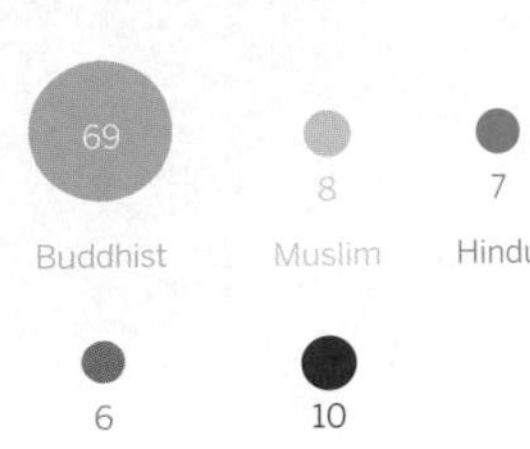

if Sri Lanka were 100 people

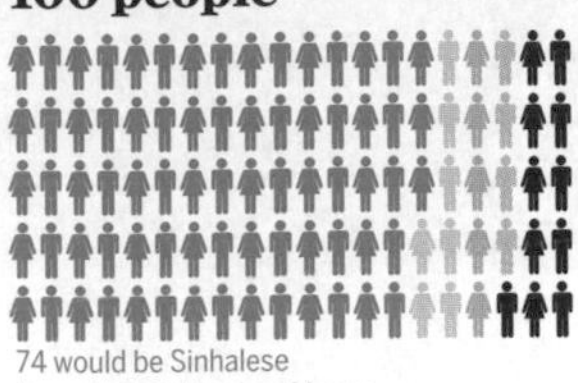

74 would be Sinhalese
7 would be Sri Lankan Moors
5 would be Indian Tamil
4 would be Sri Lankan Tamil
10 would be other

Optimism across the nation is replacing the relief that was pervasive immediately after fighting stopped. Literally gazing down on it all is the president, Mahinda Rajapaksa, whose moustached visage adorns huge billboards everywhere. His challenge is to steer the nation into reconciliation while so much pain remains.

Tourist Boom

A record number of tourists (over 800,000) visited Sri Lanka in 2011, an increase of almost 40% from the year before. And as most people in the industry will tell you, that's just the start. The physically much smaller Bali in Indonesia, by comparison, had 2.4 million tourists in 2011 and Sri Lankan boasters will tell you that surpassing Bali is a mid-term goal.

Sri Lanka, with its amazing beaches, beautiful Hill Country, eight Unesco World Heritage Sites, ancient cultures, tooting choo-choo trains and much more (elephants and leopards, anyone?) is a visitor's dream that was regularly overlooked by travellers during the war years.

New guesthouses and hotels are being built and in places like Galle and Ella, businesses aimed right at backpackers – like travellers' cafes – are opening their doors for the first time. It's a time of dizzying change and it's bound to continue.

For Europeans looking for a new warm-weather spot during the interminable winters, Sri Lanka is a couple of hours closer than Thailand and not quite as far as the Caribbean. It's hoped that a new international airport being built in the South will prove the ideal landing strip for hordes of holidaymakers.

Sri Lanka does well in the shorter one-day and 20-20 forms of cricket, and won the Cricket World Cup in 1996 and were runners-up to Australia in 2007. The sport is national religion, even if success was elusive going into 2012.

Documentaries

» The 2008 BBC documentary *Hot Spots: Sri Lanka* details the country's history of ethnic tensions.

» A 2011 report by the UK's Channel Four, *Sri Lanka's Killing Fields*, examines events in the final months of the war.

Top Websites

Ceylon Today (www.ceylon today.lk) News, sports and entertainment; general interest; exchange rates.

Daily Mirror (www.dailymirror.lk) Best of the newspaper sites; a good selection of opinion pieces plus cultural coverage.

Gossip Lanka (www.english.gossiplankanews.com) Gossip and entertainment news; plus investigative reporting. *Kotthu*-stand chatter.

Indi.ca (www.indi.ca) News, opinion and culture by an excellent local journalist.

History

Sri Lanka's history is a source of great pride to both Sinhalese and Tamils, the country's two largest ethnic groups. The only problem is, they have two completely different versions. Every historical site, religious structure, even village name seems to have conflicting stories about its origin, and those stories are, in turn, blended over time with contrasting religious myths and local legends. The end results are often used as evidence that the island is one group's exclusive homeland; each claims first dibs.

In fact, the island's location – its position along hundreds of ancient trade routes and its proximity to India – has resulted in a potpourri of visitors, immigrants, invaders, missionaries, traders and travellers, mostly from India, but also from East Asia and the Middle East. Many stayed on, and over the generations they assimilated and intermarried, converted and converted back again. The island's history, like that of its ethnicities, is one of constant flux and shifting dominance. Nonetheless, the contemporary Sri Lankan take on history is deeply political and marked by deep ethnic divides – divides that may be totally artificial.

Veddah Place Names

» Gal Oya National Park

» Nanu Oya

» Kelaniya Ganga

Prehistory & Early Arrivals

Legend and history are deeply intertwined in the early accounts of Sri Lanka. Did the Buddha leave his footprint on Adam's Peak (Sri Pada) while visiting the island that lay halfway to paradise? Or was it Adam who left his footprint embedded in the rock while taking a last look at Eden? Was the chain of islands linking Sri Lanka to India the same chain that Rama crossed to rescue his wife Sita from the clutches of Rawana, demon king of Lanka, in the epic Ramayana?

Whatever the legends, the reality is that Sri Lanka's original inhabitants, the Veddahs (Wanniyala-aetto, called Yakshas in the Pali chronicles), were hunter-gatherers who subsisted on the island's natural bounty. Much about their origins is unclear, but anthropologists generally believe that they are descended from people who migrated from

TIMELINE

Pre 6th century BC

The island is inhabited by Veddahs (Wanniyala-aetto), a group of hunter-gatherers who anthropologists believe were descendants of a society that existed on Sri Lanka since 32,000 BC.

6th century BC

Vijaya, a shamed North Indian prince, is cast adrift, but makes landfall on Sri Lanka's west coast. He settles around Anuradhapura and establishes the island's first recorded kingdom.

4th century BC

India's first poet pens the Hindu epic the Ramayana, in which the god Rama conquers Lanka and its demon-god Rawana. The sandbars off Mannar Island are described as Rama's Bridge.

India, and possibly Southeast Asia, and existed on the island as far back as 32,000 BC. It's also likely that rising waters submerged a land bridge between India and Sri Lanka in around 5000 BC.

Historians and archaeologists have differing interpretations of its origins, but a megalithic culture emerged in the centuries around 900 BC with striking similarities to the South Indian cultures of that time. Also during this Early Iron Age, Anuradhapura began to grow as a population centre.

Objects inscribed with Brahmi (an ancient 'parent' script to most South Asian scripts) have been found from the 3rd century BC; parallels to both North Indian and South Indian Brahmi styles have been made, though Tamil words are used in many of those found in the north and east of the island. Sri Lankan historians debate these details fiercely, as do many Sri Lankans, but rather than there being two distinct ethnic histories, it is more likely that migrations from West, East and South India all happened during this time and that those new arrivals all mixed with the indigenous people.

Anuradhapura

The 5th-century-AD Pali epic, the Mahavamsa, is the country's primary historical source. But although it is a somewhat faithful record of kingdoms and Sinhalese political power from around the 3rd century BC, its historical accuracy is much shakier – and indeed full of beautiful myths – before this time. Nonetheless, many Sinhalese claim that they are descended from Vijaya, an immoral 6th-century-BC North Indian prince who, according to the epic, had a lion for a grandfather and a father with lion paws who married his own sister. Vijaya was banished for bad behaviour, with a contingent of 700 men, on dilapidated ships from the subcontinent.

Rather than drowning, they landed near present-day Mannar, supposedly on the day that the Buddha attained enlightenment. Vijaya and his crew settled around Anuradhapura, and soon encountered Kuveni, a Yaksha (probably Veddah) who is alternately described as a vicious queen and a seductress who assumed the form of a 16-year-old maiden to snag Vijaya. She handed Vijaya the crown, joined him in slaying her own people and had two children with him before he kicked her out and ordered a princess – along with wives for his men – from South India's Tamil Pandya kingdom. (That, by this account, the forefathers of the Sinhalese race all married Tamils is overlooked by most Sri Lankans.) His rule formed the basis of the Anuradhapura kingdom, which developed there in the 4th century BC.

Buddhism arrived from India in the 3rd century BC, transforming Anuradhapura and possibly creating what is now known as Sinhalese culture. Today the mountain at Mihintale marks the spot where King Devanampiya Tissa is said to have first received the Buddha's teaching.

Possible Early Iron Age Sites

» Sigiriya
» Kantarodai
» Tissamaharama

3rd century BC

Indian emperor Ashoka sends his son and daughter to the island to spread the Buddha's teachings. Anuradhapuran king Devanampiya Tissa accepts them.

205–161 BC

Reign of Chola king Elara, described in the Mahavamsa as a just leader. Although Tamil and Hindu, he offers alms to Buddhist monks and employs both Sinhalese and Tamils.

103–89 BC

Five Tamil kings from India invade Anuradhapura and rule for 14 years. King Valagambahu is forced to flee and shelters in the caves around Dambulla.

1st century BC

The Fourth Buddhist council is held in Aluvihara. The collection of the Buddha's teachings, previously preserved by oral tradition, is written down for the first time.

The earliest Buddhist emissaries also brought to Sri Lanka a cutting of the bodhi tree under which the Buddha attained enlightenment. It survives in Anuradhapura, now garlanded with prayer flags and lights. Strong ties gradually evolved between Sri Lankan royalty and Buddhist religious orders. Kings, grateful for monastic support, provided living quarters, tanks (reservoirs) and produce to the monasteries, and a symbiotic political economy between religion and state was established, a powerful contract that is still vital in modern times.

Buddhism underwent a further major development on the island when the original oral teachings were documented in writing in the 1st century BC. The early Sri Lankan monks went on to write a vast body of commentaries on the teachings, textbooks, Pali grammars and other instructive articles, developing a classical literature for the Theravada (doctrine of the elders) school of Buddhism (p285) that continues to be referenced by Theravada Buddhists around the world. The arrival of the tooth relic of the Buddha at Anuradhapura in AD 371 further reinforced the position of Buddhism in Sinhalese society. Buddhism gave the Sinhalese a sense of national purpose and identity, and inspired the development of their culture and literature.

Early Anuradhapura History

- Mannar
- Mihintale
- Sri Maha Bodhi
- The tooth relic

The Anuradhapura kingdom covered the whole island during the 2nd century BC, but it frequently fought, and coexisted with, other dynasties on the island over the centuries, especially the Tamil Cholas. The boundaries between Anuradhapura and various South Indian kingdoms were frequently shifting, and Anuradhapura was also involved in conflicts in South India. A number of Sinhalese heroes arose to repel South Indian kingdoms, including Vijayabahu I (11th century AD), who finally decided to abandon Anuradhapura and make Polonnaruwa, further southeast, his capital.

For centuries the kingdom was able to rebuild after its battles through rajakariya, the system of free labour for the king. This free labour provided the resources to restore buildings, tanks and irrigation systems and to develop agriculture. The system was not banished from the island until 1832, when the British passed laws banning slavery.

Polonnaruwa

The next capital, at Polonnaruwa, survived for more than two centuries and produced two more notable rulers. Parakramabahu I (r 1153–86), nephew of Vijayabahu I, was not content simply to expel the South Indian Tamil Chola empire from Sri Lanka, but carried the fight to South India and even made a raid on Myanmar. He also constructed many new tanks around the island, and lavished public money to make Polonnaruwa a great Asian capital.

His benevolent successor, Nissanka Malla (r 1187–96), was the last king of Polonnaruwa to care for the well-being of his people. He was followed

4th century AD

Buddhism is further popularised with the arrival in Anuradhapura of the sacred tooth relic of the Buddha. It becomes a symbol of both religion and sovereignty over the island.

5th century

After engineering his father's death and expelling his older brother Mugalan, King Kasyapa constructs the rock fortress at Sigiriya. With the assistance of Indian mercenaries, Mugalan finally retakes the throne.

5th century

The Mahavamsa (Great Chronicle) epic poem is written by Buddhist monks. It recounts the Buddhist and royal history of the island, interwoven with supernatural tales.

5th century

Indian scholar-monk Buddhaghosa arrives in Sri Lanka and writes the Visuddhimagga, a manual for the Buddha's teachings. His explications become part of the Theravada canon and are still studied today.

TANK-BUILDING

The science of building tanks, studying gradients and constructing channels is the key to early Sri Lankan civilisation. The tanks, which dot the plains of the ancient dominions of Rajarata (in the north-central part of the country) and Ruhuna (in the southeast), probably started as modest structures. But by the 5th century BC they reached such dimensions that local legends say they were built with supernatural help. It is claimed that Giant's Tank near Mannar Island was built by giants, while other tanks were said to have been constructed by a mixed workforce of humans and demons.

The irrigation system, developed on ever-greater scales during the millennium before the Common Era, ranks with the ancient *qanats* (underground channels) of Iran and the canals of Pharaonic Egypt in sophistication. These dry-zone reservoirs sustained and shaped Sri Lanka's civilisation for more than 2500 years, until war and discord overtook the island in the 12th to 14th centuries AD.

by a series of weak rulers, and with the decay of the irrigation system, disease spread and Polonnaruwa was abandoned. The lush jungle reclaimed the second Sinhalese capital in just a few decades.

After Polonnaruwa, Sinhalese power shifted to the southwest of the island, and between 1253 and 1400 there were another five different capitals, none of them as powerful as Anuradhapura or Polonnaruwa. Meanwhile, the powerful kingdom of Jaffna expanded to cover a huge part of the island. When Arab traveller Ibn Batuta visited Ceylon in 1344, he reported that it extended south as far as Puttalam.

The bodhi tree in Anuradhapura has a 2000-year history of human care and custody, making it the world's oldest tree of this kind.

With the decline of the Sinhalese northern capitals and the ensuing Sinhalese migration south, a wide jungle buffer zone separated the northern, mostly coastal Tamil settlements and the southern, interior Sinhalese settlements. For many centuries, this jungle barrier kept Sinhalese and Tamils largely apart, sowing the seeds for Sri Lanka's ethnic dichotomy.

Trade & Conquest

Enter the Portuguese

At the heart of the Indian Ocean, Sri Lanka had been a trading hub even before Arab traders arrived in the 7th century AD with their new Islamic faith. Gems, cinnamon, ivory and elephants were the valued items of commerce. Early Muslim settlements took hold in Jaffna and Galle, but the arrival of a European power, focused as much on domination as trade, forced many Muslims inland to flee persecution.

When the Portuguese arrived in 1505, Sri Lanka had three main kingdoms: the Tamil kingdom of Jaffna, and Sinhalese kingdoms in Kandy and Kotte (near Colombo). Lorenço de Almeida, the son of the

7th–15th century

Arab traders settle in Sri Lanka, marrying locally and establishing Islam on the island. They maintain trade with the Middle East and coexist peacefully with both Tamils and Sinhalese.

11th century

Weary of continued conflict with Tamil neighbours, King Vijayabahu I defeats the Cholas and moves the Sinhalese capital southeast to Polonnaruwa; a brief golden age follows.

1216

As Polonnaruwa declines, the Tamil kingdom of Jaffna is established and briefly becomes a feudatory of South India's Pandya kingdom before gaining independence. It survives for four centuries.

» Atadage (p195), Polonnaruwa

Portuguese Viceroy of India, established friendly relations with the Kotte kingdom and gained a monopoly on the valuable spice trade. The Portuguese eventually gained control of the Kotte kingdom.

Tamil-Portuguese relations were less cordial and Jaffna successfully resisted two Portuguese expeditions before falling in 1619, at which point the Portuguese destroyed Jaffna's many beautiful Hindu temples and its royal library. Portugal eventually took over the entire west coast, then the east, but the Kandyan kingdom in the central highlands steadfastly resisted domination.

The Portuguese brought along religious orders, including the Dominicans and Jesuits. Many coastal communities converted, but other resistance to Christianity was met with massacres and the destruction of local temples. Buddhists fled to Kandy, and the Hill Country city assumed its role as protector of the Buddhist faith, a sacred function solidified by another three centuries of unsuccessful attempts at domination by European powers.

BAILAS

Descendants of Mozambican slaves brought to Sri Lanka by the Portuguese are almost totally assimilated. Their most obvious contributions to modern Sri Lankan culture are the folk tunes called *bailas*, love songs founded on Latin melodies and African rhythms.

The Dutch & the British

In 1602 the Dutch arrived, just as keen as the Portuguese on dominating the lucrative traffic in Indian Ocean spices. In exchange for Sri Lankan autonomy, the Kandyan king, Rajasinha II, gave the Dutch a monopoly on the spice trade. Despite the deal, the Dutch made repeated unsuccessful attempts to subjugate Kandy during their 140-year rule.

The Dutch were more industrious than the Portuguese, and canals were built along the west coast to transport cinnamon and other crops. Some can be seen around Negombo today. The legal system of the Dutch era still forms part of Sri Lanka's legal canon.

The British initially viewed Sri Lanka in strategic terms, and considered the eastern harbour of Trincomalee as a counter to French influence in India. After the French took over the Netherlands in 1794, the pragmatic Dutch ceded Sri Lanka to the British for 'protection' in 1796. The British moved quickly, making the island a colony in 1802 and finally taking over Kandy in 1815. Three years later the first unified administration of the island by a European power was established.

The British conquest unsettled many Sinhalese, who believed that only the custodians of the tooth relic had the right to rule the land. Their apprehension was somewhat relieved when a senior monk removed the tooth relic from the Temple of the Sacred Tooth Relic, thereby securing it (and the island's symbolic sovereignty) for the Sinhalese people.

Sinhalese angst grew further when British settlers began arriving in the 1830s. Coffee and rubber were largely replaced by tea from the 1870s, and the island's demographic mix was profoundly altered with an influx of Tamil labourers – so called 'Plantation Tamils' – from South India. (These 'Plantation Tamils' were – and still are – separated by geography,

1505

Following Polonnaruwa's decline, Sinhalese power is with the Kotte in the southwest. The Portuguese arrive and conquer the entire west coast, but Kandy defeats their advances.

1658

Following a treaty with the Kandyan kingdom, the Dutch, who arrived in 1602, establish a monopoly on the spice market and wrest control of coastal Sri Lanka from the Portuguese.

1796

The Netherlands, under French control, surrenders Ceylon to the British. The shift is initially thought to be temporary, and the British administer the island from Madras, India.

1802

After the decline of the Dutch, Sri Lanka becomes a British colony. The island is viewed as a strategic bulwark against French expansion, but its commercial potential is soon recognised.

history and caste from the Jaffna Tamils.) Tamil settlers from the North made their way south to Colombo, while Sinhalese headed to Jaffna. British colonisation set the island in a demographic flux.

The Road to Independence

Growing Nationalism

The dawning of the 20th century was an important time for the grassroots Sri Lankan nationalist movement. Towards the end of the 19th century, Buddhist and Hindu campaigns were established with the dual aim of making the faiths more contemporary in the wake of European colonialism, and defending traditional Sri Lankan culture against the impact of Christian missionaries. The logical progression was for these groups to demand greater Sri Lankan participation in government, and by 1910 they had secured the minor concession of allowing Sri Lankans to elect one lonely member to the Legislative Council.

By 1919 the nationalist mission was formalised as the Ceylon National Congress. The Sinhalese-nationalist activist Anagarika Dharmapala was forced to leave the country, and the mantle for further change was taken up by a variety of youth leagues, some Sinhalese and some Tamil. In 1927 Mahatma Gandhi visited Tamil youth activists in Jaffna, providing further momentum to the cause.

Further reform came in 1924, when a revision to the constitution allowed for representative government, and again in 1931, when a new constitution finally included the island's leaders in the parliamentary decision-making process and granted universal suffrage. Under the constitution no one ethnic community could dominate the political process, and a series of checks and balances ensured all areas of the government were overseen by a committee drawn from all ethnic groups. However, both Sinhalese and Tamil political leaders failed to thoroughly support the country's pre-independence constitution, foreshadowing the problems that were to characterise the next eight decades.

From Ceylon to Sri Lanka

Following India's independence in 1947, Ceylon (as Sri Lanka was then called) became fully independent on 4 February 1948. Despite featuring members from all of the island's ethnic groups, the ruling United National Party (UNP) really only represented the interests of an English-speaking elite. The UNP's decision to try to deny the 'Plantation Tamils' citizenship and repatriate them to India was indicative of a rising tide of Sinhalese nationalism.

In 1956 this divide further increased when the Sri Lankan Freedom Party (SLFP) came to power with an agenda based on socialism, Sinhalese nationalism and government support for Buddhism. One of

Sir James Emerson Tennent's affable nature shines through in his honest and descriptive writing about 19th-century Sri Lanka, now serialised at www.lankaweb.com/news/features/ceylon.html.

European-era Forts

- Batticaloa
- Jaffna
- Matara
- Trincomalee

1815

Determined to rule the entire island, the British finally conquer the Kandyan kingdom. It's the first (and only) time all of Sri Lanka is ruled by a European power.

1832

Sweeping changes in property laws open the door to British settlers. English becomes the official language, state monopolies are abolished and capital flows in, funding the establishment of coffee plantations.

1843–59

Unable to persuade the Sinhalese to labour on plantations, the British bring in almost one million Tamil labourers from South India. Today 'Plantation Tamils' are 5% of the population.

late 19th century

The Arwi language, a combination of Tamil and Arabic that evolved among Sri Lankan Moors, is at its peak with the publication of several important religious works.

WHAT'S IN A NAME?

Changing the country's name from Ceylon to Sri Lanka in 1972 caused considerable confusion for foreigners. However, for the Sinhalese it has always been known as Lanka and for the Tamils as Ilankai; the Ramayana, too, describes the abduction of Sita by the king of Lanka.

The Romans knew the island as Taprobane and Muslim traders talked of Serendib, meaning 'Island of Jewels' in Arabic. The word Serendib became the root of the word 'serendipity' – the art of making happy and unexpected discoveries. The Portuguese somehow twisted Sinhala-dvipa (Island of the Sinhalese) into Ceilão. In turn, the Dutch altered this to Ceylan and the British to Ceylon.

In 1972 'Lanka' was restored, with the addition of 'Sri', a respectful title.

the first tasks of the SLFP leader SWRD Bandaranaike was to fulfil a campaign promise to make Sinhala the country's sole official language. Under the British, Tamils became capable English speakers and were overrepresented in universities and public service jobs, which created Sinhalese resentment, especially during the slow economy of the 1950s. The main political parties played on the Sinhalese fear that their religion, language and culture could all be swamped by Indians, perceived to be natural allies of Sri Lankan Tamils. The Tamils, whose Hindu identity had also become more pronounced in the lead-up to independence, began to find themselves in the position of threatened minority.

The Sinhala-only bill disenfranchised Sri Lanka's Hindu and Muslim Tamil-speaking population: almost 30% of the country suddenly lost access to government jobs and services. Although tensions had been simmering since the end of colonial rule, this decision marked the beginning of Sri Lanka's ethnic conflict.

A similar scenario played out in 1970, when a law was passed favouring Sinhalese for admission to universities, reducing numbers of Tamil students. Then, following an armed insurrection against the government by the hardline anti-Tamil, student-led People's Liberation Front (Janatha Vimukthi Peramuna or JVP), a new constitution (which changed Ceylon's name to Sri Lanka) gave Buddhism 'foremost place' in Sri Lanka and made it the state's duty to 'protect and foster' Buddhism.

Unrest grew among northern Tamils, and a state of emergency was imposed on their home regions for several years from 1971. The police and army that enforced the state of emergency included few Tamils (partly because of the 'Sinhala only' law), creating further division and, for Tamils, an acute sense of oppression.

1870s

The coffee industry drives the development of roads, ports and railways, but leaf blight decimates the coffee industry, and plantations are converted to growing tea or rubber.

1919

Following the British arrest in 1915 of Sinhalese leaders for minor offences, the Ceylon National Congress unifies Sinhalese and Tamil groups to further nationalist and pro-independence goals.

1931

A new constitution introduces power sharing with a Sinhalese-run government. Universal suffrage is introduced as the country is the first Asian colony to give women the right to vote.

1948

Ceylon becomes an independent member of the Commonwealth six months after neighbouring India. The United National Party (UNP) consolidates power by depriving the Plantation Tamils of citizenship.

Birth of the Tigers

In the mid-1970s several groups of young Tamils, some of them militant, began advocating for an independent Tamil state called Eelam (Precious Land). They included Vellupillai Prabhakaran, one of the founders of the Liberation Tigers of Tamil Eelam (LTTE), often referred to as the Tamil Tigers.

Tamil had been elevated to the status of 'national language' for official work, but only in Tamil-majority areas. Clashes between Tamils and security forces developed into a pattern of killings and counter-reprisals, all too often with civilians in the crossfire. Passions on both sides rose, and a pivotal moment came in 1981, when a group of Sinhalese men (some say government forces) burnt down Jaffna's library, which contained, among other things, various histories of the Tamil people, some of which were ancient palm-leaf manuscripts.

Small-scale reprisals followed, but the world only took notice two years later, in 1983, when, in response to the Tigers' ambushing and killing of 13 soldiers in the Jaffna region, full-scale anti-Tamil massacres erupted in Colombo. In a riot now known as Black July, between 400 and 3000 Tamils were clubbed, beaten, burned or shot to death, and Tamil property was looted and burned. Several Tamil-majority areas, including Colombo's Pettah district, were levelled, and the violence spread to other parts of the country.

The government, the police and the army were either unable or unwilling to stop the violence; some of them assisted. Hundreds of thousands of Tamils left the country or fled to Tamil-majority areas in the North or East – and many joined the resistance. (Many Sinhalese, meanwhile, moved south from the North and East.) The horror of Black July prompted a groundswell of international sympathy for Tamil armed resistance groups, and brought funding from fellow Tamils in southern India, as well as from the government of Indira Gandhi.

Revenge and counter-revenge attacks continued, and grew into atrocities and massacres – on both sides. The government was widely condemned for acts of torture and disappearances, but it pointed to the intimidation and violence against civilians, including Tamils and Muslims, by the Tamil fighters.

Implementation of a 1987 accord, which would offer limited Tamil autonomy, alongside officialising Tamil as a national language, never happened, and the conflict escalated into a 25-year civil war that would eventually claim upwards of 100,000 lives.

Enemy Lines: Warfare, Childhood, and Play in Batticaloa, by Margaret Trawick, is a poignant memoir of living and working in eastern Sri Lanka and witnessing the recruitment of teenagers to the LTTE cause.

1956

The Sri Lankan Freedom party (SLFP) defeats the UNP on a socialist and nationalist platform. Protests, ethnic riots and conflict break out after a 'Sinhala only' language law is passed.

1959

Despite coming to power in 1956 with a Sinhalese-nationalist manifesto, SWRD Bandaranaike begins negotiating with Tamil leaders for a federation, resulting in his assassination by a Buddhist monk.

1959

Widow Sirimavo Bandaranaike assumes her late husband's SFLP post, becoming the world's first female prime minister. She is appointed prime minister several more times before her death in 2000.

» Sirimavo Bandaranaike

Attempts at Peace

Indian Peacekeeping

In 1987 government forces pushed the LTTE back into Jaffna. In an attempt to disarm the Tamil rebels and keep the peace in northern and eastern Sri Lanka, the prime minister, JR Jayawardene, struck a deal with India for an Indian Peace Keeping Force (IPKF). A single provincial council would be elected to govern the region with substantial autonomy for a trial period.

It soon became clear the deal suited no one. The LTTE complied initially before the Indians tried to isolate it by promoting and arming other Tamil rebel groups. Opposition to the Indians also came from the Sinhalese, a revived JVP and sections of the sangha (community of Buddhist monks and nuns), leading to violent demonstrations. In 1987 the JVP launched a second revolution with political murders and strikes, and by late 1988 the country was terrorised, the economy crippled and the government paralysed. The army struck back with a ruthless counter-insurgency campaign. The insurrection was put down, but not before tens of thousands died.

Not an easy read but an important one, *When Memory Dies*, by A Sivanandan, is a tale of the ethnic crisis and its impact on one family over three generations.

By the time the Indian peacekeepers withdrew, in March 1990, they had lost more than 1000 lives in just three years. But no sooner had they left than the war between the LTTE and the Sri Lankan government escalated again. By the end of 1990 the LTTE held Jaffna and much of the North, although the East was largely back under government control. In May 1991 Rajiv Gandhi was assassinated by a suicide bomber; it was blamed on the LTTE, presumably in retaliation for consenting to the IPKF arrangement.

The 2002 Ceasefire

Although most Tamils and Sinhalese longed for peace, extremists on both sides pressed on with war. President Premadasa was assassinated at a May Day rally in 1993. The LTTE was suspected but never claimed responsibility. The following year, the People's Alliance (PA) won the parliamentary elections; its leader, Chandrika Bandaranaike Kumaratunga, the daughter of former leader Sirimavo Bandaranaike, won the presidential election. The PA had promised to end the civil war, but the conflict continued in earnest.

At least one million land mines were laid during Sri Lankan hostilities in the 1990s. Efforts to clear the mines have meant that thousands of displaced people have been resettled.

In 2000 a Norwegian peace mission brought the LTTE and the government to the negotiating table, but a ceasefire had to wait until after the December 2001 elections, which handed power to the UNP. Ranil Wickremasinghe became prime minister, and economic growth was strong while peace talks appeared to progress. Wickremasinghe and President Chandrika Bandaranaike Kumaratunga, however, were from different parties, and circled each other warily until 2003, when Kumaratunga dissolved parliament and essentially ousted Wickremasinghe and his UNP.

In 2002, following the Norway-brokered ceasefire agreement, a careful optimism reigned. In the North, refugees, internally displaced persons

1972

A new constitution is created. It changes Ceylon's name to Sri Lanka, declares, once again, Sinhalese to be the official language and gives Buddhism 'foremost place' among the island's religions.

1970s

Young Tamils begin fighting for an independent Tamil state called Eelam (Precious Land) in Sri Lanka's north. The strongest group becomes the Liberation Tigers of Tamil Eelam (LTTE).

1981

Jaffna's Public Library, home to many ancient Tamil works and a symbol of Tamil culture and learning, is burnt down by Sinhalese mobs, galvanising the Tamil separatist movement.

1983

The ambush of an army patrol near Jaffna ignites widespread ethnic violence. Up to 3000 Tamils are estimated killed by Sinhalese mobs in what is now known as Black July.

and long-absent émigrés began to return, bringing an economic boost to devastated Jaffna. Nongovernmental organisations startled tackling, among other things, an estimated two million land mines.

But peace talks stumbled, and the situation became ever more fraught. Accusations of bias and injustice were hurled from all sides. In October 2003 the US listed the LTTE as a Foreign Terrorist Organisation (FTO). Some believed this to be a positive move; others saw it as an action that would isolate the LTTE, thereby causing further strain and conflict. In early 2004 a split in LTTE ranks pitched a new dynamic into the mix, and with killings, insecurity, accusations and ambiguities, the Norwegians went home. At that stage almost all of Sri Lanka, including most of the Jaffna peninsula, was controlled by the Sri Lankan government. The LTTE controlled a small area south of the Jaffna peninsula and pockets in the East, but it still had claims on land in the Jaffna peninsula and in the northwest and northeast of the island.

William McGowan's *Only Man is Vile* is an incisive, unrelenting account of ethnic violence in Sri Lanka, penetrating deeply into its complexities.

After the Tsunami

An event beyond all predictions struck the island on 26 December 2004, affecting not only the peace process but also the entire social fabric of Sri Lanka. As people celebrated the monthly *poya* (full moon) festivities, the waves of a tsunami cast their fury, killing 30,000 people and leaving many more injured, homeless and orphaned. Initially there was optimism that the nation would come together in the face of catastrophe, but this soon faded into arguments over aid distribution, reconstruction, and land tenure and ownership.

Meanwhile Kumaratunga, seeking to extend her presidential term, sought to have the constitution altered. Her plans were thwarted by a Supreme Court ruling that directed that presidential elections occur in 2005. Among the numerous contenders, two candidates were the most likely victors – the then prime minister, Mahinda Rajapaksa, and the opposition leader, Ranil Wickremasinghe. With a LTTE boycott on voting, Rajapaksa won by a narrow margin. The LTTE's motives for the boycott were unclear, but their actions cost Wickremasinghe an expected 180,000 votes and the presidency and, perhaps, a better chance at peace. President Rajapaksa pledged to replace the Norwegian peace negotiators with those from the UN and India, renegotiate a ceasefire with the LTTE, reject Tamil autonomy and refuse to share tsunami aid with the LTTE. Such policies did not auger well for future peace. Meanwhile LTTE leader Prabhakaran insisted on a political settlement during 2006, and threatened to 'intensify' action if this did not occur. Tensions were high, and once again Sri Lanka was perched on a precipice. Killings, assaults, kidnappings and disappearances occurred on both sides, and commentators predicted the worst.

The 2004 Indian Ocean tsunami killed more than 225,000 people in 14 countries. The waves, which were in some places more than 30m tall, travelled as far as the East African coast.

July 1987

An accord is signed, with India's involvement, granting Tamils an autonomous province in the country's north, but disagreements over its implementation prevent it from being put into effect.

1987

Government forces push the LTTE back into Jaffna. An Indian Peace Keeping Force (IPKF) attempts to establish stability, but is also dragged into conflict with the LTTE.

1987–89

The JVP launch a second Marxist insurrection, and attempt a Khmer Rouge–style peasants' rebellion in the countryside. When the uprising is finally crushed, up to 60,000 people have died.

1991

A Black Tiger (an LTTE fighter trained in suicide missions) kills former Indian prime minister Rajiv Gandhi, presumably to protest the IPKF, in the world's first female suicide bombing.

The End of the War

Another ceasefire was signed in early 2006, but cracks began to appear almost at the start, and by mid-year the agreement was in tatters. Major military operations by both sides resumed in the North and East, and a wave of disappearances and killings in 2006 and 2007 prompted human-rights groups and the international community to strongly criticise all belligerents. By August the fighting in the northeast was the most intense since the 2002 ceasefire, and peace talks in Geneva failed again. The optimistic days of negotiation and ceasefire seemed more distant than ever.

Anil's Ghost, by Booker Prize–winner Michael Ondaatje, is a haunting novel about human rights amid the turmoil of late-20th-century Sri Lanka. The book has received much international commendation and some local condemnation.

In January 2008 the Sri Lankan government officially pulled out of the ceasefire agreement, signalling its dedication to ending the 25-year-old civil conflict by military means. When the LTTE offered a unilateral ceasefire in support of the South Asian Association for Regional Co-operation (SAARC) in Colombo, the government response was an emphatic no. Defence Secretary Gotabhaya Rajapaksa (the younger brother of the president) called the offer a 'ploy by the LTTE…to strengthen it militarily under the guise of holding negotiations'.

A change in military strategy saw the Sri Lankan security forces fight fire with fire with an increase in guerrilla-style attacks, and by August the Sri Lankan Army (SLA) had entered the LTTE's final stronghold, the jungle area of the Vanni. The Sri Lankan government stated that the army was on track to capture the LTTE capital Kilinochchi by the end of 2008. Faced with a series of battleground defeats, the LTTE struck back with another suicide bomb in Anuradhapura, killing 27 people.

In September 2008 the Sri Lankan government ordered UN agencies and NGOs to leave the Vanni region, saying it could no longer guarantee their safety. This may have been true, but their withdrawal denied a beleaguered population of Tamils access to humanitarian support and the security of a human-rights watchdog. The departure of the NGOs, and barring of independent journalists from the conflict region, made (and continues to make) it impossible to verify claims made by either side about the final battles of the war, which were now starting in earnest.

Although its authorship and veracity have been disputed, *Tamil Tigress*, by Niromi de Soyza, tells the engrossing story of a former Tamil Tiger child soldier who left school at 17 to join the movement.

Government and LTTE forces remained dug in around Kilinochchi – the de facto capital of the unofficial Tamil Eelam state since 1990 – until the SLA declared victory there in January 2009. This was followed rapidly by claims of control throughout the Vanni, and by February, the LTTE had lost 99% of the territory it had controlled just 12 months earlier.

Government advances pushed remaining LTTE forces and the 300,000 Tamil civilians they brought with them to an increasingly tiny area in the northeast near Mullaittivu. Amid growing claims of civilian casualties and humanitarian concerns for the noncombatants hemmed in by the fighting, foreign governments and the UN called for an immediate ceasefire in Feb-

1994

President Chandrika Kumaratunga comes to power pledging to end the war with the LTTE. Peace talks are opened, but hostilities continue. In 1999 she survives a suicide bomb attack.

1995–2001

Hostilities between the Sri Lanka military and the LTTE intensify; following more failed attempts at negotiation, the LTTE bombs Kandy's Temple of the Sacred Tooth Relic in 1998.

2002

After two years of negotiation, a Norwegian peace mission secures a ceasefire. Sri Lankans, especially in the north and east, return to a new normal; many émigrés return.

2004

A tsunami devastates coastal Sri Lanka, leaving 30,000 people dead. It's thought the disaster will bring unity, but the government and LTTE are soon wrangling over aid distribution and reconstruction.

A FLAG FOR COMPASSION

Sri Lanka's flag was created in 1948 and took on many changes over the years. The core element was the lion on a crimson background, which had been used on flags throughout Sri Lankan history, beginning with Prince Vijaya, who is believed to have brought a lion flag with him from India. The lion, then, represented the Sinhalese people, and the gold is said to signify Buddhism. The flag was adopted in 1950, and as Sri Lanka settled into independence, it evolved: in 1951 green and orange stripes were added to signify Sri Lanka's Muslims and Hindus, respectively, and in 1972 four bo leaves were added to represent *metta* (loving-kindness), *karuna* (compassion), *upekkha* (equanimity) and *muditha* (happiness).

ruary 2009. Military operations continued, but escape routes were opened for those fleeing the fighting to move to no-fire zones, where there was to be further transport to welfare centres. The military, claiming that attacks were being launched from within the safe zones, then shelled them for days.

With claims that the Sri Lankan military was bombing civilians in the 'safe areas', and counter-claims that the LTTE was using Tamil civilians as human shields and stopping them from leaving the conflict zone, the UN High Commissioner for Human Rights Navi Pillay accused both sides of war crimes. But the international community remained largely quiet.

The Bitter End

By April, tens of thousands of Tamil civilians along with LTTE fighters were confined to a single stretch of beach, where they were bombarded from all sides. The LTTE offered the Sri Lankan government a unilateral ceasefire, but given that the Sri Lankan military's objectives were so close to being fulfilled it was naturally dismissed as 'a joke' by the Sri Lankan Defence Secretary. Other efforts by Swedish, French and British diplomats to inspire a truce were also dismissed by a Sri Lankan government with ultimate battleground success in its sights after three decades.

Crucible of Conflict: Tamil and Muslim Society on the East Coast of Sri Lanka, by Dennis McGilvary, reinforces that future healing must recognise the country's cultural diversity.

The government forces finally penetrated the LTTE and implored trapped war refugees to move to safe areas. The Tigers allegedly blocked many from leaving and killed others, while many refugees reported that government forces raped and executed many who surrendered. The end finally came in May when the Sri Lankan military captured the last sliver of coast and surrounded the few hundred remaining LTTE fighters. The LTTE responded by announcing they had 'silenced their weapons' and that the 'battle had reached its bitter end'. Several senior LTTE figures were killed, including leader Vellupillai Prabhakaran, and the war that terrorised the country for 26 years was finally over.

AFP / GETTY IMAGES ©

» Children's tsunami artwork

2005

Sinhalese nationalist Mahinda Rajapaksa wins presidential elections. Before the election Rajapaksa signs a deal with the Marxist JVP party, rejects Tamil autonomy outright and denies tsunami aid to the LTTE.

2008

The government pulls out of the 2002 ceasefire agreement, signalling a single-minded focus on a military solution. From 1983 to 2008, an estimated 70,000 people have died in the conflict.

May 2009

After almost 30 years, Asia's longest-running war ends in May when the LTTE concedes defeat after a bloody last battle at Mullaitivu. Legitimate Tamil aspirations and grievances remain.

Environmental Issues

Sri Lanka's superlatives extend to its natural world. Conservation International has identified Sri Lanka as one of the planet's 25 biodiversity hotspots, which means the island is characterised by a very high level of 'endemism' (species unique to the area). Sure enough, Sri Lanka tops the charts, with endemism in 23% of the flowering plants and 16% of the mammals. On the other hand, hotspots are targeted as habitats seriously at risk. One could hardly summarise the Sri Lankan situation more succinctly.

At the beginning of the 20th century about 70% of the island was covered by natural forest. By 1998 this had shrunk to about 29%. Worse, in recent years Sri Lanka has had one of the highest recorded rates of primary-forest destruction in the world: an 18% reduction in forest cover and 35% loss of old-growth tracts. You only need see the huge old-growth trees being cut up at the roadside lumber mills between Matale and Dambulla to understand that threats to the rainforest are ongoing.

What Tree Is That? by Sriyanie Miththapala and PA Miththapala contains handy sketches of common trees and shrubs in Sri Lanka, and includes English, Sinhala and botanical names.

Chena (shifting cultivation) is blamed for a good part of this deforestation, but irrigation schemes, clearance for cultivation and land 'development', armed conflict, and, obviously, illegal logging have all been contributing factors.

The boom in Sri Lanka's economy after peace is also bound to put even more pressure on the environment. With tourism increasing rapidly, new construction projects are proliferating. And the track record is not good: after the 2004 tsunami, laws were put in place that banned construction of hotels and restaurants within 100m of the high-tide line yet at Unawatuna and many other coastal areas, new buildings were built virtually at the water's edge.

Pear-shaped Treasure

Looking a lot like a plump pear, the island country of Sri Lanka dangles into the Indian Ocean off the southern end of India. At roughly 66,000 sq km it's slightly smaller than Ireland, but sustains 4.5 times as many people. That's 22 million in a space stretching 433km from north to south and only 244km at its widest point – like the entire population of Australia taking up residence in Tasmania.

ENDANGERED SPECIES

The International Union for Conservation of Nature's Red List of Threatened Species counts over 60 species in Sri Lanka as critically endangered and endangered. They include the Asian elephant, purple-faced langur, red slender loris and toque macaque. All five of Sri Lanka's marine turtle species are threatened, as are the estuarine crocodile and the mild-mannered dugong, all of which are killed for their meat. Also under threat are several species of birds, fish and insects.

Thrust up out of the encircling coastal plains, the southern centre of the island – the core of the pear – is dominated by mountains and tea-plantation-covered hills. The highest point is broad-backed Mt Pidurutalagala (Mt Pedro; 2524m), rising above the Hill Country capital city of Nuwara Eliya. However, the pyramid profile of 2243m-high Adam's Peak (Sri Pada) is better known and far more spectacular.

Hundreds of waterways channel abundant rain from the south-central wet-zone uplands – haven of the country's surviving rainforests – down through terraced farms, orchards and gardens to the paddy-rich plains below. The Mahaweli Ganga, Sri Lanka's longest river, has its source close to Adam's Peak and runs 335km to Koddiyar Bay, the deep-sea harbour of Trincomalee.

North-central Sri Lanka is home to high, rolling hills, including some fantastically dramatic landscapes like the area around the Knuckles Range. These hills give way to plains that extend to the northern tip of the island. This region, portions of the southeast and most of the east comprise the dry zone.

Horagolla National Park is a recently designated 13-hectare preserve of wet-zone forest near Nittambuwa, 40km northeast of Colombo on the A1.

Sri Lanka's coastline consists of hundreds of mangrove-fringed lagoons and marshes – some now protected wetlands – interspersed with fine white-sand beaches, the most picturesque of which are on the southwest, south and east coasts. A group of low, flat islands lies off the Jaffna peninsula in the north.

In terms of animals, it's not just elephants – although they are awesome; Sri Lanka has a huge range of animals for such a small island. And where Africa has its famous 'Big Five' (lion, leopard, elephant, rhino and Cape Buffalo), Sri Lanka has a 'Big Four' plus one (leopard, elephant, sloth bear and wild Asiatic water buffalo plus the ginormous blue whales found offshore). See p35 for details.

Plants

The southwestern wet zone is home to the country's surviving tropical rainforest, characterised by dense undergrowth and a tall canopy of hardwood trees, including ebony, teak and silkwood. The central hill zone has cloud forests and some rare highland areas populated by hardy grasslands and elfin (stunted) forests.

Other common trees are the banyan, bodhi (also known as bo or peepu), flame, rain, Ceylon ironwood and neem, an assortment of names as colourful as their barks, leaves and especially flowers. There are traditional medicinal uses for almost all of them. In the Hill Country don't be surprised by the eucalypts planted to provide shade at tea estates.

The sacred bodhi tree was brought from India when Mahinda introduced the teachings of the Buddha to Sri Lanka in the 3rd century BC. Most Buddhist temples have a bodhi tree, but the most famous is the Sri Maha Bodhi of Anuradhapura, the oldest historically authenticated tree in the world.

Native fruit trees such as mangoes, tamarinds, wood apples and bananas grow in many private gardens, supplemented by introduced species like papayas and guavas. The jackfruit and its smaller relative, the *del* (breadfruit), will certainly catch your eye. The jackfruit tree produces the world's largest fruit; green and knobbly skinned, it weighs up to 30kg and hangs close to the trunk.

Sri Lanka's Elephants

Elephants occupy a special place in Sri Lankan culture. In ancient times they were Crown property and killing one was a terrible offence. Legend has it that elephants stamped down the foundations of the dagobas (stupas) at Anuradhapura, and elephant iconography is common in Sri Lankan art. Even today elephants are held in great affection. Of those in captivity, the Maligawa tusker, who carries the sacred tooth relic for the Kandy Esala Perahera, is perhaps the most venerated of all. In the wild, one of Sri Lanka's most incredible wildlife events is 'the Gathering' in Minneriya National Park (p201).

Despite being held in high regard, Sri Lanka's elephant population has declined significantly. Their plight has become a powerful flashpoint in the ongoing debate about human–animal conflict.

Save the Elephants

» Don't feed them in the wild.

» Don't patronise places where they're in chains.

» Do visit them in national parks to support conservation.

Dwindling Numbers

At the end of the 18th century an estimated 10,000 to 20,000 elephants lived unfettered across Sri Lanka. By the mid-20th century small herds of the decimated population (perhaps as few as 1000) were clustered in the low-country dry zone. Natural selection had little to do with that cull: under the British big-game hunting delivered a mighty blow to elephant life expectancy. Today experts disagree about whether numbers are increasing or diminishing, but the population is believed to be between 3000 and 4000 in the wild, half of which live on protected land, plus about 300 domesticated animals.

Human–Elephant Conflict

Farmers in elephant country face an ever-present threat from animals that may eat or trample their crops, destroy their buildings and even take their lives. During the cultivation season, farmers maintain round-the-clock vigils for up to three months to scare off unwelcome raiders. For farmers on the breadline, close encounters with wild elephants are a luxury they can't afford.

Meanwhile, elephants, who need about 5 sq km of land each to support their 200kg-per-day appetites, no longer seem to have sufficient stock of food staples in the small wildlife safety zones where they are protected. Hunger (and perhaps curiosity) is driving them to seek fodder in other areas – manmade ones abutting their 'secure' habitats. The resulting conflict pits elephants against farmers – both just trying to secure their own survival.

TURTLES

Everything you ever wanted to know about sea turtles, including when and where to see them lay eggs, can be found at www.tcpsrilanka.org, the website of the Turtle Conservation Project of Sri Lanka.

Contributing to the vicious circle is unfortunate behaviour on both sides. Electric fences installed in the national parks to contain elephants have been knocked down by famers seeking to graze their cattle illegally on park land. Elephants leave the parks through the compromised fences and bedevil the farmers. Also, as can be seen at Uda Walawe National Park, vendors have set up fruit stands where the park borders the highway, so that tourists can feed the elephants. An increasing number of elephants now hang out all day by the roadside waiting for their tasty handouts. The idea of actually foraging for their normal diet is soon forgotten.

Possible Solutions

Some people are looking for long-term solutions to the conflict. One involves fencing *humans in*; or, rather, elephants out of human areas. This

SRI LANKA'S UNESCO WORLD HERITAGE SITES

» Cave temples at Dambulla (p185)

» Dutch fortifications at Galle (p94)

» Medieval capital of Polonnaruwa (p192)

» Royal city of Kandy (p133)

» Sacred city of Anuradhapura (p202)

» Sigiriya rock monastery (p188)

» Sinharaja Forest Reserve (p178)

» Central Highlands, encompassing the Sri Pada Peak Wilderness Reserve (p150), Horton Plains National Park (p163) and Knuckles Range (p150)

GREEN RESOURCES

For information on environmental issues in Sri Lanka, see the following websites.

» **Environment Sri Lanka** (www.environmentlanka.com) The Department of Forestry & Environmental Science at the University of Sri Jayewardenepura has info on Sri Lankan wildlife and essays on key environmental issues.

» **Green Movement of Sri Lanka** (www.greensl.net) A consortium of 150 groups that are involved in natural-resource management. Among the projects highlighted are the ongoing reports of the environmental threats posed by Sri Lanka's massive road-building schemes.

» **Lakdasun** (www.lakdasun.org) Visit the helpful forums on this website to get up-to-date information from knowledgeable Sri Lankan locals on how to 'Discover, explore and conserve the natural beauty of Sri Lanka'.

» **Sri Lanka Wildlife Conservation Society** (SLWCS; www.slwcs.org) Recognised by the UN in 2008 for community-based projects that made a tangible impact on poverty, the SLWCS has opportunities for volunteering. See p309 for more information on volunteering in Sri Lanka.

approach has been proven effective by the **Sri Lanka Wildlife Conservation Society** (SLWCS; www.slwcs.org), an award-winning wildlife conservation group. Another is to give farmers alternative livelihood solutions and land practices that incorporate elephants. The collection and commercial use of elephant dung is one such possible enterprise (you can see the resulting products at the Cottage Craft shop in Colombo). Spreading around the economic benefits that come from scores of visitors coming to see elephants is another solution.

The Nature of Sri Lanka, with stunning photographs by L Nadaraja, is a collection of essays about Sri Lanka by eminent writers and conservationists.

Responsible Travel in Sri Lanka

The best way to responsibly visit Sri Lanka is to try to be as minimally invasive as possible. This is of course easier than it sounds, but consider the following tips:

» **Demand green** Sri Lanka's hotel and guesthouse owners are especially accommodating and as visitor numbers soar, most are keen to give the customers what they want. Share your environmental concerns and tell your hosts that their green practices – or lack thereof – are very important to you.

» **Watch your use of water** Travel in the Hill Country of Sri Lanka and you'll think the island is coursing with water, but demand outstrips supply. Take up your hotel on its offer to save itself big money, er, no, to save lots of water, by not having your sheets and towels changed every day. Also, stay at places without pools. If you want a dip, stay at the beach; tell your host that you appreciate there *not* being a pool.

» **Don't hit the bottle** Those bottles of water are convenient but they add up and are a major blight. Still, you're wise not to refill from the tap, so what to do? Ask your hotel if you can refill from their huge containers of drinking water.

» **Conserve power** Sure you want to save your own energy on a sweltering afternoon, but using air-con strains an already overloaded system. Electricity demand in Sri Lanka is soaring. Try to save as much energy as possible and act as if you are paying your own electricity bill.

» **Don't drive yourself crazy** Can you take a bus or, even better, a train, instead of a hired car? Even Colombo is more walkable than you think, it's a very interesting stroll all the way from Cinnamon Gardens to Fort and it's better for the environment than a ride in an exhaust-spewing three-wheeler. And encourage the recent trend of hotels and guesthouses providing bikes for guests. Large swaths of Sri Lanka are best toured during the day on two wheels.

» **Bag the bags** Just say no to plastic bags (and plastic straws too). The clerk might look at you funny but you'll be doing your bit.

Largest surviving tracts of rainforest

» Peak Wilderness (250 sq km)

» Knuckles Range (175 sq km)

» Sinharaja (90 sq km)

People of Sri Lanka

Visitors to Sri Lanka notice first the gentleness of the land and people. White-domed dagobas (stupas) and rainbow-coloured Hindu temples pierce cobalt-blue skies, mosques call the faithful to prayer at dawn, and swaths of mist cling to rolling hills blanketed with tea plantations. People wander with flowers to temples, rows of women in yellow saris walk to *puja* (prayers) bringing offerings to their gods, and people greet visitors with warmth and hospitality.

Every so often, things are less gentle. Rivers swell, inundating the land and snatching lives. Ethnic violence explodes and more lives are lost and shattered, and poverty coexists uneasily with luxury. But Sri Lankans continue to balance this chaos and duality, and exude an alluring charm after having welcomed visitors for millennia. Different faiths and ethnicities have mixed and married, yet fascinating distinctions still exist. For the visitor, the overriding memory will be a nation of generosity and hospitality.

Tradition & Ethnicity

Traditional Sri Lankan life was centred on the *gamma* (village), a highly organised hub of activity, where everyone fulfilled specific roles. Agriculture was the mainstay, and some villages focused on particular products – even today you might pass through a 'cane-furniture *gamma*'. Every village had a protector deity (or several), usually associated with aspects of nature.

Veddahs

To understand historical and contemporary Veddah life and customs, see www.vedda.org.

The Veddahs (Hunters), also called the Wanniyala-aetto (People of the Forest), are Sri Lanka's original inhabitants. Each wave of migration to Sri Lanka left the Veddahs with less forest on which to subsist. Today they are fewer than 2000, and only a tiny percentage of those identify themselves as Veddah and retain a semblance of their old culture, which comprises a hunter-gatherer lifestyle and close relationships to nature and their ancestors. The Kele Weddo (jungle-dwelling Veddahs) and Can Weddo (village-dwelling Veddahs) live mainly in the area between Badulla, Batticaloa and Polonnaruwa.

Sinhalese

The predominantly Buddhist Sinhalese sometimes divide themselves into 'low country' and 'high country' (ie Kandyan). The Kandyan Sinhalese are proud of the time when the Hill Country was a bastion of Sinhalese rule, and still consider Kandy to be the island's spiritual hub. Although the Buddha taught universalism, the Sinhalese have a caste system, with everyone falling somewhere along the spectrum between aristocrat and itinerant entertainer.

Tamils

Most Tamils are Hindu and have cultural and religious connections with South Indian Tamils across the water, though they generally see themselves as discrete groups. So do Jaffna Tamils, who live mostly in the North and East, and 'Plantation Tamils', who were brought by the British from India in the 19th century to work on tea farms. For Hindus, caste is very important. Jaffna Tamils are mainly of the Vellala caste (landlords and blue bloods), while Plantation Tamils mainly come from lower castes. Times are changing, however, and traditional caste distinctions among both Sinhalese and Tamils are gradually eroding.

Want to understand more about people's names in Sri Lanka? It's all revealed at http://asiarecipe.com/srinames.html.

Muslims

The island's Muslims - called Sri Lankan Moors - are descendants of Arab or Indian traders who arrived around 1000 years ago. To escape Portuguese persecution, many moved into the Hill Country and the east coasts, and you'll still see predominantly Muslim towns like Hakgala near Nuwara Eliya.

Burghers

The Burghers are Eurasian descendants of the Portuguese, Dutch and British. Even after independence, Burghers had a disproportionate influence over political and business life, but as growing Sinhalese nationalism reduced their role in Sri Lankan life, many Burghers emigrated. Look out for surnames like Fernando, de Silva and Perera.

Religion

Religion has been the cause of much division in Sri Lanka, but the often-overlooked reality is that Sri Lanka's many religions mix openly. Buddhists, Hindus, Muslims and Christians visit many of the same pilgrimage sites, a Catholic may pay respect to a Hindu god, and Sri Lankan Buddhism has Hindu influences and vice versa. Think of it as spiritual insurance.

Equal-Opportunity Pilgrimages

- Adam's Peak
- Kataragama
- Nainativu

Buddhism

Buddhism is the belief system of the Sinhalese and plays a significant role in the country, spiritually, culturally and politically. Sri Lanka's literature, art and architecture are all strongly influenced by it. Strictly speaking, Buddhism is not a religion but a practice and a moral code espoused by the Buddha. Although now 'Buddhist' is a deeply entrenched cultural and ethnic identifier, the Buddha taught meditation to people of various religions, and emphasised that no conversion was necessary (or even recommended) to benefit from his teachings, also known as the Dhamma.

Born Prince Siddhartha Gautama in modern-day Nepal around 563 BC, the Buddha abandoned his throne to seek a way out of suffering. After many years of rigorous training, the Buddha discovered the 'Four Noble Truths': existence itself is suffering; suffering is caused by craving for sensual and material pleasures as well as existence itself; the way out of suffering is through eliminating craving; and craving can be eliminated by following a path of morality and the cultivation of wisdom through meditation. After many states of spiritual development - and probably, many lifetimes - nirvana (enlightenment, or *nibbana* in Pali) is achieved, bringing freedom from the cycle of birth and death.

Religious Hubs

- Nallur Kandaswamy Kovil, Jaffna
- Temple of the Sacred Tooth Relic, Kandy
- Kechimalai Mosque, Beruwela
- Our Lady of Madhu Church, Madhu

Historical Buddhism

King Devanampiya Tissa's acceptance of the Buddha's teaching in the 3rd century BC (p269) firmly implanted Buddhism in Sri Lanka, and a strong relationship developed between Sri Lanka's kings and the Buddhist clergy.

POYA DAYS

Poya, or *uposatha*, days, fall on each full moon and have been observed by monks and laypeople since the time of the Buddha as times to strengthen one's practice. Devout Buddhists visit a temple, fast after noon and abstain from entertainment and luxury. At their temple they may make offerings, attend teachings and meditate. *Poya* days are public holidays in Sri Lanka, and each is associated with a particular ritual.

Some notable days:

Durutu (January) Marks the Buddha's first supposed visit to the island.

Vesak (May) Celebrates the Buddha's birth, enlightenment and *parinibbana* (final passing away).

Poson (June) Commemorates Buddhism's arrival in Sri Lanka.

Esala (July/August) Sees the huge Kandy festival, which commemorates, among other things, the Buddha's first sermon.

Unduwap (December) Celebrates the visit of Sangamitta, who brought the bodhi tree sapling to Anuradhapura.

Worldwide there are two major schools of Buddhism – Theravada and Mahayana. Theravada (meaning 'way of the elders') scriptures are in Pali, the language spoken in North India in the Buddha's time, while Mahayana (Greater Vehicle) scriptures are in Sanskrit. Theravada is regarded as more orthodox, and Mahayana more inclusive of later traditions.

Mahayana Buddhism is practised in Sri Lanka, but the Theravada tradition is more widely adopted. Several factors have consolidated Buddhism (especially the Theravada stream) in Sri Lanka. Firstly, Sinhalese Buddhists attach vital meaning to the words of the Mahavamsa (Great Chronicle; one of their sacred texts), in which the Buddha designates them as the protectors of the Buddhist teachings. This commitment was fuelled by centuries of conflict between the Sinhalese (mainly Buddhist) and Tamils (mainly Hindu). For some Sinhalese, Mahayana Buddhism resembled Hinduism – and indeed was followed by many Tamils in early times – and therefore defence of the Theravada stream was considered crucial. Many Buddhist sites in India were destroyed in the 10th century AD, around the time of a Hindu resurgence (and a popular Hindu text that described the Buddha as a wayward incarnation of Vishnu), further reinforcing the Sinhalese commitment to protect the tradition.

Buddhist Nationalism

In *Buddhism: Beliefs and Practices in Sri Lanka*, Lynn de Silva combines lucid writing, fascinating information and a scholarly (but accessible) approach to shed light on the island's Buddhist tradition.

Since the late 19th century an influential strand of 'militant' Buddhism has developed in Sri Lanka, centred on the belief that the Buddha charged the Sinhalese people with making the island a citadel of Buddhism in its purest form. It sees threats to Sinhalese Buddhist culture in Christianity and Hinduism. Sri Lankan Buddhism is historically intertwined with politics, and it was a Buddhist monk, dissatisfied with Prime Minister SWRD Bandaranaike's 'drift' from a Sinhala-Buddhist focus, who assassinated him in 1959, in contradiction of the very first Buddhist precept against killing.

Today some Buddhist monks strongly oppose compromise with the Tamils. Hardline monks are also at the vanguard of Sinhalese nationalism, and in 2007 achieved a significant position of leverage in the Sri Lankan government through the Jathika Hela Urumaya (JHU or National Heritage Party). Conversely, many other monks are dedicated to the spirit of Buddhism, and are committed to the welfare of devotees.

Hinduism

Tamil kings and their followers from South India brought Hinduism to northern Sri Lanka, although the religion may have existed on the island well before the arrival of Buddhism, as a result of the island's proximity to India and the natural cultural exchange that would have taken place. Today Hindu communities are most concentrated in the tea plantation areas, the North and the East.

Hinduism is a complex mix of beliefs and gods. All Hindus believe in Brahman: the myriad deities are manifestations of this formless being, through which believers can understand all facets of life. Key tenets include belief in ahimsa (nonviolence), samsara (the recurring cycle of births and deaths until one reaches a pure state), karma (the law of cause and effect) and dharma (moral code of behaviour or social duty).

Hindus believe that living life according to dharma enhances the chance of being born into better circumstances. Rebirth can also take animal form, but it's only as a human that one may gain sufficient self-knowledge to escape the cycle of reincarnation and achieve moksha (liberation).

For ordinary Hindus, fulfilling one's ritual and social duties is the main aim of worldly life. According to the Hindu text Bhagavad Gita, doing your duty is more important than asserting your individuality.

For more information on Hinduism, see www.bbc.co.uk/religion/religions/hinduism or www.hinduismtoday.com.

The Hindu pantheon is prolific, and some estimates put the number of deities at 330 million. The main figures are Brahma, who created the universe, and his consort Saraswati, the goddess of wisdom and music; Vishnu, who sustains the universe, is lawful and devout, and his consort Lakshmi, the goddess of beauty and fortune; and Shiva, the destroyer of ignorance and evil, and his consort, Parvati, who can be the universal mother or the ferocious and destructive Kali. Shiva has 1008 names and takes many forms: as Nataraja, lord of the *tandava* (dance), his graceful movements begin the creation of the cosmos.

Islam

There are 1.8 million Sri Lankan Muslims, descendants of Arab traders who settled on the island from the 7th century, not long after Islam was founded in present-day Saudi Arabia by the Prophet Mohammed. Islam is monotheistic, and believes that everything has been created by Allah.

After Mohammed's death the movement split into two main branches, the Sunnis and the Shiites. Sunnis emphasise following and imitating the words and acts of the Prophet. They look to tradition and the majority views of the community. Shiites believe that only imams (exemplary leaders) can reveal the meaning of the Quran. Most of Sri Lanka's Muslims are Sunnis, although small communities of Shiites have migrated from India.

All Muslims believe in the five pillars of Islam: the shahada (declaration of faith: 'there is no God but Allah; Mohammed is his prophet'); prayer (ideally five times a day); the zakat (tax, usually a donation to charity); fasting during the month of Ramadan; and the haj (pilgrimage) to Mecca.

In Hindu mythology elephants are seen as symbols of water, life and fortune. They also signify nobility and gentleness, the qualities achieved when one lives a good life. In Sri Lanka, only the elephant gets to parade with sacred Buddhist relics and Hindu statues.

Christianity

Christianity in Sri Lanka potentially goes back to the Apostle Thomas in the 1st century AD, and it's certain that in the early centuries AD small numbers of Christians established settlements along the coast.

With the Portuguese in the 16th century, Christianity, specifically Roman Catholicism, arrived in force and many fishing families converted. Today Catholicism remains strong among western coastal communities. The Dutch brought Protestantism and the Dutch Reformed Church, mainly present in Colombo. Evidence of the British Christian denominations are seen in the quaint stone churches that dot the Hill Country landscape.

In recent years groups of radical Sinhalese nationalist Buddhist monks have been implicated in attacks on Christian churches and communities.

Sri Lankan Tea

But for misfortune, the world might be drinking 'Ceylon coffee' instead of tea.

Tea came to Sri Lanka when extensive coffee plantations were decimated by disease in the 19th century. The first Sri Lankan tea was grown in 1867 at the Loolecondera Estate southeast of Kandy by James Taylor (*not* the musician). Plantation owners discovered that the Hill Country combines warm climate, altitude and sloping terrain: a winning trifecta that's perfect for growing tea.

Tea actually first came to Sri Lanka in 1824 as part of a botanical exhibit planted by the British. Nobody had any idea what this would lead to.

Shipments of Ceylon tea began filling London warehouses in the 1870s. The public's thirst for a cuppa proved nearly unquenchable. Fortunes were made by the early growers, which included a name still famous worldwide today: Thomas Lipton. Read more about him in the boxed text, p164.

During the next several decades, tea production spiralled upwards. Rainforests were cleared and plantations greatly expanded. A running war was fought with various pests and diseases that afflicted the crops, and all manner of chemicals were created to keep the tea plants looking serene and green.

In a probably unintentional bit of honesty, Ceylon's main tea producers banded together and funded a marketing arm in 1932: it was called the Ceylon Tea Propaganda Board.

Sri Lanka overtook Kenya as the second most important tea-producing nation in 2008, with an annual production of 330 million kilograms. Sri Lankan tea (branded internationally as 'Ceylon' tea) enjoys a premium positioning and its auction sale prices are more than 50% higher than main rival and market leader India. The annual value of the Sri Lankan tea crop is nearing US$1 billion and it represents 15% of the economy.

Tea plantations cover about 1900 sq km. This is primarily in the Hill Country and adjoining regions, especially in the South.

Despite the British roots of the industry, most Ceylon tea today is exported to Eastern Europe and the Middle East, where the product is in enormous demand.

Besides the various forms of ubiquitous black tea, Sri Lanka produces green tea, which is known for its more pungent flavour, and white tea, which is among the most premium of teas and is often called 'silver tips'.

Regular commercial teas are usually made by blending various types to achieve a particular flavour associated with a product or brand.

Tea Workers

Sri Lanka's tea industry is responsible for more than one million jobs – about 5% of the entire population. Wages for tea pickers remain very low – around US$3 per day (two-thirds the minimum wage for government employees) – and the hardworking pickers must pick a minimum of 20kg of leaves per day. Compulsory pension and funeral payments erode already low wages, and many families live in seriously substandard housing. You see these barracks-like buildings down in gullies amid the plantations as you pass by on trails, roads or rail.

DRINKING TEA

Although tea is pretty forgiving, there are still right and wrong ways to prepare a cup. For maximum enjoyment, keep the following points in mind.

» Store tea in an airtight container, whether it is lose or in tea bags. It's prone to absorbing odours, which are especially harmful to some of the delicate blends or flavoured teas.

» Use fresh water and boil it (water that's been boiling for a while or which was previously boiled gives you a flat-tasting cup of tea).

» Too accustomed to tea bags? With loose tea, it's one teaspoon per average-sized cup plus one extra if you're making a pot.

» Let the tea brew. It takes three to five minutes for tea to fully release its flavour.

» Conversely, once the tea is brewed, toss the tea leaves, whether they were loose or in a tea bag. Tea leaves quickly get bitter once brewed.

» For milk tea, pour the milk into the cup and then add the tea: the flavours mix better.

The vast majority of tea workers are Tamils. Originally the British tea barons of the 1870s intended to hire Sinhalese but the work was unappealing to the locals, so the plantation owners looked to India. Huge numbers of Tamils were brought over and today, most tea workers are Tamils.

Seeing Tea

A great introduction to the endless rolling green fields of the Hill Country's tea plantations is riding the train from Ella to Haputale. In just a few hours you'll see dozens of plantations and their emerald-green carpets of plants. Amid it all you'll see the brightly garbed workers toiling under the sun, busily meeting their quotas for the day.

Tea factories and plantations throughout the Hill Country provide tours to explain the process, usually using machinery and technology that are largely unchanged since the 19th century. Some of our favourite places to get up close and smell the tea are listed on p290.

Sleeping with Tea

Near Adam's Peak in the Hill Country, you can stay in a variety of colonial-era cottages that were used by tea-plantation managers. Located in beautiful settings, they are attractive and evocative places to sleep somewhere out of the ordinary; see the boxed text, p153.

Many more guesthouses, bungalows and hotels located in the midst of tea plantations can be found throughout the Hill Country chapter.

Getting Active with Tea

There are all manner of hikes, treks and rides through the Hill Country's tea regions. Here some of our favourites.

» A 10km bicycle ride through tea plantations that begins in Nuwara Eliya.

» A 7km walk through tea plantations to mountain-lookout Lipton's Seat near Haputale.

» A 4.5km walk through lush tea plants and verdant hills to the lookout at Little Adam's Peak near Ella.

The health benefits of drinking tea are considerable. Organic green tea has more than six times the level of antioxidants than spinach or cauliflower. Pretty good news if you're not a big fan of vegetables.

Buying Tea

Tea is inexpensive, easy to pack and much loved by most everyone so it makes an excellent gift for others at home – or yourself. The tea factories and plantations in the Hill Country have a bewildering array of options on offer. There are also many good shops in Colombo; other highly recommended tea stores are listed on p293.

Producing Tea

Tea bushes are pruned back to around 1m in height and squads of Tamil tea pluckers (all women) move through the rows of bushes picking the leaves and buds. These are then 'withered' (demoisturised by blowing air at a fixed temperature through them) either in the old-fashioned multistorey tea factories, where the leaves are spread out on hessian mats, or in modern mechanised troughs. You'll spot the huge factory buildings throughout tea-growing country. Many are over 100 years old.

The partly dried leaves are then crushed, starting a fermentation process. The green leaves quickly turn a coppery brown as additional heat is applied. The art in tea production comes in knowing when to stop the fermentation, by 'firing' the tea at an even higher heat to produce the final, brown-black leaf that will be stable for a reasonable length of time.

The workers who regulate the myriad variables to take a day's pickings and produce proper tea, which will demand the premium prices Sri Lankan tea producers count on, are high up the ladder on the plantations. There is a definite art to the process that has been refined over decades.

From the time tea is picked until it is finished being processed and placed in bags for shipment takes only 24 hours.

1

BEST TEA PLANTATIONS & FACTORIES

» **Tea Museum** Near Kandy, an informative early stop in your tea tour of Sri Lanka (p137)

» **Labookellie Tea Factory** A factory well positioned by the Nuwara Eliya road if you're in a hurry (p155)

» **Pedro Tea Estate** Also near Nuwara Eliya, has tours of the factory, which was originally built in 1885 (p156)

» **Dambatenne Tea Factory** Near Haputale; built by Sir Thomas Lipton in 1890 and offers full-on tours (p166)

Clockwise from top left

1. Plucked tea leaves **2.** Tea fields around Maskeliya **3.** Bags of fresh tea leaves **4.** Tea awaiting distribution

2

KEVIN CLOGSTOUN / LONELY PLANET IMAGES ©

3

KIMBERLEY COOLE / LONELY PLANET IMAGES ©

1

3

KIMBERLEY COOLE / LONELY PLANET IMAGES ©

GILLIANNE TEDDER / LONELY PLANET IMAGES ©

Types of Tea

The many varieties of tea are graded by size (from cheap 'dust' through fannings and broken grades to 'leaf' tea) and by quality (with names such as flowery, pekoe or souchong). Obviously tea sized as dust is rather inferior. Anything graded in the leaf category is considered the minimum designation for respectable tea. In terms of quality designations, whole leaves are best and the tips (the youngest and most delicate tea leaves) are the very best.

The familiar name pekoe is a superior grade of black tea. Interestingly, there is no definitive record of where the 'orange' in the popular orange pekoe moniker comes from. It definitely has nothing to do with flavour but rather is either an artefact of a designation used by early Dutch tea traders or a reference to the colour of the leaves when dried. Either way, orange pekoe is a very superior grade of Ceylon black tea.

But tea grading doesn't stop there. It is further categorised into low-grown, mid-grown or high-grown. The low-grown teas (under 600m) grow strongly and are high in 'body' but low in 'flavour'. The high-grown teas (over 1200m) grow more slowly and are renowned for their subtle flavour. Mid-grown tea is something between the two.

Nuwara Eliya is at the heart of high-grown tea country. The teas produced around Kandy define mid-grown tea, while those found in the hills just inland of the south coast are low-grown.

BEST TEA SHOPS

» **Sri Lanka Tea Board Shop** In Colombo, has a wide range of teas from most of the country's producers (p69)

» **Mlesna Tea Centre** High-quality teas and a cafe in Bandarawela (p169)

» **Orchid House** In Galle, a fine tea shop with good incense too (p102)

» **Chaplin Tea Centres** In Bentota and Unawatuna; have a good range of teas

Clockwise from top left

1. Fresh tea leaves **2.** Dried tea leaves **3.** Tea tasting

A Taste of Sri Lanka

Sri Lanka boasts a unique and exciting cuisine, shaped by the island's bounty and the influence of traders, immigrants and colonisers. In a world awash with more well-known cuisines, like Indian, Thai and Vietnamese, Sri Lankan cuisine is little known. If the rest of the world had the chance to revel in a great rice and curry, that would surely change, but until then...

The distinctiveness of the island's cuisine comes from the freshness of its herbs and spices and the methods used to grind, pound, roast, temper and combine them. Roasting the spices a little more, or a little less, delivers a very different outcome. The oil that distributes the flavours may be vegetable, sesame or, for a richer taste, coconut. Varieties of rice offer unique textures, fragrances and flavours. Curries may be prepared within delicious sauces, or they may be 'dry'.

Dos & Don'ts

» Always use your right hand for eating.

» Hold a glass in your left hand.

» Remove your shoes before a meal at a home.

Regional differences in cuisine are more about availability of ingredients than ethnicity. In the North the palmyra tree reigns, and its roots, flowers, fruits and seeds produce dishes ranging from curries to syrups, sweets, cakes and snacks. In the South rice is considered indispensable; fish and jackfruit are popular, too. In the fertile Hill Country there are vegetables and mutton, but fewer fish and spices.

In all parts of the country, the influence of outsiders is never far from the menu. Muslim restaurants serve up perfect flatbreads and samosas introduced by Arab traders. Celebratory cakes often have a Dutch or Portuguese touch, and deliciously sweet desserts concocted from jaggery (brown sweet made from the *kitul* palm), coconut milk, cloves and cardamom are redolent of Malay traders from the spice islands further east.

The Joy of Rice

Rice is the staple of Sri Lankan cuisine, and it is usually served at every meal – plain, spiced, in meat juices, with curd (buffalo-milk yoghurt) or tamarind, or with milk. Different varieties are cooked with subtle spices.

Rice flour is the basis of two popular dishes: hoppers (also called *ah-ppa* or *appam*), which are bowl-shaped pancakes, and dosas *(thosai)*. These paper-thin pancakes are usually served stuffed with spiced vegetables.

Popular breakfasts include hoppers, bread dipped in curry, and *pittu*, a mixture of rice flour and coconut steamed in a bamboo mould. *Kola kanda* (porridge of rice, coconut, green vegetables and herbs) is very nutritious.

Rice & Curry

On almost every menu, Sri Lankan rice and curry comprises small spiced dishes made from vegetables, meat or fish, and served with chutneys and *sambol,* a condiment made from ingredients pounded with chilli.

Most curries include chilli, turmeric, cinnamon, cardamom, coriander, *rampe* (pandanus leaves), curry leaves, mustard, tamarind and coconut milk. Dried fish is also frequently used to season dishes.

Because Sri Lankan food takes time to prepare, order early in the day and leave the cooks to work their magic. Also note that many restaurants only serve rice and curry at lunch so if you want it for dinner, you'll need to arrange it.

Once the plethora of little dishes that comprise a rice and curry arrive, deciding what to sample first will be a major challenge. It's a freshly prepared personal banquet, and the variation of dishes from one cook to the next is astonishing. Maybe the sweet-and-sour eggplant, the surprisingly subtle garlic curry, the velvety dhal, the marinated long beans...

Vegetarian Food

» Widely available.

» Curries made from banana, banana flower, breadfruit, jackfruit, mangoes, potatoes, beans and pumpkins.

» Many short eats, including *rotti* and samosas, have vegetarian versions.

Fish & Seafood

Excellent fish and prawns are widespread, and in many coastal towns you'll find crab and lobster. Seer, a tuna-type fish, is a favourite. A southern speciality is the popular *ambulthiyal* (sour fish curry), made with *goraka,* a sour fruit. A simple grilled fish is usually a less challenging alternative than the fiery flavours of Sri Lankan cuisine.

Other Specialities

Chilli lovers will thrive on 'devilled' dishes, where meat is infused with chilli. A great snack with a cold Lion beer is a bowl of devilled cashews. Even the simplest cafe will often prepare these hot and fresh, or look for them sold by roadside vendors.

Lamprais is made from rice, meat and vegetables, all slowly baked in a banana leaf; open the leaf to release the aroma and tempt the senses. The name comes from the Dutch word *lomprijst,* and the dish dates back to the first Dutch settlers in the 17th century.

Simple restaurants – confusingly called 'hotels' – cater to locals with a basic but utterly tasty menu of rice and curry.

Desserts & Sweets

Wattalappam (*vattalappam* in Tamil), a coconut-milk and egg pudding with jaggery and cardamom, is a favourite dessert, while curd with *kitul* (syrup from the *kitul* palm; also called treacle) is good at any time.

SPICY SRI LANKA

Sri Lankan food has a reputation for being absurdly spicy, a label that seems to have been perpetuated by generations of visitors unaccustomed to fiery tingles.

Having endured centuries of tourist complaints about spicy food, Sri Lankans have tempered it for Western palates. In fact connoisseurs of authentically seasoned food may have a bit of a struggle to get their meals prepared in local style. Just asking for 'hot' will get a knowing smile from the server and slightly more heat. To get things truly authentic, you may have to show your great joy at spiciness at one meal by using all the spicy condiments and then return for another meal while requesting that the food be cooked as the server or chef likes it.

Some Sri Lankan dishes may be spicy but in terms of heat, you'll find the same level of heat in cuisines worldwide. If you feel the urge to add some spice to your food, ask for these two condiments (and earn the respect of your server):

» **Pol sambol** A savoury chilli and coconut creation that is dry and powdery.

» **Chilli paste** A delicious mix of chilli seeds, spices and often a little fruit that is heated on a hot skillet to release the flavours.

DRINKS

Sri Lanka's heat means that refreshing beverages are an important – and vital – part of the day's consumption.

» Tea with spoonfuls of sugar is the locally preferred way to drink the indigenous hot drink. If you don't have a sweet tooth, be very assertive about lowering the sugar dose. For more on tea, see p288.

» Coffee, while not traditionally favoured, is now literally a hot commodity in Colombo and some other large towns. Cafes with full-on espresso machines are popular. Elsewhere, be prepared for instant, or something fresh that tastes like instant.

» Lime juice is excellent. Have it with soda water, but ask for the salt or sugar to be separate. If not, you could be in for another serious sugar hit.

» Indian restaurants and sweet shops are a good spot for a *lassi* (yoghurt drink).

» Ginger beer is old school, very British and offers refreshment with a zing – look out for the Elephant or Lion brands.

» *Thambili* (king coconut) juice still in the husk is on sale at roadside stalls everywhere.

Alcoholic Drinks

» Locally brewed Lion Lager is a crisp and refreshing brew that is widely sold.

» Three Coins and Anchor are less delicious local lagers. The licensed versions of international brands like Carlsberg, Heineken and Corona offer no surprise at all.

» Lion sells a very good stout, with coffee and chocolate flavours and a hearty 8% alcohol content.

» Toddy, a drink made from the sap of palm trees, has a sharp taste, a bit like cider. There are three types: toddy made from coconut palms, toddy from *kitul* palms and toddy from palmyras.

» Arrack is fermented and (somewhat) refined toddy. It can have a powerful kick and give you a worse hangover. The best mixer for arrack is the local ginger ale.

Hardened *kitul* is jaggery, a candy and all-purpose sweetener. Little freshly made sweets sold as snacks are hugely popular and their variations are infinite. Don't miss the popular Bombay-style candy shops on Galle Rd in Colombo.

Fruit

Sri Lanka's largely tropical climate supports many fruits, including avocados, mangoes (those in the north are considered the juiciest), melons, pineapples and guavas. At breakfast don't forget to add a squeeze of lime to your morning papaya.

The beautifully produced *Sri Lankan Flavours* by talented chef Channa Dassanayaka offers recipes and personal stories of Sinhalese people and food.

The wooden-shelled woodapple is used for refreshing drinks, dessert toppings and jam. British writer Anthony Burgess reckoned the spiky-skinned durian tasted 'like eating sweet raspberry blancmange in the lavatory' – definitely an acquired taste, but worth trying by adventurous foodies. Rambutan is so prized that growers guard their trees to outwit poachers.

In season from July to September, mangosteen tastes like strawberries and grapes combined. The jackfruit, with its orange-yellow segments, is the world's biggest fruit. It tastes good fresh, or cooked up in a curry where it assumes the consistency of chicken.

You'll find these fruits and more at the central food markets found in almost every town. Just look for the enormous bunches of bananas that add a huge swath of yellow to the roadside.

Short Eats

The midday joy of Sri Lankan cuisine, short eats are meat-stuffed rolls, meat-and-vegetable patties (called cutlets), pastries and *vadai* (deep-fried snacks made from lentil flour and spices).

You order short eats from a counter and take them away, or you can sit down – if there are chairs. At some places, a plate of short eats is placed on your table, and you're only charged for what you eat. Most bakeries run on a 'two batches a day' system, with piping-hot baked goodies coming out of the wood-fired ovens around 7.30am and 2pm daily. However, the best and most popular places (many reviewed in this book) have new batches appearing throughout the day.

Don't miss the wildly popular local fast food *kotthu rotti,* a doughy pancake (*rotti*) that is chopped and fried with fillings ranging from chilli and onion to vegetables, bacon and egg. Outlets abound; one of the best is Hotel De Pilawoos in Colombo (p65). Elsewhere, look for streetside huts (called *kadé* or boutiques by the Sinhalese, and *unavakam* by Tamils). You'll soon become attuned to the evening chop-chop sounds of the *kotthu rotti* maker. Along with the nasal whine of a three-wheeler, it's one of the sounds that will define your trip to Sri Lanka.

Also available from the *kadé* and bakeries are lunch packets. These self-contained food parcels are sold all over the country between 11am and 2pm. Inside you'll usually find rice, curry (generally chicken, fish or beef, though if you're vegetarian, you'll get an egg), curried vegetables and *sambol.* Expect to pay around Rs 125 to 200.

CINNAMON

Cinnamon is native to Sri Lanka, and was exported to China and Egypt by Arab traders as early as 2000 BC. More than 80% of the world's cinnamon is still grown in Sri Lanka.

Celebrations

As a symbol of life and fertility, rice is the food for festivities. The Buddha is said to have derived energy from *kiri bath* (coconut-milk rice). *Kiri bath* is a baby's first solid food, and is also the food newlywed couples feed each other.

Dumplings are popular for celebrations, and in northern Sri Lanka the revelry includes gently dropping *kolukattai* (dumplings with edges pressed to resemble teeth) on a toddler's head while the family make wishes for the infant to develop healthy teeth. Sweet dumplings, *mothagam,* are offered to Ganesh in prayer.

Hindus celebrate the harvest at Thai Pongal in January. *Pongal* (milk boiled with rice and jaggery) is offered to the sun god in thanksgiving. The rice is then eaten in celebration of the harvest and its life-sustaining qualities.

Ramadan ends with the breaking of the fast and the Eid-ul-Fitr festival. Muslims eat dates in memory of the Prophet Mohammed, and then *congee* (rice cooked with spices, coconut milk and meat). On Eid-ul-Fitr, Muslims share food with family, friends and neighbours.

Aurudu (Sri Lankan New Year) is another time for celebration. After the sacred activities, feasting begins with *kiri bath* followed by *kaung* (oil cake), a Sri Lankan favourite. Food is always shared at New Year, stressing harmony among family, friends and neighbours.

Alcohol isn't sold on *poya* (full-moon) holidays. You can stock up in advance and keep your beer cold in your room's fridge, or some especially affable guest-houses will sell you a beer 'under the table'.

Scrumptious Sri Lanka

With an island as rich in spices and ingredients as Sri Lanka, it's no surprise its foods burst with a panoply of flavours. Celebrating food is part of the culture and people spend many hours producing extraordinary dishes that are a key part of everyday life.

Hoppers

1 These bowl-shaped pancakes are a joy to behold. Skilled cooks artfully use rice flour to create these delicate bowls. Crispy and wafer-thin, they are the ideal venue for all manner of savoury fillings.

Short Eats

2 A traveller's best friend at lunch, these ubiquitous snacks are sold across the country in dizzying variety. Typically deep-fried and sold at stands, stalls or from street vendors, short eats can be samosas, crispy patties, stuffed rolls and more.

Curry & Rice

3 The national dish is anything but a cliché. It's a banquet for the masses – you're presented with up to a dozen (or even more) small dishes of vegetables and usually meats that have been prepared myriad ways.

Wattalappam

4 The signature dessert of Sri Lanka's north, *wattalappam* is a delicious pudding made from coconut milk and eggs. Various spices such as cardamom give it a flavour that's both unique and addictive. It's an important part of Tamil ceremonies.

Kotthu Rotti

5 There is no one way to make this favourite national dish. You start with some *rotti* and chop it up before it goes in the frying pan; after that, what's best added to the mix is endlessly debated.

Clockwise from top left
1. Hopper with egg and *sambol* **2.** Vegetable-filled *rotti*
3. Breakfast of string hopper, egg curry and potato curry

2

OLIVER STREWE / LONELY PLANET IMAGES ©

RHONDA GUTENBERG / LONELY PLANET IMAGES ©

Survival Guide

Directory A–Z

Accommodation

Sri Lanka has all types of accommodation ranging from rooms in family homes to five-star resorts. As tourism booms, expect the range and quality of choices to increase right along with prices. Wherever you stay be sure to bargain over the price as negotiation is common. Online booking sites mostly represent higher-end choices, although this too is changing.

Rates are very seasonal, particularly at beach resorts. The prices quoted in this guide are typical high-season rates; look for good discounts in the low season. The high season is December to April on the west and south coasts, and April to September on the east coast.

Some midrange and top-end hotels quote room prices in US dollars or euros, but accept the rupee equivalent. Note that a service charge of 10% will usually be added to the rate you're quoted. At more expensive hotels an additional Value Added Tax (VAT) of 15% is added. Reviews in this book include the addition of both service charge and VAT.

Types of Accommodation

Guesthouses and hotels provide the majority of places to sleep in Sri Lanka. In rural areas, almost every place is a guesthouse. The difference is that hotels will usually be larger and offer more services beyond a friendly person minding the desk. Often guesthouses are family-run. Their budget siblings are family stays, where you literally stay in a family compound which has a couple of budget rooms for travellers.

Almost every place to stay can provide meals. Note that it's easy to stumble upon places that are quite inferior, whether it's guesthouses renting rooms by the hour or top-end hotels that have ossified. There are almost always better choices nearby, so look around.

BUDGET

There are budget guesthouses and a few budget hotels across Sri Lanka; they vary widely in standards and price.

Expect the following amenities:

» fans in most rooms, air-con in only one or two, if any (fans are fine in the Hill Country and right on the beach)

» maybe hot water

» private bathroom with shower and sit-down flush toilet

» simple breakfast

» laissez-faire but cheery staff.

MIDRANGE

Midrange guesthouses and hotels are the most common choices throughout Sri Lanka. Most provide a decent level of comfort, although some can be quite nice with a range of services and views. Look for well-run colonial-era places, of which a few are left.

PRICE RANGES

The following price ranges refer to a double room with bathroom in high season. Unless otherwise stated, rooms come with a fan, and tax is included in the price.

$ less than Rs 2500
$$ Rs 2500 to 8000
$$$ more than Rs 8000

BOOK YOUR STAY ONLINE

For more accommodation reviews by Lonely Planet authors, check out http://hotels.lonelyplanet.com. You'll find independent reviews, as well as recommendations on the best places to stay. Best of all, you can book online.

Expect the following amenities:

» maybe a balcony/porch/patio
» satellite TV
» small fridge
» air-con in most if not all rooms
» maybe wi-fi
» maybe a pool.

TOP-END HOTELS

Top-end hotels range from small stylish boutique affairs in colonial mansions to lavish five-star resorts.

Expect the following amenities:

» good service
» usually enticing views – ocean, lush valleys and rice fields or private gardens
» usually a pool
» spa.

Villa rentals are in their infancy but you'll find some along the south coast with many more likely to follow. Speciality accommodation includes the former homes of British tea-estate managers in the Hill Country, which have been converted into guesthouses or hotels, often with beautiful gardens and antique-stuffed living rooms.

Business Hours

In this book it is assumed that standard hours are as follows. Significant variations are noted in listings.

Banks 8am to 3pm Monday to Friday

Government and private offices, post offices 8am to 4.30pm Monday to Friday (but they are not standardised)

Restaurants and cafes 7am to 10pm daily, especially in areas popular with travellers

Shops 10am to 7pm Monday to Friday, 10am to 3pm Saturday

Shops and services catering to visitors 9am to 8pm

Bars usually close by midnight and last call is often a sobering 11pm.

Customs Regulations

Sri Lanka has the usual list of prohibited imports, including drugs, weapons, fresh fruit and anything remotely pornographic.

Items allowed:

» 0.25L of perfume
» 1.5L of alcohol.

There are duty-free shops in the arrivals area before you reach baggage claim at the airport.

For more details, check **Sri Lanka Customs** (www.customs.gov.lk).

Discount Cards

An International Student ID Card is not widely recognised in Sri Lanka.

Electricity

The electric current is 230V, 50 cycles. Plugs come in a bewildering range of variations. Besides the primary plug type shown here, you may well find US, EU and British-style plugs in your room.

Adaptors are readily available at markets, supermarkets and tourist shops for under Rs 100.

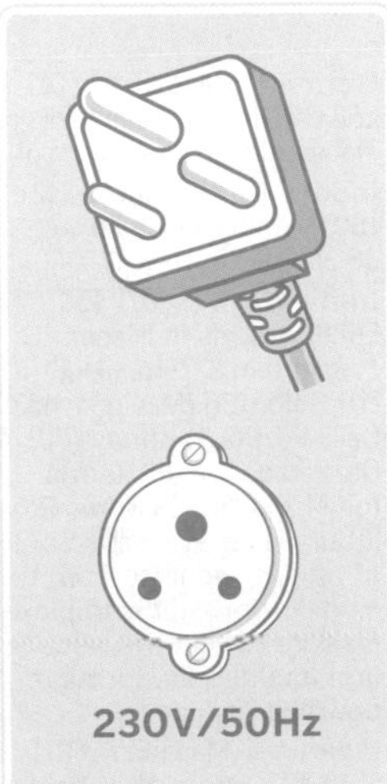

Embassies & Consulates

It's important to realise the limits to what your embassy can do if you're in trouble. Generally speaking, their hands are tied if you've broken Sri Lankan law. In real emergencies you might get some assistance, but only if all other channels have been exhausted. Embassies can recommend hospitals and dentists.

Unless indicated, the following embassies are in Colombo:

Australia (Map p54; ☎011-246 3200; www.srilanka.embassy.gov.au; 21 Gregory's Rd, Col 7)

Canada (Map p54; ☎011-532 6232; www.srilanka.gc.ca; 33-A 5th Lane, Col 03)

France (Map p54; ☎011-269 8815; www.ambafrance-lk.org; 89 Rosmead Pl, Col 7)

THE VERY TOP END

Sri Lanka has some beautiful rental villas, old colonial mountain retreats and other luxurious and exclusive accommodation options. Three local agents are good places to start you browsing/dreaming:

Boutique Sri Lanka (www.boutiquesrilanka.com)
Carolanka (www.carolanka.co.uk)
Sri Lanka In Style (www.srilankainstyle.com)

PRICE RANGES

The following price rangers refer to a standard main course.

$ less than Rs 250

$$ Rs 250 to 800

$$$ more than Rs 800

Germany (Map p54; ☎011-258 0431; www.colombo.diplo.de; 40 Alfred House Ave, Col 3)

India (Map p54; ☎011-242 1605; www.hcicolombo.org; 36-38 Galle Rd, Col 3)

India Visas (☎011-450 5588; www.vfs-in-lk.com; ⏲8am-1pm & 2-4pm Mon-Fri) Colombo (Map p54; 433 Galle Rd, Col 3) Kandy (701/A Old Peradeniya Rd) Jaffna (off Map p250; 89 Brown Rd) Indian visas are issued out of offices separate from the high commission complex. Be sure to visit the website first as there are forms to download online.

Maldives (Map p62; ☎011-551 6302; www.maldiveshighcom.lk; 25 Melbourne Ave, Col 4)

Netherlands (Map p54; ☎011-251 0200; http://srilanka.nlambassade.org; 25 Torrington Ave, Col 7)

UK (British High Commission; Map p54; ☎011-539 0639; http://ukinsrilanka.fco.gov.uk; 389 Bauddhaloka Mw, Col 7)

USA (Map p54; ☎011-249 8500; http://colombo.usembassy.gov; 210 Galle Rd, Col 3)

Food

See A Taste of Sri Lanka (p294) for information about Sri Lankan food.

Gay & Lesbian Travellers

Male homosexual activity is illegal in Sri Lanka (there is no law against female homosexuality), and the subject is not discussed publicly. No one has been convicted for over 60 years, but it pays to be discreet.

The situation is changing, and Colombo has a low-key scene. You can be more open in cosmopolitan areas like Col 1, Col 3 and Col 7.

Equal Ground (☎011-567 9766; www.equal-ground.org), a Colombo-based organisation supporting gay and lesbian rights, sponsors pride events, offers counselling services and has useful online publications.

Health

While the potential dangers of Sri Lankan travel may seem ominous, most travellers experience nothing more serious than an upset stomach. Travellers tend to worry about contracting infectious diseases, but infections rarely cause *serious* illness or death in travellers. Note that hygiene standards are casual at best and downright bad at worst in many kitchens throughout the country.

Availability & Cost of Health Care

Medical care is hugely variable in Sri Lanka. Colombo has some good clinics aimed at expats; they may be more expensive than local medical facilities, but they're worth using because a superior standard of care is offered.

Self-treatment may be appropriate if your problem is minor (eg traveller's diarrhoea). If you think you may have a serious disease, especially malaria, do not waste time: travel to the nearest quality facility to receive attention. It is always better to be assessed by a doctor than to rely on self-treatment.

Before buying medication over the counter, always check the use-by date and ensure the packet is sealed. Colombo and larger towns all have good pharmacies; most medications can be purchased without a prescription.

Health Insurance

Even if you're fit and healthy, don't travel without health insurance: accidents do happen. A travel or health insurance policy is essential. You may require extra cover for adventure activities, such scuba diving. If your normal health insurance doesn't cover you for medical expenses abroad, get extra insurance. If you're uninsured, emergency evacuation is expensive, and bills of more than US$100,000 are not uncommon.

Vaccinations

Specialised travel-medicine clinics stock all available vaccines and can give specific recommendations for your trip. The doctors will consider factors including past vaccination history, your trip's duration, activities you may be undertaking and underlying medical conditions such as pregnancy.

REQUIRED VACCINATIONS

The only vaccine required by international regulations is yellow fever. Proof of vaccination will only be required if you have visited a country in the yellow-fever zone within the six days before entering Sri Lanka.

RECOMMENDED VACCINATIONS

The World Health Organization (WHO) recommends the following vaccinations for travellers to Sri Lanka (as well as being up to date with measles, mumps and rubella vaccinations).

Adult diphtheria and tetanus Single booster recommended if none in the previous 10 years.

Hepatitis A Provides almost 100% protection for up to a year.

Hepatitis B Now considered routine for most travellers.

Polio Incidence has been unreported in Sri Lanka for several years but must be assumed to be present.

Rabies Three injections in all. A booster after one year will then provide 10 years' protection.

Typhoid Recommended for all travellers to Sri Lanka, even if you only visit urban areas.

Varicella If you haven't had chickenpox, discuss this vaccination with your doctor.

Water

The water is not safe to drink from any tap. Use bottled or filtered water; for the former, look for the small round 'SLSI' logo which shows the water has been tested by the government's Sri Lanka Standards Institution (about two-thirds of local brands).

PRACTICALITIES

» Sri Lanka has several daily newspapers in English, they can be entertaining reads, whether intentionally so or not. Try a few to find your favourite.

» Sri Lanka government-run stations dominate the radio and TV broadcast channels. Midrange and more expensive hotels usually have satellite TV with international networks.

» Sri Lanka uses the international metric system, though some Sri Lankans still express distance in yards and miles. The term *lakh* is often used in place of '100,000'.

» Smoking is not common in Sri Lanka, mostly due to the cost. Smoking is outlawed on buses, trains and public places. Bars and restaurants are legally required to have separate smoking and nonsmoking sections, although these often merge. The legal age for purchasing tobacco products is 21.

Insurance

Unless you are definitely sure that your health coverage at home will cover you in Sri Lanka, you should take out travel insurance – bring a copy of the policy as evidence that you're covered.

Worldwide travel insurance is available at www.lonelyplanet.com/travel_services. You can buy, extend and claim online anytime – even if you're already on the road.

Internet Access

Internet facilities are available across Sri Lanka. In the smallest of towns, look around the bus stand.

Access in Colombo and provincial towns and cities is cheap (around Rs 100 per hour); in tourist areas and on the coast costs can increase to around Rs 150 per hour.

Wi-fi in guesthouses and hotels is becoming common in Colombo and touristed areas of the coasts and inland areas. It's often free, except at some top-end places which can charge excessive rates. Connection speeds are acceptable – but don't expect to stream a film.

In the North and more remote areas elsewhere, guesthouses may only have a 3G dongle for your internet connection. This requires that your device has a USB port.

Legal Matters

Sri Lanka's legal system is a complex, almost arcane mix of British, Roman-Dutch and national law. The legal system tends to move slowly, and even a visit to a police station to report a small theft can involve a whole lot of time-consuming filling out of forms. The tourist police in major towns and tourist hotspots should be your first point of contact in the case of minor matters such as theft.

Drug use, mainly locally grown marijuana, but also imported heroin and methamphetamine, is common in tourist centres such as Hikkaduwa, Negombo and Unawatuna. Dabbling is perilous; you can expect to end up in jail if you're caught using anything illegal.

Maps

Basic free maps can be found among brochure racks at hotels; however, their usefulness is limited. If you are touring, you may wish for something more detailed and accurate. Consider the following, which are sold internationally:

» Nelles Verlag *Sri Lanka*
» Periplus *Sri Lanka*

You can find good maps at Colombo's bookshops (p70), otherwise sourcing maps locally will be difficult. Most Colombo bookshops sell the highly useful *A to Z Colombo,* which also has details for other Sri Lankan cities.

Money

The Sri Lankan currency is the rupee (Rs), divided into 100 cents, although these days pricing in cents is rare. Rupee coins come in denominations of one, two, five and 10 rupees. Notes come in denominations of 10, 20, 50, 100, 200, 500, 1000 and 2000 rupees.

ATMs

ATMs are common in Colombo and other cities such as Kandy. Larger towns will have at least one and often more. ATMs often issue Rs 500 and 1000 notes. Try and break them as soon as possible as small vendors may not accept large notes:

you can usually do this inside the bank that operates the ATM.

Cash

Any bank or exchange bureau will change major currencies in cash, including US dollars, euros and British pounds. Change rupees back into hard currency at the airport (before security) prior to leaving, as even nearby countries may not exchange Sri Lankan currency.

Credit Cards

MasterCard and Visa are the most commonly accepted credit cards. Amex and Diners Club are also accepted. Cards are generally accepted at some midrange and most top-end hotels and restaurants.

Moneychangers

Moneychangers can be found in Colombo and major tourist centres. They generally don't charge commission and their rates are competitive. Unlicensed moneychangers trade currency at slightly better rates than officially licensed moneychangers. They're not worth the very real risk in getting ripped off. ATMs are safer and more reliable.

Tipping

Although a 10% service charge is added to food and accommodation bills, this usually goes straight to the owner rather than the worker. Drivers expect a tip, as do people who 'guide' you through a site (in these cases you should make certain that a fee is discussed in advance). A rule of thumb is to tip 10% of the total amount due. Also appropriate is Rs 20 for the person who minds your shoes at temples, and Rs 50 for a hotel porter.

AYURVEDA

Ayurveda (eye-your-veda) is an ancient system of medicine using herbs, oils, metals and animal products to heal and rejuvenate. Influenced by the system of the same name in India, Ayurveda is widely used in Sri Lanka for a range of ailments.

Ayurveda postulates that the five elements (earth, air, ether, water and light) are linked to the five senses, which in turn shape the nature of an individual's constitution – his or her *dosha* (life force). Disease and illness occurs when the *dosha* is out of balance. The purpose of Ayurvedic treatment is to restore the balance.

For full-on therapeutic treatments, patients must be prepared to make a commitment of weeks or months. It's a gruelling regimen featuring frequent enemas and a bare minimum diet of simple vegetable-derived calories.

Much more commonly, tourists treat themselves at Ayurvedic massage centres attached to major hotels and in popular tourist centres. Full treatments take up to three hours and include the following relaxing regimens:

» Herbal saunas (Sweda Karma) are based on a 2500-year-old design. The plaster walls are infused with herbal ingredients, including honey and sandalwood powder. The floor of the sauna is covered with herbs. Like a European sauna, a steady mist of medicinal steam is maintained with water sprinkled onto hot coals.

» The steam bath (Vashpa Swedanam) looks like a cross between a coffin and a torture chamber. Patients lie stretched out on a wooden platform, and a giant hinged door covers the body with only the head exposed. From the base of the wooden steam bath, up to 50 different herbs and spices infuse the body.

» The so-called Third Eye of the Lord Shiva treatment (Shiro Dhara) is the highlight for many patients. For up to 45 minutes, a delicate flow of warm oil is poured slowly onto the forehead and then smoothed gently into the temples by the masseuse.

The standards at some Ayurvedic centres are low. The massage oils may be simple coconut oil and the practitioners may be unqualified, except in some instances where they may even be sex workers. As several poisoning cases have resulted from herbal treatments being misadministered, it pays to enquire precisely what the medicine contains and then consult with a conventional physician.

For massage, enquire whether there are both male and female therapists available; we've received complaints from female readers about sexual advances from some male Ayurvedic practitioners. In general it's not acceptable Ayurvedic practice for males to massage females and vice versa.

Photography

» Memory cards and other supplies are easily bought in Colombo (p70).

» Most Sri Lankans love getting their picture taken, but it's common courtesy to ask permission. A few business-oriented folk like the stilt fishermen at Koggala or the mahouts at the Pinnewala Elephant Orphanage will ask for payment.

» It's forbidden to film or photograph dams, airports, road blocks or anything associated with the military. You'll still find areas where photography is sensitive in the Fort area of Colombo and in the North and East.

» Never pose beside or in front of a statue of the Buddha (ie with your back to it) as this is considered extremely disrespectful. Flash photography can damage ages-old frescoes and murals, so respect the restrictions at places like Dambulla and Sigiriya.

Public Holidays

New Year's Day 1 January
Independence Day 4 February
Labour Day 1 May
Good Friday March/April
Christmas Day 25 December

Note also that all *poya* days are public holidays (see boxed text, p23) and much is closed.

Safe Travel

Almost all of Sri Lanka is open for travel and at the time of research there were no hostilities of any kind. You can check the security situation in advance at government websites. Parts of the North may remain sensitive for some time, so you may encounter road blocks, security zones and a few areas still off limits, but there has overall been a sea change since the war.

For more on how to travel safely in the North, see p249.

Sri Lanka does not present any extraordinary concerns about safe travel, although women will want to read about certain concerns (p309).

Telephone

Sri Lanka country code	+94
International access code	+00

Mobile Phones

Mobile coverage across Sri Lanka is good in built-up areas and cheap. GSM phones can usually be used, but confirm this with your home carrier (and check roaming fees, which can be higher here than other countries) in advance.

Local mobile-phone costs using a Sri Lankan SIM card:

SIM card Rs 200
Local calls Rs 1 to 2 per minute
Calls to Australia/UK/US Rs 13/5/2 per minute
Unlocked mobile phone Rs 1500 to 3000

Mobile companies have booths in the arrivals area of Bandaranaike International Airport. Major providers:

Dialog (www.dialog.lk)
Hutch (www.hutch.lk)
Mobitel (www.mobitel.lk)

Phone Codes

All regions have a three-digit area code followed by a six- or seven-digit number. Mobile numbers usually begin with 07 or 08 and have up to 12 digits.

Time

Sri Lanka's time, being 30 minutes off the top of the hour used in much of the world, bedevils many a traveller. Sri Lanka is 5½ hours ahead of GMT (the same as India), 4½ hours behind Australian EST and 10½ hours ahead of American EST.

Toilets

All top-end and midrange accommodation will have sit-down flush toilets. Only budget places that don't get a lot of tourists will have squat toilets and lack toilet paper. Public toilets are scarce (and are grim when they exist); use restaurants, hotels and attractions like tea plantation visitor centres.

Tourist Information

The Colombo main office of the **Sri Lanka Tourist Board** (SLTB; Map p54; ☎011-243 7059; www.srilankatourism.org; 80 Galle Rd, Col 3; ⏰9am-4.45pm Mon-Fri, to 12.30pm Sat) has useful glossy brochures and staff can help with hotel bookings.

For useful websites, see p267.

GOVERNMENT TRAVEL ADVICE

Government advisories often are general and guaranteed to allow for bureaucratic cover should trouble occur. However, the following sites also have useful tips:

» **Australia** (www.smartraveller.gov.au)
» **Canada** (www.voyage.gc.ca)
» **New Zealand** (www.safetravel.govt.nz)
» **UK** (www.fco.gov.uk)
» **US** (www.travel.state.gov)

SHOPPING

Sri Lanka has a wide variety of attractive handicrafts on sale. Markets in major towns are good places to start. Top-quality vanilla beans, for example, are sold very cheaply.

Colombo offers a great and growing range of places to shop (p68). Elsewhere, interesting shops and boutiques are beginning to open in tourist areas. Laksala, a government-run store found in most cities and tourist towns, has items of reasonable quality. Tea is a very popular purchase; see p288.

Bargaining

Unless you are shopping at a fixed-price shop, you must bargain. Before you hit the open markets, peruse the prices in a fixed-price shop for an idea of what to pay. Generally, if someone quotes you a price, halve it. The seller will come down about halfway to your price, and the last price will be a little higher than half the original price. Try and keep a sense of perspective. Chances are you're arguing over less than US$1.

Batik

Originally introduced by the Dutch in colonial times, the Indonesian art of batik is very popular in Sri Lanka. Some of the best and most original batik is made in the west-coast towns of Marawila, Mahawewa and Ambalangoda, and there are also several worthwhile outlets in Kandy.

Gems

You'll find showrooms and private dealers all across Sri Lanka. In Ratnapura, the centre of the gem trade, it seems that everybody is a part-time gem dealer. Your challenge is the same here as elsewhere in the world: make sure what you're being offered is not worthless glass. The best way to avoid the myriad gem scams is to avoid buying any.

Masks

Sri Lankan masks are a popular collector's item. They're carved at a number of places, principally along the southwest coast. Look for shops from Galle and to the East.

Spices

Spices are integral to Sri Lanka's cuisine and Ayurvedic traditions. A visit to a spice garden is an excellent way to discover the alternative uses of familiar spices.

Travellers with Disabilities

Sri Lanka is a challenge for travellers with disabilities, but the ever-obliging Sri Lankans are always ready to assist. If you have restricted mobility, you may find it difficult, if not impossible, to get around on public transport. Buses and trains don't have facilities for wheelchairs. Moving around towns and cities can also be difficult for those in a wheelchair and for the visually impaired because of the continual roadworks and very ordinary roads; don't expect many smooth footpaths. The chaotic nature of Sri Lankan traffic is also a potentially dangerous challenge. A car and driver is your best transport option. If possible, travel with a strong, able-bodied person.

Apart from some top-end hotels, accommodation is not geared for wheelchairs. However, many places can provide disabled travellers with rooms and bathrooms that are accessible without stairs.

Visas

Beginning in 2012, Sri Lanka did away with its free visas, which had been issued on arrival. To nearly universal criticism, an online visa system was introduced. At time of research, this system was still being refined (eg after the number of people doing a short stopover plummeted, the visa fees were waived for certain 48-hour visits).

Obtaining a Visa

Before visiting Sri Lanka you should do the following to obtain a 30-day visa:

» Visit the **Sri Lanka Electronic Travel Authorization System** (www.eta.gov.lk) several days before arriving.

» Follow the online application process and pay with a credit or debit card.

» Once approved, print out the visa confirmation.

You can still obtain visas at Sri Lankan embassies abroad and there is a counter at Bandaranaike International Airport for people who arrive without a visa, although you'll have to wait with the other visa-less masses and pay a small penalty.

Visa Fees

The visa fees are as follows:

Transit visa good for 48 hours	Free
Tourist visa good for 3-7 days	US$10
Standard 30-day tourist visa	US$20

Visas secured at Bandaranaike International Airport cost US$5 more. You can pay in rupiah, euros, UK pounds and Australian dollars in addition to US dollars.

Visa Extensions

For stays in Sri Lanka beyond the usual 30-day visa, contact the **Department of Immigration and Emigration** (www.immigration.gov.lk). They are not hard to get but require jumping through some bureaucratic hoops.

Volunteering

Following the tsunami in 2004, Sri Lanka became a focus for many volunteer efforts and organisations. Post-tsunami relief work is greatly decreased but several local organisations still accept volunteers.

Some local Sri Lankan organisations:

Millennium Elephant Foundation (www.millenniumelephantfoundation.org)

Rainforest Rescue International (www.rainforestrescueinternational.org)

Sewalanka Foundation (www.sewalanka.org)

Turtle Conservation Project (www.tcpsrilanka.org)

Women Travellers

Few Sri Lankan women travel unchaperoned, so women travelling alone may experience uncomfortable levels of male attention. The relative isolation caused by the Sri Lankan civil war and exposure to more open and provocative Western media have created a small group of Sri Lankan men lacking the fundamentals in how to deal with Western women.

Outside of Colombo, it is a good idea to cover your legs and shoulders, though you'll be stared at no matter what you wear. Tight tops are a bad idea. And away from the tourist beaches of the South and West, consider swimming in a T-shirt and shorts.

In Colombo you can relax the dress code a little and get away with wearing sleeveless shirts. 'Are you married?' could be the snappy conversation starter you hear most often, so consider wearing a fake wedding ring and carrying a few pics of your imaginary partner back home.

Women travelling alone may be hassled while walking around day and night, or while exploring isolated places. Physical harassment (grabbing and groping) can occur anywhere. Single women may be followed, so try to be connected with larger groups of people. There have also been cases of solo women being attacked by guides at heritage sites; again, don't go alone.

However, don't imagine travelling in Sri Lanka is one long hassle. Such unpleasant incidents are the exception, not the rule. Women travellers have the opportunity to enter the society of Sri Lankan women, something that is largely out of bounds for male travellers. On the other hand, there are many social environments that are almost exclusively male in character – local bars, for example. If you feel uncomfortable in local eateries or hotels, try to find one where women are working or staying.

Stock up on tampons as they can be hard to find outside large Colombo supermarkets.

Bus & Train Travel

Women travelling solo will find buses and trains trying at times. In Colombo ordinary buses are so packed that sometimes it's impossible to avoid bodily contact with other passengers. Stray hands on crowded buses and trains happen; this is something that local women are also subjected to. Change your seat or sit with a local woman. If you gesture to a local woman to sit next to you, she'll understand why. You can try standing at the front near the driver if you can't get a seat.

We strongly suggest not travelling on trains alone, as we've received warnings from women who have been sexually assaulted on such trips. Consider finding a travelling companion.

Transport

GETTING THERE & AWAY

Sri Lanka is still catching up in terms of air service. It's hoped that choices will multiply as the aviation infrastructure expands.

Flights, tours and rail tickets can be booked online at lonelyplanet.com/bookings.

Entering the Country

Immigration at Bandaranaike International Airport is straightforward although fluid visa regulations have complicated matters, see p308.

Passport

You must have your passport with you at all times in Sri Lanka. Before leaving home, check that it will be valid for at least six months after you plan to return home.

Air

Airports & Airlines

Sri Lanka's only international airport is **Bandaranaike International Airport** (www.airport.lk) at Katunayake, 30km north of Colombo. There are 24-hour money-changing facilities in the arrivals and departures halls as well as ATMs. Compared to years past, the airport is much more orderly now and the throngs of touts that once greeted passengers are gone. Transit passengers and those checking in early should note, however, that the terminals remain quite spartan in terms of amenities.

Sri Lanka is ripe for additional airline service. In the meantime, international service is provided by the following airlines.

Air Asia (www.airasia.com)

Cathay Pacific (www.cathaypacific.com)

Emirates (www.emirates.com)

Etihad (www.etihadairways.com)

Indian Airlines (www.indian-airlines.nic.in)

Jet Airways (www.jetairways.com)

Kuwait Airways (www.kuwait-airways.com)

Malaysia Airlines (www.malaysia-airlines.com)

Qatar Airways (www.qatarairways.com)

Singapore Airlines (www.singaporeair.com)

Sri Lankan Airlines (www.srilankan.aero)

Thai Airways (www.thaiairways.com.lk)

Tickets

Shop around online; there is limited charter service to Sri Lanka for now. Sri Lankan Airlines and others often have their best prices only on their own websites.

CLIMATE CHANGE & TRAVEL

Every form of transport that relies on carbon-based fuel generates CO_2, the main cause of human-induced climate change. Modern travel is dependent on aeroplanes, which might use less fuel per kilometre per person than most cars but travel much greater distances. The altitude at which aircraft emit gases (including CO_2) and particles also contributes to their climate change impact. Many websites offer 'carbon calculators' that allow people to estimate the carbon emissions generated by their journey and, for those who wish to do so, to offset the impact of the greenhouse gases emitted with contributions to portfolios of climate-friendly initiatives throughout the world. Lonely Planet offsets the carbon footprint of all staff and author travel.

Asia

Sri Lanka is well served by major Asian carriers, including Malaysian budget favourite Air Asia. Service from India is competitive between several carriers.

MALDIVES

Many visitors combine a visit to Sri Lanka with the Maldives. Sri Lankan Airlines and Emirates fly between Colombo and Malé.

Australia & New Zealand

Connections are on Asian carriers such as Singapore Airlines and Thai Airways. Using Emirates requires major back-tracking.

Europe

Sri Lankan Airlines links Colombo nonstop with Frankfurt, London, Paris and Rome. But nonstop service by a European airline remains a holy grail of Sri Lankan tourism. Connecting through on a Middle Eastern carrier such as Emirates, Etihad Airways, Kuwait Airways and Qatar Airways is common.

North America

You're literally going halfway around the world from Canada and the USA; from the west coast connect through Asia, from the east coast connect through the Middle East or India.

Sea

Plans to resume ferry services between Mannar in northwest Sri Lanka and India have been rumoured for many years, but have yet to materialise.

In 2011 **Flemingo Liners** (www.flemingoliners.com) began a much-hyped new service linking Colombo and Tuticorin (Tamil Nadu) in India. The overnight sailings were economical and popular. However, a dispute with a vendor caused the service to be suspended at the end of 2011.

MATTALA INTERNATIONAL AIRPORT

Sri Lanka is on track to get a second international airport as early as 2013. **Mattala International Airport** (www.airport.lk/hia/hia.php) is being built 15km north of Hambantota near the south coast. The first phase will have a runway long enough to handle the largest jets flying nonstop to/from Europe. Service details were not clear at time of research but once open, it will be interesting to see how many people wish to fly directly to the southern end of the country. What seems likely, initially, is that Sri Lankan Airlines will launch true domestic service linking to Bandaranaike International Airport near Colombo, and some charter flights filled with sun-seeking holidaymakers may fly direct from other nations.

Don't be surprised if the airport is formally named after a politician before it opens.

GETTING AROUND

Domestic flights in Sri Lanka are quite limited (service between Colombo and Jaffna is the most regular) but with the boom in tourism, this may change.

Travelling on public transport is therefore mostly a choice between buses and trains: both are cheap. Trains can be crowded, but it's nothing compared with the seemingly endless numbers of passengers that squash into ordinary buses. Trains are a bit slower than buses, but a seat on a train is preferable to standing on a bus. Even standing on a train is better than standing on a bus.

On the main roads from Colombo to Kandy, Negombo and Galle, buses cover around 40km to 50km per hour. On highways across the plains, it can be 60km or 70km an hour. In the Hill Country, it can slow to just 20km an hour.

All public transport gets crowded around *poya*

GETTING AROUND OPTIONS

Your options for getting around Sri Lanka are many. Broadly, the options and considerations are as follows:

	PROS	CONS
bus	cheap frequent go everywhere	very crowded uncomfortable no room for luggage slow
car & driver	comfortable flexible efficient	more expensive than buses and trains
train	tickets in all classes are cheap some routes beautiful 1st class comfortable	not frequent slow 2nd & 3rd class crowded and uncomfortable limited destinations

(full-moon) holidays and their nearest weekends, so try to avoid travelling then.

Air

Options for flying within Sri Lanka are limited and there is no domestic connecting service at Bandaranaike International Airport near Colombo, although this may change with the opening of Mattala International Airport on the south coast; see p311 for details.

Very limited domestic service operates at times from Ratmalana Air Force Base, 15km south of Fort. If you are flying from here, consult with your airline for transport options to/from the airport.

Helitours (www.airforce.lk) The commercial arm of the Sri Lankan Air Force was conducting limited passenger flights – on military planes – primarily between Jaffna's Palali Airport and Ratmalana Air Force Base.

Sri Lankan Airlines Air Taxi (www.srilankan.lk) The national airline flies services using floatplanes offering scenic jaunts between various lakes in the country.

Bicycle

Cycling around historic areas such as Anuradhapura and Sigiriya are the best and most enjoyable ways to see these important sites. More and more accommodation has bicycles guests can hire (rent).

Hire

» Simple cheap mountain bikes make up much of the rentals you'll find in guesthouses and hotels. Rates average about Rs 300 to 500 per day.

» If your accommodation doesn't hire bikes, they can usually hook you up with someone who does. Many places rent bikes to nonguests.

» Bikes available for day use typically are not suitable for long-distance riding. Bike-rental shops offering quality long-distance machines are rare. Consider bringing your bike from home if you plan serious cycle touring.

Bike Tours

Tour and outfitting companies organise cycling tours of Sri Lanka and may also help you get organised for independent travel.

Adventure Asia (www.ad-asia.com),

Adventure Sports Lanka (www.actionlanka.com)

Eco Team (www.srilankaecotourism.com)

Long-Distance

» Keen long-distance cyclists will enjoy Sri Lanka, apart from the steeper areas of the Hill Country and the busy roads exiting Colombo. When heading out of Colombo in any direction, take a train to the edge of the city before you start cycling.

» Start early in the day to avoid the heat, and pack water and sunscreen. Your daily distances will be limited by the roads; be prepared for lots of prudent 'eyes down' cycling as you negotiate a flurry of obstacles from potholes to chickens. Remember, too, that speeding buses, trucks and cars use all parts of the roadway and shoulder, so be very cautious and wear very visible clothing.

» If you bring your own bicycle, also pack a supply of spare tyres and tubes. These suffer from the poor road surfaces, and replacement parts can be hard to obtain. The normal bicycle tyre size in Sri Lanka is 28in by 1.5in. Some imported 27in tyres for 10-speed bikes are available but only in Colombo and at high prices.

» Keep an eye on your bicycle at all times and use a good lock.

» When taking a bicycle on a train, forms must be filled out, so deliver the bicycle at least half an hour before departure. At Colombo Fort train station you may want to allow up to two hours. It costs about twice the 2nd-class fare to take a bicycle on a train.

Purchase

Expect to pay US$125 to US$350 for a new bike, depending on the quality. Most are made in India or China. There are several bike shops (rentals not available) along Dam St in the Pettah market area of Colombo.

Bus

Bus routes cover about 80% of the nation's 90,000km of roads. There are two kinds of bus in Sri Lanka:

Central Transport Board (CTB) buses These are the default buses and usually lack air-con, they ply most long-distance and local routes. You'll also see buses with a Sri Lanka Transport Board (SLTB) logo.

Private buses Independent bus companies have vehicles ranging from late-model Japanese coaches used on intercity-express runs to ancient minibuses on short runs between towns and villages. Private air-con intercity buses cover some major routes. For long-distance travel they are far more comfortable and faster than other bus services. Note that completion of the Southern Expressway has sparked the introduction of new express services in fully modern air-con coaches. Expect more of these services as roads are completed.

Bus travel in Sri Lanka can be interesting and entertaining. Most locals speak at least some English, so you may have some enjoyable interactions. Vendors board to sell snacks, books and gifts on long-distance routes. Note, however, that women travelling alone may be hassled; see p309.

Important considerations for bus travel:

» Important routes will have service several times an hour during daylight hours.

» Finding the right bus at the chaotic bus stations of major cities and towns can be challenging, although almost all buses now have part of their destination sign in English.

» There is usually no central ticket office; you must locate the right parking area and buy your bus ticket either from a small booth or onboard the bus.

» You *may* be able to reserve a seat on a bus in advance; check at the station.

» 'Semi-comfortable' buses are run by private companies and have larger seats and window curtains compared to CTB buses, but lack the air-con of the best intercity buses.

» Most people at bus stations and on buses will help you with your questions.

» Luggage space is limited or non-existent; you may have to buy a ticket for your bag.

» The first two seats on CTB buses are reserved for 'clergy' (Buddhist monks).

» To guarantee a seat, board the bus at the beginning of its journey.

» When you arrive at your destination, confirm the departure details for the next stage of your journey.

» It's expected that private bus companies will proliferate in the coming years and that more services such as reservations will be offered and that buses will get more comfortable.

Costs

In most cases, private bus companies run services parallel to CTB services. Intercity expresses charge about twice as much as CTB buses, but are more than twice as comfortable and usually faster. Fares for CTB buses and ordinary private buses are very cheap.

Car & Motorcycle

Self-drive car hire is possible in Sri Lanka, though it is far more common to hire a car and driver. If you're on a relatively short visit to Sri Lanka on a midrange budget, the costs of hiring a car and driver can be quite reasonable.

When planning your itinerary, you can count on covering about 35km/h in the Hill Country and 55km/h in most of the rest of the country.

Motorcycling is an alternative for intrepid travellers. Distances are relatively short and some of the roads are a motorcyclist's delight; the trick is to stay off the main highways. The quieter Hill Country roads offer some glorious views, and secondary roads along the coast and the plains are reasonably quick. But you will have to make inquiries as motorcycle and motorbike rental is nowhere near as commonplace as it is in much of the rest of Asia.

New expressways are revolutionising how people get around Sri Lanka.

Throughout Sri Lanka, Mw is an abbreviation for Mawatha, meaning 'Avenue'.

Driving Licence

An International Driving Permit (IDP) can be used to roam Sri Lanka's roads; it's valid for three months to one year and is sold by auto clubs in your home country. Note that many travellers never purchase an IDP and have no problems.

Hiring a Car & Driver

A car and a driver guarantee maximum flexibility in your travels and while the driver deals with the chaotic roads, you can look out the window and – try to – relax.

You can find taxi drivers who will happily become your chauffeur for a day or more in all the main tourist centres. Guesthouses and hotels can connect you with a driver, which may be the best method. Travel agencies also offer various car and driver

SRI LANKA'S NEW HIGHWAYS

Various new expressways are opening over the next few years. Most will be toll roads, with relatively cheap tolls.

Colombo–Kandy Highway Approved in 2012, this road is expected to open in 2015 and reduce travel time to close to an hour.

Colombo–Katunayake Highway Running some 25km from the airport to a point just northeast of Fort, this could cut travel time to under 30 minutes. It is expected to be open in 2013.

Outer Circular Highway This beltway will link the Colombo–Katunayake Hwy with the Southern Expressway, which will put Galle and the South within two hours of the airport, revolutionising travel patterns. It should be fully open by 2015.

Southern Expressway The first new expressway completed. It is 126km long and runs from Colombo's southern suburb of Kottawa, near Maharagama, to Pinnaduwa, near Galle. It costs Rs 400 to Galle. Until linking roads are complete, it can take as long to get from Fort to the expressway entrance as it does from there to Galle – or even longer. Travel time to/from the airport can take two hours. Plans call for the road to eventually reach Hambantota.

schemes, although these can cost considerably more.

COSTS

Various formulas exist for setting costs, such as rates per kilometre plus a lunch and dinner allowance and separate fuel payments. The simplest way is to agree on a flat fee with no extras. Expect to pay Rs 5500 to 7000 per day, excluding fuel, or more for a newer, air-con vehicle. Other considerations:

» Most drivers will expect a tip of about 10%.

» Meet the driver first as you may sense bad chemistry.

» Consider hiring a driver for only two or three days at first to see if you fit.

» You are the boss. It's great to get recommendations from a driver but don't be bullied.

» Unless you speak absolutely no English or Sinhala, a guide in addition to the driver is unnecessary.

Drivers make a fair part of their income from commissions. Most hotels and guesthouses pay drivers a flat fee or a percentage, although others refuse to. This can lead to disputes between you and the driver over where you're staying the night, as the driver will literally wish to steer you to where the money is. Some hotels have appalling accommodation for drivers; the smarter hotels and guesthouses know that keeping drivers happy is good for their business, and provide decent food and lodgings.

Recommended drivers include the following (there are many more; the Lonely Planet Thorn Tree forum is a good source of driver recommendations):

Milroy Fernando (☎077 857 0343; milroy@ancientlanka.com)

Dimuthu Priyadarshana (☎077 630 2070; dimuthu81@hotmail.com)

Nilam Sahabdeen (☎081 238 4981; http://srilankatour.wordpress.com/)

Self-Drive Hire

Colombo-based company **Quickshaws Tours** (☎011-258 3133; www.quickshaws.com; 3 Kalinga Pl, Col 5) offers self-drive car hire. A Nissan Sunny costs US$266 per week, while a larger Toyota Corolla costs US$280 per week. Both have air-con and include 700km per week.

Road Conditions

You may see a number of accidents during your time on the road; driving requires constant attention to the road. Country roads are often narrow and potholed, with constant pedestrian, bicycle and animal traffic to navigate. Note, however, that Sri Lanka's massive road-building program is improving roads across the nation.

Punctures are a part of life here, so every village has a repair expert.

It's dangerously acceptable for a bus, car or truck to overtake in the face of oncoming smaller road users. Three-wheelers, cyclists, or smaller cars and vans simply have to move over or risk getting hit. To announce they are overtaking, or want to overtake, drivers sound a shrill melody on their horns. If you're walking or cycling along any kind of main road, be very alert.

Road Rules

» Speed limit 56km/h in towns, 72km/h in rural areas and 100km on the new expressways.

» Driving is on the left-hand side of the road, as in the UK and Australia.

Hitching

Hitching is never entirely safe in any country in the world, and we don't recommend it. In any case, Sri Lanka's cheap fares make it an unnecessary option.

Local Transport

Many Sri Lankan towns are small enough to walk around. In larger towns you can get around by bus, taxi or three-wheeler.

Bus

Local buses go to most places, including villages outside main towns, for fares from Rs 10 to 40.

Taxi

Sri Lankan taxis are common in all sizable towns, and even some villages. Only a few are metered (mostly in Colombo), but over longer distances their prices are comparable to those of three-wheelers, and they provide more comfort and security. Radio taxis are available in Kandy and Colombo. You can count on most taxi rides costing around Rs 60 to 100 per kilometre.

Three-wheeler

Three-wheelers, known in other parts of Asia as tuk-tuks, *bajajs* or autorickshaws, are literally waiting on every corner. Use your best bargaining skills and agree on the fare before you get in. Some keen drivers will offer to take you around Mars and back, and we've heard of travellers who have gone from Kandy to Nuwara Eliya in a three-wheeler, which would be a slow five hours or so.

As a rule of thumb, a three-wheeler should cost no more than Rs 100 per kilometre, but this can prove elusive depending on your negotiating skills. Note that three-wheelers with meters are becoming popular in Colombo.

Three-wheelers and taxis waiting outside hotels and tourist sights expect higher-than-usual fares. Walk a few hundred metres to get a much better deal.

Tours

Sri Lanka has many inbound travel companies providing tours. Many of the tours are focused on a particular interest or activity.

A Baur & Co Ltd (www.baurs.com) Wildlife-watching tours.

Adventure Asia (www.ad-asia.com) White-water rafting, kayaking, hot-air ballooning and bicycling tours.

Adventure Sports Lanka (www.actionlanka.com) White-water rafting, hiking, mountain biking, canoeing and diving.

Boutique Sri Lanka (www.boutiquesrilanka.com) Specialises in interesting accommodation, Ayurvedic retreats, and luxury resorts, guesthouses and small, heritage hotels.

Eco Team (www.srilankaecotourism.com) Wide range of wilderness-based active adventures, including white-water rafting, hiking and wildlife safaris.

Jetwing Eco (www.jetwingeco.com) Wildlife- and birdwatching tours.

Rainforest Rescue International (www.rainforestrescueinternational.org) One-day tours of ecologically fascinating areas and longer stays on organic farms and projects.

Red Dot Tours (www.reddottours.com) Everything from golf and cricket to wildlife and wellness.

Sri Lanka Expeditions (www.srilankaexpeditions.com) Activity-based tours, including rock climbing, trekking, mountain biking and white-water rafting.

Sri Lanka In Style (www.srilankainstyle.com) Splurge-worthy and unique accommodation.

Train

Sri Lanka's railways are a great way to cross the country. Although they are slow, there are few overnight or all-day ordeals to contend with. A train ride is almost always more relaxed than a bus ride. Costs are in line with buses: even 1st class doesn't exceed Rs 1000.

There are three main lines:

South from Colombo Newly renovated, runs past Aluthgama and Hikkaduwa to Galle and Matara.

East from Colombo To the Hill Country, through Kandy, Nanu Oya (for Nuwara Eliya) and Ella to Badulla. A beautiful route, the portion from Haputale to Ella is one of the world's most scenic train rides.

North from Colombo Through Anuradhapura to Vavuniya, plans are to restore the line to Jaffna. One branch reaches Trincomalee on the east coast, while another serves Polonnaruwa and Batticaloa.

Other Lines The Puttalam line runs along the coast north from Colombo, although rail buses run between Chilaw and Puttalam. The Kelani Valley line winds 60km from Colombo to Avissawella.

Trains are often late. For long-distance trains, Sri Lankans sometimes measure the lateness in periods of the day: quarter of a day late, half a day late and so on. Other considerations:

» Most stations have helpful information windows.

» The **Sri Lankan Railways** (www.railway.gov.lk) website has a useful trip planner.

Classes

There are three classes on Sri Lankan trains:

1st Class Comes in three varieties: coaches, sleeping berths and observation saloons (with large windows). The latter are used on the line east from Colombo and are the preferred means of travelling this scenic line. Some have large rear-facing windows and vintage interiors. Reserve 1st-class seats in advance.

2nd Class Seats have padding and there are fans. On many trains these seats can be reserved in advance.

3rd Class Seats have little padding and there are no reservations. The cars accommodate as many as can squeeze in and conditions can be grim.

In addition private companies have begun running comfortable train cars, which are attached to regular trains (Colombo–Kandy is the first route, fares average US$12). Although the 1st-class observation cars are more charming – and cheaper – these private cars offer air-con, snacks and may have seats available when regular trains are already fully booked.

Private car operators:

Expo Rail (☎011-522 5050; www.exporail.lk)

Rajadhani Express (☎071 035 5355; www.rajadhani.lk)

Reservations

» You can reserve places in 1st class and in 2nd class on intercity expresses.

» Always make a booking for the 1st-class observation saloons, which are very popular.

» Reservations can be made at train stations up to 10 days before departure. You can book a return ticket up to 14 days before departure.

» If travelling more than 80km, you can break your journey at any intermediate station for 24 hours without penalty. You'll need to make fresh reservations for seats on the next leg.

Language

WANT MORE?

For in-depth language information and handy phrases, check out Lonely Planet's *Sinhala Phrasebook* and *India Phrasebook*. You'll find them at **shop.lonelyplanet.com**, or you can buy Lonely Planet's iPhone phrasebooks at the Apple App Store.

Sinhala and Tamil are national languages in Sri Lanka, with English commonly described as a lingua franca. It's easy to get by with English, and the Sri Lankan variety has its own unique characteristics – 'You are having a problem, isn't it, no?' is one example. However, while English may be widely spoken in the main centres, off the beaten track its spread thins. In any case, even a few words of Sinhala or Tamil will go a long way.

SINHALA

Sinhala is officially written using a cursive script. If you read our coloured pronunciation guides as if they were English, you shouldn't have problems being understood. When consonants are doubled they are pronounced very distinctly, almost as separate sounds. The symbols t and d are pronounced less forcefully than in English, th as in 'thin', dh as the 'th' in 'that', g as in 'go', and r is more like a flap of the tongue against the roof of the mouth – it's not pronounced as an American 'r'. As for the vowels, a is pronounced as the 'u' in 'cup', aa as the 'a' in 'father', ai as in 'aisle', au as the 'ow' in 'how', e as in 'met', i as in 'bit', o as in 'hot', and u as in 'put'.

Basics

Hello.	aayu-bowan
Goodbye.	aayu-bowan
Yes.	owu
No.	naha
Please.	karuna kara
Thank you.	istuh-tee
Excuse me.	samah venna
Sorry.	kana gaatui
Do you speak English?	oyaa in-ghirisih kata karenawa da?
What's your name?	oyaaghe nama mokka'da?
My name is ...	maaghe nama ...

Accommodation

Do you have any rooms available?	kaamara thiyanawada?
How much is it per night?	ek ra-yakata kiyada
How much is it per person?	ek kenek-kuta kiyada
Is breakfast included?	udeh keh-emath ekkada?
for one night	ek rayak pamanai
for two nights	raya dekak pamanai
for one person	ek-kenek pamanai
for two people	den-nek pamanai
campsite	kamping ground eka
guesthouse	gesthaus eka
hotel	hotel eka
youth hostel	yut-hostel eka

Eating & Drinking

Can we see the menu?	menoo eka balanna puluvandha?
What's the local speciality?	mehe visheshayen hadhana dhe monavaadha?

I'd like rice and curry, please.	bahth denna
I'm a vegetarian.	mama elavalu vitharai kanne
I'm allergic to (peanuts).	mata (ratakaju) apathyayi
No ice in my drink, please.	karunaakarala maghe beema ekata ais dhamanna epaa
That was delicious!	eka harima rasai!

Please bring a/the...	... karunaakarala gennah
bill	bila
fork	gaarappuvak
glass of water	vathura veedhuruvak
knife	pihiyak
plate	pingaanak

bowl	vendhuwa
coffee	koh-pi
fruit	palathuru
glass	co-ppuwa
milk	kiri
salt	lunu
spoon	han-duh
sugar	seeni
tea	thay
water	vathura

Numbers – Sinhala

0	binduwa
1	eka
2	deka
3	thuna
4	hathara
5	paha
6	haya
7	hatha
8	atta
9	navaya
10	dahaya
100	seeya
200	deh seeya
1000	daaha
2000	deh daaha
100,000	lakshaya
1,000,000	daseh lakshaya
10,000,000	kotiya

Emergencies

Help!	aaney!/aaeeyoh!/ammoh!
Call a doctor!	dostara gen-nanna!
Call the police!	polisiyata kiyanna!
Go away!	methanin yanna!
I'm lost.	maa-meh nativelaa

Shopping & Services

What time does it open/close?	ehika kiyatada arinneh/vahanneh?
How much is it?	ehekka keeyada?
big	loku
medicine	behe-yat
small	podi/punchi

bank	bankuwa
chemist/pharmacy	faahmisiya
... embassy	... embasiya
market	maakat eka
my hotel	mang inna hotalaya
newsagency	pattara ejensiya
post office	tepal kantohruwa
public telephone	podu dura katanayak
tourist office	sanchaaraka toraturu karyaalayak

Time & Dates

What time is it?	velaave keeyada?
morning	udai
afternoon	havasa
day	davasa
night	raah
week	sumaanayak
month	maasayak
year	avuurudeh
yesterday	ee-yeh
today	ada (uther)
tomorrow	heta

Monday	sandu-da
Tuesday	angaharuwaa-da
Wednesday	badaa-da
Thursday	braha-spetin-da
Friday	sikuraa-da
Saturday	senasuraa-da
Sunday	iri-da

Signs – Sinhala

ඇතුල්වීම	**Entrance**
පිටවීම	**Exit**
විවෘතව ඇත.	**Open**
වසා ඇත.	**Closed**
තොරතුරු දැන්වුම	**Information**
තහනම් වෙ.	**Prohibited**
පොලිස් ස්ථානය	**Police Station**
කාමර ඇත.	**Rooms Available**
කාමර නැත.	**No Vacancy**
වැසිකිළි	**Toilets**
පුරුෂ	**Men**
ස්ත්‍රී	**Women**

Transport & Directions

When does the next ... leave/arrive?	meelanga ... pitaht venne/paminenne?
boat	bohtuwa
bus (city)	bus eka
bus (intercity)	bus eka nagaraantara
train	koh-chiya

I want to get off.	mama methana bahinawa
I'd like a one-way ticket.	mata tani gaman tikat ekak ganna ohna
I'd like a return ticket.	mata yaam-eem tikat ekak ganna ohna

1st class	palamu veni paantiya
2nd class	deveni paantiya
3rd class	tunveni paantiya
bus stop	bus nevathuma
ferry terminal	totu pala
timetable	kaala satahana
train station	dumriya pala

I'd like to hire a ...	mata ... ekak bad-dhata ganna ohna
bicycle	baisikeleya
car	kar (eka)

Where is a/the ...?	... koheda?
Go straight ahead.	kelinma issarahata yaanna
Turn left.	wamata harenna
Turn right.	dakunata harenna
near	lan-ghai
far	durai

TAMIL

The vocabulary of Sri Lankan Tamil is much the same as that of South India – the written form is identical, using the traditional cursive script – but there are marked differences in pronunciation between speakers from the two regions. In this section we've used the same pronunciation guides as for Sinhala.

Basics

Hello.	vanakkam
Goodbye.	poytu varukirehn
Yes.	aam
No.	il-lay
Please.	tayavu saydhu
Thank you.	nandri
Excuse me.	mannikavum
Sorry.	mannikavum
Do you speak English?	nin-gal aangilam paysu-virhalaa?
What's your name?	ungal peyr en-na?
My name is ...	en peyr ...

Accommodation

Do you have any rooms available?	ingu room kideikkumaa?
How much is it per night/person?	oru iravukku/aalukku evvalavur?
Is breakfast included?	kaalei unavum sehrtha?
for one/two nights	oru/irandu iravukku
for one/two people	oruvarukku/iruvarukku

Signs – Tamil

வழி உள்ளே	**Entrance**
வழி வெளியே	**Exit**
திறந்துள்ளது	**Open**
அடைக்கப்பட்டுள்ளது	**Closed**
தகவல்	**Information**
அனுமதி இல்லை	**Prohibited**
காவல் நிலையம்	**Police Station**
அறைகள் உண்டு	**Rooms Available**
காலி இல்லை	**No Vacancy**
மலசலகூடம்	**Toilets**
ஆண்	**Men**
பெண	**Women**

campsite	mukhaamidum idahm
guesthouse	virun-dhinar vidhudheh
hotel	hotehl
youth hostel	ilainar vidhudheh

Eating & Drinking

Can we see the menu?	unavu pattiyalai paarppomaa?
What's the local speciality?	ingu kidaikkak koodiya visheida unavu enna?
I'd like rice and curry, please.	sorum kariyum tharungal
I'm a vegetarian.	naan shaiva unavu shaappidupavan
I'm allergic to (peanuts).	(nilak kadalai) enakku alejee
No ice in my drink, please.	enadu paanaththil ais poda vendaam
That was delicious!	adhu nalla rushi!

Please bring a/the...	... konda varungal
bill	bill
fork	mul karandi
glass of water	thanni oru glass
knife	kaththi
plate	oru plate

bowl	kooppai
coffee	kahpee
fruit	paadham
glass	glass
milk	paal
salt	uppu
spoon	karandi
sugar	seeree
tea	te-neer/plan-tea
water	than-neer

Emergencies

Help!	udavi!
Call a doctor!	daktarai kuppidunga!
Call the police!	polisai kuppidunga!
Go away!	pohn-goh!/poi-vidu!
I'm lost.	naan vali tavari-vittehn

Shopping & Services

What time does it open/close?	et-thana manikka tirakhum/mudhum?

Numbers – Tamil

0	saifer
1	ondru
2	iranduh
3	muundruh
4	naan-guh
5	ainduh
6	aaruh
7	ealluh
8	ettu
9	onbaduh
10	pat-tuh
100	nooruh
1000	aayirem
2000	irandaayirem
100,000	oru latcham
1,000,000	pattuh lat-chem
10,000,000	kohdee

How much is it?	adhu evvalavu?
big	periyeh
medicine	marunduh
small	siriyeh

bank	vanghee
chemist/pharmacy	marunduh kadhai
... embassy	... tudharalayem
market	maarket
my hotel	enadu hotehl
newsagency	niyuz paper vitku-midam
post office	tafaal nilayem
public telephone	podhu tolai-pessee
tourist office	toorist nilayem

Time & Dates

What time is it?	mani eth-tanai?
morning	kaalai
afternoon	pit-pahel
day	pahel
night	iravu
week	vaarem
month	maadhem
year	varudem
yesterday	neh-truh
today	indru
tomorrow	naalay

Monday	tin-gal
Tuesday	sevvaay
Wednesday	budahn
Thursday	viyaalin
Friday	vellee
Saturday	san-nee
Sunday	naayiru

Transport & Directions

When does the next ... leave/arrive?	eththanai manikku aduththa ... sellum/varum?
boat	padakhu
bus (city)	baas naharam/ul-loor
bus (intercity)	baas veliyoor
train	rayill
I want to get off.	naan iranga vendum
I'd like a one-way ticket.	enakku oru vahly tikket veynum
I'd like a return ticket.	enakku iru vahlay tikket veynum
1st class	mudalahaam vahuppu
2nd class	irandaam vahuppu
bus/trolley stop	baas nilayem
luggage lockers	porul vaikku-midam
timetable	haala attavanay
train station	rayill nilayem
I'd like to hire a ...	enakku ... vaadakhaikku vaynum
bicycle	sai-kul
car	car
Where is it?	adhu en-ghe irukkaradhu?
Where is a/the ...?	... en-ghe?
Go straight ahead.	neraha sellavum
Turn left.	valadhur pakkam tirumbavum
Turn right.	itadhu pakkam thirumbavum
near	aruhil
far	tu-rahm

SRI LANKAN ENGLISH

Greetings & Conversation

Go and come. – farewell greeting, similar to 'See you later' (not taken literally)

How? – How are you?

Nothing to do. – Can't do anything.

What to do? – What can be done about it? (more of a rhetorical question)

What country? – Where are you from?

paining – hurting

to gift – to give a gift

People

baby/bubba – term used for any child up to about adolescence

batchmate – university classmate

peon – office helper

uncle/auntie – term of respect for elder

Getting Around

backside – part of the building away from the street

bajaj – three-wheeler

bus halt – bus stop

coloured lights – traffic lights

down south – the areas south of Colombo, especially coastal areas

dropping – being dropped off at a place by a car

get down – to alight (from bus/train/three-wheeler)

normal bus – not a private bus

outstation – place beyond a person's home area

petrol shed – petrol/gas station

pick-up – 4WD utility vehicle

seaside/landside – indicates locations, usually in relation to Galle Rd

two-wheeler – motorcycle

up and down – return trip

up country/Hill Country – Kandy and beyond, tea plantation areas

vehicle – car

Food

bite – snack, usually with alcoholic drinks

boutique – a little, hole-in-the-wall shop, usually selling small, inexpensive items

cool spot – traditional, small shop that sells cool drinks and snacks

hotel – a small, cheap restaurant that doesn't offer accommodation

lunch packet/rice packet – rice/curry meal wrapped in plastic and newspaper and taken to office or school for lunch

short eats – snack food

Money

buck – rupee

last price – final price when bargaining

purse – wallet

GLOSSARY

ambalama – wayside shelter for pilgrims

Aurudu – Sinhalese and Tamil New Year, celebrated on 14 April

Avalokitesvara – the *bodhisattva* of compassion

Ayurveda – traditional system of medicine that uses herbs and oils to heal and rejuvenate

bailas – folk tunes based on Portuguese, African and local music styles

baobab – water-storing tree *(Adansonia digitata)*, probably introduced to Mannar Island and the Vanni in northern Sri Lanka by Arab traders

bodhi tree – large spreading tree *(Ficus religiosa)*; the tree under which the Buddha sat when he attained enlightenment, and the many descendants grown from cuttings of this tree

bodhisattva – divine being who, although capable of attaining *nirvana*, chooses to reside on the human plane to help ordinary people attain salvation

Brahmi – early Indian script used from the 5th century BC

bund – built-up bank or dyke surrounding a *tank*

Burgher – Sri Lankan Eurasian, generally descended from Portuguese-Sinhalese or Dutch-Sinhalese intermarriage

cadjan – coconut fronds woven into mats and used as building material

Ceylon – British-colonial name for Sri Lanka

chetiya – Buddhist shrine

Chola – powerful ancient South Indian kingdom that invaded Sri Lanka on several occasions

CTB – Central Transport Board, the state bus network

dagoba – Buddhist monument composed of a solid hemisphere containing relics of the Buddha or a Buddhist saint; a *stupa*

devale – complex designed for worshipping a Hindu or Sri Lankan deity

dharma – the word used by both Hindus and Buddhists to refer to their respective moral codes of behaviour

eelam – Tamil word for precious land

gala – rock

ganga – river

gedige – hollow temple with thick walls and a corbelled roof

gopuram – gateway tower

guardstones – carved stones that flank doorways or entrances to temples

Hanuman – the monkey king from the *Ramayana*

Jataka tales – stories of the previous lives of the Buddha

juggernaut – decorated temple cart dragged through the streets during Hindu festivals (sometimes called a 'car')

kachcheri – administrative office

kadé – Sinhalese name for a streetside hut (also called boutiques); called *unavakam* by Tamils

Karava – fisherfolk of Indian descent

karma – Hindu-Buddhist principle of retributive justice for past deeds

Kataragama – see *Murugan*

kiri bath – dessert of rice cooked in coconut milk

kolam – meaning costume or guise, it refers to masked dance-drama; also the rice-flour designs that adorn buildings in Tamil areas

kovil – Hindu temple dedicated to the worship of Shiva

kulam – Tamil word for *tank*

lakh – 100,000; unit of measurement in Sri Lanka and India

lingam – phallic symbol; symbol of Shiva

LTTE – Liberation Tigers of Tamil Eelam, also known as the Tamil Tigers; separatist group fighting for an independent Tamil Eelam in the North and the East

Maha – northeast monsoon season

Mahaweli Ganga – Sri Lanka's longest river, starting near Adam's Peak and reaching the sea near Trincomalee

Mahayana – later form of Buddhism prevalent in Korea, Japan and China; literally means 'greater vehicle'

Mahinda – son of the Indian Buddhist emperor Ashoka, credited with introducing Buddhism to Sri Lanka

mahout – elephant master

Maitreya – future Buddha

makara – mythical beast combining a lion, a pig and an elephant, often carved into temple staircases

makara torana – ornamental archway

mandapaya – a raised platform with decorative pillars

masala – mix (often spices)

moonstone – semiprecious stone; also a carved 'doorstep' at temple entrances

mudra – symbolic hand position of a Buddha image

Murugan – Hindu god of war; also known as *Skanda* and *Kataragama*

naga – snake; also applies to snake deities and spirits

nirvana – ultimate aim of Buddhists, final release from the cycle of existence

nuwara – city

ola – leaves of the talipot palm; used in manuscripts and traditional books

oruva – outrigger canoe

oya – stream or small river

Pali – the language in which the Buddhist scriptures were originally recorded

palmyra – tall palm tree found in the dry northern region

perahera – procession, usually with dancers, drummers and elephants

pirivena – centre of learning attached to monastery

poya – full-moon day; always a holiday

puja – 'respect', offering or prayers

rajakariya – 'workers for the king', the tradition of feudal service

Ramayana – ancient story of Rama and Sita and their conflict with *Rawana*

Rawana – 'demon king of Lanka' who abducts Rama's beautiful wife Sita in the Hindu epic the *Ramayana*

relic chamber – chamber in a *dagoba* housing a relic of the Buddha or a saint and representing the Buddhist concept of the cosmos

Ruhunu – ancient southern centre of Sinhalese power near Tissamaharama that survived even when Anuradhapura and Polonnaruwa fell to Indian invaders

samudra – large *tank* or inland sea

Sangamitta – sister of *Mahinda;* she brought the sacred *bodhi tree* sapling from Bodhgaya in India

sangha – the community of Buddhist monks and nuns; in Sri Lanka, an influential group divided into several nikayas (orders)

Sanskrit – ancient Indian language, the oldest known member of the family of Indo-European languages

sari – traditional garment worn by women

Sinhala – language of the Sinhalese people

Sinhalese – majority population of Sri Lanka; principally Sinhala-speaking Buddhists

Skanda – see *Murugan*

stupa – see *dagoba*

Tamils – a people of South Indian origin, comprising the largest minority population in Sri Lanka; principally Tamil-speaking Hindus

tank – artificial water-storage lake or reservoir; many of the tanks in Sri Lanka are very large and ancient

Theravada – orthodox form of Buddhism practised in Sri Lanka and Southeast Asia, which is characterised by its adherence to the *Pali* canon

unavakam – Tamil name for a streetside hut; called kadé or boutiques by the Sinhalese

vahalkada – solid panel of sculpture

vatadage – circular relic house consisting of a small central *dagoba* flanked by Buddha images and encircled by columns

Veddahs – original inhabitants of Sri Lanka prior to the arrival of the Sinhalese from India; also called the *Wanniyala-aetto*

vel – trident; the god *Murugan* is often depicted carrying a *vel*

vihara, **viharaya** – Buddhist complex, including a shrine containing a statue of the Buddha, a congregational hall and a monks' house

Wanniyala-aetto – see *Veddahs*

wewa – see *tank*

Yala – southwest monsoon season

behind the scenes

SEND US YOUR FEEDBACK

We love to hear from travellers – your comments keep us on our toes and help make our books better. Our well-travelled team reads every word on what you loved or loathed about this book. Although we cannot reply individually to postal submissions, we always guarantee that your feedback goes straight to the appropriate authors, in time for the next edition. Each person who sends us information is thanked in the next edition – the most useful submissions are rewarded with a selection of digital PDF chapters.

Visit **lonelyplanet.com/contact** to submit your updates and suggestions or to ask for help. Our award-winning website also features inspirational travel stories, news and discussions.

Note: We may edit, reproduce and incorporate your comments in Lonely Planet products such as guidebooks, websites and digital products, so let us know if you don't want your comments reproduced or your name acknowledged. For a copy of our privacy policy visit lonelyplanet.com/privacy.

OUR READERS

Many thanks to the travellers who used the last edition and wrote to us with helpful hints, useful advice and interesting anecdotes:

Keith Abraham, Mark Aggleton, Laura Airaksinen, Han Andre Iluk, Hiroko Aoki, Marcelina Arabucka, Crista Arangala, Sue Arnold, David Ashby, Trineke Bakker, Suus Baltussen, Bettina Bauer, Melle Bijlsma, Kitty Bijsterveld, Alex Blothner, Kalpana Boodhoo, Sally Burnett, Michael Byrne, Christian Cantos, Reid Casner, Sean Chambers, Stephen Champion, Danny Childs, Huang Chun-yang, Annick Claesen, Richard Colbey, Leonard Cox, Youri Curfs, KP Cyril Ananda, Louis D Botha, Brian Dandy, Lyn Davis, Ashley De Silva, Ingrid De Bruin, Matthew De Lange, Medha De Alwis, Randie Denker, Annechien Deurloo, Anna Dudek, Alexandru Dumitru, Ann Dupre Rogers, Carl Eastwood, Lynn Edwards, Yura, Matt & Eileen Erskine, Claas Feye, Mark Flinn, Yuji Fujimoto, Barbara Gamage, Simon Gasser, Giancarlo Gianfranchi, Walter Gillies, Sonja Gobec, Rob Gomes, Vanessa Gouloumet, Caroline Gowan, Dan Green, Steve Hall, Lesley Hampshire, Chullaka Hapuarachchi, Sarah Haq, Kane Harris, Keith Hockly & Suzie Lee, Henrik Hofmeister, Alan Holden, Maria Holzscheiter, J Hoon Kim, Nicky Hope, Sona Houskova & Nick Vodicka, Anna Houston, Petr Hruska, Niki Huber, David Hughes, Barbara Huwiler, Georgie Hyams Vn, Ali Jaffee, Ansh Jain, Gerbert Jansen & José Groothuis, Cecilia Jensen, Anja Kainz, Shinhyun Kang, Elena Katsorchis, Joseph Kelly, Rene Kerkhof, Ralf Kleiber, Friederike Klotz, Veronia Kohne, Jackie Koper & Adrian Lachowski, Mari-ann Kucharek, Bronwen Lambert, Kees Langeveld, Mary Leathwood, Tang Lee, Martin Lemberger, Mike Levine, Sonny Lindner, Kimberley Lorimer, Robert Malies, Kim Markwell, David Marsden, Andrew Matheson, Kip Mckay, Brian Mcmanus, Vinod Moonesinghe, Steve Morgan, Jim Moulton, Sabine Mueller, Elizabeth Mulleneux, Ursa Nakrst, Tamara Nanayakkara, Nagulan Nesiah, Paul Nevin, Donatella Pallocci, Ellen Pavlovic, Maggie Pendleton, Richard Perry, David Phillips, Peter Phillips, Sara Pierri, Annemarie Pot, John Punter, Daisy Radevsky, Sarah Reglar, Jonathan Rohman-Jancovich, Mark Ross, Bram Roziers, Martin Ruyant, Liam Salter, Stefan Samuelsson, Mark Sawyer, Jennifer Scanlan, Gerald Schlamp, Christian Schuetzinger, Michael Stokes, Dan Straw, Patricia Sulewski, Kay Sutton, Jan Swart, Desmond Tang, Katie Taylor, Raffaella Taylor-Seynour, Tim Thijssen, Gareth Thomas, Judie Tierney, Mark Tissot, Jonna Toft, Ruth Tsang, Nicola Turner, Hagai Tzur, Brenda Van Eeden, Caroline Van Frankenhuyzen, Daisy Van Essen, Jan Van

Den Bosch, Koen Van Laar, Liz Vance, Joris Vergragt, Caroline Viitanen, Hamish Wallace, Dilsiri Welikala, Charles Westaway, Edgar Westerhuys, Beate Wichary, Adam Wiesner, Laurence Wild, Sarah Wood, James Woods, Monica Worsley, Sifaan Zavahir, Jeltje Zuiderveld.

AUTHOR THANKS

Ryan Ver Berkmoes

Thanks to all who made my time in Sri Lanka a delight and shared valuable insights: Milroi Janaka, Dimuthu Priyadarshana, the great blogger Indi Samarajiva, the geographically brilliant Charitha Jithendra Jith and my old pal Juliet Coombe. At LP I thank Kate Morgan and Andrea Dobbin for giving me the chance to both work on the book and appear literate (plus a big piña colada to Stuart). And vast gratitude to Janine Eberle for helping me finish the gin.

Stuart Butler

Thanks again to Dimuthu Priyadarshana for everything, as well as Milroy Fernando and HA Anura. Thanks to Sena and Rashinika Kolambahewage for the loan of the baby bed and toys, Stephanie and Palitha, Juliet Coombe in Galle, Ramyadava Gunasekara and Jai and Sumana (all in Midigama), Sue and family at Sharon Inn in Kandy, Hannah Jenkins, Sarah Benbernou, Alexandre Gellert and Eve Morelli for good company and, most importantly, thanks again to Heather and Jake for being brilliant travel companions.

Amy Karafin

I'm very grateful to the Sri Lankan people for answering so many questions, especially the bus- and train-station guys and the many friendly Hindu priests who blessed me along the way. Thanks also to Kate, Suzannah, Ryan, Stuart and Brigitte, all the readers who sent tips, Akash Bhartiya, Meera Sriskanthan, Gaya Sriskanthan, Shanthi Sachithanandam, Sherine Xavier, Dhuvarahan Balasubramaniam, Siddiq Issath, SK Sitrampalam, Venerable Bhikkhu Bodhi, Jessica Wolfendale, Clare McConnachie, and SN Goenka and everyone at Dhamma Kuta. *Bhavatu sabba mangalam.*

ACKNOWLEDGMENTS

Climate map data adapted from Peel MC, Finlayson BL & McMahon TA (2007) 'Updated World Map of the Köppen-Geiger Climate Classification', *Hydrology and Earth System Sciences*, 11, 163344.

Cover photograph: Thuparama Dagoba, Anuradhapura, Reinhard Schmid, 4Corners. Many of the images in this guide are available for licensing from Lonely Planet Images: www.lonelyplanetimages.com.

THIS BOOK

This 12th edition of Lonely Planet's *Sri Lanka* guidebook was researched and written by Ryan Ver Berkmoes (coordinating author), Stuart Butler and Amy Karafin. The previous edition was written by Brett Atkinson (coordinating author), Michael Kohn, Ethan Gelber and Stuart Butler. This guidebook was commissioned in Lonely Planet's Melbourne office, and produced by the following:

Commissioning Editors Kate Morgan, Glenn van der Knijff
Coordinating Editors Carolyn Bain, Andrea Dobbin
Coordinating Cartographer Xavier Di Toro
Coordinating Layout Designer Wendy Wright
Managing Editor Brigitte Ellemor
Senior Editor Susan Paterson
Managing Cartographers Shahara Ahmed, Adrian Persoglia
Managing Layout Designer Jane Hart
Assisting Editors Kate James, Helen Koehne, Kristin Odijk, Sam Trafford
Assisting Cartographer Mick Garrett
Assisting Layout Designer Jacqui Saunders
Cover Research Naomi Parker
Internal Image Research Aude Vauconsant
Language Content Annelies Mertens
Thanks to Ryan Evans, Andi Jones, Shawn Low, Trent Paton, Gerard Walker

index

000 Map pages
000 Photo pages

000 Map pages
000 Photo pages

000 Map pages
000 Photo pages

Y

INDEX W-Y

000 Map pages
000 Photo pages

how to use this book

These symbols will help you find the listings you want:

Driving | Hiking | Biking

These symbols give you the vital information for each listing:

- Telephone Numbers
- Opening Hours
- Parking
- Nonsmoking
- Air-Conditioning
- Internet Access
- Wi-Fi Access
- Swimming Pool
- Vegetarian Selection
- English-Language Menu
- Family-Friendly
- Pet-Friendly
- Bus
- Ferry
- Metro
- Subway
- Tram
- Train

Reviews are organised by author preference

Look out for these icons:

TOP CHOICE — Our author's recommendation

FREE — No payment required

A green or sustainable option

Our authors have nominated these places as demonstrating a strong commitment to sustainability – for example by supporting local communities and producers, operating in an environmentally friendly way, or supporting conservation projects.

Map Legend

Sights
- Beach
- Buddhist
- Castle
- Christian
- Hindu
- Islamic
- Jewish
- Monument
- Museum/Gallery
- Ruin
- Winery/Vineyard
- Zoo
- Other Sight

Activities, Courses & Tours
- Diving/Snorkelling
- Canoeing/Kayaking
- Skiing
- Surfing
- Swimming/Pool
- Walking
- Windsurfing
- Other Activity/Course/Tour

Sleeping
- Sleeping
- Camping

Eating
- Eating

Drinking
- Drinking
- Cafe

Entertainment
- Entertainment

Shopping
- Shopping

Information
- Bank
- Embassy/Consulate
- Hospital/Medical
- Internet
- Police
- Post Office
- Telephone
- Toilet
- Tourist Information
- Other Information

Transport
- Airport
- Border Crossing
- Bus
- Cable Car/Funicular
- Cycling
- Ferry
- Metro
- Monorail
- Parking
- Petrol Station
- Taxi
- Train/Railway
- Tram
- Other Transport

Routes
- Tollway
- Freeway
- Primary
- Secondary
- Tertiary
- Lane
- Unsealed Road
- Plaza/Mall
- Steps
- Tunnel
- Pedestrian Overpass
- Walking Tour
- Walking Tour Detour
- Path

Geographic
- Hut/Shelter
- Lighthouse
- Lookout
- Mountain/Volcano
- Oasis
- Park
- Pass
- Picnic Area
- Waterfall

Population
- Capital (National)
- Capital (State/Province)
- City/Large Town
- Town/Village

Boundaries
- International
- State/Province
- Disputed
- Regional/Suburb
- Marine Park
- Cliff
- Wall

Hydrography
- River, Creek
- Intermittent River
- Swamp/Mangrove
- Reef
- Canal
- Water
- Dry/Salt/Intermittent Lake
- Glacier

Areas
- Beach/Desert
- Cemetery (Christian)
- Cemetery (Other)
- Park
- Forest
- Sportsground
- Sight (Building)
- Top Sight (Building)

OUR STORY

A beat-up old car, a few dollars in the pocket and a sense of adventure. In 1972 that's all Tony and Maureen Wheeler needed for the trip of a lifetime – across Europe and Asia overland to Australia. It took several months, and at the end – broke but inspired – they sat at their kitchen table writing and stapling together their first travel guide, *Across Asia on the Cheap*. Within a week they'd sold 1500 copies. Lonely Planet was born.

Today, Lonely Planet has offices in Melbourne, London and Oakland, with more than 600 staff and writers. We share Tony's belief that 'a great guidebook should do three things: inform, educate and amuse'.

OUR WRITERS

Ryan Ver Berkmoes

Coordinating Author, Colombo, The Ancient Cities Ryan Ver Berkmoes first visited Sri Lanka in 2005 after the tsunami, when he covered the aftermath as a journalist. Impressed then at Sri Lankans' resilience, he's only more impressed now as the island emerges from its long time in the shadows. On his visits since, he has criss-crossed this beautiful island looking for the best rice and curry ever. He's had some great ones but this sort of quest should never end. Off-island, Ryan lives in Portland, Oregon and writes about travel and more at ryanverberkmoes.com.

Read more about Ryan Ver Berkmoes at:
lonelyplanet.com/members/ryanverberkmoes

Stuart Butler

West Coast, The South, The Hill Country English-born Stuart Butler first hit Sri Lanka during a long trans-Asia surf trip many years ago. One wave and one curry and he was hooked. Since then the food, beaches, wildlife, waves, people and hills have called him back many times. He now calls the beaches of southwest France home. In addition to Sri Lanka his travels have taken him across South Asia and beyond, from the desert beaches of Pakistan to the coastal jungles of Colombia. He still waxes lyrical over Sri Lankan curries. Read about his travels on http://stuartbutler-journalist.blogspot.com.

Read more about Stuart Butler at:
lonelyplanet.com/members/stuartbutler

Amy Karafin

The East, Jaffna & the North For almost 20 years Amy Karafin has been meditating and reading the ancient Pali texts first written down in Sri Lanka. She's also been fascinated by Tamil culture since living in a hut in Tamil Nadu on her first South Asia journey in 1996. The North and East, with their long histories of spiritual exchange, were a natural fit for her, and she jumped at the chance to be among the first travellers to visit islands, beaches, temples and natural springs that had been closed to civilians for decades. When not on the road, Amy lives in Brooklyn, New York.

Read more about Amy Karafin at:
lonelyplanet.com/members/amykarafin

Published by Lonely Planet Publications Pty Ltd
ABN 36 005 607 983
12th edition – July 2012
ISBN 978 1 74179 700 8

10 9 8 7 6 5 4 3 2 1
Printed in China